AN INTRODUCTION TO
GOVERNMENT & POLITICS

A Conceptual Approach

NINTH EDITION

MARK O. DICKERSON
University of Calgary

THOMAS FLANAGAN
University of Calgary

BRENDA O'NEILL
University of Calgary

NELSON

NELSON

An Introduction to Government and
Politics: A Conceptual Approach,
Ninth Edition
by Mark O. Dickerson, Thomas
Flanagan, and Brenda O'Neill

**Vice President, Editorial
Higher Education:**
Anne Williams

Acquisitions Editor:
Anne-Marie Taylor

Marketing Manager:
Ann Byford

Senior Developmental Editor:
Linda Sparks

**Photo Researcher and Permissions
Coordinator:**
Natalie Russell

**Senior Content Production
Manager:**
Natalia Denesiuk Harris

Production Service:
MPS Limited

Copy Editor:
Gillian Watts

Proofreader:
MPS Limited

Indexer:
MPS Limited

**Senior Production
Coordinator:**
Ferial Suleman

Design Director:
Ken Phipps

Managing Designer:
Jennifer Leung

Interior Design Modifications:
Cathy Mayer

Part Opener Images:
Katrina Leigh/Shutterstock

Cover Design:
Cathy Mayer

Cover Image:
Ann Cutting/Botanica/
Getty Images

Compositor:
MPS Limited

**Library and Archives Canada
Cataloguing in Publication Data**

Dickerson, M. O., 1934–
    An introduction to
government and politics : a
conceptual approach / Mark O.
Dickerson, Thomas Flanagan,
Brenda O'Neill. — 9th ed.

Includes bibliographical references
and index.
ISBN 978-0-17-650788-6

    1. Political science—
Textbooks. 2. Canada—Politics
and government—Textbooks.
I. Flanagan, Thomas, 1944–
II. O'Neill, Brenda, 1964– III. Title.

JC131.D52 2013   320
C2012-907064-5

ISBN-13: 978-0-17-650788-6
ISBN-10: 0-17-650788-4

Brief Contents

Contents

Preface

Brenda O'Neill, who joined our writing team for the eighth edition, continues with us for the ninth edition. Dr. O'Neill's expertise in political engagement, gender and politics, political culture, and democratic procedures is reflected in extensive changes to the chapters on those topics. As always, we have had the benefit of extensive feedback on the text initiated by Nelson Education Ltd. While our conceptual approach remains, the feedback has prompted a number of changes both in content and in format; but, while updating the material and presentation, we have tried to remain faithful to the basic approach that seems to have worked well over the past eight editions.

MAJOR CHANGES FOR THE NINTH EDITION

The text has been updated throughout to take account of recent events, including the Great Recession of 2008 and the accompanying ideological debates, the Arab Spring, the Occupy movement, and the 2011 Canadian election, which produced a majority government for the first time since 2004. Beyond that, we have revised certain chapters in greater depth:

- Chapter 1, "Government and Politics," now takes account of research on primate politics, situating human political behaviour in a wider context.

- Chapter 8, "Cooperation under Anarchy" (formerly "International Order"), has been shortened and now emphasizes current illustrative case studies.

- Chapter 10, "Liberalism," now discusses the Great Recession and the revival of Keynesianism.

- Chapter 18, "Transitions to Democracy," has been updated.

- Chapter 24, "Communications Media," now has a discussion of social media.

- Chapter 29, "The Judiciary," has a discussion of new appointment procedures for the Supreme Court of Canada.

- All the end-of-chapter "Further Reading" sections have been reviewed and revised.

- Many of the discussion questions have been revised or elaborated upon.

- New boxes include
  - Chapter 2, Historical Perspectives: "Crush on Obama"
  - Chapter 3, International Perspectives: "The Failed State of Somalia"
  - Chapter 13, World View: "New Nation-States Created after the Collapse of Communism in Eastern Europe, 1991"
  - Chapter 14, World View: "The Gender Gap"
  - Chapter 17, World View: "The Arab Spring"
  - Chapter 24, World View: "Blogs and Politics"
  - Chapter 27, Canadian Focus: "Prime-Ministerial Government?"
- All end-of-chapter Internet links have been updated and are also available live on the student website, at **www.nelson.com/intropolitics9e.**

PEDAGOGICAL APPROACH

The essence of our approach is the pedagogical method that E. D. Hirsch calls "selective exemplification." That is, we try to provide readers with "a carefully chosen but generous sampling of factual data that are set forth in a meaningful web of inferences and generalizations about the larger domain."[1] According to Hirsch, educational research shows that this method yields better results than either an abstract discussion of general principles or an encyclopedic recitation of isolated facts. Of course, selective exemplification will work only if the examples make sense to students; so, as with each previous edition, we have taken care to update our examples to make them as current as possible.

This text is for a first-year course in political science. Although designed for use in Canadian universities and colleges, it does not focus solely on Canadian government. We use Canadian illustrations of general principles together with examples from many other countries, but particularly the British and American political systems—both of which are historically of great importance to Canada.

Historical and Contemporary Perspective

In many years of teaching introductory courses in political science, we have encountered thousands of students. This experience has taught us something about the virtues and vices of the present approach to social studies in Canadian schools. On the positive side, many students come to university with an active curiosity about politics and a healthy skepticism about orthodox opinions. They are eager to learn more about a field they recognize as important.

At the same time, many students are handicapped by certain deficiencies in the social studies curriculum:

- They have been offered little historical information and historical perspective on events. History has suffered perhaps more than any other discipline through being integrated into social studies. Students without a historical perspective are adrift intellectually. They lack the important bearings that make sense of Canada's unique history, as well as the development of Western civilization and the rise and fall of other civilizations.

- They have little specific information about the institutions of Canadian government. Most students entering university are unable to say how a judge is appointed or what an order-in-council is. Their knowledge of government is focused more on current affairs, with heavy emphasis on issues as portrayed in the mass media.

- They are accustomed to discussing politics but not to using rigorously defined concepts. They are used to applying looser reasoning than is required for an academic discipline.

Our textbook addresses each of these problems. We can do relatively little about students' lack of historical background, since the course for which this book is designed cannot replace the systematic study of history. However, we do attempt to put important topics in a historical or developmental perspective and we supply some information about watershed events such as the French and Russian Revolutions. Also, we refer whenever possible to authors, from Plato to Keynes, whose reputations are established and who are important historical figures in their own right.

We can spend only limited time on the details of Canadian political institutions, for those would require a course in Canadian government; rather, we have chosen to emphasize concepts. The material in this book follows a careful sequence: concepts are introduced one at a time, discussed at length, and then used as a basis for explaining further ideas. Important terms are boldfaced where they first occur or where they are thoroughly explained; these terms are used consistently throughout the text and are listed alphabetically at the back of the book for easy reference. We believe that this will equip the student with a comprehensive and logically consistent vocabulary for the study of politics. In the last part of the book, we offer a method for conceptualizing the process of politics and for organizing or arranging the many ideas and concepts introduced in the earlier parts. Thinking about politics as a coherent process is an essential first step in becoming a student of politics, evaluating politics, and becoming a critic of one's own political system. We hope that this approach will be of value not only to students who intend to major in political science but also to those who are seeking a shorter path toward becoming informed political observers (and, of course, participants).

Key Terms and Concepts

We are keenly aware that this effort at consistency means simplifying the meaning of some important terms. Political scientists often disagree on the meaning and use of many significant political terms: *politics, nation-state,* and *democracy* are a few well-known examples of this problem. Our experience has been that students at the introductory level cannot absorb all these debates about meaning, especially when they are subjecting these terms to serious analysis for the first time. For this reason we have narrowed the meaning of many terms—without, we hope, departing from the mainstream of current usage. Readers will undoubtedly criticize our handling of this or that concept, but we hope the pedagogical benefit of applying a consistent vocabulary will compensate for any resulting problems. It is a considerable advantage to be able to explain, for example, liberalism in terms of previously established concepts, such as society, state, and coercion, that the student has already assimilated.

Organization

The book is divided into four parts that together constitute what we believe is a logical way to begin the study of government and politics. Part One defines those terms, ideas, and concepts that are basic to political science. An understanding of terms such as *state* and *society, authority* and *legitimacy,* and *law* and *sovereignty* is essential to a systematic study of politics. Part Two discusses the ideological basis of modern political systems. Liberalism and socialism, the fundamental ideological systems in the modern world, are discussed in the context of the political spectrum that runs from communism to fascism. The emergent ideologies of feminism and environmentalism are also discussed here and placed in context. Part Three looks at forms of government. Here we discuss different types of political systems: liberal-democratic, authoritarian, and totalitarian; parliamentary and presidential; federal and unitary. In Part Four we examine government as a process. A complex interaction of individuals and political institutions produces law and public policies for a society, and we try to view this interaction as a systemic process. The model of politics we offer is hypothetical; however, we draw examples from Canada, the United Kingdom, the United States, and other countries to illustrate how the process works in reality.

Our work is meant to be objective and dispassionate, but that does not mean it is value-free or without commitment. We consistently try to point out the value of the leading ideas of the Western world's political traditions. We pay particular attention to two different and sometimes conflicting groups of ideas, both of which are of great importance. One group centres on constitutionalism and includes notions such as the rule of law and individual freedom; the other centres on democracy and allied concepts such as majority rule and popular sovereignty. For the past two centuries the Western world has tried to combine these two clusters of ideas into the system of government known as constitutional or liberal democracy, in which majorities rule within a legal framework intended to prevent the oppression of minorities. This form of government has been most stable and successful in the countries of Western Europe and North America where it originated. In Canada, where liberal democracy seems securely established, we are apt to take it for granted, but it is far from being an obvious or universal form of government. We hope that better understanding of liberal democracy will help it to flourish.

ANCILLARIES

The Nelson Education Teaching Advantage (NETA) program delivers research-based instructor resources that promote student engagement and higher-order thinking to enable the success of Canadian students and educators.

Instructors today face many challenges. Resources are limited, time is scarce, and a new kind of student has emerged: one who is juggling school with work, has gaps in his or her basic knowledge, and is immersed in technology in a way that has led to a completely new style of learning. In response, Nelson Education has gathered a group of dedicated instructors to advise us on the creation of richer and more flexible ancillaries and online learning platforms that respond to the needs of today's teaching environments. Whether your course is offered in-class, online, or both, Nelson is pleased to provide pedagogically-driven, research-based resources to support you.

NETA Assessment relates to testing materials. Under *NETA Assessment*, Nelson's authors create multiple-choice questions that reflect research-based best practices for constructing effective questions and testing not just recall but also higher-order thinking. Our guidelines were developed by David DiBattista, a 3M National Teaching Fellow whose recent research as a professor of psychology at Brock University has focused on multiple-choice testing. All Test Bank authors receive training at workshops conducted by Prof. DiBattista. A copy of *Multiple Choice Tests: Getting Beyond Remembering*, Prof. DiBattista's guide to writing effective tests, is included with every Nelson Test Bank/Computerized Test Bank package.

- **Instructor's Resources:** These include the test bank, computerized test bank, PowerPoint® presentation, image bank, and Day One slides. All are available under "Instructor Resources" on the website, at **www.nelson.com/intropolitics9e.**

- **NETA Assessment:** The Test Bank includes multiple-choice questions written according to NETA guidelines for effective construction and development of higher-order questions. Also included are true/false, fill-in-the-blank, and short answer questions. Test Bank files are provided in Word format for easy editing and in PDF format for convenient printing whatever your system.

- **Computerized Test Bank in ExamView®** This computerized testing software helps instructors create and customize exams in minutes. It contains all the questions from the printed test bank. Instructors can easily edit and import their own questions and graphics, change test layouts, and reorganize questions. It is available for both Windows and Macintosh.

- **Microsoft® PowerPoint® Presentation** This presentation features important concepts and key points from the textbook and is provided to professors for classroom use to add colour and interest to lectures.

- **Image Bank** Most of the figures and tables from the text are available in this image bank, which can be used for slides or transparencies.

- **DVD (978-0-17-665307-1)** Nelson Education offers a compilation of current CBC news clips covering a wide range of topics. The videos include suggested discussion questions for use in class, making these videos a great enhancement to lectures. Ask your Nelson Education sales representative for more information on how to order the DVD.

ACKNOWLEDGMENTS

Special thanks are due to Jim Keeley and Gavin Cameron for (yet again) revising Chapter 8, which is now titled "Cooperation under Anarchy." Tyson Kennedy gave us indispensable help in updating the Internet references and bibliographies and revising the glossary. We extend our appreciation to Anne-Marie Taylor, Linda Sparks, and Ann Byford at Nelson Education Ltd, and to Jitendra Kumar of MPS Limited. We would also like to thank the readers retained by Nelson Education to review the eighth edition and give us suggestions for the ninth:

Christopher Erickson, University of British Columbia

Louise Carbert, Dalhousie University

Carlos Pessoa, St. Mary's University

Lavinia Stan, St. Francis Xavier University

Todd Always, McMaster University

John Soroski, Grant MacEwan University

Gaelan Murphy, Grant MacEwan University

Visit the Website

For discussion questions, web links by chapter, glossary, and other resources, visit the text's website at **www.nelson.com/intropolitics9e.**

The Study of Political Science

Political science is the systematic study of *government* and *politics*, terms that are defined at greater length in Chapter 1. But before getting into the subject matter, students may find it useful to learn something about the discipline itself.

HISTORY OF POLITICAL SCIENCE

The origins of political science lie in the classical period of Greek philosophy, whose greatest writers were Plato and Aristotle. The Greek philosophers did not approach political science as a specialized discipline in the modern sense, but they thought and wrote systematically about government. They were concerned above all with how politics can contribute to a life of excellence and virtue. The long quotation from Aristotle printed in Historical Perspectives I.1 gives some idea of how this great philosopher saw political science as a moral endeavour committed to the betterment of the human condition. Greek philosophy, and with it the habit of systematic reflection upon government, became part

---

Historical Perspectives I.1

Aristotle on Political Science

Now it would be agreed that [the Supreme Good, the purpose of human existence] must be the object of the most authoritative of the sciences—some science which is pre-eminently a mastercraft. But such is manifestly the science of Politics; for it is this that ordains which of the sciences are to exist in states, and what branches of knowledge the different classes of the citizens are to learn, and up to what point; and we observe that even the most highly esteemed of the faculties, such as strategy, domestic economy, oratory, are subordinate to the political science. Inasmuch then as the rest of the sciences are employed by this one, and as it moreover lays down laws as to what people shall do and what

things they shall refrain from doing, the end of this science must include the ends of all the others. Therefore, the Good of man must be the end of the science of Politics. For even though it be the case that the Good is the same for the individual and for the state, nevertheless, the good of the state is manifestly a greater and more perfect good, both to attain and to preserve. To secure the good of one person only is better than nothing; but to secure the good of a nation or a state is a nobler and more divine achievement.

Source: Aristotle, *The Nicomachean Ethics* 1.2.4–8, trans. H. Rackham, rev. ed. (London: William Heinemann, 1934; Loeb Classical Library, vol. 19), 5–7.

of the cultural tradition of the Western world. Political science continued to exist as a branch of moral philosophy, and important contributions were made by authors who also wrote in other areas of philosophy, such as Thomas Aquinas, Thomas Hobbes, and John Locke. Such writings, extending over more than two millennia, constitute a rich body of wisdom that is still the foundation of political science.

In the eighteenth century, political science started to differentiate itself from moral philosophy—not yet as an independent study but as part of the new science of political economy. Writers such as Adam Smith, who held the chair of moral philosophy at the University of Glasgow, began to study and write about the workings of the market. They did not do this in a vacuum; in the society of the time, market processes were being freed from mercantilist policies predicated on governmental control of the economy. The study of government was a junior partner in the new science of **political economy,** which emphasized market forces. Government was seen as a limited auxiliary that could carry out a few functions not performed well in the marketplace. In the late eighteenth and early nineteenth centuries, universities established chairs of political economy. During this period, much work that today we would call political science was also done in faculties of history and law, especially under the guise of comparative and constitutional law.

Economics and political science began to diverge in the second half of the nineteenth century as scholars began to specialize. The discovery of the principle of marginal utility in the 1870s made it possible for economics to become mathematical, and hence more specialized and remote from the everyday concerns of government and politics. Universities in the United States took the lead in establishing autonomous departments of political science, which united the work of professors who might previously have gravitated to political economy, history, and law. Political science in its modern academic form thus stems from developments in the United States in the late nineteenth century. The first American department of political science was founded at Columbia University in 1880; by the outbreak of World War I in 1914, there were 40 such departments in U.S. universities.[1]

Why in the United States? Partly because this rapidly expanding country was opening scores of new universities that were not bound by old traditions about academic specialties. But the more important reason is that the United States—a nation founded on a political act of revolution—has always been fascinated with government. Political science at the university level was a logical extension of the civics education that was so important in the public schools. Also, those early political scientists tended to be moralistic crusaders for governmental reform—a good example being Woodrow Wilson, the only political science professor ever to become an American president.

In the first half of the twentieth century, political science as an academic discipline remained largely an American phenomenon, with only a few chairs being established in universities in other countries. Of course, the substance of political science was pursued elsewhere, but it was usually conducted within departments of law, political economy, economics, and history. However, after World War II, political science was adopted as an independent discipline around the world. This was partly in imitation of the American cultural behemoth. A deeper reason, perhaps, was the tremendous expansion of the scope of government in the second half of the twentieth century. The small state of the laissez-faire era could be understood fairly easily within the study of political economy; the large, interventionist state of the present era seems to demand its own specialized discipline.

Political science in Canada must be seen in this historical context. In 1950 there were only about 30 political scientists in Canada, most of them employed in university departments of political economy.[2] Their main periodical was the *Canadian Journal of Economics and Political Science* (CJEPS). In the 1960s, as enrollments increased and more staff were hired to cope with an unprecedented expansion of universities, these departments began to split into separate departments of economics and political science. In 1967 the CJEPS was split into the *Canadian Journal of Economics* (CJE) and the *Canadian Journal of Political Science* (CJPS), while two separate professional associations also emerged: the Canadian Economics Association (CEA) and the Canadian Political Science Association (CPSA). Some years later, as part of the general movement of Quebec nationalism, political scientists in that province formed their own association, the Société québécoise de science politique, with its own journal, *Politique et sociétés*. The two associations maintain cooperative relations with one another and there is a good deal of cross-membership, but in political science, as in so many other areas, the reality of Canada is that Quebec is a "distinct society."

The term *political economy* no longer embraces the entire territory of economics and politics as it once did. It now has several special uses. In some circles it refers to the study of certain narrower subjects—such as economic intervention by government—that require information and insights from both disciplines in order to be understood. In other circles it denotes a historical–materialist approach to the study of politics that draws heavily, though not exclusively, on the thought of Karl Marx and other writers in the Marxist tradition. Within the Canadian political-science community, the practitioners of political economy in this latter sense are a recognized subgroup whose members tend to work together with like-minded historians, economists, and sociologists. Together they maintain their own academic network and help to support an interdisciplinary journal, *Studies in Political Economy*, which is based at Carleton University in Ottawa.

APPROACHES TO POLITICAL SCIENCE

When political science achieved academic autonomy, its practitioners brought to it the methods of their forebears in philosophy, political economy, law, and history. These methods were chiefly the narrative, chronological, and descriptive study of political institutions, complemented by philosophical reflection about matters of good and evil in the sphere of government. Great changes have taken place since that beginning.

In the 1940s, sociology and social psychology began to exert enormous influence, and political scientists became familiar with methods of research common in those disciplines, such as attitude scales, sample surveys, and statistical analysis. The rapidly increasing use of these methods was closely tied to a shift in emphasis away from formal constitutional structures and toward political parties, pressure groups, elections, and collective behaviour. This transition—often referred to as the **behavioural revolution**—brought political science closer to the other social sciences.

A second phase of the behavioural revolution began in the 1950s and is still far from ending. It is characterized by the influence of rational-choice models of analysis that were first developed in economics and mathematics. Increasingly, political scientists are using deductive models derived from branches of mathematics, such as game theory and information theory, to explain the data gathered in their empirical investigations. This phase is more abstract and theoretical in nature than the first and is drawing political science closer to natural sciences such as biology and cybernetics, which often use similar mathematical models.

There were acrimonious divisions within the discipline in the 1950s and 1960s, between supporters and opponents of the new methods, with many extreme claims being made on both sides. That furor, however, has largely subsided. Political scientists who use quantitative methods now coexist peacefully with colleagues who rely on the old techniques of description and reflection. It seems to be accepted that political science is inherently pluralistic, and united not by adherence to a single method but by concern with a common subject. Because different questions of politics and government lend themselves to different approaches, political scientists may resemble philosophers, sociologists, historians, lawyers, economists, or anthropologists in their research methods; yet all feel that they are united in a joint enterprise to understand the many facets of government and politics.

The methodological battles have subsided but they have been followed by equally noisy ideological strife. In the late 1960s, political economists and others rooted in the Marxist tradition enunciated a vigorous challenge to what they saw as the capitalist bias of most political science. Their criticism was soon augmented by distinctive new points of view such as environmentalism, feminism, and multiculturalism, each arguing in its own way that fragile and ill-defended assumptions amounting to bias exist in conventional political science. There is no immediate prospect for consensus on such issues, and political science remains what it has always been—an inherently pluralistic discipline in which different points of view clash and final victory is never achieved.

In this respect, political science is very different from the natural sciences. At any given time, probably 99 percent of physicists, chemists, or biologists agree on about 99 percent of the contents of their respective disciplines. They may disagree heatedly about research on the frontiers, but overall the areas of such disagreement are small.

Those who challenge the fundamentals of such disciplines are often regarded as cranks and banished to the periphery. In contrast, political science is an ongoing debate in which honest differences of opinion over fundamental issues are the norm.

Nonetheless, in spite of such deep-seated divisions, there are large areas of agreement. Although feminist and conservative political scientists may disagree profoundly on the larger implications, they should be able to agree on how many women sit in the House of Commons, on what the statistical trend has been over time, and on at least some of the reasons why the percentage (1) used to be extremely low, (2) rose rapidly from the 1960s to the mid-1990s, and (3) levelled off with the election of 1997 at about 21 percent, with an upward spike to 25 percent in the 2011 election—still far below the level for women in the legislatures of several European countries. Such agreement is important in itself, even if it is immersed in vigorous polemics about whether the trends are good or bad and whether additional measures ought to be enacted to accelerate changes.

To introduce some technical terminology, political scientists can hope for agreement on **empirical** (i.e., factual) questions, such as the shape of the political world and how that world functions. Although disagreement on such questions always exists, it can in principle be overcome by more research and better evidence. But disagreement on **normative** (i.e., evaluative) questions is harder—perhaps impossible—to resolve because it may stem from different value commitments. To go back to the preceding example, even after feminist and conservative political scientists reach agreement on a host of empirical issues relating to the representation of women in the House of Commons, they might continue to disagree on the normative question of whether one ought to take steps to increase that level of representation.

Pulling these strands of historical background together, one can identify four leading contemporary approaches within the discipline of political science. These are not the only ones, to be sure, but they are so widespread that everyone studying political science must be aware of them. Few political scientists would maintain that any of these approaches is the only correct one, but in practice most political scientists depend on one of them most of the time in the research they do. Consequently, the discipline as a whole consists of an aggregate of these different and sometimes conflicting approaches to the study of politics.

Institutionalism

Institutionalism focuses on detailed, systematic analysis of the workings of political organizations such as legislatures, cabinets, political parties, interest groups, and courts. Obviously, any political scientist has to be an institutionalist to some extent because the political world consists of institutions, and you cannot understand politics without knowing what these institutions are and how they work. You could, for example, hardly presume to speak about American politics without understanding that the U.S. Congress is divided into two branches called the Senate and the House of

Representatives, that legislation must be approved by both branches, that the president has the right to veto legislation, and that the Congress can override a presidential veto under certain circumstances. Institutionalism, however, is sometimes criticized for being nothing more than formalistic description, devoid of deeper insight into political processes. Dissatisfaction with institutionalism, which was the dominant approach to political science up to the 1950s, led to the development of behaviouralism.

Behaviouralism

Behaviouralism focuses on the behaviour of individuals rather than on the structure of institutions. Behaviouralists typically study topics such as political culture and socialization, public opinion, and voting—where people think and make decisions as individuals, not as cogs in the wheel of an organization. They often use methods such as sample surveys, which allow them to ask people questions and record their responses as individual-level data, after which they use statistical methods to find correlations among variables. This type of research can tell you, for example, which categories of people tend to vote for the candidates of the various political parties—information that is not only interesting in itself but also of great practical importance to the strategists who craft the appeals that parties make to voters during elections.

Behaviouralism has undoubtedly made great contributions to the development of political science, but it has some obvious limitations. Public opinion and elections are interesting and important, but in themselves they do not decide anything except who will fill elected political office. Those elected officeholders are the ones who actually make decisions, and they do so not as unconstrained individuals but as role-players in institutions. A balanced view, therefore, would see institutionalism and behaviouralism as complementary rather than contradictory approaches to the study of politics, both being necessary for a complete explanation of political outcomes.

Public Choice

Public choice is sometimes called the "economics of politics." It represents the application of assumptions about human behaviour that are standard in economics—rationality and the maximization of individual utility—to the explanation of political phenomena. In its purest form, public-choice analysis begins with abstract reasoning to devise a model of how rational, self-interested utility-maximizers would act in stipulated political circumstances, and of how their behaviour would respond to changes in those circumstances. Would such people vote for Party A or Party B? Would they join a political party? Would they bother to vote at all? The predictions of the model are then tested against data collected from the real world of politics.

One of the great advantages of public choice is its applicability to both individual behaviour and institutional structure. Practitioners of public choice analyze institutions as aggregations of individual choices. To the extent that this approach works, it has the potential to overcome the split between behaviouralism and institutionalism. Another advantage of public choice is that it operates with a single, explicit theory of human nature, which helps to give it consistency across different applications. However, the critics of public choice believe that interpreting human behaviour as self-interested utility maximization is too narrow and too dependent upon the capitalist theory of economics, from which public choice was imported into political science. Many critics denounce public choice as simply an ideological rationalization for a conservative, market-oriented brand of politics.

Even though we admit the significance of some of the criticisms of public choice, the authors of this book have been influenced by it, and one of us has even written a book attempting to interpret Canadian politics in public-choice terms.[3] Public-choice interpretations, therefore, crop up here and there throughout this text. But we do not believe that public choice is the only valid way of doing political science, and the text draws as much, if not more, on the findings of researchers committed to institutionalism and behaviouralism.

Political Economy

Political economy, like public choice, is also an application of economic theory to the explanation of political life, but it mobilizes a different version of economics. Political economy, at least as the term is generally understood today in Canada, derives from the Marxist view that politics is conditioned by and expresses class struggle, and that the ruling class uses organized government as a tool to maintain its position of dominance. Starting from this premise, practitioners of political economy refuse to analyze politics and government as such; they believe that satisfying explanations can be found only by linking political phenomena to the underlying realities of class conflict.

As part of its Marxist heritage, political economy also rejects the notion of value neutrality that tends to dominate in other contemporary approaches to political science. Political economists do not see themselves merely as value-free analysts of political life; on the contrary, they hope that by exposing the realities of class conflict they will hasten the approach of a less exploitive, more egalitarian form of economy and society.

The strengths and weaknesses of political economy are in some ways like those of public choice. Political economy transcends the divide between behaviouralism and institutionalism, and its explicit theory of human nature as a product of social circumstances, particularly of the class struggle, gives it rigour and consistency. But as with public choice, those who question the underlying economic premises will have further doubts about the validity of applying them to the interpretation of politics.

ORGANIZATION OF THE DISCIPLINE

Political science, like all academic disciplines, has become so large that internal specialization is necessary. Political scientists typically think of themselves as working in one or two particular fields, and university and college departments of political science organize their course offerings accordingly. The following, most common way of carving up the discipline is based more on convenience than on any profound intellectual rationale:

- Political philosophy
- Canadian politics
- Comparative politics
- International relations

Political philosophy, which goes back to Plato and Aristotle, is treated as a separate field because it has its own long tradition and because its methods are mainly reflective and conceptual rather than empirical. Yet political philosophy often generates empirical hypotheses that can be tested against evidence in all of the other fields.

Canadian politics is treated as a field simply because we live in Canada: the requirements of citizenship make it important to understand the politics of the country where we live. Each country treats its own national politics as a distinct field. Thus American and British universities have separate fields of American and British politics and teach Canadian politics (if they do at all) as part of comparative politics.

It is important to note that Canadian politics does not operate only at the national level. Provincial and municipal governments are important political arenas that for many students are closer to their own experience than the more remote field of national government. Recent developments in Aboriginal self-government have further enriched the field of local government. At one time, Aboriginal communities were simply administered by the Department of Indian Affairs and thus were not of much interest to political scientists. However, the more than 600 Indian bands (today usually called First Nations) now have governments that are just as worthy of study as other local governments in Canada.

Comparative politics is the study of politics in different countries. Canadian universities teach American and British politics as part of comparative politics, even though these would be considered separate fields in the United States and Great Britain respectively. This is mainly a matter of convenience. Politics has many similarities and differences all around the world, and people can understand their own national politics better through comparison with those of other countries. This book, while written for Canadian students, tries to include comparative material from many other countries, particularly the United States and Great Britain, to give Canadians a better understanding of their own system.

Comparative politics can also be conceptualized as a method of analysis. Studying multiple cases and looking for both similar and divergent features helps to build a body of knowledge applicable to the entire world, not just to the country in which you happen to live.

International relations studies the way in which independent states relate to one another. As explained at greater length in Chapter 8, international politics is characterized by the absence of overall sovereignty, which makes it a unique field of study. In fact, it is so different that some universities have separate programs or even departments of international relations.

Beyond this traditional fourfold division of political science, still found in almost every university catalogue, a variety of fields and subfields crop up more or less widely. The department of political science in which you are studying may group courses under headings such as public administration, public law, public policy, political behaviour, and research methods. These groupings usually cut across the traditional divisions among the four fields described above. Public policy—for example, the study of government's role in health care—will be both Canadian and comparative. Researchers study the origin and implementation of such policies and also attempt to evaluate their effectiveness in attaining their stated objectives. Policy studies thus have both philosophical and empirical dimensions to the extent that values are involved and evaluations of effectiveness are made. The field of public policy is of particularly practical importance because many positions in government are filled by graduates of public policy programs. A well-known Canadian example of this kind of work is *How Ottawa Spends*, an annual series produced by the School of Public Administration at Carleton University in Ottawa.

When we debated these matters in our department at the University of Calgary, someone proposed the metaphor of "fields and streams," based on the title of a well-known hunting and fishing magazine. The four traditional areas can be thought of as expansive territorial divisions (the fields) while the special concerns, such as public policy, can be seen as streams meandering through all the fields. Don't take it too seriously, though—it's just a metaphor; but we have found it helpful in organizing our research and teaching in political science.

HOW SCIENTIFIC IS POLITICAL SCIENCE?

The answer to this question depends upon what you mean by *science*. If you take highly mathematical, theoretical disciplines such as physics and chemistry as the model, political science does not measure up very well. Those sciences operate according to the hypothetico-deductive method, in which hypotheses are logically derived from abstract theories and then tested against real-world data. A famous example is the verification of Einstein's theory of relativity—in itself merely a complex mathematical model—by testing its prediction that the path of light passing close to the sun will be bent by the enormous force of its gravitational field.

Among contemporary approaches to political science, public choice makes the loudest claims to applying the hypothetico-deductive method. Yet many public-choice predictions, including some of the best-known ones, have not been supported very well by empirical evidence.[4] Because of discrepant data, public choice has had to refine its predictions so often that many of them begin to look less like broad generalizations and more like specific descriptions of particular cases—in other words, not scientific in the sense of physics or chemistry.

Political science stacks up better against disciplines such as biology and geology, in which systematic observation and careful description still play a larger role than abstract model-building. Just as biologists can demonstrate how differences in precipitation or soil nutrients affect the growth of plant species, political scientists can show how changes in the electoral system affect the competition of political parties in democracies. Just as geologists can offer a plausible explanation of many features of the earth's surface in terms of plate tectonics, political scientists can explain elections in terms of the formation and breakup of political coalitions. Geology cannot predict the timing of an earthquake in advance, and political science cannot predict when a realignment of coalitions will take place, but both disciplines can offer enlightening after-the-fact explanations. Political scientists often disagree among themselves about many topics, but meteorologists, geologists, and biologists also sometimes disagree strenuously—for example, about whether global warming is a reality, what its causes might be (if indeed it exists), and how it might be combated (if indeed it ought to be combated).

Political scientists have much to be modest about. The history of the discipline is filled with failed predictions, unsubstantiated claims to scientific rigour, and unproductive ideological controversy. Nonetheless, it is not an unrealistic aspiration for political scientists to build a body of knowledge composed of careful description together with well-tested generalizations about political phenomena.

WHY STUDY POLITICAL SCIENCE?

There are at least four answers to this question.

1. There is no professional category of political scientist as there is of economist, chemist, or geologist. Nonetheless, the knowledge imparted by political science is highly useful in several professions, and many students major in political science as a sort of pre-professional degree. One can take political science as a preparation for studying law, entering the civil service, or working in party politics. Political science is an obvious springboard for anyone interested in these professions, although other disciplines such as history and economics can also serve the same purpose.

2. Political science is a form of education for citizenship. Everyone in the modern world lives under the jurisdiction of a government and is a potential participant in politics. Even those who are not particularly interested in politics—and not everyone is or needs to be—are required to pay taxes and encouraged to vote. Studying political science can help you become a more effective citizen by enhancing your understanding of the environment in which you operate.

3. The study of political science can be part of a broad liberal arts education. Political philosophy is particularly useful in this respect. Systematic reflection on government has natural linkages to other liberal disciplines such as philosophy, history, and literature.

4. For a few who have the time, inclination, and ability to go on to postgraduate studies, political science can lead to careers in research and teaching in universities, colleges, and research institutes. Someone who takes this path becomes part of the same type of scientific community that exists for all disciplines. It is a life dedicated to the advancement of knowledge in your chosen field.

All of the above are valid reasons for studying political science. Whatever your own reasons (you probably have more than one), we hope this book provides an entry into the discipline. It's just a first step, not the last word. Take what you learn and build on it. We, as its authors, will feel more than compensated if you remember an aphorism of the philosopher Friedrich Nietzsche: "You badly repay your teacher if you always remain a student."

Questions for Discussion

1. Why do you think Aristotle said that politics is not a proper study for young people? Do you agree with him? Why or why not?

2. What is the difference between an empirical statement and a normative statement? Give an example of a normative statement. Do you think such statements merely reflect personal preferences, or do they have some stronger foundation?

3. In what ways is the study of political science useful? Would you personally want to major in political science? Why or why not?

Internet Links

1. Nelson Education Political Science Resource Centre: **www.polisci.nelson.com**. A comprehensive reference site maintained by Nelson Education, the publisher of this book. Includes many links to various topics.

2. Canadian Political Science Association website: **www.cpsa-acsp.ca**.

3. American Political Science Association website: **www.apsanet.org**.

4. The Ultimate Political Science Links Page: www.upslinks.net. Many links to various topics.

5. IPSA Portal: **ipsaportal.unina.it**. The top 300 websites for political science students. A publication of the International Political Science Association.

6. National Newswatch: **www.nationalnewswatch.com**. Gateway to top stories in current events in Canada and around the world.

Further Reading

Archer, Keith, et al. *Parameters of Power: Canada's Political Institutions.* 3rd ed. Toronto: Nelson Canada, 2002.

Baxter-Moore, Nicolas, Terrance Carroll, and Roderick Church. *Studying Politics: An Introduction to Argument and Analysis.* Toronto: Copp Clark Longman, 1994.

Brooks, Stephen. *Canadian Democracy.* 7th ed. Don Mills, ON: Oxford University Press, 2012.

Clement, Wallace, ed. *Understanding Canada: Building on the New Canadian Political Economy.* Montreal: McGill-Queen's University Press, 1997.

Dahl, Robert Alan, and Bruce Stinebrickner. *Modern Political Analysis.* 6th ed. Englewood Cliffs, NJ: Prentice Hall, 2003.

Dyck, Rand. *Canadian Politics: Critical Approaches.* 6th ed. Toronto: Nelson, 2011.

Goodin, Robert E., ed. *The Theory of Institutional Design.* Cambridge: Cambridge University Press, 1996.

Goodin, Robert E., and Hans-Dieter Klingemann, eds. *A New Handbook of Political Science.* Oxford: Oxford University Press, 1996.

Guy, James John. People, Politics and Government. Political Science: A Canadian Perspective. 7th ed. Toronto: Pearson, 2010.

Howlett, Michael, Alex Netherton, and M. Ramesh. *The Political Economy of Canada: An Introduction.* Don Mills, ON: Oxford University Press, 1999.

Johnson, David B. *Public Choice: An Introduction to the New Political Economy.* Mountain View, CA: Mayfield Publishing, 1991.

Jones, Laurence F., and Edward C. Olson. *Political Science Research: A Handbook of Scopes and Methods.* New York: Longman, 1996.

MacLean, George A., and Brenda O'Neill, eds. *Ideas, Interests, and Issues: Readings in Introductory Politics.* 2nd ed. Toronto: Pearson, 2009.

Marsh, David, and Gerry Stoker, eds. *Theory and Methods in Political Science.* London: Macmillan, 1995.

Mueller, Dennis, ed. *Perspectives on Public Choice: A Handbook.* Cambridge: Cambridge University Press, 1997.

Richter, Melvin. The History of Political and Social Concepts: A Critical Introduction. New York: Oxford University Press, 1995.

Rowley, Charles K., and Friedrich Schneider, eds. *The Encyclopedia of Public Choice.* Dordrecht, Netherlands: Kluwer Academic Publishers, 2004.

Shively, W. Phillips. *The Craft of Political Research.* Upper Saddle River, NJ: Prentice Hall, 2002.

Stoker, Gerry. *Why Politics Matters: Making Democracy Work.* New York: Palgrave MacMillan, 2006.

White, Louise G. *Political Analysis: Technique and Practice.* 3rd ed. Belmont, CA: Wadsworth, 1994.

PART 1

BASIC CONCEPTS

CHAPTER 1
Government and Politics

The English word **politics** is derived from the Greek word *polis,* usually translated as "city-state." The *polis* was essentially a self-governing city surrounded by some agricultural hinterland. It has given us a set of related words about government, including *politics, political, politician, policy,* and *police.* The Roman equivalent of *polis* was *civitas,* and the Latin word for "citizen"—a member of the *civitas*—is *civis.* From Latin also we derive an important set of words about government, including *civic, civil, citizenship,* and *city.* Knowing these linguistic roots underscores the fact that politics and the study of politics are not new inventions but an ancient part of human culture.

For a contemporary definition, go to Wikipedia, where you will read that politics is the "process by which groups of people make collective decisions. The term is generally applied to the art or science of running governmental or state affairs."[1] (Some snobbish professors look down on Wikipedia, but we think it's a wonderful thing, as long as you treat it as a jumping-off spot, not a resting place.) That's a good beginning. Often when people speak of politics, they are indeed referring to the process of making decisions for human communities—what the criminal law should be, whether or not to go to war, where to build roads and harbours, and so on. So it's fair to say that, in one sense, *politics* means about the same thing as **government**.

But there's more to it because we also sometimes distinguish between politics and government. For example, democracies have two quite different types of people who work in government: civil servants, who are full-time employees and who are expected to be politically neutral, and elected politicians, who are expected to set policy to be carried out by the civil servants working in government. In this usage, government and politics seem to be not the same thing but two different things.

At this point you may be thinking of the famous dialogue between Alice and Humpty Dumpty:

> "When I use a word," Humpty Dumpty said in rather a scornful tone, "it means just what I choose it to mean—neither more nor less."
>
> "The question is," said Alice, "whether you can make words mean so many different things."
>
> "The question is," said Humpty Dumpty, "which is to be master—that's all."[2]

Or, for a more learned reference, you could go to the seventeenth-century philosopher Thomas Hobbes, who wrote, "Words are wise men's counters, they do but reckon by them: but they are the money of fools."[3]

We spend a lot of time on words in this book because words are labels for concepts, and concepts are the mental tools by which we think about politics, and about anything else. Like Humpty Dumpty or Hobbes's wise man, you have to become the master of the words with which you think, not just take them for granted, like Hobbes's fool.

How, then, can *government* and *politics* mean both the same thing and different things? The short answer is that the meaning depends on the context, which usually furnishes sufficient cues for understanding. The longer answer will take us through an interesting detour into human nature.

The first book written by world-renowned primatologist Frans de Waal was titled *Chimpanzee Politics*.[4] Chimpanzees are our closest biological relatives: the human and chimpanzee genomes are about 99 percent the same. But what sense does it make to speak of "chimpanzee politics"? Chimpanzees don't have language, they don't engage in deliberation over community issues, and they don't make collective decisions binding on their group. Yet they are political in another sense, which is also relevant to human behaviour.

The research of de Waal and others has shown that chimpanzees, who live together in communities of a few dozen adults and infants, maintain separate ranking systems for females and males. Female rank is a bit fuzzy, depends heavily on inheritance, and tends to be passed down from mother to daughter. Male rank, in contrast, is very strict, from the **alpha male** through beta and gamma down to the lowest. Males fight for rank, but they cannot achieve it solely by individual prowess, since most adult males are about the same size. Rather, the key to moving up the dominance hierarchy is to build supporting coalitions—cooperative groups that can intimidate even the fiercest opponent. Chimpanzees of both sexes pursue rank because it seems to confer reproductive advantage, such as better foraging opportunities, access to better-quality mates, and protection for infants. Those who achieve higher rank are likely to have more numerous and more viable offspring, so the attributes that lead to successful competition for rank get passed on across the generations.

Much of this sounds very human, suggesting that we have inherited a repertoire of political behaviour as part of our evolutionary primate heritage. Human beings are obsessed with rank. We strive to get better grades in school and university; to get promoted at work; to win athletic championships or beauty contests; to receive awards for special performance as authors, actors, or scientists. In the world of government and politics, human beings also strive for rank—to be elected to public office, to get into the cabinet, to obtain the alpha position of prime minister or president. And you can climb up the ladder of political rank only by building coalitions of support. That applies in democracies, where building a coalition means getting people to vote for you, as well as in non-democratic systems, where support may mean getting people to kill your opponents.

© Frans de Waal. Reprinted with permission.

A lower-ranking chimpanzee (centre) prostrates himself as a mark of respect to a higher-ranking male. Recognition of rank is as pervasive in chimpanzee society as it is in human society. Like chimpanzees, human beings lower themselves to recognize rank. Bowing, curtsying, kneeling, genuflection, and prostration are well-known signs of deference to authority in politics and religion.

When we speak of politics as distinct from government, this is what we mean: building coalitions of support to obtain rank. If we think of government as a machine that exists to steer the community by making decisions for it, then politics is the process that determines who gets to run the machine. Those who can build the biggest and most effective coalitions win the highest positions and thus get to make the decisions. From this point of view, government is the prize and politics is the struggle to win it.

But that level of analysis, while true, is a bit oversimplified, because politics is required to get things done in government even after winning control of the decision-making positions. It takes politics to make policy. You have to get people, both inside and outside of government, onside with what you want, and that means building coalitions of support. So you can't just do politics to get into government and then stop, as if the contest were over. People in government have to keep on building and maintaining their coalitions of support, or they will not achieve anything even if they are theoretically in charge of the government machine, and they will soon find themselves out of government.

That's why we have titled this textbook *An Introduction to Government and Politics*—because the two are always found together. When we want to emphasize the machinery of decision-making, we speak of government, and when we want to emphasize the process of building supportive coalitions, we speak of politics. The politics of our chimpanzee cousins is concerned only with achieving rank for reproductive advantage because they do not make collective decisions. But human beings are endowed with high intelligence, language, and the faculty of collective deliberation.

We don't just live together like a primate troop. We think about who should be in our community and who should be out, and how you have to act if you are going to be a member. We argue about these things, sometimes passionately, sometimes even to the point of lethal violence. So our politics does bear a family resemblance to that of chimpanzees, but it also entails a kind of conscious collective decision-making found in no other species on earth.

OTHER VIEWS OF POLITICS

Because of the complexity of human politics, political scientists have looked at it in many different ways and have said many different things about it. It's a bit like the old parable of multiple blindfolded people touching various parts of an elephant and then trying to generalize about the beast. It's interesting to look at a few of these views, because they each capture, in a different way, part of the reality of human politics.

One definition comes from a French writer, Bertrand de Jouvenel. According to Jouvenel, "We should regard as 'political' every systematic effort, performed at any place in the social field, to move other men in pursuit of some design cherished by the mover."[5] For him, politics is the activity of gathering and maintaining support for human projects.

Jouvenel's conception of politics emphasizes support. Another common approach is to equate politics with conflict. J. D. B. Miller writes that politics "is about disagreement or conflict."[6] Alan Ball carries this even further; for him, politics "involves disagreements and the reconciliation of those disagreements, and therefore can occur at any level. Two children in a nursery with one toy which they both want at the same time present a political situation."[7]

Ball's definition is not too far from Jouvenel's, for in real life, mobilizing supporters for a project almost always involves overcoming conflicts of opinion or desire. Certainly conflicts arise that do not seem political in any usual sense; there is conflict if a mugger tries to take my wallet, but it is a simple crime, not a political action, because no collective project is envisioned. To be political, a crime must be linked to some vision of reordering society. It is thus a political act—as well as a crime—for a revolutionary group to kidnap a politician in the hope of exciting the people to rise against the government.

Yet another conception of politics is expressed in the title of Harold Lasswell's famous book *Politics: Who Gets What, When, How.*[8] In Lasswell's view, politics is the distribution of the good things of earthly life, such as wealth, comfort, safety, prestige, and recognition. David Easton means the same thing when he says that politics is the "authoritative allocation of values"—*values* meaning not moral ideals but those valuable things in life that people desire to enjoy.[9] There is certainly much merit in this approach, in that it draws attention to the fact that the winners in a conflict—that is, those who succeed in mobilizing support for their projects—usually allocate to themselves and their followers a generous share of material and social benefits. At the same time, however, the distributive approach tends to risk merging politics with other activities. Wealth, for example, can be distributed through the impersonal economic transactions of buying and selling, which are not in themselves political acts because they do not involve mobilizing support for seeking rank. I do not have to be a supporter of Tim Hortons to buy a doughnut and a double-double; I just have to be hungry and have a little money to spend in order to engage in an act of exchange.

Politics has been called the art of the possible and the art of compromise, because it must resolve disagreements among people with different opinions and desires. Compromise is usually necessary if violence and coercion are to be avoided. Political problems rarely have a satisfying solution; usually the best that can be obtained is a settlement—that is, an arrangement that makes no one perfectly happy but with which everyone can live.[10] When this is achieved, politics approximates the definition put forward by the English political scientist Bernard Crick: "The activity by which different interests within a given unit of rule are conciliated by giving them a share in power in proportion to their importance to the welfare and the survival of the whole community."[11] Citing Aristotle, Crick argues that politics is not unity but harmony— that is, the peaceful and cooperative coexistence of different groups, not their reduction to a single imposed pattern. This is a good description of politics as it can be and sometimes is practised, but in reality, harmony often breaks down and people resort to coercive measures.

COALITIONS: POLITICS IN ACTION

A fundamental part of politics is the **coalition**, defined as "the joining of forces by two or more parties during a conflict of interest with other parties."[12] Coalitions involve both conflict and cooperation. They draw a boundary within which cooperation takes place to defeat or gain advantage over an external opponent. Political coalitions are formed precisely to exclude others and thereby exercise power over them.

There are at least three kinds of coalitions. The first kind is similar to the personal, face-to-face coalitions found in chimpanzee societies, while the other two are distinctively human.

1. In small-scale settings, coalitions are based on personal relationships among individuals. For example, in any parliamentary system the prime minister must keep the support of the party caucus—the party's elected members of parliament—in order to remain in office. Some prime ministers, as was reported of Brian Mulroney, spend a lot of time "stroking" caucus members—inviting them to dinner, talking to them individually after caucus meetings, calling them on the phone. Others, like Stephen Harper, are more personally reserved and rely on treating members of caucus fairly in the distribution of rewards—chiefly appointments to the cabinet or committee

chair positions. But no matter how it is done, caucus must be kept onside or the prime minister will lose his position, as happened to Canadian prime minister John Diefenbaker in 1963 and British prime minister Margaret Thatcher in 1990.

2. Coalitions can also be formal alliances of organizations. The North Atlantic Treaty Organization (NATO) is a coalition of 28 European and North American countries that have agreed to defend each other in case of attack. In domestic politics, cabinets are sometimes formed by coalitions when no single party has a majority of seats in the elected legislature. The party caucuses, acting through their leaders, make an explicit agreement to support each other and to divide up the seats in the cabinet. The cabinets of many European democracies—for example, Germany, Italy, Denmark, and the Netherlands—are routinely put together in this way. The most recent Canadian example is the Liberal–NDP coalition cabinet formed in Saskatchewan, after the 1999 provincial election left the NDP with exactly half the seats, one seat short of a controlling majority. That coalition lasted until the election of 2003, at which time the NDP won a narrow majority (30–28) over the opposing Saskatchewan Party and the Liberals failed to win any seats at all. More recently, in 2008 the federal Liberals and New Democrats agreed to make a coalition, supported by the Bloc Québécois, to overthrow the governing Conservatives, but they were out-manoeuvred by Prime Minister Harper and never came to power.[13] The Conservatives then won a majority of seats in the 2011 election, so the coalition issue is dead for the time being, but it is sure to revive sooner or later.

3. Less formally, the building of coalitions is a characteristic of the mass politics of modern democracies. Party leaders form electoral coalitions by proposing policies to attract certain groups of voters. Each party tends to be backed by a distinctive array or coalition of groups defined by geography or demography. For example, major elements in the Republican coalition in American national politics are white Southerners, suburban and rural voters (especially in the Great Plains and Rocky Mountain states), private-sector businesspeople, and (increasingly) Roman Catholics. The Democratic coalition, in contrast, emphasizes blacks, Latinos (except Cubans, who tend to vote Republican), Jews, organized labour (especially teachers and other government employees), and urban voters (especially in the Northeast and on the Pacific coast). Of course, these divisions are not absolute: the Democrats get 90 percent of the black vote in presidential races while the Republicans get only about 10 percent, but even 10 percent of this large group is still a lot of people.

The individuals or groups that make up any type of coalition are not necessarily permanent partners. Southern whites and Roman Catholics used to support Democrats in American politics but have changed allegiance over time, as have blacks, who used to vote Republican. In Canada, a dominant coalition virtually monopolized federal politics between 1946 and 1984; as a result, Liberal governments were elected for 32 of those 38 years. Significant groups in this coalition included Quebeckers, both francophone and anglophone; immigrants and ethnic minorities in many parts of the country; Roman Catholics; and many individuals in the media and in the academic community. One factor holding these disparate groups together was a belief in the state's ability to guide change, progress, and economic development in Canadian society. When those years produced expensive bureaucracies and programs that did not always work as intended, the stage was set for the breakup of the dominant coalition. The Conservatives in 1984 seized the opportunity to create a new one, which in turn fell apart in the early 1990s.

CONCLUSION

To recapitulate, government and politics are universal aspects of human existence. Government and politics both arise from the need for people to live in societies; for a society to succeed, people must settle conflicts and abide by common rules in such a way that the community is not endangered. Government and politics involve coercion, but not for its own sake. One reason why rulers resort to force is to lessen the use of force by private individuals against each other.

Government and politics become more and more indispensable as civilization advances. The more complicated our way of life becomes, the less we can afford to have our plans upset by random intrusions of others on our person, property, or expectations. Government can be the great guarantor of stability of expectations and the force that makes it possible for other human endeavours, such as religion, art, science, and business, to flourish. When a government is working well, the political process continually and unobtrusively resolves those conflicts that might otherwise tear society apart. In fact, politics may work so well that the ordinary person may take it for granted and have very little need to be concerned with it.

Even though government is essential, we are not always reconciled to it. There is a persistent belief that we may someday attain a perfectly harmonious, conflict-free society in which government will be unnecessary. One form of this belief is the Judeo-Christian tradition of the Kingdom of the Saints or the Kingdom of God on earth.[14] According to this idea, human conflict will cease with the advent (Judaism) or return (Christianity) of the Messiah, and there will be no ruler except this divinely authorized figure. Related ideas in Islam involve the appearance of the Mahdi or the return of the Twelfth Imam, enlightened teachers who presage the coming of the Last Days.

Secular versions of this scenario also exist.[15] The early French socialist Henri de Saint-Simon (1760–1825) wrote that eventually "the government of men" would be replaced by the "administration of things"—a formula later echoed by Lenin.[16] They both hoped that in a future world where everyone was comfortable and gross inequalities had vanished, people would become so peaceable that governmental coercion would be unnecessary. The same expectation is embodied in the Marxist doctrine

Canadian Focus 1.1

Conservative Coalition-Building

When Jean Chrétien was prime minister of Canada (1993–2003), the conservative side of the spectrum in federal politics was represented by two political parties, the Reform Party of Canada (later renamed the Canadian Alliance) and the Progressive Conservative Party of Canada. Neither party could get enough votes to wrest control of the government from the Liberals until, in 2003, Alliance leader Stephen Harper invited PC leader Peter MacKay to form a coalition. However, the two leaders, with the support of their party members, agreed to go even further and merge. The new Conservative Party of Canada went on to bring the Liberals down to a minority in the 2004 election, win a minority government in the 2006 and 2008 elections, and form a majority government in 2011.

These events illustrate coalition-building at all three levels described in the text. First, Stephen Harper and Peter MacKay had to build a personal coalition between the two of them before anything else could happen. Then the members of the two parties had to approve a merger of organizations. Finally, voters who were used to supporting the old merger partners had to play follow-the-leader and support the new Conservative Party in federal elections, thus building a mass electoral coalition that could defeat the other parties and win control of the government.

of "the withering away of the state," which teaches that government will eventually become obsolete after a communist revolution.[17] But none of these visions has ever come to pass, and still we must rely on politics and government to mediate the conflicts that arise among self-interested individuals.

Questions for Discussion

1. Can you think of examples of political conflicts that you have encountered outside of government, for example, in school, clubs, or athletic teams? How were these issues resolved?

2. Have you ever felt excluded from benefiting fully in an organization that seemed to be dominated by a powerful clique (coalition)? Have you ever excluded others from a coalition? Describe the experiences.

3. Have you ever participated in building a coalition to accomplish some objective? Describe the kind of coalition you were involved in and how you went about building it.

Internet Links

1. Government of Canada home page: **www.gc.ca**. Links to all departments of the government of Canada.

2. Wikipedia, The Free Encyclopedia: **http://en.wikipedia.org**. A vast storehouse of information. Search for articles on key terms such as *government, politics, primitive government,* and so on.

3. Worldwide Governments on the WWW: **http://www.gksoft.com/govt/en/world. html**. Gateway to information on all the world's governments.

Further Reading

Ball, Alan R., and B. Guy Peters. *Modern Politics and Government.* 7th ed. London: Palgrave Macmillan, 2005.

Bateman, Thomas M. J., Manuel Mertin, and David M. Thomas, eds. *Braving the New World: Readings in Contemporary Politics.* Scarborough, ON: Nelson Canada, 1995.

Blakeley, Georgina, and Valerie Bryson. *Contemporary Political Concepts.* Sterling, VA: Pluto Press, 2002.

Brodie, M. Janine, ed. *Critical Concepts: An Introduction to Politics.* Toronto: Prentice Hall, 2002.

Evans, Peter, ed. *State–Society Synergy: Government and Social Capital in Development.* Berkeley: University of California at Berkeley, International and Area Studies, 1997.

Flanagan, Thomas. *Game Theory and Canadian Politics.* Toronto: University of Toronto Press, 1998.

Franks, C. E. S., et al. *Canada's Century: Governance in a Maturing Society. Essays in Honour of John Meisel.* Montreal: McGill-Queen's University Press, 1995.

Hawkesworth, Mary, and Maurice Kogan. *Encyclopedia of Government and Politics.* 2nd ed. London: Routledge, 2004.

Klosko, George. *The Principle of Fairness and Political Obligation.* 2nd ed. Savage, MD: Rowman & Littlefield, 2003.

Leftwich, Adrian, ed. *What Is Politics? The Activity and Its Study.* Oxford: Blackwell, 2004.

MacLean, George A., and Brenda O'Neill, eds. *Ideas, Interests and Issues: Readings in Introductory Politics.* Toronto: Pearson Prentice Hall, 2006.

McMenemy, John. *The Language of Canadian Politics: A Guide to Important Terms and Concepts.* 3rd ed. Waterloo, ON: Wilfrid Laurier University Press, 2001.

Pierson, Paul. *Politics in Time: History, Institutions, and Social Analysis.* Princeton, NJ: Princeton University Press, 2004.

Putnam, Robert D. *Bowling Alone: The Collapse and Revival of American Community*. New York: Simon and Schuster, 2004.

Roninger, Luis, and Ayse Gunes-Ayata, eds. *Democracy, Clientelism, and Civil Society*. Boulder, CO: Lynne Rienner, 1994.

Russell, Peter, Francois Rocher, Debra Thompson, and Linda White, eds. *Essential Readings in Canadian Government and Politics*. Toronto: Emond Montgomery, 2010.

Tansey, Stephen D. *Politics: The Basics*. 2nd ed. London: Routledge, 2000.

Tarrow, Sidney. *Power in Movement: Social Movements, Collective Action and Politics*. Cambridge: Cambridge University Press, 1994.

Tremblay, Reeta Chowdhary. *Mapping the Political Landscape: An Introduction to Political Science*. Toronto: Nelson, 2004.

Walsh, David F. *Governing Through Turbulence: Leadership and Change in the Late Twentieth Century*. Westport, CT: Praeger, 1995.

CHAPTER 2
Power, Legitimacy, and Authority

Power in the broadest sense is the capacity to achieve what you want. The word is related to the French verb *pouvoir*, "to be able." Power can be the physical ability to perform a task such as lifting or running, the intellectual capacity to solve a problem, or the social ability to induce others to do what you want.

In political science, *power* has this last meaning. Political science is centred on the study of political power, seeking answers to questions such as the following: Who has power and who does not? Are those who exercise power held accountable in some way to those who do not? Can those who wield power be replaced peacefully or only with violence? What beliefs justify the distribution and exercise of power in political systems?

Power is to politics what money is to economics: the medium of exchange, the universal common denominator. Political power, however, is not a homogeneous quantity like money, and it does not have a simple unit of measurement such as dollars. There are, in fact, three main forms of power—influence, coercion, and authority—which have to be discussed separately.

INFLUENCE

Influence is the ability to persuade others to do your will, to convince them to want to do what you want them to do. The important point is that the targets of persuasion act voluntarily; they are not conscious of restraints on their will because they have freely chosen to agree. Of course, they may agree either because they have come to think that the action is right and justified or because they think they will reap personal benefit from it. Influence takes many forms, which in the hard light of reality often overlap:

- Appeals to the intellect (convincing people that a given action is intrinsically best)

- Appeals to the passions (persuading people to act by playing directly on the emotions)

- Appeals to self-interest (persuading people to support a cause because of "what's in it for them")

- Appeals to group solidarity (persuading people to work on behalf of a community to which they belong)

Because there are so many ways to influence others, there are also many resources that can be deployed in the task. The following list, while by no means exhaustive, enumerates some possibilities:

- Intelligence, knowledge, and research can be used to construct convincing arguments.
- People with money and expertise can produce effective advertising.
- People who control wealth can offer financial inducements (such as bribes).
- People with organizational connections can offer career prospects (jobs, contracts, patronage in all its forms).
- Officials who control the apparatus of government can offer what political scientists call "policy outputs," or promises to legislate in ways that will benefit their supporters.

Influence is always at work in government. Candidates for office in a democratic system win elections by persuading their fellow citizens to vote for them. Once in office, they are in turn besieged by individuals and groups who want government to do something on their behalf—for example, to build a road along one route rather than another, or to lower their taxes. For its part, government seeks to influence the behaviour of the electorate. For example, the government of Canada has run extensive advertising campaigns exhorting Canadians to exercise more, stop smoking, drink less alcohol, conserve energy, and support Canadian unity.

Democratic politics is a giant web of influence and persuasion. Consider the position of the Conservative government of Canada elected on 2 May 2011. They got to that position by persuading 39.6 percent of eligible voters to vote for them. In order to accomplish that feat, they had to persuade new members to join the party, activists to work during the campaign, and donors to contribute money. Having gotten elected through this exercise of influence, the Conservative government became subject to all sorts of influence from those wanting action of various kinds. Business, labour, and agricultural groups lobby for legislation to benefit their members. Advocacy groups, such as Greenpeace, carry out campaigns to steer public opinion in one way or another, with the ultimate aim of influencing government to do something those groups desire. Also, opposition parties attempt to persuade the Conservatives to make changes in their legislative proposals after they are introduced in Parliament. And of course all parties hope to influence voters to support them in the next election, whenever that will come.

COERCION

Coercion is the deliberate subjection of one will to another through fear of harm or threats of harm. When coercion is applied, compliance is not voluntary: it results from fear of unpleasant consequences.

Coercion can take many forms. **Violence** involves physical harm, such as beatings, torture, and murder. Imprisonment, while not directly violent, is enforced by violence if the prisoner tries to leave custody. Other forms of coercion include monetary penalties (e.g., fines imposed by government) and strikes, in which workers combine to threaten employers with losses in the marketplace. The number of ways of harming or threatening people is infinite, but most methods ultimately rely on violence. We must pay a fine for a traffic violation to avoid imprisonment. Employers must submit to the economic setback of a legal strike. If they repudiated their agreements to bargain collectively with the unions, discharged their workers, and tried to hire a new workforce, they would be breaking the law and could be fined or even imprisoned.

Modern governments try to control most forms of outright coercion, especially violence. Ordinary people are prohibited from violently assaulting each other or seizing property. They are supposed to refrain from violence except in self-defence, and limits are enforced even in such situations. Government uses its near-monopoly on violence to protect society from external attack and to enforce rules of conduct and punish those who violate them. To these ends, every government has developed a complex apparatus of armed forces, police forces, prisons, and courts.

One partial exception to the governmental control of coercion involves industrial relations. During the twentieth century, governments accepted that collective bargaining is an arena in which employees and employers may resort to economic coercion to achieve their objectives. Yet the exception is perhaps not as great as it seems: collective bargaining was introduced to civilize labour relations, which were for a long time marked by a great deal of overt violence. Governments now try, more or less successfully, to legalize a degree of economic coercion and thus keep both sides from resorting to violence.

Government forbids all individuals and groups to use violence against it. Whatever their other differences, all governments are identical in their resistance to acts of political violence, because such acts undermine the very existence of the state. The use of force and the threat to use force against government are defined as political crimes. A government that cannot resist such threats will not survive long. Liberal democracies define political crimes narrowly as the use of force, or the advocacy of such use, against the state. Totalitarian and authoritarian regimes extend the definition to include peaceful opposition to or criticism of the state. How a political crime is defined is an almost infallible test for the genuineness of liberal democracy.

Coercion is a powerful tool, but no government can depend on it entirely. Society has so many members engaging in so many different activities that everything cannot be coercively directed. Even if it were possible, it would be too expensive because coercion is so labour-intensive. In any case, it is logically impossible for everything to depend on coercion, because there must be a coalition of the coercers to get the job done. What holds them together? More coercion? If so, who provides it? At some point societies must go beyond coercion to a principle that holds its followers together for joint action and that makes it possible for them to coerce others—in a word, *authority.*

The Chinese communist leader Mao Zedong (1893–1976) expressed this truth when he wrote, "Political power grows out of the barrel of a gun. Our principle is that the Party commands the gun; the gun shall never be allowed to command the Party."[1] (The first sentence of this statement is often quoted out of context, as if coercion were the ultimate reality of politics.) To be sure, the gun is significant, as was demonstrated at Tiananmen Square in 1989, when the Chinese government used tanks to put down the democracy movement. But it is noteworthy that the army did nothing until the Communist Party had sorted out its internal disagreements and resolved upon a repressive course of action. Until there was clear direction from the party, the army was unwilling to use its firepower against unarmed civilians. The point is that coercion is not the ultimate form of power but rather a highly useful adjunct to authority.

AUTHORITY

Authority is a form of power in which people obey commands not because they have been rationally or emotionally persuaded or because they fear the consequences of disobedience, but simply because they respect the source of the command. The one who issues the command is accepted as having a right to do so, and those who receive the command accept that they have an obligation to obey. The relationship between parents and young children is a model of authority. Sometimes the parents will persuade the child to do something, and occasionally they may have to resort to coercion, but most of the time they can command with the expectation of being obeyed.

All governments possess at least some authority and strive to have as much as possible, for obvious reasons. Something more than influence is necessary to guarantee predictable results. Coercion produces compliance but it is also very expensive and, furthermore, is possible only if a substantial number of agents of coercion are held together by authority. Clearly, authority is an inescapable necessity of government.

It is safe to say that most people, most of the time, are acting in deference to authority when they do what their government wishes. They stop at red lights and file tax returns because they realize that such actions have been commanded. Of course, they may have other motives as well. Perhaps their consciences bother them if they disobey authority. How else can we explain such obedience even in circumstances where punishment is highly unlikely? Most drivers obey traffic lights even at 3 a.m. on a deserted street, and not solely because they fear a hidden police cruiser—almost certainly they would feel a little uncomfortable about violating an authoritative rule.

Nevertheless, not everyone is always deferential to authority, which is why coercion is extremely useful—it motivates by fear those who are not susceptible to feelings of obligation. Coercion is present as a background threat, as with a soldier who may be prompted to obey out of fear of a court-martial. But this coercion, though important, is only a tool of authority. Coercion by itself could not produce the united action necessary to hold a court-martial. On the other hand, authority without powers of coercion to back it up is likely to become ineffectual. We have seen this situation in "failed states" such as Somalia, where the government, though still recognized internationally, has lost effective control. In such cases, authority becomes purely nominal and is no longer a form of real-world power.

We must also distinguish between natural and public authority. The former exists whenever one person spontaneously defers to the judgment of another. Little children tagging after big children, and students seeking out teachers in the early days of the medieval university, are instances of **natural authority**. Every individual is always surrounded by numerous natural authorities—friends, relatives, colleagues—and acts as an authority to others on occasion. Natural authority is simply another term for the human tendencies to follow and imitate as well as to lead and initiate. These are some of the bonds that hold society together.

Public authority, in contrast, is deliberately created by human agreement. The English language recognizes the difference between natural and public authority in an interesting way. We say that an expert on baseball statistics is "an authority" in his chosen field, but not that he is "in authority" in that field. But when we describe, for example, a police officer, we do not say she is "an authority" by virtue of any personal quality, but rather that she is "in authority" by virtue of the power entrusted to her by government. Her uniform is a visible sign of the public, or artificial, authority that she wields. To be a natural authority, you must have special personal qualities; to hold public authority, you have only to be in a position or office that carries with it rights of command.

What is the relationship between public authority and social order? Power is required to order any society, but it must be more than coercive power if a given society is to be open and free. An advantage of authoritative power over coercive power is that most individuals voluntarily submit to it. But why would people submit to any power that restricts their freedom of action? The answer is not easy to find; political philosophers have grappled with the question for centuries, searching for the roots of consent to authority. One writer has put the issue this way:

> the authority of government does not create the order over which it presides and does not sustain that order solely by its own fiat or its accredited power. There is authority beyond the authority of government. There is a greater consensus without which the fundamental order of the community would fall apart.[2]

LEGITIMACY

Although we often speak of *having* or *possessing* authority, that usage is misleading because it makes authority sound like a quality that some people have, like red hair or a deep voice. In fact, authority is a social relationship; an individual has it only if others respect and obey it. Authority is one pole of a relationship in which the other pole is **legitimacy**. When we emphasize the right to command, we speak of authority; when we emphasize the acceptance of command, we speak of legitimacy. Authority is focused in the one who commands; legitimacy is the feeling of respect for authority that exists in those who obey—it is what makes authority possible. It is the same type of relationship as exists between leaders and followers. Neither makes sense without the other: you can't exercise leadership if no one is willing to follow you.

Both authority and legitimacy are moral or ethical concepts; that is, they involve perceptions of right and wrong. We feel that someone in authority has a right to command. Similarly, we feel that it is right to obey, that we have a duty or obligation to do so. Governmental power without legitimacy is only coercion or force; with legitimacy, power becomes authority.

Legitimacy creates a sense of obligation, as illustrated in the following diagram:

Authority	**Legitimacy**	**Obligation**
RIGHT OF COMMAND	BELIEF IN RIGHTNESS OF GOVERNMENT	SENSE OF DUTY

We feel obligated to respond to commands when we are convinced that those who exercise authority are justified in doing so.

Public authority survives only as long as it has some degree of legitimacy in society. It is not necessary that literally everyone, or even a numerical majority, accept the legitimacy of a particular government, but there must be at least a loyal minority, strong and united, to withstand potential opposition. If such a minority exists and is willing to use coercion, it can sustain itself in power for a surprisingly long time in the face of widespread popular opposition.

It was obvious for decades that the numerical majorities in the Republic of South Africa and in the communist countries of Eastern Europe would have chosen other rulers if they had been effectively consulted. Yet those governments were in little danger of falling as long as they maintained their weapons monopoly and the political support of a determined minority. These regimes finally changed when reform movements were established within the governments themselves. In each case, substantial elements of the ruling elite, led by the head of government, decided to break with the past. In each case, the system had long ago lost its legitimacy, but this in itself was not sufficient to topple the structure of authority.

Starting in 2011, the Arab world became convulsed with uprisings against undemocratic governments. A particularly violent case was Libya, where a group of NATO powers, including the United States, Great Britain, France, and Canada, used air power to stop troops loyal to leader Muammar al-Gaddafi from defeating dissidents based in eastern Libya. The point in this context is that the rebels no longer saw Gaddafi as a legitimate authority. They resorted to force in order to overthrow him, while some of his troops still respected his authority and were willing to fight on his behalf. Such a contest over legitimacy is typical of revolutionary situations.

Legitimacy rests upon beliefs and values that are not static. These things change over time, and legitimacy is challenged when government actions no longer correspond with them. According to Carl Friedrich,

> The process of aging leadership in consensual power situations is usually associated with the disintegration of authority. The actions of the "old one" are no longer understood, because they make no sense in terms of the altered values and beliefs; his capacity for reasoned elaboration is declining and finally is gone. This often carries with it a decline of power, though just as often the power continues, but it gradually becomes more coercive, less consensual.[3]

Power, authority, and legitimacy are integral components of government and politics. Power without legitimacy represents coercion—naked force. Power combined with legitimacy represents authoritative force—the force required to order a diverse society.

One of the great advantages of democracy is that regular, nonviolent changes of government are possible at periodic intervals. If a government ignores ongoing changes in beliefs and values, it can be voted out of office. Democracy provides a safety valve that enables voters to change governments without having to change the nature of the political system. Legitimacy is maintained for the system as a whole even as authority is transferred within it.

Because authority and legitimacy are so central to political life, they are an important focus of study in political science. One of the most important contributions to understanding them was made by the German sociologist Max Weber (1864–1920), who identified three kinds of authority/legitimacy: *traditional, legal,* and *charismatic.*[4] These "ideal types," as Weber called them, are always found mixed together in political systems. They are intellectual models that never exist in pure form in the real world, yet they help observers to understand what they see.

TRADITIONAL AUTHORITY

Traditional authority is domination based on inherited position. Hereditary monarchs are a good example of traditional authority. They hold the right of command not because of extraordinary personal qualities or because they have been chosen by others but because they have inherited a position from a parent or other relative. The arrangement is regarded as legitimate because it has the sanction and prestige of tradition: things have been done that way from time immemorial. The principle of inherited authority also draws support from its similarity to the workings of the family, the most fundamental social institution.

The feudal system of medieval Europe was based mainly on traditional authority. At the apex of authority were the hereditary monarchs. They appointed judges, administrators, and military commanders who owed them personal allegiance; their authority was only an extension of the monarch's. Many governmental functions were performed by members of the nobility, whose social positions also stemmed from right of birth. The system depended on the work of the common people, who were born into a social position out of which it was extremely difficult to rise. Throughout the system, command and obedience were associated with inherited social rank and sanctified by tradition. Similar arrangements characterized much of the rest of the world until very recently, and traditional authority still prevails in Saudi Arabia and other Gulf sheikhdoms, where authority is vested in the royal family and a number of related clans. It is also worth noting that about half the First Nations in Canada are governed by chiefs who have obtained their positions by inheritance rather than through contesting elections.

LEGAL AUTHORITY

The central concept of **legal authority** is that of general rules binding on all participants in the system. Authority is exercised only when it is called for by these rules. It is not associated with individuals who inherit their status but with legally created offices that can be filled by many different incumbents. It is, to quote an ancient phrase, the "rule of law, not of men" (see Chapter 7 for a further discussion of this phrase).

In Canada and Great Britain, authority is primarily legal, although the external symbolism is still traditional. A hereditary monarch reigns but does not rule, while actual power is wielded by politicians who are elected to office under a strictly defined system of laws. A prime minister is in authority while in office but has no personal status once retired. Those who work for government are no longer the personal servants of the monarch; their allegiance to the Crown means loyalty to the government as a whole, not to a particular person within it. There is no longer a hereditary class of nobles carrying out governmental functions. The House of Lords still survives in Great Britain, but it is mainly a symbolic reminder of the vanished age of traditional authority. The system derives its legitimacy not from the acceptance of status or from loyalty to personal authority but from loyalty to the constitution, which is a legal system stronger than any individual.

However, some traditional elements still survive within contemporary legal authority. Law itself is hallowed by tradition. As rule-following animals, we quickly build up habits of compliance to those in power. Over time it begins to seem right to obey, simply because that is the way things have been done in the past. It is undoubtedly true that habit is a powerful source of governmental legitimacy. We obey because we are accustomed to do so, because we have always done so. Reflective thought is not necessarily involved.

Such habits of obedience are necessary, for if we continually had to reconsider the legitimacy of government we would have time for little else. Those habits break down in times of revolutionary transition, when one form of authority is replaced by another. But they quickly re-establish themselves as part of the new government's legitimacy.

The great trend of development in modern political history is for traditional authority to be replaced by legal authority. This long, slow, and painful process began in Great Britain and its American colonies in the seventeenth century, continued in Europe in the eighteenth and nineteenth centuries, and engulfed the entire world in the twentieth century. It is the political aspect of the wider social process known as **modernization**. Social changes gradually and cumulatively modified people's notions of political legitimacy; this process was punctuated at certain times by the dramatic collapse of a traditional regime and its replacement by a new system of legal authority. The great popular revolutions of modern history must be seen in this context:

1688	Glorious Revolution	Stuarts overthrown by English Parliament
1776	American Revolution	American colonies declare independence from British Crown
1789	French Revolution	Bourbon dynasty replaced by a republic
1911	Chinese Revolution	Manchu dynasty replaced by a republic
1917	Russian Revolution	Romanov dynasty overthrown; Russian Empire becomes Soviet Union

These are only a few of the many revolutions that in three centuries have transformed the political face of the globe. Together they make up what is often called the "world revolution." The French writer Alexis de Tocqueville, who made an extended tour in 1831–32 of the United States and Canada and noted the great social inequality in the traditional order of Europe, memorably stated the essence of the transition from traditional to legal authority:

> On the one side were wealth, strength, and leisure, accompanied by the refinements of luxury, the elegance of taste, the pleasures of wit, and the cultivation of the arts; on the other were labor, clownishness, and ignorance. But in the midst of this coarse and ignorant multitude it was not uncommon to meet with energetic passions, generous sentiments, profound religious convictions, and wild virtues. The social state thus organized might boast of its stability, its power, and, above all, its glory. But the scene is now changed. Gradually the distinctions of rank are done away; the barriers which once severed mankind are falling down; property is divided, power is shared by many, the light of intelligence spreads and the capacities of all classes are equally cultivated.[5]

The social equalization described by de Tocqueville is inseparable from legal authority, in which individuals are governed by universal rules applicable to all. It cannot coexist for long with the hereditary classes and ranks of traditional authority. The worldwide transition from traditional to legal authority is the single most important political event of our times, and it furnishes the context in which everything else takes place.

The collapse of communism in the Soviet Union and Eastern Europe was a further development in this direction. Communism as an ideology promised the benefits of legal authority and social equalization, but the communist regimes never came close to attaining these goals. In practice they resembled a kind of bureaucratic feudalism, with great emphasis on the personal authority of the party leaders and disregard for impersonal legal norms. The party leaders constituted an elite as privileged and oppressive as any traditional aristocracy.

CHARISMATIC AUTHORITY

Charismatic authority is based on the projection and perception of extraordinary personal qualities. Weber defined charisma as "a certain quality of an individual personality by virtue of which he is set apart from ordinary men and treated as endowed with supernatural, superhuman, or at least specifically exceptional powers or qualities."[6]

Charisma was originally a theological term, derived from the Greek word for "grace" or "spiritual favour." Generally speaking, charismatic leaders are prophets, saints, shamans, or similar figures. Their legitimacy does not depend on tradition or law but on their followers' belief that they speak to them directly from God. Their transcendental claim to authority often places them in conflict with traditional or legal authorities. Some of our most striking and well-known historical figures were charismatic in this sense: the biblical prophets of the Hebrews, as well as Joan of Arc, whose heavenly visions inspired her to help drive the English from France. (For a Canadian example of charisma, see Historical Perspective 2.1 on Louis Riel.)

The term *charisma* is also applied to political leaders who base their claim to rule on an alleged historical mission. Adolf Hitler, for example, believed that he had a special mission to restore Germany's greatness. He came to this conviction as he lay in hospital in 1918, having been blinded by a British gas attack on the Western Front. His blindness coincided with Germany's surrender; when he recovered his sight, he became convinced that he might also be the means of Germany's restoration to greatness. The title he always preferred was *Führer*, the German word for "leader"; it emphasized that his authority radiated from his personality, not from any office that he happened to occupy.

Charisma is sometimes collectively shared, as in the political thought of Ayatollah Khomeini (1900–89), the symbol and leader of the revolution that swept the shah of Iran from power in 1979. Khomeini was a jurist who specialized in the study of the *shari'a*, the Islamic law. "The jurists," according to Khomeini, "have been appointed by God to rule."[7] The state, he said, must also have secular legislative and executive authorities, but the jurists as a group have an overriding and divinely given power and responsibility to ensure that all government is carried on within the principles of the *shari'a*. Khomeini saw himself less as a special individual than as the most prominent representative of a charismatic class. This class of jurists still exercises considerable power in the contemporary Islamic Republic of Iran, though it is also paralleled by a more conventional structure of legal authority based on a written constitution and elections.

Historical Perspectives 2.1

Louis Riel

Louis Riel is Canada's best-known example of a charismatic leader. On 8 December 1875 he experienced a mystical illumination that convinced him he was the "Prophet of the New World." He saw himself as endowed by God with a personal mission to create a new religion in North America, in which his people, the Métis, would be a chosen people like the Hebrews. Riel wanted the Métis to adopt certain Old Testament practices such as polygamy and the Saturday sabbath; these would eventually be merged with a revised version of Roman Catholicism. Riel preached this novel doctrine to the Métis at Batoche during the North-West Rebellion of 1885. The rebels formed a sort of provisional government, but Riel did not hold office in it—he preferred to be recognized as a prophet. Each morning he assembled the Métis forces to tell them of the divine revelations he had received during the night.

He promised his followers that God would work a miracle to defeat the expeditionary force sent by the government of Canada.

The miracle did not happen and the uprising was crushed. Riel was later convicted of high treason. He went to the scaffold believing that he, like Christ, would rise from the dead on the third day after his hanging. His execution served as a form of martyrdom that ensured his reputation would persist and grow across subsequent generations of history.

In eastern Canada, Riel seemed like a madman, and in fact his friends and relatives in Montreal had him committed to a lunatic asylum in the years 1876–78. But the Métis saw him as charismatic. His inspiration played off the desperation of the buffalo-hunting Métis, who were being increasingly marginalized by the opening of the Canadian West to agricultural immigration and economic development.

The term *charisma* is also often applied in a looser sense to politicians who have never made claims such as those of Louis Riel or Joan of Arc. The best recent example is Barack Obama in his 2008 campaign for the American presidency. Young, well-educated, and an eloquent orator, he stirred up unusual adulation on the campaign trail, with a particular attraction to young people. His exotic ancestry (a father from Kenya and a mother from Kansas) helped contribute to the perception that he was not cut from ordinary cloth. He deliberately used slogans—such as "Yes we can" and "We are the change that we have been looking for"—that heightened expectation that things would be fundamentally different if he were elected. He enjoyed a type of adulation usually reserved for movie stars, rock musicians, and professional athletes (see Historical Perspectives 2.2), though he never claimed to be anything more than an officeholder in a structure of legal authority. Certainly he never claimed a right to rule on the basis of divine inspiration or a world-historical mission. If political leaders such as Obama are to be called charismatic, it should be remembered that this is a looser use of the term than when it is applied to genuinely charismatic authorities such as Louis Riel.

Historical Perspectives 2.2

"Crush on Obama"

In 2007, when Barack Obama was running against Hillary Clinton for the Democratic presidential nomination, a saucy video titled "I've Got a Crush on Obama" was posted on YouTube. It featured an amply endowed, scantily clad young woman singing seductively of her love for Obama. Although Obama repudiated it and said it had hurt his daughters' feelings, it quickly went viral. It caught on because it captured in a semi-humorous, semi-serious way the charismatic effect that Obama had on many Americans.

The video is still on YouTube and can be found by searching for "Crush on Obama." Check it out or, better yet, ask your professor to play it for group discussion if your classroom has an Internet connection.

Charisma, like authority in general, is not a thing that a leader has; it is a social relationship based on the followers' perception of the legitimacy of the leader's claims. The most important question is not how Joan of Arc, Louis Riel, or Adolf Hitler could utter such extraordinary claims about themselves, but how they could find such a receptive audience. The short answer is that charismatic leaders are accorded legitimacy in times of crisis or grave unrest, when other forms of authority appear to have failed. Joan of Arc came to the rescue of France during the Hundred Years' War, at a time when England had the upper hand and France was in danger of being conquered. The traditional authority of the French monarch seemed incapable of meeting the challenge. Riel preached his radical gospel to the Métis at a time when the disappearance of the buffalo and the replacement of ox-trains by railways and steamboats threatened to destroy the Métis way of life. It was a challenge that the traditional Métis authorities—the patriarchs of the clans—were helpless to meet. Hitler came to power during a turbulent phase of German history. The traditional authority of the Kaiser had been destroyed by Germany's defeat in World War I, and the legal authority of the Weimar Republic, never deeply rooted, was gravely shaken by runaway inflation in the early 1920s and the international depression of the early 1930s. Driven to desperation, the German people, particularly the middle class, listened eagerly to Hitler's promises of salvation.

Similar considerations apply to Barack Obama, even if he did not make the type of claims made by true charismatic leaders. In 2007–08, the United States was embroiled in unpopular wars in Afghanistan and Iraq, the housing market had collapsed, and then the stock market fell dramatically in October 2008 as the so-called Great Recession began. There was a strong sense of political and economic crisis in the country throughout the presidential campaign.

If charisma is a response to crisis, it is difficult to see how it can be very long-lasting. As stability is restored, we would expect a return to traditional or legal authority. Weber was well aware of this tendency, which he called the "routinization of charisma."[8] The more success prophets or leaders have in creating a following, the more either they or their followers find it necessary to create an enduring structure of authority that can exist over generations. If Riel had been successful in the North-West Rebellion, he would eventually have had to take on some role other than prophet. Once the Shah was overthrown, Khomeini approved a new Iranian constitution that institutionalized and regularized the authority of the Islamic jurists, who have carried on since his death. And by the time of the congressional elections of 2010, observers were remarking how ordinary and human President Obama seemed as he tried to cope with the difficulties of his office. Political history seems to alternate short, intense upheavals of charismatic authority with longer periods of normalcy.

Questions for Discussion

1. Some people talk about hunger, poverty, and disease as forms of violence directed against the poor. Would you agree or disagree with extending the concept of violence to cover these things? Why or why not?

2. The traditional model of authority presents government as a sort of extended family. Based on your experience, what similarities and differences do you perceive between government and the family?

3. Politicians and rock stars can both be said to be charismatic. What do they have in common? How does this usage differ from the original way the term was used?

Internet Links

1. "Charismatic authority": Use this as a search term. The Internet will give you dozens of discussions of the subject, in both general and specific contexts.

2. Nelson Education Ltd. Political Science Resource Centre: **www.polisci.nelson.com.** Links to studies of political violence.

3. Stanford Encyclopedia of Philosophy: Much of this chapter is based on the work of Max Weber. For an informative site on Weber, visit **http://plato.stanford.edu/ entries/weber/.** The page also contains other useful links to pages on Weber.

Further Reading

Aberbach, David. *Charisma in Politics, Religion and the Media: Private Trauma, Public Ideals.* New York: New York University Press, 1996.

Beetham, David. *The Legitimation of Power.* London: Macmillan, 1991.

Chemers, Martin M., and Roya Ayman, eds. *Leadership Theory and Research: Perspectives and Directions.* San Diego, CA: Academic Press, 1993.

Dowding, Keith. *Power*. Minneapolis: University of Minnesota Press, 1996.

Franck, Thomas M. *The Power of Legitimacy among Nations*. New York: Oxford University Press, 1990.

Harris, Paul, ed. *On Political Obligation*. London: Routledge, 1990.

Hurd, Ian. *After Anarchy: Legitimacy and Power in the United Nations Security Council*. Princeton, NJ: Princeton University Press, 2007.

Jaffe, Erwin. *Healing the Body Politic: Rediscovering Political Power*. Westport, CT: Praeger, 1993.

Kittrie, Nicholas N. *The War Against Authority: From the Crisis of Legitimacy to a New Social Contract*. Baltimore: Johns Hopkins University Press, 1998.

Lukes, Steven. *Power: A Radical View*. 2nd ed. London: Palgrave Macmillan, 2005.

Madsen, Douglas, and Peter G. Snow. *The Charismatic Bond: Political Behavior in Time of Crisis*. Cambridge, MA: Harvard University Press, 1991.

Mumford, Michael D. *Pathways to Outstanding Leadership: A Comparative Analysis of Charismatic, Ideological, and Pragmatic Leaders*. Philadelphia: Lawrence Erlbaum Associates, 2006.

Nelson, Daniel N. *After Authoritarianism: Democracy or Disorder?* Westport, CT: Greenwood Press, 1995.

Pfeffer, Jeffrey. *Managing with Power: Politics and Influence in Organizations*. Cambridge, MA: Harvard Business School Press, 1992.

Potts, John. *A History of Charisma*. New York: Palgrave Macmillan, 2009.

Raz, Joseph, ed. *Authority*. Oxford: Blackwell, 1990.

———. *The Authority of Law: Essays on Law and Morality*. 2nd ed. Oxford: Oxford University Press, 2009.

Russell, Bertrand. Power: *A New Social Analysis*. New York: Routledge, 2004.

Waldron, Jeremy. *Law and Disagreement*. New York: Oxford University Press, 1999.

Zartman, I. William, ed. *Collapsed States: The Disintegration and Restoration of Legitimate Authority*. Boulder, CO: Lynne Rienner, 1995.

CHAPTER 3
Sovereignty, State, and Citizenship

SOVEREIGNTY

The term **sovereign,** derived from the Latin *super*, meaning "above," literally denotes one who is superior. Human beings naturally associate superiority with the physical quality of elevation. We put kings and queens on high thrones to make them taller, and we picture God, the highest of all authorities, as living in the heavens above the earth. Conversely, we lower ourselves to recognize authority. We bow or curtsy when we address royalty, and we kneel or even prostrate ourselves when we pray.

Sovereignty was first used in its modern sense by the French author Jean Bodin toward the end of the sixteenth century. Writing at a time of fierce wars between Catholics and Protestants, Bodin sought to obtain civil peace by establishing the king as the supreme authority whose will could decide such disputes. Bodin's idea was that in any community there ought to be a single highest authority who is not subject to other human authority. He wrote in *Six livres de la république* (1576) that "sovereignty is the absolute and perpetual power of a commonwealth. The sovereign Prince is only accountable to God … Sovereignty is not limited with respect to power, scope, or duration … The Prince is the image of God."[1]

Bodin, who was a student of Roman law, was trying to revive the idea of centralized power in an age when it did not exist or existed only in an imperfect way. To understand why this was so, we must recall some facts about the feudal society of medieval Europe. Everyone was subject to a feudal overlord, but there was no effective pyramid of authority with the monarch at its peak. For all practical purposes, the nobles were often autonomous, as were many city-states in Italy and along the Rhine. The pope exercised a claim to rule in religious matters through his bishops. The Church maintained its own system of ecclesiastical courts; it even had the power to gather taxes, by which means money flowed to Rome. Nowhere was there a single sovereign—a highest authority—and, indeed, except for the authority of God, the concept did not exist. This helps to explain why the religious wars of the Protestant Reformation were so protracted. Various nobles gave their support to one side or the other and there was no effective central power to keep them all in check. Bodin's idea of the sovereign took hold at a time of revulsion against this warfare and became well established in the seventeenth and eighteenth centuries. This was the age of *absolute monarchs*—so called not because they could do whatever they pleased but because there was no human authority superior to theirs.

However, it is less the person than the power that is of interest here. Sovereignty is the authority to override all other authorities. Family, employer, church—all social authorities—must yield to the sovereign's power when it is turned in their direction. More concretely, sovereignty is a bundle of powers associated with the highest authority of government. One is the power to enforce rules of conduct—by establishing tribunals, compensating victims, punishing offenders, and so on—and includes the power of life and death. Another is the power to make law; that is, to create new law, amend existing law, and repeal old law. Sovereignty also includes control of all the normal executive functions of government such as raising revenue, maintaining armed forces, minting currency, and providing other services to society. In the British tradition sovereignty also implies an underlying ownership of all land. Private ownership of land "in fee simple" is a form of legal delegation from the sovereign, who can reclaim any parcel of land through expropriation. In Canada, compensation to the private owner is mandated by legislation but not required by the constitution. Finally, sovereignty always means the power to deal with the sovereigns of other communities, as well as the right to exercise domestic rule free from interference by other sovereigns.

Sovereignty was exercised by individual sovereigns in the Age of Absolutism, in the seventeenth and eighteenth centuries, but it can also be placed in the hands of a small group or an entire people. In England, the Stuarts' claims to absolute monarchy were decisively defeated by Parliament in the Glorious Revolution of 1688. This victory ultimately led to the theory of **parliamentary sovereignty**, articulated by William Blackstone in his *Commentaries on the Laws of England* (1765–69). Blackstone held that the supreme authority in England was Parliament, defined as the Commons, Lords, and Crown acting together under certain procedures.

Parliamentary sovereignty is still the main principle of the British constitution. It means that Parliament may make or repeal whatever laws it chooses; one Parliament cannot bind its successors in any way. Parliament is still the highest court in the land and cannot be overruled by the judiciary. The executive authority of government symbolized by the Crown can be exercised only by ministers who are responsible to Parliament.

A century ago, A. V. Dicey, one of the greatest British constitutional experts, claimed facetiously that "Parliament can do anything except make a man into a woman." The invention of sex-change surgery has now removed even that limitation! However, in other ways Parliament has conceded some of its sovereignty in recent years. By entering into the European Union (EU), Britain has voluntarily subjected itself to decisions of the EU bureaucracy and the European Court of Justice. Britain could leave the EU, but as long as it remains a member, the sovereignty of Parliament is functionally limited.

While Blackstone was developing the theory of parliamentary sovereignty, the French philosopher Jean-Jacques Rousseau's book *The Social Contract* (1762) set forth the great alternative of **popular sovereignty.** Rousseau taught that supreme authority resided in the people themselves and could not be delegated. Laws should be made by the people meeting in direct-democratic fashion, not by electing representatives to legislate for them (indirect democracy). "The people of England," wrote Rousseau, "deceive themselves when they fancy they are free; they are so, in fact, only during the election of members of Parliament: for, as soon as a new one is elected, they are again in chains, and are nothing."[2]

Because Rousseau's ideal of direct democracy is extremely difficult to attain in a commonwealth of any great size, subsequent writers have kept alive the notion of popular sovereignty by softening the definition. For example, the American Declaration of Independence (1776) states that governments derive "their just powers from the consent of the governed." This moderate formulation of popular sovereignty, which stresses consent rather than direct rule, underlies modern representative democracy.

The three alternatives of personal, parliamentary, and popular sovereignty are not mutually exclusive. All three have to be examined to explain the present reality of, for example, British government. Queen Elizabeth II is still sovereign in the symbolic sense that she represents the power of the state; she "reigns but does not rule," as the saying goes. Parliament is legally sovereign in its control over legislation and all aspects of government, but Parliament does not exist in a political vacuum. The most important part of Parliament is the House of Commons, whose members are elected by the people at large. Interpreters of the British system argue that popular sovereignty exists in the political sense that Parliament depends on public support. If Parliament uses its legal sovereignty in a way that runs counter to public opinion, the people will elect new members to the House of Commons when the opportunity arises. In the long run, popular sovereignty is as much a fact of British politics as is parliamentary sovereignty.

The British situation is complex, and the Canadian one even more so. Canada has a heritage of representative democracy based on the British model, and Canadians share the same balance of personal, parliamentary, and popular sovereignty. The Queen is the sovereign of Canada, as she is of Great Britain and of some other members of the Commonwealth, and Canada has a legally sovereign Parliament whose political composition is determined by a voting population. But Canada's political system also divides power among levels of government. The national Parliament and the provincial legislatures all have a share of sovereign lawmaking power. The provinces, for example, have control of education but cannot issue money or raise an army. The government of Canada controls trade and commerce but not property and civil rights, which are provincial matters. In other words, Canadian sovereignty is divided, not concentrated. This arrangement is vastly different from Bodin's original conception of sovereignty as a single, undivided centre of power.

The same is true in the United States, where sovereign power is also divided among levels of government. A further complexity of the American constitution is that the president, who is the chief executive officer, must cooperate with Congress in order to make law, wage war, and perform other governmental acts.

Sovereignty may also be delegated to administrative agencies or even private bodies. Marketing boards enforcing production quotas, professional associations licensing practitioners, corporations exploiting mineral rights obtained from the Crown, and trade unions requiring all employees to abide by a collective agreement are exercising a small, delegated share of sovereignty. Much of modern politics consists of a competitive struggle among organized groups to get the government to delegate a share of sovereign power to them, so that they may use it to benefit their members.

Clearly, Bodin's original desire to locate sovereignty entirely in one place has not been fully realized. The bundle of sovereign powers that exists conceptually may be divided among different hands. Some fragmentation of power helps to ensure that sovereignty is exercised within the rules established by the constitution. It is perhaps better for a free society that power be divided in this way, for concentrated, unopposed power is a standing temptation to abuse by those who wield it.

It might even be best to abandon the concept of sovereignty altogether for purposes of domestic politics and to admit that no person or group is sovereign in the original sense of the term. Metaphorically, we might say that the constitution is sovereign; that is, that all political power is constrained by constitutional rules that establish and limit the exercise of public authority. Different authorities exercise sovereign power at different moments in the political process: the people in voting for candidates to office, parliamentarians in voting on legislation, the head of state in giving assent to legislation. Each exercise of power takes place within constitutional limits, so that no one group or person is sovereign in the original sense.

However, even if sovereignty is internally constrained, divided, and delegated within the state, it still makes sense to inquire whether a government is able to control a certain population on a given territory, free from interference by other governments. This is actually the most frequent use of the term today—that is, to denote autonomy from outside control in international affairs. Sovereignty in this sense is claimed by all governments and recognized by international law.

THE STATE

The preceding discussion of sovereignty makes it possible to develop the concept of **state**, which has been mentioned previously but not fully explained. A state is defined by the joint presence of three factors: population, territory, and sovereignty. A state exists when a sovereign power effectively rules over a population residing within the boundaries of a fixed territory. As the sociologist Max Weber put it, "a state is a human community that (successfully) claims the *monopoly of* the *legitimate use of physical force* within a given territory" [Weber's emphasis].[3]

Canada is a state, as are Great Britain and France. Quebec, on the other hand, is not a full-fledged state in this sense; it has people and territory but not a sovereign government (except to the limited extent to which a province in the Canadian system has a share of sovereignty). It is the program of the Bloc Québécois and the Parti Québécois to turn Quebec into a state by attaining full sovereignty, but that is a project for the future, not a current reality.

International Perspectives 3.1

The Failed State of Somalia

Somalia, strategically located on the Horn of Africa, has been without an effective national government since civil war broke out in 1991. The so-called transitional federal government enjoys international recognition but it best controls only the capital, Mogadishu. Two parts of the country, Somaliland and Puntland, have declared themselves to be autonomous but have not achieved international recognition. The Islamist al-Shabaab movement, related to al-Qaeda, controls much of Somalia's territory. The lack of effective sovereignty explains why piracy based in Somalia continues to flourish. Most of the world's major nations have sent warships to patrol the waters off Somalia, but they have been unable to stamp out piracy. Another consequence of state failure in Somalia is famine, which began in earnest in 2011 after years of drought. Al-Shabaab has often blocked the delivery of relief by international organizations, fearing that foreign aid might interfere with its control of territory.

The state is the universal form of political organization in the modern world. The earth's entire land mass, with the exception of Antarctica, is divided into territories under the control of sovereign states. At the time of writing, 193 states are members of the United Nations. It is difficult to say precisely how many states there are in total, because of certain anomalous cases. Some mini-states such as Monaco, Andorra, and San Marino do not carry on a full range of relationships with other states; their foreign policy is conducted by larger neighbours. Other difficult cases include *governments-in-exile*, states that lack universal recognition—for example, Taiwan—and puppet or buffer states. Also important are **failed states,** such as Somalia, which have an apparatus of government but have lost the ability to effectively control the territory over which they claim sovereignty (see International Perspectives 3.1). Various states claim portions of Antarctica, but the claims conflict and have never been resolved. Despite all this, we tend to take the state for granted as the only conceivable form of political organization, even though the combination of people, territory, and sovereignty that we call the state is, historically speaking, a fairly recent invention.

Governmental processes in tribal societies are carried on without the state form of organization. Like hunting societies, the earliest agricultural societies were also **stateless**. Farming took place in autonomous villages that could handle their collective affairs without a specialized machinery of government. How, then, did the state arise? The answer almost certainly lies in warfare. Armed clashes between hunting tribes do not lead to the formation of a state as long as the losers can migrate to new hunting grounds; roughly the same is true of primitive agriculturalists, as long as arable land is available. But where new land is not readily accessible, warfare produces a social hierarchy of victors and vanquished that is enforced by coercion. A specialized state machinery of armies, courts, tax gatherers, and other officials evolves as the conquerors enrich themselves at the expense of the conquered.[4] When a strong monarch consolidates conquered territory, the state form of organization emerges.

Research in anthropology and human biology has stressed that reproductive competition was interwoven with competition for land and other resources in the rise of the early states.[5] Tribes victorious in warfare commonly killed or enslaved the men seized among their conquered opponents while making wives or concubines of the captured women. Chiefs and headmen used their power to take and support a larger number of wives. Early states were almost all characterized by polygamy in the upper classes, with kings and powerful noblemen maintaining harems of remarkable size. The Hebrew king Solomon reputedly had 700 wives and 300 concubines.[6]

Once created, the state was a powerful and expansive force. It easily prevailed over neighbouring agricultural communities if these had not formed their own states. It found tougher opposition in warlike nomads, who at times overran even territorial states, as happened often in the history of Europe and Asia. Over thousands of years, tribe after tribe of invaders from the steppes of Eurasia descended upon the empires of China, India, the Middle East, and Europe. Often the conquerors did not destroy the state; rather, they took it over and installed themselves as rulers, and they were sometimes able to extend the state's territories. At other times, the conquest was such a shock that the state machinery deteriorated and required a long period to be rebuilt.

The modern European states arose from such an interregnum after invasions by Germans and other peoples destroyed the highly developed Roman Empire. The invaders installed themselves as rulers in medieval Europe but did not initially create a full-fledged state system. There were rudimentary specialized structures of government, but territorial boundaries between authorities were not clear. The Norman conquest of England in 1066 led to a situation that seems bizarre by today's standards. For hundreds of years England's Norman kings were nominally feudal vassals of the French kings, because they still had important territorial holdings in France. The Roman Catholic Church in all parts of Europe carried on activities, such as raising revenue and conducting court trials, which today would be considered governmental. The political history of modern times is the history of the emergence of separate, sovereign states out of the overlapping, interlocking jurisdictions of medieval Europe. For more on the development of European states, see Historical Perspectives 3.1.

CITIZENSHIP

Remember that the state is defined as a sovereign authority exercising a legitimate monopoly of physical force as it rules over a population inhabiting a fixed territory. Just as the legal boundaries of the state mark the limits of its territory, so the concept

Historical Perspectives 3.1

The Development of European States

The development of the state runs like a thread through the familiar epochs into which Western history is customarily divided. Although the subject is far too big for a complete discussion here, we can at least mention some of the main stages.

During the Renaissance (in the fifteenth and sixteenth centuries) there was a great revival of interest in classical antiquity. Knowledge of Latin and Greek became more widespread, and many forgotten works of art, literature, and science were recovered. This revival culminated in *humanism*, one of the great contributions of the Renaissance. One consequence of this was a heightened knowledge of Roman law, whose concept of *imperium* helped clear the way for sovereignty. Legal advisers trained in Roman law guided monarchs toward assertion of centralized control over their territories.

The Reformation (in the sixteenth and seventeenth centuries) broke the political power of the Roman Catholic Church. In England and parts of Germany, new Protestant churches were created that were firmly subordinated to the state. (The Queen is still head of the Church of England, for example.) In countries such as France and Spain, which remained Roman Catholic, church administration was shorn of independent political power and the pope lost the ability to intervene in internal political disputes. Another aspect of the Reformation—the increased use of vernacular languages rather than Latin—strengthened the developing states of Europe by fostering the notion of

a different official language for each state. The dialect of Paris became the language of France, the "King's English" became the standard speech of Britain, and so on.

The Enlightenment (in the eighteenth century) saw a relaxation of religious tensions. Exhausted by more than a century of religious warfare, people turned their energies to secular matters. Science and philosophy flourished under the patronage of kings, who founded institutions such as the Royal Society of London to promote the advancement of learning. Scepticism, science, and individual freedom contributed to the development of the name by which the Enlightenment is best known: the Age of Reason. Hope and optimism became the qualities of a civilization that perceived itself as peaceful and reasonable.

Interestingly, the Enlightenment in its political aspect is often known as the Age of Absolutism. The European continent was now more or less clearly divided into territorial states ruled by strong monarchs, who established standing armies, court systems, and police forces and in other ways developed a virtual monopoly of law enforcement and armed coercion. Further, they founded a professional bureaucracy that was capable of raising money through taxes and of offering public services to the population, such as the construction of harbours and highways and the promotion of agriculture. It was in the

(continued)

eighteenth century that the state first took on a shape we would recognize if we could return to that era.

There was an important contradiction between the political thought of the Enlightenment, which was generally individualistic, and the political practices of that age, which were absolutist and monarchical. "*L'état c'est moi* [I am the State]," said Louis XIV, emphasizing his personal sovereignty. In England this contradiction had been partly resolved through the establishment of parliamentary sovereignty in 1688. On the continent of Europe the revolution was delayed for a century and was correspondingly more violent when it came. The year 1789 saw a popular uprising against the French monarchy that proved to be the beginning of the end of personal sovereignty and traditional authority. Since then, all the great royal dynasties have been overthrown or made merely symbolic, as in Britain. Yet the age of popular revolutions did not abolish the states created by the absolute monarchs; on the contrary, it extended and perfected those states. Modern governments control armies, police, and bureaucracies that Louis XIV could never have imagined.

of citizenship marks its demographic boundaries. The modern state is not just an organized structure of governmental power; it is also an association of members. **Citizenship** is membership in the state.

When the concept of citizenship first arose in the world of the classical *polis*, its meaning was somewhat different than it is today. Citizenship in the *polis* meant the right to participate in public affairs, to vote and hold public office; it was restricted to a minority of those residing in the city. Only free adult males—not slaves, women, or children—could be citizens. Also, ancient cities typically contained large numbers of resident aliens who lived and worked in the city but did not possess citizenship unless it was granted as a special favour.

Modern citizenship, in contrast, is universal. Citizens are not a special category within the state; they are the state. The essential feature of modern universal citizenship is the right to live within the territorial boundaries of the state. In Canada this is now protected by Section 6 of the Canadian Charter of Rights and Freedoms: "Every citizen of Canada has the right to enter, remain in and leave Canada." Non-citizens require special permission to become permanent residents, and as long as they do not become citizens, they can be deported for reasons such as having entered the country under false pretences or being convicted of a serious criminal offence.

Beyond this minimal right of residence, modern citizenship has also come to include and universalize the classical notion of the right to participate in politics. This happened by degrees as the rights to vote and run for office were gradually extended to women as well as to men who were not property owners. Today, except in a very few countries where democratic institutions do not exist, political rights are seen as an attribute of citizenship. The relationship is protected in Section 3 of the Canadian Charter of Rights and Freedoms: "Every citizen of Canada has the right to vote in an election of members of the House of Commons or of a legislative assembly and to be qualified for membership therein." Many other imputed attributes of citizenship, both rights and obligations, also appear in public discussion. People often speak of the payment of taxes, military service, reception of economic benefits, and freedom from discrimination as if these things were part of citizenship, but there is in fact considerable variation in these matters among political communities. They are not nearly as universal as the right of residence and the right to participate in politics.

There is also a great deal of variation in the rules that different communities use to determine who is qualified for citizenship, either by birth or by **naturalization,** the procedure by which an adult is granted citizenship. Amid all the variations, however, one can discern two basic principles, known by their Latin names: ***jus soli*** (right of soil) and ***jus sanguinis*** (right of blood). According to *jus soli*, which is the basic principle of citizenship law in the United Kingdom, France, Canada, the United States, and most other states in the New World, anyone born within the boundaries of the state automatically becomes a citizen. Thus women from Mexico occasionally go to great lengths to have their baby born during a visit to the United States, so that the child will be able to claim citizenship, including the right of residence, at the age of eighteen. In much of Europe, in contrast, the basic principle is *jus sanguinis* (right of blood), which means that only the children of citizens acquire citizenship by birth.[7] In Germany, which is quite strict in applying *jus sanguinis*, millions of Turkish and other foreign workers do not have German citizenship even though they were born in Germany. Most states have elements of both *jus soli* and *jus sanguinis* in their citizenship law, but the balance may be tilted quite far toward one side or the other.

The category of Canadian citizenship did not exist until 1 January 1947, when the first Citizenship Act came into effect. Prior to that time, the key status was that of "British subject," which supposedly carried with it not only the right to vote but also the right to live anywhere within the British Commonwealth (in practice, immigration to Canada from non-white countries such as India was restricted to almost nothing). Before 1947, residents of Britain, Australia, and New Zealand could without limitation immigrate to Canada whenever they chose and could vote or run for office immediately upon taking up residence; Canadians had the same right to move to those countries and exercise political rights. The establishment of a separate Canadian citizenship was an important step in the emergence of a Canadian state distinct from the rest of the British Commonwealth. Canadian Focus 3.1 provides a guide to the types of Canadian citizenship.

As a summary, let us link together the four key concepts that have been discussed thus far: society, state, politics, and government. *Society* is the voluntary, spontaneously emerging order of relationships in which we coexist with and serve the needs of one another. It is what makes possible human comfort and even survival. The *state* is the community organized and armed with coercive power to protect the social order from internal disruption and external attack, and to provide certain public services to the

---

Canadian Focus 3.1

Canadian Citizenship

According to the Citizenship Act, the following categories of people are deemed Canadian citizens:

- A person born in Canada (*jus soli*).
- A person born outside of Canada if at least one parent is a Canadian citizen (*jus sanguinis*). Such people lose their Canadian citizenship unless they apply for it and live in Canada for a year before they become 28.

- An immigrant who, after living in Canada for three of the past four years, applies for citizenship, demonstrates knowledge of French or English, and passes a test of knowledge about Canada (*naturalization*). Dependent children receive citizenship along with their parents.

---

community. *Government* is the decision-making structure and process of the state, while *politics* is the never-ending struggle for support in the public realm. Social factions put pressure on public authorities, hoping to influence their decisions in certain ways, and provide support if the desired decisions are made.

Although the concepts of state and government overlap to a considerable extent, there is a subtle distinction of emphasis between them. Government is the process of decision-making and the structure of offices that sustain the process. The state is the entire territorial community, organized for collective action through its government. The state is a more abstract and permanent entity. Governments come and go as politicians and civil servants change in office, but the state remains, unless it is destroyed through civil war, conquest, or annexation by another state.

Questions for Discussion

1. Economists often speak of "consumer sovereignty," by which they mean that, in a competitive market, producers will be able to sell only those goods and services that consumers are willing to pay for. Compare this to the meaning of *sovereignty* as used in the study of government and politics. Do you see any important differences?

2. Politicians in Quebec routinely refer to their provincial government as *"l'état du Québec* [the Quebec state]." How does this way of speaking differ from the definition of state offered in this chapter?

3. Under current law, Canadians can hold dual citizenship. Do you think this lessens one's commitment to Canada? Regardless of your personal view, what advantages and disadvantages do you see in allowing dual citizenship?

Internet Links

1. Bloc Québécois: **www.blocquebecois.org**, and Parti Québécois: **www.pq.org**. These two sites will give you access to documents explaining Quebec separatists' understanding of sovereignty.

2. Citizenship and Immigration Canada: **www.cic.gc.ca**. Gateway to information about Canadian citizenship.

3. Dual Citizenship FAQ: **www.richw.org/dualcit**. Highly informative, non-technical source of information about dual citizenship in United States law. This could be of practical significance to you if you are one of the many Canadians who would like to work in the United States or who have an American family background. The author is now updating his FAQs on Wikipedia.

4. Failed States Index: **http://www.foreignpolicy.com/failedstates**. Published annually by the American think-tank Fund for Peace and the magazine *Foreign Policy*, the index ranks failed states based on social, economic, and political indicators.

5. United Nations: **www.un.org**. By following the links, you can get an up-to-date list of member states (193 at time of writing).

Further Reading

Albo, Gregory, David Langille, and Leo Panitch. *A Different Kind of State? Popular Power and Democratic Administration.* Toronto: Oxford University Press, 1993.

Boyer, Pierre, Linda Cardinal, and David Headon, eds. *From Subjects to Citizens: A Hundred Years of Citizenship in Australia and Canada.* Toronto: University of Toronto Press, 2004.

Camilleri, Joseph. *The End of Sovereignty? The Politics of a Shrinking and Fragmenting World.* Aldershot, UK: Elgar, 1992.

Courchene, Thomas J., and Donald J. Savoie. *Art of the State: Governance in a World Without Frontiers.* Montreal: Institute for Research on Public Policy, 2003.

Elkins, David J. *Beyond Sovereignty: Territory and Political Economy in the Twenty-first Century.* Toronto: University of Toronto Press, 1995.

Esberey, Joy E., and L. W. Johnston. *Democracy and the State: An Introduction to Politics.* Peterborough, ON: Broadview Press, 1994.

Gidengil, Elisabeth, André Blais, Neil Nevitte, and Richard Nadeau. *Citizens.* Vancouver: University of British Columbia Press, 2004.

Gill, Graeme. *The Nature and Development of the Modern State.* London: Palgrave Macmillan, 2003.

Godfrey, Sima, and Frank Unger, eds. *The Shifting Foundations of Modern Nation-States: Realignments of Belonging.* Toronto: University of Toronto Press, 2004.

Greven, Michael Th., and Louis W. Pauly, eds. *Democracy Beyond the State? The European Dilemma and the Emerging Global Order.* Lanham, MD: Rowman & Littlefield, 2000.

Guehenno, Jean-Marie. *The End of the Nation-State.* Translated by Victoria Elliott. Minneapolis: University of Minnesota Press, 1995.

Harding, Alan. "The Origins of the Concept of the State," *History of Political Thought* 15 (Spring 1994).

Harmes, Adam. *The Return of the State: Protestors, Power-Brokers and the New Global Compromise.* Vancouver: Douglas & McIntyre, 2004.

Held, David. *Democracy and the Global Order: From the Modern State to Cosmopolitan Governance.* Stanford, CA: Stanford University Press, 1995.

———. *Models of Democracy.* 3rd ed. Cambridge, UK: Polity Press, 2006.

Keohane, Robert O., ed. *Power and Governance in a Partially Globalized World.* New York: Routledge, 2002.

Magocsi, Paul Robert. *The End of the Nation-State? The Revolution of 1989 and the Future of Europe.* Kingston, ON: Kashtan Press, 1994.

Pierson, Christopher. *The Modern State.* New York: Routledge, 2004.

Poggi, Gianfranco. *The State: Its Nature, Development, and Prospects.* Stanford, CA: Stanford University Press, 1990.

Sorell, Tom, and Luc Foisneau, eds. *Leviathan after 350 Years.* New York: Oxford University Press, 2004.

CHAPTER 4
The Nation

What we described in the previous chapter as the modern, legal, participatory state, many authors prefer to call the **nation-state**. The word *nation* is added to *state* to emphasize that the state is participatory—that it is an association of citizens, not just an organized system of power within a certain territory. For reasons that will become clear later in this chapter, the term *nation-state* raises all sorts of problems in Canada, and we prefer to use it sparingly. However, the term is widely employed in political science, and you will undoubtedly encounter it many times. Why does the word *nation* have these connotations of voluntary consent and active participation when it is added to *state*?

First of all, *nation* can be almost a synonym for *state*. The United Nations is an organization to which only states can belong, which means that bodies such as the Palestine Liberation Organization can have only observer status. Could the United Nations just as well have been called the United States if that name had not already been taken by our southern neighbour? Probably not, for "United States" suggests an association of governments, whereas "United Nations" suggests an association of the peoples of the world. They may communicate with each other through their governments, but if the term means anything, they are also involved as peoples.

This brings us to the nub of the issue. There are social realities called nations that are conceptually distinct from states. Typical nations are the Americans, the French, and the Germans. Who exactly are the Germans? They are not simply those who speak the German language, for German is also spoken in Austria and parts of Switzerland, Luxembourg, and Belgium. Nor can the Germans be identified with reference to a single state, for after the Second World War there were two German states—the German Democratic Republic (East Germany) and the Federal Republic of Germany (West Germany)—which did not merge until 1990. Nor is religion the explanation, for the Germans are about equally divided between Protestants and Catholics.

The French writer Ernest Renan explored this topic in 1882 in a well-known essay, "Qu'est-ce qu'une nation? [What Is a Nation?]". He wrote:

> A nation is a soul, a spiritual principle ... A nation is a great solidarity, created by the sentiment of the sacrifices which have been made and of those which one is disposed to make in the future. It presupposes a past; but it resumes itself in the present by a tangible fact: the consent, the clearly expressed desire to continue life in common. The existence of a nation is a plebiscite of every day, as the existence of the individual is a perpetual affirmation of life.[1]

In more contemporary language, we would say that a **nation** is an identity shared by a large number of people based on, but not reducible to, objective factors such as common race, language, religion, customs, and government.

The nation, like the participatory state, is a product of modern European history. It did not exist in medieval Europe. People in that era thought of themselves in both broader and narrower terms: on the one hand as Christians or subjects of the Holy Roman Empire, on the other in terms of limited local identities. The first discernible nations to emerge were the English, French, and Spanish, and in each instance the pattern was similar. A strong monarchy established a stable territorial state, within which local identities were merged over centuries into a wider national identity. The language of the royal court became current throughout the realm while local dialects were marginalized or even suppressed. The monarch's religion was made a state religion, and nonconforming groups were stripped of power or even expelled (Huguenots from France, Jews and Moors from Spain). Social disparities between the nobility and the common people were gradually reduced as the monarchy, employing many commoners in its official service, stripped away the privileges of the aristocracy. The estates of medieval society—nobility, clergy, freemen, and serfs—were levelled into the single category of citizens. Out of this sometimes brutal exercise of state power emerged nations conscious of a common identity and destiny. Events in France after the revolution of 1789 indicate the emergence of the French nation. With the king overthrown and Austria and Prussia—the traditional enemies of France—threatening war, the French rose to defend *la nation française*. With the introduction of military conscription, huge armies of citizen-soldiers overran Europe, defeating the professional and mercenary armies of other states.

It was the French Revolution more than anything else that awakened the spirit of nationality in Europe. Other peoples began to think of themselves as nations, even though they were not associated with a single strong state like the French or the English. The Italians and the Germans, for example, had lived for centuries divided among many large and small states. Now movements of unification began, which eventually resulted in the formation of the Kingdom of Italy (1861) and the German Empire (1871). Other peoples, such as the Irish and the Greeks, who had long been ruled by foreign masters began to assert their nationhood in popular uprisings. One of the great themes of European history since 1789 has been the emergence of nations demanding their own nation-states. The process is now largely complete in Western Europe, though a few small groups, such as the Basques, Scots, and Bretons, remain submerged minorities. A striking political phenomenon of recent decades has been the "mini-nationalism" of such small groups—their attempts to assert themselves as full-fledged nations, even to the point of demanding political independence.[2] For a discussion of nation and state in Eastern Europe, see World View 4.1.

Colonization also created new nations elsewhere in the world. European immigrants flocked to the United States, Canada, Australia, New Zealand, and Latin America. In different ways and at different times, these nations gained independence, and political

World View 4.1

Nation and State in Eastern Europe

Until the First World War, Eastern Europe was controlled by four multinational empires—the German, Russian, Austro-Hungarian, and Ottoman. With the Peace of Versailles (1919), the victorious Allied powers broke up these empires with the announced purpose of creating nation-states. But demographic reality did not correspond to political aspiration. None of the peoples of Eastern Europe lived in neatly bounded territories; centuries of conquest and migration had produced a colourful checkerboard of diverse peoples. Hence all the new nation-states, from Poland on the Baltic Sea through Yugoslavia on the Mediterranean to Bulgaria on the Black Sea, contained large and often unhappy minorities.

At enormous human cost, the Second World War led to the "solution" of some of these minority problems, particularly in the northern part of the region. Millions of Jews were killed and millions of Germans were driven out of Poland and Czechoslovakia. But other minority problems remained unresolved, and they went into suspended animation when the Soviet Union imposed communism upon its East European satellites.

The struggle to define national identities resumed with a vengeance after half a century of suppression under communist rule. The 1993 break-up of Czechoslovakia into Slovakia and the Czech Republic; the three-cornered war among Serbs, Croats, and Muslims in Bosnia, followed by fighting between Serbs and Albanians in Kosovo; the war between ethnic Russians and ethnic Romanians in Moldova; the numerous wars in the Caucasus Mountains, of which the struggle of Chechnya for independence is one example—these and many other conflicts in the area since the 1990s continue the long process of sorting out nations and boundaries.

autonomy became the focus of new national identities. These are open, synthetic nations composed of immigrants of varied origins, whereas the traditional European nations are more closed, having evolved over centuries of common history.

A major development of the twentieth century was the spread of European-style nationalism to the rest of the world. The rapid pace of global change that continues today has made the nation the chief source of political legitimacy by weakening traditional social institutions such as the family, tribe, and village. It has also meant the destruction of ancient empires and the emergence of new nations from the wreckage. Related to this is the attempt to fuse tribal identities into nationalities. In the nineteenth century most of Africa was divided by the European powers on more or less arbitrary lines that bore little relation to patterns of tribal habitation. The European powers are now gone but their colonial boundaries remain as the borders between sovereign African states. In most of these states, tribal identities are far more important than national ones. The tragic civil war between Hutu and Tutsi tribes in Rwanda is one example of such tribal conflict; another is the disintegration of the Democratic Republic of the Congo into several warring tribal factions, each receiving some degree of military assistance from neighbouring states. Over time, at least some of these new states may develop viable national identities. In the meantime, many have been devastated by chronic civil war among tribes, and the continent of Africa is troubled with millions of refugees who have been driven from their homes by political violence.

This brief historical survey confirms that nationality is not tied to any single objective factor. National identity is usually based on some combination of language, race, religion, and government, but none of these is either necessary or sufficient. The Swiss as a nation are divided by religion between Protestant and Catholic and are linguistically divided among speakers of German, French, Italian, and Romansch; the focus of national identity is government itself. Government is also the focus in the United States, which is a multiracial nation with European, African, Asian, and Native American elements; also, there are about 40 million Americans whose first language is not English but Spanish. In contrast to Switzerland and the United States, the small country of Lebanon, where all are of the same race and all speak Arabic, might seem well favoured to develop a coherent nationality, yet for much of the 1980s that country was torn by civil war among Christians and several sects of Muslims. One must look at each case separately to see what factors contribute to or work against the growth of national identity. The only safe generalization is that there is no universal formula. As a form of identity, the nation is a subjective or psychological reality that transcends objective factors. That is what Renan meant when he called it "a plebiscite of every day"—nations are created by human will. Ultimately, identity is a matter of what you wish to call yourself and what you can get others to accept.

Against this backdrop, the noted Canadian scholar (and former leader of the Liberal Party of Canada) Michael Ignatieff has introduced a useful distinction between ethnic and civic nations.[3] **Ethnic nations** are those in which the national identity depends primarily on objective factors such as language, race, or religion. Where the national identity is ethnic, outsiders may live in the community for decades or even generations without coming to share that identity—think of the Koreans in Japan or the Turkish "guest workers" in Germany. **Civic nations**, in contrast, have an identity that depends primarily on acceptance of the political order. In these circumstances, exemplified by Canada and the United States, newcomers may take on the national identity within very few years.

The contrast, however, should not be overdrawn. Civic nations always have ethnic underpinnings; think of the role of American popular culture, expressed in the English language, in reinforcing the American national identity. The Super Bowl and Hollywood movies are arguably as important as the Statue of Liberty and the Star-Spangled Banner in producing the identity of being American. And ethnic nations always have some civic aspects. European nations such as France, Italy, and Germany have, in fact, socialized millions of immigrants and their children to the new national identity, even though the process may be slower than in North America. It is, moreover, not the case that ethnic nations are bad and civic nations are good. Both are valid ways of generating the identity of a political community.

PROBLEMS OF ETHNICITY

Nations are rarely homogeneous; they almost always contain significant minorities whose identity can conflict or overlap with the dominant national identity. Such minorities are often called **ethnic groups**, but that term itself needs further specification. Let us mention three categories of great importance to Canada, all drawn from a more extended classification proposed by the Canadian philosopher Will Kymlicka:[4]

- **Substate nations**, such as the francophones of Canada. Originally the dominant settler group, they were traded by France to the British Empire as part of a complex deal in the Treaty of Paris (1763), and subsequently they became outnumbered by new waves of anglophone settlers. Since substate nations could have become sovereign nations if history had turned out differently, it is not surprising that the members of substate nations cling tenaciously to their identities and continue to insist upon their national status, even if they have been incorporated into a larger state.

- **Indigenous or Aboriginal peoples**, such as the North American Indians. Indigenous peoples did not originally describe themselves as nations, for that whole vocabulary is a product of European history. But, once subordinated to a colonial political system, they may adopt that vocabulary and begin to claim national status as a way of obtaining greater political power.

- **Immigrants**, such as Italian Canadians or Chinese Canadians. Immigrants may come from well-established national communities such as the Italians or Chinese, but when they voluntarily move to another country, they are generally thought to have given up any claim to national status in their new homelands. Immigrant groups usually make claims for speedier integration into the nation to which they have moved, rather than recognition of a distinct national status of their own. (African Americans don't fit very well into this tableau because most of them did not come voluntarily to the Americas; their ancestors were brought as slaves.)

Let us look at some North American examples of strategic claims to national status. In the United States the religious movement popularly known as the Black Muslims (their most famous adherent is the boxer Muhammad Ali) maintains that African Americans are a nation—to be precise, the "Nation of Islam."[5] This assertion is tied to the demand that, as a nation with a full-fledged identity, African Americans should have their own sovereign state. Critics of the Black Muslims counter that African Americans are a special group within, but still part of, the American nation. In Canada, the Dene, the indigenous people of the Northwest Territories, elevated themselves to national status in the Dene Declaration of 1975: "We the Dene of the Northwest Territories insist on the right to be regarded by ourselves and the world as a nation."[6] In this they followed the Métis, who have insisted for a century and a half that they too are a nation, the "New Nation." Native Indians in Canada now refer to themselves as the "First Nations,"[7] and that position was roundly endorsed by the 1996 report of the Royal Commission on Aboriginal Peoples, which called for "nation rebuilding and nation rec-ognition" of Aboriginal peoples as "a crucial first component" in restructuring Canada as a multinational confederacy.[8] Today, First Nations terminology is routinely used in public, not only by aboriginal leaders but also by politicians of all parties.

French Canadians are often regarded by English Canadians as an ethnic group, although, at least in Quebec, they generally regard themselves as the Québécois nation, one of the two so-called "founding nations" of Canada. The issue came to a head in the House of Commons in fall 2006, when Bloc Québécois (BQ) leader Gilles Duceppe introduced a motion recognizing Quebec as a nation. Prime Minister Stephen Harper responded by amending the motion to affirm that "the Québécois form a nation within a united Canada"; all parties supported the amended motion, though the BQ would have preferred the original wording.[9] This was more than just quibbling over words. A nation is potentially a self-governing community, perhaps even potentially a sovereign state.[10] The BQ introduced its original motion precisely to serve as a platform for further efforts to separate Quebec from Canada. Insertion of the phrase "within a united Canada" was meant to derail that plan, and use of the word *Québécois* rather than *Quebec* was meant to emphasize that the nation was a community of people, not a state ruled by a particular government.

Objectively, there is no precise definition of a nation. It is not a scientific issue but a strategic one, relating to whether one social group has the power and the right to assert itself against others. What counts are not objective criteria but the respect and influence that go along with being called a nation.

NATIONS AND STATES

Let us now return to the relationship between nation and state. There are several typical situations. Nation-states exist where the limits of common identity coincide with the boundaries of sovereign authority. Clear contemporary examples are Iceland, Sweden, and Poland, in which the state contains a relatively homogeneous population. Perhaps more numerous are those nation-states where one nation is clearly preponderant but minorities are significant. The United States contains the Nation of Islam and other black nationalists, as well as some Hispanic activists who dream of reunion with Mexico. Great Britain has to deal with important nationalist movements in Northern Ireland, Scotland, and Wales. Spain contains significant Basque and Catalan minorities, some of whom aspire to independence. When minorities accept the legitimacy of the state, they can be regarded as ethnic groups within the nation, whether as substate nations, indigenous peoples, or immigrant communities. But in many cases the minorities are not content to be ethnic groups; they struggle vigorously for national status, union with a neighbouring state, or even a nation-state of their own.

A second situation is that of the **binational** or **multinational state**. In such cases, two or more nations coexist under a single government. From one point of view, Canada is a binational state, a partnership of English Canadians and French Canadians that is enriched by the presence of indigenous peoples as well as immigrant communities. Belgium might also be considered a binational state, a partnership of Flemings and Walloons. India is a vast multinational state, as were the Soviet Union and the Austro-Hungarian, Ottoman, and Russian Empires.

If there are multinational states, there are also multi-state nations. Prime examples are the German people, who were divided into East and West Germany from 1945 to 1990; the Koreans, who are still split into North and South Korea; the Poles, whose state was split up among Russia, Austria, and Prussia at the end of the eighteenth century; and the Basques, who straddle the border between France and Spain. Nations can live submerged for hundreds of years with no state of their own and then suddenly reappear, as the Poles did after the First World War when their state was reconstituted.

Overall it seems safe to say that the world is such a complicated place that homogeneous nation-states are and will continue to be a small minority. Most states comprise multiple identity groups whose members either have to work out ways of peacefully sharing a government or else will be fated to engage in conflicts that may tear the state apart. The emergence of the nation as the paradigm of political community has not changed the fundamental challenge of politics, which is always to achieve a tolerable degree of harmony among people with different interests, identities, and worldviews.

IS CANADA A NATION?

Those who created the Dominion of Canada in 1867, the so-called "Fathers of Confederation," imagined Canada as a single nation. Acutely aware of linguistic, religious, and regional cleavages, they tried to define the new national identity in political terms as allegiance to the government. Quebec's leading spokesman, George-Étienne Cartier, called the new Dominion a "political nationality,"[11] by which he meant that the existence of a common government would create an identity transcending linguistic and regional differences, although these differences would continue to exist and would be reflected in provincial governments. Canadians, like the Swiss, would constitute a single nation, even if they spoke more than one language and worshipped God in different churches.

But there was always a view in Quebec that Canada was a partnership of two nations, French and English, and this view re-emerged forcefully in the 1960s during the Quiet Revolution. Quebec nationalists articulated the ***deux nations*** view of Canada, which both the Progressive Conservative Party and the New Democratic Party adopted for a time. The Liberal Party, however, under the leadership of Pierre Trudeau, continued to insist that Canada was a single nation, albeit bilingual and multicultural. The Meech Lake Accord, proposed but not adopted in the late 1980s, referred to Quebec as a "distinct society." Proponents of the Accord saw this as a justifiable accommodation of Quebec's uniqueness, while opponents, including Pierre Trudeau, saw it as code for "two nations." However, that period of Liberal opposition to any talk of "two nations" ended in 2006, when the Liberals supported Prime Minister Harper's motion to affirm that "the Québécois form a nation within a united Canada."

One of the complexities here is that, if Canada consists of two nations, they are of quite different types. The identity of being Québécois is primarily an ethnic one, depending on language, culture, and a common sense of history, whereas the identity of being Canadian is primarily civic, depending on allegiance to the political system. There simply is no English-Canadian nation in the same sense as there is a French-Canadian (or Québécois) nation. English-speaking Canadians have never thought of themselves as a collective entity in opposition to French-speaking Canadians; their identity is intrinsically pan-Canadian and inclusive of Quebec. "My Canada includes Quebec," as the saying goes.

In the meantime, while Canada and Quebec were going through this prolonged identity crisis, Aboriginal people started using national terminology to describe themselves. As described above, the Métis, in fact, had long spoken of a "Métis Nation," and in 1982 the National Indian Brotherhood transformed itself into the Assembly of First Nations. Curiously, politicians who always refused to speak of Quebec as a nation rushed to adopt the new practice of referring to Indian bands as "First Nations." But this was perhaps due more to the weakness than the strength of the Aboriginal position. More than 630 First Nations are small, with an average population of slightly more than 1000, and scattered across the whole of Canada. Although politically influential in some circumstances, they are not in a position to break up the Canadian state. Quebec, in contrast, is a single province strategically located in the middle of Canada. With more than eight million people, it is certainly large enough to become a viable state in its own right.

That these are vital political issues, not just conceptual quibbles, was obvious during the Canadian referendum campaign of 1992. Supporters of the Charlottetown Accord often spoke of "two founding nations"—English and French—or even three—English, French, and Aboriginal (lumping all Aboriginal peoples together for this purpose). They saw the Accord, with its proposals for special guarantees for Quebec and a "third order" of government for Aboriginal Canadians, as a means of representing these national differences in Canada's political institutions. In contrast, many opponents of the Accord spoke of the "equality" of individuals and provinces within Canada. In their view, Canada was a single nation of equal citizens, and no group required elaborate protections.

The "one Canada" view won the referendum, but that does not mean the debate is over. The views that there are two or three or several hundred nations will remain alive because they articulate the political aspirations of significant social groups with robust identities. Their leaders, like all political leaders, will continue to use words as weapons in their struggle to attain political power.

Questions for Discussion

1. How do you personally think of Canada—as one nation, two nations, or many nations? What is the most important factor in the way you think about Canada?

2. Is Canada truly a political nationality, as G.-E. Cartier maintained, or is the national identity also dependent on aspects of language and culture?

3. Canada has experienced massive immigration in the period since World War II. How do you think this immigration has affected the Canadian national identity(ies)?

Internet Links

1. Assembly of First Nations: **www.afn.ca**. Information about the main organization of First Nations in Canada.

2. The Nationalism Project: **www.nationalismproject.org**. Bibliography on nations and nationalism, plus links to other sites.

3. Nation of Islam Online: **www.noi.org**. Information about a leading black nationalist movement in the United States.

4. Statistics Canada: **www.statcan.ca**. Data about the population of contemporary Canada, including ethnic composition.

Further Reading

Ajzenstat, Janet, Paul Romney, Ian Gentles, and William D. Gairdner, eds. *Canada's Founding Debates.* Toronto: University of Toronto Press, 2003.

Anderson, Benedict. *Imagined Communities.* New York: Verso, 2006.

Behiels, Michael D., and Marcel Martel, eds. *Nation, Ideas, Identities: Essays in Honour of Ramsay Cook.* Don Mills, ON: Oxford University Press, 2000.

Breuilly, John. *Nationalism and the State.* 2nd ed. Chicago: University of Chicago Press, 1994.

Calhoun, Craig. *Nationalism.* Minneapolis: University of Minnesota Press, 1997.

Conlogue, Ray. *Impossible Nation: The Longing for Homeland in Canada and Quebec.* Stratford, ON: Mercury Press, 1996.

Connor, Walker. *Ethnonationalism: The Quest for Understanding.* Princeton, NJ: Princeton University Press, 1994.

Dahbour, Omar. *Illusion of the Peoples: A Critique of National Self-Determination.* Lanham, MD: Lexington Books, 2003.

Flanagan, Tom. *First Nations? Second Thoughts.* 2nd ed. Montreal: McGill-Queen's University Press, 2008.

Friesen, Gerald. *Citizens and Nation: An Essay on History, Communication and Canada.* Toronto: University of Toronto Press, 2000.

Gellner, Ernest. *Nations and Nationalism.* 2nd ed. Ithaca, NY: Cornell University Press, 2006.

Granatstein, Jack. *Yankee Go Home: Canadians and Anti-Americanism.* Scarborough, ON: HarperCollins Canada, 1996.

Grant, George. *Lament for a Nation: The Defeat of Canadian Nationalism.* 40th anniversary ed. Montreal: McGill-Queen's University Press, 2005.

Halliday, Fred. *Nation and Religion in the Middle East.* Boulder, CO: Lynne Rienner, 2000.

Hobsbawm, E. J. *Nations and Nationalism Since 1780: Programme, Myth, Reality.* Cambridge: Cambridge University Press, 1990.

Ignatieff, Michael. *Blood and Belonging: Journeys into the New Nationalism.* Toronto: Penguin Books Canada, 1993.

Miller, David. *On Nationality.* Oxford: Oxford University Press, 1995.

Paul, T.V., G. John Ikenberry, and John A. Hall. *The Nation-State in Question.* Princeton, NJ: Princeton University Press, 2003.

Romney, Paul. *Getting It Wrong: How Canadians Forgot Their Past and Imperilled Confederation.* Toronto: University of Toronto Press, 1999.

Schulze, Hagen. *States, Nations, and Nationalism: From the Middle Ages to the Present.* Translated by William E. Yuill. Oxford: Blackwell, 1996.

Smith, Anthony D. *The Nation in History: Historiographical Debates about Ethnicity and Nationalism.* Hanover, NH: University Press of New England, 2000.

Spira, Thomas. *Nationalism and Ethnicity Terminologies: An Encyclopedic Dictionary and Research Guide.* Gulf Breeze, FL: Academic International Press, 1999.

CHAPTER 5
Political Culture and Socialization

The study of politics requires an understanding of the concepts associated with its institutional elements, such as nations and states, and its use of power, including the key concepts of legitimacy and authority. Also important is an understanding of the psychological element of politics: how citizens think about politics and government and why this matters. *Culture,* like so many terms used in the social sciences, has many different meanings. One writer calls it "one of the two or three most complicated words in the English language."[1] In everyday conversation it often refers to the fine arts, including "high culture" (opera, classical music, painting and sculpture, poetry and fiction, live theatre), and to "popular culture" (network television, Hollywood movies, magazines and comic books, popular fiction). However, when social scientists speak of **culture,** they are referring to the pattern of beliefs, preferences, and practices of a people, shaped by the family, religion, and politics itself. *Culture* has become an umbrella term that reflects institutional arrangements as well as the attitudes, beliefs, and values that accompany them.

Observers have long noticed that the different peoples of the world possess varying cultural traits. Canadians are seen to be overly polite, the Japanese very hard-working, and Americans strongly nationalistic. Cultural stereotypes, which can sometimes contain a kernel of truth regarding a group of people, can nevertheless sometimes rest on exaggerated differences or, worse, on differences that no longer exist. These can at times be perpetuated because they serve some purpose or because of our information-processing biases. In the aftermath of 9/11, increasing Islamophobia—defined as prejudice against all Muslims and Islam based on misinformation—has been argued by some to be an inevitable response to the scale of the tragedy, and by others to legitimize the American government's adoption of public policies that have significantly eroded civil liberties. As individuals, we are much less likely to pay attention to information that challenges our stereotypes, but when what we see or hear reinforces them, we are much more likely to notice. Yet not all cultural differences are stereotypes or exaggerations. The difficulty is identifying which cultural differences rest in fact rather than in perception or exaggeration.

The part of culture having to do with government and politics is known, not surprisingly, as **political culture**. It includes the attitudes, beliefs, values, and norms that people have developed toward government and politics, a concept employed to help explain why and how politics varies between peoples and states. As with culture in general, popular stereotypes—sometimes but not always containing a kernel of truth—exist about different political cultures. Germans, for example, are sometimes thought to be very respectful of public authority. While such a generalization is interesting and perhaps contains a kernel of truth, it cannot explain all of German politics and is likely not true of all Germans. The expectation is, however, that the values and beliefs in a political culture will be widely shared and relatively coherently held among the members of that community. Beyond that, important political subcultures may also exist. Canada has been said to consist of several regional political cultures. The earliest argument along these lines came in the 1970s from Richard Simeon and David Elkins, who argued that the provinces contained political cultures that reflected unique provincial institutions.[2] More recent examinations have confirmed that provincial subcultures remain an important dynamic in Canadian politics.[3]

Political culture represents the psychological dimension of politics.[4] It encompasses how people think about politics and thus can help us to understand differences in how politics is practised across states. Because it includes attitudes, beliefs, values, and norms regarding government and politics, it is simultaneously rational, emotional, and judgmental.

Political culture encompasses ideology—notions about what government is and what it ought to be. An example may clarify the relationship between political culture and ideology: Belief in individual freedom is a fundamental part of the political culture of the Western world. At the same time, within the ideology of liberal democracies, we not only value individual freedom but also believe that maintaining it should be a primary goal of governments. Freedom of political action is the basis on which individuals and groups can become involved in the political process. Without political freedom, there would be little opportunity to participate in politics. Thus the liberal-democratic ideology is an integral part of our political culture. Most Canadians think it quite reasonable to engage in peaceful protest against a law or policy with which they disagree; as part of the wider global movement, the recent Occupy protests in a number of Canadian cities generated relatively little opposition, at least in their early stages.[5] Canadians believe that political protest, while never guaranteeing a government response, is a legitimate mechanism for voicing public opposition.

By way of contrast, Latin American political systems are influenced by Iberic-Latin traditions that include, among other things, a society that is hierarchical, stratified, and authoritarian.[6] Although democratization has gained a foothold in the region, recent history is littered with failed attempts at challenging authoritarianism's hold. Public opinion surveys suggest that while there is general support for democracy among Latin Americans, political corruption, heightened crime levels, and lack of trust in governments have led to a loss of support for many of the region's regimes, which hinders the introduction of democracy.[7]

Political culture researchers grapple with the question of whether a democratic political culture is required for a stable democratic system to take root. Many now agree that while democratic values can help ensure the success of democracy, it is also the case that a democratic regime itself is integral to instilling those values in citizens.[8] Importantly, political cultures can change, but this occurs only very slowly because values and beliefs adopted early in life are tremendously durable. Generational replacement is generally agreed to be the primary mechanism through which political cultures change. A single generation is unlikely to experience a significant change in political values and attitudes; across two generations—comparing parents and their children—however, changes are more likely.

Studies of public opinion have sought to identify a typology of political cultures with a goal of better understanding their role in the practice of politics. A five-nation empirical study undertaken in the early 1960s by Gabriel Almond and Sydney Verba established three basic categories of political culture: parochial, subject, and participatory.[9] In a **parochial culture**, people hold rather negative views of government and as a result participate little in the political system. In a **subject culture**, people hold more positive opinions about government but remain largely uninvolved. In a **participatory culture**, people expect to participate in politics and that government will be responsive to citizen demands. Almond and Verba argued that a "civic culture"— one that ensured a stable democracy—consisted of a mix of these three types so as to ensure that challenges to authority would be offset by the obedience of others, and that the participation of some would be offset by the apathy of others. Too much participation and too many challenges to authority are as threatening to democratic stability as too little participation and too much deference.

A more modern typology for political culture distinguishes between polyarchal, fragmented, and collectivist cultures.[10] **Polyarchal cultures** are unified, which means there is broad agreement on basic social values and active citizen engagement based on a strong sense of efficacy. People in such cultures agree on the key rules of the political game and participate in it actively, given that such activity is believed to pay off. Disagreements do not lead to violence because they occur at the level of policy (on the goals to pursue), not at the more fundamental level of how to decide on the goals, and because people in these cultures treat others, including political opponents, with respect. Canada, the United States, and France fall into the polyarchal culture category.

Fragmented cultures, on the other hand, are ones that display similarly high levels of citizen engagement, but these are combined with relatively low levels of agreement on the rules of the game. Disagreements and disunity are the norm, as are relative distrust and suspicion of others. Politics in such cultures is often violent, brutal, and deadly, and governments are rarely stable. *Coups d'état,* ethnic cleansing, and political assassinations are commonplace because the lack of trust makes political compromise and accommodation impossible. Two examples of fragmented political cultures are Rwanda and Bosnia, although politics in both countries has been relatively calm in recent years.

A third type, **collectivist culture**, exhibits the broad agreement on social values of polyarchal cultures, but this is combined with little in the way of citizen engagement. The lack of engagement in collectivist cultures stems from the knowledge that engagement is fruitless and that it can sometimes be dangerous. Citizens in political systems that express little support for political and civic freedoms learn to keep quiet or risk imprisonment, or worse. Citizen engagement in such states is akin to cheerleading on the sidelines of the real political game, providing moral support to the players but having relatively little effect on the overall outcome of the contest. North Korea and Cuba are examples of collectivist political culture. This typology provides a shorthand method for understanding at a basic level why the politics that takes place in a country happens the way that it does: people's political values, beliefs, and norms shape their participation in politics.

TRENDS IN POLITICAL CULTURE

Recent investigations in political culture have focused on trends that affect many societies simultaneously. A prime example is the growth of **post-materialism** in the political culture of the Western world. According to Ronald Inglehart, who pioneered research on post-materialism, the years since World War II have seen a gradual but profound shift of values. Relying on two hypotheses—the scarcity hypothesis, which argues that things in short supply are more desirable than things that are abundant, and the socialization hypothesis, which argues that one's values are shaped and set relatively early in life—he argues that recent generations have grown up taking their physical and economic security for granted and, as a result, their priorities differ from those of previous generations. Previous generations are predominantly **materialists**, as Inglehart uses the term, concerned with physical and economic security, whereas more recent generations are **post-materialists**, concerned with self-fulfillment and self-expression. With generational replacement, the electorate is becoming increasingly concerned with self-expression and less inclined to leave politics to politicians and to accept the necessity of pragmatic compromises.[11] There have been several political results. One is a decrease in voter loyalty to particular parties and a corresponding increase in vote switching from election to election. Another is the rise of single-issue movements (feminist, pro-choice, pro-life, environmentalist, ethnic, linguistic, gay rights, rights for the disabled, and so on) that are reluctant to submerge their causes within a single political party. More recently, Inglehart's work has expanded to the role played by economic development in the shaping of political culture, and in particular beliefs regarding individual autonomy and gender equality.[12]

An important book by the Canadian political scientist Neil Nevitte, titled *The Decline of Deference,* examines this process of value change in Canada against the backdrop of similar changes in other liberal democracies in Western Europe and North America.[13]

Nevitte's data, as summarized in Figure 5.1, suggest that by 1990 post-materialism had become the dominant value type in Europe and North America among people under 45, whereas older people were more likely to be materialists.

Another important branch of research looking at political culture has identified the importance of social capital for understanding democratic outcomes. **Social capital** consists of the social networks and levels of trust and reciprocity that exist in a community. In a nutshell, the greater the level of community interaction and trust, the greater the democratic health of that community is likely to be. Robert Putnam's book *Bowling Alone* argues that the increasing disconnectedness of Americans has caused a decline in civic health.[14] The importance of this research is in highlighting the role of social activity for determining civic health: political culture does not develop on its own but rather stems at least in part from the day-to-day connections between citizens that may have nothing at all to do with politics. Fewer Americans are joining bowling leagues and similar associations, which means they spend less time with their neighbours and have smaller social networks. One result, argues Putnam, is less trust in others, less willingness to engage in the community, and an overall

Figure 5.1 Value Type by Age Group: Europe and North America, 1990

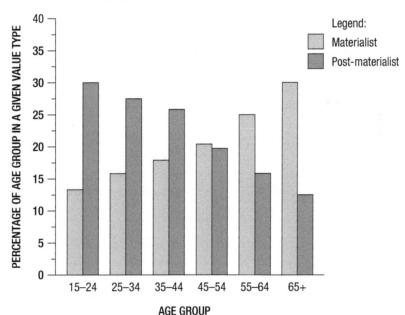

Note: Value type by age group among the publics of France, Britain, West Germany, Italy, Netherlands, Denmark, Belgium, Spain, Ireland, Northern Ireland, the United States, Canada, and Mexico (1981: N = 16 043; 1990: N = 20 464). Value type not available for the United States, 1981.

Source: 1981 and 1990 World Values Surveys. From R. Inglehart, *Modernization, Cultural Change and Democracy.* (Cambridge University Press, 2005) p. 100.

decline in civic health. Putnam points to a number of factors that help to explain why the current generation of Americans is more disconnected: increasingly busy lifestyles, two-career families, the spread of suburbia, and the increased use of television and the Internet.

Social connections and networks are central to integration in a community, but so too is where one happens to live. Urban areas, which are often made up of a mixture of ethnic communities, make it more difficult to build stocks of social capital than more rural and less diverse ones. Urban residents are more likely to isolate themselves from others in communities that are highly diverse.[15] And while research on this question is still in its early stages, a potential mechanism linking diversity and social capital might be identity: how people identify themselves and others shapes how they behave within their community. Seeing others as like you in some way (as Canadian or American, for example), in spite of other differences, likely leads you to trust them more than you otherwise would and to engage in the community with them.

The level of diversity found in communities can be closely linked to immigration patterns: the higher the level of immigration in a community, the greater the level of diversity it is likely to exhibit. The integration of immigrant and diverse cultures is both difficult to address and of great consequence for politics; the riots that took place in November 2005 in Paris suburbs populated mainly by African immigrants attest directly to its importance.[16] Multiculturalism policies in Canada have attempted to assist cultural groups in overcoming barriers so as to allow them to integrate more fully into society (see Canadian Focus 5.1). Assistance in learning one of the two official languages has been one of the planks of the policy. With one of the highest levels of per capita immigration in the world—according to the 2006 census, one in five Canadians is foreign-born—and with 95 percent of immigrants settling in urban areas, integration and national unity are key issues on the political agenda.[17] The challenge is to find a balance between accommodating immigrant cultures and maintaining a strong sense of national unity while at the same time ensuring respect for key values such as equality, rights and freedoms, and tolerance. A debate in Quebec during the 2007 provincial election—over whether women wearing a burqa or niqab had to reveal their faces in order to vote—shows how difficult the balance can be to achieve.

Striking a balance can be especially difficult when the values in question stem from religious beliefs. Social scientists have argued in the past that the process of **secularization**—that is, the decreasing importance assigned to religion in the modern world—meant that religion would cease to be a factor of much importance over time. Recent events have challenged this thinking, however, with the events of 9/11 in particular stimulating renewed interest in the relationship between religion and politics.[18] Unlike a number of countries around the world, Canada and the United States endorse the principle of separation of church and state, but this does not mean that religion is divorced from politics. Public funding for certain religious schools in some Canadian provinces and the prominent role of religious groups in the American

Canadian Focus 5.1

Multiculturalism in Canada

Pierre Trudeau's Liberal government initiated the policy of multiculturalism in 1971. Multiculturalism was also recognized in 1982, in Section 27 of the Canadian Charter of Rights and Freedoms: "This Charter shall be interpreted in a manner consistent with the preservation and enhancement of the multicultural heritage of Canadians." Brian Mulroney's Progressive Conservative government passed the Multiculturalism Act in 1988 and also created a Department of Multiculturalism, whose functions now reside in Citizenship and Immigration Canada. Canada currently stands as one of the world's most multicultural societies.

The goals of multiculturalism included recognizing and accommodating cultural diversity; promoting equal participation by all groups; and encouraging intercultural exchange and acquisition of Canada's official languages. The accommodation and recognition of diversity has to be balanced, however, by a strong belief in a common identity, a sense of solidarity. Canada appears to be succeeding in this regard, at least in terms of the lack of strongly negative attitudes toward immigration numbers, as shown below.

Such attitudes are driven in part by the adoption of the points system for identifying potential immigrants

Figure 5.2 Public Opinion on Immigration, 1988–2006

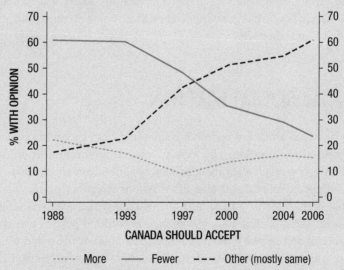

Source: From Banting, Keith G., "Is There a Progressive's Dilemma in Canada?" in *The Canadian Journal of Political Science*, 43(4), © 2010. Cambridge Journals Online. (*continued*)

Canadian Focus 5.1 *(continued)*

to Canada; the result is that once in the country, immigrants have relied less on social welfare programs than they might have otherwise—a key source of conflict in other countries. Research also suggests that the political integration of immigrants, at least in terms of political participation levels, is very strong.

Yet evidence can be found that suggests the balance between diversity and solidarity has not been completely achieved. Recent events in Quebec, including proposed legislation to ban the wearing of the niqab when accessing provincial government services, highlight the tension in attempting to accommodate diversity within a liberal secular state. Moreover, while only a small share of Canadians believe that we should reduce immigration numbers, a strong majority of over 70 percent agrees that immigrants must adapt to Canada society once they arrive.

See Keith Banting, "Is There a Progressive's Dilemma in Canada? Immigration, Multiculturalism, and the Welfare State," *Canadian Journal of Political Science* 43, no. 4 (2010): 797–820.

---

civil rights movement are but two examples of the interrelationship between religion and politics. Religious beliefs and values directly influence political values and political behaviour. These can reinforce democratic values, such as equality and freedom, and democratic behaviour such as voting, but they can also run up against them, as in the case of the Fundamentalist Latter-Day Saints sect, which practises the subordination of women to men in polygamous marriages. The identity, beliefs, and values stemming from religious beliefs can incite an intolerance that may sometimes lead to violence, terrorist activity, and genocide.

POLITICAL SOCIALIZATION

The means by which a political culture is transmitted from generation to generation is known as **political socialization**. The focus of research on this topic is on determining where and how young people learn about politics, become interested in politics, and decide whether to engage in political and civic life.[19] As one researcher noted, "Good citizens are made, not born."[20] At the macro level, the political system itself will influence what individuals learn about politics. How government responds to political events and crises, the importance of and respect shown for human and political rights and freedoms, and the nature of transitions in government will necessarily shape what people believe about their government and the political system. At the individual level, the main agents of political socialization conveying values, beliefs, and attitudes across generations are the family, schools, friends and peer groups, and the media. Let us say a brief word about each.

It seems intuitively obvious that the family would play an important role in political socialization, if for no other reason than that government is a system of authority and the family is where children first encounter authority. Yet families introduce children to more than simply a system of authority. For many young people, the family setting is where one first learns about politics and government, first hears discussions concerning politics and policy, and first witnesses individual political action. Research shows that if family members regularly discuss politics and participate in political activities, then the children in those families are more likely to become politically interested and active as adults.[21] These early lessons about the importance of politics appear to be crucial for the development of future generations' political engagement.

Schools are also central to learning about government and politics, and in recent years schools in North America have significantly increased their efforts to educate students for future citizenship, attempting to stimulate positive attitudes about civic responsibilities such as voting and paying taxes. Part of the spark for this renewed effort at civics education lies in the dropping levels of voter turnout recorded in many Western democracies in recent years; another is research suggesting that citizenship education can be particularly important for levels of political knowledge. Service learning—sometimes facetiously referred to as "mandatory volunteering"—has been adopted in a number of schools to develop civic engagement as a lifelong habit.[22]

Although the importance of friends and peer groups for political socialization has always been understood, research in this area has recently begun to re-examine the topic.[23] In line with the increased interest in social capital, the importance of social activity for many aspects of political socialization, including civic knowledge and civic attitudes, is now accepted, and how these processes might work during the adolescent years has become a new area of inquiry. Friends and memberships in organizations can play a central role in shaping what we value and what we believe; in adolescence, how many friends we have, who they are, and what and how many groups we have joined are all linked in some way to the attitudes that we possess and to the importance that we assign to civic and political participation throughout our lives. The Boy Scouts and Girl Guides, for example, promote environmental protection when they organize outdoor activities, and they teach lessons about community engagement when they organize bottle drives and cookie sales.

The media, finally, are omnipresent today in all phases of socialization; it would be difficult to overemphasize their importance. Television, radio, newspapers, and magazines are often listed as key sources of information about government and politics. The Internet is fast becoming a rival to these sources, particularly among younger generations.[24] And unlike more traditional sources of news and information, its speed, its ability to facilitate the creation of virtual communities, and its lack of formal gatekeepers set it apart. Research has yet to determine the precise impact that increased use of social-networking Internet sites such as Facebook, MySpace, and other sites such as YouTube is having on political socialization, but it is clearly having an effect. The importance attached to social media in a number of recent election contests—most famously the American presidential election in 2008—undoubtedly suggests that its importance will only increase.

Questions for Discussion

1. What are your basic political values and beliefs? How do these shape whether and how you participate in politics?

2. Do you agree with Inglehart's thesis that the difference between materialists and post-materialists is largely generational? Think of some examples in your everyday life that support or reject Inglehart's finding. Do you think you are more a materialist or a post-materialist?

3. Think about how agents of political socialization have influenced the development of your own political views. Which agent has had the most significant influence? How do you think the Internet has changed political socialization?

Internet Links

1. Environics Research Group: **www.environics.ca**. A major Canadian polling company that conducts research on values.

2. Multiculturalism Program, Citizenship and Immigration Canada: **www.cic.gc.ca/english/multiculturalism/index.asp**.

3. ThisNation.com: **www.thisnation.com**. An American website on politics with information links to resources on political culture and socialization.

4. World Values Survey: **www.worldvaluessurvey.org**. A worldwide research project on post-materialism.

Further Reading

Adams, Michael. *Fire and Ice: The United States, Canada and the Myth of Converging Values*. Toronto: Penguin Canada, 2003.

———. *Unlikely Utopia: The Surprising Triumph of Canadian Pluralism*. Toronto: Viking Canada, 2007.

Almond, Gabriel A., and Sydney Verba. *The Civic Culture Revisited*. Boston: Little, Brown, 1980.

Bloemraad, Irene. *Becoming a Citizen: Incorporating Immigrants and Refugees in the United States and Canada*. Berkeley: University of California Press, 2006.

Burns, Nancy, Kay Lehman Schlozman, and Sidney Verba. *The Private Roots of Public Action: Gender, Equality, and Political Participation*. Cambridge, MA: Harvard University Press, 2001.

Carpini, Michael X. Delli, and Scott Keeter. *What Americans Know about Politics and Why It Matters*. New Haven, CT: Yale University Press, 1996.

Cristi, Marcela. *From Civil to Political Religion: The Intersection of Culture, Religion and Politics*. Waterloo, ON: Wilfrid Laurier University Press, 2001.

Crothers, Lane, and Charles Lockhart, eds. *Culture and Politics: A Reader*. New York: St. Martin's Press, 2000.

Diamond, Larry Jay, ed. *Political Culture and Democracy in Developing Countries*. Boulder, CO: Lynne Rienner, 1993.

Inglehart, Ronald. *Culture Shift in Advanced Industrial Society*. Princeton, NJ: Princeton University Press, 1990.

Inglehart, Ronald, and Pippa Norris. *Rising Tide: Gender Equality and Cultural Change around the World*. New York: Cambridge University Press, 2003.

Inglehart, Ronald, and Christian Welzel. *Modernization, Cultural Change and Democracy: The Human Development Sequence*. New York: Cambridge University Press, 2005.

Nevitte, Neil. *The Decline of Deference*. Peterborough, ON: Broadview Press, 1996.

Putnam, Robert. *Bowling Alone: The Collapse and Revival of American Community*. London: Simon and Schuster, 2000.

———. *Making Democracy Work: Civic Traditions in Modern Italy*. Princeton, NJ: Princeton University Press, 1993.

Smith, T. Alexander, and Raymond Tatalovich. *Cultures at War: Moral Conflicts in Western Democracies*. Peterborough, ON: Broadview Press, 2003.

Thomas, David M., and Barbara Boyle Torrey, eds. *Canada and the United States: Differences That Count*. 3rd ed. Peterborough, ON: Broadview Press, 2003.

Verba, Sidney, Kay Lehman Schlozman, and Henry E. Brady. *Voice and Equality: Civic Voluntarism in American Politics*. Cambridge, MA: Harvard University Press, 1995.

Woshinsky, Oliver H. Explaining Politics: Culture, Institutions and Political Behavior. New York: Routledge, 2008.

PART 1

CHAPTER 6
Law

Law in the broadest sense means a rule or regularity in the behaviour of any element in the universe. The laws of gravitation describe the motion of falling bodies on the earth and of the planets in the heavens; the laws of evolution describe changes over time in living species; the laws of supply and demand describe human behaviour in dealing with scarce resources. Laws or regularities such as these make the universe intelligible. Law is also the foundation of society, which is essentially a group of people living together under the same laws or rules of conduct.

Although law is all-embracing, it is not monolithic. There is a subtle change in the character of law as one moves from inanimate objects through plant and animal life to human beings. The higher levels have a greater element of self-guidance or freedom in the way they follow laws. Planets stay in their orbits exactly. Crops grow under certain conditions, but only the average yield can be predicted, not the growth of a particular plant. Animals mate at certain times of the year but not with clockwork regularity. People usually try to buy cheap and sell dear in the marketplace, but any individual may depart from this model for personal reasons.

The variability of human behaviour raises the problem of enforcement (a problem that does not exist for inanimate objects and lower life forms but may have parallels among the higher, social animals). From now on, when we use the term **law**, we shall mean a rule of human conduct that is enforced by the community, by means of coercion or violence if necessary.

Law is only one of several kinds of rules that we follow. Our behaviour is guided by instincts of which we may not even be aware. Innate desires to sleep, find nourishment, and reproduce surely contribute to regularities of human behaviour. However, these basic impulses are always mediated by higher forms of rules. A purely personal rule of conduct is usually called a **habit.** We must all drink, but some of us habitually drink coffee while others take tea at certain times of the day. Habit gradually merges with **custom** as social forces come more into play. Most adults in the Western world drink either coffee or tea because they see others drink the same beverages. In other spheres, the social element is even more influential. Such things as politeness, appropriate clothing, and table manners are elaborate codes of conduct, learned through imitation and parental instruction, that every society has.

Habits and customs create regularities in human behaviour without coercive enforcement in situations where the incentives to violate or ignore them are small or nonexistent. Language, for example, is what theorists call a coordination game; its purpose is to communicate with others. We suffer a disadvantage if we depart from its rules because we will not be understood. It does not matter what the rules are; once they exist, it is to our advantage to abide by them. The conventions are more or less self-enforcing. Similarly, we lose out when we flout normal customs of politeness because others avoid the company of those who create unpleasantness. In these instances there is no true enforcement—only a spontaneous reaction that helps keep our conduct within accustomed channels.

Some things, however, cannot be left to spontaneous self-correction. Typically, enforcement is required when the rules are of primary importance to peaceful cooperation and when the rewards of breaking the rules are attractive relative to the costs. Ordered society demands that, at the very least, we know which family we belong to and which material things are within our control. That is why all societies have rules about the family and property that are coercively enforced. Violating table manners makes one incur heavy social penalties for little apparent gain, so enforcement is unnecessary; stealing someone's property, on the other hand, can be such an attractive proposition that sanctions against such behaviour become necessary.

The enforcement of law performs a number of functions for society that can be conveniently remembered as the four Rs: retribution, restitution, rehabilitation, and restraint. **Retribution** is the punishment of those who violate the norms of society. **Restitution** is the provision of compensation to those who have been harmed by rule-breakers. **Rehabilitation** is a change in conduct that will prevent lawbreaking in the future. And **restraint** is roughly the same as deterrence—the fear we instill in those who cannot be swayed by influence or authority.

Two general points about rules are worth noting. First, we do not need to know what a rule is in order to follow it—we only need to know how to act. Language, for example, is a complex system of rules. We all learn to speak by imitation before we acquire the ability to read those rules in grammar books. Similarly, children learn what kind of behaviour is fair long before they develop a conscious understanding of the rules of justice. A child of three or four, who does not even know the word *justice*, can obey a rule not to grab other children's toys. Second, rules are not necessarily designed by conscious intelligence. They may also grow over time in an evolutionary process of trial and error, as is true of habits, customs, and a great many laws.

CUSTOMARY LAW AND COMMON LAW

These observations help to explain the two main kinds of law. The older kind of law, found in all societies, is evolutionary or **customary law**; this sort of law arises gradually and cannot be traced to an identifiable moment in time. The newer kind of law, **legislation**, is consciously formulated and deliberately constructed. Both kinds of law are equally enforceable and so equally valid. Let us first consider customary law.

All human communities have enforceable rules of conduct. They may not be written down and no one may be able to articulate them as abstract propositions; even so, they exist and are enforced. Such laws are an embodiment of the experience a community has gained in its struggle to survive. With the passage of time, the actors discover methods of cooperation, that is, rules that promote internal order and external strength.

Tribal societies repel or kill external attackers, but their most severe method of enforcement against internal rule-breakers is usually ostracism. To be permanently cast out of the small hunting and gathering band, to lose the support of one's family and kin, is tantamount to a death sentence. To be temporarily shunned is usually enough to make the rule-breaker return to accepted norms of conduct.

Laws of this type represent reason—tacit reason—rather than command because no one has ever issued them. Typically the community attributes divine origin to them. According to the Old Testament, Moses received the Law atop Mount Sinai, enveloped in fire and smoke. God himself wrote the Ten Commandments on two tablets of stone, and the face of Moses shone as he brought the tablets down from the mountain.[1] From the political scientist's point of view, attributing divine origin to law is a way of saying that law does not depend just on the will of people alive today and that its importance transcends mere individual preferences.

Society took a step toward assuming conscious control of law when laws began to be written down instead of merely being honoured in practice and entrusted to collective memory. This deliberate recording of laws, however, should not be confused with true legislation. Early legal systems, such as the laws of Hammurabi in Babylon and the Twelve Tables in Rome, were regarded not as a new creation by the sovereign but as a recording of ancient laws that had existed from time immemorial.[2] These laws, said the rulers, had always been valid, but they were now being recorded to avoid misunderstanding and dispute.

A rather similar attitude underlies the **common law** of the English-speaking peoples. Before the Norman Conquest (1066), there were several bodies of law in the different regions of England. The Norman kings set up a unified system of courts throughout the realm that for a time competed with older local courts. The traditional courts gradually fell into disuse as the English found the king's justice to be fairer and more predictable. The king's courts, for their part, continued to interpret the old customary laws, many of which were generally acceptable and became common to all the courts of the realm. Thus there was never a radical break with the past.

Common law is essentially the sum of a vast number of cases decided by English courts since the Middle Ages. Most of these cases were decided not by reference to a written law but by a process of reasoning based on the needs of ordered liberty. Certain principles, such as security of possession of private property and the enforcement of contracts, can be applied to a multitude of disputes. Application yields results, which then serve as models or **precedents** for later cases. The courts generally observe the rule of ***stare decisis***, "to stand by what is decided"—that is, to follow precedent. Adherence to the example of past decisions allows the law to grow in an orderly and predictable way. By studying prior cases, one can gain a fair idea of how future disputes will be decided. This is how an enforceable body of law can develop over centuries without ever having been issued as general commands. It is judge-made law, although *made* is perhaps not the best word. It might be better to speak of *finding* the common law, as was done in the Middle Ages. The law—the abstract rule—is gradually discovered through experience with a number of concrete cases.

The great advantage of common law is its flexibility, in the sense that it can forever be applied to new situations. It need never become obsolete so long as judges are reasonably free to follow precedents. For example, the law faced a novel situation when radio waves began to be used commercially early in the twentieth century. Questions arose, such as whether one could broadcast on a frequency already used by another transmitter. Judges immediately began to cope with these problems, reasoning by analogy with other forms of property.

Common law, having been developed in England, was transported to the British colonies and is still very much alive in Canada, the United States, Australia, and New Zealand. It has a big impact on our lives in areas such as personal property, contracts, and family relationships. But, valuable as it is, it has certain inherent limitations. At any given time it is liable to contain conflicting precedents on unsettled points of law, and conflict means uncertainty. It may become very complex as precedents multiply over the centuries, and complexity is another source of uncertainty. Finally, there is no guarantee that the common-law process will produce desirable results. Judges may box themselves in through a series of undesirable decisions and in doing so create an impasse that may take decades or even centuries to resolve.

LEGISLATION

One solution to these problems is to codify an existing body of customary law in a way that reveals its principles in greater clarity. An example of this is Justinian's Code, produced in the sixth century CE by order of Justinian, emperor of the surviving, eastern half of the Roman Empire. This code systematized the results of a thousand years of Roman customary law, state practice, and imperial edicts. In the early years of the nineteenth century, Justinian's Code served as a model for the French lawyers whom Napoleon had summoned to codify the complex body of French customary law. The Napoleonic Code is an all-encompassing system that forms the basis of law in France as well as in Italy, Spain, and most other European and Latin American countries.[3]

The production of legal codes is a final step toward deliberate control of law. This conscious creation of law is legislation. It may result in a **statute**, which is a particular piece of legislation, or in a legal **code**, which is a comprehensive set of interrelated rules.

As might be expected, Canada, being derived from two colonial powers, has a mixed legal system. The private law of the province of Quebec was systematized in the **code civil** of 1866;[4] private law in the other nine provinces remains an uncodified extension of the common law (**private law** deals with the relationships of individuals with one another, such as contracts). In effect there are two systems of private law in Canada, which is reflected in our constitutional provision that three judges on the Supreme Court of Canada must be from Quebec in order to deal with appeals from that province. The criminal law, in contrast, is unified in the Criminal Code, an act of Parliament passed in 1892 to replace the common law in those matters.

The general rule is that common law retains its validity until the state displaces it with statutory law. In Canada, large sections of common law have been replaced by legislated statutes or codes. One good example is labour relations. In the nineteenth century, relations between employer and employee were regulated by the common law of contracts, employment being considered the contractual exchange of money for work. But all the provinces of Canada, as well as the federal government, have now replaced the common law with comprehensive labour-relations codes. They have established a framework for collective bargaining—negotiations, strikes, arbitration, certification of bargaining agents, and so forth—that is far different from what existed under the common law.

The expansion of legislation has certain advantages. Legislators can foresee situations and try to prevent conflicts. In contrast, common-law adjudication must wait for conflicts to arise. Also, legislation can be created or changed in a relatively short time; in common law it may take decades for solutions to evolve. As well, legislation may offer greater certainty because the law is not inferred from precedent but is clearly laid down.

This certainty, however, is somewhat illusory. However perfectly designed statutes may be, ambiguity of language can never be completely avoided. Also, statutes are soon overtaken by the course of events and need to be adapted to new situations. Continual legislative amendment is not practical; the statutes must be interpreted in particular disputes as they are brought before the courts. A sequence of cases will arise in which the courts will usually follow precedent according to the rule of *stare decisis,* so legislation becomes interpreted through a body of case law. In this way, legislation becomes subject to the same sort of evolutionary forces that guide the development of common law. See Law Focus 6.1 for a discussion of the development of law through delegated legislation.

NATURAL LAW AND HUMAN RIGHTS

Since the time of the Stoics in late antiquity, many writers on law and government have argued that a **natural law** exists that transcends the **positive law** put in place ("posited") by the state and the will of the sovereign. These writers have held that there is an order in the universe that creates certain principles of conduct binding on all

Law Focus 6.1

Delegated Legislation

In a democracy, the primary source of legislation is the representative assembly, such as the Parliament of Canada or the provincial legislatures. But many of the statutes they pass set up a framework for other bodies to create legally enforceable rules, known as *delegated legislation*. The main forms of delegated legislation are

- **Orders-in-council**—formal decisions of the cabinet.

- **Regulations**—rules created by a minister of a government department or by an independent agency such as the Canadian Human Rights Commission.

- **By-laws**—rules passed by local governments, for example, parking ordinances.

All of these forms of delegated legislation are just as much a part of law as the statutes passed by elected assemblies. The courts will enforce them and levy penalties upon people who flout them. But orders-in-council, regulations, and by-laws have to be made under a grant of authority from the representative assembly, that is, in conformity to a statute giving subordinate lawmaking authority to cabinet, ministers, agencies, or city councils. Thus the assembly remains the ultimate source of all legislation even when it delegates rule-making authority.

human beings, at all times, wherever they live. There are many versions of natural-law theory. Some have an explicitly religious foundation, such as that of the thirteenth-century theologian Saint Thomas Aquinas; others are totally secular, such as that of the eighteenth-century philosopher David Hume. All versions agree that there exists a higher law that can be used as a criterion to judge laws made by the state, and that in certain cases disobedience to laws of the state can be justified by appeal to this higher law. Thus Thomas Jefferson invoked "the laws of nature and of nature's God" in the American Declaration of Independence, when he justified the rebellion of the Thirteen Colonies against laws made by Parliament.

The terminology of natural law is infrequently used in twentieth-century political discourse, except at the academic level; however, a very similar idea has taken strong new root in the contemporary field of human rights. **Human rights** are the rights that all human beings are supposed to enjoy simply by virtue of being human. Freedom of religion, freedom to marry and have children, and freedom from torture and arbitrary imprisonment are examples of human rights that are widely accepted in theory (though often violated in practice). These and other such rights are held up in the international community as standards against which the laws and practices of nations are evaluated, and governments that violate them come under pressure to conform.

The idea that a constitution is a proper restraint upon the lawmaking ability of the state (this issue will be explored in depth in the next chapter) is also rooted in the tradition of natural law and human rights.

What natural law and human rights have in common is the view that law is not just the command of the sovereign enforced by the machinery of the state, and that the state can be held to account before higher standards of morality.

Questions for Discussion

1. Would you follow the law if there were no coercive enforcement mechanisms to encourage compliance? Are there any laws you would be tempted to ignore if there were no consequences for breaking them? Why?

2. Changing the law through judicial interpretation is sometimes faster than waiting for legislation to be passed. If that is an advantage of judicial change, can you think of any advantages of legislative change?

3. Is natural law an empirical or a normative concept? Why? What about human rights?

Internet Links

1. Civil Code of Quebec: **www.justice.gouv.qc.ca/english/sujets/glossaire/code-civil-a.htm**. Complete text (in English) of Quebec's unique body of civil law, as well as a brief history of the code.

2. Department of Justice Canada: **canada.justice.gc.ca**. By following the links you can get access to all Canadian federal legislation.

3. Supreme Court of Canada decisions: **scc.lexum.org/en/index.html**. You can quickly read recent decisions by typing the name of the case into the search engine.

Further Reading

Benson, Bruce L. *The Enterprise of Law: Justice Without the State*. San Francisco: Pacific Research Institute for Public Policy, 1990.

Bogart, W. A. *Consequences: The Impact of Law and Its Complexity*. Toronto: University of Toronto Press, 2002.

———. *Courts and Country: The Limits of Litigation and the Social and Political Life of Canada*. Toronto: Oxford University Press, 1994.

Bork, Robert. *The Tempting of America: The Political Seduction of the Law*. New York: Simon and Schuster, 1990.

Boyd, Neil. *Canadian Law: An Introduction*. Toronto: Harcourt Brace, 1995.

Friedland, Martin L. *A Place Apart: Judicial Independence and Accountability in Canada.* Ottawa: Canadian Judicial Council, 1995.

Greene, Ian, Carl Baar, Peter McCormick, George Szablowski, and Martin Thomas. *Final Appeal: Decision-Making in Canadian Courts of Appeal.* Toronto: James Lorimer, 1998.

Hart, H. L. A. *The Concept of Law.* 2nd ed. Oxford: Clarendon Press, 1994.

Hausegger, Lori, Matthew Hennigar, and Troy Riddell. *Canadian Courts: Law, Politics, and Process.* Don Mills, ON: Oxford University Press, 2009.

Horner, Jessie. *Canadian Law and the Canadian Legal System.* Toronto: Pearson Education Canada, 2006.

Loughlin, Martin. *The Idea of Public Law.* Toronto: Oxford University Press, 2004.

Malleson, Kate, and Peter Russell. *Appointing Judges in an Age of Judicial Power: Critical Perspectives from around the World.* Toronto: University of Toronto Press, 2006.

Marshall, T. David. *Judicial Conduct and Accountability.* Scarborough, ON: Carswell, 1995.

McCormick, Peter. *Canada's Courts.* Toronto: James Lorimer, 1994.

McCormick, Peter, and Ian Greene. *Judges and Judging: Inside the Canadian Judicial System.* Toronto: James Lorimer, 1990.

Morton, F. L., ed. *Law, Politics and the Judicial Process in Canada.* 3rd ed. Calgary: University of Calgary Press, 2002.

Paciocco, David M. *Getting Away with Murder: The Canadian Criminal Justice System.* Toronto: Irwin Law, 1999.

Roberts, Julian V., and Loretta J. Stalans. *Public Opinion, Crime, and Criminal Justice.* Boulder, CO: Westview Press, 1997.

Russell, Peter H., ed. *Canada's Trial Courts: Two Levels or One?* Toronto: University of Toronto Press, 2007.

Russell, Peter H., and David M. O'Brien, eds. *Judicial Independence in the Age of Democracy: Critical Perspectives from around the World.* Lynchburg, VA: University Press of Virginia, 2001.

Tremblay, Luc B. *The Rule of Law, Justice, and Interpretation.* Montreal: McGill-Queen's University Press, 1997.

PART 1

CHAPTER 7

Constitutionalism

A **constitution** is a set of fundamental rules and principles by which a state is organized. These rules and principles generally

a. establish the powers and responsibilities of the legislative, executive, and judicial branches of government;

b. allocate powers to different levels of government, such as federal, provincial, and local;

c. enumerate the rights of citizens in relationship to each other and to the government, as in a bill of rights; and

d. stipulate procedures for amending the constitution.

The term *fundamental rules* is used advisedly because a constitution comprises not only laws that are enforceable in the courts but also customs, or conventions, that are enforceable only in the sense that a government may lose political support by violating them. A **convention** is a practice or custom that is consistently followed by those in government even though it is not legally required. According to a leading authority, a convention is not just any custom that happens to be observed. To be considered a convention, a practice must exist for a good reason and those who follow it must be aware that they are following a rational rule.[1]

Conventions exist at several different levels: there are strong ones that are essential to the constitution, and weak ones that are really no more than usages. For example, it is essential in a parliamentary democracy that the head of state confer the task of forming a government to a politician who commands a working majority in the representative assembly—otherwise, the democratic principle of majority rule would be jeopardized. This convention is of the strongest type. In contrast, there is no intrinsic importance to the practice, rigorously followed in Canada, of the Commons adjourning to the Senate to witness royal assent to legislation. The head of state could just as well perform this function in private, as is done in Quebec and Australia. This convention is of the weakest type and could be changed on short notice without damage to the Constitution.[2]

Although useful, the distinction between law and convention is not as solid as it appears because courts have no power to enforce anything unless judges are obeyed by those who control the coercive apparatus of the state. This obedience is itself no more than a convention (albeit of the strongest type) based on politicians' belief that public opinion wishes the courts to be obeyed.[3] In the last analysis, law and convention are two related manifestations of the same spirit of constitutionalism and the rule of law.

THE BRITISH UNWRITTEN CONSTITUTION

The older type of constitution, which used to be very common but now survives in only a few countries such as Great Britain and New Zealand, is usually called **unwritten**. It is essential for Canadians to have some understanding of the unwritten British Constitution, for it is the source of our own. However, the term *unwritten* is not entirely accurate, for most of the British Constitution is written down. It is simply not written in a single place; rather, it must be pieced together from many different sources. *Unwritten* in this context really means uncodified. Also, there exist as part of the British Constitution many conventions that are not written down at all.

Much of the British Constitution consists of statutes of the King-in-Parliament. The oldest such text is the **Magna Carta** (Great Charter), which King John was forced to sign in 1215, before Parliament even existed, and which was later adopted by Parliament in statutory form. It established the principle that the sovereign had to rule within the law of the land. Further restrictions on royal power were established in the Bill of Rights (1689), which, among many other provisions, prevented the Crown from levying taxes without the consent of Parliament. The Act of Settlement (1701), as well as fixing the succession to the throne, protected the independence of judges by making it impossible for the king to dismiss them without cause. The Parliament Act (1911) imposed several restrictions on the powers of the House of Lords, and in doing so strengthened the Commons.

These, as well as many other statutes passed over hundreds of years, make up the legal framework of the British Constitution. But more than statutory law is involved. Since statutes always raise problems of interpretation when they are applied, the body of case law that has developed around the statutes must be considered part of the constitution. Also, the very existence of Parliament rests not on statutes but on the common-law or **prerogative** powers of the kings who first established the practice of calling Parliaments for consultation. In an important sense, the statutory structure of the British Constitution has a common-law foundation.

Many of the most important institutions of British government rest not on law but on convention. The cabinet and prime minister are mentioned briefly in some statutes, but the offices were never deliberately created by legislation. Similarly it is conventional that the Crown not refuse assent to a bill passed by Parliament, that the leader of the majority party be invited to form a cabinet, and so on.

This short sketch of the British Constitution suggests one of its important characteristics: flexibility. The written part—that is, constitutional law—is no different from any other type of law; all law, constitutional or otherwise, may be changed by an act of

Parliament. An act of Parliament cannot be unconstitutional as long as specified procedures are adhered to, and Parliament could free itself from existing procedures if it chose. Constitutional conventions are even more flexible than constitutional law, since they are essentially usages that are constantly evolving. This peculiar flexibility of the British unwritten constitution has led some observers to say that it is not a constitution at all; indeed, it may be thought of as a synonym for the ensemble of governmental institutions at any given moment.

THE AMERICAN WRITTEN CONSTITUTION

The British Constitution differs strikingly from the American one, which is the world's oldest surviving written constitution. The core of the U.S. Constitution consists of one systematic, deliberately designed document drawn up at the Constitutional Convention in Philadelphia in 1787. In fewer than 6,000 words this text arranges the legislative, executive, and judicial powers of the state; divides government into federal and state levels; and deals with some other necessary matters. The rights of the individual are enumerated in the Bill of Rights, which includes the first ten amendments to the Constitution, adopted in 1791. The amending process was intentionally made arduous so that the Constitution could not be changed lightly by the transitory desires of whoever happened to be in power. Amendments must be approved by a two-thirds majority in both houses of Congress and subsequently ratified by three-quarters of the states. Not surprisingly, this very difficult procedure has been used successfully only 27 times since 1787.

The rather rigid amending process has not hampered constitutional evolution in the United States as much as might be expected because the courts have taken on the function of declaring the meaning of the Constitution in specific applications. A large body of case law has grown up that is indispensable to understanding the Constitution, and this case law is flexible in much the same way as common law. For example, the U.S. Supreme Court held in 1896 in *Plessy v. Ferguson* that it did not conflict with the Constitution for states to require racially segregated coaches on railway trains.[4] According to the court, as long as the facilities were "separate but equal" the situation did not violate the equal-protection clause of the Fourteenth Amendment. But in 1954 the same court departed from this precedent in the famous case of *Brown v. Board of Education*, holding that segregated schools were necessarily injurious to the minority and thus contrary to the Fourteenth Amendment principle of equal protection of the law.[5] Strictly speaking, the Supreme Court did not overrule *Plessy v. Ferguson;* rather, it distinguished *Brown v. Board* from the earlier precedent because it dealt with education rather than transportation. But the political effect was the same as a change in the Constitution. The point here is that the U.S. Constitution is, to a large extent, what the courts say it is.

Although *convention* is not used as a technical term in American constitutional law, there is inevitably something like it in the U.S. Constitution. The power of the courts to declare legislation unconstitutional is not mentioned in the text of 1787. Chief Justice

John Marshall first claimed this right in the seminal case of *Marbury v. Madison* (1803); it ultimately rests on the acquiescence of Congress.[6] Another example was the practice established by George Washington, the first president, that no chief executive should serve more than two terms. This precedent was followed until World War II, when Franklin Roosevelt, citing the dangerous international situation, chose to run for a third and then a fourth term. His violation of the practice touched off such a reaction that the Twenty-Second Amendment, ratified in 1951, officially wrote the two-term principle into the Constitution. Usage, having proved insufficient, was thus translated into constitutional law.

The contrast between the British and American Constitutions is instructive. The former is unwritten and flexible, the latter written and rigid. The former can be amended by simple statute, the latter only by an elaborate amending process. Judicial decisions play a role in both but have a far larger role in the American model, where they supply the flexibility that is missing in the constitutional text.

THE CANADIAN HYBRID

The Canadian Constitution may be seen as a blend of the written and unwritten models. Although there is no central, systematic document of the American type, the Canadian Constitution does have a substantial written core. As with the British model, this core consists of a series of statutes enacted over a long period of time. But, contrary to the British Constitution, these statutes can no longer be amended or repealed by a simple act of Parliament. See Canadian Focus 7.1 for a further comparison of the Canadian and American constitutions.

The starting point for finding the written constitution is now the Constitution Act, 1982. Schedule I of the Act lists 30 statutes and orders-in-council (formal decisions of Cabinet), some Canadian and some British in origin, that are now assured of constitutional status and can therefore be amended only by approved procedures. The most important of these 30 items is the British North America (BNA) Act, 1867, now renamed the Constitution Act, 1867. This British statute created the Dominion of Canada in 1867 and set up the federal system as well as the legislative, executive, and judicial institutions of government, all of which still exist today. Many of the 30 items consist of amendments to the BNA Act made by the British Parliament at the request of Canada between 1867 and 1982. These amendments have all been restyled "the Constitution Act, 1871," or "1940," or whichever year applies. Other scheduled items include the statutes and orders-in-council by which Canada was enlarged to its present boundaries— for example, the Manitoba Act, the British Columbia Terms of Union, and the Alberta and Saskatchewan Acts. These have all retained their original names. Finally there is the Statute of Westminster, 1931, a piece of British legislation by which Britain renounced the right to legislate for Canada except to amend the Canadian Constitution—a duty that Britain retained by necessity until 1981, when the federal government and all the provinces except Quebec reached agreement on an amending formula.

Canadian Focus 7.1

Constitutional Preambles

The preambles to the American Constitution and to the Canadian Constitution Act, 1867, give some idea of the differences between the two documents. Note that the American preamble characterizes the making of the Constitution as an act of "the people," whereas the Canadian preamble is an introduction to a piece of British legislation, which is an act of the Crown taken with the advice and consent of Parliament. The people as such do not figure in the British/Canadian model. Also, the American preamble describes a new legal construction, whereas the Canadian preamble emphasizes continuity ("a Constitution similar in Principle to that of the United Kingdom").

Preamble to the American Constitution

We the People of the United States, in Order to form a more perfect Union, establish Justice, insure domestic Tranquility, provide for the common defence, promote the general Welfare, and secure the Blessings of Liberty to ourselves and our Posterity, do ordain and establish this Constitution for the United States of America.

Preamble to the Constitution Act, 1867

WHEREAS the Provinces of Canada, Nova Scotia, and New Brunswick have expressed their Desire to be federally united into One Dominion under the Crown of the United Kingdom of Great Britain and Ireland, with a Constitution similar in Principle to that of the United Kingdom:

And whereas such a Union would conduce to the Welfare of the Provinces and promote the Interests of the British Empire:

And whereas on the Establishment of the Union by Authority of Parliament it is expedient, not only that the Constitution of the Legislative Authority in the Dominion be provided for, but also that the Nature of the Executive Government therein be declared:

And whereas it is expedient that Provision be made for the eventual Admission into the Union of other Parts of British North America … .

The Constitution Act, 1982, not only enumerated and confirmed the pre-existing parts of the written Constitution but also introduced important new substance, particularly in the first 34 sections, known as the Canadian Charter of Rights and Freedoms. In establishing limits to the powers of the federal and provincial legislatures and governments, the Charter radically transformed the nature of the Constitution, which previously had not contained any statement of the fundamental rights of Canadians. Civil liberties, such as freedom of religion and speech, and political rights, such as the right to vote and run for office, are now entrenched in the Constitution. This in turn has enhanced the political power of the courts, which are the natural interpreters of the Constitution.

The rest of the Constitution Act, 1982, addresses Aboriginal and treaty rights of Native peoples, future constitutional conferences, ownership and control of natural resources, and—most important for this discussion—the process to be followed in amending the Constitution. Before 1982, some parts of the written Constitution could be amended only by the British Parliament. The normal procedure was for a joint address of the Canadian Senate and House of Commons to request that the king or queen have the British cabinet introduce the needed amendment into the British Parliament—a request that was never refused. Although the mechanics of the procedure were under federal control, it became a matter of convention to seek provincial agreement to amendments affecting the provinces. This usually, but not always, meant getting the unanimous consent of the provincial governments.

The Act has transferred constitutional amendment from the realm of convention to that of law. There are now three main ways of changing the Canadian Constitution:

- **Unanimous procedure**. For certain fundamental matters, such as the existence of the monarchy and the composition of the Supreme Court, the agreement of all provincial legislative assemblies must be added to that of the Senate and the House of Commons.

CP Photo/stf

Queen Elizabeth II and Prime Minister Pierre Trudeau sign the Constitution Act, 1982.

- **General procedure.** Most other questions require resolutions of the legislatures of at least two-thirds of the provinces, containing among themselves 50 percent of the population of the provinces, and the consent of the Senate and House of Commons.
- **Bilateral procedure.** This third option exists for situations that affect only one province. In such a case, approval is required from the legislature of the province in question as well as from the House of Commons and the Senate. The bilateral procedure was used in 1993 to entrench official bilingualism in New Brunswick, in 1997 to remove the constitutionally guaranteed rights of Newfoundland's church-administered schools, and in the same year to change Quebec's school system from a religious to a linguistic basis.

In all three procedures, the Senate has only a suspensory veto. If the Senate does not agree to the resolution, it can be proclaimed by the governor general if it is passed again by the House of Commons after a waiting period. This happened in the case of the Newfoundland schools amendment. The amendment was rejected in the Senate the first time around but then passed a second time in the House of Commons after the required six-month waiting period, so it acquired constitutional force without ever being passed by the Senate.

Quebec refused to ratify the 1982 constitutional amendments for several reasons. It was not in the interest of the Parti Québécois, which governed Quebec at the time, to sign on to any form of renewed federalism, for that would have conflicted with its own hopes for separation. But opposition in Quebec went far beyond Parti Québécois circles. At the procedural level, many Quebeckers claimed (although the Supreme Court of Canada disagreed) that their province held a veto under a constitutional convention requiring unanimous provincial consent. At the substantive level, many francophones objected to the fact that the Charter, by guaranteeing certain rights of official-language minorities, reduced traditional provincial powers over education and language.

JUDICIAL INTERPRETATION

Whatever happens with the formal amending procedures, the most important mechanism of constitutional change in Canada now is judicial interpretation. This has been true since 1867 with respect to the allocation of powers between the federal and provincial governments, as set forth in Sections 91 to 95 of the Constitution Act, 1867. It is only by virtue of court decisions that we know, for example, that the federal government has the power to legislate a national system of wage and price controls under conditions of economic emergency.[7] This is the case even though such power is not specifically mentioned in the Act itself. Since 1982, the interpretive function of the courts in constitutional matters has become much wider because the Canadian Charter of Rights and Freedoms, which is a constitutional text, covers so much territory. The courts now not only allocate power (i.e., rule whether the federal or provincial government has the right to legislate on a particular matter) but also deny power (i.e., rule whether a federal or provincial government may abridge freedom of the press or take away the right to vote, and so on).[8] Canada is now very close to the United States in the extraordinary importance of the courts in defining what the Constitution means.

In another way, however, we remain close to Great Britain. The preamble to the Constitution Act, 1867, states that Canada desires to have "a Constitution similar in Principle to that of the United Kingdom." These words have imported into Canada a large body of British constitutional convention relating to the use of the royal prerogative, the appointment of a prime minister and cabinet, the need to maintain support in the House of Commons, and many other matters. The working machinery of parliamentary government in Canada is based largely on these conventions. Because the Constitution Act, 1867, does not even mention the words *prime minister* and *cabinet*, an uninformed reader of the Act might conclude that the governor general and the Queen's Privy Council for Canada are the chief executive authorities in Canada. Even in 1867 that was far from true, and it is not at all true today. But the outmoded language of the written constitution is meaningful because it is supported by many conventions such as the existence of Cabinet as the working committee of Privy Council and the reliance of the governor general upon the advice of cabinet ministers.

CONSTITUTIONALISM

All constitutions, whether of the British unwritten, the American written, or the Canadian hybrid type, ultimately manifest an underlying spirit of **constitutionalism**. This is the belief that government is not the controlling force of society but an instrument within it. It exercises the powers of authority and coercion for the general welfare by doing things that other agencies cannot do, but it is still part of society, not elevated above it. The society has, to use another common expression, a **limited state**. The constitution expresses government's limitations by stipulating which powers will be exercised by which person or body. Perhaps more important, it also states which powers are *not* to be exercised by anyone in government but are to be left to the people, such as the power to decide how to worship. The constitution of an unlimited state would be mere camouflage, for if government could do whatever it chose, its actions would not be restricted by rules and its discretion would be complete.

RULE OF LAW

Closely related to constitutionalism and the limited state is the concept of the **rule of law.** This phrase is more readily understood if it is approached as a shortened form of the ancient expression "the rule of law, not of men." It means that, to the greatest extent possible, people should not be subject to the unhindered discretion of others, but that all—rulers and ruled alike—should obey known, predictable, and impartial rules of conduct. It is a shield that protects citizens against the abuse of power "by laying down a set of procedures governing the use and alleged misuse of coercive power."[9] It has always been part of the Canadian Constitution to the extent that the Constitution is "similar in Principle to that of the United Kingdom," and it has now been made explicit in the short preamble to the Charter: "Whereas Canada is founded upon principles that recognize the supremacy of God and the rule of law." We can distinguish several layers of meaning in the idea of the rule of law.

Maintenance of Law and Order

At the most elementary level, the government must maintain law and order so that people are, as much as possible, prevented from attacking each other. The enforcement of law in this sense allows us to count on security of person and property. Yet it is not enough for sovereigns to restrain us from despoiling each other if they themselves are not so restrained. Simple law and order must be complemented by restrictions upon government itself. The ideal of the rule of law leads logically to constitutionalism and the limited state.

No Punishment Without Law

The subject should be liable to punishment by government only for violation of law. "No punishment without law" is an old maxim of English common law. It prevents rulers from using their coercive power arbitrarily against those who are the object of their dislike. People cannot be punished just for being who they are; they must commit specified acts that violate known laws. This aspect of the rule of law is an important safeguard of individual freedoms because it means that people are free to do anything not explicitly forbidden by law. The opposite of this principle is exemplified in the following 1935 law of the German Nazi regime:

> Any person who commits an act which the law declares to be punishable or which is deserving of penalty according to the fundamental conceptions of a penal law and sound popular feeling, shall be punished. If there is no penal law directly covering such an act it shall be punished under the law of which the fundamental conception applies most nearly to the said act.[10]

Under such broadly drawn provisions, one could be punished for any action disliked by someone in authority. The meaning of the rule of law is entirely subverted, even if the form of legislation is preserved.

Discretion

Not all government activity can be reduced to impartial enforcement of rules. There is also the large and important element of **discretion**. This flexibility to decide something within the broader framework of rules appears in law enforcement when the judge assigns a sentence to a convicted offender, and it is even more prominent in the service activities of the state. If government is to defend the country from external enemies, it must have discretion to locate military bases in suitable spots, choose effective weaponry, and promote capable officers. If government is to build roads, it must plan their location, acquire land, and let contracts for grading and construction; none of these things can be achieved without discretion.

But discretion need not be complete; it can and must be hedged with limiting rules. Government, for example, must have the discretion to acquire land, but there can be rules ensuring that owners will be compensated at fair market value and that they may appeal to the courts if they are dissatisfied with the state's offer. Similarly, government's discretion in letting contracts can be controlled by requiring contractors to tender bids in an open competition. The rule of law requires that where governmental discretion is necessary, it should be exercised within a framework of rules that discourage arbitrary decisions and offer recourse if such decisions are made.

Government Subject to Law

Government and its employees must be as subject to law as the people who are ruled. This is the great principle that was established in the English-speaking world by the Magna Carta. It means today that the powers of government must be founded on either common law or legislation. For example, it may seem necessary in the interests of national security to open the mail of individuals suspected of treasonous or seditious activities, but this is a power that common law gives neither to government nor to private citizens. If it is to be exercised at all, the rule of law requires that it be explicitly approved by legislation setting forth the appropriate conditions. See Law Focus 7.1 for a discussion of the Supreme Court's role in the rule of law.

Recognized Procedure

Law must be made by known and accepted procedures and is binding only if these procedures are followed. In the common-law system, if a judge violated accepted rules of procedure—for example, by not allowing one side to speak—the resulting decision would be reversed on appeal and would not become a precedent contributing to the law. Similarly, legislation can be created only if Parliament follows all its rules of procedure. An attempt by the House of Commons to legislate without the assent of the Senate and the governor general would be contrary to the rule of law. Of course, these legislative procedures are not immutable; they are contained in the Constitution, which can be amended. But amendment itself requires that fixed procedures be followed.

Law Focus 7.1

The Supreme Court and the Rule of Law

The foundational case on the rule of law in Canada is *Roncarelli v. Duplessis*.[11] In 1946, when Maurice Duplessis was premier and attorney general of Quebec, he ordered the Quebec Liquor Commission to revoke the liquor licence of Frank Roncarelli, who owned a small restaurant in Montreal. The only reason given was that Roncarelli, an active Jehovah's Witness, had furnished bail money for other Witnesses who had run afoul of Quebec's laws against distribution of religious literature. The Supreme Court of Canada ultimately concluded that Duplessis had acted without legal authority, because Roncarelli's religious activities were unconnected with the statute under which his liquor licence had been granted. Duplessis was required to pay financial compensation to Roncarelli for the damage caused to his business. His position as premier did not confer on him any immunity for actions taken outside the law.

The 1985 *Operation Dismantle* case extended judicial enforcement of the rule of law even further.[12] A coalition of peace groups known as Operation Dismantle tried to use the courts to prevent testing of cruise missiles in Canadian airspace, arguing that such testing violated the "security of the person" guaranteed by Section 7 of the Charter, in that it made war and attack on Canada more likely. The testing took place under an order-in-council pursuant to Canada's participation in NATO. Although the Supreme Court of Canada refused Operation Dismantle's request for an injunction to halt the cruise tests, it ruled that orders-in-council are governed by the rule of law and must conform to the Constitution, as interpreted in judicial review.

This was an important ruling, for orders-in-council are the chief means by which the political executive acts in a parliamentary democracy. Thousands are passed every year in Canada in the course of meetings of federal and provincial cabinets. *Operation Dismantle* reaffirmed the principle that those who control the government are not above or beyond the law.

CHALLENGES TO THE RULE OF LAW

Important as the rule of law is, it is not the only principle governing political behaviour. Laws are human contrivances, and as such it is always possible that they can be imperfect and unfair. That is particularly true when not everyone can participate in politics, so the lawmakers come from restricted circles. In the nineteenth century, when only men could vote, it no doubt seemed quite reasonable to most of them that women should not have the same right. But had women been effectively consulted about it? Not really, because they were excluded from politics at the time. In theory, law should be changed by rational discussion leading to legislative amendment in the elected assembly or reinterpretation in the courts, but sometimes these institutions seem unresponsive, and groups in society—such as the **suffragists** (advocates of women's right to vote)—will challenge the law in an attempt to change it.

One way in which dissatisfied groups challenge the law is through peaceful protest—rallies, marches, demonstrations, sit-ins, boycotts, strikes, and so on. These activities involve speech but they go beyond speech because they also involve human bodies in action. They may be completely legal or they may involve temporary flouting of the law, such as holding up traffic on roads or blocking access to office buildings. Even when protests are non-violent, because they mobilize masses of people, they suggest the possibility of physical force if demands are not met.

Such forms of protest are not new, but they have recently been re-energized by social media. Facebook can quickly alert people to a protest action; Twitter can move protestors around a city faster than police can keep up; YouTube can post videos of arrests and beatings if the authorities resort to repression. Social media were deeply involved in the massive protests that brought down the autocratic governments of Tunisia and Egypt in early 2011. There were isolated violent clashes with the authorities, but by and large it was peaceful protest rallies, sustained over days and weeks, that brought down these regimes. It must be noted, however, that the Tunisian and Egyptian governments, perhaps sensing that they could not rely on their armies and police forces, did not make serious resort to violence. Other Arab regimes, such as Saudi Arabia, struck hard in response to similar protests and were able to put them down.

One special form of protest is known as **civil disobedience**, exemplified by sit-ins in the American South in the 1960s. Black activists, sometimes with white supporters, went into restaurants, buses, and other places where they could not be legally present and remained until they were arrested. Indeed, being arrested was the goal. Civil disobedience works through voluntary acceptance of the legal penalties that may be imposed for breaking unjust laws, thus highlighting the coercive nature of the regime. Passive resistance to authority is crucial, such as allowing oneself to be dragged out by police without fighting back. Violent resistance cedes the moral high ground on which civil disobedience depends.

The greatest theorist of civil disobedience was Mahatma Gandhi, who used it in his decades-long struggle for obtaining the independence of India from the British Empire. Gandhi in turn influenced Martin Luther King Jr. and Nelson Mandela in their struggles for Black rights in the United States and South Africa. Gandhi spoke of **satyagraha**, "the power of truth." The point was not to defeat one's opponents but to convert them through non-resistance, thus demonstrating the power of moral conviction.

Civil disobedience had noted successes in India and the American South because the authorities were constrained by a working constitutional government. Acts of civil disobedience served to remind the authorities that they were violating the general principles of their own constitution. The rule of law could be cited as a standard against which racial discrimination or imperial subjection had to be condemned. In a general climate of constitutionalism, civil disobedience can have a powerful effect by highlighting ways in which the society is not living up to its professed principles.

In contrast, civil disobedience, like other forms of peaceful protest, has not been successful against autocratic regimes determined to use as much violence as necessary to put down protest. Civil disobedience can work upon public opinion if protestors are arrested in front of television cameras, tried in open courtrooms, and sentenced to determinate prison terms. But it can't work if protestors are secretly arrested in the middle of the night and subsequently disappear because they have been either murdered or sent to remote prison camps. Against regimes that pay no heed to constitutionalism and the rule of law, revolutionary force may be the only option.

Questions for Discussion

1. Would Canada be better off if our political conventions were written into the Constitution? What are some advantages of a hybrid constitution? Disadvantages?

2. Can you give an example from current public affairs where you think the rule of law is not being observed? What particular facet of the rule of law is being violated?

3. Approving constitutional amendments by means of referendums has the obvious virtue of demonstrating popular consent. Can you think of any possible negative aspects to using the referendum procedure?

Internet Links

1. The Constitution Society: **www.constitution.org**. All sorts of information about the United States Constitution.

2. Liberty Library of Constitutional Classics: **www.constitution.org/liberlib.htm**. A large collection of online texts of classic works on constitutionalism and political philosophy.

3. Richard Kimber's Political Science Resources: **www.politicsresources.net**. Follow the links to texts of past and present constitutions of all the world's countries.

4. Solon Law Archive: **www.solon.org**. A veritable treasure trove that gives access to all the Canadian constitutional documents listed in the schedule to the Constitution Act, 1982, plus subsequent amendments; the Meech Lake and Charlottetown Accords; and constitutions of several other countries, including the United States, Mexico, and Australia.

5. U.S. State Constitutions: **www.constitution.org/cons/usstcons.htm**. Texts of the constitutions of all the American states.

Further Reading

Ajzenstat, Janet, et al., eds. *Canada's Founding Debates.* Toronto: Stoddart, 1999.

Alexander, Larry, ed. *Constitutionalism: Philosophical Foundations.* Cambridge: Cambridge University Press, 1998.

Beard, Charles Austin. *The Supreme Court and the Constitution.* Mineola, NY: Dover Publications, 2006.

Cardinal, Linda, and David Headon, eds. *Shaping Nations: Constitutionalism and Society in Australia and Canada.* Toronto: University of Toronto Press, 2002.

Cook, Curtis, ed. *Constitutional Predicament: Canada after the Referendum of 1992.* Montreal: McGill-Queen's University Press, 1994.

Cummings, Milton C. Jr., and David Wise. *Democracy under Pressure: An Introduction to the American Political System.* Orlando, FL: Harcourt, 1996.

Heard, Andrew. *Canadian Constitutional Conventions: The Marriage of Law and Politics.* Toronto: Oxford University Press, 1991.

Hogg, Peter W. *Constitutional Law of Canada.* 4th ed. Scarborough, ON: Carswell, 1997.

Hurley, James Ross. *Amending Canada's Constitution: History, Processes, Problems and Prospects.* Ottawa: Canada Communication Group, 1996.

James, Patrick, Donald E. Abelson, and Michael Lusztig. *The Myth of the Sacred: The Charter, the Courts, and the Politics of the Constitution in Canada.* Montreal: McGill-Queen's University Press, 2003.

Kelly, James B., and Christopher Manfredi, eds. *Contested Constitutionalism: Reflections on the Canadian Charter of Rights and Freedoms.* Vancouver: University of British Columbia Press, 2009.

Knopff, R., and F. L. Morton. *Charter Politics.* Scarborough, ON: Nelson Canada, 1992.

Licht, Robert A., ed. *Is the Supreme Court the Guardian of the Constitution?* Washington, DC: AEI Press, 1993.

Mandel, Michael. *The Charter of Rights and the Legalization of Politics in Canada.* Rev. ed. Toronto: Thompson Educational Publishing, 1994.

Manfredi, Christopher. *Judicial Power and the Charter: Canada and the Paradox of Liberal Constitutionalism.* Toronto: McClelland & Stewart, 1993.

McCormick, Peter. *Supreme at Last: The Evolution of the Supreme Court of Canada.* Toronto: James Lorimer, 2000.

Milne, David. *The Canadian Constitution.* Rev. ed. Toronto: James Lorimer, 1991.

Monahan, Patrick. *Meech Lake: The Inside Story.* Toronto: University of Toronto Press, 1991.

PART 1

Russell, Peter H. *Constitutional Odyssey: Can Canadians Become a Sovereign People?* Toronto: University of Toronto Press, 2004.

Russell, Peter H., Rainer Knopff, Thomas M. J. Bateman, and Janet L. Hiebert. *The Court and the Constitution:* Leading Cases. Toronto: Emond Montgomery Publications, 2008.

Saywell, John T. *The Lawmakers: Judicial Power and the Shaping of Canadian Federalism.* Toronto: University of Toronto Press, 2004.

Sheldon, Charles H. *Essentials of the American Constitution: The Supreme Court and the Fundamental Law.* Boulder, CO: Westview Press, 2002.

Waldron, Jeremy. *Law and Disagreement.* New York: Oxford University Press, 1999.

Webber, Jeremy H. A. *Reimagining Canada: Language, Culture, Community and the Canadian Constitution.* Kingston, ON: McGill-Queen's University Press, 1994.

CHAPTER 8
Cooperation under Anarchy

James F. Keeley and Gavin Cameron

States must deal not only with other states but also with non-state actors such as **international organizations, non-governmental organizations** (NGOs), businesses, religious movements, armed groups, and individuals. They engage with other states and non-state actors in the traditional realm of military–political relations but also in a wide range of economic, demographic, and cultural transactions. They must also cope with physical processes, such as climate change, that reach across national boundaries. Financial and budgetary crises in one country may have effects around the world, so that an earthquake in Japan or a flood in Thailand can disrupt automotive industry supply chains in North America.

States could try to cope with this complex environment without cooperation, but some forms of interdependence cannot be avoided or are too costly to reduce. Thus, while the extent of cooperation among states may be less than many people might hope for, there is far more cooperation than could be explained if the international realm were merely a Hobbesian "war of all against all."

Because states are sovereign—acknowledging no legal superior—the international state system is a formal **anarchy,** a decentralized system without a true government. International law exists *between* states, not above them, and interstate cooperation is cooperation between states. So we find scholars talking not about "international government" but about "governance without government" as states attempt to manage the implications of international interdependence. After noting some mechanisms through which states try to manage interdependence under anarchy, we will look briefly at three illustrations of international cooperation.

MECHANISMS

By allocating jurisdictional competencies among states, **international law** tells states what limits are set on their actions by the legal rights of other actors. It provides mechanisms through which states can settle disputes with each other. Through **treaties**—legally binding international agreements—states may specify obligations and powers vis-à-vis each other and other actors, as well as create intergovernmental organizations (specifying their composition, mandates, rules, powers, and resources) to deal with challenges they confront. The body of international law governing **diplomacy** also shapes the mechanisms through which governments interact with each other.

Intergovernmental organizations help states pool their resources and information, coordinate their activities, provide collective action, and discuss problems. (This is increasingly done with input from NGOs claiming to speak on behalf of "global civil society.") The practices of "parliamentary diplomacy"—committees, resolutions, votes—and the existence of administrative secretariats in these organizations allow the organization to act in the name of the entire membership. But while these mechanisms may lead some to think of these bodies as embryonic "world governments," that considerably overstates their position. Even where they may have some degree of independence, these organizations must operate within the limits of the legal powers granted them by member states. Less formal networks, including meetings of officials from various governments such as finance ministers, or the G8 and G20 meetings, may also serve as vehicles for discussion and coordination, though they are much more dependent on voluntary action by the states concerned.

The numbers and the significance of such coordination efforts, and the wide range of issues that they cover, have stimulated a particular branch of theory in the discipline of international relations: the theory of **international regimes.** International regimes may be formalized in law or associated with intergovernmental organizations, or they may be much less formal and consist primarily of concepts of problems, solutions, and modes of behavior shared among a number of states. While the effectiveness of such regimes is still widely debated, the significance of the regime concept for "governance without government" seems well-established.

PROBLEMS AND LIMITS

If the phrase "cooperation under anarchy" now seems widely accepted, it is also widely accepted that it faces limitations and problems. Although proponents of international cooperation are often keen to assert the necessity of collective action to address international problems and are quick to decry failures to act as they desire, cooperation may not occur automatically. It requires the adjustment of interests among participants, which may limit effectiveness.

Action to deal with an international problem requires a workable agreement on the nature of the problem, on the possible solutions, and on the distribution of the costs and benefits of effective action. Obtaining agreement may be a complex and lengthy process, requiring compromises that could influence the effectiveness of whatever collective action results. Even for issues that seem to affect the entire globe, states will have different perceptions of how their interests will be affected. They will generally seek to avoid costs and to reap significant and especially more immediate benefits. They will particularly seek to avoid paying immediate high costs, especially in exchange for uncertain longer-term benefits, even if the latter may ultimately be greater. They may be reluctant to grant extensive authority or resources to international bodies, or resist being strongly guided by plans produced at the international level rather than pursuing agreed targets through means more adapted to their local conditions and capabilities.

The task of achieving coordination can be hard enough if an international body already exists to provide a framework for action; it is more difficult still if a new body needs to be created. Coordination problems are especially difficult if large numbers of states must agree or if consensus is the decision-making mechanism. Problems may also exist if certain significant states must be brought on board for the effort to be effective, giving those states veto power. Some of these problems may be reduced if effective action can be accomplished by agreement among a few highly capable states. This means, however, that only the problems those few think are significant will get addressed and the solutions they prefer will tend to be favoured. Inequalities in power may permit action but also affect what action is taken, and they may create resentments and threats of non-cooperation among other states.

For implementation at the national level, some states may lack the necessary capability and may need both time and assistance in order to do their part. National governments may vary in their willingness to act, and agencies of government will have different concerns and interests that they want to defend. There may be strong political pressures to defend significant domestic actors from external forces. Some local actors may complain about a "democratic deficit," claiming that the wishes of the state's people are being overridden to fulfill international obligations. Such domestic forces often affect the course and outcome of negotiations.

THE LAW OF THE SEA

Many fundamental principles of the modern law of the sea—such as the right of all states to sail the high seas (freedom of navigation), the exclusive jurisdiction of states over vessels registered under their flag on the high seas, the limitations on jurisdictional claims by coastal states, and the status of piracy under international law—date back hundreds of years. In fact, until the later 1950s, the law of the sea was essentially customary international law. That is, it existed as a set of practices that states had, over time, come to regard as legally binding, even though they were not set down in a **treaty.** An international conference held in 1958 produced four conventions: on territorial seas and contiguous zones, on the high seas, on the continental shelf, and on fisheries on the high seas. In 1967 the UN General Assembly created a Seabed Committee to start examining problems caused by increasing technological access to resources under the seabed. Meanwhile, competition for access to fisheries led to disputes between coastal states and states with long-range fishing fleets. The Third United Nations Conference on the Law of the Sea (UNCLOS III) opened in 1973 after a second conference, in the 1960s, failed to reach agreement. In 1994 the treaty resulting from unclos III received enough ratifications to come into force. The United States has never ratified it but is still bound by the earlier conventions to which it was a party, as well as by existing customary law.

The UN **Law of the Sea** tells coastal states and states with vessels sailing the seas what rights and obligations they have. It especially gives coastal states a complex set of jurisdictional zones, overlapping both physically and in terms of their other legal properties. It tries to meet the interests of these coastal states while at the same time meeting the interests of maritime states—states with large navies and merchant fleets—by preserving freedom of navigation. It must cope with an ever larger number of states and contending interests, especially as new technologies permit greater use of ocean resources. The shift from customary to treaty-based law is one way of responding to these problems in a relatively quick and coherent manner, rather than waiting for accepted practices to accumulate over time, with the risk of serious disputes occurring while this is going on. While major portions of unclos III are based on customary principles, large sections of it, dealing with fisheries and seabed mining, are quite new. The Law of the Sea thus presents a good example of cooperation under anarchy in adapting to changing circumstances.

While the United Nations sponsored the conferences that produced the modern Law of the Sea, the Law of the Sea exists apart from the UN as an organization. That it took fifteen years to negotiate unclos III, starting with the Seabed Committee, and another twelve to come into force, and that some countries such as the United States are still not parties indicates the difficult character of the issues behind the treaty, such as seabed resources, fisheries, and jurisdictional zones.

Access to mineral resources was a major issue, pitting those states capable of mining the deep seabed against states without such capability, and against dry-land producers of the same minerals. The problems were handled in part by extending the concept of the continental shelf, giving coastal states exclusive and sovereign rights over the resources on and under the seabed up to 200 nautical miles from their coasts. This massive "privatization" of the seabed brought many areas thought to have mineral wealth within national jurisdictions. The prospect of oil and gas resources under the Arctic Ocean has led states bordering it to advance continental-shelf claims based on the geology of the seabed, which overlap with one another. These claims remain to be worked out among the states.

On the deep ocean floor beyond these national jurisdictional zones, a different solution was sought. Rather than simply allowing states with the necessary mining technology to reserve the benefits for themselves, developing states wanted a share. This approach was initially indicated by a General Assembly resolution calling the resources of the deep seabed "the common heritage of mankind." An International Seabed Authority was created under unclos III to govern mining in "the Area" (the deep ocean floor beyond national continental shelves), granting licences to companies to mine—or engaging in mining itself—and receiving part of the revenue, which would be used for "the general benefit of mankind." This approach and a desire of developing states to obtain access to the necessary mining technology became key points of dispute with technologically capable states. The latter naturally wished to ensure that they, and private firms operating under their protection, would obtain the hoped-for profits. They also objected to some of the technology-transfer provisions sought by developing states, which could be seen as giving other states access, under unfairly favourable terms, to capabilities developed elsewhere at great expense. So the United States and other technologically capable states initially did not sign UNCLOS III but instead sought to develop rules to apply among themselves. However, seabed mining has not developed to the extent anticipated, which has postponed the legal and political difficulties of relations with these "holdout" states. Since 1994 some of the technologically capable states have ratified UNCLOS III. The legal tribunal that deals with continental-shelf claims will soon become busy, as Canada, Russia, and others are preparing claims regarding their continental shelves to bring before the tribunal in a year or so.

Growing pressures on fisheries also led to difficulties. Coastal states sought to protect their fisheries from foreign competition while states with long-range fishing fleets sought access to those resources. An initial response by coastal states was to declare exclusive fishing zones extending as far as 100 miles or more from their coasts, or indeed simply to extend their territorial seas (in which foreign fishing is prohibited without permission). This led to clashes such as the "cod wars" between Britain and Iceland. Even as the Third Conference was taking place, however, a consensus developed that coastal states had preferential, though not exclusive, rights over fisheries beyond their territorial seas. UNCLOS III gives coastal states an **exclusive economic zone (EEZ)** extending 200 nautical miles from their shores, with preferential rights over the resources of the water column in that zone. Since this practice developed and became accepted even as UNCLOS III was being negotiated, many writers on international law regard it as having status in customary law as well as under the treaty. Fish stocks that straddle the high seas and EEZs still present significant management problems, however.

A central issue in the Law of the Sea has been how to protect the interests of coastal states while preserving rights of navigation for other states. The general strategy adopted has been to develop jurisdictional zones that give coastal states the authority they need for specific purposes without otherwise hampering ocean-going traffic. The result is a complex set of zones that can overlap both geographically and legally. Over its internal waters—ports, harbours, bays, and river mouths—a coastal state has sovereign authority, including over foreign merchant shipping, and the right even to deny access to its ports. In its territorial sea (up to 12 nautical miles from its coast) it has strong regulatory powers, but foreign ships are protected to a degree under the principle of "innocent passage." Passage through international straits, even within a state's territorial sea, has additional protections. In a further zone of up to 12 nautical miles (the "contiguous zone"), the coastal state may enforce its rules against smuggling, pollution, and the like. The eez, as noted, gives the coastal state special rights over living and non-living resources for up to 200 nautical miles outwards, while its legal continental shelf gives it sovereign and exclusive rights to resources on and under the seabed for at least 200 nautical miles. In these various zones the coastal state has suitable enforcement powers, including a right to pursue and capture vessels that break the rules (other than foreign naval vessels, which are immune from its jurisdiction). Otherwise, however, the coastal states do not have rights to disrupt peaceful navigation of the oceans by other states.

Beyond such zones, on the high seas, a crucial general rule is that only the flag state—the state in which a vessel is registered—has jurisdiction over a vessel. There are exceptions in the case of piracy (a crime under universal jurisdiction: any state may capture and punish a pirate on the high seas) and if a vessel is suspected of hiding its registration or of not sailing under any flag because only states (and thus only vessels properly registered with a state) have the right to sail the seas. However, states may also agree to grant boarding rights to each other, for example, to suppress the drug trade.

The Law of the Sea has been relatively successful as an area of interstate cooperation, in part because of the long-standing customary law on which it is based. Where this did not address state interests adequately or had been rendered obsolete by technology, it had to be updated and modified. A primary strategy, largely successful, has been to extend national jurisdictions to serve specific interests of coastal states. By subdividing these jurisdictional zones in both subject matter and physical extent, an accommodation with competing interests of international navigation has largely been reached. Governing the international commons of the high seas and the deep ocean floor, however, has been more challenging. While the fundamental rules of ocean navigation remain intact, issues of technological access have hampered the acceptability of the seabed mining regime, and the fate of international fish stocks is still in question.

COLLECTIVE SECURITY AND PEACEKEEPING

At the end of World War I, the victorious Allied powers created the League of Nations. Its primary objective was to remove the threat of another catastrophic conflict by creating a mechanism to marshal overwhelming power against any state threatening the peace. The idea that all states had an interest in preserving the peace, and would organize themselves to deter and punish breaches of the peace, underpinned the principle of **collective security.** This, rather than the failed concept of a **balance of power,** was seen as a way of preventing another major war. Initially the League had some success, but by the 1930s it was increasingly incapable of meeting its challenges as Japan invaded China and Italy invaded Ethiopia. The Great Powers in particular were divided: Germany, Italy, and Japan were fascist, the Union of Soviet Socialist Republics was communist, and the United States had refused to join the League. That left only Britain and France as major supporters.

The League was dismantled at the end of World War II, but the principle of collective security was preserved and given new life in the United Nations. The five Great Powers at the end of the war—the United States, the USSR, the United Kingdom, France, and China—designed the collective security elements of the new organization's charter, giving themselves permanent membership and a veto in the **Security Council,** and they were also expected to provide the vast bulk of forces if a threat to the peace developed. The veto would prevent the Security Council from acting against their interests. The privileged position of these states was the price of an effective collective security mechanism.

With the development of the **Cold War,** the collective security mechanism provided for in the Charter of the United Nations fell apart because the required agreement among the five permanent members of the Security Council was not forthcoming. As a result, there are only two major examples of collective security after 1945: the Korean War (1950–53) and the Gulf War of 1991. In neither case did the collective security mechanism actually operate along the lines laid down in the Charter. When North Korea invaded South Korea, only the absence of the USSR from key Security Council meetings permitted the UN to cobble together a response, and that was under the leadership of the United States rather than the UN Military Staff Committee. When Iraq invaded Kuwait in 1990, the earlier ending of the Cold War (and a degree of Soviet dependence on Western goodwill) allowed the Security Council to react forcefully and immediately, demanding that Iraq leave Kuwait, imposing sanctions, and threatening military measures if it did not obey. In the brief war that followed, Iraq was driven from Kuwait and was placed under continuing sanctions after a ceasefire was signed, while its weapons of mass destruction and its ability to produce them were systematically destroyed. Again, however, the UN enforcement action was led by the United States, which merely informed the Security Council of what it was doing rather than being organized through the essentially defunct Military Staff Committee. The record shows that the UN can undertake enforcement actions—including major collective security operations—but only under the relatively rare circumstances of unity among the five permanent members, and also that it has not used the precise mechanisms provided for in the Charter.

However, the UN has found new ways to respond to security challenges. One of these was the "Uniting for Peace" mechanism. Under the Charter, only "substantive" resolutions in the Security Council are subject to veto. The Uniting for Peace mechanism permitted the Security Council—under a procedural resolution—or the General Assembly if the Security Council was deadlocked, to shift an issue from the Security Council to the General Assembly. The General Assembly could then recommend action to the UN membership (only the Security Council could require action). This was the device used in the Korean War when the USSR returned to Security Council meetings and began using its veto there. Additionally, beginning in the later 1940s and drawing on some early League experience, the UN experimented with sending small groups of observers to monitor ceasefire agreements in some conflicts.

These two mechanisms came together in the Suez Crisis of 1956, when Britain, France, and Israel attacked Egypt; the attack faltered because of American and Soviet opposition and general dismay among other states in the UN. When action in the Security Council was blocked by vetoes, the scene shifted, through the Uniting for Peace mechanism, to the General Assembly. There, Lester Pearson of Canada and Dag Hammarskjöld, the UN **Secretary-General**, put together a proposal for a UN force to separate the combatants and maintain a ceasefire while diplomats sought a resolution. This **peacekeeping** force would be drawn not from the Great Powers but from smaller and middle-power states such as Canada. Excluding forces from the Great Powers would help prevent them from being drawn into the dispute more directly. Peacekeeping thus offered a number of advantages: it stopped fighting and created a chance for peaceful settlement of the dispute; it gave less powerful states a significant role in the maintenance of peace; and it allowed the United States and the USSR to limit their involvement. Peacekeeping—a very different and less ambitious task than collective security, and one not specifically provided for in the Charter—became the major instrument employed by the UN to preserve international peace. There were 12 peacekeeping operations during the Cold War, and there have been 50 since it ended.

The next great peacekeeping operation took place in 1960–64, when public order disintegrated in the former Belgian Congo (now the Democratic Republic of the Congo) after independence. This was a different sort of operation—within a state rather than involving two or more opposing states—and was a matter of restoring public order rather than separating two well-organized military forces. It was complicated by a secessionist movement in one part of the country and further hampered when the West and the USSR backed opposing sides. This led to a financial crisis within the UN, when the USSR refused to pay its share of the expenses of the operation, and to a political crisis when Secretary-General Hammarskjöld was accused by the USSR of favouring the West in his management of the operation.

The Middle East peacekeeping operation in 1967, UNEF I, demonstrated some of the limitations of the peacekeeping concept when it was forced to withdraw shortly before the outbreak of the June war between Israel and Egypt. While it had successfully separated the combatants after the Suez Crisis, it could operate only with their agreement, and in the years following, a diplomatic resolution had not been reached. When a new UN force, UNEF II, was put in place after the 1967 war, it faced the same limitations. In 1974 a UN peacekeeping force was put into Cyprus to separate Greek and Turkish Cypriots, but it has shown the same diplomatic limitation; the Cyprus question has continued, unresolved, since that date. A peacekeeping force can, if the disputants are willing, help to keep a situation from flaring up, but it cannot of itself solve the political problems that sustain the dispute; instead it may simply shield the disputants from the effects of their intransigence.

Nonetheless, peacekeeping was a useful technique to help maintain and restore peace. After the end of the Cold War there was a new round of peacekeeping operations when civil disorder and secessionist movements broke out in Yugoslavia, Somalia, and elsewhere. There, however, the pattern was that of the Congo operation of the 1960s, not the interstate UNEF operations. Handling these "internal war" situations proved to be far more complex and ambitious than monitoring ceasefires between organized forces. Large forces were needed for long periods of time to carry out relief and other operations (for example, protecting civilians) as well as to monitor ceasefires. They needed not just to restore basic law and order in a situation of turmoil but also to support humanitarian relief for a vulnerable civilian population and to provide basic services while trying to build up basic state capacities and demobilize armed groups. These efforts require not only a greater array of skills and resources than "classic" peacekeeping but also larger UN operations over a longer period of time. The parties to such internal disputes are generally not well-organized, well-disciplined militaries, and indeed they may not be under any central control at all. The disputants are often intermingled, so that a ceasefire line—if one can be established at all—is complex to handle. The parties to the conflict may have little interest in seeking a political solution or in moderating their hostilities, and they may even see a UN intervention force as favouring the other side rather than as a neutral actor.

UN operations depend on the willingness of states to provide adequate resources, whether financial contributions, personnel, equipment, logistical support, or a legal mandate. Unwillingness to do this or to grant sufficient freedom of action to a UN commander in the field hinders the UN's ability to respond to a crisis. Faced with a fast-changing situation, the Secretary-General might ask the UN Security Council for a large force, only to see that requirement reduced by the unwillingness of states to commit adequate forces in a timely fashion. The UN sent a force to Rwanda, but it had neither the troop strength nor the mandate to prevent the genocide that occurred in 1994. Such operations highlighted various defects in the setup and management of peacekeeping operations, not only in the field but also at UN headquarters. Following the Brahimi Report of 2000, the UN headquarters in New York has attempted to strengthen its management of peacekeeping operations to provide better support to field operations. But while the need to reform and strengthen UN operations is recognized, progress has been slow and limited. The realities of complex operations in the field combine with the political realities at the centre to challenge high hopes of quick and effective reforms.

UN peacekeeping and collective security operations, especially the former, have shown the organization's ability to adapt to new demands and to political circumstances that could well have condemned the organization to early irrelevance. Despite its limits and defects, and despite the more ambitious nature of its field operations since the end of the Cold War, the United Nations presents a significant record of state cooperation. Central to both its adaptive capability and its limits have been the ability of dominant groups of states to find ways around obstacles (such as the Uniting for Peace mechanism and the technique of peacekeeping itself) and a political willingness to use the UN constructively to manage crises. As an association of sovereign states, the UN reflects in its operations the ambitions, interests, and resources of its membership. It also reflects their unwillingness or inability to overcome their particular interests and ambitions, and their dislike of granting strong independent powers and resources—which might then be used against their interests—to an international organization.

CLIMATE CHANGE

Environmental issues offer one of the clearest examples of the difficulties states face in cooperating under anarchy. The 1972 Stockholm Conference (officially the United Nations Conference on the Human Environment), the first serious international attempt to establish supranational environmental governance principles, created the UN Environment Programme (UNEP). By the late 1980s an epistemic community—a transnational community of experts who shared knowledge and information and were trying to reach a common consensus—had emerged on climate change. This community increasingly raised concerns about the extent and speed of global warming. The widespread burning of fossil fuels has released a variety of gases, including carbon dioxide and methane, that reinforce the Earth's natural tendency to trap some of the infrared sunlight reflected back from its surface and over time may increase the average temperature of the world (the "greenhouse effect").

In 1988 the Intergovernmental Panel on Climate Change (IPCC) was created to assess climate change and its potential effects. In its 2007 report, the IPCC stated that the likelihood of climate change's being caused by human actions was over 90 percent. In response to earlier reports, a key aspect of the 1992 Rio Earth Summit was creation of the UN Framework Convention on Climate Change (UNFCCC), which included a non-binding commitment by developed states to try to reduce their greenhouse gas emissions to 1990 levels by 2000. The UNFCCC also bound participants to a continuing series of meetings to review progress. The second review meeting occurred in 1997 in Kyoto. The Kyoto Protocol to the UNFCCC sought to reduce greenhouse gas emissions from developed countries as a means of limiting adverse changes to the global climate system. Unlike at Rio, the Kyoto Protocol imposed specific limits on states that signed and ratified the agreement. It entered into effect in 2005, when 156 of the participants (representing 55 percent of global greenhouse gas emissions) ratified the agreement.

The Kyoto Protocol committed 37 developed countries to reduce their greenhouse gas emissions by 5 percent on average, based on 1990 emission levels. However, the precise size of the reduction for each country was the product of negotiation. For example, the European Union agreed to cuts of 8 percent while Canada and Japan both agreed to reductions of 6 percent. Such reductions were to occur by 2012, with penalties attached for failure to meet the targets.

The greatest challenge to implementation of the Kyoto Protocol was that it represented a mismatch of certain short-term costs and uncertain long-term benefits. The agreement applied only to developed countries, which would have to alter their behaviour, but as global warming affects all countries, the gains from such changes would be enjoyed universally. This mismatch of individually incurred costs and collective benefits is a phenomenon known as "the tragedy of the commons." It occurs where there is an unregulated, openly accessed, and commonly held resource, such as the atmosphere, that is not owned by anyone. Actors have an interest in seeing a mutually beneficial agreement fulfilled but may hope that it can be achieved without their participation or payment of costs. Although the Kyoto Protocol included penalties for failure to meet emissions-reduction targets, without an international authority beyond the state level, enforcement mechanisms for such agreements are generally weak. If it is possible for a state to do nothing and enjoy the benefits of costs borne by other states (if enough countries act to mitigate climate change), so it is also possible for a state to incur the costs and gain no benefit if an insufficient number of countries participate. This creates an incentive for inaction, even if the gains to be made from successful cooperation and implementation of an agreement are very high and the costs of not achieving such implementation are clearly understood by all participants.

Even before the Kyoto Protocol was signed, it faced extensive challenges and skepticism over its implementation. Doubters questioned the extent of climate change, the role of human activities in causing such global warming, and the likelihood of alterations in human behaviour reversing such change. These problems were exacerbated by the scale of change necessary for countries such as Canada and the United States to achieve their Kyoto targets. Encompassing, at the very least, power generation, agriculture, transportation policy, energy conservation, and reduction of industrial emissions, these moves would require substantial financial investment and political will, combined with long-term popular support, to implement. Moreover, any costs would also be unevenly borne within a country. Certain industrial sectors, such as the oil and gas industry in Alberta, would find it a struggle to accommodate Canada's Kyoto commitments, and, given the province's dependence on that industry, attempts to implement that commitment would likely have severe regional economic effects.

Attempts at implementation also saw many examples of localism, with opposition by residents to, for example, nuclear power facilities or wind farms. Opponents argued that these facilities created their own types of environmental damage, that wind farms caused noise and visual pollution and that nuclear energy could not be considered either environmentally friendly (because of the need to dispose of nuclear waste) or safe (because of fears about nuclear accidents). Such disputes made the politics of Kyoto implementation more complicated, even in countries where there was widespread support for its provisions.

The ease of implementation varied considerably among participants of the Kyoto Protocol. The choice of baseline year enabled Russia to achieve its goal (to maintain emissions at 1990 levels, a reduction target of zero) by closing large parts of its inefficient, "dirty" Soviet-era industry. Similarly, the economics-driven trend from heavy to light industry in parts of Western Europe in the years since 1990 facilitated implementation there. By contrast, countries such as Canada that retained large-scale primary or secondary industries had a harder time achieving the Kyoto goals.

Opposition to the Kyoto Protocol within countries also centred on fears of economic damage, decreasing international competitiveness, and job losses resulting from implementation. Since the Protocol applied only to developed countries, there were concerns that industries elsewhere would enjoy an advantage. The United

States Senate made it clear, even before an agreement at Kyoto was reached, that U.S. ratification of an emissions control agreement would happen only if that agreement included developing countries such as China and India. In 2001 the Bush administration formally renounced the Kyoto Protocol on this same basis, a move that was almost universally condemned by the rest of the world. In purely economic terms, this position has some merit: at least some of China's increase in greenhouse gas emissions can be attributed to the movement of industrial processes to that country from developed states. However, emissions control regulations represent only a part of the reason why, in a globalized world, some industries have moved from developed to developing countries.

The future of the climate change regime depends on participation by key developing states such as China and India. China is already the largest emitter of carbon dioxide in the world, and India's emissions are also growing rapidly. But the participation of states such as China would alter part of the logic created by the Kyoto Protocol: that developed countries should take responsibility for reducing emissions, not simply because of current emissions levels but also because of the historical legacy of 150 years of post-industrialization. Developing countries lack this historical legacy; should they be treated as peers of the developed world, fully accountable for reducing current emissions, or as still-developing states that consequently deserve some leniency on emissions?

The difficulties in achieving the goals of the Kyoto Protocol, and in addressing climate change more generally, reflect the challenges of achieving international cooperation when costs and benefits are not fully aligned. This problem goes beyond simple ideas of fairness because the costs within developed countries could include economic losses, significant changes in how people in that country live (for example, what type of transport they use, which might in turn alter where they choose to live), and potentially even reductions in living standards. Governments therefore face an awkward political choice over implementing emissions control agreements such as Kyoto. No matter how great the future cost of global warming, it still requires considerable political will and popular support for national governments to implement the necessary changes.

CONCLUSION: THE GLASS IS HALF—WHAT?

There is clearly more cooperation in the formal anarchy of the interstate system than a purely Hobbesian vision can explain. Collective management can occur in the absence of a central government. International interdependence is clearly increasing, creating greater pressures for coordinated action. Hence states may willingly enter into collaborative agreements to manage interdependence. Even in those cases, however, neither success nor sustainability can be assured. Even where traditional interstate realms of action are involved, such as in collective security and peacekeeping or in the Law of the Sea, states may have difficultly agreeing on joint action or pursuing it effectively. Where the challenges of interdependence reach more deeply into the domestic affairs—and thus the domestic politics—of states, the resulting number and complexity of interests, actors, and political systems make concerted international action more difficult. Even where failure to cooperate effectively might exact a great cost, the costs of achieving a higher degree of cooperation may be so great that states respond by accepting failure (for example, an increase in carbon emissions).

Cynically, one could say of the extensive system of international cooperation now in existence that the wonder is that it works at all. Less cynically, we might be reminded of a comment by the German sociologist Max Weber, who described politics as a "slow boring of hard boards." International cooperation under anarchy is no easy task, and for that reason, any degree of success is no trivial accomplishment.

Questions for Discussion

1. Is the United Nations a success story? Why or why not? Can you see any common factors in cases where international cooperation has been achieved? What about cases where cooperation has been unsuccessful?

2. Are the difficulties faced by attempts to cooperate explained by the notion of a Hobbesian anarchy—a "war of all against all"—or do they instead suggest other problems, for example, in the internal politics of states?

3. What changes would make it easier for states to cooperate with one another, and what are the barriers to making such changes?

Internet Links

1. United Nations: **www.un.org**.

2. United Nations Department of Peacekeeping Operations: **www.un.org/en/peacekeeping/about/dpko**.

3. United Nations Division for Ocean Affairs and the Law of the Sea: **www.un.org/depts/los/index.htm**.

4. United Nations Framework Convention on Climate Change: **unfccc.int/2860.php**.

5. United Nations Law of the Sea Treaty Information Center: **www.unlawoftheseatreaty.org**.

Further Reading

Adler, Emmanuel. "Constructivism and International Relations." In Walter Carlsnaes, Thomas Risse, and Beth Simmons, eds., *Handbook of International Relations.* London: Sage, 2002.

Axelrod, Regina S., Stacey VanDeveer, and David Leonard Downie, eds. *The Global Environment: Institutions, Law, and Policy.* 3rd ed. Washington, DC: CQ Press, 2010.

Axelrod, Robert. *The Complexity of Cooperation: Agent-Based Models of Competition and Collaboration.* Princeton, NJ: Princeton University Press, 1998.

Baldwin, David A., ed. *Neorealism and Neoliberalism: The Contemporary Debate.* New York: Columbia University Press, 1993.

Barnett, Michael, and Martha Finnemore. *Rules for the World: International Organizations in Global Politics.* Ithaca, NY: Cornell University Press, 2004.

Chasek, Pamela, David L. Downie, and Janet Welsh Brown. *Global Environmental Politics.* 5th ed. Boulder, CO: Westview, 2010.

Fortna, Virginia Page, and Lise Morjé Howard. "Pitfalls and Prospects in the Peacekeeping Future." *Annual Review of Political Science* 11 (2008): 283–301.

Hasenclever, Andreas, Peter Mayer, and Volker Rittberger. *Theories of International Regimes.* Cambridge: Cambridge University Press, 1997.

Howard, Lise Morjé. *UN Peacekeeping in Civil Wars.* Cambridge: Cambridge University Press, 2008.

Keohane, Robert O., and Joseph Nye. *Power and Interdependence.* 4th ed. New York: Longman, 2011.

Malanczuk, Peter. *Akehurst's Modern Introduction to International Law.* London: Routledge, 1997.

O'Neill, Kate. *The Environment and International Relations.* New York: Cambridge University Press, 2009.

Pushkina, Darya. "A Recipe for Success? Ingredients of a Successful Peacekeeping Mission." *International Peacekeeping* 13, no. 2 (2006): 133–49.

Sandholtz, Wayne. "Globalization and the Evolution of Rules." In Aseem Prakash and Jeffrey A. Hart, eds., *Globalization and Governance,* 77–102. London: Routledge, 1999.

Sandholtz, Wayne, and Alec Sweet. "Law, Politics, and International Governance." In Christian Reus-Smit, ed., *The Politics of International Law,* 238–71. Cambridge: Cambridge University Press, 2004.

Slaughter, Anne-Marie. *A New World Order.* Princeton, NJ: Princeton University Press, 2004.

Victor, David G. "Toward Effective International Cooperation on Climate Change: Numbers, Interests and Institutions." *Global Environmental Politics* 6, no. 3 (2006): 90–103.

Wendt, Alexander. "Constructing International Politics." *International Security* 20 (1995): 71–81.

PART 2

IDEOLOGY

CHAPTER 9
Ideology

Part One showed that government's authority and legitimacy rest on a network of beliefs about human nature, society, and the purpose of government. Speculation about these matters—known as *political philosophy or political theory*—was the first aspect of political science to emerge, having been cultivated by the Greek thinkers of classical antiquity. What is said of philosophy in general—that "all philosophy is a footnote to Plato"—is equally true of the special field of political philosophy. All the great issues had already been addressed in the writings of Plato and his pupil Aristotle.

But only a few people read philosophical works. Most of us discuss politics with concepts that have been greatly simplified in comparison to their philosophical origins. The contemporary word for such simplified systems of political thought is **ideology**, which is described in a well-known textbook in the following terms:

> An ideology is a value or belief system that is accepted as fact or truth by some group. It is composed of sets of attitudes towards the various institutions and processes of society. It provides the believer with a picture of the world both as it is and as it should be, and, in so doing, it organizes the tremendous complexity of the world into something fairly simple and understandable ... An ideology must be a more or less connected set of beliefs that provide the believer with a fairly thorough picture of the world.[1]

Remember that politics means gathering and maintaining support for collective projects. Support may be obtained by offering bribes or making threats, but in the long run it has to rest on conviction. Ideology furnishes a basis for political persuasion by providing certain assumptions and values that may be held in common. More specifically, it has the following attributes:

1. Ideology is not mere personal opinion but a social belief accepted by large numbers of people and passed on by the normal channels of cultural transmission.

2. Ideology always involves a mixture of factual and moral beliefs. Because governmental legitimacy is an inherently ethical problem, ideology always includes beliefs about how people should act and what they should consider right and wrong.

3. Ideology, as a mass belief, is somewhat simplified. It reduces the infinite complexity of the world to simpler ideas that can be understood by large numbers of people who, after all, must devote most of their time to concerns other than the study of politics.

4. An ideology is not a random collection of opinions but a more or less organized system of beliefs that fit together logically. It is important to say "more or less" because the integration is never perfect. All of us have some surprising contradictions in our opinions. However, there is a big difference between an orderly, interrelated set of ideas and an assortment of unrelated opinions.

In this sense, ideologies are espoused by intellectuals in politics: by lawyers, teachers, journalists, and politicians who carry on public debate in ideological terms. It is doubtful whether many ordinary people, even among a well-educated populace, can be said to have ideologies.[2] They are more likely to believe in an assortment of somewhat conflicting ideological fragments—to be conservative on some points, liberal on others, and socialist on still other matters. It does not bother them to be inconsistent in this way because they probably spend relatively little time pondering social and political questions. Examples of contradictory thinking frequently turn up in public-opinion polls. It is routine, for example, for respondents to say that taxes are too high while simultaneously demanding higher levels of public spending on education and medical care.

One interesting aspect of the term *ideology* is the negative connotations it carries. The word is often used as a weapon to degrade ideas with which one disagrees. Dismissing ideas as "mere" ideology is a common tactic in argument. It is worth knowing why this is possible.

The word *ideology* was coined in 1796 by the French philosopher Antoine Destutt de Tracy, who gave it a meaning quite different from what it bears today. For him, "ideology" was to be the name of a new science—the study of human consciousness in all its aspects. Destutt de Tracy had once supported Napoleon; when he began to criticize him, the emperor responded by ridiculing his new science as an obscure doctrine and branding those who espoused it as "ideologues." The concept of ideology would probably have died out if Marx and Engels had not rescued it and redefined it to bolster their theory that all human thought has an economic basis—that art, science, literature, law, and political thought reflect the underlying economic conditions of their creators. Marx wrote that one should always distinguish between the "economic conditions of production," which are the essence of class conflict, and "the legal, political, religious, aesthetic, or philosophic—in short, ideological—forms in which men become conscious of this conflict and fight it out." Economic relations are the "foundation, on which rise legal and political superstructures and to which correspond definite forms of social consciousness."[3]

Marx's view was bound to give the concept of ideology a bad name because he regarded his theory not as ideology but as science—scientific socialism. In other words, the beliefs of others were ideology, whereas his were science. Marx had a profound, although debatable, reason for thinking this, but it is easy to see how the word could become a mere polemical weapon in the hands of others. Moreover, there is much that is obviously true in Marx's insight: the intellectual world does have some relation to its economic milieu. Marx's insight was so significant that the term he used to express it was bound to become popular.

However, as often happens, the word has become detached from the particular theory that gave it currency. Today when a belief system is branded an ideology, the detractors might mean any of several things. They might be implying that the beliefs have not really been thought through and would not withstand comparison to a well-developed philosophy (such as their own!). Or they might mean that the beliefs are a not very subtle expression of self-interest on the part of some group that is trying to assert itself. Or, following the sociologist Karl Mannheim, they might mean that the beliefs are a rationalization of the status quo, and thus inherently conservative in function.[4]

Our use of the term is not intended to have any of these special implications. We use *ideology* simply as a convenient contemporary word for political ideas in action—ideas not as they are found in the philosopher's study but as they motivate large numbers of people. However, students should be aware of the many other connotations of the term that they will certainly encounter elsewhere.

Part Two will emphasize the four main ideologies that have dominated politics since the nineteenth century: liberalism, conservatism, socialism, and nationalism. It will also take a briefer look at two more recent ideologies—feminism and environmentalism—that acquired global significance in the latter part of the twentieth century. Ideologies are never static; it is essential to have some sense of their rise and decline.

Up to a point, it is useful to analyze ideologies as systems of ideas or beliefs. But remember that all ideologies are abstractions. They do not really exist; real people with their individual thoughts, and organizations that adopt statements or programs, are what exist. It is unlikely that the beliefs of any person or organization perfectly fit any of the descriptions given here of particular ideologies. Yet common tendencies and common concerns unite diverse thinkers, even if they do not agree on every point. Think of ideologies as broad tendencies of thought existing over long periods of time. No two people identified as liberals or socialists or feminists think identically, but there are certainly recognizable patterns in their ideas. Above all, do not think of ideologies as fixed creeds from which a thinker who varies on any point is excommunicated. Ideologies are more like families of ideas; as in any real family, resemblances are strong but disagreements can be heated. When this proviso is kept in mind, the concept of structured ideologies can be a helpful device for showing how ideas are connected to one another.

The six ideological families to be discussed in this book are all peculiarly modern systems of thought. Although they have earlier roots, they have taken on their distinctive forms only in the past two hundred years. The terms *liberalism, conservatism, socialism,* and *nationalism* were never used to denote systems of thought before the early decades of the nineteenth century, while feminism and environmentalism crystallized as worldviews only in the last two decades of the twentieth century. These "isms" provide terms of discourse about politics in the modern world, but they are not a universal and permanent vocabulary of political discourse.

All six ideologies are secular in orientation. Belief in God can be and has been combined with each of them, but it is not essential. All modern Western ideologies (except for some varieties of environmentalism) are humanistic—not in the sentimental sense of kindness or generosity but in the philosophical sense of being human-centred, taking human happiness on earth as an unquestioned goal. Although each has a different way of arriving there, the goal remains the same. Jeremy Bentham (1748–1832), an early liberal, expressed the goal when he said, "The business of government is to promote the happiness of the society, by punishing and rewarding,"[5] not to fulfill the will of God or to prepare people for the next life. Marx was even more aggressive in his humanism, stating that belief in God was a hindrance to humanity's struggle to create happiness. "Religion," wrote Marx, "is only the illusory sun about which man revolves so long as he does not revolve about himself."[6] The humanism of the other ideologies is not always as forceful as in Marx's teachings, but it is a common trait. This means that the arguments among them focus on the best means of achieving the agreed-upon goal, which is human happiness on earth. On this point, the only dissent among the ideologies is found in the "ecocentric" varieties of environmentalism, which hold that humanity has no special claim to the planet, that all species have equal rights under the principle of "biocentric equality."[7]

Also, all the ideologies we study presuppose that society is something people attempt to change, reform, or mould according to their desires. All except conservatism have programs or agendas of social change for government to undertake. Conservatism differs in that it believes society is too complex to be easily improved by human design. However, conservatism would not exist as a self-conscious ideology except for the challenges posed by the other worldviews. If it had never occurred to anyone that we could take charge of and deliberately improve society, there would have been no occasion to develop a conservative ideology in reaction against such programs. In this sense the modern confidence in social improvement is the backdrop to all contemporary ideologies.

The four older ideologies stem from the same historical situation, symbolized by the French Revolution: the transition from traditional to legal authority and legitimacy. We can see the central values of these ideologies in the famous slogan of that revolution—*liberté* (liberalism), *égalité* (socialism), *fraternité* (nationalism). Broadly speaking, liberalism celebrates the onset of legal authority as human emancipation from bondage. Socialism is ambiguous about it, welcoming the demise of traditional authority and also fearing that the freedom created by legal authority will produce a new aristocracy of wealth even more oppressive than the old aristocracy of inherited privilege. Nationalism also welcomes the transition to legal authority but seeks to establish a new form of political identity to replace traditional ones. Conservatism is suspicious of pure legal authority, fearing that the accumulated wisdom of the past will be lost if the transition from traditional authority is too abrupt.

It is no accident that the great ideologies of our age appeared on the political scene almost simultaneously at the end of the eighteenth century. The French Revolution and the Napoleonic Wars were the most visible signs of a vast social change. These events in Europe proved to be a rehearsal for similar changes throughout the world. This is the unifying theme of our era, often called the Age of Ideology.

A WIDER PERSPECTIVE

The preceding section applies to ideology in the Western world, which, beginning with the so-called Enlightenment of the eighteenth century, has undergone a comprehensive process of secularization. Religion is still very important, but most people in the West now understand religion as a set of personal beliefs that give meaning to life and guide personal conduct but do not directly structure the social order. Indeed, the religious pluralism of the Western world makes that impossible. Multiple religions can coexist peacefully only if there is separation between church and state.

Western ideas, including the secularization of society and the separation of church and state, have spread widely around the world, so Western political ideologies are no longer just Western but also global. But the triumph of Western modes of thought is far from complete. Particularly in the Islamic world, a religious worldview that does not recognize the separation of mosque and state is still powerful. A good example would be the Muslim Brotherhood, the world's largest Islamic organization, which was founded in Egypt in 1928 by the Islamic scholar Hassan al-Banna. The two main pillars of the Muslim Brotherhood's worldview are described on their website as follows:

1. The introduction of the Islamic Shari'ah as the basis controlling the affairs of state and society.

2. Work to achieve unification among the Islamic countries and states, mainly among the Arab states, and liberating them from foreign imperialism.[8]

Shari'ah is the Arabic word for the law of God as revealed in the Koran and in the collected sayings of Muhammad. Saying that shari'ah should be "the basis controlling the affairs of state and society" is like saying in a Christian context that the Bible should be the law of the land. A few Christians do actually believe this—in Canada and the United States their view is known as "Dominion theology."[9] But the number of such Christian believers is small, and they have no political parties capable of electing people to office in Western countries. In contrast, shari'ah is now embedded in the constitution of several Islamic states, and the belief that it should be the basis of civil law is advocated by parties or movements in every Islamic country.

There are, of course, many versions of Islamic political thought. The Islamic Republic of Iran is very different from the Wahabi regime of Saudi Arabia, and both differ from the revolutionary al-Qaeda movement, which organized the famous September 11, 2001, attack on the United States. But there is a common factor, namely that none of them thinks in terms of Western ideologies. Terms such as *liberal* and *conservative, socialist* and *communist,* simply do not apply. Indeed, they would not recognize the validity of the whole concept of ideology as denoting a secular system of beliefs. They believe in revelation and religion, not secular ideologies. In that sense, Islamic politics now is like Christian politics was before the Enlightenment.

LEFT, RIGHT, AND CENTRE

Are ideologies related to each other in a sufficiently systematic way that we can array them along a single dimension? The answer is a qualified yes as far as conservatism, liberalism, and socialism are concerned, but it becomes much more complicated when nationalism, feminism, and environmentalism are considered. Here we try to relate all these ideologies to each other. You may wish to return to this section after completing Part Two has given you a better idea of what these ideologies mean.

Conservatism, liberalism, and socialism are often depicted as lying along a spectrum whose ends are designated left and right. Many observers agree more or less on the following construction:

Left		Centre		Right	
Communism	Social democracy	Reform liberalism	Classical liberalism	Conservatism	Fascism

Although this spectrum corresponds to common perception, it is not easy to say precisely what it means. Is the left for change and the right against it? That simplistic explanation will hardly do, for everything depends on who is in power. In a communist state, classical liberalism would be an ideology of radical change. In constitutional democracies, both communism and fascism represent radical change. As a yardstick, freedom is not much help either. All ideologies, even fascism, claim to be for freedom, but they define it in different ways. Nor does using democracy as a measure solve the problem because the democratic centralism of Marxism-Leninism is in reality just as antithetical to popular government as fascism is.

Considering the circumstances in which the words *left* and *right* first began to be used as political labels sheds some light on the subject. The usage arose shortly after 1789 in the National Assembly, in the early days of the French Revolution. Those factions that favoured retaining substantial powers for the monarchy, such as the right to appoint judges and to veto legislation, sat to the right of the chairman of the Assembly. Those who favoured reducing the monarch to a purely symbolic figure, letting the elected representatives of the people exercise all political power, sat to the left of the chairman. The basic issue was popular sovereignty. The left held that all political power emanated from the people, the right believed that God conferred political power upon the king through inheritance, and the centre sought a compromise or balance between those two approaches.[10]

This political difference between left and right soon took on an economic dimension when socialism assumed a prominent role in European politics. The term *left* was then applied to those who favoured equalization of property through political action. Socialists proposed to replace the market process, which is not under the control of any identifiable individual or group, with a system of state planning. Socialism thus extended popular sovereignty from the political to the economic sphere.

Many ambiguities of the left–right terminology arise from this double origin. Advocates of popular sovereignty do not inevitably favour socialist planning; they may be sincerely convinced that the market principle will in the long run be of more benefit to ordinary working people. It is also not inevitable that advocates of socialist planning will support popular sovereignty with equal warmth, for the desires of the real, existing people (as opposed to the hypothetical reformed people) may obstruct the plan. In short, the political and the economic left coincide often but not always.

In contemporary usage the economic factor predominates, though not entirely. Going back to our common-sense listing of ideologies on the left–right spectrum, we can now give an approximate interpretation in terms of the meanings of equality that will be discussed at greater length in Part Two. Let us now redraw the spectrum, adding the various forms of equality and inequality that the ideologies claim as their own:

Left		Centre		Right	
Equality of condition	Equality of opportunity	Equality of right		Aristocracy	Hierarchy
Communism	Social democracy	Reform liberalism	Classical liberalism	Conservatism	Fascism

This picture is better than the first, but it can still be seriously misleading without appropriate qualifications. Communists advocate long-run equality of result in the sense of the equality of happiness that would be produced by implementing the motto "From each according to his ability, to each according to his needs." In the short run they claim to equalize conditions somewhat but not absolutely. Social democrats and reform liberals are not exclusively wedded to equality of opportunity. Their use of the progressive income tax as a levelling measure is also an approach to equality of result. The classical liberal commitment to equality of right is not especially problematic in this context, but the conservative position easily causes confusion. Early conservatives such as Edmund Burke saw hereditary aristocracy as a socially useful institution. Twentieth-century conservatives no longer defend the hereditary principle but may argue that the wealthy will perform some of the same useful functions as a hereditary aristocracy—philanthropy, public service, and so on. Obviously this position shades into classical liberalism; the difference is only a matter of whether we emphasize the equality of universal rules or the unequal results arising from them. Finally, fascists tend to think of hierarchy not as social transmission through legal inheritance but as biological transmission of racial qualities. For Adolf Hitler, Germans were the master race (*Herrenvolk*) while Jews and Slavs were subhuman (*Untermenschen*). This is the most absolute type of inequality that can be imagined because there is no conceivable way of altering it. Fascists also reject the constitutional principle of rule of law, which is another formulation of equality of right.

This underlying dimension of egalitarianism is not an absolute scale of measurement that allows us to assign a precise value to an ideology from any time or place. However, it does make a limited amount of sense to say of two ideologies at a certain place and time that one is to the left or right of the other. The same applies to the adherents of ideologies. Thus it is reasonable to say that in recent Canadian politics the New Democratic Party (NDP), as a party of social democracy, is usually to the left of the Liberal Party. Yet the difference is chiefly one of degree. Liberal prime minister Louis St. Laurent said of the CCF, the predecessor of the NDP, that they were just "Liberals in a hurry." That numerous quasi-socialist measures, such as national health insurance and a publicly owned oil company, were proposed by the CCF/NDP and ultimately legislated by the Liberal Party shows the kinship between the two parties. Similarly, the Liberals, as a reformist party, are generally to the left of the Conservatives. But again there is much overlap. It is, therefore, best to think of political parties as occupying overlapping positions on the ideological spectrum:

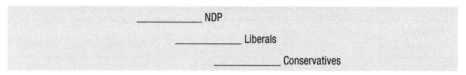

Note that, except for fascism, we have not attempted to place nationalism on the left–right scale. Nationalism can be allied with any one of liberalism, conservatism, or socialism because commitment to the nation-state does not automatically dictate a position on issues of equality. It is worth noting here that in times of war, normal political differences are suspended. Parties of the left and right often come together in a coalition government of national unity to carry out the war effort. This illustrates how support for the nation is on a different level than other political issues. When the threat to the nation is past, the distinction between left and right reasserts itself and governments of national unity soon fall apart (as happened in Canada after World War I and Great Britain after World War II).

The Bloc Québécois furnishes another example of how nationalism does not fit onto the standard left–right spectrum. The Bloc, formed in 1990 by former Conservative Lucien Bouchard as a protest against delays in ratifying the Meech Lake Accord, is essentially a single-issue movement devoted to the goal of turning Quebec into a sovereign state. The MPs who joined the Bloc defected from both the Conservative and the Liberal Parties, and they were joined in the 1993 election by candidates who had previously worked for other parties in Quebec such as the NDP. Gilles Duceppe, leader of the BQ from 1997 to 2011, was at one time a Communist. Although the party takes a generally social democratic position, its true program is the independence of Quebec, and it thus attracts some nationalist voters who are not really social democratic in ideology.

The varieties of feminism can be aligned partially, though not completely, with the left–right spectrum. Liberal feminists and socialist feminists can, without too much distortion, be seen as liberals and socialists who happen to be particularly concerned with a certain set of problems. Overall, their thinking fits into familiar liberal and socialist categories. Radical feminism, however, is much more difficult to place. As a transformation of Marxism, it seems to belong on the left, and when radical feminists get involved in electoral politics, they do so with parties of the left. But their over-riding concern with patriarchy is fundamentally different from the concerns with popular sovereignty and economic equality that characterize positions on the left–right spectrum, so that we might think of radical feminism as belonging on a dimension that cuts perpendicularly across the left–right dimension. This helps to explain what might otherwise be seen as some strange political coalitions. For example, radical feminists have frequently worked together with conservatives in law-enforcement agencies on issues such as pornography, sexual abuse, and violence against women. The two groups conceptualize the issues in quite different ways but they agree on the desirability of harsher criminal penalties. Liberals who are thought of as quite left-wing—for example, members of the Canadian Civil Liberties Association—can find themselves on the opposite side on these issues even though they may think of themselves as favourable to feminism.

The situation with environmentalism is similar. Generally we can comfortably sort out environmentalists by examining the means they advocate to achieve their ends. Free-market environmentalists clearly belong with the classical liberals, while many advocates of human welfare ecology just as clearly prefer the more interventionist tools of reform liberalism and social democracy. But "deep ecology," like radical feminism, is really on a different dimension because it rejects the materialist goals of the other ideologies.

The left–right spectrum, though often useful, is unidimensional. Real-world ideologies are multidimensional—that is, they are concerned not only with inequality and equality but also with many other political values. For example, it would be possible to map ideologies on a continuum according to their views on the scope of state control of society:

Maximum			Minimum
Communism	Social democracy	Classical liberalism	
Fascism	Reform liberalism	Conservatism	Anarchism

Communists and fascists favour the total identification of state and society. Social democrats and reform liberals favour active government regulation and intervention but do not wish to subject all of society to state control. Conservatives and classical liberals desire a very limited state to carry out certain restricted functions; otherwise, they want society to evolve according to its own laws. **Anarchists** believe that society can exist without any government at all.

The above is as valid as the conventional left–right approach, but it expresses another aspect of the reality of ideologies and thus does not coincide with the conventional left–right spectrum. To speak of left and right is a useful shorthand way of referring to ideologies, as long as the limitations of this approach are kept in mind. Left and right are only convenient labels; they are no substitute for a detailed understanding of a point of view. Difficulties quickly become apparent when we try to apply the notion of a left–right continuum to concrete issues. To illustrate, let us look at several issues from the realms of economics, society, and politics.

Among economic issues, the left–right spectrum fits very well with the debate about progressive taxation. Those furthest to the left are the most vociferous in their desire to "make the rich pay," as the Communist Party of Canada used to put it. Those in the centre accept the principle of progressive taxation but may worry that the marginal rate is so high as to interfere with productivity; they wish the state to act in a redistributive way but not to "kill the goose that lays the golden eggs." Those on the right reject progressive taxation in favour of a flat tax, that is, one whose rate is the same for all. The issue of taxation can be readily mapped onto the left–right continuum because the underlying question is one of egalitarianism.

On social issues, the left seems to favour a position of individual libertarianism— abortion on demand, legalization of marijuana, abolition of movie censorship—and the right seems to uphold traditional standards of morality. But this seeming unidimensionality exists only in liberal democracies where the extreme left is weak, as in North America. Communists and other revolutionary leftists are in fact rather puritanical in their outlook on many moral questions. Marijuana and other mind-altering drugs were rigorously forbidden in communist countries, as were many mildly obscene books and movies that would hardly raise an eyebrow in the Western world. Freedom of individual choice is not a high priority for the revolutionary left.

Even with all these nuances and exceptions, the terms *left* and *right* are convenient for categorizing ideological tendencies. Most of the inconsistencies disappear if we restrict the application of the terms to stable constitutional democracies in which the extreme right and left are weak or nonexistent. Under those conditions, *left* and *right* stand for relatively coherent ideological positions—reform liberalism and social democracy on the one side, classical liberalism and conservatism on the other. The more moderate forms of feminism and environmentalism can be fitted into this tableau without too much strain, but if radical feminism and deep ecology ever become dominant ideologies, *left* and *right* will have to be either redefined or abandoned altogether as practical labels.

For more on the multidimensionality of politics, see Concept Box 9.1. The matrix is borrowed from the Vote Compass results featured on the CBC website in the 2011 federal election. It shows the approximate location of the main political parties as measured by their positions on 30 issues mentioned in their platforms. The Conservatives favoured a combination of traditional morality and free-market economics, while the Liberals advocated more government intervention on economic issues but freedom of choice on social issues. The New Democrats, Greens, and Bloc Québécois went even further than the Liberals in combining economic interventionism with social permissiveness.

Concept Box 9.1

Multidimensional Scaling

Many of the difficulties of employing left–right terminology arise from the fact that politics is multidimensional, which is to say that people have different opinions about many different issues and that these issues do not all line up neatly on the same dimension. In Canadian politics today there is a cluster of economic issues, including the level of taxation and provision of public services, on which the dimension of difference runs from the free market on the right to government provision on the left. Then there is another cluster of so-called social issues, including abortion and gay rights, on which the dimension of difference runs from traditional morality on the right to individual choice on the left. Combining these into a two-dimensional matrix enables the analyst to make a more accurate classification of where people actually stand.

Note that the New Democrats and the Bloc Québécois seem similarly positioned when we consider only these two dimensions, but they would be much farther apart if we brought in a third dimension, of national unity.

Figure 9.1 Multidimensional Ideologies among Canadian Voters, 2011

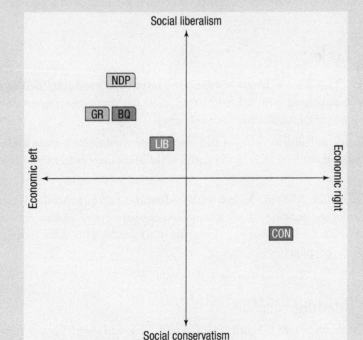

Source: Vote Compass, http://votecompass.ca. Reproduced with permission.   *(continued)*

The NDP favours the continuance of Canada within its present boundaries, whereas the BQ advocates the separation of Quebec from Canada, by unilateral means if necessary. Considering three or even more dimensions of difference brings gains in analytical accuracy, but the resulting diagrams are difficult to reproduce in the two-dimensional world of the printed page.

Questions for Discussion

1. Have you ever used one of these ideological labels to characterize your own political views? Based on what you have read thus far, do you think you were using the right label?

2. Can you locate your own views in the two-dimensional matrix shown in Concept Box 9.1? Do you support the political party located nearest your own views? (Don't worry if there is a discrepancy; there are many other valid reasons for supporting a particular party.)

3. Before reading this chapter, had you ever used the word *ideology* in your own conversation? Can you remember whether you used it as a neutral or a pejorative term?

Internet Links

1. Ideology: The War of Ideas: **www.zmangames.com/products/Ideology**. This website is associated with a board game in which participants attempt to gain worldwide acceptance of a particular ideology.

2. Keele Guide to Political Thought and Ideology on the Internet: **www.keele.ac.uk/depts/por/ptbase.htm**. A comprehensive set of bibliographic links to thinkers and topics.

3. World's Smallest Political Quiz: **www.theadvocates.org/quiz.html**. Measure your own ideological position, using a two-dimensional scheme somewhat similar to that shown in Concept Box 9.1. Compare your results with those of others who have taken the quiz.

Further Reading

Ajzenstat, Janet, and Peter J. Smith, eds. *Canada's Origins: Liberal, Tory, or Republican?* Ottawa: Carleton University Press, 1997.

Baldwin, Douglas. *Ideologies*. Scarborough, ON: McGraw-Hill Ryerson, 1992.

Ball, Terence, and Richard Dagger. *Ideals and Ideologies: A Reader*. 8th ed. New York: Pearson, 2010.

———. *Political Ideologies and the Democratic Ideal*. 8th ed. New York: Pearson, 2010.

Baradat, Leon P. *Political Ideologies: Their Origins and Impact*. 11th ed. New York: Pearson, 2011.

Boaz, David. *Libertarianism: A Primer*. New York: Free Press, 1997.

Bobbio, Norberto. *Left and Right: The Significance of a Political Distinction*. Translated by Allan Cameron. Cambridge, UK: Polity Press, 1996.

Campbell, Colin, and William Christian. *Parties, Leaders, and Ideologies in Canada*. Toronto: McGraw-Hill Ryerson, 1996.

Cheles, Luciano, Ronnie Ferguson, and Michalina Vaughan, eds. *The Far Right in Western and Eastern Europe*. White Plains, NY: Longman, 1995.

Desai, Meghnad. *Rethinking Islamism: The Ideology of the New Terror*. London: I. B. Tauris, 2006.

Eagleton, Terry. *Ideology: An Introduction*. London: Verso, 1991.

Ebenstein, Alan O., William Ebenstein, and Edwin Fogelman. *Today's Isms: Socialism, Capitalism, Fascism, Communism*. 10th ed. Englewood Cliffs, NJ: Prentice Hall, 1994.

Freeden, Michael. *Ideologies and Political Theory: A Conceptual Approach*. Oxford: Oxford University Press, 1996.

———. *Ideology: A Very Short Introduction*. Oxford: Oxford University Press, 2003.

Gentile, Giovanni. *Origins and Doctrine of Fascism: With Selections from Other Works*. Piscataway, NJ: Transaction, 2004.

Gibbins, Roger, and Loleen Youngman. *Mindscapes: Political Ideologies Towards the 21st Century*. Toronto: McGraw-Hill Ryerson, 1996.

Heywood, Andrew. *Political Ideologies: An Introduction*. 5th ed. London: Palgrave Macmillan, 2012.

Holmes, Stephen. *The Anatomy of Antiliberalism*. Cambridge, MA: Harvard University Press, 1993.

Hoover, Kenneth, et al. *Ideology and Political Life*. Fort Worth, TX: Harcourt College Publishers, 2001.

Kaase, Max, and Kenneth Nentin. *Beliefs in Government*. Oxford: Oxford University Press, 1995.

Macridis, Roy C., and Mark Hulliung. *Contemporary Political Ideologies*. 6th ed. New York: Pearson, 1996.

McLellan, David. *Ideology*. 2nd ed. Minneapolis: University of Minnesota Press, 1995.

PART 2

Liberalism

The word *liberal* comes from the Latin *liber*, meaning "free." It was first used as a political term in Spain during the Napoleonic Wars and became common later in the nineteenth century with the establishment of the Liberal Party in Britain. The ideas of liberalism, however, are older than the name. Broadly speaking, liberalism grew out of the English Whig tradition of liberty under law. Prominent Whig thinkers were John Locke (1632–1704) in England, Adam Smith (1723–90) and David Hume (1711–76) in Scotland, and Thomas Jefferson (1743–1826) and James Madison (1751–1836) in America. These men never called themselves liberals, but they elaborated the principles later known as liberalism. They were followed by such writers as John Stuart Mill (1806–73) and his French contemporary Alexis de Tocqueville (1805–59), who did call themselves liberals.

THE HISTORY OF LIBERALISM

The history of **liberalism** reveals four principles, all of which relate to the broad concept of freedom: personal freedom, limited government, equality of right, and consent of the governed. These principles were mentioned earlier in our discussion of constitutionalism; indeed, political liberalism is really the same thing as constitutionalism:

1. **Personal freedom**, as understood by liberals, refers to the absence of coercion in the various realms of life. It includes free speech, religious liberty, the right of private property, and the right of political opposition.

2. **Limited government** means that the state is an instrument that serves a particular function in society and is not in general charge of all society.

3. **Equality of right** implies that all must abide by the same laws, which the state enforces with impartiality.

4. **Consent of the governed** means that government emanates from the people, is responsible to them, and may be changed by them—a moderate and practical statement of the doctrine of popular sovereignty.

These four principles mark the entire liberal tradition from Locke to the present day. Indeed, there is such wide acceptance of these principles today that almost everyone in the Western world pays at least lip service to them. However, there is also a deep division within liberalism that must be carefully examined. From this point on we will distinguish the older, classical liberalism from the newer, reform liberalism.

Classical liberalism was the dominant ideology in the nineteenth century in North America, Britain, and much of Western Europe. It accepted the four principles in a straightforward and literal way. In particular, it identified personal freedom with a free-market or laissez-faire economy. **Reform liberalism,** which began as a reform movement within the British Liberal Party at the end of the nineteenth century, later became dominant, though there was some revival of classical liberalism in the late twentieth century. Reform liberalism favours using the state to modify the market system without abolishing it altogether and advocates a larger role for the state in providing equality of opportunity.

Note that the two types of liberalism discussed in this text are only loosely connected with the "capital L" Liberal Party of modern Canada. Over its long history, the Liberal Party has sometimes inclined to one side, sometimes to the other. Under the leadership of Pierre Trudeau (1968–84), the party clearly tilted toward reform liberalism and became quite interventionist in its economic policies. However, the Liberal government of Jean Chrétien (1993–2003) moved some distance back toward classical liberalism, downsizing or even dismantling some of the interventionist programs of the Trudeau era.

Personal Freedom

For classical liberals, freedom is simply the absence of coercion. Without totally rejecting this definition, reform liberals try to add another dimension. They usually think of freedom in terms of our capacity to achieve our goals in life, arguing that freedom from coercion means little unless the means of attaining a decent life are provided. The Canadian journalist Pierre Berton expressed this position in his book *The Smug Minority:*

> A poor man is not free and a destitute man is as much a prisoner as a convict; indeed a convict generally eats better. A man who can't afford a streetcar ticket, let alone real travel, who can exercise no real choice in matters of food, clothing, and shelter, who cannot follow the siren song of the TV commercials, who can scarcely afford bus fare to the library let alone a proper education for himself or his children—is such a man free in an affluent nation?[1]

According to this view, the poor are not really free, even though they are not actively coerced, because the lack of financial means limits their opportunities in life as effectively as if they were kept down by force.

This difference in the understanding of freedom is not a trivial matter; it is at the heart of the difference between the old and the new liberalism. Classical liberals emphasize the absence of coercion—freedom in the sense of being left alone to do what you want, as long as it does not infringe on the freedom of others to do likewise. Reform liberals, on the other hand, wish to use governmental power to reduce the freedom of some in order to provide opportunities for others. They justify this in terms of freedom, arguing that they are increasing the amount of real liberty in society by furnishing people with the means to achieve their goals. The two kinds of liberals use the same words but do not speak the same language. Their differing conceptions of freedom have resulted in differing ideas about the role of the state in economic life. In particular, economic freedom and the market system are not accorded the same primacy in reform liberalism as in classical liberalism.

While reform liberalism now differs significantly from classical liberalism, the former can be seen as a logical outgrowth of the latter. If freedom is the absence of coercion, the individual will—the right to do what you want—must be fundamental to freedom. Reform liberalism purports to be a more effective way of enabling more people to obtain the objects of their desire, using the power of the limited state if necessary. Both versions of liberalism agree (and differ from other ideologies) in celebrating the fulfillment of individual desire as the highest good.[2]

Limited Government

Classical liberals see the state in negative terms: its role is primarily to prevent people from harming each other through force or fraud. To this end, classical liberalism accepts the use of force to protect the community from external attack and to punish those who commit acts of aggression or deception against others. Beyond these functions, the state should do relatively little, leaving people to work out their own destinies within society. This classical liberal idea of government has been caricatured as a "night-watchman state," as merely the caretaker of society.

Reform liberals accept that the state has caretaking functions, but they wish to add to them the interventionist role of promoting freedom in the additional sense of capacity. They want the state to be a positive force that ensures the availability of leisure, knowledge, and security for those who might not otherwise acquire them. The two different views of freedom lead to two different conceptions of the duties of the state.

Equality of Right

For classical liberals, equality of right means only that all abide by the same rules. It definitely does not imply **equality of result** in the outcomes of social and economic processes. Classical liberals accept that there will always be inequality of wealth, status, and power. One might even say that for them, equality of right is the right to become unequal.[3] Reform liberals, while not committed to a wholesale equalization of results, wish to reduce economic and social differences. They have often adopted what was originally a socialist formula, **equality of opportunity.**

Opportunities by themselves are never equal. One child is born to wealthy parents, another to poor ones. One child is born to parents who encourage diligence in school, another is born to parents who care nothing for learning. Obviously the state can do little about many such inequalities, but if equality of opportunity is to have any meaning, the state must take positive steps to address those circumstances that cannot reasonably be blamed on the child. Thus government may provide public schools, trying to ensure that all children start with the same sort of education, and offer grants and low-interest loans to help young people obtain professional training that their parents might not be able to provide. Such measures go much further than the classical liberal conception of equality of right.

Consent of the Governed

Classical liberals in the nineteenth century often favoured a **property franchise,** which required citizens to own a stipulated amount of property before receiving the right to vote. Viewing government as based largely on the protection of property, they felt it was reasonable to entrust government to those who possessed substantial amounts of property and who paid most of the taxes supporting the state. Reform liberals, in contrast, are strongly democratic. Since they put so much emphasis on using the state positively to provide for the common welfare, they naturally feel it is important that everyone have a share of political power.

Reform liberalism has much in common with democratic socialism. For historical reasons the term *socialist* has been unpopular in North America, whereas it is more respected in Europe. Many who are known as liberals in contemporary North America might be called socialists or social democrats if they lived in Europe.

CLASSICAL LIBERALISM

Liberalism grew out of the struggle of Parliament with the Stuart kings in seventeenth-century England. At the level of political power, the Glorious Revolution of 1688 established the supremacy of Parliament over the monarchy. At the level of ideas, the Revolution established that public authority is not derived directly from God, as the Stuarts had tried to maintain, but ultimately resides in the people themselves, who delegate it to the sovereign. The sovereign must rule within the law of the land, as made by Parliament and interpreted by the courts. In Max Weber's terms, this was the triumph of legal over traditional authority.

The ideas animating the Glorious Revolution were given classic expression by John Locke in *The Second Treatise of Government* (1690). Locke argued that the people deliberately create government by agreement among themselves in order to achieve a reliable, impartial enforcement of law. The purpose of government is fundamentally to protect them in their "life, health, liberty, or possessions."[4] Government is not authorized "to destroy, enslave, or designedly to impoverish the subject."[5] Arbitrary rule by the Stuarts had this result, according to Locke, so the English were right to resist and depose them:

> Wherever law ends, tyranny begins if the law be transgressed to another's harm. And whosoever in authority exceeds the power given him by the law, and makes use of the force he has under his command to compass that upon the subject which the law allows not, ceases in that to be a magistrate and, acting without authority, may be opposed as any other man who by force invades the right of another.[6]

Locke's arguments were repeated in the American Declaration of Independence of 1776. This text, drafted by Thomas Jefferson, is the most concise and memorable statement of the political theory of classical liberalism:

> We hold these truths to be self-evident, that all men are created equal, that they are endowed by their creator with certain unalienable rights; that among these are life, liberty and the pursuit of happiness; that to secure these rights governments are instituted among men, deriving their just powers from the consent of the governed; that whenever any form of government becomes destructive of these ends, it is the right of the people to alter or to abolish it, and to institute new government.[7]

Similar ideals animated the early days of the French Revolution of 1789. In August of that year, the National Assembly adopted the Declaration of the Rights of Man and of the Citizen, which stated:

> The end of all political associations is the preservation of the natural and imprescriptible rights of man; and these rights are liberty, property, security, and resistance of oppression. The nation is essentially the source of all sovereignty; nor can any individual, or any body of men, be entitled to any authority which is not expressly derived from it.[8]

The political theory of classical liberalism called for equality before the law and equality of right in respect to person and property, but not equality of political participation. In the early stages of the French Revolution, a distinction was made between passive citizens (who had full legal and civil rights but not political rights) and active citizens (who could also vote and hold elective office). The incorporation of democracy into liberalism occurred later; it will be discussed in the section on reform liberalism.

The demand that government be bound by law was part of a larger concern for freedom of the individual. This was worked out first in the area of religion; many of the disputes between Parliament and the Stuarts had a religious basis. Locke's *A Letter Concerning Toleration* (1689) held religion to be a private matter: "The care of souls cannot belong to the civil magistrate because his power consists only in outward force;

but true and saving religion consists in the inward persuasions of the mind, without which nothing can be acceptable to God."[9] His conclusion was that the state should tolerate all religions as long as they did not disturb civil peace by meddling in politics.

Regarding religion as a private matter was congenial to the increasingly secular outlook of the Enlightenment. It also coincided with a growing feeling that communication ought to be as free as possible. The First Amendment to the American Constitution (1791) established a wide freedom of speech and the press:

> Congress shall make no law respecting an establishment of religion, or prohibiting the free exercise thereof; or abridging the freedom of speech or of the press; or the right of the people peaceably to assemble, and to petition the government for a redress of grievances.[10]

At about the same time, the Declaration of the Rights of Man and of the Citizen enunciated an even broader principle: that not only thought and speech but also conduct should be left alone by the state as long as it did not coercively invade the rights of others:

> Political liberty consists in the power of doing whatever does not injure another. The exercise of the natural rights of every man, has no other limits than those which are necessary to secure to every other man the free exercise of the same rights; and these limits are determinable only by law.[11]

John Stuart Mill brought all these themes together in his book *On Liberty* (1859), which is perhaps the best-known statement in the English language of the value of freedom. *On Liberty* asserted "one very simple principle": "The only purpose for which power can be rightfully exercised over any member of a civilized community, against his will, is to prevent harm to others. His own good, either physical or moral, is not a sufficient warrant."[12] Mill tried to prove in his book that in the long run we would all be better off if the state were restrained from prohibiting "experiments in living," provided they were not coercive of others. Freedom to experiment with new ideas and new ways of doing things would encourage progress through discovery of better alternatives to present practices.

In the economic sphere, classical liberalism is identified with the free market. Locke did not have a fully developed theory of the market, but he helped lay the foundations for one by stressing that a major purpose of government is the protection of private property. The principles of the market were brought to light in the eighteenth century by numerous writers, of whom the most famous is Adam Smith. His book *The Wealth of Nations* (1776) used the metaphorical term "invisible hand" to describe what happens when an individual seeks to promote his own self-interest:

> He intends only his own security; and by directing that industry in such a manner as its produce may be of the greatest value, he intends only his own gain, and he is in this, as in many other cases, led by an invisible hand to promote an end which was no part of his intention. Nor is it always the worse for the society that it was no part of it. By pursuing his own interest he frequently promotes that of the society more effectually than when he really intends to promote it.[13]

PART 2

John Stuart Mill, 1806–73, one of the most important philosophers of liberalism.

Smith articulated in this passage a central belief of classical liberalism: that the common good can be served in the economic sphere by individual initiative without state direction. Much the same thing was meant by Anne-Robert-Jacques Turgot, a French contemporary of Smith, who coined the term **laissez-faire** ("let alone"). The terms *invisible hand* and *laissez-faire* both imply that human needs are best served by free competition in the economic marketplace. Government has to enforce the rules of property and agreements that make competition possible, but it need not otherwise direct the process.

A more modern exposition of classical liberalism and its leading idea—freedom as the absence of coercion—can be found in the works of two Nobel Prize–winning economists, Milton Friedman and Friedrich Hayek.[14] Their argument for freedom runs approximately as follows: People must live in communities in order to survive and to live well. The efforts of each contribute to the welfare of all. How can all these individual efforts best be coordinated for the common good? One obvious answer is to set up a central source of direction. But people make better use of their talents if they are left to solve their own problems in their own way. Society is so complex that no central power can direct it efficiently; individuals can do better through mutual adjustment to one another's initiatives. While freedom may seem inefficient, in the long run it is the most effective basis for social life, for there is no intelligence that can look after people's affairs better than they themselves can.

Individual initiative does not preclude cooperation. As the eighteenth-century philosopher David Hume pointed out in a famous example, two men would quickly discover how to row a boat across a river. Trial and error would show them how to work the oars together.[15] Society is a great self-regulating order whose parts are continually adjusting to each other through processes of communication and exchange. Cooperation exists, but it is decentralized cooperation achieved through mutual consent, not directed from above. Order emerges as the many members of society, pursuing their own good in their own way, respond to the initiatives of others. Hayek called this emergent decentralized, voluntary order **spontaneous order**.[16]

The economic marketplace is a spontaneous order since it is not under the control of any one individual or committee. Freely moving prices are the signals by which participants communicate to each other the relative abundance or scarcity of commodities. The science of economics focuses on the ability of the market to clear itself—that is, to bring supply and demand into equilibrium. Producers and consumers use the information conveyed by prices to adjust their expectations so that the quantity produced equals the quantity desired.

This view of markets assumes that there are many buyers and sellers who are trading freely without coercion and who know what they want and what goods and services are available; that entry to the market is relatively open, so that new participants can always undermine any collusion among present participants; and further, that there is a legal framework to protect property and enforce contracts. Under these conditions, it is argued, all exchanges are mutually beneficial. Because participants have a variety of choices, they do not engage in transactions unless they find them more worthwhile than the available alternatives. As we will see later, those who criticize the spontaneous market order often do so not because they oppose its intrinsic logic but because they believe that one or more of these factual assumptions are, in practice, false.

To prevent mutual coercion, the market order requires that behaviour be limited by rules of conduct. Such rules include respect for individuals and their property as well as the keeping of agreements and contracts. Those who violate rules while expecting others to abide by them are known in the jargon of contemporary economics as **free riders.** Tax evasion, for example, is usually free riding because it is not a protest against government as such but merely an attempt to enjoy the benefits of government without paying for them. It is the essential role of government to make spontaneous order possible by enforcing those general rules of conduct that are necessary to it.

Adam Smith offered a succinct classical liberal description of the duties of government:

> According to the system of natural liberty, the sovereign has only three duties to attend to; three duties of great importance, indeed, but plain and intelligible to common understandings: first, the duty of protecting the society from the violence and invasion of other independent societies; secondly, the duty of protecting, as far as possible, every member of the society from the injustice or oppression of every other member of it, or the duty of establishing an exact administration of justice; and, thirdly, the duty of erecting and maintaining

certain public works and certain public institutions, which it can never be for the interest of any individual, or small number of individuals, to erect and maintain; because the profit could never repay the expense to any individual or small group of individuals, though it may frequently do much more than repay it to a great society.[17]

Smith's third duty of government embraced certain activities that are not profitable in a free market because it is difficult to charge for them. For example, it would not pay for an entrepreneur to beautify a city because it is difficult if not impossible to charge people for looking at sculptures, parks, and grand buildings. Similarly, it seldom pays for an entrepreneur to subsidize basic scientific research because profitable application is so uncertain. In contemporary economics, such things are known as **collective** (or **public**) **goods.** They are defined as goods and services that are not divisible among individuals but are enjoyed in common, and from which it is difficult to exclude consumers. A street light, for example, shines for all who are near the road. The fact that one person sees the light does not make it less available for others. Contrast this with food or clothing, which cannot be used simultaneously by more than one person.

Collective goods have an inherent free-rider problem. When people feed and clothe themselves, they have to pay for what they consume, but it is tempting for them to hold back their share of the cost of a collective good in the hope that others will pay for it and that they will be able to enjoy the benefits free of charge. How many street lights would there be if they were supported by voluntary contributions?[18] The state helps to provide collective goods through ensuring that we all pay our fair share. The state's monopoly on coercion can be used to collect taxes to pay for harbours, roads, scientific research, urban beautification, and many other desirable things. The liberal justification of this procedure is that, in providing collective goods, government is being used to help people attain what they actually want, not to impose goals upon them that are contrary to their own desires.

Classical liberals have always recognized the category of collective goods, but they have not usually been eager to provide many of them through the state. Adam Smith had only a few such items in mind when he wrote *The Wealth of Nations*. Classical liberals have generally been confident that private ingenuity will find ways to offer in the market the goods and services that substitute for government provision of collective goods. For example, a movie is a sort of collective good, since many people can enjoy it at once, but it can be marketed by the simple expedient of selling the right to a seat.[19]

One crucial tenet of classical liberalism is that, beyond the three functions of government mentioned by Smith, the state has no mandate to correct the results of the marketplace by transferring wealth or income from rich to poor. Classical liberals see a degree of inequality as an inevitable result of free competition. In the long run, they think, it will benefit even the poor as capital is reinvested to create new opportunities for employment and production. The classical liberal believes that economic advances may initially benefit only a restricted few, but that over time those benefits will become more widely disseminated. Such innovations as television, computers, and mobile phones were at first expensive luxuries but eventually became articles of mass consumption.

Classical liberals object to state **redistribution** of wealth and income because they believe it is economically inefficient. For the market to work properly, the agreements made in it must be based on the data about supply and demand that prices furnish. An individual who gains wealth by responding to these price signals is regarded as contributing to the welfare of others, not as taking away from them wealth that must be repossessed by the state. Classical liberals would see nothing untoward in the fact that Bill Gates, one of the richest men in the world, at one time had a fortune of more than US$100 billion. Rather, they would emphasize the incalculable benefits that his Microsoft software has conferred upon all those who use personal computers.

Although classical liberalism was not egalitarian in the sense of equality of result, it was an important force for promoting equality before the law. When the ideology crystallized in the seventeenth and eighteenth centuries, there were many grossly unequal institutions, such as slavery, even in the freest countries. Classical liberals fought against both slavery and the privileges of the nobility, against discrimination imposed on ethnic or religious minorities, against monopolies and tariffs that favoured corporations and producer cartels, and against government patronage in employment and public works. Since many of these goals have now been largely achieved in the Western democracies, classical liberalism today seems conservative, a force for preserving the status quo; indeed, classical liberals in this century are often called, and call themselves, conservatives (more on this later).

Although classical liberalism is logically consistent in its views on government, many observers say it lacks concern for those not favoured by ability or good fortune. The classical liberal's confidence that, in the long run, free enterprise and the market system will raise the living standards of all does not do much now for those who are less well off. And even if the economic inequalities generated by the market are no greater than in other systems, many critics object to classical liberalism's willingness to accept these inequalities. It should be possible, they say, to do better—to keep the admittedly useful aspects of the market while using government to ensure that all citizens have a decent standard of living, adequate medical care, and education for their children, and that there is financial security for the injured, the sick, the unemployed, and the old. Sentiments such as these have encouraged reform-minded liberals to develop a more activist conception of government's role in society.

REFORM LIBERALISM

The American sociologist Paul Starr refers to classical liberalism as "constitutional liberalism" because of its emphasis on constitutional government and the rule of law, and to reform liberalism as "modern democratic liberalism." According to Starr,

> The relationship between liberalism in these two phases has been predominantly cumulative: while rejecting laissez-faire economic policy, modern democratic liberalism

continues to take the broader tradition of constitutional liberalism as its foundation. That is why it is possible to speak not only of the two separately, but also of an overarching set of ideas that unites them.[20]

John Stuart Mill, perhaps the best-known exponent of classical liberalism, was also one of the pioneers of reform liberalism. One aspect of his thought that pointed toward the future was its emphasis on democracy. Mill advocated the extension of voting rights to all adults—men and women alike. Fearful that this new mass of uninstructed voters might use the franchise for selfish purposes, such as the confiscation of property, he proposed that the educated be entitled to multiple votes; however, in historical perspective his support of democracy was on the whole more politically significant than his reservations about it.

The democratization of liberalism began, but did not end, with the expansion of the right to vote. The ballot was made secret so that ordinary voters cannot be pressured or intimidated by their employers, creditors, or landlords. Salaries of elected officials have been raised so that one does not have to be independently wealthy to run for office. Entry to careers in the civil service now depends on ability rather than on family connections. Limits have been placed on campaign expenditures by political parties so that a "plutocracy" of big donors cannot simply buy an election.

Democratization of the political system tends to affect the economy. The vote is a form of political power. Once ordinary people gain access to that power, they naturally want to use it to improve their economic status. Though J. S. Mill remained committed to the free market, he was deeply pained by economic inequalities. In 1848 he wrote, in *Principles of Political Economy:*

> If the institution of private property necessarily carried with it as a consequence, that the produce of labour should be apportioned as we now see it, almost in an inverse ratio to the labour—the largest portions to those who have never worked at all, the next largest to those whose work is almost nominal, and so in a descending scale, the remuneration dwindling as the work grows harder and more disagreeable, until the most fatiguing and exhausting bodily labour cannot count with certainty on being able to earn even the necessaries of life; if this or Communism were the alternative, all the difficulties, great or small, of Communism would be but as dust in the balance.[21]

The decisive step toward reform liberalism in Britain was taken by T. H. Green (1836–82), a professor of philosophy at Oxford University. It was Green who redefined the concept of freedom to include not only the absence of coercion but also the presence of means or capacity:

> When we speak of freedom, we should consider carefully what we mean by it. We do not mean merely freedom from restraint or compulsion … we mean a positive power or capacity of doing or enjoying something worth doing or enjoying and that, too, something that we do or enjoy in common with others.[22]

Green argued that the state would have to regulate liberty of contract in order to secure a higher standard of living for the less fortunate. He achieved lasting influence by explaining the quest for equality of result in terms of the attainment of freedom. In doing so, he made it possible for liberalism to incorporate equality of result, which previously had been seen as a socialist issue.

Green and like-minded professors at English universities educated a generation of students who later rose to prominence within the Liberal Party of Great Britain and laid the foundations of the **welfare state** when they came to power in the first decade of the twentieth century. They adopted the income tax as a means of redistribution; involved the state in unemployment insurance, old-age pensions, and other social insurance programs; and encouraged, through permissive legislation, the rise of organized labour.

In Canada, William Lyon Mackenzie King was nourished on the same ideas. While he chose to move slowly through the complexities of Canadian federalism, by the time he retired as prime minister in 1948 he had launched the Canadian welfare state. Other Liberal prime ministers, notably Lester Pearson and Pierre Trudeau, built on and expanded his reforms. Their governments expanded unemployment insurance and welfare payments and initiated a national medical insurance scheme. The thrust of these reforms was to guarantee, through state action, the financial security of all residents of Canada.

Another vital player in the development of reform liberalism was the British economist John Maynard Keynes. His *General Theory of Employment, Interest and Money* (1936) argued that the spontaneous order of the market had a fatal flaw. Because of this flaw, the economy could fall into a permanent depression characterized by high unemployment of labour and underuse of other resources. Government could compensate for this flaw by applying appropriate fiscal and monetary measures (see Comparative Perspectives 10.1). Keynes did not make government the central planner demanded by socialism, but he did call for it to be much more than the rule-enforcer of classical liberalism. It was now responsible for maintaining prosperity and full employment through fiscal and monetary policy, duties that were explicitly accepted by the governments of Britain, Canada, and the United States at the close of World War II.

A striking feature of reform liberalism is that, while it no longer promotes the laissez-faire economic freedom of classical liberalism, it has preserved and even intensified its commitment to individual choice in other spheres of life—for example, legalizing mind-altering drugs and all types of sexual relations between consenting adults. Pierre Trudeau's famous remark that "the state has no place in the bedrooms of the nation" is a fair statement of the attitude of reform liberals in these matters.

This apparent paradox in reform liberalism can perhaps be explained as a function of the individualistic character of all liberal thought, whether classical or reform. All liberals see society as essentially a means for enabling individuals to do what they want without preventing others from doing likewise. Reform liberals believe that their

Comparative Perspectives 10.1

Keynesian Economics

The economist John Maynard Keynes and his followers believed that governments could guarantee full employment without taking over the economy altogether. All that was necessary was to follow what they saw as enlightened fiscal and monetary policies. **Fiscal policy** refers to government spending and taxation, and **monetary policy** refers to control over interest rates and the supply of money. In Canada, the minister of finance controls taxes and spending through preparation of the annual budget, whereas the Bank of Canada controls interest rates and the supply of money.

To simplify somewhat, the basic idea of Keynesianism was that governments should coordinate both fiscal and monetary policy in a countercyclical direction. That is, in times of economic recession, government should force down interest rates (monetary policy)—thus making it easier for people to borrow money—and spend more than it collected in taxes (fiscal policy). Both measures would tend to put more money in the hands of consumers, which would in turn stimulate business activity. In times of prosperity, government should steer in the opposite direction, raising interest rates and collecting a surplus of taxation over expenditure, thus damping down the economy. In theory the public budget would be balanced, not necessarily in any one year but over the course of the business cycle.

In practice, Keynesianism was often contaminated by political considerations. Politicians found it much easier to lower interest rates than to raise them, and to run **deficits** rather than surpluses. As consumers got used to stimulative measures, they had to be ratcheted upward to have any effect, thus setting off an upward spiral of inflation and deficit spending. In the 1970s, most economists and governments appeared to renounce Keynesianism as a long-term guide to fiscal and monetary policy. However, Keynesian countercyclical spending made a comeback with the Great Recession of 2008: governments all over the Western world ran stimulative deficits to avoid economic collapse. Most countries are now in the stage of trying to get back to balanced budgets.

economic interventions will help individuals to satisfy their desires. Their general outlook remains individualistic and libertarian even when they advocate increased state involvement in the economy.

Ideologies do not undergo such profound changes without cause. The rise of reform liberalism was chiefly motivated by concern about the new working class during the Industrial Revolution. The rural poor of Great Britain flocked to cities such as Birmingham, Manchester, and London to work in factories. The new working class, concentrated in industrial towns and cities, was far more visible than the rural poor dispersed across the countryside. Extensive urban slums created a widespread belief that the market system caused poverty and wretched living conditions. The new developments in liberalism were an attempt to share the wealth more widely and, in the minds of some, to stave off the socialist revolution that would occur if the conditions of the working class did not improve.

Reform liberalism was the dominant ideology of the Western world throughout much of the twentieth century, with adherents in parties of all labels. However, the reform liberal consensus that had prevailed since the end of World War II broke down in the 1980s. Keynesianism became discredited in practice because politicians used it to legitimize recurrent deficit spending with inflationary effects. There was a revival of classical liberalism in both the United Kingdom and the United States under the governments of Margaret Thatcher and Ronald Reagan, respectively. Thatcher and her advisers were particularly influenced by the writings of Friedrich Hayek, Reagan and his advisers by the works of Milton Friedman. Both administrations spoke of reducing the size of government and deregulating the economy, of privatizing government-owned enterprises, of inaugurating a new era of free-market growth, and of lessening our preoccupation with social security and equality of result.

Because of their belief that government action can improve society, reform liberals are often caricatured as naïve idealists.

The revival of market-oriented classical liberalism came later in Canada and was enacted less enthusiastically. Pierre Trudeau's last government (1980–84) was highly interventionist in economic affairs. Brian Mulroney's government (1984–93) took steps in the direction of deregulating the economy and privatizing or downsizing government operations, but his initiatives were cautious compared with those in the United States, the United Kingdom, Australia, and New Zealand. The Liberal government of Jean Chrétien, elected in 1993, turned even further toward classical liberalism by accepting that the federal budget must be balanced. Repudiation of deficit financing caused the Chrétien government to reduce spending on many government programs such as unemployment insurance (renamed "employment insurance") and social assistance, which reform liberals had previously thought to be untouchable. The Keynesian Moment appeared to have passed.

Then the worldwide recession of 2008 led to a dramatic revival of the Keynesian version of reform liberalism, which sees government as the guarantor of prosperity through its control over monetary and fiscal policies (interest rates and budgets). Many commentators feared that the world was about to re-enact the Great Depression of the 1930s. Leading world governments—whether nominally socialist, liberal, or conservative—quickly agreed on a coordinated Keynesian response, built on three main policies:

1. Stem the emergency by bailing out financial institutions. This meant advancing huge government loans to threatened financial institutions, or even in some cases putting banks under partial or full public ownership. The goal was to stop the domino effect caused by bad loans and restore financial liquidity to the world's economy.

2. Let the "automatic stabilizers" work. In an economic recession, government tax revenues fall because fewer people are employed, incomes fall, and sales volumes decline. Meanwhile, government expenditures increase for social assistance, unemployment insurance, and pensions for older workers forced out of the labour market. Rising expenditures and falling revenues produce a budget deficit without the need for an explicit decision to pursue one.

3. Budget for a "stimulus package" by deliberately increasing the deficit. The stimulus packages adopted in various countries involved temporary tax cuts, accelerated spending on infrastructure such as roads and utilities, and subsidies to targeted industries. The theory is that deliberate deficit spending adds to the stimulus effect of the automatic stabilizers and helps keep workers employed who might otherwise be laid off.

Initially it seemed as if the recession might bring a long-term shift to the left, with more government regulation and Keynesian management of the economy, but as the downturn levelled out, governments began stressing that their bailouts and stimulus packages were temporary interventions, not long-term policy shifts. It now seems that the revival of Keynesianism should be seen as a short-term phenomenon in response to an emergency. As of fall 2012, it seemed that further steps might be necessary to prevent the collapse of the European banking system, but that is not the same thing as the revival of Keynesianism.

The ebb and flow of ideologies has had considerable effect on the taxes we pay because classical and reform liberalism differ in their approach to taxation. Classical liberals generally favour **proportional taxes,** in which the rate is the same for everyone. We still have many of these taxes in Canada today, for example, the federal GST, with a rate of 5 percent. The more goods and services you purchase, the more tax you pay, but the rate is the same for all payers. Reform liberals, however, generally advocate **progressive taxes,** such as the federal income tax. In a progressive income tax, the rate is graduated so that it rises as the amount of income rises. Reform liberals consider that proportional taxes weigh more heavily on lower-income earners, who spend a greater proportion of their income on necessities, and argue that proportional taxes violate **social justice.** In 2012 the Canadian federal personal income tax had a progressive structure with four rates:

Structure of Canadian Federal Income Tax, 2011

Taxable Income	Applicable Rate
First $42 707	15%
From $42 707 to $85 414	22%
From $85 414 to $132 406	26%
Above $132 406	29%

The structure is more steeply progressive than it appears in the table, for the provinces also levy income taxes in tandem with the federal tax. The top federal–provincial combined rate ranges from 39 percent in Alberta to more than 45 percent in some provinces. That is, depending on where they live, Canadians in 2012 paid tax of 39 percent or more on their taxable income above $132 406. In Canada, as in many other countries, the graduated tax structure used to be steeper; it has been flattened somewhat with the revival of classical liberal thinking. Steep progressive taxes are generally thought to be a deterrent to work effort ("Why should I work harder to earn an additional dollar if the government is going to take 70 or 80 percent of it?"). On the other hand, there still seems to be wide popular support for some degree of progressivity in the tax system. Progressive income taxes are a means of redistribution because those who earn more pay proportionally more to fund government services that are equally available to all. Such taxes, therefore, mesh with the reform liberal strategy of using the state to promote equality of opportunity.

Classical and reform liberalism are extreme ideal types within the liberal family of ideas. For intellectual purposes it is useful to organize ideologies into coherent and consistent positions, but in the actual world of politics, many people see merit in both positions and try to combine them in one way or another or stake out some intermediate position. The portraits of classical and reform liberalism presented in this chapter can be used as tools for analyzing what people say in political discourse, but do not expect to find such clarity and consistency in real life.

Questions for Discussion

1. Critics of reform liberalism often assert that welfare programs such as employment insurance and social assistance create dependency and reduce incentives for self-help. Reform liberals argue, in contrast, that such programs, by giving help when needed, assist people in looking after themselves. Based on your own experience and observations, which view do you think is more accurate?

2. Critics of the progressive income tax often claim that high taxes are a major cause of the so-called "brain drain"—that is, of the tendency of Canadians with high earning potential to move to the United States. Do you know any Canadians who have made such a move? Do you think tax avoidance was crucial to their decision, or were other factors more important?

3. If you had a magic wand to wave, would you move Canada in a reform-liberal or in a classical-liberal direction? Why? In your mind, is this a question of the values you hold or of your assessment of the best way to attain values that most people hold?

Internet Links

1. American Civil Liberties Union: **www.aclu.org**. More consistently reform liberal (left) than the Canadian Civil Liberties Association.

2. Brookings Institution: **www.brook.edu**. The largest and best-known reform-liberal research institute in North America.

3. Canadian Civil Liberties Association: **www.ccla.org**. Takes an interesting mix of classical-liberal and reform-liberal positions.

4. International Society for Individual Liberty: **www.isil.org**. Has a large number of links to classical-liberal authors, publishers, and research institutes.

5. Laissez Faire Books: **www.laissezfaire.org**. An American bookseller specializing in works with a classical-liberal perspective.

6. Liberal International: **www.liberal-international.org**. The international organization of liberal parties, including the Liberal Party of Canada.

7. Liberal Party of Canada: **www.liberal.ca**.

8. Ludwig von Mises Institute: **www.mises.org**. Online editions of the books of famous liberal economist Ludwig von Mises, who was the teacher of Friedrich Hayek.

Further Reading

Allen, R. T. *Beyond Liberalism: The Political Thought of F. A. Hayek and Michael Polanyi.* New Brunswick, NJ: Transaction Publishers, 1998.

Amadae, S. M. *Rationalizing Capitalist Democracy: The Cold War Origins of Rational Choice Liberalism.* Chicago: University of Chicago, 2003.

Berlin, Isaiah. *Four Essays on Liberty.* 2nd ed. London: Oxford University Press, 2002.

Blais, Andre, Elisabeth Gidengil, Richard Nadeau, and Neil Nevitte. *Anatomy of a Liberal Victory: Making Sense of the Vote in the 2000 Canadian Election.* Peterborough, ON: Broadview Press, 2002.

Gray, John. *Liberalism.* 2nd ed. Minneapolis: University of Minnesota Press, 1995.

———. *Two Faces of Liberalism.* New York: New Press, 2000.

Hayek, F.A. *The Constitution of Liberty: The Definitive Edition.* Chicago: University of Chicago Press, 2011.

Hellsten, Sirkku. *In Defense of Moral Individualism.* Helsinki: Philosophical Society of Finland, 1997.

Higgs, Robert, E. C. Pasour, Carl P. Close, and Randal Ray Rucker, eds. *The Challenge of Liberty: Classical Liberalism Today.* Washington, DC: Independent Institute, 2006.

Hunter, Albert, and Carl Milofsky. *Pragmatic Liberalism: Constructing a Civil Society.* New York: Palgrave Macmillan, 2007.

Ignatieff, Michael. *The Rights Revolution.* Toronto: House of Anansi, 2000.

Josephson, Peter. *The Great Art of Government: Locke's Use of Consent.* Lawrence: University of Kansas Press, 2002.

Mandle, Jon. *What's Left of Liberalism? An Interpretation and Defense of Justice as Fairness.* Lanham, MD: Lexington Books, 2000.

Meadowcroft, James, ed. *Hobhouse: Liberalism and Other Writings.* Cambridge: Cambridge University Press, 1994.

Morefield, Jeanne. *Covenants Without Swords: Idealist Liberalism and the Spirit of Empire.* Princeton, NJ: Princeton University Press, 2004.

PART 2

Mulhall, Stephen. *Liberals and Communitarians.* 2nd ed. Oxford: Blackwell, 1996.

Owen, J. Judd. *Religion and the Demise of Liberal Rationalism: The Foundational Crisis of the Separation of Church and State.* Chicago: University of Chicago Press, 2001.

Paul, Ellen Frankel, Fred D. Miller Jr., and Jeffrey Paul. *Natural Rights Liberalism from Locke to Nozick.* Cambridge: Cambridge University Press, 2005.

Rawls, John. *Political Liberalism.* New York: Columbia University Press, 1993.

Sandel, Michael J. *Liberalism and the Limits of Justice.* 2nd ed. Cambridge: Cambridge University Press, 1997.

Starr, Paul. *Freedom's Power: The True Force of Liberalism.* New York: Basic Books, 2007.

CHAPTER 11
Conservatism

To *conserve* means to save or preserve. Thus a conservative is a person who wishes to keep society as it is and who is skeptical about change. **Conservatism** in this sense is a disposition "to prefer the familiar to the unknown ... the tried to the untried, fact to mystery, the actual to the possible, the limited to the unbounded, the near to the distant, the sufficient to the superabundant, the convenient to the perfect, present laughter to utopian bliss," said Michael Oakeshott, a twentieth-century British political theorist and well-known conservative writer.[1] Or, as critics of conservatism have said with a touch of exaggeration, a conservative is a person who never wants to do anything for the first time.

This preference for the existing present over the conjectural future rests upon a sober assessment of human nature. The Canadian historian W. L. Morton put it this way:

> To the theologian, this is the belief in original sin, the belief that man is by nature imperfect and may be made perfect only by redemption and grace. In philosophic terms, it is a denial of the fundamental liberal and Marxist belief that human nature is inherently perfectible, and that man may realize the perfection that is in him if only the right environment is created.[2]

According to conservative thinking, the limitations of human nature make it imprudent for society to embark on large-scale ventures of social transformation. Much that is good may be lost, with little likelihood of reaching "utopian bliss."

This attitude can also be defended with arguments drawn from social science, particularly from the idea of spontaneous order. The main point is that spontaneous order acts as a vast filter for selecting desirable and discarding undesirable innovations. Such an order consists of millions of intelligences freely cooperating under suitable rules. Any innovation—a new theory in science, a new trend in art, or a new product in business—is subjected to the repeated independent scrutiny of countless individuals who must decide whether to accept, imitate, or purchase. Any individual may make a poor decision, but there is a strong presumption that in time the right decision or course of action will emerge. This is especially true since the testing process continues over generations.

So there is some reason to assume that the present way of doing things is socially useful. If a better way existed, the chances are that it would already have been adopted. But this is only a probability, not a certainty. The fact that progress occurs shows that some innovations do have value, even if most do not. This is why the conservative tends to adopt a cautious attitude toward changes, waiting to see their usefulness demonstrated before adopting them. This is not hostility to change or improvement as such, but rather respect for wisdom inherited from the past combined with caution in the face of an unknown future.

Social reformers, whose proposals seem so obviously beneficial in their own eyes, are naturally impatient with this conservative attitude. Conservatives reply in their own defence that existing institutions already have the tacit approval of millions of minds over generations. That is a strong counterweight to reformers' confidence in their own ideas. They may in fact be correct, but they must bear the burden of proof.

An interesting facet of conservatism is respect for habits and customs whose rationale may not be immediately apparent. Conservatives assume that there is tacit wisdom in inherited patterns of behaviour. People may not understand all the reasons for what they do, but they may still be doing the right thing in following custom. Reformers, in contrast, are often quick to condemn what they do not understand, preferring conscious reason over inarticulate habit.

The conservative theory of change is closely associated with the ideas of the Anglo-Irish parliamentarian Edmund Burke (1729–97), who was moved to reflect on change by the outbreak of the French Revolution. In 1789, Louis XVI convened the Estates-General, a medieval type of consultative body that had not met since 1614. The king's goal was to raise new taxes, but events quickly escaped from royal control. The Estates-General converted itself into a National Assembly and declared France a constitutional monarchy. Change followed change with dizzying rapidity. The National Assembly adopted the Declaration of the Rights of Man and of the Citizen, created a form of representative government, abolished the last remnants of feudalism, nationalized the property of the Roman Catholic Church, and replaced the old provinces with geometrically drawn *départements*. Even weights and measures were affected as the National Assembly commissioned the preparation of what became the metric system. All this, as well as much more, was done quickly in an exalted spirit of reform: the rationalism of the Enlightenment, finally put into practice, would remodel society.

The results were not what had been expected. Within four years France was under the dictatorship of Maximilien Robespierre and the Revolution had entered a phase later known as the Terror. France also went to war with the rest of Europe. Louis XVI and Marie Antoinette had been put to death by the guillotine, a new form of execution. Thousands of other opponents of Robespierre also went to the guillotine, and the dictator himself was finally removed from power in the same way. Political stability was restored only by Napoleon, who ruled at least as autocratically as any of the Bourbon kings had done, though far more effectively.

Edmund Burke (1729–97), the most important philosopher of conservatism.

Burke wrote *Reflections on the Revolution in France* (1790) before the worst excesses began, but he correctly predicted that turmoil and despotism would grow out of such a radical break with the past. We are not wise enough to remake society all at once, he asserted; we must rely on the accumulated wisdom of the past, contained in customs, traditions, and practices:

> We are afraid to put men to live and trade each on his own private stock of reason; because we suspect that this stock in each man is small, and that the individuals would do better to avail themselves of the general bank and capital of nations and ages. Many of our men of speculation, instead of exploding general prejudices, employ their sagacity to discover the latent wisdom which prevails in them. If they find what they seek, and they seldom fail, they think it more wise to continue the prejudice, with the reason involved, than to cast away the coat of prejudice, and to leave nothing but the naked reason; because prejudice, with its reason, has a motive to give action to that reason, and an affection which will give it permanence.[3]

The contemporary reader is struck by Burke's praise of prejudice, which is today a negative term implying unfair discrimination. For Burke, *prejudice* meant literally the sort of "prejudgment" that contains the latent wisdom of past experience. People are not able to think their way through each new situation, so they must fall back on rules of thumb that have served them well in the past. Past experience, limited as it may be, is better than nothing as a guide to the future. The conservative view expressed by Burke is that prejudice is not just an irrational closing of the mind but a necessary way of dealing with a world in which complete information is rarely available.

As the psychologist Gordon Allport has pointed out, "the human mind must think with the aid of categories ... Once formed, categories are the basis for normal prejudgment."[4] Such prejudgments are necessary and useful; they "become prejudices [in the pejorative sense] only if they are not reversible when exposed to new knowledge."[5] The challenge for conservatism is to combine open-mindedness about new developments with attachment to traditional values.

Burke did not oppose change as such—he had earlier spoken in defence of the American Revolution—but he wanted it to be gradual, so that the inherited wisdom of the past would not be lost:

> We must all obey the great law of change. It is the most powerful law of nature, and the means perhaps of its conservation. All we can do, and that human wisdom can do, is to provide that the change shall proceed by insensible degrees. This has all the benefits which may be in change, without any of the inconveniences of mutation. This mode will, on the one hand, prevent the unfixing old interests at once: a thing which is apt to breed a black and sullen discontent in those who are at once dispossessed of all their influence and consideration. This gradual course, on the other hand, will prevent men, long under depression, from being intoxicated with a large draught of new power, which they always abuse with a licentious insolence.[6]

The conservative attitude toward change is perhaps best expressed in the old adage "If it is not necessary to change, it is necessary not to change." In the absence of some compelling reason for innovation, it is desirable not to tamper with the status quo, which has shown at least some degree of viability. Alternatives that are attractive in theory may turn out to be much worse in practice. In evaluating proposed reforms, conservatives are aware that they are comparing things that exist and whose faults are therefore apparent with ideas that have not yet been tested and whose faults may be unsuspected.

Conservatism is a prejudice (in Burke's sense) against using the state's coercive power to sponsor large-scale experiments in social change. The conservative will eventually give grudging approval to change that has occurred spontaneously through the cautious accumulation of many individual decisions, but to use the state as an agency of rapid reform short-circuits this process and may commit society to beautiful but unworkable visions.

Conservatism is conveniently described as an attachment to the present or status quo, but that is an oversimplification in one important respect. Conservatives are often highly critical of present trends, comparing them unfavourably with their image of the past. This is not incompatible with their view of gradual change, for the testing period of complex innovations may well extend over decades or generations. Conservatives often feel that we are heading in the wrong direction and should return to the ways of the past before it is too late. Therefore, they can find themselves in the position of making proposals that are themselves innovative vis-à-vis present arrangements. When conservatives refer to the status quo, they mean the present seen not as an isolated moment in time but as an extension of a long past. It is the prolonged experience of the past that the conservative values, not the mere present existence of a custom, practice, or institution.

Burke expressed this unity of past, present, and future by metaphorically speaking of the state as a partnership across generations:

> It is a partnership in all science; a partnership in all art; a partnership in every virtue and in all perfection. As the ends of such a partnership cannot be obtained in many generations, it becomes a partnership not only between those who are living, but between those who are living, those who are dead, and those who are to be born.[7]

No one since has more clearly stated the conservative's sense of continuity. For Burke, this continuity was further buttressed by a belief in divine order as the foundation of social order. Other conservatives have reversed this relationship, seeing religion more as a useful support of society than as its basis. But whatever their differences of religious faith, conservatives all revere the social order as something larger and more important than the individual. They are always mistrustful of the rationalistic intellectual's confidence in individual judgment; they put more trust in the collective wisdom of society as expressed in customs, usages, and institutions.

As presented here, conservatism is an attitude, not a full-fledged ideology with a whole set of beliefs about human nature, society, and government. By the conservative's own admission, the status quo is always changing, never the same from year to year. Paradoxically, conservatism's commitment to the status quo entails gradual acceptance of new principles as the present reality changes. In this way conservatism differs markedly from liberalism and socialism, both of which are built around certain ideas regarded as universal truths. Classical liberals believe that the market is the most effective means of meeting human wants; socialists believe the same of central planning. They defend their systems where they exist and work for their introduction where they do not. They regard the status quo as a secondary factor that merely affects the speed with which desired goals may be achieved; they derive the goals themselves from principles and have no commitment to what exists simply because it does exist.

All of this means that there is no single, unchanging body of doctrine that can be identified as conservative. Nonetheless, conservative thinkers do have certain traits in common. Russell Kirk, a leading American writer on conservatism, lists six such common characteristics:

1. Belief in a transcendent order, or body of natural law, which rules society as well as conscience....

2. Affection for the proliferating variety and mystery of human existence, as opposed to the narrowing uniformity, egalitarianism, and utilitarian aims of most radical systems....

PART 2

3. Conviction that civilized society requires orders and classes, as against the notion of a "classless society."...

4. Persuasion that freedom and property are closely linked: separate property from private possession, and the Leviathan becomes master of all....

5. Faith in prescription and distrust of "sophisters, calculators, and economists" who would reconstruct society upon abstract designs....

6. Recognition that change may not be salutary reform: hasty innovation may be a devouring conflagration, rather than a torch of progress.[8]*

Here we must confine our view largely to the Anglo-American tradition.[9] In continental Europe, *conservatism* has often referred to the ideology of those who have not accepted the legal type of authority and legitimacy, who have wished to cling to the practices that were widespread in Europe before the French Revolution: a hereditary aristocracy, established religion, and a monarchy unchecked by representative government—in general terms, to a traditional society of inherited status.

Though Anglo-American conservatism also began with reaction against the French Revolution, that reaction was not as total and violent, because the status quo in England in 1789 was far removed from that in continental Europe. The so-called Glorious Revolution of 1688 had already established parliamentary supremacy and religious toleration in Britain. Although a powerful aristocracy existed, it was closely tied to the business or mercantile class. In the newly independent American colonies there was no aristocracy at all, the monarchy had been abolished, and religious freedom was nearly absolute. England and America in 1789 already were, to a great extent, what the early reformers of the French Revolution wished to create. Anglo-American conservatism, epitomized by Burke, rejected sudden, state-directed change, but it could not have rejected many of the aspirations of those reformers without rejecting itself.

A brief look at some of Burke's opinions suggests the complexities of being a conservative in a society whose traditions are largely liberal. Burke's economic views were almost identical to those of Adam Smith. He praised the market in these terms: "Nobody, I believe, has observed with any reflexion what market is, without being astonished at the truth, the correctness, the celerity, the general equity, with which the balance of wants is settled."[10] Correspondingly, Burke strongly advocated private property and totally rejected the redistributive state. Politically Burke was a Whig— that is, a member of the party that, in broad terms, supported the rights of Parliament. He revered the memory of the Glorious Revolution and he spoke in favour of the American colonies in their dispute with England, because he thought they were being deprived of the traditional English right of self-government. All of these positions sound very liberal, seeming to support freedom, constitutionalism, and the rule of

*From the book *The Conservative Mind* by Russell Kirk. Copyright © 1985. Published by Regnery Publishing, Inc. All rights reserved. Reprinted by special permission of Regnery Publishing Inc., Washington, D.C.

law. On the other hand, Burke was a strong advocate of hereditary aristocracy, though he himself was not of that class. To ensure that the nobility, together with merchants of great property, retained control of English government, he opposed any extension of the right to vote, which in his day was quite narrowly restricted. He thought that society was divided necessarily into hierarchical levels and that this was something for government to protect because of the hierarchy's contribution to social stability.

Burke accepted a degree of economic liberalism in combination with his social and political conservatism. The precise nature of that combination is intelligible only in the context of the issues of his day. Since then, Anglo-American conservatives have held various ideas, depending on when and where they lived, but they have generally followed Burke's example in combining market economics with respect for the past. Two of the founders of Canada—John A. Macdonald and George-Étienne Cartier—fit this description well. Both were thoroughly committed to the market system. Macdonald eventually adopted a protective tariff—which violates the concept of free trade—but only because he could not conclude a reciprocity (free trade) agreement with the United States. Both were opposed to universal suffrage and regarded the United States as an instructive example of democracy run amok. Both were strong supporters of the British Empire and the Crown, seeing a constitutional monarchy as a valuable source of social stability. It has been said of these two statesmen: "It was not that the founders of the Canadian nation despised freedom; indeed, they revered it. But, for them, freedom arises from order, from restraint, not from unconstrained passions. The world they desired was the Burkean world, the world of order, restraint, sterner virtues and prudence."[11]

In comparison with American conservatism, the Canadian variety is less imbued with the virtues of free enterprise and more willing to resort to collectivist economic schemes. By any measure, American society and American thought are more individualistic than their Canadian counterparts, and Canadian conservatism reflects this general difference. Also, there is in Canada a tradition of conservatism that is rather skeptical of the competitive-market philosophy of classical liberalism. Thinkers in this vein are often called **Red Tories** because they combine some traditionalist views with others that may seem interventionist or even socialist. The best-known Red Tory is the philosopher George Grant, whose 1965 book *Lament for a Nation* has become a classic of Canadian political thought. Grant was stirred to write his book by the collapse of John Diefenbaker's government over the issue of whether Canada should accept American nuclear warheads on its soil. In Grant's view, Lester Pearson's subsequent decision to accept the weapons showed that Canada had been pulled irretrievably into the American orbit. Grant's objection was based not merely on sentiments of Canadian nationalism but also on philosophical considerations: "The impossibility of conservatism in our era is the impossibility of Canada. As Canadians we attempted a ridiculous task in trying to build a conservative nation in the age of progress, on a continent we share with the most dynamic nation on earth. The current of modern history was against us."[12]

The dynamism to which Grant refers is the individualistic market orientation of American society. He touches here upon a profound truth—that the market is the great dissolver of customs, traditions, and all the things to which conservatives are temperamentally attached. The profit-and-loss psychology of the market often undermines the heritage of the past. No ideology is ever free of internal contradictions. The most obvious contradiction of conservatism is that in accepting the competitive market, which is really a classical liberal idea, it threatens many of its own values relating to tradition, stability, and social cohesion. Nonetheless, contemporary conservatism as a practical, real-world ideology tries to ride both horses, so to speak: it accepts the laissez-faire economic policy of classical liberalism along with a traditionalist view of social customs, morality, and political institutions.

SOCIAL CONSERVATISM AND LIBERTARIANISM

Modern conservatism is a not-always-consistent blend of Burkean conservatism and classical liberalism. The classical emphasis on limited government and free markets is today largely accepted by conservative political parties and advocacy groups. Politics, however, is not just about economics. Government also has to deal with many other issues of human conduct that are not reducible to profit and loss. Below are a few examples currently being debated in Canada, the United States, and many other countries:

- To what degree should abortion be regulated? Is the fetus merely tissue within a woman's body, over which she should have complete control, or is it an unborn child with rights that the state should protect?

- Should government continue to criminalize possession and sale of drugs such as marijuana, cocaine, and heroin?

- Gambling used to be prohibited or heavily restricted but is now widely available and even used as a fundraising tool by governments. Is this trend simply legal recognition of a harmless amusement or have we gone too far in making it easy for people to squander their savings?

- Television and movies now routinely display levels of violence, profanity, and sexuality that would have been unthinkable 30 years ago. Does this represent laudable progress toward freedom of expression or the degradation of public decency?

Many who call themselves conservatives would answer these and similar questions in the direction of greater restraint on individual behaviour. They believe that abortions should be more difficult to obtain, that mind-altering drugs should be criminally prohibited, that gambling should be severely restricted, and that government should restrain the commercial exploitation of sex and violence. The common denominator in all these positions is a belief that a good society cannot be merely a collection of pleasure-seeking individuals. Social existence demands that human behaviour be restrained by institutions such as the family, the church, the school, and—if all else fails—the state. Conservatives who espouse this Burkean view about the restraint of individual desire in the name of the common good are today often called **social conservatives**.

Other conservatives see things rather differently. While not actually advocating abortion, drug use, gambling, and pornography, they fear the enlargement of the state that may ensue when government is called upon to prohibit or regulate such activities. Some who take this approach prefer to call themselves not conservatives but **libertarians**. They are really classical liberals in the spirit of John Stuart Mill. They follow Mill's argument in *On Liberty* that it is better to leave people alone to make their own mistakes as long as they are not inflicting direct harm upon others. Libertarians might prefer to call themselves liberals, except that in modern usage that term has become closely identified with interventionist reform liberalism. Libertarians strive for intellectual consistency around the values of personal freedom and individual choice. They argue that if freedom and choice are essential in the economy, they are just as important in all other areas of social existence.

Struggling libertarian parties exist in Canada and the United States, but they are not really a political force. The importance of libertarianism is more as an intellectual current within the broader political movement of conservatism. For example, several prominent conservative authors came out in favour of decriminalizing the possession of marijuana and other psychoactive drugs—for example, Milton Friedman, winner of the Nobel Prize in economics and a major source of economic policy ideas for all conservative thinkers; William F. Buckley, former publisher of the influential conservative magazine *National Review*; and Michael Walker, former president of the Fraser Institute, the largest and most influential conservative research institute in Canada. Meanwhile, however, other conservatives continue to advocate Burkean ideas about the role of government in restraining individual desires.

In a way, this internal split within the conservative camp mirrors the division in the liberal camp between classical and reform liberals. Classical liberals believe in freedom across the board, while reform liberals believe in government restraint of individual choice—within the economy. Libertarians also believe in freedom across the board, whereas social conservatives believe in government restraint of individual choice *outside* the economy. To see where you fall in this debate, take the "World's Smallest Political Quiz" at http://www.theadvocates.org/quiz.

CONSERVATISM IN CONTEMPORARY POLITICS

The "heroic age" of modern conservatism was definitely the 1980s. Things had not gone well in the Western world in the 1970s. Unemployment was rampant, inflation was high, budget deficits were spiralling out of control, and the Soviet Union was acquiring more client states in the Third World. Against this backdrop, a new generation of conservative leaders was elected to office—Margaret Thatcher in Great Britain, Ronald Reagan in the United States, and Brian Mulroney in Canada. Their messages were clear, powerful, and politically polarizing: reduce inflation by restricting growth in the supply of money; **downsize** government by contracting out services and **privatizing** publicly owned businesses; let the market function more freely by deregulating industries; decrease deficit spending with a goal of balancing government budgets; and build up military armaments to counter Soviet expansionism.

Some of these goals were met. Most notably, an American military build-up contributed to the collapse of the Soviet Union in 1991. Inflation was wrestled down from 12–13 percent to more acceptable figures of 2–3 percent annual growth in the consumer price index. Many business activities were **deregulated**, so that today it seems hard to imagine that airfares or telephone rates were ever set by decisions of government commissions. Publicly owned corporations such as Air Canada and Petro-Canada were sold to investors in the private sector. Other goals were harder to reach. Deficit spending remained a difficult problem. Nor did conservatives in power dare to touch the most popular spending programs of the welfare state, such as universal health care, old-age pensions, unemployment insurance, free public education, and social assistance. Overall, however, the conservative revival of the 1980s did experience considerable success.

There is an old saying that imitation is the sincerest form of flattery. Parties of the left—liberals and social democrats—came back into power in the 1990s by adopting and even extending the most successful conservative initiatives. In the United States, Democratic president Bill Clinton balanced the budget, after conservative presidents Ronald Reagan and George Bush had failed to do so, and introduced a sweeping reform of welfare. In Great Britain, Tony Blair proclaimed a "Third Way" for Labour that preserved most of Margaret Thatcher's reforms. In Canada, Jean Chrétien balanced the federal budget, which Brian Mulroney's Conservatives had not been able to do; accepted Mulroney's goal of free trade with the United States and Mexico (free trade is a form of deregulation); continued the sell-off of Crown corporations; and in general governed like a moderate conservative, at least on economic issues.

As the new millennium dawned, this convergence between parties of the left and right led conservatives to wonder what would come next. Tax reduction proved to be a popular conservative theme; it was pursued enthusiastically by George W. Bush in the United States and Stephen Harper in Canada, but liberal parties also moved in the same direction. More recently, however, the Great Recession of 2008 led to clearer differentiation between conservatives and liberals. In general, conservatives were now preaching the necessity of rebalancing the budget after the surge of Keynesian spending brought on by the recession. In Great Britain, the Conservative–Liberal Democrat coalition led by David Cameron announced a draconian austerity program that would lead to painful cuts in public services and was denounced by the opposition Labour Party. In the United States, where the scale of federal deficit spending was truly frightening, the Republicans, particularly the Tea Party ("Taxed Enough Already") faction, seemed much more concerned about moving toward a balanced budget than the Democrats, led by the liberal President Barack Obama. And in Canada the Conservatives, led by Stephen Harper, wanted to balance the budget without tax increases, whereas the other parties proposed to balance it by increasing corporate taxes, which would also allow them to pay for some new social programs.

So the political battle between liberals and conservatives goes on, seemingly without end. Maybe Gilbert and Sullivan were right when they wrote in their comic opera *Iolanthe:*

> I often think it's comical—Fal, lal, la!
> How Nature always does contrive—Fal, lal, la!
> That every boy and every gal
> That's born into the world alive
> Is either a little Liberal
> Or else a little Conservative!
> Fal, lal, la![13]

Questions for Discussion

1. Older people are typically more conservative than younger people. Can you explain why this should be so, in light of Edmund Burke's theory of conservatism?

2. Many proverbs, such as "A bird in the hand is worth two in the bush," embody a Burkean view of human behaviour. Can you think of other such proverbs and explain the Burkean element in them?

3. Do you think Canada is better off or worse off as a result of the conservative (classical liberal) economic policies adopted during the 1980s and 1990s? Has your view been altered by the Great Recession of 2008? How should governments respond to the recession as they go forward?

Internet Links

1. American Enterprise Institute: **www.aei.org**. A large American conservative foundation.

2. Canadian Conservative Forum: **www.conservativeforum.org**. Essays by conservative writers, plus many links.

3. Cardus: **www.cardus.ca**. A Canadian think-tank with a social conservative orientation.

4. Conservative Party of Canada: **www.conservative.ca**.

5. Fraser Institute: **www.fraserinstitute.ca**. A Vancouver-based think-tank whose goal is "the redirection of public attention to the role of competitive markets in providing for the well-being of Canadians." Tends toward the libertarian side of conservatism.

6. Heritage Foundation: **www.heritage.org**. Another large American conservative foundation.

7. International Democrat Union: **www.idu.org**. The international organization of conservative parties, including the Conservative Party of Canada.

Further Reading

Betz, Hans-Georg. *Radical Right-Wing Populism in Western Europe*. New York: St. Martin's Press, 1994.

Boaz, David. *Libertarianism: A Primer*. New York: Free Press, 1997.

Crowley, Brian Lee. *Fearful Symmetry: The Fall and Rise of Canada's Founding Values*. Toronto: Key Porter, 2009.

DeMuth, Christopher, and William Kristol. *The Neoconservative Imagination: Essays in Honor of Irving Kristol*. Washington, DC: AEI Press, 1995.

Diamond, Sara. Roads to Dominion: *Right-Wing Movements and Political Power in the United States*. New York: Guilford Press, 1995.

Doherty, Brian. Radicals for Capitalism: *A Freewheeling History of the Modern American Libertarian Movement*. Jackson, TN: PublicAffairs, 2007.

Dorrien, Gary. *The Neoconservative Mind*. Philadelphia: Temple University Press, 1993.

Drury, Shadia B. *Leo Strauss and the American Right*. New York: St. Martin's Press, 1997.

Flanagan, Tom. *Harper's Team: Behind the Scenes in the Conservative Rise to Power*. 2nd ed. Montreal and Kingston: McGill-Queens University Press, 2009.

———. *Waiting for the Wave: The Reform Party and the Conservative Movement*. Montreal and Kingston: McGill-Queens University Press, 2009.

Frum, David. *Comeback: Conservatism That Can Win Again*. New York: Doubleday, 2008.

Gairdner, William D., ed. *After Liberalism: Essays in Search of Freedom, Virtue, and Order*. Toronto: Stoddart, 1998.

Grant, George. *Lament for a Nation: The Defeat of Canadian Nationalism*. 40th anniversary ed. Montreal and Kingston: McGill-Queens University Press, 2005.

Hamowy, Ronald, ed. *The Encyclopedia of Libertarianism*. Thousand Oaks, CA: Sage Publications, 2008.

Honderich, Ted. *Conservatism*. London: H. Hamilton, 1990.

Jeffrey, Brooke. *Hard Right Turn: The New Face of Neo-conservatism in Canada.* Toronto: HarperCollins, 1999.

Kristol, Irving. *Neoconservatism: The Autobiography of an Idea.* New York: Free Press, 1995.

Lakoff, George. *Moral Politics: What Conservatives Know That Liberals Don't.* Chicago: University of Chicago Press, 1996.

Murray, Charles. *What It Means to Be a Libertarian.* New York: Broadway Books, 1997.

Panichas, George A. *Restoring the Meaning of Conservatism: Writings from* Modern Age. Wilmington, DE: ISI Books, 2008.

Schneider, Gregory L. *Conservatism in America Since 1930: A Reader.* New York: New York University Press, 2003.

Wilson, Francis Graham. *The Case for Conservatism.* Piscataway, NJ: Transaction Publishers, 1990.

PART 2

12

Socialism and Communism

Like liberalism and conservatism, **socialism** is not a single ideology. We use the term here as a concept that includes communism, democratic socialism, social democracy, anarchism, syndicalism, and other ideologies that bear a family resemblance to one another. Four of their common traits are particularly important, although this is not to suggest that there ever has been, or is now, a unified world socialist movement. In particular, communism and social democracy are worlds apart in political orientation, even though they have grown from the same family tree (see Figure 12.1).

COMMON ELEMENTS OF SOCIALIST IDEOLOGIES

Planning

Socialists repudiate the profit-motivated market economy, believing that society can emancipate itself from impersonal market processes and take conscious control of its economic affairs by deliberately planning them to maximize human happiness.

Common Ownership

Socialists condemn private ownership of productive property such as land, factories, stores, and the means of transportation and communication. They believe that such assets should be owned by the community, supposing that the benefits will then flow to all, not just to a restricted circle of private owners. However, they generally accept private ownership of consumer goods.

Equality of Result

Socialists aspire to a high degree of equality of result. While recognizing that people cannot be literally equal in all respects, they believe that much can be done to reduce major inequalities of wealth, income, social position, and political power. They see a planned economy and common ownership as important means to this end.

Figure 12.1 The Socialist Family Tree

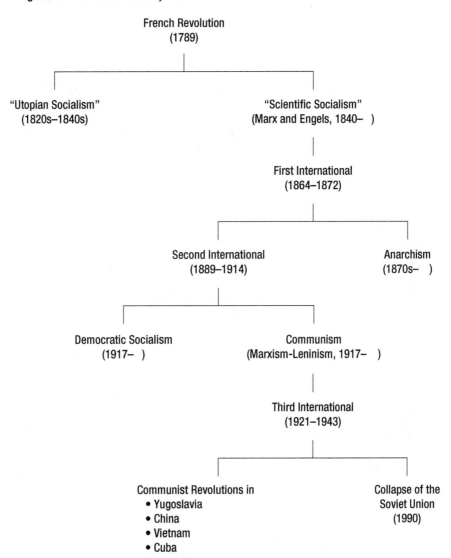

Selflessness

Socialists regard selfishness not as an innate human characteristic but as the product of flawed social institutions. They are convinced that appropriate social change can produce a new "socialist man" who is less self-interested and more concerned about the welfare of the collectivity.[1] Change in human behavior will result from and at the same time support the first three objectives.

HISTORICAL OVERVIEW

Common ownership of property is an ancient topic of philosophical speculation. Plato's *Republic* (ca. 380 BCE) portrayed a *polis* in which the intellectual and military classes shared property and wives, although the ordinary people continued to have private property and families. Thomas More's *Utopia* (1516) went further and extended common property to an entire society, but it was a satire on the England of More's day, not a serious proposal for implementation. Other philosophers toyed with socialism from time to time, but it was not viewed as realistic until the nineteenth century.

There is also a long religious history to socialism. The Bible's Acts of the Apostles reports that in the first Christian community of Jerusalem, "the whole body of believers was united in heart and soul. Not a man of them claimed any of his possessions as his own, but everything was held in common."[2] Community of goods has repeatedly been reintroduced by Christian sects, particularly those who believe that the second coming of Christ to earth is imminent. In Canada today, this kind of Christian socialism is represented by the Hutterites, who collectively own and operate large farms in the western provinces.

Like so much else in modern politics, secular, political socialism made its debut during the French Revolution, when a journalist named François-Noël Babeuf organized an abortive communist uprising in 1796.[3] Its practical significance at the time was nil because the police broke up the plot and Babeuf was sentenced to death. But the events, and particularly the speech Babeuf made at his trial, began the story that leads to Marx, Lenin, and the socialist revolutions of the twentieth century.

Babeuf's plan was for a short, successful insurrection in Paris on the model of several that had been attempted since 1789. Having seized the French state at the centre, he would institute a provisional government to crush the enemies of the people. Private property would be confiscated, and a "Grand National Economy" would replace the market system of allocation with a central storehouse where goods would be deposited, then distributed to all as needed:

> It will be composed of all in complete equality—all rich, all poor, all free, all brothers. The first law will be a ban on private property. We will deposit the fruits of our toil in the public stores. This will be the wealth of the state and the property of all. Every year the heads of families will select stewards whose task will be the distribution of goods to each in accordance with his needs, the allotment of tasks to be performed by each, and the maintenance of public order.[4]

Babeuf did not desire or expect this system to create great wealth. He quoted with approval the words of Rousseau that "all luxury is superfluous—everything is superfluous above and beyond the sheerest of physical necessities."[5] To ensure that luxury did not creep into this spartan society, he would have banned money and foreign trade.

Babeuf's conspiratorial and insurrectionary approach survived his death, but it was complemented in the first decades of the nineteenth century by the **utopian socialism** of writers such as Robert Owen (1771–1858) and Charles Fourier (1772–1837). They proposed not to seize the state by force but to teach by example—to found small-scale communities in which productive property would be jointly owned, all would join in performing necessary labour, and living standards would be more or less equalized. Unlike Babeuf, they did not seek to impose a regime of universal poverty; they believed that their communes would allow everyone to enjoy the luxuries previously reserved for the rich. Literally hundreds of these communes, based on various models, have been tried out. Some of the experiments became quite famous, such as New Harmony, Indiana, run by Robert Owen, and Brook Farm, in Massachusetts, modelled on the ideas of Fourier.[6] The utopian strategy of showing the world the merits of socialism on a small scale has not been fully successful, but neither has it been without effect—the Israeli kibbutz is a direct descendant of these early experiments.

Karl Marx (1818–83) and Friedrich Engels (1820–95) gave the ideology of socialism its classic formulation. Their greatest innovation was to transform socialism into the doctrine of a single class, the industrial working class, which they renamed the **proletariat**. They labelled their predecessors as utopian for having aimed at the

Karl Marx (1818–83), the most famous philosopher of socialism.

betterment of humanity through appeals to reason. The proletariat, as the "universal class," embodied the future hopes of humanity; its political struggle would furnish the "material weapons" needed by socialist philosophy.[7]

Marx's emphasis on the working class gives the impression that for him the central issues were poverty, equality, and living standards, but the discovery of unpublished manuscripts written in his youth has put the matter in a different light. "An enforced increase in wages," wrote Marx in 1843, "would be nothing more than a *better remuneration of slaves*, and would not restore, either to the worker or to the work, their human significance and worth."[8] To the young Marx, the true issue was what he called alienation. A market system, he argued, reverses the right order of human priorities. Work, which ought to be people's highest activity, the expression of their creative powers, becomes in such a system merely a means for people to keep themselves alive. Instead of valuing human activity for its own sake, people become acquisitive, obsessed with accumulation. They lose control over what they produce as their products are bought and sold on the market. Property owners are equally dehumanized, even if they escape the impoverished condition of the proletariat. The social alienation between owners—the **bourgeoisie**, in Marx's vocabulary—and proletarians was only one aspect of the larger alienation of all people from their human essence. Of course, that did not make class differentials less odious, and Marx depicted them with all his rhetorical power:

> Labour certainly produces marvels for the rich but it produces privation for the worker. It produces palaces, but hovels for the worker. It produces beauty, but deformity for the worker. It replaces labour by machinery, but it casts some of the workers back into a barbarous kind of work and turns the others into machines. It produces intelligence, but also stupidity and cretinism for the workers.[9]

Marx offered not only a principled critique of society but also an analysis of the course of history. He wanted to show not just that capitalism ought to be destroyed but that it would destroy itself through its internal contradictions. Marx and Engels called their doctrine **scientific socialism** because they thought it was not only a morally attractive alternative but also an empirically based guide to what was bound to happen.

Although the subject is much too complex to summarize here, we can indicate the main lines of the capitalist breakdown that Marx foresaw.[10] One was the polarization of society. Capitalism would create a large working class, who would become the "gravediggers" of the system. The proletariat was doomed to impoverishment—perhaps not in absolute terms, but in comparison with the rapidly increasing affluence of the bourgeoisie. The working class, led by socialist intellectuals such as Marx himself, would eventually seize the state and use it to abolish capitalism. Indeed, when the proletariat came to power, it would find that the system had already virtually abolished itself. The market process would have generated industrial monopolies, as only a few giant firms would have survived the rigours of competition. Without many competitors, the market would not work, even on its own terms. The new proletarian state would simply have to confiscate those monopolies from their bourgeois owners and set them to work under central planning.

Marx held that the ultimate victory of socialism was certain but not automatic; it also required a deliberate political struggle. He proposed (and helped to bring about) the representation of the working class by organized political parties. In constitutional states with a parliamentary system, the workers might struggle for the universal franchise. Once the vote was achieved for all, socialists could expect to be elected to power, for the proletariat would be a majority of the electorate; in other words, socialism would be a natural outgrowth of democracy. Simultaneously, Marx also proposed a revolutionary seizure of power, particularly where constitutionalism and the rule of law did not exist. Such a rising would produce a workers' government, the **dictatorship of the proletariat.** In a situation equivalent to civil war, the proletarian dictatorship would have to ignore the niceties of the rule of law, at least until its power was secure. This dual approach to gaining power was to prove fateful for the subsequent history of socialism. The two approaches, united in Marx, would eventually split into the two mutually antagonistic movements known as socialism and **communism.**

Because of their emphasis on the collapse of capitalism and the proletarian seizure of power, neither Marx nor Engels wrote much about socialism itself. What one finds is mostly abstract and rather enigmatic sayings, such as the dictum that socialism means "the ascent of man from the kingdom of necessity to the kingdom of freedom."[11] However, some scattered passages give a rough idea of what Marx and Engels expected to happen after the workers came to power. It is striking to read the list of transitional measures given in the *Communist Manifesto* (1848), most of which have subsequently been adopted by liberal and even conservative governments (see Historical Perspectives 12.1). The ones marked with an asterisk have been at least partly implemented in most Western democracies.

Accomplishing these and other measures would supposedly make the state master of the economy, able to conduct central planning. But full equality of result would take a long time to achieve. There would have to be an interim period during which equality would mean, in effect, "equal pay for equal work." All workers would be employed by the state, and ownership of property would no longer allow the wealthy to escape labour; but some would work more effectively and diligently than others, and they would be rewarded for doing so.

Beyond this stage, Marx's thoughts on the future became visionary. The state, even though it would have to be large and powerful in order to conduct central planning, would lose its coercive character. As Engels put it, in a biological metaphor, the state would "wither away." Marx preferred to say that the state would be "transcended"— that people would learn to conduct their affairs without a centralized apparatus of coercion.

The transcendence of the state was linked to what Marx called the "higher phase of communist society," where "equal work for equal pay" would give way to a nobler form of equality: "From each according to his ability, to each according to his needs."[12] Work would become a freely creative activity performed for its own sake, not to be bought and sold. People would express themselves in all directions, utilizing their

Historical Perspectives 12.1

Transitional Measures from the *Communist Manifesto*

1. Abolition of property in land and application of all rents of land to public purposes.

2. A heavy progressive or graduated income tax.*

3. Abolition of all right of inheritance.

4. Confiscation of the property of all emigrants and rebels.

5. Centralization of credit in the hands of the state, by means of a national bank with state capital and an exclusive monopoly.*

6. Centralization of the means of communication and transport in the hands of the state.*

7. Extension of factories and instruments of production owned by the state; the bringing into cultivation of wastelands, and the improvement of the soil generally in accordance with a common plan.*

8. Equal liability to all of labour. Establishment of industrial armies, especially for agriculture.

9. Combination of agriculture with manufacturing industries; gradual abolition of the distinction between town and country, by a more equable distribution of the population over the country.

10. Free education for all children in public schools. Abolition of children's factory labour in its present form. Combination of education with industrial production.*[13]

* indicates measures that have been at least partially implemented in Western democracies

repertoire of human powers; in the socialist "kingdom of freedom" there would be no economic necessity forcing them to be narrow specialists. In an almost lyrical passage, Marx and Engels wrote:

> For as soon as the distribution of labour comes into being, each man has a particular, exclusive sphere of activity, which is forced upon him and from which he cannot escape. He is a hunter, a fisherman, a shepherd, or a critical critic, and must remain so if he does not want to lose his means of livelihood; while in communist society, where nobody has one exclusive sphere of activity but each can become accomplished in any branch he wishes, society regulates the general production and thus makes it possible for me to do one thing today and another tomorrow, to hunt in the morning, fish in the afternoon, rear cattle in the evening, criticize after dinner, just as I have a mind, without ever becoming hunter, fisherman, shepherd or critic.[14]

In addition to being theorists, Marx and Engels were also political activists who contributed to the political struggle of the working class. Their first organization, the Communist League, is remembered chiefly because Marx and Engels wrote the *Communist Manifesto* to be its program. More important was the International Workingmen's Association (1864–72), commonly known as the **First International**, in which Marx and Engels were deeply involved. A loose association of socialist parties and labour unions in Western Europe, with headquarters in London, it split into hostile wings in 1872 when old factional differences became too strong to contain. The split was partly a clash of personalities between Marx and the Russian Mikhail Bakunin (1814–76), but there was also an important ideological issue. Bakunin and his followers, who subsequently became known as **anarchists**, thought that Marx was infatuated with the state. They believed that the state could be destroyed quickly in the aftermath of the workers' revolution, whereas Marx envisioned a period of state socialism leading up to a true classless society and the higher phase of communism. The anarchists feared, with considerable foresight, that the Marxian socialist state might turn out to be permanent rather than temporary.[15]

Although the First International collapsed, socialist parties continued to exist in various European states. They were reunited, excluding the anarchists, in the **Second International**, founded in Paris in 1889 to celebrate the centennial of the French Revolution.[16] Marx had died in 1883, so Engels became the elder statesman of the new organization, and Marxism became its ideology. With the Second International, socialism came of age in Europe. Socialist and labour parties thrived by following Marx's evolutionary strategy. None ever won a majority in an election, but all succeeded in electing substantial blocs of representatives wherever liberal and constitutional values kept politics open. The Second International expressed itself in revolutionary rhetoric, but its political practices were overwhelmingly evolutionary and constitutional.[17]

Because the czar ruled the Russian Empire autocratically, the absence of a parliament and constitution made the evolutionary strategy inapplicable there, forcing the Russian Social Democratic Party to work illegally, secretively, and conspiratorially. Vladimir Ilyich Lenin (1870–1924), leader of the wing of the party known as the Bolsheviks, was led by these conditions—so different from those in Western Europe—to create a new style and a new theory of party leadership. Marx had expected the revolution to grow from spontaneous class-consciousness of the workers, whereas Lenin, faced with a backward country and a small working class, tended to think of revolutionary consciousness as something transmitted by bourgeois intellectuals to the workers. This seemingly minor difference implied a new approach to party organization. The party had to be firmly controlled from the top because the leadership could not rely on the workers' spontaneity. Lenin's theory of the disciplined party—**democratic centralism**—moulded the party into an effective revolutionary weapon suited to survival in the autocratic Russian setting.[18]

Lenin, incidentally, is associated with another major innovation in socialist ideology. Marx had always insisted that the socialist revolution would be a world revolution. His view of the world was centred on Western Europe, and he apparently thought that the European nations would drag their empires with them into socialism. Because he emphasized Europe, Marx thought the revolution would occur soon, because capitalism, which was fated to put an end to itself, was well advanced on that continent. But when World War I broke out, he had been dead for 30 years and socialists had still not come to power anywhere.

Lenin spent most of the war in exile in Switzerland; he used this period of enforced leisure to write a pamphlet explaining the delay. *Imperialism: The Highest Stage of Capitalism* (1917) argued that the advanced nations had managed to postpone the revolution by amassing colonial empires. Overseas investments counteracted the downward tendency of the rate of profit, while colonial markets temporarily solved the problem of overproduction. Merciless exploitation of the colonies could buy off the proletariat at home, creating a "labour aristocracy" of well-paid workers at the centre of the empire. World War I, however, showed that the imperialists had begun to quarrel with each other. The socialist revolution would arise not from a business crash, as Marx had been inclined to believe, but out of the turmoil of war. Lenin thus decisively broadened the scope of socialism from a European to a global movement, and in so doing bolstered his own revolutionary optimism. "Capitalism," he wrote, "has grown into a world system of colonial oppression and of the financial strangulation of the overwhelming population of the world by a handful of 'advanced' countries."[19]

World War I sounded the death knell for the Second International. Most of the workers in the combatant states supported the war effort, effectively pitting the International against itself. In February 1917 the czar was toppled and a constitutional democracy created. In October of the same year, the Bolsheviks, led by Lenin, seized control of the state through insurrections of armed workers in St. Petersburg and Moscow, creating a dictatorship of the proletariat in which their party played the dominant role. They outlawed political opposition—even socialist opposition. These events were an agonizing test for the socialists of Western Europe, who had yearned for a revolution for generations. Now, as they witnessed this successful one, they were appalled by its undemocratic aspects.

The eventual result of the Russian Revolution was an irreparable split in the world socialist movement. Those who approved of Lenin and his methods formed **communist** parties in every country and gathered themselves in the **Third International**, or **Comintern** (short for "Communist International"). In practice, the Comintern soon became an extension of the Soviet state for foreign-policy purposes. Although Stalin dissolved it in 1943 as a gesture of cooperation with the Allies during World War II, the individual communist parties continued to be closely tied to Moscow. After the end of the war, the organizational emphasis shifted to the Soviet satellite states. In 1947 these were bound together into the **Cominform** (Communist Information Bureau), which in 1956 was in turn replaced by the Warsaw Treaty Organization. The latter was dissolved in 1991 as part of the general de-communization of Eastern Europe. Today the term *communist* is rarely encountered. The organizations that used to call themselves communist parties still exist, but they have adopted new names that emphasize concepts such as labour or democracy.

Those who opposed Lenin regrouped under the general name of **social democrats**, often merging with moderate socialists who had been outside the Marxist consensus of the Second International. These social-democratic parties still exist as the Labour Party of Great Britain, the Social Democratic Party of Germany, and so on. They have kept to the course of constitutionalism and are well integrated into their respective political systems. They form governments when they win elections and resign from office when they lose.

Socialism, in the form of social democracy, is a familiar part of contemporary politics. Its ideology has, over decades, become considerably diluted relative to the Marxist thought from which it sprang, so that social democrats today can be hard to distinguish from reform liberals. Both espouse, to a limited degree, the typical socialist goals of central planning, common ownership, and equality of result. Social democrats call for government to guide the economy by pulling the levers of spending, taxation, and regulation. They wish some major enterprises to be publicly owned—that is, they call for a **mixed economy**—but they do not advocate wholesale nationalization of all business.

Several small socialist parties existed in Canada before the great split between communists and social democrats, but none was ever very significant. The first important party of the social-democratic type was the Co-operative Commonwealth Federation (CCF), founded in Calgary in 1932. It drew together remnants of the old socialist parties, trade unionists, farmer activists, and intellectuals who had been influenced by British socialist thought. The party's first platform was the Regina Manifesto, adopted in 1933. It repudiated "change by violence" and promised to promote the socialist cause "solely by constitutional methods." Although the means would be peaceful, the end was declared to be far-reaching:

> We aim to replace the present capitalist system, with its inherent injustice and inhumanity, by a social order from which the domination and exploitation of one class by another will be eliminated, in which economic planning will supersede unregulated private enterprise and competition, and in which genuine democratic self-government, based upon economic equality, will be possible ... We aim at a planned and socialized economy in which our natural resources and the principal means of production and distribution are owned, controlled and operated by the people.[20]

The CCF achieved some political successes, most notably the election of the first socialist government in North America, in Saskatchewan in 1944, but its electoral support eroded badly during the 1950s. In 1961 it restructured itself as the New Democratic Party, with greatly strengthened ties to organized labour. Tellingly, the word *socialism* did not appear in the New Party Declaration it adopted.[21] As in other countries, social democracy now presented itself not as a full alternative to the market system but rather as a means of using the state as a reforming agency.

Ed Broadbent expressed the rapprochement of social democracy with the market when he announced his resignation as federal leader of the NDP in 1989:

> The serious debate about the future is not about the desirability of a market economy. For most thoughtful people that debate is now closed ... We New Democrats believe in the marketplace including private investment decisions, reduced tariffs, private property, the free disposal of assets, the right to make a profit, decentralized decision making ... As the world evolves so must our policies.[22]

From this perspective, social democracy, like reform liberalism, consists of government efforts to "correct" the market—to change some of its results rather than to replace it outright. Not surprisingly, the contemporary NDP has dropped almost the entire vocabulary of class. Its platform in the 2011 federal election promised to provide benefits for "your family," not for the working class.[23]

Marx had a grudging admiration for the market system as a means of accumulating wealth but regarded it as a temporary phase of human development. Socialism, he thought, would be able to make much more humane use of the productive powers unleashed by capitalism. But in fact, socialism, except in the watered-down form of social democracy, has been least likely to come to power in precisely those countries that have been most capitalistic and, by Marx's reasoning, most ready for socialism. In the industrialized countries, socialism has been most effective in a diluted form— that is, as social democracy; in such cases it represents a reformist impulse within the system, not a polar alternative. The stronger form of communism came to dominance in the economically backward Russian Empire; the Soviet Union imposed it by force on the nations of Eastern Europe. Authentic communist revolutions (i.e., not the result of Soviet initiatives) also took place in Yugoslavia, China, and Vietnam. The latter two revolutions were almost the opposite of what Marx would have anticipated: they happened in pre-industrial societies in which capitalism had barely gotten underway.

We now move on to a more conceptual analysis of the socialist family of ideologies.

PLANNING

In varying degrees, socialists are generally hostile to the market, condemning it as anarchic, inefficient, and inequitable. Even contemporary social democrats, while accepting the market in principle, think it needs a good deal of correction in practice. Socialists particularly condemn the pursuit of profit; in the words of the Regina Manifesto, the principle of a socialist society "will be the supplying of human needs and not the making of profits."[24] But the classical liberal and conservative view is that profit in the market system is not antithetical to need but rather the means by which needs are met. That people need food, clothing, shelter, and recreation and are willing to pay for them induces entrepreneurs to seek a profit by offering these goods for sale. The central issue is not need versus profit but the most effective means of discovering and satisfying human needs. Is it the market system, with competition, floating prices, and the profit motive, or is it a **planning** system, in which a central authority decides what to produce and allocates products to consumers?

The market, while hardly a perfect system, demonstrably performs a job of matching production and consumption across a large number of commodities. Early socialists were quite naïve about how difficult this task is. Babeuf's central storehouses could scarcely have coped with the problem, but he probably would not have cared because he wanted all to live in spartan simplicity. Marx simply ignored the problem by refusing to speculate on the practical consequences of a socialist society. Through the pain of much trial and error, the Soviet Union and other socialist states developed state planning machinery that was actually a hybrid of the planning principle and the market principle. The State Planning Committee, as it was called in the Soviet Union, developed and updated a national plan that specified tonnes of coal and steel of various grades, kilowatt hours of electricity, tonnes of wheat, and other production quantities to be produced by the various industries. One industry supplied another as part of this plan rather than by market auction. But markets connected the industrial complex to the inhabitants of the country, who purchased the output at retail stores owned by the state and sold their labour to the state as employer. By this partial use of markets, the state refrained from trying to directly control the daily affairs of hundreds of millions of people.

These markets, however, were heavily controlled by the state. The labour market was restricted by lack of mobility; for example, a worker on a collective farm was not allowed to leave that farm to seek work in the city. Also, prices in markets for both labour and consumer goods did not float according to supply and demand but were administered by the state. When price is not used to ration scarce commodities, other forms of rationing must intervene. One is direct assignment by authority, as was used to distribute housing. Another is queuing: as a means of acquiring goods, the ability to spend time waiting replaced the ability to spend money. Still another form of rationing was evasion of the law. Those with more money than time frequently resorted to bribery and black markets. Indeed, life in Eastern Europe would scarcely have been possible without the black market, because many goods and services needed in daily life were not available at any price in the state stores.

Although it produced a low standard of living in comparison with the Western market economy, the communist planned economy did work after its own fashion. In the Soviet Union it brought many people considerable improvement in living standards relative to czarist days. Jobs were guaranteed for all, inflation was repressed, and food, clothing, shelter, and other basic commodities were available at low prices. Education was universal and in some ways of excellent quality; low-tech medical care was generally accessible; and retired people could count on modest state pensions. Taxes were low because the state derived most of its revenue from its ownership of the economy. Daily life was often uncomfortable, inconvenient, and monotonous, but at least it was predictable.

Eastern European communism started to collapse in the late 1980s when the Soviet leader Mikhail Gorbachev attempted to reform the system. Worried that his regime was failing in economic and military competition with the West, he tried to introduce elements of the market economy and individual freedom. But the reform process quickly got out of his control, leading to the fall of all the communist governments in Eastern Europe in the late 1980s and early 1990s. Subsequently these socialist economies were marketized, with the introduction of private property, freely moving prices, and foreign trade and investment. Free-market capitalism has not created a utopia in Eastern Europe, and some people are nostalgic for communism, but hardly anyone in a position of power wants to go back.

PART 2

In the People's Republic of China, the Communist Party still exercises firm political control but has largely privatized agriculture, which the majority of China's people are still engaged in. Moreover, it has allowed massive foreign investment in enterprise zones in the provinces bordering Hong Kong. By some estimates, the economy of China is now more than half capitalist, even though the regime is still nominally communist.[25] For all intents and purposes, the Chinese economy, now second in size only to that of the United States, is part of the global open-market system (see Figure 12.2).

Social democrats in the Western world used to have a vision of full-fledged planning. For example, *Social Planning for Canada*, written in 1935 by the leading intellectuals in the CCF, called for a national planning commission modelled on the Soviet example.[26] Today, neither the NDP nor other social democratic parties advocate full-scale planning. Instead they see the state as a means for guiding the market toward particular objectives such as full employment, location of industry in depressed areas, and

Figure 12.2 China's Rapid Growth

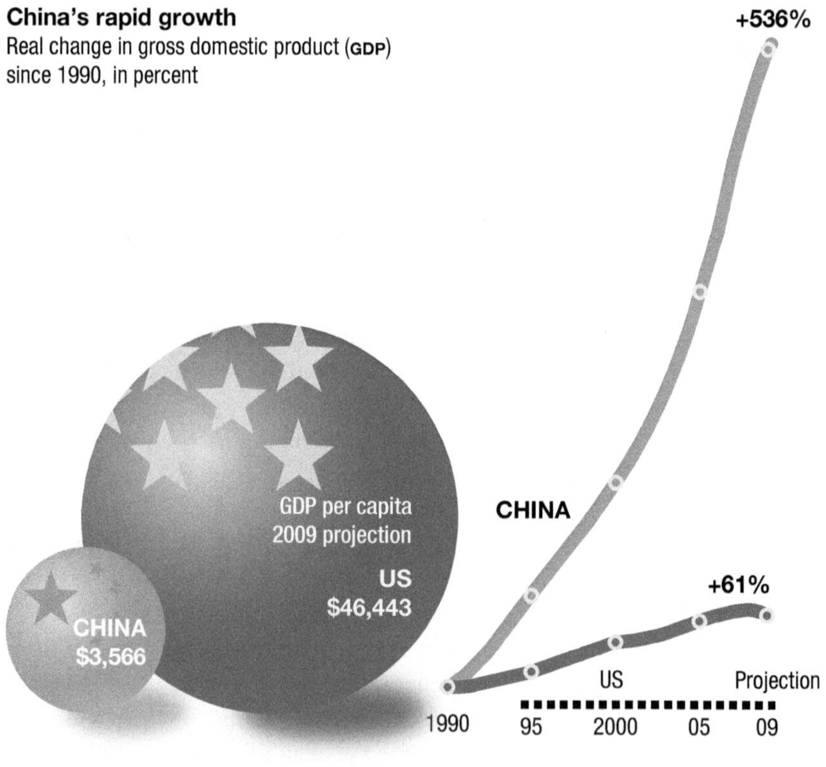

China's rapid growth
Real change in gross domestic product (GDP)
since 1990, in percent

+536%

GDP per capita
2009 projection

US
$46,443

CHINA
$3,566

CHINA

+61%

US   Projection

1990   95   2000   05   09

Note: China's per capita economy has been growing rapidly but is still much smaller than that of the United States.

Source: DER SPIEGEL, 11 November 2009, http://www.spiegel.de/international/world/reluctant-partners-global-crisis-makes-us-more-dependent-on-china-than-ever-a-660432.html.

advancement of disadvantaged minorities. To achieve these goals, the state may employ taxation, subsidies, monopoly concessions, regulatory legislation, price controls, adjustments in interest rates, and other interventionist tools. A program of such interventions is sometimes called a plan, but it is not planning in the original sense of the term.

COMMON OWNERSHIP

Except in times of war or other emergency, central planning cannot work without a high degree of common ownership. The central plan requires investment decisions other than those that private owners would spontaneously make; otherwise there would be no need for the plan. Productive property has to be publicly owned to remove these potential conflicts between the plan and private property rights.

Common ownership can be achieved in a number of ways. In the Third World it can be appended to existing communal traditions. If a peasant village already holds grazing, timber, or water rights in common, collective ownership of the surrounding arable land may not be a drastic step. Another approach to common ownership is the voluntary cooperative, utilized to organize either producers or consumers. A great many cooperatives—credit unions, wheat pools, housing co-ops—already exist in Canada, where they function as part of the market economy, but they could also become part of a socialist economy. Another possibility is for the workers to own their own factory or other workplace. A variant of socialism known as **syndicalism** (from the French *syndicat,* "association") takes this approach. No one has ever tried a fully syndicalist economy, but there were elements of syndicalism in the Yugoslavian version of socialism, in which workers' councils had some say in the running of enterprises.

These options are interesting and important, but in the socialist mainstream, common ownership has meant state ownership. Socialization or nationalization of property means a takeover by the state, which then owns and administers the property as an agent of the people. This ownership can be direct (as in the case of the Canadian Forces, operated as part of a government department under ministerial supervision) or indirect (as in the case of Canada Post and the Canadian Broadcasting Corporation, which are Crown corporations owned by the state but operating more or less autonomously under their own boards of directors).

In the Soviet Union, the state owned all factories, railways, and other means of production, as well as all schools, hospitals, and retail stores. It also owned all natural resources and all land, which it leased to entities such as collective farms and housing cooperatives. Private ownership was confined almost entirely to consumer goods.

The Regina Manifesto exempted farms from public ownership but called for nationalization of the entire financial industry, as well as the transportation, communications, and electric power sectors, "and all other industries and services essential to social planning."[27] The latter would have included many firms in the resource sector. The logic of the list was that these industries represented "the commanding

PART 2

heights of the economy."[28] All other businesses—manufacturing, wholesaling, retailing, personal services, and so on—need access to credit, transportation, communications, energy, and natural resources. If the government owned and controlled these indispensable industries, it would be able to compel or induce other industries to work toward politically chosen goals. Manufacturing firms, for example, could be persuaded to locate in depressed areas by offers of low-interest loans or cheap transportation.

EQUALITY OF RESULT

One of the attractive goals of socialism has been to reduce the material inequalities that are part of a market economy. These inequalities are unseemly to socialists (as well as to many others), who have sought to overcome them through a planned economy and public ownership of property. However, while it is easy to call for equality of result, it is much harder to state precisely what that means. We differ so much in our aptitudes, needs, and desires that it would be absurd to say we should all have the same number of shoes or square metres of housing.

One approach is equality of opportunity: using the state to ensure that everyone can have certain chances in life, but allowing individuals to keep the rewards of their own efforts. This social-democratic idea, now widely accepted by reform liberals, fits in well with the contemporary welfare state, which is supposed to educate us as children and protect us against contingencies as adults. Its safety net allows us to bounce back from sickness, accidents, and unemployment but does not in itself guarantee a very desirable standard of living. We have to achieve that on our own initiative.

A related approach to equality is to reduce the range of inequality by raising the floor and lowering the ceiling, so that extremes of wealth and poverty vanish but some variation remains. This partial egalitarianism is widely accepted today, not just by socialists but also by reform liberals and many others who have no definable ideology. It can be attempted in the market system through progressive taxation, redistribution, and the abundant services of the welfare state. Or, as in the Soviet style of planned economy, it can be approached by setting wages and salaries on an egalitarian basis.

By some statistical indices, the communist states appeared to equalize living standards. Published data on incomes showed smaller differentials between manual workers and professionals than in the West, and of course large pools of capital no longer existed in private hands. Statistics, however, did not tell the whole story, because the communist systems instituted significant forms of non-monetary privilege. For example, high officials of the Communist Party, as well as leading scientists, athletes, managers, and artists, had access to special housing, shopping, and medical care; could often avoid waiting lists for things such as automobiles; and had the privilege of foreign travel.[29]

The ultimate in equality is still as stated in the Marxian slogan "from each according to his ability, to each according to his needs." This noble sentiment expresses the operating principle of a happy family, one in which parents assess the needs and abilities of their children. But can an entire society of adults operate like a single family? If we let people assess their own needs and set their own contributions, is it not likely that they will estimate the former on the high side and reduce the latter below what is reasonable? It seems hard to avoid the requirement for a central authority to decide such things (indeed, parents are almost all-powerful in relation to their children). This casts serious doubt on the premise that the state will wither away, which is what is supposed to occur in the highest stage of communism.

SELFLESSNESS

The discussion in the preceding paragraph assumes that human behaviour will remain self-interested. The situation would be different if selfishness arose only from the effects of a market economy, which encourages people to put their own interests first. Socialists have often assumed that conflict is typical of capitalism and that cooperation would be typical of a socialist system. However, to contrast cooperation with conflict is misleading. Spontaneous order depends on cooperation voluntarily achieved through mutual pursuit of self-interest, as in Adam Smith's metaphor of the invisible hand. A planned economy calls for cooperation directed from above. The important question is not whether we shall have cooperation, for obviously we must; it is whether mutual coordination is a more effective means of achieving it than authoritative direction.[30]

In contrast to socialism, both liberalism and conservatism accept human beings as they are, with all their flaws, and seek to understand the social order that inevitably follows. They assume that society is and always will be composed of individuals and groups that are in conflict with one another. They hope to contain that conflict within a peaceful framework, not abolish it altogether. Contemporary socialists, to the extent that they have reduced some of their earlier and more visionary expectations about planning, public ownership, and equality, have also become pessimistic about the possibility of an easy, quick change in human nature.

GOVERNING

We have discussed at some length the differences between communists and social democrats in their approach to obtaining power. The distinction between constitutional and unconstitutional methods is also reflected in the way socialist states are governed. Social democrats, in their rapprochement with liberalism, have adopted the constitutional philosophy of the limited state and the rule of law. Communists, in contrast, use constitutionalism only as a means of achieving power.

PART 2

Central planning and state ownership of the means of production put the entire economy at the disposal of the government. This produced such an unparalleled concentration of power that observers had to invent a new term, *totalitarianism,* to describe the resulting system. This expansion of the state posed thorny problems for the ideologists of Marxism-Leninism. Marx's dictatorship of the proletariat was meant to be a transitional regime, even if Marx did not say how long it would last. It was also supposed to preside over the dissolution of social classes, thereby rendering itself unnecessary; a permanent dictatorship of the proletariat would have been a contradiction in terms.[31]

Soviet thinkers maintained that the Soviet state was "a state of the whole people." In the words of Nikita Khrushchev to the Twenty-Second Congress of the Communist Party of the Soviet Union,

> With the victory of socialism and the country's entry into the period of full-scale communist construction, the working class of the Soviet Union has on its own initiative, consistent with the tasks of communist construction, transformed the state of proletarian dictatorship into a state of the whole people. That, comrades, is a fact unparalleled in history! Until now the state has always been an instrument of dictatorship by this or that class. In our country, for the first time in history, a state has taken shape which is not a dictatorship of any one class, but an instrument of society as a whole, of the entire people.[32]

This solved one problem but created others by contradicting Marx's view that all states are means by which one class rules over others, and undercutting his idea of a state that could be unlimited because it was temporary and transitional.

CONCLUSION

As was true of liberalism, the general family of socialism gave rise to a number of different movements, the two most important being social democracy and communism. The definitive split between these two branches of socialism in the 1920s led to very real differences in ideology, of which the five listed below are particularly significant.

Social Democrats	Communists
See socialism as an evolutionary process.	See socialism as a revolutionary process.
Achieve power through constitutional means; accept the limited state and the rule of law.	Achieve power unconstitutionally; reject the limited state and the rule of law as a bourgeois mystification.
Advocate a mixed economy.	Advocate a state-owned and -directed economy.
Accept a pluralistic society of self-interested individuals and groups.	Envision a future harmonious society of selfless individuals.
Advocate the competition of political parties.	Advocate a one-party state.

These fundamental differences mean that social democracy and communism became separate ideologies, even though they grew from common roots. Communism is today the official ideology of only a few governments—North Korea, Cuba, China, and Vietnam—and in the latter two cases the adherence to communism is more theoretical than real. Nor is communism a powerful revolutionary movement anywhere in the world today. Social democracy, however, has become an integral part of modern politics; so, to some extent, we are all the heirs of Marx and Engels.

Questions for Discussion

1. Canada has a mainly market economy, but there are also some sectors, such as public education, that are set up along socialist lines of public ownership and control. Can you think of three other such sectors?

2. Why do you think these semi-socialist sectors were created? What benefits do they offer? Why were Canadians not content just to leave them to the market?

3. What characteristic problems do these socialist sectors face? That is, are there recurrent patterns in the complaints that people make about them?

Internet Links

1. Canadian Centre for Policy Alternatives: **www.policyalternatives.ca**. A social-democratic think-tank supported by organized labour in Canada.

2. Einstein, Albert, "Why Socialism?": **http://monthlyreview.org/2009/05/01/ why-socialism**. This 1949 essay by the great scientist explains why he was drawn to socialism.

3. Mao Zedong's "Red Book": **http://www.marx2mao.com/PDFs/QCM66.pdf**. Online reproduction of *Quotations from Chairman Mao Tse-Tung*, a major influence on early Chinese communism.

4. Marxists Internet Archive: **www.marxists.org**. Online texts of hundreds of Marxist classics, including books by Marx, Engels, Lenin, and so on.

5. Museum of Communism: **www.gmu.edu/departments/economics/bcaplan/ museum/musframe.htm**. Historical information about communism.

6. New Democratic Party: **www.ndp.ca**. Canada's social-democratic political party.

7. Socialist International: **www.socialistinternational.org**. The worldwide association of socialist parties, including Canada's New Democratic Party.

Further Reading

Angus, Ian. *Canadian Bolsheviks: The Early Years of the Communist Party of Canada*. 2nd ed. Victoria, BC: Trafford Publishing, 2004.

PART 2

Archer, Keith. *Political Choices and Electoral Consequences: A Study of Organized Labor and the New Democratic Party.* Montreal and Kingston: McGill-Queens University Press, 1990.

Archer, Keith, and Alan Whitehorn. *Political Activists: The NDP in Convention.* Toronto: Oxford University Press, 1997.

Beilharz, Peter. *Labour's Utopias: Bolshevism, Fabianism, Social Democracy.* London: Routledge, 1992.

Blackburn, Robin. *After the Fall: The Failure of Communism and the Future of Socialism.* London: Verso, 1991.

Campbell, J. Peter. *Canadian Marxists and the Search for a Third Way.* Montreal and Kingston: McGill-Queen's University Press, 1999.

Draper, Hal. *Socialism from Below.* Atlantic Highlands, NJ: Humanities Press, 1992.

Furet, François. *The Passing of an Illusion: The Idea of Communism in the Twentieth Century.* Translated by Deborah Furet. Chicago: University of Chicago Press, 2000.

Giddens, Anthony. *A Contemporary Critique of Historical Materialism.* 2nd ed. Basingstoke, UK: Macmillan, 1995.

Gwertzman, Bernard. *The Collapse of Communism.* New York: Times Books, 1992.

Kitschelt, Herbert. *The Transformation of European Social Democracy.* Cambridge: Cambridge University Press, 1994.

Kornai, János. *The Socialist System: The Political Economy of Communism.* New York: Oxford University Press, 1992.

Laxer, James. *In Search of a New Left: Canadian Politics after the Neoconservative Assault.* New York: Viking Press, 1996.

Le Blanc, Paul. *From Marx to Gramsci: A Reader in Revolutionary Marxist Politics, Historical Overview and Selection.* Atlantic Highlands, NJ: Humanities Press, 1996.

Muravchik, Joshua. *Heaven on Earth: The Rise and Fall of Socialism.* Landham, MD: Encounter Books, 2004.

Penner, Norman. *From Protest to Power: Social Democracy in Canada, 1900–Present.* Toronto: James Lorimer, 1992.

Schumpeter, Joseph A. *Capitalism, Socialism and Democracy.* New ed. London: Routledge, 2006.

Stiglitz, Joseph E. *Whither Socialism?* Cambridge, MA: MIT Press, 1994.

Whitehorn, Alan. *Canadian Socialism: Essays on the CCF–NDP.* Toronto: Oxford University Press, 1992.

Woodcock, George. *Anarchism and Anarchists.* Kingston, ON: Quarry Press, 1992.

CHAPTER 13
Nationalism

The nation, it will be remembered, is a specific type of political community that evolved out of feudal Europe. The decline of universal institutions—the Roman Catholic Church and the Holy Roman Empire—coupled with the erosion of parochial or regional loyalties to manor, village, city, or province, resulted in large aggregates of people sharing common identities. The nation, which arose in Western Europe, has now become the model of community for the rest of the world as well.

Nationalism, at the level of emotions, is a feeling of loyalty to one's nation, recognizing ties with other members of one's group. The pride Canadians feel when a Canadian wins a medal at the Olympics and the sense of recognition that Canadians may experience when they happen to meet other Canadians in a foreign land are manifestations of nationalism. Writing about the *polis*, Aristotle said that "friendship ... seems to hold states together."[1] Nationalism is the equivalent of friendship in communities that are so large we can never actually know more than a tiny proportion of the other members. A common national identity leads us to care about people with whom we are personally unacquainted.

NATIONAL MYTHOLOGY

Loyalty to a nation rests on the fundamental human need for group identification. It is fostered by **national mythology**, that is, by stories about the common history and destiny of the nation. The model for such national myths in the Western world is the historical self-awareness of the Hebrews. Their understanding of themselves as a chosen people, bound to God by a special covenant, recurs in the myths by which other nations justify their existence. No nation has a single myth or story; rather, each has a complex mythology or set of stories existing at different levels, ranging from folklore to deliberate creations by intellectuals writing history in order to further national consciousness.

A fine example of the latter is a book by L.-F. R. Laflèche, Bishop of Trois-Rivières, *Quelques considérations sur les rapports de la société civile avec la religion et la famille* (1866). Laflèche wrote: "Providence has allotted each and every nation its own mission to fulfil."[2] The French-Canadian people, in his view, were a nation among the human family of nations, with their homeland in the valley of the St. Lawrence. Their special calling was "basically religious in nature … to convert the unfortunate infidel local population to Catholicism, and to expand the Kingdom of God by developing a predominantly Catholic nationality."[3]

Laflèche's sketch of the history of French Canada emphasized missionary work among the Native people. With that period largely past, he wrote, the new calling was to be a devout Catholic enclave in Protestant North America, setting an example that might lead others to Rome. The Catholic faith would be reinforced by adherence to the French language. The historical theory was well suited to preserving the identity of a minority, with its call for an intertwining of language, religion, and customs into a protective whole. Laflèche did not create French-Canadian nationalism; rather, he articulated historical symbols to express more clearly what the people already felt. His myth entered the wider mythology, to which many other writers also contributed.

Of course, mythologies change over time. Today, after the Quiet Revolution of the 1960s secularized Quebec society, Laflèche's religious formulation does not express very well the aspirations of Québécois nationalists, who speak about the unique value of their culture and language rather than about religion. The contemporary version of the Québécois mission is to maintain an island of francophone national culture amid the anglophone sea of North America; hence the need for provincial legislation to make French the official language of Quebec, to create a "French face" by regulating the language of public signs, and to restrict access to English schools. The mission is now linguistic and cultural rather than religious, but the underlying idea is still the same: the nation has a special role to play in the drama of human history.

The national mythology of English Canada is more diffuse than that of French Canada because the community itself is less well defined. English-speaking Canada is not a single entity but an alliance of several colonies founded in different circumstances. Massive immigration has further complicated an already complex situation. However, there is one constant theme in the interpretations that Canadians give to their collective existence: to be Canadian is to be not American. Initially, of course, there was no Canada and no Canadian identity, only several British colonies in North America that for ideological reasons shared in the rejection of the American Revolution. Indeed, these colonies were populated largely by descendants of the United Empire Loyalists, who left the United States during or shortly after the American Revolution. The union of these separate colonies in 1867 was impelled less by positive feelings of friendship for one another than by a collective fear that if they remained separate, they would inevitably fall into the orbit of the United States.

Not surprisingly, statements about the meaning of Canada almost always involve a comparison with the United States. During the nineteenth century and much of the twentieth, these comparisons usually interpreted Canada as a more conservative, orderly, and peaceful country than its neighbour. Common themes of self-congratulation were the superiority of constitutional monarchy over republicanism, the British tradition of social deference, an orderly frontier protected by the North-West Mounted Police, and generous treatment of Canada's Aboriginal peoples. Today the topics of comparison are different but the mental process is much the same.[4] Canadians believe that they are fortunate to have less crime than the United States, less racial hostility, a more pristine natural environment, and a more compassionate society. They lay particular stress on Canadian public policies (the key one being national health insurance) that do not exist in the United States. Again it is obvious that the structure of Canadian national mythology serves to protect the group's distinctiveness by discouraging absorption into a larger neighbour. The logic of the situation compels both English- and French-Canadian national mythologies to be defensive in nature.

The character of American nationalism differs from both Canadian nationalisms. The American national identity rests on the political ideas that animated the revolution of 1776. Ever since that time, Americans have interpreted themselves as participants in a social experiment of vast importance to all humanity—testing the limits of liberty. Thomas Jefferson wrote in 1802:

> It is impossible not to be sensible that we are acting for all mankind; that circumstances denied to others, but indulged to us, have imposed on us the duty of proving what is the degree of freedom and self-government in which a society may venture to leave its individual members.[5]

American national mythology plays endlessly on the theme of freedom and interprets everything else in relation to it. In this perspective, modern mass democracy, which first appeared in the United States, is not just majority rule, and capitalism is not just a form of economic organization; both are the means by which a free people conducts its affairs. The Declaration of Independence, the Constitution, and the Bill of Rights are not just political documents; they are sacred texts for the inspiration of all humanity.

This characteristic of American national mythology perhaps helps to explain why American ventures in international politics often tend to become crusades: in contests with other nations, freedom itself is at stake. Woodrow Wilson brought the United States into the First World War "to make the world safe for democracy." Franklin Roosevelt interpreted American participation in the Second World War in a similar way. Cold War rivalry with the Soviet Union was defence of the "free world." George W. Bush responded to the 11 September 2001 terrorist attack on New York and Washington, D.C., not just by retaliating against the terrorists but also by denouncing an international "axis of evil" composed of Iraq, Iran, and North Korea. He then invaded Iraq not just to punish a hostile state but also to bring democracy to the Middle East. In contrast, policymakers in other nations are more likely to see international politics in less moralistic terms.

The point is not that one nation's myths are false while another's are true. It is that every nation worthy of the name has a mythology that supports its national identity by lending meaning to its collective history. Without such a source of meaning, the nation, which is ultimately a psychological reality—an "imagined community,"[6] as Benedict Anderson has called it—could not exist. Space has permitted only a brief look at a few examples, but similar myths exist for all nations.

PART 2

As shown in Chapter 4, there are two rather different ways of "imagining" the nation. Civic nations are imagined in political terms: the key factor is allegiance to a common government. Ethnic nations, in contrast, are imagined in cultural terms: the key factor is a common background involving some combination of language, race, religion, and customs. The distinction is not absolute, because civic nations always have some cultural underpinnings and ethnic nations always have aspects of political allegiance in addition to their emphasis on cultural identity. But distinctions can be useful even when they are not absolute. There is in practice a world of difference between being Canadian or American (primarily civic) and being Lithuanian or Albanian (primarily ethnic).

Nationalism is not a single ideology. The details of each nationalism are unique because each nation is unique. However, there are common factors in the various structures of belief, because national mythologies serve similar purposes for the various nations. Most broadly, nationalism is "the making of claims in the name, or on behalf, of the nation."[7] The claims commonly arise under two headings: loyalty to the nation and the quest for the nation-state.

Loyalty to the Nation

In the nationalist worldview, loyalty to the nation should transcend other loyalties such as allegiance to family, region, or ethnic group. The nation is taken to be the primary social group, outranking all others. This presupposition is so deeply entrenched today that we often do not recognize its significance. Why, for example, do we keep economic statistics on a national basis? In fact, economic relationships do not necessarily coincide with national sentiments. To say that the unemployment rate in Canada is 6 percent obscures the fact that it may be 11 percent in Newfoundland and 5 percent in Saskatchewan. What the national figures mean is rather unclear, yet we religiously compute them. Similarly, athletes can compete in the Olympic Games only as members of a national team; they cannot represent themselves, a city, or a club. Yet sport has intrinsically as little to do with the nation as does economics.

Quest for the Nation-State

That the nation and the state should coincide in the nation-state is not a universal belief of nationalism. The traditional posture of French-Canadian nationalism, for example, was defence of the French-Canadian nation within the Canadian binational state, which in practice meant heavy emphasis on provincial autonomy. That being said, the demand for the nation-state tends to be a recurring one. Thus, French-Canadian nationalism gave rise to separatism in the early 1960s. Interestingly, René Lévesque, the first separatist premier of Quebec, once defended separatism by saying that it was "natural" for a nation to aspire to statehood. The word *natural* reflects the predominance of the nation-state in contemporary thinking.

Opinion about the inevitability of the nation-state is divided. Because freedom depends on voluntary acceptance of legitimate authority, John Stuart Mill argued that in the long run a free society is possible only in a nation-state. He wrote in *Considerations on Representative Government* (1861):

> Free institutions are next to impossible in a country made up of different nationalities. Among a people without fellow-feeling, especially if they read and speak different languages, the united public opinion, necessary to the working of representative government, cannot exist.[8]

Mill feared that in a multinational state one nation would always end up coercively oppressing the others. National antagonism would require such a strong government that individual freedom would be impossible. Indeed, the problem that Mill perceived destroyed the Soviet Union. The reform program introduced by Mikhail Gorbachev allowed for reassertion of national identities that had long been politically suppressed, first by the Russian Empire and then by the Soviet state. Lithuanians, Latvians, Estonians, Ukrainians, and many other nationalities demanded political independence until nothing was left of the Soviet Union.

A contrary view was maintained by Mill's younger contemporary Lord Acton (1834–1902), who wrote that "those states are substantially the most perfect which, like the British and Austrian Empires, include various distinct nationalities without oppressing them."[9] The existence of different nationalities was a positive blessing, according to Acton, because it provided a bulwark against too much state domination of society. Smaller nations within the state, fearful that the government might become controlled by the larger nations, would be reluctant to assign too many functions to the central authorities. Sensitive matters such as education and culture would tend to remain with local governments or perhaps even in private hands.

Acton's beliefs greatly influenced the political thought of Pierre Trudeau and formed the philosophical basis of his linguistic and constitutional policies, which were intended to make Canada a pluralistic state in which neither the French nor the English would feel oppressed by each other. Trudeau's vision of Canada as a culturally pluralistic state was expressed in his often-quoted essay "The New Treason of the Intellectuals":

> Without backsliding to the ridiculous and reactionary idea of national sovereignty, how can we protect our French-Canadian national qualities? … We must separate once and for all the concepts of state and of nation, and make of Canada a truly pluralistic and polyethnic society. Now in order for this to come about, the different regions within the country must be assured of a wide range of local autonomy, such that each national group, with an increasing background of experience in **self-government**, may be able to develop the body of laws and institutions essential to the fullest expression and development of their national characteristics.[10]

Official **bilingualism** and **multiculturalism** became for Trudeau the institutional means of allowing Canada's peoples to coexist under political condominium.

TYPICAL FORMS OF NATIONALISM

The two general concerns of nationalism—loyalty to the nation and the quest for the nation-state—manifest themselves in a bewildering variety of complex phenomena. We will draw attention to a few of the typical situations in which nationalism appears.

Separatism

A substate nation may seek to separate from the state that rules it in order to establish a nation-state, as illustrated by separatist movements in Quebec and among the Welsh and Scots in Great Britain. Sometimes the minority might have to separate from two or more states; examples of this are the Basques, who are now ruled by France and Spain, and the Kurds, who are divided among Turkey, Iraq, Syria, and Iran.

Oppression of Minorities

A national majority that controls the government may use its political power to suppress, assimilate, or expel minorities that do not fit the nation-state's image of itself. In the early 1970s, the African states of Uganda, Kenya, and Tanzania expelled most of their substantial East Indian minorities. These people were vilified as alien exploiters who had been given an unfair position of economic advantage by the British colonialists. More recently, the Albanian-speaking majority of Kosovo drove out most of the Serbian minority, albeit in retaliation for earlier Serbian oppression of the Albanians.

Irredentism

A nation-state may claim fragments of territory adjacent to its borders on the grounds that they constitute a historical part of the nation. The preamble to the 1978 constitution of the People's Republic of China says: "Taiwan is China's Sacred Territory. We are determined to liberate Taiwan and accomplish the great cause of unifying our motherland."[11] Because of this aspiration, before it would join the United Nations, China insisted that Taiwan be expelled, and it discourages, as strongly as it can, other states from maintaining diplomatic relations with Taiwan. The technical name for this sort of claim is **irredentism**. Another example is the unsuccessful Serbian attempt in the 1990s to annex parts of Croatia and Bosnia that had significant Serbian minorities.

Imperialism

A large and powerful nation may create an empire by imposing itself on its neighbours. German nationalism between the two world wars began with irredentist claims to German-populated territories such as the Sudetenland in Czechoslovakia, which had once been part of the Austrian Empire but had been taken away by the Treaty of Versailles. From there it went on to demand *Lebensraum* ("living space") and to subjugate the neighbouring states of Central and Eastern Europe. Nationalism can thus transcend the nation-state and lead to a multinational empire under the rule of a dominant nation.

Protectionism

The nation-state may try to insulate itself from external influences that are perceived as threatening it in some way. This can mean blockading ideas, for example, censoring foreign publications, jamming broadcast signals, or interfering with the Internet. It can also mean erecting barriers against the movement of goods, such as import quotas or protective tariffs, in the belief that such measures not only stimulate the domestic economy but also protect the integrity of the nation. During the 1988 federal election in Canada, opponents of the Free Trade Agreement with the United States expressed many fears for Canada's future. They claimed that free trade not only would harm Canadian industries but also would reduce the autonomy of the Canadian state, force Canada to adopt American social policies, and destroy Canada's cultural distinctiveness.[12] Such fears were debatable, but they were understandable in the context of the long-term defensive posture of nationalism in Canada.

HISTORICAL OVERVIEW

The relationship between nationalism and other ideologies is complicated. History shows that one can be a nationalist while simultaneously being liberal, conservative, or socialist. This is because nationalism has a different fundamental concern than the three other ideologies. They focus on the question of what the role of government in society should be, whereas nationalism addresses itself to the question of the proper limits of the political community. Three French nationalists can agree that France ought to be a sovereign nation-state, *une et indivisible*, while adhering otherwise to conservative, liberal, or socialist views about the functions of government. The relationship between nationalism and other ideologies is not merely a matter of chance; it is structured, as the historian Hans Kohn has shown, according to the course of modern historical development.[13]

Initially, nationalism and liberalism seemed to be natural allies. Great Britain, the first modern nation to emerge, was also the home of liberal constitutionalism. The United States, the first European colony to achieve independence, was constituted in 1776 as a reaffirmation of the principles of the Glorious Revolution. France proclaimed the concept of nationhood in 1789 as part of the liberal freedoms enunciated in the Declaration of the Rights of Man and of the Citizen.

The political situation in the first half of the nineteenth century strengthened the assumption that nationalism and liberalism were two sides of the same coin. Nationalism chiefly meant struggles to liberate small European nations from rule by large empires: the Irish from the British Empire, the Greeks from the Ottoman Empire, the Poles and Finns from the Russian Empire. With the notable exception of the British Empire, all European empires were based on traditional authority rather than legal constitutionalism. Those who struggled for national emancipation had to struggle at the same time for elected parliaments, freedom of the press, religious toleration, and other liberal goals. It was assumed that the peoples of the earth, once liberated from alien rule, would comprise a family of nations living side by side, peacefully and freely. The alliance between liberalism and nationalism reached its peak in 1848, when a wave of attempted revolutions swept across Europe, all having the same goal of creating liberally governed nation-states. But the empires were able to reassert themselves—not least by playing the different nationalities against one another—and the liberal nationalist dream did not become reality.

Liberal nationalism continued to exist after 1848, but it was increasingly displaced by a more militaristic, state-oriented kind of nationalism. The national unification of Italy (1861) and of Germany (1871), long a goal of liberal nationalism, was achieved less by liberal methods of voluntary agreement than by military conquest. The new nation-states of Italy and Germany almost immediately began acquiring colonial empires, especially in Africa, where Britain and France, which had long possessed overseas empires, also joined in. Even the United States, which had previously been critical of European imperialism, acquired overseas colonies—Puerto Rico, Cuba, and the Philippines—after a war with Spain in 1898. By the end of the nineteenth century, nationalism had come to imply much less the liberation of small nations than the imperial aggrandizement of powerful nations. Numerous writers extolled the virtues of military service and loyalty to the state. This was also the period when racial theories became allied with nationalism. Writers of the various large nations justified their policies of imperial expansion by claiming biological superiority for Anglo-Saxons, French, or Germans, who had to rule the "coloured" races for their own good as well as that of humanity in general.

This aggressive form of nationalism fostered the growth of anti-Semitism. Jews, who lived dispersed in many European states, were attacked as alien elements in the national community. The German composer Richard Wagner wrote:

> The Jew speaks the language of the nation in whose midst he dwells from generation to generation, but he always speaks it as an alien ... Our whole European art and civilization, however, have remained to the Jew as a foreign tongue; for, just as he has taken no part in the evolution of the one, so he has taken none in that of the other; but at most the homeless wight [an archaic word for "creature"] has been a cold, nay more, a hostile on-looker.[14]

One of the most important expressions of this mood of anti-Semitism was *The Protocols of the Elders of Zion*, a forged document first published in 1903 and often reprinted thereafter.[15] Written by an agent of the czarist secret police in order to encourage anti-Semitism in Russia, it purported to prove there was a Jewish conspiracy to enslave the entire world. It interpreted Jewish achievements in science, international finance, and the socialist movement not as unrelated developments but as part of a calculated plot to gain ascendancy over the gentiles (non-Jews). *The Protocols* were to have a fateful influence on Adolf Hitler later in the twentieth century. The myth of an international Jewish conspiracy continues to this day to lead a subterranean existence, surfacing from time to time, as in the 1980s in Canada, when Ernst Zundel and Jim Keegstra were prosecuted for fomenting hatred against Jews. Both men attracted attention for asserting that the Holocaust—the murder of six million Jews during World War II—had never taken place and was a creation of Jewish propaganda. Holocaust revisionism, as it is called, is based on the notion of the *Protocols*—that there exists a supremely powerful Jewish cabal capable of perpetrating such a massive hoax upon the world.[16]

In the late nineteenth century, European Jews reacted to the growing wave of anti-Semitism by developing their own form of nationalism. **Zionism** taught that the Jews would never achieve respect until they became a nation-state, and that the Jewish population must therefore gather itself into a single territory under the control of a sovereign Jewish state.

The aggressive nationalism of the late nineteenth and early twentieth century led to World War I, when Britain, France, Russia, and Italy fought in alliance against the German, Austro-Hungarian, and Ottoman Empires. At first the outcome of this bloody war seemed to be a revival of liberal nationalism. The Treaty of Versailles dismembered the empires that had ruled Central and Eastern Europe and replaced them with nation-states equipped with liberal constitutions. Poles, Czechs, Hungarians, Lithuanians, Finns, and other peoples emerged with their own states for the first time in modern history. But nationalism and liberalism soon parted company. Each of these new nation-states had important national minorities, such as the Germans in Czechoslovakia and the Hungarians in Romania. Nationalistic conflict and irredentism raised the temperature of politics to the point where individual freedoms seemed of minor concern relative to the security of the national community. In the 1920s and 1930s, constitutional government was overthrown in almost all these new states of Europe, from Italy and Germany eastward. Nationalism then made an even more aggressive appearance in the new ideology of **fascism**.

Shortly after World War I, Benito Mussolini—an ardent socialist who had nevertheless rallied to the support of Italy in the war—launched a political movement with a unique mixture of ideological themes. Rejection of liberal individualism and constitutional government was paramount. There would no longer be a private sphere of life exempt from governmental intrusion. He extolled the state as the highest expression of the nation and praised war as bringing "all human energies to their highest tension and setting a seal of nobility on the peoples who have the virtue to face it."[17]

The symbol of Mussolini's movement, and the source of its name, was the *fasces*, a bundle of rods containing an axe with the blade projecting, which had been a Roman symbol of authority. The rods and axe represented the threatening power of coercion (i.e., beating or beheading); the fact that they were bound together symbolized the unity of the nation. Italy, for the third time, would emerge as the leader of humanity. After the Rome of the Caesars and the Rome of the Popes would come the "Third Rome," the "Rome of the People." To these nationalist motifs Mussolini added elements of socialism. The state, while not nationalizing property, would guide the economy for collective purposes. Mussolini had also learned from Lenin that an elite, disciplined party could seize power in a constitutional state and maintain its hold thereafter by ruthlessly suppressing opposition. Conspicuously absent were the egalitarian ideals of socialism, except in the sense that all were equally exhorted to follow the charismatic leadership of the *duce* (leader).

Like Mussolini's fascism, Adolf Hitler's doctrine of "national socialism" was a combination of left-wing and right-wing motifs, with the substitution of German for Italian nationalism. Hitler's goal was to create the Third Reich, a new German Empire to succeed the medieval Holy Roman Empire and the empire Bismarck had created in 1871. Also, while Mussolini was not anti-Semitic, Hitler made anti-Semitism the centre of his ideology by blaming the German defeat in World War I on the Jews—the "stab in the back" theory, which he arrived at after reading *The Protocols of the Elders of Zion*—and by promising to make Germany *Judenrein* (free from Jews). Similar ideologies sprang up elsewhere in Europe. Their adherents came to power in Spain, with the help of Italian and German intervention, and became influential in such Central European countries as Hungary and Romania.[18]

Fascism survives today in small political parties and movements in many countries. Although nowhere near coming to power, these so-called **neo-fascist** groups can sometimes cause considerable turmoil through street violence, crime, and terrorism. For example, Timothy McVeigh, who blew up the federal building in Oklahoma City in 1995, killing 167 people, was inspired by a novel called *The Turner Diaries*. He followed detailed instructions in the book for constructing a powerful bomb out of fertilizer and diesel fuel. *The Turner Diaries* depicts an all-out race war in the United States between Jews and blacks on one side and a secret order of white super-patriots on the other side. The book is distributed by the National Alliance, which claims to represent the ideological legacy of Adolf Hitler. Many European countries also have neo-fascist parties, such as the National Democratic Party of Germany.

WORLDWIDE NATIONALISM

While discrediting fascism, World War II ushered in a historical period in which nationalism became truly a worldwide force. British, French, Italian, Portuguese, American, Dutch, and Japanese colonies all attained independence, leaving the Soviet Union and its sphere of influence as the last of the great multinational empires until it dissolved itself in 1991. (See World View 13.1.)

World View 13.1

New Nation-States Created After the Collapse of Communism in Eastern Europe, 1991

Estonia	Czech Republic	Montenegro
Latvia	Slovakia	Moldavia
Lithuania	Slovenia	Armenia
Belarus	Croatia	Georgia
Russia	Serbia	Azerbaijan
Ukraine	Kosovo	

The world is now a society of nation-states, even if many of the new nations are still rather tentative aggregations of tribal, ethnic, and regional groups. The most important new manifestation of nationalism in the postwar period was the struggle of these new nations for independence. In several instances—for example, in Vietnam, Algeria, Angola, and Mozambique—the colonial power was reluctant to surrender its sovereignty and did so only after a prolonged war of national liberation.

In the Third World, the mentality of national liberation is still strong and its symbolism is still potent. The new nations have achieved political sovereignty, but in economic terms many of them are in difficult straits. They commonly blame their low standard of living not only on the colonial past but also on what they perceive as continuing economic domination by the capitalist nations of the Western world, especially the United States. Not surprisingly, since they believe their problems to be caused by the market system, many of the new nations have turned to socialism (see Chapter 12). A recent example is the "*bolivarismo*" of Venezuelan President Hugo Chávez, named after Símon Bolívar, the "liberator" whose rebellion in the early nineteenth century led to the emancipation of Latin American nations from the Spanish empire. Chavez's *bolivarismo*, combining socialist economics with anti-American nationalism, led him to make common cause with Cuba, Iran, and any other country that had hostile relations with the United States.

The recurrent alliance between nationalism and socialism in the Third World may prove itself very long-lasting because the two ideologies have one important affinity: both see the state as the central institution in society. For socialists it is the planner of society and for nationalists it is the expression of national identity; in contrast, for liberals and conservatives it is only a limited instrument with special purposes. Socialist and nationalist uses of the state are not incompatible and, indeed, can reinforce each other, as when nationalization of a multinational corporation is touted as an assertion of sovereignty as well as a measure to benefit the local working class.

PART 2

This rapprochement between nationalism and socialism is mildly ironic in that the early socialists had little use for the nation-state. Marx sympathized with the national aspirations of the Irish and the Poles, not for their own sake, but because he thought national liberation would weaken the political system that helped maintain capitalism. Marx believed that all states, including nation-states, would ultimately disappear. The socialist parties of the Second International were also anti-nationalistic, believing that aggressive nationalism distracted proletarians from the true issue of the class struggle. But the global proliferation of nation-states in this century is a political fact to which ideologies must adjust if they are to survive. Socialists have managed to make the transition by focusing on the state rather than on those parts of their original doctrine that anticipated the passing away of the state.

Nationalism today is critical to the process of building a sense of loyalty and identity among diverse ethnic groups in a given nation-state. At the same time, rabid nationalism can be a destructive force, as can be seen in the series of civil wars in the former Yugoslavia, the repression of the Kurds in Iraq and Turkey, and the ongoing struggle of the Chechens to achieve and maintain independence from Russia. In each case, old animosities have triggered atrocities on all sides. These incidents point out the ugly side of nationalism and the enormous problems involved in reconciling differences through politics.

Questions for Discussion

1. What national myths do you think sustain the Canadian identity? How have they informed your own view of what it means to be Canadian? Can you give some concrete examples of how debates about issues of public policy in Canada tend to become debates about Canadian identity and American influence?

2. Belief in a world Jewish conspiracy, as described in *The Protocols of the Elders of Zion,* is a prime example of conspiracy thinking. Have you encountered any other examples of conspiratorial thinking? What are the common characteristics of this mode of thought?

3. Some authors think that nationalism is becoming less important because of increases in international communication, travel, investment, trade, and immigration. Do you find this to be true of people your own age? Do you think they are less nationalistic than older people, or not?

Internet Links

1. Institute for Historical Review: **http://ihr.org**. A major purveyor of Holocaust revisionism with a pretence of academic respectability.

2. Israel Ministry of Foreign Affairs, "Zionism": **http://www.mfa.gov.il/MFA/ History/Modern+History/Centenary+of+Zionism/**. An informative overview of the subject, with links to many sources on Zionism.

3. Italian Life under Fascism: **www.library.wisc.edu/libraries/dpf/Fascism**. Exhibits from the University of Wisconsin special collections, with lots of interpretation.

4. The Nationalism Project: **www.nationalismproject.org**. Literature and links to many sources on nationalism.

Further Reading

Anderson, Benedict. *Imagined Communities: Reflections on the Origin and Spread of Nationalism*. New ed. London: Verso, 2006.

Beiner, Ronald, ed. *Theorizing Nationalism*. Albany: State University of New York Press, 1999.

Bremmer, Ian, and Ray Taras, eds. *New States, New Politics: Building the Post-Soviet Nations*. 2nd ed. Cambridge: Cambridge University Press, 1997.

Brubaker, Rogers. *Nationalism Reframed: Nationhood and the National Question in the New Europe*. Cambridge: Cambridge University Press, 1996.

Canovan, Margaret. *Nationhood and Political Theory*. Cheltenham, UK: Edward Elgar, 1996.

Chennells, David. *The Politics of Nationalism in Canada: Cultural Conflict Since 1760*. Toronto: University of Toronto Press, 2001.

Comaroff, John L., and Paul C. Stern, eds. *Perspectives on Nationalism and War*. Amsterdam: Gordon and Breach, 1995.

Cook, Ramsay. *Canada, Quebec, and the Uses of Nationalism*. 2nd ed. Toronto: McClelland & Stewart, 1995.

Dahbour, Omar, and Micheline R. Ishay. *The Nationalism Reader*. Atlantic Highlands, NJ: Humanities Press, 1995.

Eley, Geoff, and Ronald Grigor Suny, eds. *Becoming National: A Reader*. New York: Oxford University Press, 1996.

Farnen, Russell F., ed. *Nationalism, Ethnicity, and Identity: Cross-National and Comparative Perspectives*. Piscataway, NJ: Transaction Publishers, 2004.

Flanagan, Tom. *First Nations? Second Thoughts*. 2nd ed. Montreal and Kingston: McGill-Queen's University Press, 2008.

Gellner, Ernest. *Nations and Nationalism*. 2nd ed. Ithaca, NY: Cornell University Press, 2006.

Goldberg, Jonah. *Liberal Fascism: The Secret History of the American Left from Mussolini to the Politics of Meaning*. New York: Doubleday, 2007.

Griffiths, Richard. *Fascism*. New York: Continuum International Publishing, 2005.

Hobsbawm, E. J. *Nations and Nationalism Since 1780: Programme, Myth, Reality*. Cambridge: Cambridge University Press, 1990.

PART 2

Ichijo, Atsuko, and Gordana Uzelac, eds. *When Is the Nation? Towards an Understanding of Theories of Nationalism.* New York: Routledge, 2005.

Ignatieff, Michael. *Blood and Belonging.* Toronto: Penguin Books Canada, 1993.

Keating, Michael, and John McGarry, eds. *Minority Nationalism and the Changing International Order.* Toronto: Oxford University Press, 2001.

Minahan, James. *Nations Without States: A Historical Dictionary of Contemporary National Movements.* Westport, CT: Greenwood Press, 1996.

Moore, Margaret. *The Ethics of Nationalism.* Toronto: Oxford University Press, 2001.

Motyl, Alexander, ed. *Encyclopedia of Nationalism.* 2 vols. San Diego, CA: Academic Press, 2001.

Smith, Anthony D. *Ethnicity and Nationalism.* The Netherlands: Brill, 1992.

———. *Nationalism.* 2nd ed. Cambridge, UK: Polity Press, 2010.

Snyder, Louis L. *The New Nationalism.* Piscataway, NJ: Transaction Publishers, 2003.

Tully, James. *Strange Multiplicity: Constitutionalism in an Age of Diversity.* Cambridge: Cambridge University Press, 1995.

Watson, Michael. *Contemporary Minority Nationalism.* London: Routledge, 1990.

CHAPTER 14
Feminism

In the past 50 years the ideological picture has become increasingly complex, with the rise to prominence of new systems of thought, especially feminism and environmentalism. Liberalism, conservatism, socialism, and nationalism are all primarily concerned with questions of power, such as who is going to control human communities, and to what end. **Feminism** adds an additional dimension to this debate by focusing on the relationship between power and gender, that is, by introducing the concept of patriarchy into the discussion. The rise of **post-materialism** after World War II (see Chapter 5) has produced a climate favourable for ideologies that go beyond concerns of public order and material prosperity.

Some might be forgiven for thinking that feminism is dead, given the media's tendency to declare its demise and the relative invisibility of much of its work. Evidence of its existence was particularly visible, however, in the wave of "SlutWalk" protests that occurred worldwide in 2011. The trigger for this most recent round of activism was a police officer's suggestion, at a women's safety forum at York University in Toronto, that women "should avoid dressing like sluts in order not to be vicitmized."[1] The resulting protests, focused partly on legitimizing the word *slut,* underscored an argument with a long feminist history: that women should feel safe from violence regardless of what they wear. Put differently, rape victims cannot and should not be held responsible for the assaults on them. The protests received extensive media coverage and were controversial, even among feminists. Ideologies are dynamic and ever changing, and debates over ideas and the actions of activists in the feminist movement are one source of this continuous evolution.

FEMINISM

The term *feminism* is derived from the Latin *femina,* which means "woman" or "female." As the name suggests, the ideology is centred on the position of women in society. It should be noted in passing that *feminist* is a label both for certain ideas and for people who hold such ideas. It is not a synonym for *woman.* Some men are feminists (John Stuart Mill was an influential feminist of the nineteenth century) and not all women are feminists. Younger women, for example, are less likely than other women to identify themselves as feminist, even when they hold attitudes that are consistent with feminism.[2]

Feminism is not an entirely new ideology. Its roots go back to the seventeenth century; like liberalism, conservatism, socialism, and nationalism, it belongs to the family of ideologies produced by the French Revolution. It may have seemed new when the contemporary feminist movement burst onto the political stage in the late 1960s, but in fact this was the "second wave" of active feminism. An earlier feminist movement, commencing in the second half of the nineteenth century, had as one of its main goals women's suffrage, which was attained in most Western countries by the end of World War I. The "new" ideology of feminism was the rekindling of a fire that had once burned brightly and never gone out.

As with all ideological trends, there were objective reasons for the "second wave" revival of feminism. A crucial factor was the birth rate, which peaked in the late 1950s and declined rapidly throughout the 1960s. This decline was associated with, though not entirely due to, the introduction of effective oral contraceptives. Lower birth rates meant smaller families, which in turn meant that many women were starting to spend more of their adult lives working in the paid labour force and engaging in public activities such as politics. These objective developments made it pressing to re-examine sex roles in society, because laws and social institutions had traditionally assumed that women's lives would be private and domestic, centred on home and family, while men would predominate in the public spheres of the economy and politics.

Like other ideologies, feminism is a family of belief systems with certain concerns and ideas in common but with many internal differences. The central concern is easily stated: all feminists hold the belief that society is disadvantageous to women, systematically depriving them of individual choice, political power, economic opportunity, and intellectual recognition. Within this broad perspective are many schools of thought about the causes of and remedies for this situation. We will look at three varieties of feminism often mentioned in the literature: liberal feminism, Marxist feminism, and radical feminism.

LIBERAL FEMINISM

Starting in the late seventeenth century, books and pamphlets began to appear arguing that women had the same intellectual and moral capacities as men and should have the same legal rights. The best-known of these early works is *A Vindication of the Rights of Woman* (1792) by Mary Wollstonecraft. A largely self-educated schoolteacher and author, Wollstonecraft is also known for being the mother of Mary Wollstonecraft Shelley, who wrote the novel *Frankenstein*.

The context of the *Rights of Woman* is significant. It was printed very soon after Wollstonecraft's earlier pamphlet *The Rights of Men* (1790), which was an attack on Edmund Burke's *Reflections on the Revolution in France*. Wollstonecraft was an ardent defender of the French Revolution, particularly its egalitarian aspects. In her view, equality for women was a logical corollary of the attempt to create a political system based on equality before the law. She argued that women should have the right to vote, to own property, and to pursue whatever profession they chose, and also to be educated in the liberal arts and sciences like men, not just in the arts of running a household. Like feminists ever since, she argued that political and legal equality had to be rooted in equality within the family. But, unlike some contemporary radical feminists, she did not challenge the traditional procreative role of women. "Make women rational creatures and free citizens," she wrote, "and they will quickly become good wives and mothers."[3]

The general theme of **liberal feminism** is equality of rights, or the extension of men's rights to women. This is vividly expressed in the "Declaration of Sentiments" (1848), drafted by Elizabeth Cady Stanton and modelled closely on the American Declaration of Independence:

> When, in the course of human events, it becomes necessary for one portion of the family of man to assume among the peoples of the earth a position different from that which they have hitherto occupied, but one to which the laws of nature and of nature's God entitle them, a decent respect for the opinions of mankind requires that they should declare the causes that impel them to such a course. We hold these truths to be self-evident; that all men and women are created equal; that they are endowed by their Creator with certain inalienable rights; that among these are life, liberty and the pursuit of happiness; that to secure these rights governments are instituted, deriving their just powers from the consent of the governed.[4]

The underlying presupposition of this text and others in the tradition of liberal feminism is that liberalism would be an adequate ideology if it took itself seriously and extended its view to include both halves of the human race on equal terms. The objective is to modify, rather than replace, the existing political system.

The liberal feminist view was systematically worked out in John Stuart Mill's essay *The Subjection of Women* (1869), written with the help of his wife, Harriet Taylor Mill. The subordination of women, wrote Mill, "ought to be replaced by a principle of perfect equality, admitting no power or privilege on the one side, nor disability on the other."[5] The dependence of women was nothing but "the primitive state of slavery lasting on,"[6] and just as men had been liberated from slavery, so should women. The subjection of women might appear natural, but "was there ever any domination which did not appear natural to those who possessed it?"[7]

The emancipation of women, argued Mill, was in everyone's interest, for "any limitation of the field of selection deprives society of some chances of being served by the competent, without ever saving it from the incompetent."[8] That is, everyone, men and women alike, would profit if women were given a fair chance to develop their abilities

PART 2

and put them to use. Although it might be true that there are natural differences between men and women, Mill claimed that we could not know this for certain because of the dependence in which women had been kept. But that did not matter:

> One thing we may be certain of—that what is contrary to women's nature to do, they never will be made to do by simply giving their nature free play. The anxiety of mankind to interfere in behalf of nature, for fear lest nature should not succeed in effecting its purpose, is an altogether unnecessary solicitude. What women by nature cannot do, it is quite superfluous to forbid them from doing. What they can do, but not so well as the men who are their competitors, competition suffices to exclude them from; since nobody asks for protective duties and bounties in favor of women.[9]

This quotation underscores the liberal character of Mill's approach, a kind of laissez-faire argument applied to the relationship between the sexes.

Mill advocated complete legal equality for women. He also thought marriage should be an equal partnership, and was eloquent about how this would increase the happiness of men as well as women. But, as was typical of early liberal feminists, he seems to have taken for granted that the traditional division of labour between the sexes would continue as the social, although not the legal, norm. Men would continue to be more concerned with public life, married women with the household and private life. Individual women should be perfectly free to devote themselves to the public life of work and government, but it would not be the normal state of affairs:

> When the support of the family depends not on property but on earnings, the common arrangement, by which the man earns the income and the wife superintends the domestic expenditure, seems to me in general the most suitable division of labour between the two persons. If, in addition to the physical suffering of bearing children, and the whole responsibility of their care and education in early years, the wife undertakes the careful and economical application of the husband's earnings to the general comfort of the family; she takes not only her fair share, but usually the larger share, of the bodily and mental exertion required by their joint existence ... In an otherwise just state of things, it is not, therefore, I think, a desirable custom, that the wife should contribute by her labour to the income of the family.[10]

Mill's words illustrate the paradox of the early phase of liberal feminism: it advocated equality of rights for women in a legal sense and accepted the validity of individual women's choosing to pursue careers in the public domain, but it also took for granted a sexual division of labour in which women, although with exceptions, would freely choose to devote themselves primarily to child-bearing and child-rearing for most of their adult lives. Thus reappeared the typical classical-liberal tension between equality of right and equality of outcome: men and women would have equal rights but the conditions of their lives would be very different; it was men who would continue to have greater control over wealth and power in the public realm, while most women would remain in the private sphere of the household.

When Mill wrote *The Subjection of Women*, there was already an active political movement of women, usually known as **suffragism** because of its emphasis on attaining suffrage, or the right to vote, for women. But women's emancipation was much broader than this issue; it included the struggle for legal and political equality in all forms, such as the right to hold public office, to attend university and enter the learned professions, to own property in marriage, and to receive custody of children in cases of divorce or separation. These goals were gradually attained in most Western countries toward the end of the nineteenth and the beginning of the twentieth centuries. Some leading Canadian feminists of that era were Dr. Emily Howard Stowe, Canada's first female physician, who founded the Canadian Women's Suffrage Movement in Toronto in 1876; Emily Murphy, a journalist who was appointed a police magistrate in Edmonton in 1916, the first such appointment in the British Empire; and Nellie McClung, also a journalist, who was elected to the Alberta legislature in 1921.[11] Historical Perspectives 14.1 lists some other important milestones in the political progress of Canadian women.

The contemporary phase of liberal feminism in North America was signalled by publication in 1963 of Betty Friedan's best-selling book *The Feminine Mystique*. Friedan, an American journalist, devoted her book to "the problem that has no name," namely

> ... a strange stirring, a sense of dissatisfaction, a yearning that women suffered in the middle of the twentieth century in the United States. Each suburban wife struggled with it alone. As she made the beds, shopped for groceries, matched slipcover material, ate peanut butter sandwiches with her children, chauffeured Cub Scouts and Brownies, lay beside her husband at night—she was afraid to ask even of herself the silent question—"Is this all?"[12]

Friedan's answer at that time was unambiguous: no, domestic life was not enough; women had to become complete participants in the public world of politics and the economy:

> There is only one way for women to reach full human potential—by participating in the mainstream of society, by exercising their own voice in all the decisions shaping that society. For women to have full identity and freedom, they must have economic independence.[13]

In her pursuit of these goals, Friedan went on to become a founding member and first president of the National Organization for Women (NOW)—an American feminist advocacy group—and a leading figure in the American women's movement.

Her book *The Second Stage,* published in 1981, examined some of the difficulties arising out of women's attempts to play a full role in economic and political life. In the book, she quotes a young woman who is attending Harvard Medical School:

> I'm going to be a surgeon. I'll never be a trapped housewife like my mother. But I would like to get married and have children, I think. They say we can have it all. But how? I work thirty-six hours in the hospital, twelve off. How am I going to have a relationship, much less kids, with hours like that? I'm not sure I can be a superwoman.[14]

PART 2

Canadian Women's Political Milestones

1897 Clara Brett Martin is admitted to the Law Society of Upper Canada.

1916 Manitoba, Alberta, and Saskatchewan grant women the right to vote in provincial elections.

1918 Women obtain the right to vote in federal elections.

1929 In the *Persons* case, the Judicial Committee of the Privy Council rules that women are legal persons and may be appointed to the Senate.

1930 Cairine Wilson is appointed to the Senate.

1940 Women get the right to vote in Quebec provincial elections.

1957 Ellen Fairclough becomes the first woman to serve in the federal cabinet.

1960 The right to vote is granted unconditionally to First Nations, including women.

1982 Bertha Wilson becomes the first woman appointed to the Supreme Court of Canada.

1984 Jeanne Sauvé becomes Canada's first female Governor General.

1985 Bill C-31 restores status to First Nations women who had lost their official Aboriginal status by marrying non-status men.

1989 Audrey McLaughlin is elected leader of the New Democratic Party, the first woman to lead a federal party.

1993 Kim Campbell becomes the first woman prime minister of Canada.

1995 Alexa McDonough succeeds Audrey McLaughlin as leader of the New Democratic Party.

2000 Beverley McLachlin becomes the first female Chief Justice of the Supreme Court of Canada.

2004 Two new appointments raise the number of women on the Supreme Court of Canada to four out of nine.

2011 The leader of the Green Party, Elizabeth May, wins the party's first and only seat in the House of Commons.

Three provinces (British Columbia, Alberta, and Newfoundland) are headed by female premiers.

Friedan's answer to this dilemma was "the restructuring of our institutions on a basis of real equality for women and men."[15] Concretely, this would mean changes in sex roles within the family, with both men and women working outside the home while sharing the tasks of housework and child care. It would also require innovations in public policy, such as public support for daycare to facilitate women's participation in the workforce.

This approach sits comfortably within the tradition of reform liberalism. If government can provide old-age pensions and medical care in the name of equality, then why not daycare as well? But such demands collided with the conservative revival of the 1980s and the fiscal pressures of the 1990s, and many aspects of the contemporary liberal feminist agenda remain unfulfilled in North America. Friedan's brand of liberal feminism also rested squarely on the experiences of white middle-class, heterosexual women, for which it was heavily critiqued.

MARXIST FEMINISM

Feminism has always been an important theme in socialist thought. Many of the utopian socialists believed in restructuring the relationships between the sexes. Charles Fourier wrote:

> It is known that the best nations have always been those which concede the greatest amount of liberty to women. As a general proposition: Social progress and changes of period are brought about by virtue of the progress of women towards liberty, and social retrogression occurs as a result of a diminution in the liberty of women.[16]

The Israeli kibbutz, remotely based on the ideas of Fourier, tried to revolutionize the status of women by introducing collective housekeeping and child-rearing arrangements. Another early utopian, Robert Owen, also proposed easier divorce and other reforms of the family. Philosophically, Owen's great theme was the malleability of human nature, by which he meant that individual behaviour could be changed by alterations in the social environment:

> the character of man is, without a single exception, always formed for him ... it may be, and is, chiefly, created by his predecessors ... they give him, or may give him, his ideas and habits, which are the powers that govern and direct his conduct. Man, therefore, never did, nor is it possible he ever can, form his own character.[17]

If this is true, the relationship between the sexes can be put on the table for social reform along with everything else—there is nothing natural about any particular family structure.

Marx did not write a great deal about the position of women in society, but a few passages show that he made a connection between the family and private property. In *The German Ideology* (1845), he referred to the family as a kind of "latent slavery"—as the first form of property, in that it gave the husband "the power of disposing of the labour-power of others" (i.e., of the wife and children).[18] In *The Communist Manifesto*, Marx and Engels predicted that the family would be revolutionized under communism:

> With the transfer of the means of production into common ownership, the single family ceases to be the economic unit of society. Private housekeeping is transformed into a social industry. The care and education of children becomes a public affair; society looks after all children alike, whether they are legitimate or not.[19]

After Marx's death, Engels explored the theme of the family further in *The Origin of the Family, Private Property and the State* (1884), in which he tried to integrate recent anthropological research with his Marxist ideology. Among his conclusions were the following:

> The modern individual family is founded on the open or concealed domestic slavery of the wife, and modern society as a mass is composed of these individual families as its molecules ... Within the family, he is the bourgeois, and the wife represents the proletariat ... the peculiar character of the supremacy of the husband over the wife in the modern family, the necessity of creating real social equality between them and the way to do it, will only be seen in the clear light of day when both possess legally complete equality of rights. Then it will be plain that the first condition for the liberation of the wife is to bring the whole female sex back into public industry, and that this in turn demands that the characteristic of the monogamous family as the economic unit of society be abolished.[20]

Thus arose the standard Marxist position on what the nineteenth century called "the woman question": that the legal equality so beloved of liberal feminists such as Mill was essential but insufficient. The true emancipation of women could be achieved only through communist revolution. To change the relationship between the sexes in a thoroughgoing way would necessitate socializing the means of production and abolishing the economic system of capitalism. As August Bebel, a leading German Social Democrat, put it in *Women under Socialism* (1883), "the solution of the woman question [would be] identical with the solution of the social question."[21]

Marxist feminists challenged the notion that patriarchy would be abolished along with capitalism, given that the sexual division of labour within the family predates it; the transhistorical nature of patriarchy is not easily reconciled with the historical and cultural requirements of Marxism. They also worked to develop a theoretical understanding of patriarchy within the Marxist framework. For some, this involved examining female domestic labour as a key element of production and capital (including women's role in reproduction), while for others it involved examining how women's labour-market participation replicated their domestic roles, leading to the sexual division of labour in the workplace and to their treatment as a reserve army of labour. Ultimately, the difficulty of reconciling a focus on gender with the primacy of class in Marxism led many feminists to move away from Marxist orthodoxy, toward a socialist feminism that eschews revolution in favour of reform.

Communist regimes in the Soviet Union and elsewhere did, however, act on the implications of Marxist theory. Quickly after coming to power, communist governments legislated legal equality between men and women and also made efforts to destroy "the monogamous family as the economic unit of society." Women were encouraged, indeed virtually required, to take paid employment outside the home. Inexpensive and publicly operated daycare facilities were made easily available to facilitate women's entry into the labour force. Under most communist regimes, divorce, birth control, and abortion were also readily available, which encouraged a sharp drop in the birth rate—this in what before the revolution had been largely agrarian societies with high birth rates.

These were real and significant changes, and many Western feminists were initially enthusiastic about the effect of communism upon women's lives. Doubts arose, however, as the decades went by. Communism brought women into the labour market but it did not liberate them from housework, and the lives of ordinary women were filled with overwork and exhaustion. Women entered and even came to dominate certain prestigious professions such as medicine, but in those professions they earned less than (largely male) factory workers. The rise of women through the administrative and political hierarchies also seemed to stall. No communist regime has ever had a female head of state, head of government, or head of the Communist Party. Women were always represented on the highest committees, but in a token way, never exercising leadership. And while communist states sponsored mass political organizations for women, these were always carefully controlled; no independent women's movement was allowed to emerge.

For all of these reasons, Marxist feminism of the traditional type has little weight today in North America. While Marxist feminist writings continue to exercise some influence among intellectuals, their influence on the contemporary women's movement is minimal. A third branch of feminism, however, called radical feminism, with roots in the 1960s, continues to exercise a remarkable influence on contemporary politics and public policy.

RADICAL FEMINISM

Women writing at the end of the 1960s and beginning of the 1970s developed what has since been labelled the ideology of **radical feminism**. Many had participated in the New Left movement of the 1960s, which was a non-communist, anti-authoritarian revival of Marxism. The radical feminists broke with the New Left because the men in that movement regarded women as subordinate and did not take their concerns seriously. When they departed, they gave up orthodox Marxism but took with them a certain Marxist style of thought that served as a framework for their new categories.

In radical feminist analysis, women and men constitute separate "sexual classes." History is the story of class struggle between these two sexual classes—not, as the Marxists would have it, between the economic classes of owners and employees. The central concept in radical feminism is not capitalism but **patriarchy.** In the words of Kate Millet, the author of *Sexual Politics*, "When one group rules another, the relationship between the two is political. When such an arrangement is carried out over a long period of time it develops an ideology (feudalism, racism, etc.). All historical civilizations are patriarchies: their ideology is male supremacy."[22]

In one way this was a definite break with Marxism because it no longer saw property relations as the fundamental variable in human history. The New York Radical Feminists stated in a manifesto that "we do not believe that capitalism, or any economic system, is the cause of female oppression, nor do we believe that female oppression will disappear as a result of a purely economic revolution."[23] Another break with Marxists, who see the wage relationship as the chief means of exploitation, comes from radical feminists' focus on personal, face-to-face relationships between men and women. "Women have very little idea of how much men hate them," wrote Germaine Greer in *The Female Eunuch* (1971).[24]

Radical feminists analyze certain behaviours—usually regarded previously as social pathologies—as typical forms of male control over females. In *Against Our Will: Men, Women and Rape* (1975), Susan Brownmiller wrote that rape is "nothing more or less than a conscious process of intimidation by which all men keep all women in a state of fear."[25] Many radical feminists see rape, as well as sexual harassment and violence against women, as widespread, almost universal means of social control. Some radical feminists apply a similar analysis to pornography, which they condemn not because it openly portrays sexual conduct but because it degrades and oppresses women. "Pornography is the undiluted essence of anti-female propaganda," in Brownmiller's words.[26] By identifying the harmful impact to women of relationships, activity, and policy within the private sphere, radical feminism introduced the argument "the personal is the political."

The problem is not just male misconduct but the family itself. "The tyranny of the biological family" must be ended, according to Shulamith Firestone in *The Dialectic of Sex* (1971).[27] For Ti-Grace Atkinson, "the phenomenon of love is the psychological pivot in the persecution of women"[28] because it leads them to define themselves in relation to men. For some leading radical feminists, emancipation from male domination leads directly to lesbianism, which is a political statement, not just a sexual preference. For radical feminists such as Adrienne Rich, the adoption of political lesbianism is essential to feminism in that it requires a commitment to women as an expression of solidarity. Moreover, it directly challenges traditional notions of family and motherhood—both important elements in the oppression of women.

Firestone's *Dialectic of Sex* goes furthest in developing the idea of revolution against supposedly natural sex roles. Whereas orthodox Marxists emphasize the importance of production, Firestone makes reproduction the key issue. Women will never obtain their liberation until they can give up the "barbaric" function of pregnancy and reject the myth that children need their mothers. Child-bearing must be rejected in favour of a combination of test-tube fertilization and artificial placentas, or perhaps the implantation of human fetuses in animal host uteruses. Responsibility for child-rearing must be transferred from biological families to groups of "contracting" adults not necessarily related to the child. With the end of the biological family the incest taboo could be dropped, and "humanity could finally revert to its natural polymorphous sexuality—all forms of sexuality would be allowed and indulged."[29] Where Marxists argue that freedom requires ending the capitalist mode of production, some radical feminists argue that for women it requires changing the means of reproduction. But other radical feminists, such as Mary O'Brien, have instead identified child-bearing and procreation as the source of women's strength. They have advocated reclaiming control of the process, which they believe has been captured by a male-dominated medical and scientific community.[30]

Firestone's ideas about reproduction, child-rearing, and incest may strike many readers as extreme, as may some other notions of radical feminism such as equating heterosexual intercourse with rape. Opponents of feminism often cite them in an attempt to discredit the whole ideology of feminism. These views do not represent mainstream opinion on women's place in society, but they have nevertheless powerfully affected the feminist and public policy agendas. Before the rise of radical feminism, discussion revolved mostly around the liberal agenda of legal equality for women who wanted to take their place in the world of work and politics; typical issues were discrimination in employment, admission to professional schools, and nomination as candidates for political parties. While radical feminism did not reject the importance of such issues, it added a new dimension of "sexual politics." The key issues now became rape, violence against women, the sexual abuse of children, sexual harassment, pornography, and the rights of gays and lesbians.

In Canada, as in many other countries, radical feminism has already had a significant impact on public policy. Human rights law has been amended to incorporate sexual harassment as a form of discrimination—a conceptual merger between the liberal and radical views. Rape crisis shelters have been established, and Parliament has changed the law and procedures relating to sexual assault to make convictions easier to obtain. The Supreme Court has removed the statute of limitations on incest and child abuse, again increasing the possibility of conviction. And in the *Butler* case (1992), which upheld the criminalization of pornography, it also accepted the radical feminist position that pornography is harmful because it is degrading to women, not because it is sexually explicit. No political observer writing before the emergence of radical feminism could have predicted these legal and political trends.

PERENNIAL QUESTIONS OF FEMINISM

It is typical of ideologies that their most central questions seem to have no final answers. Liberals have disagreed for centuries over what freedom *really* means, and there is no general consensus among nationalists as to which groups are *really* nations. Similarly, certain issues in the feminist movement have never been resolved. Two of these are discussed below.

How Different are Men and Women?

Liberal and Marxist/socialist feminists have generally emphasized the fundamental similarity of men and women as human beings, arguing that the two sexes have the same mental and moral capacities and can do the same kinds of work. They generally regard physical differences of size and strength as not very important in an increasingly technological world. To the extent that there are more important physical differences associated with reproductive biology, they have often proposed to ameliorate the effects of those differences by changing social arrangements. Relevant examples are the provision of daycare facilities to encourage women's participation in the paid labour force and the policy of some law firms to reduce the "billable hours" expectations for female lawyers during the years when they have young children. The purpose of these and similar proposals is to allow women to compete on as equal terms as possible in occupations that have long been dominated by men. The underlying assumption is that clearing the field of obstacles will allow all the players to compete and be judged on the basis of individual performance.

Since the publication of Friedan's *The Second Stage* in 1981, feminists have increasingly emphasized the ways in which women differ from men. Carol Gilligan's *In a Different Voice* (1983) argued that men and women approach moral questions differently: men thinking in terms of abstract rights and rules, women in terms of networks and mutual support. Another widely read book is Deborah Tannen's *You Just Don't Understand* (1990), which documents the different conversational styles of women and men. Others go even further in arguing that women are not only different from men but also morally superior to them, and therefore they must develop their differences in a separate "womanculture."

This "feminism of difference," as it has been called, poses difficult problems for the liberal strategy of integration based on the assumption of a fundamental similarity between men and women. If there really are subtle and deep-seated differences in areas such as moral reasoning and conversational style, it may be much harder than liberal feminists originally assumed for women and men to play the same roles in the public world of work and government. Different solutions are conceivable—perhaps women need to change; perhaps men need to change; perhaps the two sexes will become more like each other; perhaps the differences will remain and ways will be found to make them more complementary and harmonious—but this will obviously be more complex than simply legislating equal opportunity.

What is the Origin of the Differences?

Are the differences between women and men biological or cultural? Feminists have given different answers to these questions. For Shulamith Firestone the difference is essentially biological: women can never be emancipated until they no longer have to bear children. Other radical feminists, however, insist that the differences are fundamentally cultural and as such can be overcome by social and political action:

"By destroying the present society, and building a society based on feminist principles, men will be forced to live in the human community on terms very different from the present. For that to happen, feminism must be asserted by women, as the basis of revolutionary social change."[31] In this view, women are oppressed by male culture but they also have their own (now subordinated) "womanculture," which can be asserted through political activism and which will eventually reshape society.

No one would deny that there are cultural differences between men and women related to their upbringing and the way they are educated in school, depicted in the media, treated by employers, and so on. And no one would deny that these cultural differences are affected by cultural developments. Clearly women can learn to be plumbers and men can learn to be nurses. But what if men and women tend to learn some things more readily than other things? That is, it may be that the members of either sex can learn to play almost any role, but left to their own devices, they may tend to learn some roles more readily than others. If that is true, any program of eradicating or minimizing gender differences may require a degree of compulsion that will make at least liberal feminists uncomfortable.

WOMEN IN POLITICS

Women make up half or more of the voting-age population in modern Western societies. Thus extension of the suffrage and other political rights to women at the end of World War I suddenly doubled the size of democracy. What effect has this expansion had upon the political system?

Women do indeed use their political rights: the percentage of women who vote in elections is the same as that for men. Survey evidence reveals, however, that women on average are less interested in and less knowledgeable about politics than men— differences that cannot be explained by differences in education and income, nor by the greater demands that are often made on women's time.[32]

When the working class gained the vote in the nineteenth century, the immediate result was creation of social-democratic parties that were largely dependent on the labour vote. In contrast, the entry of women into the political system did not lead to the formation of women's parties. It turned out that women, like men, have a variety of political views and vote for a variety of political parties. There are, however, some interesting differences in the political behaviour of women and men. Up to about 1970, women in most democracies were more likely than men to vote for parties of the centre right, particularly those with a religious aspect, such as the Christian Democratic Parties of Europe and Latin America. But this pattern started to change in the 1970s, first in the United States, then in other countries. Today the general pattern in established democracies is that women are more likely to vote for parties of the centre left. This is not true, however, of emerging democracies in the Third World or in the post-communist areas of Eastern Europe, although things may evolve that way as time goes on.[33]

This voting **gender gap**—the difference between the percentage of women and the percentage of men voting for a given candidate—can range from small to quite large. In the 2008 election in the United States, 56 percent of women favoured the Democrat Barack Obama for president while only 49 percent of men did the same—a gap of 7 percentage points, similar to that recorded in the two previous presidential elections. By international standards this would be considered a moderate difference but one that was both statistically and practically significant.

Significant gender differences in support for Senators Hillary Clinton and Barack Obama in the 2008 Democratic primaries suggest that gender effects can be primed by the gender of candidates. The situation is somewhat more complicated in Canada because of the existence of five major parties. In recent elections, parties on the right of the electoral spectrum have been less likely to attract the votes of women, while the opposite tends to be the case among parties on the left. In the 2006 federal election, a gender gap of 10 percentage points appeared for the Conservative Party. The NDP, on the other hand, has a similarly sized gender gap, although it attracts more support from women than from men.

Explanations for the gender gap include that women in contemporary society are more dependent than men on government programs and thus more likely to vote for parties that favour the welfare state rather than those criticize it. Partly because of pregnancy, childbirth, and the complexity of the female reproductive system, women visit doctors and hospitals more than men do. In most families, mothers are more directly involved with the health care and education of children than are fathers. In the case of divorce, women are more likely to get custody of small children and to be supported by social assistance payments. Finally, women, because of their longer life expectancy, are statistically likely to spend more years being supported by old-age pensions. For all these reasons, it is logical for women to be more concerned than men about the generosity and dependability of health care, education, social assistance, and pensions in the welfare state. The gender gap, of course, depends as much on male as upon female voting behaviour. The relative swing of women to the left in the past two decades also reflects the fact that men have been more responsive than women to the appeal of the revival of market-oriented ideology.[34]

The concept of political rights includes not only voting but also holding public office. Women's involvement was slower to develop at this level. Until the end of the 1960s, female legislators were a rarity in most jurisdictions. For example, only one woman—representing 0.4 percent of the seats—was elected to the House of Commons in the federal election of 1968. There was a gradual increase, however, in the following four decades, and 25 percent of successful candidates were female in the election of 2011. Trends in the Canadian provinces have been similar, and at lower levels of politics, such as city councils and school boards, women have been even more successful. There is much variation across the world in this regard; some democracies have a higher and some a lower percentage of female officeholders than Canada. Differences in women's political representation are due to a number of factors, including the party system, electoral rules (including the use of quotas and the type of electoral system), culture, and women's overall socioeconomic status. For a discussion of global patterns in women's equality in several arenas, see World View 14.1.

World View 14.1

The Gender Gap

The gender gap has become a concept that is widely employed to highlight disparities between women and men on a number of measures. Gender gaps of varying sizes have been recorded in labour force wages, for example, in some cases justifying the use of equal pay legislation, and in women's political representation, in some cases resulting in the use of party gender quotas.

A study in 2011 by the World Economic Forum highlighted that on most measures and across a number of countries around the world, women continue to lack equality with men.

Using a measure they developed called the "global gender gap index," computed from data collected on 135 countries around the world, the authors provide a worldwide score for women's equality with men on four measures: educational attainment, economic participation and opportunity, health and survival, and political empowerment. Each index is scored as a ratio, calculated by dividing the women's score or percentage on a measure by the men's and then averaging the score across several common measures to create the index. A score of 0 corresponds to complete inequality

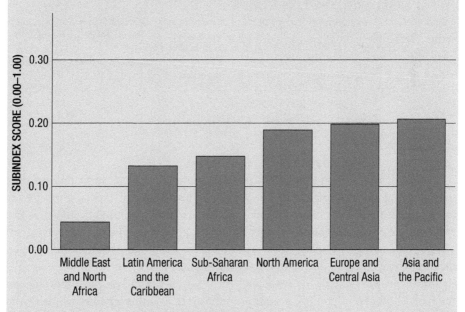

Figure 14.1 Regional Performance on the Political Empowerment Sub-index

Source: © World Economic Forum. Reprinted with permission.

(continued)

World View 14.1 *(continued)*

for women, while a score of 1 suggests complete equality; if the legislature were equally divided between women and men, for example, dividing 50 percent (women) by 50 percent (men) would result in an index score of 1.

The study's findings, which cover 90 percent of the world's population, suggest that women fare well on measures of health and survival (index score = 0.96) and in educational attainment (index score = 0.93). Men's access to economic participation and opportunity (index score = 0.59) and political empowerment (index score = 0.19) continues, however, to significantly outpace that of women. The findings are not driven by regional disparities, as shown by the regional breakdown for political empowerment in the figure above (14.1), but rather reflect a relatively global pattern. And the findings suggest that things will not naturally improve over time; tracking the index across 97 countries

over four years reveals that while 85 percent of countries showed improvement between 2008 and 2011, a full 15 percent revealed a widening of gender gaps.

Canada ranks 18th overall, with an index of 0.741. On the individual scores it ranks 10th on economic participation and opportunity (index score = 0.776), 31st on educational opportunities (index score = 0.999), 36th on political empowerment (index score = 0.210), and 49th on health and survival (index score = 0.978). The top four index scores were earned by Iceland, Norway, Finland, and Sweden, with each country scoring more than 0.80. In contrast, the country with the lowest ranking across the 135 countries was Yemen, which received an overall score of 0.49.

Source: Ricardo Hausmann, Laura D. Tyson, and Saadia Zahidi, The Global Gender Gap Report 2011 (Geneva: World Economic Forum, 2011). Available online at www.weforum.org/reports/global-gender-gap-report-2011.

Finally, it should also be emphasized that there is much more to politics than simply voting and running for office. Women's presence in the media, given its key role in reporting the news and commenting on developments in public affairs, is also of interest. Women's success in creating important interest groups and advocacy organizations—ranging in Canada from the once strong National Action Committee on the Status of Women on the left to REAL Women of Canada on the right—is especially significant in the light of the neoliberal turn. Given the increasing importance of the judicial process in politics, it is also significant to examine whether women enter the legal profession in more or less the same numbers as men. As of 2011, the Chief Justice of the Supreme Court of Canada and three other members of that court were female, giving women a powerful presence in the highest legal authority in Canada.

As many feminists would point out, however, not all women are feminist, and the advancement of women's interests can be argued to require more than simply reaching parity with men.

Questions for Discussion

1. Think of some differences you have observed in the behaviour of men and women. Think of a possible explanation in terms of inherited genetic differences, and another possible explanation in terms of culture and environment. What kind of evidence would help you decide which explanation is correct?

2. Do you consider yourself a feminist? If no, is it because you disagree with certain tenets of feminism or for other reasons? If yes, what type of feminist?

3. Should programs such as gender quotas be implemented in Canada to promote greater representation for women in the legislative branch of government? Why or why not?

4. Why do you think women have had more success at being elected to municipal councils and school boards than to provincial legislatures and the federal parliament?

Internet Links

1. Equal Voice: **www.equalvoice.ca**. A Canadian group working to increase women's electoral representation in Canada.

2. The F-Word: **www.thefword.org.uk/features/category/feminism**. The website of a U.K. collective of grassroots feminist activists.

3. Status of Women Canada: **www.swc-cfc.gc.ca**. The federal department responsible for women's issues; includes online publications.

4. Women's Legal Education and Action Fund (leaf): **www.leaf.ca**. This Canadian women's interest group intervenes in court cases relevant to women and girls, providing a feminist perspective.

Further Reading

Arneil, Barbara. *Politics and Feminism.* Oxford: Blackwell, 1999.

Backhouse, Constance. *Challenging Times: The Women's Movement in Canada and the U.S.* Montreal: McGill-Queen's University Press, 1992.

Baumgardner, Jennifer, and Amy Richards. *Manifesta: Young Women, Feminism, and the Future.* New York: Farrar, Straus, and Giroux, 2000.

PART 2

Beauvoir, Simone de. *The Second Sex*. New York: Vintage Books, 1989.

Bryson, Valerie. *Feminist Political Theory: An Introduction*. 2nd ed. New York: Palgrave Macmillan, 2003.

Donovan, Josephine. *Feminist Theory: The Intellectual Traditions of American Feminism*. New York: Ungar, 1985.

Faludi, Susan. *Backlash: The Undeclared War Against American Women*. New York: Crown, 1991.

Ferree, Myra Marx, and Aili Mari Tripp. *Global Feminism: Transnational Women's Activism, Organizing, and Human Rights*. New York: NYU Press, 2006.

Friedan, Betty. *The Feminine Mystique*. New York: Dell, 1983.

Hirsh, Marianne. *Conflicts in Feminism*. New York: Routledge, 1990.

Inglehart, Ronald, and Pippa Norris. *Rising Tide: Gender Equality and Cultural Change around the World*. Toronto: Cambridge University Press, 2003.

Lovenduski, Joni, and Pippa Norris, eds. *Gender and Party Politics*. London: Sage, 1993.

Mill, John Stuart. *The Subjection of Women*. Arlington Heights, IL: AHM Publishing, 1980.

Newman, Jacquetta A., and Linda A. White. *Women, Politics, and Public Policy: The Political Struggles of Canadian Women*. Toronto: Oxford University Press, 2006.

Phillips, Anne, ed. *Feminism and Politics*. Oxford: Oxford University Press, 1998.

Rendall, Janet. *The Origins of Modern Feminism*. London: Macmillan, 1985.

Sharpe, Sydney. *The Gilded Ghetto: Women and Political Power in Canada*. Toronto: HarperCollins, 1994.

Sommers, Christina Hoff. *Who Stole Feminism? How Women Have Betrayed Women*. New York: Simon and Schuster, 1994.

Sperling, Liz. *Women, Political Philosophy and Politics*. Edinburgh: Edinburgh University Press, 2001.

Steinem, Gloria. *Outrageous Acts and Everyday Rebellions*. New York: Holt, Rinehart and Winston, 1983.

Stetson, Dorothy McBride. *Abortion Politics, Women's Movements, and the State*. Toronto: Oxford University Press, 2001.

Tong, Rosemarie. *Feminist Thought: A More Comprehensive Introduction*. 3rd ed. Boulder, CO: Westview Press, 2009.

Tremblay, Manon, and Linda Jean Trimble, eds. *Women and Electoral Politics in Canada*. Toronto: Oxford University Press, 2003.

Young, Lisa. *Feminists and Party Politics*. Vancouver: University of British Columbia Press, 2000.

CHAPTER 15
Environmentalism

Like feminism, **environmentalism** is not a single belief system but a family of ideologies, linked by their focus on the environment but divided by profound internal differences. Also like feminism, environmentalism has old roots, although it has gained significant momentum since the 1970s. Some versions of environmentalism can be traced back about a century. Older traces of environmental thinking also exist, such as the speculations of Thomas Malthus about the inevitability of overpopulation, but those are probably best interpreted as environmental reflections within a liberal context rather than the beginning of a new ideology. The genuine tradition of environmentalism began a little more than a century ago with the conservationist movement.

CONSERVATIONISM

Conservationism is the attempt to manage natural resources so that human users, including future generations, derive maximum benefit over a long period of time. The emergence of the discipline of forestry in the nineteenth century was one important development in conservationism. Another was the national parks movement. In 1872 the U.S. Congress passed the Yellowstone Park Act to create the first national park, and Canada followed suit in 1885 with the creation of Banff National Park. Human use was clearly the driving force in the national parks movement; for example, Banff National Park was established around hot springs and promoted by the Canadian Pacific Railway as a tourist destination and health resort.

Banff National Park has recently assumed international leadership for its role in the study and development of wildlife highway crossings. The Trans-Canada Highway— the main east-to-west commercial highway in the province of Alberta—directly bisects Banff National Park, and its presence has, not surprisingly, had a significantly negative impact on wildlife habitat and mortality. Over the past 30 years, a series of structures—overpasses, underpasses, and fencing—has been developed in combination with extensive highway twinning so as to mitigate the environmental and wildlife impact of transportation routes through the park. The objective is to both protect and present the park for this and future generations. Other aspects of the conservation movement along these lines include flood control, reforestation, and soil reclamation.

The use of resources by humans is the common aim of all these efforts. For instance, many hunters contribute time and money to Ducks Unlimited in an effort to conserve and restore prairie wetlands, with the long-term goal of improving duck hunting. The hunters work to improve wildlife habitat but they are thinking mainly of human recreation, not of any intrinsic value of wildlife apart from human use.

HUMAN WELFARE ECOLOGY

The rise of **human welfare ecology** began, most observers agree, in 1962, when Rachel Carson's book *Silent Spring* raised the alarm about the effects of pesticides, particularly DDT, on the reproduction of birds. This movement began as an extension of conservationism in that it originally focused on wildlife management. At the same time it transcended the economic dimension of traditional conservationism by directly addressing the environment's value to human health and happiness. Since *Silent Spring*, environmental concerns have broadened and now embrace an infinity of issues—air and water quality, carcinogens, the ozone layer, global warming, overpopulation, solid-waste disposal, nuclear radiation, and so on—but in all cases the theme is the effect of environmental degradation on human welfare. For example, human welfare ecologists fear that the thinning of the ozone layer may lead to an increase in the incidence of skin cancers, and that global warming may cause flooding of coastal cities as well as desertification of currently productive agricultural lands. Like conservationism, human welfare ecology is basically anthropocentric (i.e., human-centred).[1] In practical political terms, the human welfare brand of ecology has led to the passage of environmental legislation, the creation of departments of the environment, and the rise of new regulatory processes such as environmental impact studies and public hearings on the construction of dams, high-tension power lines, and other major projects.

Both conservationism and human welfare ecology can be understood to some degree as extensions of liberalism. They are chiefly concerned with phenomena that we discussed earlier under the heading of public goods. They typically see problems such as the waste of resources or the pollution of the environment as resulting from "market failure." A famous essay along this line is "The Tragedy of the Commons" (1968) by Garret Hardin. The title comes from an illustration Hardin used: a common pasture that is bound to be overgrazed as long as the livestock owners pursue their individual self-interest without coordination. It is in the interest of each owner to allow his livestock to graze as much as possible on the pasture; a herder who holds his flock back will not get any benefit because others will simply let their animals graze even more. The herders would like to conserve the pasture but cannot do so without a mechanism to prevent free riding. It is in their interest to limit their own herd's grazing only if they can count on others to do likewise. For more on the tragedy of the commons, see Issues Box 15.1.

Issues Box 15.1

The Tragedy of the Commons

Imagine a grazing area owned in common by 10 ranchers, each of whom uses it to pasture 10 head of cattle. The carrying capacity of the pasture is exactly 100 cattle; that is, with that degree of grazing, the grass can renew itself and the cattle can feed indefinitely.

Now put yourself in the position of one of the owners. If you add one more cow to the commons, you increase your personal herd by 10 percent (10 plus 1). True, you degrade the commons, but only by 1 percent (100 plus 1). The costs of the overgrazing, which will be manifested in diminished grass production, will be borne by all the owners together, whereas you will get all the benefit of selling the additional cow.

Thus you have an incentive to add livestock beyond the pasture's carrying capacity, and so do all the other owners. If all the owners follow their incentives for private gain, the result will be destruction of the commons through overgrazing. With ironical reference to Adam Smith, theorists call this "the back of the invisible hand." In situations of common property, unregulated pursuit of individual interest produces collective loss rather than the common benefit that Smith described in *The Wealth of Nations.*

There are two standard responses to the tragedy of the commons, both of which involve aligning private and collective interest: (1) Privatize the commons and give each owner his or her own little pasture, which they will then have incentives to preserve. (2) Set up a regulatory regime to ensure that owners do not go beyond sustainable limits. Such a regime could be either formal (government) or informal (social pressure), though informal regimes are likely to work only in stable situations where small numbers of people can get to know each other and monitor each other's behaviour.

The parallel with environmental dilemmas should be clear. The atmosphere, rivers, lakes, and seas are like commons with many users. Every polluter can benefit by using these commons as disposal dumps, but if too many people act this way, the volume of waste transcends the carrying capacity of the resource, with consequent degradation. Privatization may work in some situations, such as small lakes, but an authoritative management regime seems required for larger resources such as rivers and oceans.

The metaphor of the tragedy of the commons places environmental issues squarely within the liberal tradition, with its focus on individual action, profit incentives, and enforcement of rights. The remedies that arise within this perspective correspond roughly to the distinction between classical and reform liberalism.

One school of thought, analogous to classical liberalism, is known as **free-market environmentalism.** It argues that the underlying problem in public-goods situations is the failure to assign property rights. There would be no tragedy of the commons if the commons were divided up into individually owned pastures. According to this view, a problem such as air pollution arises because no one owns the atmosphere and thus has an interest in protecting it from degradation. As a result, manufacturers, power producers, drivers of automobiles—indeed, all consumers of goods and services—use the atmosphere as a seemingly free way to get rid of waste products. Free-market environmentalists believe that, while it is not feasible to create literal owners of the atmosphere, a similar result can be achieved by other means. For example, emissions trading (also known as "cap and trade") involves public regulatory authorities issuing licences to emit limited amounts of air pollution, and these licences are subsequently bought and sold in the market. In this way, atmospheric waste disposal acquires a cost, and as a costly good, it leads users to seek ways to economize on it. The market's invisible hand produces the "right" amount of air pollution—that is, the amount that can be absorbed without causing unacceptable deterioration of human amenities.

Free-market environmentalism has become more common in recent years. The European Union Emission Trading Scheme, as an example, is the world's largest greenhouse-gas emissions trading scheme, put in place in 2005. Such programs have been critiqued on a number of fronts, however, including the difficulties associated with setting emissions allowances. Nonetheless, theories of free-market environmentalism have had some success in influencing policymakers to adopt tradable pollution quotas and similar quasi-market devices.

Most environmentalists, however, believe that the tragedy of the commons can be resolved only by government direction. This view, which is closer to reform liberalism, typically leads to legislation that limits or prohibits certain acts—for example, the production of chlorofluorocarbons (which damage the ozone layer) or the use of chlorine compounds in the production of paper. Environmental debates over issues of this type expand the agenda of liberalism but do not fundamentally break with it. They are similar in principle to the myriad other debates going on all the time about whether human purposes are better served by the market or by governmental provision.

Human welfare ecology, however, tends to go beyond the liberal tradition to the extent that it is skeptical about the possibility of unlimited economic growth. Many environmentalists in this camp believe that human population and consumption must be stabilized or even reduced. An excellent example of this kind of thinking is the Kyoto Accord (1997), in which the signatory nations pledged to reduce their production of greenhouse gases, including carbon dioxide, below 1990 levels. Despite a number of international meetings since 1997, and despite broad agreement on the importance of addressing climate change, details on how specifically to implement changes continue to elude any agreements.

An organizing concept for many human welfare ecologists is **sustainable development**, defined as follows in the United Nations' Brundtland Commission Report (1987): "a form of development that meets the needs of the present without compromising the ability of future generations to meet their own needs."[2] The implication

Issues Box 15.2

Global Warming as a Tragedy of the Commons

The high-profile issue of greenhouse gas emissions and climate change is another example of a tragedy of the commons. The earth's atmosphere is a classic example of a commons—used by everyone but owned by no one. Ever since human beings discovered fire, they have discharged into the atmosphere carbon dioxide and other gases that capture heat radiated from the earth's surface. At first this hardly mattered, because the number of human beings and their consumption of fossil-fuel energy were small compared to the immensity of the atmosphere. But with the growth of population and the increase of energy-intensive technology, greenhouse gas emissions have reached the point where they contribute measurably to global warming. Most scientists agree upon the direction of the effect, though there is still much debate over its magnitude and consequences.

Global warming is a particularly difficult tragedy of the commons to deal with because the problem has two levels. Since there is no world government, each of the sovereign states must try to evolve internal policies for restricting the emission of greenhouse gases within its own jurisdiction. This is difficult enough, because it means imposing higher costs on consumers as well as on energy-intensive industries such as manufacturing, mining, and petroleum extraction. But even as a government tries to solve its internal problems by introducing new policies, it has to consider its position in the atmospheric commons. A state that introduced strict carbon regulations on its own would damage the competitiveness of its producers in world markets.

The Kyoto Protocol, negotiated in 1997, was supposed to resolve this dilemma by allowing many states to move together in regulating greenhouse gases, but it fell far short of expectations. Third World countries, including large emitters such as China, India, and Brazil, undertook no obligations, arguing that the problem had been caused by—and should be solved by—the highly industrialized countries of Europe, North America, and Japan. The United States, the world's second-largest single emitter of greenhouse gases behind China, refused to ratify the Kyoto Protocol. Other nations, such as Canada, ratified it but did not live up to their treaty obligations. The only real cuts in carbon emissions were made in countries such as the United Kingdom, Germany, and former Soviet satellites that, for other reasons, were shutting down obsolete smokestack industries.

It remains a difficult and perhaps impossible challenge to get the nearly 200 sovereign states to work together to reduce greenhouse gas emissions for the sake of the global atmospheric commons. If that pessimistic assessment is true, then adaptation to, rather than prevention of, global warming may be the only realistic alternative.

PART 2

of the concept of sustainable development is that the present generation may have to sacrifice its material standard of living for the sake of future generations. This goes beyond the classical liberal confidence in economic growth as well as the reform liberal emphasis on redistributing the results of growth along lines of social justice; it questions the very rationale of growth.

DEEP ECOLOGY

Deep ecology represents a fundamental break with liberalism, and indeed with all other ideologies, because it is "ecocentric"—that is, it posits the entire natural order, not human happiness, as its highest value. As formulated by Arne Naess and George Sessions in 1974, the basic principles of deep ecology are:

1. The well-being and flourishing of human and nonhuman Life on Earth have value in themselves (synonyms: intrinsic value, inherent value). These values are independent of the usefulness of the nonhuman world for human purposes.

2. Richness and diversity of life forms contribute to the realization of these values and are also values in themselves.

3. Humans have no right to reduce this richness and diversity except to satisfy vital needs.

4. The flourishing of human life and cultures is compatible with a substantial decrease of the human population. The flourishing of nonhuman life requires such a decrease.

5. Present human interference with the nonhuman world is excessive, and the situation is rapidly worsening.

6. Policies must therefore be changed. These policies affect basic economic, technological, and ideological structures. The resulting state of affairs will be deeply different from the present.

7. The ideological change is mainly that of appreciating life quality (dwelling in situations of inherent value) rather than adhering to an increasingly higher standard of living. There will be a profound awareness of the difference between big and great.

8. Those who subscribe to the foregoing points have an obligation directly or indirectly to try to implement the necessary changes.[3]

In such an uncompromising form, deep ecology has fewer adherents than less radical environmental belief systems. The uncompromising nature of these beliefs translates into direct, militant, and often illegal action and protest on the part of its adherents, action justified by the need for comprehensive political and social change. Deep ecology groups have included tree-sitting, property damage, tree-spiking, monkey-wrenching, and other forms of ecological sabotage ("ecotage") within their protest repertoire. Earth First!, as an example, was particularly influential in its radical defence of wilderness protection in the

United States in the 1980s, using carefully targeted action on development or logging sites to delay and hopefully end production. The tactics were important for providing activists with a means of displaying their strength of commitment to the cause, referred to as "the logic of bearing witness."[4] Equally important was their ability to impose costs on opponents of the movement, directly, through property damage, or indirectly, through loss of production and sales. Although some deep ecology activists advocate the use of violence and harm to people in defence of the cause, the tactic is not widely adopted and remains a deep source of disagreement among activists.

Another variant of deep ecology is the **animal liberation** movement, which seeks to place the rights of animals on par with those of humans and to end their status as property. Advocates challenge the use of animals for food, in research, for clothing, and in entertainment. An early influential exponent of this movement was the philosopher Peter Singer. In *Animal Liberation* (1975), he argued that any creature that feels pain possesses interests, and all interests ought to be given equal consideration. No animals, he argues, ought to suffer unnecessary pain. Using the ability to suffer as a criterion is still anthropocentric, at least by analogy, since it starts from the human desire to avoid pain and extends it to other species. Others, such as the philosopher Tom Regan, argue that some animals have rights in the same way as humans because they possess cognitive abilities; how we treat them, then, rests on their rights rather than on the degree to which we cause them to suffer. Like the environmental movement more generally, the animal liberation movement includes a number of activist groups, including People for the Ethical Treatment of Animals (PETA) and the more radical Animal Liberation Front. The animal liberation movement has had an impact, made clear by the establishment of guidelines for the ethical treatment of animals on university campuses and the now common practice of prominent labels on cosmetic products informing customers that they were "not tested on animals."

It may be a bit misleading to call deep ecology an ideology, for it is a radical challenge to the civilization that has generated all other ideologies. To the extent that it posits inherent values outside human experience, it has some resemblance to a religious revival; but if deep ecology posits a divinity, it exists in the immanent order of the universe, not in a transcendent god. In fact, deep ecologists are keenly interested in pre-Christian indigenous religious traditions, and they have tried to develop political alliances with indigenous peoples to protest against commercial development of wilderness areas. The alliance, however, is somewhat fragile, because many in Native communities favour commercial development as long as they get an appropriate share of the economic benefits. Aboriginal people, like other sectors of society, are internally divided over environmentalism.

ENVIRONMENTALISM AND POLITICS

One result of the rise of environmentalism as a family of ideologies has been the emergence of environmentalist political parties, usually known as **Green parties.** The first of these parties was the Values Party of New Zealand, founded in 1972. Since that time, a Green party has been founded in virtually every functioning democracy in the world. Although there is variation, Green party programs include a commitment to sustainable governance, grassroots democracy, and social justice.[5]

Green parties find it very difficult to elect representatives in countries such as Canada, the United States, and Great Britain, which use the first-past-the-post method of voting (for a further discussion of electoral systems, see Chapter 25). To date, only one member of a Green party—the federal party leader, Elizabeth May—has ever been elected to Parliament or to a provincial legislature in Canada. The record is slightly better for local offices such as school trustee or city councillor. Green candidates can, however, sometimes affect the outcome by taking away votes from others. Thus Ralph Nader's Green candidacy for president of the United States in 2000 may have cost Democrat Al Gore the election. Gore and his Republican opponent, George W. Bush, received almost exactly the same share of the popular vote, but the 2 percent of the vote that went to Nader would have more likely supported Gore than Bush if the Greens had not run a candidate.

To date, the Greens' biggest success in Canadian politics took place in the British Columbia provincial election of 2001, when they received 12 percent of the vote. The Greens did not win any seats but their share of the vote caused the defeat of NDP candidates in several ridings, with the result that the NDP, which had previously been in power, did not even win enough seats to be recognized as an official party in the legislature. Playing this "spoiler" role is a form of political power, to be sure, but the Greens would undoubtedly much prefer to elect representatives. Thus they went unsuccessfully to court to seek a judicial declaration that the Canadian system of first-past-the-post voting violates the guarantees of equality and political rights in the Charter of Rights and Freedoms. The Greens, perhaps more than any other political party in Canada, stand to profit from a move toward proportional representation. In the meantime, their share of votes in federal elections in Canada has ranged from 3.9 to 6.8 percent in recent years, suggesting a relatively small but consistent support base. Under legislation passed in 2003, parties receiving at least 2 percent of all valid votes qualify for a substantial grant from public funds, crucial for the ability of smaller parties to maintain their presence on the federal scene. However, the Conservative government elected in 2011 is eliminating the per vote subsidy over a three-year period, a decision that will have a significant impact on the Greens.

In countries that do have proportional representation, Green candidates are frequently elected. Green members sit today in the national parliaments of dozens of countries. There has never been a Green government as such, but under certain conditions Greens may participate in a governing coalition, as has happened in Germany, Finland, Ireland, Belgium, and France. The Greens also have a presence—and in the 2010 election once again won enough seats to hold the balance of power—in the Australian Senate, which is elected by a form of proportional representation.

Even more influential than Green political parties have been environmentalist advocacy groups, which have proliferated remarkably over the past three decades. Some of these, such as Greenpeace and Friends of the Earth, have a high media profile and operate around the world. Others, such as the Canadian Parks and Wilderness Society (formerly the National and Provincial Parks Association of Canada), are organized around issues specific to one country and operate mainly within national boundaries. Still others are local in character, having formed around a specific issue such as the location of a garbage dump or the preservation of wetlands.

Some of these Canadian advocacy groups have conducted highly influential political campaigns. An early success was the Greenpeace campaign to get the European Union to ban the sale of seal furs, thus dealing a major setback to the Newfoundland seal hunt. Greenpeace has also been successful in putting pressure on the forest products industry by convincing Europeans that British Columbia's forestry practices are environmentally unsound. And more recently the Alberta oil sands ("tar sands," in the vocabulary of environmentalists) were targeted by American opponents of the Keystone XL pipeline, who saw blocking the pipeline as a key step in preventing oil sands bitumen from coming to market. It is no exaggeration to say that today, virtually any project involving the exploitation of natural resources—mining, forestry, water storage, power generation, highway construction, pipelines—will meet some opposition from international, national, and/or local environmental advocacy groups. Environmentalists are not always successful in such contests, but their presence ensures some degree of environmental scrutiny in the decision-making system.

Even beyond the work of political parties and advocacy groups, perhaps the greatest victory of environmentalism is that it has become entrenched in the everyday machinery of government as well as in public opinion. In Canada as in other countries, older government departments with names such as "Lands and Forests," "Mines," or "Natural Resources" have long ago been folded into departments of the environment. Both legislation and government policy now require environmental reviews of government activities as well as major private-sector developments. Public opinion supports this environmental concern and would be outraged at what were not long ago common practices, such as discharging untreated sewage into rivers, clear-cutting entire mountainsides, and strip mining without reclamation.

Curing such environmental ills costs money—sometimes a great deal of money— but few today would argue that the price is too high. This willingness to pay for higher environmental standards is part of the value shift described earlier as post-materialism. When physical security and a high material standard of living seem assured, voters become more concerned about the quality of life, including the cleanliness and beauty of the physical environment.

Questions for Discussion

1. Can you think of an example from your own experience of the tragedy of the commons, that is, the degradation of a commonly owned resource by users pursuing their own self-interest? Have you personally contributed to a tragedy of the commons? What motivated you to do so?

2. There is much political conflict over national parks in Canada—for example, over the enlargement of ski resorts and town sites. Can you explain how these conflicts illustrate differences among the various forms of environmentalism discussed in this chapter?

3. As a mental experiment, ask yourself how many cents in additional tax you would be willing to pay on a litre of gasoline in order to reduce the consumption of gasoline and therefore reduce the production of greenhouse gases. How much do you think consumers in general would be willing to pay?

Internet Links

1. Canadian Parks and Wilderness Society: **www.cpaws.org**. A Canadian environmental advocacy organization.

2. Ducks Unlimited: **www.ducks.org**. This organization of hunters helps to protect wetlands and improve waterfowl habitat.

3. Friends of the Earth: **www.foei.org**. An international grassroots environmental organization with 70 national member groups and more than 5000 local activist groups on all continents.

4. Global Greens: **www.globalgreens.org**. A network of the world's Green parties and political movements.

5. Greenpeace International: **www.greenpeace.org**. The world's highest-profile environmental organization. Includes links to national Greenpeace organizations.

6. International Union for Conservation of Nature: **www.iucn.org**. A mainstream environmental organization with more than 1000 member organizations in more than 140 countries.

Further Reading

Bailey, Ronald. *Earth Report 2000: Revisiting the True State of the Planet*. New York: McGraw-Hill, 2000.

Bliese, John Ross Edward. *The Greening of Conservative America*. Boulder, CO: Westview Press, 2002.

Conca, Ken, and Geoffrey D. Dabelko, eds. *Green Planet Blues: Four Decades of Global Environmental Politics*. 4th ed. Boulder, CO: Westview Press, 2010.

Dobson, Andrew. *Green Political Thought*. 4th ed. New York: Routledge, 2007.

Doherty, Brian. *Ideas and Actions in the Green Movement*. New York: Routledge, 2002.

Drengson, Alan, and Yuichi Inoue. *The Deep Ecology Movement: An Introductory Anthology*. Berkeley, CA: North Atlantic Books, 1995.

Dunn, James R. *Conservative Environmentalism: Reassessing the Means, Redefining the Ends.* Westport, CT: Quorum, 1996.

Ehrlich, Paul R. *Betrayal of Science and Reason: How Anti-environmental Rhetoric Threatens Our Future.* Washington, DC: Island Press, 1996.

Gore, Albert. *An Inconvenient Truth: The Planetary Emergence of Global Warming and What We Can Do about It.* New York: Rodale, 2006.

Gottlieb, Roger S. *The Ecological Community: Environmental Challenges for Philosophy, Politics and Morality.* New York: Routledge, 1997.

Lomborg, Bjorn. *The Skeptical Environmentalist: Measuring the Real State of the World.* Cambridge: Cambridge University Press, 2001.

Parson, Edward A., ed. *Governing the Environment: Persistent Challenges, Uncertain Innovations.* Toronto: University of Toronto Press, 2001.

Van Nijnatten, Debora, and Robert Boardman, eds. *Canadian Environmental Policy and Politics.* 3rd ed. Toronto: Oxford University Press, 2009.

PART 2

PART 3

FORMS OF
GOVERNMENT

CHAPTER 16

Classification of Political Systems

The review of ideologies completed in Part Two leads naturally to a study of forms of government. Ideologies are not just abstract ideas; they reflect the experience of people who live under one form of government or another. This experience may express itself ideologically as acceptance of a governmental form or as rejection of it, or as a combination—partial acceptance, with proposals for modification. Also, as Marx saw, ideology is at least in part determined by the social milieu, in which government is an important factor. Finally, ideology is a determining factor of government because it establishes goals toward which people strive. For example, liberals try to fashion governmental machinery to enhance individual freedom, however they may define it, while socialists enhance the power of the state through central planning and the nationalization of industry. All this means that government and ideology are reciprocally related—each causes and is caused by the other. Part Three of this book examines the chief forms of government in relation to the ideological climate as it is emerging in the early twenty-first century.

Before one can understand a complicated set of facts, one must be able to classify them—to sort them into groups based on their position along some dimension. This process of organizing factual information about governmental systems produces broad schemes of classification usually known as **typologies.** Once such typologies are formed, one can formulate and test generalizations about the similarities and differences among the various categories.

THE CLASSICAL TYPOLOGY

One of the oldest, and still useful, typologies of government dates back to the founders of political science, Plato and Aristotle. They classified governments with two questions in mind: "Who rules?" and "In whose interest?" Possible answers to the first question were simple: rule may be exercised by a single person, by a minority ("the few"), or by a majority of the whole people ("the many"). The second question, concerning whose interests are served, is more difficult and requires a longer answer.

Figure 16.1   Platonic/Aristotelian Typology of Government

HOW IS RULE CONDUCTED?

	LAWFUL (in the common good)	LAWLESS (in private interest)
ONE	MONARCHY	TYRANNY
FEW	ARISTOCRACY	OLIGARCHY
MANY	POLITY (constitutional democracy)	DEMOCRACY

WHO RULES?

Plato held that there are two basic ways in which rule may be conducted: lawfully and lawlessly. Either the governors are bound by constitutional rules that they are not free to set aside, or they rule according to unchecked whims and emotional desires. The first possibility corresponds to what we have called the rule of law, the second to the arbitrary rule of individuals. In the words of Aristotle,

> He who bids the law rule may be deemed to bid God and Reason alone rule, but he who bids man rule adds an element of the beast; for desire is a wild beast, and passion perverts the minds of rulers, even when they are the best of men. The law is reason unaffected by desire.[1]

Aristotle added that rule by law is in the general interest of the entire community, whereas arbitrary rule represents exploitation of the ruled for the special interest of the governors. He also pointed out that rule in the common interest tends to be seen as legitimate and gives rulers authority that the ruled will obey voluntarily, while selfish government does not seem legitimate to those who are oppressed and therefore has to be sustained by coercion and fear. In sum, we have two kinds of regimes: lawful authority seeking the common good, and lawless coercion seeking private interest. Combining these two dimensions of *who* and *how* yields a six-fold typology, illustrated in Figure 16.1.

A **monarchy** for Plato and Aristotle was a regime in which sovereign authority was vested in one person who ruled within the laws of the *polis*. Its corrupt counterpart was a **tyranny,** in which one person ruled arbitrarily. An **aristocracy** was a system in which political power was held by a restricted class—usually the wealthy and those of noble ancestry—that ruled in the general interest under law. An **oligarchy,** in contrast, was a regime where the wealthy minority used its power to exploit and oppress the impoverished majority. **Democracy,** in the Greek sense of the term, was also an exploitative form of government, in the sense that the many used their political power to obtain for themselves the wealth of the rich—a majority oppressing a minority. It was the rule of the common people unchecked by legal restraints. The positive counterpart of democracy was **polity,** which today we might call constitutional democracy. The word *polity* is derived from *politeia,* the Greek word for "constitution." It expresses the idea that the rule of the many is good only if it is exercised within a fixed constitutional framework that prevents the majority from oppressing minorities. It represents the balance of public and private interests through the political process.

This raises a more general point: to the Greek philosophers, democracy, or popular government, was not necessarily a good thing. They considered any lawful regime preferable to any lawless one. The question of numbers, though not unimportant, was secondary in their minds to the question of lawfulness. This insight—that who rules is less important than how rule is conducted—is sometimes obscured because of the modern habit of regarding democracy as something good in itself. Plato and Aristotle would have said that while a polity or constitutional democracy is a good form of government, unchecked democracy is mob rule, little different in principle from tyranny or oligarchy. The nineteenth-century writers Alexis de Tocqueville and John Stuart Mill made the same point when they expressed fear that democracy could become a "tyranny of the majority."[2]

Plato and Aristotle left us a body of thought that emphasizes the rule of law—yet, paradoxically, Plato believed there was an even higher form of rule. In his famous book *The Republic* he sketched the ideal of rule by a **philosopher-king,** a man so pre-eminent in wisdom and moral virtue that he could rule by personal judgment rather than by the constraint of law. He would not be arbitrary or oppressive because his philosophic wisdom would protect him from the temptations of power. The people would consent to this form of rule because it would be in their own interest.

Plato never completely renounced his belief in the philosopher-king, but he became rather pessimistic about the possibility of finding such a man. In a later dialogue, *The Statesman,* he suggested that the rule of law was an acceptable second-best alternative in the absence of a philosopher-king. And in his last work, *The Laws,* the philosopher-king is nowhere to be found. Thus Plato, along with his pupil Aristotle, came to see the rule of law as the best political solution likely to be attained by imperfect human beings. Rule of law is second best in terms of what might be imagined but best in terms of what human beings, with their limited knowledge, can probably achieve. Yet the image of the philosopher-king who rules above law in the common good has never ceased to haunt history. Many autocratic regimes claiming superiority to the law have been based on it.

One other important point must be made. Aristotle was always careful to point out that the conflict between the few and the many was as much one of wealth as of numbers, since in practice the many are usually poor relative to the wealthy few. In

PART 3

his view, the besetting vice of democracy was the tendency of the majority to use the state's power to confiscate the property of the wealthy minority. The parallel failing of oligarchy was the desire of the wealthy few to manipulate the laws to bring about easier exploitation of the masses.

Aristotle's preference was for a polity, or constitutional democracy, where the rights of property would be protected by law. In the classical view, polity is a balancing act between two negative governmental forms: democracy and oligarchy. If both the wealthy and the poor, the few and the many, hold a share of power in the state, and if neither faction is supreme, they will check each other. Thus, in a negative way, we come back to the desired situation of the rule of law because the counterpoised factions will watch each other to make sure that neither begins to manipulate the laws to its own advantage. However, Aristotle also pointed out that the balance would probably be unstable if society were polarized into camps of extreme wealth and poverty. It would be best to have a large middle class, as this in a sense would unite numbers and property within itself. Such a class, though not itself rich, would have a stake in protecting the property of the rich—for if the rich could be despoiled, the middle class itself might be next. Aristotle's words have lost none of their wisdom after 2300 years:

> Great then is the good fortune of a state in which the citizens have a moderate and sufficient property; for where some possess much, and others nothing there may arise an extreme democracy, or a pure oligarchy; or a tyranny may grow out of either extreme.[3]

MODERN TYPOLOGIES

The classical typology of the six forms of government was the beginning of political science and is still useful today, but it is not the only approach to classification. Indeed, there can never be a definitive or final typology because classification depends on which aspect of reality we wish to emphasize. As forms of government evolve through history, schemes of classification evolve with them (see Figure 16.2 for a summary of the forms of government). The remainder of Part Three uses three different typologies, which correspond to three aspects of government in our own age.

First, we classify governments according to the relationship between state and society. The three types that appear in this classification are liberal democracies, transitional democracies, and autocracies. Second, we classify governments according to the relationship between the executive and legislative powers of government. The chief distinction here is between parliamentary and presidential systems. Third, we classify governments according to their degree of centralization or decentralization. This was not a major concern of Plato and Aristotle, who thought of government chiefly in the context of the small independent *polis*, but it is a big problem for the large states of modern times. The major types in this context are the unitary state, devolution, federalism, and confederation.

Figure 16.2   Modern Typology of Forms of Government

Basic Forms	Institutions
Liberal-democratic	Parliamentary/presidential/hybrid forms
Transitional democracies	Unitary state/devolution/federalism/ confederation
Autocratic (authoritarian, totalitarian)	

Our three classification schemes are not mutually exclusive; rather, they can be applied together for a multidimensional description of any particular government. Thus Canada would be described as a liberal-democratic, parliamentary, federal state, whereas Cuba would be autocratic, presidential, and unitary. There are inevitably many borderline cases that tend to straddle categories. For example, even though political reforms are underway, Mexico still combines certain aspects of both the liberal-democratic and autocratic forms; France represents a unique combination of parliamentary and presidential systems; and federalism in the former Soviet Union was largely overridden in practice by the overwhelming power of the Communist Party. Also because of the political transitions occurring in many countries today, nation-states can change quickly from one classification to another. For example, Chile moved from an authoritarian military dictatorship to a more liberal-democratic system of government when President Pinochet resigned in 1990. Even though all typologies will involve intermediate or ill-fitting cases, we can use these classifications as a first step in understanding how political systems work.

Questions for Discussion

1. What is the problem with democracy in the Platonic/Aristotelian typology? Can you think of some contemporary examples of the same problem in modern liberal democracies? How have modern liberal democracies tried to handle the problem?

2. What is the benefit of a classification scheme? What are the drawbacks?

3. Why is the scheme devised by Plato and Aristotle no longer fully adequate for classifying the more than 190 nation-states today? Why is it still relevant to the study of political science?

Internet Links

1. *The Economist:* **www.economist.com**. The Internet version of the famous magazine. An excellent source of current information on governments all over the world.

2. Nelson Education Political Science Resource Centre: **www.hed.nelson.com/ nelsonhed/catalog.do?courseid=PO01&disciplinenumber=20**. Many links to texts on comparative politics.

3. Organisation for Economic Co-operation and Development (OECD): **www.oecd. org**. Links to information on governments everywhere.

4. Wikipedia, "Government": **en.wikipedia.org/wiki/Government**. An informative article categorizing and defining the many different types of government.

Further Reading

Acemoglu, Daron, and James A. Robinson. *Economic Origins of Dictatorship and Democracy.* Cambridge: Cambridge University Press, 2006.

Almond, Gabriel A., G. Bingham Powell Jr., Kaare Strom, and Russell J. Dalton. *Comparative Politics Today: A Theoretical Framework.* 3rd ed. New York: Longman, 2001.

———. *Comparative Politics Today: A World View.* 9th ed. New York: Longman, 2010.

Andrain, Charles F. *Comparative Political Systems: Policy Performance and Social Change.* Armonk, NY: M. E. Sharpe, 1994.

Blondel, Jean. *Comparative Government: An Introduction.* 2nd ed. London: Prentice Hall, 1995.

Brown, Bernard E., ed. *Comparative Politics: Notes and Readings.* 10th ed. Belmont, CA: Wadsworth Publishing, 2006.

Hague, Rod, and Martin Harrop. *Comparative Government and Politics: An Introduction.* 8th ed. London: Palgrave Macmillan, 2010.

Hauss, Charles, and Miriam Smith. *Comparative Politics: Domestic Responses to Global Challenges, A Canadian Perspective.* Toronto: Nelson, 2000.

Jackson, Robert J., and Doreen Jackson. *Comparative Government: An Introduction to Political Science.* 2nd ed. Scarborough, ON: Prentice Hall, 1997.

Kesselman, Mark, Joel Krieger, and William A. Joseph, eds. *Introduction to Comparative Politics: Political Challenges and Changing Agendas.* 3rd ed. New York: Houghton Mifflin, 2003.

Lane, Ruth. *The Art of Comparative Politics.* Boston: Allyn and Bacon, 1997.

Lijphart, Arend. *Patterns of Democracy: Government Forms and Performance in Thirty-Six Countries.* New Haven, CT: Yale University Press, 1999.

McCormick, John. *Comparative Politics in Transition.* 3rd ed. New York: Harcourt College Publishers, 2001.

Moore, Barrington Jr. *Social Origins of Dictatorship and Democracy: Lord and Peasant in the Making of the Modern World.* Boston: Beacon Press, 1993.

O'Neil, Patrick H., and Ronald Rogowski, eds. *Essential Readings in Comparative Politics*. New York: W. W. Norton, 2009.

Roskin, Michael G. *Countries and Concepts: Politics, Geography, Culture.* 7th ed. Upper Saddle River, NJ: Prentice Hall, 2001.

Shugart, Matthew Soberg, and John M. Carey. *Presidents and Assemblies: Constitutional Design and Electoral Dynamics.* Cambridge: Cambridge University Press, 1992.

Tsebelis, George. *Veto Players: How Political Institutions Work.* Princeton, NJ: Princeton University Press, 2002.

Wilson, Frank Lee. *Concepts and Issues in Comparative Politics: An Introduction to Comparative Analysis.* 2nd ed. Upper Saddle River, NJ: Prentice Hall, 2001.

PART 3

CHAPTER 17
Liberal Democracy

In today's world, virtually every government claims to be democratic, and when we criticize a government, it is often for not being democratic enough. But democracy was not always so popular. Its universal acceptance stems only from the years of World War I, which was fought, in the famous words of the American president Woodrow Wilson, "to make the world safe for democracy." Despite its popularity, democracy is often misunderstood, and in recent years it has suffered from what many now refer to as "democratic malaise."

Democracy in itself is a technique, a way of making certain decisions by privileging the will of the majority. Democracy is characterized as a system that involves those affected by the decisions in the process of making them. In our view, it becomes a legitimate form of government only when it is united with the traditional Western ideals of constitutionalism, rule of law, liberty under law, and the limited state. And, conversely, it is not the only legitimate form of government. Although only a relatively small number of people could vote, aristocratic rule was not always considered oppressive. Our current democratic government carries on British constitutionalism while bringing the common people into the political realm.

The most basic conceptual problem today is that the two dimensions of the *how* and the *who* of government have become blurred in the single term *democracy*. Its current usage suggests not only majority rule but also a condition of freedom in which a limited state respects people's rights. Freedoms of expression, religion, and so on are commonly identified as democratic liberties, though they are not necessarily found in a democracy. To cloud the issue even further, democracy outside the Western world often means government allegedly "for the many" but conducted by a ruling elite, such as a vanguard party or a military **junta** (Spanish for a group of individuals that form a government, especially after a revolution), and that faces few constitutional limitations.

All of this raises so many problems that we will restrict ourselves for the moment to a discussion of Western democracy, which is in itself extremely complex. As one writer has stated,

> In the nineteenth century, democratic government was seen mainly in terms of equality of political and legal rights, of the right to vote, to express differing political opinions and to organize political opinion through political parties, of the right of elected representatives to supervise or control the activities of the government of the day. Today, much more

stress is laid upon the need for the State to guarantee to everybody certain economic and social rights, involving the elimination of educational and social inequalities.[1]

Democracy has now come to imply freedom—encompassing political, economic, and social rights—as well as the rule of the many.

Brief reflection is enough to show that these two dimensions are quite different and that no inevitable connection exists between them. Freedom is made possible by the rule of law, which minimizes arbitrary coercion and maximizes universal submission to equal laws. Yet the rule of the many, as Aristotle saw, may or may not be lawful. Specifically, a majority might take away the property, language, or religious rights of a minority unless the majority itself is restrained by the constitution. Democracy requires freedom only in the limited and partial sense that a certain amount of political freedom is necessary if the people are to choose officials: they must have a chance to nominate candidates, discuss issues, cast ballots, and so on. But beyond this necessary minimum, democracy in other realms of life could be quite oppressive.

For example, in the southern United States, white employers sometimes refused to hire Blacks. And in Canada, employers have sometimes refused to hire Aboriginal people. Such job discrimination can limit freedom in that the denial of a job possibility may be the denial of an opportunity to improve one's life. In most democracies today, the definition of democracy includes the assumption that all individuals have an equal legal right to be considered for employment.

From now on we will use the terms *constitutional* or *liberal democracy* to denote a system in which the majority chooses rulers who must then govern within the rule of law. This is what Plato and Aristotle meant by *polity*. The term *liberal democracy* refers to liberalism in the broadest sense, without distinguishing between classical and reform liberalism. Whatever their disagreements about laissez-faire, redistribution, and government intervention, classical and reform liberals are united in their support of constitutional procedures, the limited state, and a private sphere of personal freedom. Liberal democracy, based on this common ground, is broad enough to encompass different experiments in economic policy. The moderate form of socialism that we have called social democracy is also compatible with liberal democracy as a system of government. The limited amounts of nationalization, central planning, and egalitarianism advocated by social democrats are subordinated to majority rule and respect for constitutional procedure.

Communism, however, was never compatible with liberal democracy. In the people's democracies of Eastern Europe, the Leninist theory of democratic centralism, as converted into the operating philosophy of the communist state, did not allow for political freedom and the right of constitutional opposition. The uncontested elections that were the hallmark of communism in power were sharply different from the practice of liberal democracy. When democratization began in Eastern Europe in 1989, those countries repudiated communism and democratic centralism as quickly as they could. From the West they imported the entire apparatus of liberal democracy, including competitive elections, multiple political parties, an executive answerable to an elected legislature, and an independent judiciary. Based on the historical record thus far, we can say that liberal democracies are not easily transplanted, especially in countries with low economic development or where ethnic and religious interests are strongly entrenched.

Liberal democracy can be briefly defined as a system of government in which the people rule themselves, either directly or indirectly (through chosen officials), but in either case subject to constitutional restraints on the power of the majority. This definition can be expanded through an examination of four operating principles of liberal democracy: equality of political rights, majority rule, political participation, and political freedom. Let us look at these one by one.

EQUALITY OF POLITICAL RIGHTS

Equality of political rights means that every individual has the same right to vote, run for office, serve on a jury, speak out on public issues, and carry out other public functions. Obviously political rights are a matter of degree, and it was only in the twentieth century, when women and ethnic minorities obtained these rights, that full equality was approached in most Western systems. There is no hard and fast rule for determining how much political equality is enough for democracy to exist; that being said, universal adult male suffrage was an important threshold because it broke through the barrier of socioeconomic class. Prior to its introduction, suffrage was limited to a small portion of the population, made up largely of affluent men. Another important breakthrough was the extension of the **franchise** to women, which doubled the electorate.

By these criteria, the United States was the first democracy of modern times. Equality of political rights, however, was not attained all at once because the constitution of 1787 let the individual states determine the franchise. In the first decades of the nineteenth century, the states one by one adopted universal male suffrage, except in the South, where slaves were excluded. The emancipated slaves were theoretically enfranchised after the Civil War, but most were prevented from voting by various tactics until the 1960s. Women received the right to vote in federal elections at a single stroke, through the Nineteenth Amendment (1920).

Great Britain was somewhat behind the United States in providing equality of political rights. At the beginning of the nineteenth century there was still a restrictive franchise that allowed only about 200 000 male property owners to vote in elections for the House of Commons. Reforms in 1832, 1867, and 1884 gradually extended the franchise to include the middle class and the more prosperous elements of the working class. The remaining men, as well as women aged 30 and older, received the vote in 1918; women were granted suffrage on equal terms with men in 1928.

The expansion of the franchise in Canada is more difficult to describe because it was intricately involved in federal-provincial relations. Before 1885, qualifications to vote in parliamentary elections had been determined by the provinces. In that year, Sir John A. Macdonald pushed the uniform Electoral Franchise Act through Parliament, in part because he did not like the tendency of provinces to abolish the property franchise.[2] The Act of 1885 established a moderate property qualification that remained until 1898, when the government of Sir Wilfrid Laurier returned the franchise to the domain of the provinces. Most property qualifications disappeared around that time.

From 1898 to 1917, the provinces controlled the federal franchise but they could not disenfranchise particular groups of people: if people could vote in provincial elections, they could also vote in federal elections. In other words, provinces could not, through legislation, isolate certain groups demographically and deny them the right to vote in federal elections. In the Military Voters Act and the Wartime Elections Act (1917), the federal government was selective in extending and restricting the suffrage. Under the former, all men and women on active service were permitted to vote. Under the latter, conscientious objectors and those of "enemy alien" birth were denied the franchise, while the wives, widows, and female relatives of men overseas were enfranchised.[3] In 1920, with the passage of the Dominion Elections Act, the federal government resumed control of qualifications for voting in federal elections, while qualifications for voting in provincial elections remained the responsibility of provincial governments. In 1918, women aged 21 and older gained the right to vote in federal elections. Provincially, women were first enfranchised in Manitoba, in 1916; not until 1940, however, were they allowed to vote in Quebec.[4] Registered Indians received the federal franchise in 1960, although they had been allowed to vote in some earlier provincial elections.

Although each country's history is unique, the general pattern in the Western world has been a step-by-step extension of the franchise, with universal adult male suffrage being reached at the end of the nineteenth or beginning of the twentieth century. In most countries, women won the vote during or shortly after World War I. Switzerland was one exception: women received the right to vote in that country's federal elections only in 1971, and even later in some cantonal (provincial) elections. Indeed, the men of one laggard canton did not agree to grant the franchise to women until 1989.

Today the franchise could hardly be extended further in most liberal-democratic countries, except by giving it to non-citizens, children, prisoners, those with no fixed address, and the mentally disabled. In Canada this last group received the right to vote at the federal level beginning with the election of 1988. The right of prisoners to vote was reaffirmed in 2002 by the Supreme Court of Canada, when it held that the legislation depriving prisoners of the franchise unjustifiably conflicted with Section 3 of the Canadian Charter of Rights and Freedoms, which states that "every citizen has the right to vote in an election of members of the

PART 3

House of Commons or of a legislative assembly."[5] We have virtually reached the end of a process that has transformed the vote from a trust exercised by property owners or heads of families into a universal right of adult citizens.

MAJORITY RULE

Majority rule is the normal working principle of decision-making in democracies. It can be derived logically from the prior principle of political equality. If each vote is to be counted equally, the decision of the majority must be accepted because any other procedure would inevitably weigh some votes more heavily than others.

Yet in some circumstances democracies depart from majority rule. Election to public office in Canada, Britain, and the United States is normally by **plurality** rather than **majority.** In these systems, the winning candidate need only obtain more votes than any other candidate, even if the number fails to reach the "50 percent plus one" requirement for a majority. The plurality criterion is both simple and efficient. If candidates for office were always required to receive a majority, there would have to be an expensive series of runoffs to reduce the candidates to two; only then could it be guaranteed that a plurality would also be a majority of votes cast. In fact, some countries—France, for example—do employ runoff elections. The French president must receive an absolute majority of votes cast, which in practice means a two-stage election.

The majority requirement is also sometimes raised (for example, to three-fifths or two-thirds or three-fourths) in what is known as a **qualified majority.** This is done to protect the rights of minorities. Because a qualified majority is obviously harder to obtain than a simple majority, it becomes more difficult for larger groups to act against the rights of smaller ones.

The qualified majority, while a constraint upon democracy, is within the spirit of the rule of law. It is incorporated into most modern democracies as part of the process of constitutional amendment, on the assumption that the fundamental laws of the state are so important that more than a simple majority should be required to alter them. A constitutional amendment in the United States, after being passed by two-thirds of the members of the Senate and the House of Representatives, must then be ratified by three-fourths of the states. In Canada, amending most parts of the Constitution requires ratification by the Senate, the House of Commons, and the legislative assemblies of "at least two-thirds of the provinces that have, in the aggregate, according to the latest general census, at least fifty per cent of the population of all the provinces." On certain matters of fundamental importance, such as recognition of the monarchy, the consent of all provinces is required.[6] The requirement of **unanimity** offers the greatest protection for minorities because then no one could be required to do anything against their will. But the practical task of getting unanimous agreement is so formidable that it is seldom used in political systems. Balancing majority and minority rights remains one of the major challenges in a democratic system of government.

POLITICAL PARTICIPATION

Democratic institutions are founded on mass participation. The two great varieties of democracy, which differ in the nature of this participation, are **direct democracy**, the only kind known to the ancient world, and **representative democracy** (or indirect democracy, as it is sometimes called), the predominant form in modern times.

The city-states of Greece practised direct democracy. The highest authority was the assembly of all male citizens (slaves were not citizens and could not vote). Executive officers were either elected by this body or chosen by lot—a random procedure that was considered superbly democratic because it gave everyone an equal chance of being selected to serve. In either case, terms of office were very short—usually a year or less. Citizens were paid to hold office and even to attend assembly meetings so that poverty would not prevent participation.

Assembly-style direct democracy faces two obvious problems. One involves the practical difficulty of assembling more than a few thousand individuals to discuss public issues. If direct democracy was just barely possible in the Greek city-state, how could it exist in the modern nation-state, which is so much larger? The other problem concerns the quality of decisions made at large meetings, where emotional rhetoric and appeals to prejudices, emotions, and fears can easily sway votes. The democracy of Athens destroyed itself by enthusiastically voting for a disastrous military campaign against Syracuse. The best minds of antiquity, including Plato and Aristotle, were so unimpressed with direct democracy in action that they turned decisively against it.[7]

Representative democracy tries to address both problems. It overcomes the obstacles of population and distance while providing the means for choosing rulers whose talents are presumably superior to those of the people at large. These rulers are kept in check and directed by the majority through the machinery of elections. A ruler elected for life would be effectively insulated from the popular will. This is why democracy requires regular elections that those in power cannot indefinitely postpone: to ensure the accountability of government to its citizens.

The rationale behind representative government was clearly stated in 1825 by James Mill, the first important political philosopher to argue in favour of what we would today call democracy. "The people as a body," he wrote, "cannot perform the business of government for themselves."[8] What was required, he continued, was the creation of a system of "checks" that would induce rulers to act for the general benefit. Representatives elected by the community for a limited period of time would provide those checks.

PART 3

It cannot be emphasized too strongly that democratic elections do not and cannot decide questions of policy. Citizens vote for representatives but do not make policy decisions; elected representatives make those decisions for the society. Citizens probably agree with some opinions of their favourite candidates and disagree with others. Also, neither voters nor candidates can be sure of what the future will bring. Politicians are notorious for breaking campaign promises, not because they are especially dishonest but because things may look different a year or two after the election, particularly when seen from the perspective of public responsibility. Elections are much more a judgment on recent policies than a decision about the future. If voters are dissatisfied with the past record of the incumbent government, elections provide an opportunity for installing another party in power.

Many contemporary critics of representative democracy focus on the idea that elected officials have their own political agendas and disregard the wishes of the public. Such critics advocate a move toward some form of direct democracy, or at least more public involvement in the policy-making process. One way to do this would be to institutionalize direct-democratic practices such as the referendum, the initiative, and the recall.

In a **referendum,** electors are asked to vote directly on a constitutional amendment, piece of legislation, or other policy proposal. Some authors use the term **plebiscite** for a nonbinding, advisory referendum,[9] but we will not follow this usage because it is not universal. Both binding and nonbinding referendums are common around the world.

Referendums are used frequently in Switzerland at all levels of government and in the United States at the state and local levels. They are required in Australia for the approval of constitutional amendments. All Canadian provinces provide for advisory referendums in some circumstances at the local and provincial level. In the most recent provincial referendum, British Columbians voted to eliminate the Harmonized Sales Tax the province had adopted in 2010 and to reinstate the Provincial Sales Tax. There have been three federal referendums in Canada: one in 1898 on the prohibition of alcohol, one in 1942 to release Prime Minister William Lyon Mackenzie King from his promise not to send conscripted soldiers overseas, and one in 1992 on the Charlottetown Accord.

The British government has used consultative referendums to clear the air on divisive issues. In 1975 the government called a national referendum on membership in the European Economic Community. It was the first ever held in Britain. In 1979, referendums were held in Scotland and Wales as a way of deciding the issue of devolution, a proposal that both rejected. In 1997, however, voters in both Scotland and Wales accepted regional parliaments in referendums held after Tony Blair's Labour Party came to power. Scotland is likely in the near future to hold a referendum on independence.

A second form of direct democracy is the **initiative.** The mechanism is a simple one: if a minimum number of voters sign a petition dealing with a particular issue (the number would be spelled out in legislation), then the government is required to act on it. The required action may be either that the legislative body enact the proposal outlined in the petition or that it submit the proposal to voters in a referendum. A referendum originates in the legislative body and is "referred" to the electorate; in contrast, an initiative moves from the people to the legislature. The recent referendum on the HST in British Columbia took place as a result of a successful initiative drive to have the policy repealed.

Several standard arguments are made against referendums and initiatives: that legislation is too complex, that voters become fatigued when asked to decide too many issues, and that these instruments can be used to restrict the rights of minorities. Of the arguments in favour of direct democracy, the most interesting comes from former Progressive Conservative MP Patrick Boyer, Canada's leading authority on and advocate for referendums. Boyer argues that referendums are particularly useful in a parliamentary system of disciplined parties, where the legislative agenda is controlled by politicians who believe that electoral victory has given them a mandate to legislate as they please.[10]

A third and less common element of direct democracy is the **recall,** which enables voters to remove an elected representative from office.[11] The practice was introduced in the United States at the turn of the century and its purpose was to rid constituencies of representatives controlled by "political machines" (party organizations dominated by a few backroom leaders). Provisions for recall usually require a petition signed by a substantial number of voters, and a successful recall vote requires at least a simple majority of those voting. These provisions are designed to protect representatives from a minority of voters who may not like a particular stand. Recall is used in some cities and states in the United States, though less frequently today than in the 1920s. In 2003, California voters recalled Governor Gray Davis and replaced him with Arnold Schwarzenegger; Davis was only the second governor ever to be successfully recalled in the United States.

Venezuela is the only country where the head of the national government is subject to recall. The procedure was tested in 2004 with a recall campaign against President Hugo Chávez, who was considered by his opponents to be too left-wing and too close to Cuban leader Fidel Castro. Only 42 percent voted to recall President Chavez, so he remained president.

In Canada there is less support for a recall mechanism than for other forms of direct democracy. At the present time only the province of British Columbia has recall legislation, which came into effect in 1995. Since then, 20 recall petitions have been issued but none has been successful. This is partly because of the high bar set for success: the applicant has 60 days to obtain the signatures of 40 percent of registered voters in the previous election in the member's electoral district. The recall may be a fine idea in the United States, where elected officials serve fixed terms and are judged as individuals because party discipline is weak or nonexistent. But in a parliamentary system such as Canada's, elected officials are members of a team that functions collectively—the cabinet and caucus in the case of the government, the caucus in the case of the opposition.

PART 3

Today, public opinion polls also play an important advisory role in all democratic countries. An enthusiast for direct democracy will periodically remind us that it is now technically possible to connect all citizens electronically and let them decide questions of public policy. But even if such a nonstop referendum were possible, it is doubtful that it would be a good idea. Complex questions of public policy need the attention and deliberation of informed minds, and both legislators and the public need time to digest various views. Representative democracy is not just a second-best substitute for direct democracy, made necessary by the size of modern states; rather, it is a mechanism for seeking the consensus that is essential to good government. However, direct-democratic devices could be a useful supplement when such wisdom does not emerge from representative institutions.

Democratic participation involves far more than the election of representatives. It also involves influencing government policy, either through public debate or by making submissions to elected representatives. Governments today often consult extensively with the public before passing major legislation. A general policy statement may be published, followed by a draft of the statute. Often there are public hearings at which interested parties express their views. In fact, participation has expanded so much in recent years, particularly at the level of local government, that it is sometimes seen as unduly slowing decision-making and offering too much influence to vocal and well-organized minorities.

Even when they possess a strong parliamentary majority, governments will occasionally withdraw or modify policy proposals in the face of public criticism. Public participation and consultation is now an ongoing process in democratic government. Elections punctuate the process, and when governments are not responsive, voters use their votes to try to bring about a change in government.

Access to the decision-makers is a major problem in contemporary democracies; this issue will be discussed in more detail in Part Four. Critics of democracy say that powerful interests dominate the political process and that groups more marginal to the system have difficulty influencing decisions. For example, women's and environmental groups claim they have been shut out of the process in the past. The existence of elections as open contests at least offers a possibility—but not the certainty—that marginalized groups will be able to exert more influence on decision makers.

POLITICAL FREEDOM

Meaningful participation is possible only if political freedom prevails. Limited participation or directed mobilization of the masses is characteristic not of genuine democracy but of totalitarian pseudo-democracy. An infallible test for political freedom is the legitimacy of opposition: freedom is meaningful only if it extends

Brenda O'Neill

Democratic participation can sometimes take more unconventional forms, including demonstrations, protests, and occupation. The worldwide Occupy movement, shown here in Galway, Ireland, for example, targeted economic and social inequality and used as its political slogan "We are the 99%," referring to the concentration of wealth among the top 1 percent of income earners. To bring attention to the issue, protesters set up camps in public spaces.

PART 3

to those whose opinions differ from the opinions of those in authority. Freedom only to agree is no freedom at all. If freedom does not exist, public support or opposition can only be speculative, and this uncertainty can be very convenient for manipulative rulers. At the same time, the opposition in a liberal democracy must operate within the rule of law. When it resorts to unlawful means—for example, terrorist acts or plotting an insurrection—its actions are not compatible with political freedom in a liberal democracy.

Political freedom has numerous aspects: the right to speak freely, even to criticize the government; the right to form associations, including political parties that may oppose the government; the right to run for office; and the right to vote without intimidation and to choose from a slate of at least two candidates. Without these rights, democracy might be "for the people" but it is certainly not "by the people."

Extensive and important as it is, political freedom is only one aspect of the range of personal freedoms. For instance, it does not include the right to own property or to use one's chosen language. It is quite possible for very wide political freedom to coexist with, and even be the cause of, reduced freedom in other areas. An example can be taken from Quebec: all citizens have full political freedom in that province, but businesses have been restricted by legislation from posting signs in languages other than French. In 1989 the provincial government used its override power, as provided by Section 33 of the Canadian Charter of Rights and Freedoms, to reinstate its language legislation after the Supreme Court of Canada ruled that the law violated the freedom of expression guaranteed by the Charter.[12] Both the legislation and the use of the "notwithstanding clause" (as Section 33 is often called) were and remain popular with the francophone majority in Quebec. In this instance, a majority used its political freedom to reduce the linguistic freedom of minorities.

This example highlights what is sometimes seen as a general problem of liberal democracy. Can law restrain the power of the majority so that it does not use its political freedom to take away other freedoms from minorities? The tension between democracy and the rule of law is illustrated in this passage from Xenophon, a pupil of Socrates. It had just been proposed to the Athenian assembly—the democratic gathering of all male citizens—that certain alleged enemies of the regime be arrested:

> Great numbers cried out that it was monstrous if the people were to be prevented from doing whatever they wished ... Then the Prytanes [the executive committee of the assembly], stricken with fear, agreed to put the question [to a vote]—all of them except Socrates ... he said that in no case would he act except in accordance with the law.[13]

Socrates was ultimately put to death by a democracy that ignored the rule of law and heeded only its own will.

A fear first voiced by Aristotle, and echoed since by countless other writers, is that in a democracy the many would use their political power to expropriate and redistribute the wealth of the few. In the words of John Adams, the second American president, "Debts would be abolished first; taxes laid heavy on the rich, and not at all on the others; and at last a downright equal division of everything be demanded and voted."[14] In fact, the record of liberal democracy does not bear out this gloomy prediction of a dramatic clash of rich and poor.

Political freedom helps to ensure that the interests of citizens are voiced, an important step that provides governments with an ability to remain accountable to them. But political freedom, and more specifically the political participation that it encourages, can be argued to be valuable by itself. One of the values of democracy is that it encourages citizens to participate in the political process and, in so doing, encourages them to develop the skills, knowledge, and tolerance that can enhance their participation and the quality of collective decision-making.

Figure 17.1   Map of Freedom, 2011

Freedom House Map of Freedom 2011

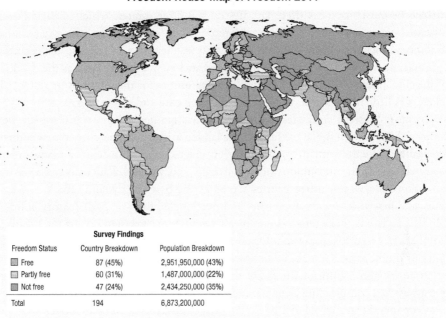

	Survey Findings	
Freedom Status	Country Breakdown	Population Breakdown
Free	87 (45%)	2,951,950,000 (43%)
Partly free	60 (31%)	1,487,000,000 (22%)
Not free	47 (24%)	2,434,250,000 (35%)
Total	194	6,873,200,000

The map of freedom 2011 provides a visual description of the three-category typology of the level of political rights and civil liberties in countries and territories around the world. While a plurality of countries (45 percent) are categorized as free, the majority (55 percent) impose some level of restriction on the rights and liberties of their citizens.

Source: Freedom House, *Freedom in the World 2011* (New York: Freedom House, 2012). Available online at http://www.freedomhouse.org/report/freedom-world/freedom-world-2011.

PROBLEMS OF LIBERAL DEMOCRACY

To paraphrase Winston Churchill, liberal democracy is not the perfect form of government; it is only the least worst. For discussion purposes we will consider two basic problems that have been present since the creation of liberal democracies: elite rule and majority versus minority rights.

Elite Rule

One common, and serious, criticism of liberal democracy is that it is elitist—that democracies are, in effect, ruled by elites and therefore undemocratic. It is true that representative democracy is a form of **elite** rule, if by elite we mean "a minority of the population which takes the major decisions in the society."[15] But to see the place of political elites in modern politics, one must compare them with the elites that were found in the traditional societies of earlier centuries. In the latter, a tiny and interlocking group of families dominated the social, economic, and political life of society. In most instances these families owned large estates, which their children inherited along with all the wealth and responsibilities that went with their status. Traditional societies were highly stratified; that is, there was a large gap between the elite and the masses. This simple dichotomized society was perpetuated as the children of the elite inherited their positions while opportunities for the masses were restricted. There was little if any social mobility between the elite and the masses.

In most Western countries this situation has gradually been transformed. The Industrial Revolution broke the hold of the landed aristocracy and created new sources of wealth and employment; mass education created opportunities for many in the lower classes; guilds and unions helped artisans and workers achieve better working conditions and wages; urban centres served as the base for dynamic marketing systems; and new attitudes about equality and freedom led to more participatory politics. Modern society is characterized more by a large middle class than it is by the polarization between wealth and poverty. Opportunities for education and jobs are extensive, and this promotes social mobility between classes. Politics is charged with new sources of authority and legitimacy. In short, the old dualism of the traditional society has given way to a complex and dynamic modern social order.

Correspondingly, the old idea of a traditional elite was replaced by the concept of pluralism. New elites began to spring up and challenge the agrarian aristocracy. An industrial elite, a commercial elite, a financial elite, a military elite, and even a political elite emerged, and each had a degree of wealth and power that posed a threat to the old guard with its roots in the land. In modern societies, elites have not disappeared; rather, they have become more numerous and more diverse. Many Marxists tend to deny that this change has really affected societies much. They still see a simple dichotomy: the rulers and the ruled. Dualism dominates their frame of reference; except in socialist societies, rulers are thought to exploit the masses. But other observers recognize that modern societies and politics have become pluralistic. The French author Raymond Aron wrote:

> Democratic societies, which I would rather call pluralistic societies, are full of the noise of public strife between the owners of the means of production, trade union leaders and politicians. As all are entitled to form associations, professional and political organizations abound, each one defending its members' interests with passionate ardour. Government becomes a business of compromises.[16]

In democracies, those who aspire to rule must build a power base. The electorate must first choose them; then, if they are to remain in office, their policies must be responsive to the needs of some coalition of groups. Contemporary theorists of democracy emphasize the competition of diverse elites. They suggest that the representative system is an instrument for ensuring that no single elite can attain power unless it reflects the desires of some fraction of the ordinary people. While it is true that powerful groups may monopolize contemporary politics, if elections are working as they were intended, there should be no contradiction between liberal democracy and elite rule.

Majority versus Minority Rights

Liberal democracies operate on the majoritarian principle. Political party nominations, elections to office, and legislative decisions are decided on the basis of a majority vote. But how do minorities fare under majoritarian government? Is it true, as the proponents of liberal democracy claim, that minority rights can be reconciled with majority rule? For example, in a multicultural society, when one or two ethnic groups (or nationalities) occupy a dominant position, can it be guaranteed that the rights of minority cultures will be protected? Can the rights of Native peoples in Canada be protected when they make up less than 4 percent of the total population? How can the rights of cultural minorities such as Chinese or West Indian Canadians, or the political rights of gays and lesbians, be guaranteed when the vast majority of Canadians are of European descent, English- or French-speaking, and heterosexual?

One argument is that all majority and minority rights are protected on the floor of the House of Commons and the Senate. This argument revolves around the assumption that most elected representatives want to be re-elected and so must appeal to a broad coalition of groups in their constituencies. They try not to alienate any voters, and certainly as few as possible if they have to legislate in a way that will alienate any. But the fact remains that winning coalitions need not be, and probably will not be, all-inclusive. Some minorities, particularly small ones, are likely to be left out, which opens up the possibility that an elected assembly could become a "tyranny of the majority" that consistently votes to override minority rights.

A second way of protecting minority rights is through a constitution and the judicial process. Since the passage of the Canadian Charter of Rights and Freedoms in 1982, individual rights for all Canadians have been spelled out in the Constitution. If a legislative assembly is perceived to have violated the rights of a minority, representatives of that minority are entitled to challenge the constitutionality of the legislation in the courts. If members of a legislative assembly choose to ignore the rights of a certain segment of society, the citizens affected have recourse through the courts. While there is no guarantee that court rulings will satisfy either the majority or the minority, the judicial system is another possible venue for reconciling majority rule with minority rights. It is also the case that recourse through the judicial system is a lengthy and expensive undertaking, and, as such, not easily accessible to all.

These classic problems are not the only ones facing liberal democracies today. Powerful interests, political party responsiveness, the influence of the media, voter apathy, representation of the electorate, and the role of the courts are challenges in most current liberal democracies. There is insufficient room in this chapter to discuss these problems individually, so each of these issues will be addressed in chapters on the political process in Part Four.

DIFFERENT PATTERNS OF POLITICS IN LIBERAL DEMOCRACIES

Liberal democracies operate in different ways. For example, within one liberal-democratic system, interest groups such as business organizations, labour unions, or farmers' associations may have a great deal of political **autonomy**—that is, they have freedom to pursue political objectives with little interference from the state. In other liberal-democratic systems, political organizations may be highly restricted in their political activity by a powerful regulatory state. Mexico, prior to political reforms instituted after 1994, is a case in point. These different patterns of politics in liberal democracies can be classified as pluralist, corporatist, or consociational (see Concept Box 17.1).

Different patterns of politics seem to follow particular cultural attributes of societies. For example, politics in the United States, a country with a strong liberal, anti-state tradition, comes close to the pluralist process that Robert Dahl described as polyarchy. In Canada and Great Britain, where elites have played a greater role in the political process, one finds traces of corporatist and consociational thinking and institutions.[17] And, until the late 1990s, in countries such as Mexico and Brazil the corporatist tradition was very strong—to the point that one can rightly ask how democratic these political systems were. The lines of demarcation between political systems can be just as porous as those between political ideologies.

CONTEMPORARY CHALLENGES

Up to this point, our discussion of liberal democracy has been mainly theoretical, with a review of some of the traditional problems encountered in this particular form of government. However, we should not give the impression that all is well with liberal democracies. Any perceptive person today knows that nothing could be further from the truth.

In most of the world's advanced democracies the greatest challenge appears to be what some are calling a **crisis of governability**. The crisis involves the inability of representative governments to respond to the demands of their citizens at a time when their action is most needed. This inability to act has only served to feed a cynicism that was already at significantly high levels, further weakening governmental legitimacy.

Concept Box 17.1

Liberal Democracies

Pluralist

Liberal democracies in which highly autonomous groups compete freely and openly in the political process are labelled **pluralist.** Robert Dahl's term for this pluralist form of liberal democracy is **polyarchy,** which means many different sources of power. For Dahl, "the characteristics of polyarchy greatly extend the number, size, and diversity of the minorities whose preferences will influence the outcome of governmental decision."[18] In a polyarchy, control of the governmental process may change hands frequently as different groups compete for political power.

Features of pluralist liberal democracies include

a. a high degree of autonomy for political interests in society to pursue their political ends;

b. equality of all groups in the political process—ideally, there is a level playing field on which political interests compete; and

c. an absence of monopoly control of government or state power by any one group. The power of groups ebbs and flows with societal conditions as coalitions are accepted or rejected by the voters.

Corporatist

Liberal democracies in which there is a significant lack of autonomy for groups are labelled "corporatist." In the corporatist pattern, the state is the dominant force in society and the activities of all interests in society are subordinate to that force. One of the principal writers on **corporatism**, Philippe C. Schmitter, has defined corporatism as follows:

> Corporatism can be defined as a system of interests representation in which the constituent units are organized into a limited number of singular, compulsory, non-competitive, hierarchically ordered and functionally differentiated categories, recognized or licensed (if not created) by the state and granted a deliberate representational monopoly within their respective categories in exchange for observing certain controls on their selection of leaders and articulation of demands and supports.[19]

Features of corporatist liberal democracies include

a. the components of the political process are arranged in a hierarchy and are not equal;

b. the components have limited autonomy, with the state restricting their actions;

c. competition is limited, in the sense that the various components are not free to compete with each other for political ends;

d. the components in the process are dependent on the state; and

(continued)

PART 3

Concept Box 17.1   *(continued)*

e. the relative power of different components may vary, depending on their relationship to the state.

Consociational

Liberal democracies in which elites and organized interests play a special and distinctive role are labelled "consociational." This form is found in several countries, including the Netherlands, Switzerland, and (to a lesser degree) Canada. Arend Lijphart suggests that the basis for **consociationalism** is a society so sharply divided along linguistic, ethnic, or religious lines that the segments have their own social institutions and live largely apart from one another.[20] The Netherlands is a classic case: although everyone speaks Dutch, the society is divided into Roman Catholic, neo-Calvinist, liberal, and socialist "spiritual families," each of which has its own schools and universities, newspapers and radio and television programs, and labour unions and recreational associations. Switzerland is similarly divided, by language as well as by religion and ideology.

Features of consociational liberal democracies include

a. each social segment has a high degree of autonomy over its internal affairs, particularly language, culture, religion, and education;

b. a rule of proportionality is followed in allocating government jobs, expenditures, and benefits among the segments;

c. all important segments have the power to veto major changes affecting their vital interests; and

d. government is carried on through a "grand coalition" of political representatives of all the main segments.

Although not the cause of the crisis, the financial calamity brought on by the 2008 U.S. sub-prime mortgage collapse, which significantly damaged global money and financial markets, underscored the consequences of changes brought on by increasing **globalization**. While governments in the 1990s focused on fiscal management and **debt** reduction, recent governments have had to balance these goals with more traditional Keynesian responses to the financial crisis. Interventions designed to limit the fallout from rising unemployment levels, to prop up failing industries such as the auto sector, and to bail out financial giants such as the Bank of America and the Royal Bank of Scotland would have been hard to imagine only 10 years earlier. Yet the pressure to return to balanced budgets continues to be felt in order to maintain investor confidence and stave off a drop in credit ratings. Balancing the two has proven especially difficult.

In some states the crisis intensified as a result of the failure of traditional policy levers to have a significant impact. In the United States, a $787 billion 2009 stimulus package may have dulled the effects of the recession, but research suggests that the proportion of people living in poverty grew by 27 percent between 2006 and 2010.[21] Global competition is partly to blame—outsourcing to cheaper labour overseas has meant fewer jobs at home.

In other states, participation in common markets has effectively removed some economic levers from national policy toolkits. Countries that are part of the eurozone, for example, have lost the ability to employ monetary policy to address the financial crisis, having handed it over to a central body. Moreover, the common currency has led to a situation in which governments have had to act to ensure its stability, often in opposition to public opinion. Where citizens of Greece cry out against austerity measures imposed upon it by its eurozone partners to maintain confidence in the euro, citizens of Germany strongly oppose bailing out a country that has practised irresponsible economic management for years.

The crisis of governability also stems from the inability of governments to address policy problems that require a level of cooperation that is increasingly unlikely as more states demand their place at the decision-making table. Globalization has opened up the West and made it economically vulnerable; at the same time, it has provided tremendous opportunities for nation-states in other parts of the world.

> Globalization was supposed to have played to the advantage of liberal societies, which were presumably best suited to capitalize on the fast and fluid nature of the global marketplace. But instead, mass publics in the advanced democracies of North America, Europe and East Asia have been particularly hard hit—precisely because their countries' economies are both mature and open to the world. In contrast, Brazil, India, Turkey and other rising democracies are benefitting from the shift of economic vitality from the developed to the developing world. And China is proving particularly adept at reaping globalization's benefits while limiting its liabilities.[22]

Increased power among a great number of states at very different levels of development has made international cooperation difficult to achieve.

Public reaction to the crisis in the Western world has spawned new political groups and movements and, in some instances, increased political polarization. In the United States, the Tea Party movement argues for reduced government, lower taxes, and reduction of the national debt. In Europe, the rise of nationalist parties, stemming from the European economic crisis and the perceived role of non-Western immigration in feeding the crisis, is evident. In Finland, for example, the True Finns party won 19.1 percent of the vote in the 2011 parliamentary election after campaigning on a platform that included significantly curtailing immigration. Worldwide, the Occupy movement has highlighted social and economic inequality, epitomized by increasing executive wages and company shares in the face of significant corporate financial losses.

In spite of these challenges, however, support for the liberal-democratic system has not wavered. Indeed, the demand for "personal dignity and responsive government" was heard more forcefully in 2011 than at any point in the recent past (see World View 17.1).[23]

PART 3

The Arab Spring

The year 2011 will be remembered for the number of revolutions that took place in the Arab world, now known as the "**Arab Spring**" or "Arab Awakening." Fuelled by a number of factors, the widespread demonstrations and protests that began in January 2011 resulted in governments being overthrown in Tunisia, Egypt, and Libya; in significant governmental change in Yemen and Bahrain; in civil war in Syria; and in more minor governmental change and protest in a number of additional countries in the region.

Epitomized by continued mass protests in Cairo's Tahrir Square in Egypt in January and February, protesters in the region demanded respect for human rights, guarantees of political freedom, and the adoption of democratic and transparent institutions—in short, liberal democracy. What they rejected included dictatorship, government corruption, high unemployment, extreme poverty, rising food prices, and concentration of wealth in the hands of a small elite, with little transparency in its distribution.

A Perfect Storm

Although dissent is not new in the region, the 2011 protests differed in their size, how long they were sustained, and their broad-based popular mobilization of a number of groups, including youth, unions, ethnic and religious groups, women, professionals, and the poor. The latter has been argued to be key to the success of such revolutions.[24] Additional important factors included the loss of elite and military support for the regime and a widespread belief that the government was a threat to the country's future. It was a "perfect storm" of factors that rarely come together; once in place, however, the combined factors are powerful in their effects.

Underlying Causes

A number of key factors have been argued to lie behind 2011's revolutions. One is unprecedented economic growth, but growth employed to enrich the wealthy few rather than the masses. In Tunisia, for example, a U.S. diplomatic cable released by WikiLeaks in 2008 underscored the fact that corruption in President Ben Ali's family had become significant enough to threaten the state's economy. Combined with rising inflation, low wages, and high unemployment among an increasingly educated population, particularly its young adults, the result was opposition that ignited quickly and spread widely.

The "tipping point" in Tunisia appears to have been the death of Mohamed Bouaziz. A young street vendor who worked to support his family, Bouaziz was regularly harassed

World View 17.1

by local police; a particularly humiliating episode in December 2010 led him to set himself on fire outside an official's office, as an act of ultimate desperation. This act and his subsequent death served to galvanize protests, aided by the use of social media such as Facebook.

Governments immediately responded to these protests with violence, increased repression, and intimidation, resulting in numerous casualties, injuries, and arrests. The Egyptian government virtually shut down Internet access for five days in January in an attempt to restrict communication through social media. Such tactics, however, were largely unsuccessful. And not all the protests have been successful. At the time of writing, demonstrations in Syria led to a crackdown on protesters that eventually led to all-out civil war; estimates have placed the number of casualties in the tens of thousands.

Aftermath

The transition to democracy is and will be a long-term process and one that is likely to be hampered by setbacks. Establishing liberal-democratic institutions, and the norms of civil society that underpin them, is slow and painful. And as the Occupy Wall Street protests suggest, opposition and demonstrations are not only instruments of revolution against autocratic regimes but also basic instruments for voicing opposition in liberal democracies.

CONCLUSION

A liberal-democratic political system, then, is one in which, on the basis of universal adult suffrage, citizens select their governors (representatives); these representatives can be changed by the electorate through periodic elections; individual or group opinions can be discussed freely without fear of retaliation by public officials or private individuals; a legal opposition is free to criticize; and an independent judiciary resolves disputes between citizens, between citizens and government, and between levels of government. If this seems excessively long for a definition, that is because it is not easy to characterize in fewer words a form of government that seeks to reconcile freedom with majority rule.

Liberal democracy is an expression of the political experience of the Western world. It is now practised in every country of Western Europe, although Spain and Portugal did not emerge from authoritarian rule until the 1970s, and Greece underwent a period of military dictatorship in the same decade. Liberal democracy is also strongly entrenched in countries that are essentially transplanted European states, for example, Canada, the United States, Australia, New Zealand, and Israel.

PART 3

While liberal democracy is a product of Western European traditions and culture, democrats believe that it can be adopted successfully outside that milieu. Two good examples are Japan and India. Both countries have ancient cultural traditions that are quite distinct from those of Western Europe, yet they have successfully operated reasonable approximations of liberal democracy for more than 50 years. There was an initial period of transplantation, to be sure—during the American occupation in Japan and the British Raj in India—but since those times, liberal democracy has continued successfully on its own. The economic contrast between Japan and India is also significant. Both countries are heavily populated. Japan is now wealthy, with a standard of living similar to Canada's. India, though growing more quickly than before, has a considerable share of its population living below the poverty line and a largely agricultural economy. Nonetheless, and in spite of severe religious differences, it has been able to make liberal democracy function. This shows that a high standard of living is not absolutely vital for liberal democracy to work. It is probably true, however, that it is more likely to succeed in countries where the economy is highly developed.

At the beginning of the twenty-first century there is good reason for optimism about liberal democracies. It still remains true that no two liberal democracies have gone to war against each other. The widespread adoption of democracy may be the best available strategy for reducing conflict in the world. Nevertheless, many analysts still believe that liberal democracies are quite fragile and need to adapt constantly to changing conditions in society. Certainly problems such as human rights, economic inequalities, political alienation, and globalization will provide major challenges for these systems of government. Stand by—politically speaking, the next few decades should be exciting times.

Questions for Discussion

1. How does liberal democracy attempt to reconcile majority and minority rights? In your opinion, have these mechanisms been successful? Can you think of situations in liberal democracies where majority rights have trumped minority rights? How about where minority rights have trumped majority rights?

2. What are the responsibilities of citizens in liberal democracies? If you had to choose one, what responsibility would you say is most important to the maintenance of liberal democracy?

3. Which constitutional devices do you see as providing the most effective protection for minority rights? Are constitutional devices themselves sufficient for minority rights protection? What else might be needed?

Internet Links

1. Center for Voting and Democracy: **www.fairvote.org**. An American centre that emphasizes elections, voting rights, and electoral systems.

2. Freedom House: **www.freedomhouse.org**. Annual rankings of all nations of the world on indicators of freedom and democracy.

3. International IDEA (Institute for Democracy and Electoral Assistance): **www.idea .int**. An intergovernmental organization promoting and supporting democracy around the world.

4. World Movement for Democracy Network of Democracy Research Institutes: **www.wmd.org**. This website is a gateway to centres for the study of democracy all over the world.

Further Reading

Ajzenstat, Janet. *The Once and Future Canadian Democracy: An Essay in Political Thought.* Montreal and Kingston: McGill-Queen's University Press, 2003.

Alexander, P. C. *The Perils of Democracy.* Bombay: Somaiya Publications, 1995.

Bachrach, Peter. *The Theory of Democratic Elitism.* Rev. ed. Washington, DC: University Press of America, 1980.

Banting, Keith, Thomas J. Courchene, and F. Leslie Seidle, eds. *Belonging? Diversity, Recognition and Shared Citizenship in Canada.* Montreal: IRPP, 2007.

Barney, Darin. *Communication Technology.* Vancouver: University of British Columbia Press, 2005.

Brooks, Stephen. *Canadian Democracy: An Introduction.* 7th ed. Toronto: Oxford University Press, 2011.

Cain, Bruce E., Russell J. Dalton, and Susan E. Scarrow, eds. *Democracy Transformed.* Toronto: Oxford University Press, 2004.

Dahl, Robert A. *On Democracy.* New Haven, CT: Yale University Press, 1998.

———. *Polyarchy: Participation and Opposition.* New Haven, CT: Yale University Press, 1971.

Dalton, Russell J. *Democratic Challenges, Democratic Choices.* Toronto: Oxford University Press, 2004.

Downs, Anthony. *An Economic Theory of Democracy.* New York: Harper and Row, 1957.

Eagles, Munro, Christopher Holoman, and Larry Johnston. *The Institutions of Liberal Democratic States.* Peterborough, ON: Broadview Press, 2004.

Elshtain, Jean Bethke. *Democracy on Trial.* Concord, ON: House of Anansi, 1993.

Esposito, John L. *Islam and Democracy.* New York: Oxford University Press, 1996.

Fischer, Mary Ellen. *Establishing Democracies.* Boulder, CO: Westview Press, 1996.

Fishkin, James S. *The Voice of the People: Public Opinion and Democracy.* New Haven, CT: Yale University Press, 1995.

PART 3

Giddens, Anthony. *The Third Way and Its Critics*. Cambridge, UK: Polity Press, 2000.

Held, David. *Models of Democracy*. 3rd ed. Cambridge, UK: Polity Press, 2006.

Keane, John. *Democracy and Civil Society*. London: Verso, 1988.

Klosko, George. *Democratic Procedures and Liberal Consensus*. Toronto: Oxford University Press, 2004.

Kymlicka, Will. *Multicultural Citizenship: A Liberal Theory of Minority Rights*. Oxford: Clarendon Press, 1995.

Lijphart, Arend. *Democracy in Plural Societies*. New Haven, CT: Yale University Press, 1977.

———. *Patterns of Democracy: Government Forms and Performance in Thirty-Six Countries*. New Haven, CT: Yale University Press, 1999.

Mackie, Gerry. *Democracy Defended*. Toronto: Cambridge University Press, 2003.

Manji, Irshad. *Risking Utopia: On the Edge of a New Democracy*. Vancouver: Douglas & McIntyre, 1997.

March, James G., and Johan P. Olsen. *Democratic Governance*. New York: Free Press, 1995.

Mouffe, Chantal. *Democracy and Pluralism: A Critique of the Rationalist Approach*. Toronto: Faculty of Law, University of Toronto, 1995.

Parry, Geraint. *Political Elites*. London: George Allen and Unwin, 1969.

Pateman, Carole. *Participation and Democratic Theory*. Cambridge: Cambridge University Press, 1970.

Plattner, Mark F. *Democracy Without Borders? Global Challenges to Liberal Democracy*. Lanham, MD: Rowman & Littlefield, 2008.

Sartori, Giovanni. *The Theory of Democracy Revisited*. Part 1, *The Contemporary Debate*. Chatham, NJ: Chatham House, 1987.

———. *The Theory of Democracy Revisited*. Part 2, *The Classical Issues*. Chatham, NJ: Chatham House, 1987.

Turner, Stephen P. *Liberal Democracy 3.0: Civil Society in an Age of Experts*. Thousand Oaks, CA: Sage, 2003.

Unger, Roberto Magabeira. *Democracy Realized: The Progressive Alternative*. New York: Verso, 1998.

Watson, Patrick, and Benjamin R. Barber. *The Struggle for Democracy*. Toronto: Key Porter, 2000.

Corporatism

Cawson, Alan. *Corporatism and Political Theory*. New York: Basil Blackwell, 1986.

———. *Organized Interests and the States: Studies in Meso-corporatism*. London: Sage, 1992.

Harrison, Reginald James. *Pluralism and Corporatism: The Political Evolution of Modern Democracies*. London: George Allen and Unwin, 1980.

Wiarda, Howard J. *Civil Society: The American Model and Third World Development*. Boulder, CO: Westview Press, 2003.

———, ed. *New Directions in Comparative Politics*. 3rd ed. Boulder, CO: Westview Press, 2002.

Wilensky, Harold, and Lawell Turner. *Democratic Corporatism and Policy Linkages: The Interdependence of Industrial, Labour Market, Incomes and Social Policies in Eight Countries*. Berkeley, CA: University of California Press, 1987.

Williamson, Peter J. *Corporatism in Perspective: An Introductory Guide to Corporatist Theory*. London: Sage, 1992.

Ziegler, L. Harman. *Pluralism, Corporatism and Confucianism: Political Associations and Conflict Resolution in the United States, Europe and Taiwan*. Philadelphia: Temple University Press, 1988.

Consociationalism

Lamy, Steven Lewis. *Consociationalism, Decentralization and Ethnic Group Equalization: The Case of Constitutional Engineering in Belgium*. Ann Arbor: University of Michigan Press, 1980.

Lijphart, Arend. *The Politics of Accommodation: Pluralism and Democracy in the Netherlands*. 2nd ed. Berkeley: University of California Press, 1975.

McRae, Kenneth Douglas, ed. *Consociational Democracy: Political Accommodation in Segmented Societies*. Toronto: McClelland & Stewart, 1974.

PART 3

CHAPTER 18
Transitions to Democracy

The collapse of the Soviet bloc and the fall of dictatorships in the Third World allowed democracies to proliferate around the globe. In his book *The Third Wave*,[1] the late Samuel P. Huntington argued that we are in the midst of the third great epoch, or "wave," of world democratization, which began in 1974 with the fall of the military regime in Portugal. Larry Diamond, one of the foremost analysts on political transitions, summarized the situation in the mid-1990s:

> Since April of 1974, when the Portuguese military overthrew the Salazar/Caetano dictatorship, the number of democracies in the world has multiplied dramatically. Before the start of this global trend, there were about forty democracies. The number increased moderately through the late 1970s and early 1980s as several states experienced transitions from authoritarian rule (predominantly military) to democratic rule. In the mid-1980s, the pace of global democratic expansion accelerated markedly. By the end of 1995, there were as many as 117 democracies or as few as 76, depending on how one counts.[2]

At the turn of this century, Freedom House data also furnished grounds for optimism. In 1974, at the beginning of the third wave, their "Annual Survey of Freedom Country Ratings" classified 33 of 146 nations (22 percent) as free. At the end of 2003, 88 of 192 carried the same classification (46 percent), 55 countries were rated as partly free (29 percent), and 49 countries were rated as not free (25 percent).[3] Their classification of *free* designates a system of government that this book would categorize as a constitutional or liberal democracy.

Today, however, analysts are more cautious. In their 2011 report on 194 countries, Freedom House noted that this was the fifth consecutive year in which "global freedom suffered a decline." In their classification, 87 countries were rated as free (45 percent), 60 partly free (31 percent), and 47 not free (24 percent).[4] Thus the momentum in favour of democracy has slowed considerably. This levelling off of the trend line has many political observers concerned. Larry Diamond, in a 2008 article titled "Democracy in Retreat," says:

> celebrations of democracy's triumph are premature. In a few short years, the democratic wave has been slowed by a powerful authoritarian undertow, and the world has slipped

into a democratic recession. Democracy has recently been overthrown or gradually stifled in a number of key states, including Nigeria, Russia, Thailand, Venezuela, and most recently Bangladesh and the Philippines.[5]

Diamond argues that in much of the developing world, abuses of power, corruption, nepotistic political parties, inaccessible judiciaries, contempt for the rule of law, and electoral malpractice have led to "predatory states" in which "the purpose of government is not to generate public goods, such as roads, schools, clinics and sewer systems [but] to produce private goods for officials, their families, and their cronies."[6]

This observation gives rise to a series of questions. Why is it so difficult to build democracies throughout the world? In the transition process, what are those institutions and practices that enhance democratization? And what are the hurdles that impede democratization? After all, most people prefer democracies; in fact, there is plenty of consensus on what democracies have to offer:

> Theorists of democracy have long noted its capacity for peaceful transitions of power and for removing many of the conditions that give rise to violent revolution. It provides for periodic changes in government which effectively prevent a given majority or group of political elites from remaining in power for too long a period.[7]

But the process of democratization is very complex. A major study of this complexity can be found in Francis Fukuyama's book *The Origins of Political Order*. Planned to be a two-volume work, its first volume was published in 2011. In it he suggests that a liberal democracy "is more than majority voting in elections; it is a complex set of institutions that restrain and regularize the exercise of power through law and a system of checks and balances."[8] The three categories of institutions to which he refers are the state, the rule of law, and accountable government.[9] The state must have the power to protect its citizens from threats within society as well as threats from other states. At the same time this state power must be limited rather than absolute. Limitations on power are found in the rule of law and accountability.

This model of liberal democracies is anything but simple. For example, Fukuyama notes: "Political institutions develop, often slowly and painfully, over time, as human societies strive to organize themselves to master their environments."[10] And the successful liberal democracy "combines all three sets of institutions in a stable balance. The fact that there are countries capable of achieving this balance constitutes the miracle of modern politics."[11] The remainder of this chapter deals with some of the more important factors, both positive and negative, involved in the transition to democracy.

PART 3

ENHANCING DEMOCRATIC TRANSITIONS

Constitutions and the Rule of Law

In Part Two we spoke of limited government as a component of classical liberalism, but it is also a fundamental principle of all good government. No government's powers should be absolute. Checks and balances have become an essential component of all democratic systems of government. Parliaments must answer to the people, cabinets and prime ministers must answer to parliament, and the laws of parliament are subject to review by the courts. These limitations on governments are enshrined in the constitution and in the concept of the rule of law, underscoring the fact that politicians and governmental officials are not above the law as spelled out in a constitution. The principle of *habeas corpus* is an example of limitations placed on governments by the rule of law: government officials cannot incarcerate individuals and leave them to languish in prison; they must be charged and tried in the courts or released.

In other words, the constitution provides the rules of the game for governing. It provides for justice and equity in the system, and it provides for freedom of the individual, human rights, and the opportunity to participate as citizens in the political process. Living within these limitations is difficult for many political leaders and does not simply occur automatically. The Russian experience in the post-Soviet period is a case in point. Peter Frank notes that in the Soviet Empire (and earlier, in czarist Russia), the regime "atomized society ... to make it terrified and submissive." In addition, the Soviet regime provided "cohesion in a vertically ordered society" through the dictates of the party. Together these factors led to an "unshakable structure."[12] It is not easy for a society to shake off hundreds of years of hegemonic cultural tradition and move to a free and more open society. Nor is it easy to establish limits on governing officials when they have never existed before. While constitutions and the rule of law are critical to democratic transitions, it may take a long time to nurture a working relationship between democratic values and democratic governance.

Free and Fair Elections

Conducting free and fair elections is another crucial component of democratic transitions. It is an important component because an election is the only peaceful method through which citizens of a polity can change their government. Between 2003 and 2005, massive street demonstrations led to the removal of authoritarian governments and a turn toward democracy in three states of the former Soviet Union—Georgia, Ukraine, and Kyrgyzstan. While these events showed how widespread the desire for free elections is, and suggest that the movement toward democracy in the former Soviet Union still has momentum, contrary trends are in evidence elsewhere.

For example, after the 2008 elections in Zimbabwe, Robert Mugabe refused to accept what most observers saw as the defeat of his government. While a runoff was scheduled, he and his supporters used violence and intimidation to terrify the opposition. Mugabe's opponent, Morgan Tsvangirai, eventually withdrew from the runoff because he feared for his own safety and that of his supporters. Such a refusal to accept the verdict of a free election is a refusal to accept the rule of law, and it undermines the confidence of citizens in their governmental process.

For elections to work, they not only have to be free and fair but citizens must also have confidence that the process is legitimate and that it will make leaders accountable to voters. Elections and accountability are there to "control political power."[13] They contribute to the public's support for the system of governance by creating a sense of legitimacy.

Strong Civil Society

The creation of a strong and viable **civil society** is another important factor in the transition to democracy. Larry Diamond defines civil society as "the realm of organized social life that is open, voluntary, self-generating, at least potentially self-supporting, autonomous from the state, and bound by a legal order or set of shared rules."[14] In short, civil society means social pluralism, with numerous voluntary autonomous organizations that seek their own interest in addition to the public interest as they understand it.

The strength of powerful autonomous groups can offset the dominating force of a powerful state—a state that may be tempted to use power arbitrarily to suppress opposition. By the same token, a strong civil society can enhance public participation in the political process and nurture the democratic dialogue essential in a successful transition to democracy. A dynamic deliberative process is one of the cornerstones of democracy.

While civil society is a crucial factor in democratization, according to Iris Marion Young it can pose a real dilemma for democracies: "Some argue that the fragmentation and plurality of civil society can undermine the trust and solidarity necessary for self-determining democracy." In other words, powerful associations in society can distort the public interest by overpowering other groups in the political process. Therefore, "democratic state institutions ... have unique and important virtues for promoting social justice."[15] Consequently, in any transitional process—and in a full-fledged practising democracy—there must be balance between a strong civil society and the state.

Economic Development

Fifty years ago the American sociologist Seymour Martin Lipset noted a correlation between economic development and democracy, in as much as democratic political systems were also the most developed economic systems.[16] Indeed, much of the push for economic development and globalization assumes that these changes will lead to economic growth and that economic growth will enhance democratic transitions:

While economic growth is systematically associated with poverty reduction, the rate at which growth translates into lower poverty depends on the initial level of income inequality in the distribution of income and how that distribution changes over time. Growth—and its effectiveness in reducing poverty—also depends on sound, stable government. So confronting socioeconomic inequalities and building sound institutions can be important both for providing a socially sustainable basis for overall growth and for ensuring that poor people gain substantially from that growth.[17]

Developing "sound, stable government," however, may be easier said than done. We now know that entrenching democratic values and institutions in nations transitioning to democracy is no easy task. Building a system of governance that individuals see as legitimate and that they will support requires a lot of political engineering. What is involved in the "consolidation" process by which democracy takes root and becomes formalized? To better understand how economic development may influence democratic consolidation, it is essential to see how different analysts deal with the problem.

One of those analysts is the Finnish scholar Tatu Vanhanen, who has investigated the problem discussed by Lipset, that is, the connection between economics and politics. Vanhanen describes his study as a "resource distribution theory of democratization."[18] In effect he is explaining reasons for a successful democracy as one might explain reasons for one team's winning a hockey game. In hockey the explanatory variables may be coaching, personnel, financial resources, team spirit, and so on. With democracies, he is seeking a variable or variables that explain successful democracies:

> If the resources used as sources of power are concentrated in the hands of one group, the same group will be the most powerful group. If the resources used as sanctions are distributed widely among several groups, it is reasonable to expect that power also becomes distributed among several groups.[19]

In an introductory textbook we cannot provide a complete discussion of Vanhanen's statistical approach, but we can report his major finding: "It was found that the major explanatory factor of the study, the distribution of power resources, explained about 66 percent of the variation in degree of democracy."[20] In other words, the distribution of power resources in society is strongly correlated with the degree of democratization.

Amartya Sen, a Nobel Prize winner in economics, offers another comprehensive way of examining the process of development. His concept of development includes the social, economic, and political changes occurring in non-industrial societies, connecting the developmental process with freedom of the individual: "The analysis of development presented in this book treats the freedom of individuals as the basic building blocks. Attention is thus paid particularly to the expansion of the capabilities of persons to lead the kind of lives they value."[21] Sen's argument is that development means "expanding the real freedom that people enjoy," and expanding it for all segments in society. "Human development is first and foremost an ally of the poor, rather than the rich and the affluent."[22]

Sen sees the **capitalist** system as one of the causes of development in affluent societies:

> While capitalism is often seen as an arrangement that works only on the basis of the greed of everyone, the efficient working of the capitalist system is, in fact, dependent on powerful systems of values and norms. Indeed, to see capitalism as nothing other than a system based on a conglomeration of greedy behaviour is to underestimate vastly the ethics of capitalism, which has richly contributed to its redoubtable achievements.[23]

Nevertheless, the use of a capitalist system for development has its limitations, especially in dealing with "economic inequality, environmental protection and the need for cooperation of different kinds that operate outside the market."[24]

For Sen, one critical factor in achieving the economic development of a society is development of "human capabilities." These capabilities are fostered by social development, for example, in "education, better health care, finer medical attention and other factors that causally influence the effective freedoms that people actually enjoy."[25] Sen is synthesizing economic growth in society with development of the human capabilities of all individuals in that society. This dual process of development then creates true individual freedom. Thus an essential step in the fostering of democracy is the development of human capabilities.

Another important work explaining transitions to democracy is by Hernando de Soto, president of the Institute for Liberty and Democracy in Peru. Soto makes a straightforward argument about the failure of capitalism in most non-industrial states.[26] He sees capital as a critical component of the developmental process. Capital is the "lifeblood" of capitalism; it provides "the means to support specialization and the production and exchange of assets in the expanded market."[27] In addition, says Soto, "even in the poorest countries, the poor save. The value of savings among the poor is, in fact, immense—forty times the foreign aid received throughout the world since 1945."[28] However, few in developing systems are able to "transform their assets and labour into capital." They lack the "implicit legal infrastructure hidden deep within their property structure" that Western nations have developed. The key to change in the non-industrial world is to develop the means for converting property rights to capital. This legalized contractual process will, according to Soto, enable the poor to harness their resources and use the capitalist system to develop freedom and opportunity.[29]

In concrete terms, Soto is referring to the difficulty that people have in obtaining legal title to land in much of the Third World. Great cities such as Lima, Bombay, and Cairo are thronged with millions of people who are squatting on publicly owned land. Governments cannot drive these squatters out and also have not created legal procedures for them to regularize their possession. Without proof of ownership, these people cannot use their houses as collateral to borrow money from financial institutions. They also have no legal address and thus often tap into water and electricity services without paying for them. The resulting economic inefficiency and disorder drags down the

PART 3

World View 18.1

Summary of Hernando de Soto's Argument in *The Mystery of Capital*

- The situation and potential of the poor need to be better documented.

- All people are capable of saving money.

- What the poor are missing is the legally integrated property systems that can convert their work and savings into capital.

- Civil disobedience and the mafias of today are not marginal phenomena but the result of people marching by the billions from life organized on a small scale to life on a big scale.

- In this context, the poor are not the problem but the solution.

- Implementing a property system that creates capital is a political challenge because it involves getting in touch with people, grasping the social contract, and overhauling the legal system.

Source: Hernando de Soto, *The Mystery of Capital* (New York: Basic Books, 2001), 277.

whole system. Soto argues that transitional democracies in the Third World should do what the United States and Canada did in the nineteenth century: recognize the title that squatters acquire by possession so they can enter the economy on a legitimate basis. For more on Soto's argument, see World View 18.1.

Obviously, no single factor can fully explain the success of the complex processes of democratization, nation-building, and political development. The difficulties are enormous, as illustrated by attempts to create a new democratic system in Iraq after the United States and its allies conquered that country in 2003 and embarked on the task of "regime change." It is a simplistic assumption that overthrowing autocratic regimes will lead to democracy. Sectarian violence, hatred for the Americans as intruders in the region, corruption, and the problem of security are only a few of the complications to any transition to democracy in Iraq. Even though the United States withdrew most of its military forces in 2011, there is still no guarantee of a favourable outcome in the country's struggle for democracy.

IMPEDIMENTS TO DEMOCRATIC TRANSITIONS

Ethnic and National Violence

Ethnic and national violence (sometimes referred to as **ethnonational violence**) is an obvious impediment to any democratic transition. The concern for preservation of ethnic or national identity engenders strong emotions. Ensuing conflicts, within or between nation-states, can be not only brutal but also self-destructive for emerging democracies. More often than not the loss of life is extensive, the economy is torn to shreds, and the political system becomes dysfunctional. One can look in almost any of the four corners of the world and find examples of destructive violence.

Unfortunately, Africa offers too many examples. The Democratic Republic of the Congo is one of the worst. In the decade prior to 2006, conflicts there involved "three Congolese rebel movements, 14 foreign armed groups, and countless militias; killed over 3.3 million Congolese; and destabilized most of central Africa."[30] An agreement in 2003 and elections in 2006 were supposed to bring peace to the country. "Yet over two million more Congolese have died since the official end of the war."[31]

Ethnonational violence is also a problem in Asia. Sri Lanka gained its independence in 1948, and since that time the country has struggled with the secessionist movement of the Tamil Tigers. There are about 20 million people in the country; 74 percent of Sri Lankans are Buddhist Sinhalese and about 18 percent are Hindu Tamils. The Tamils have been fighting for independence or more autonomy since 1948. A civil war in the 1980s and 1990s took as many as 60,000 lives. The Sri Lankan government defeated the Tamil Tigers, but a great deal of tension remains between Tamils and Sinhalese.

In Eastern Europe, ethnic violence between Serbs and Albanians in the province of Kosovo has been intense. Before the breakup of Yugoslavia in the 1990s, the violence was so appalling that the North Atlantic Treaty Organization (NATO) felt compelled to intervene by sending troops to separate the two sides. And even in 2008, when Kosovo, supported by most of the nations of the world, declared independence, Serbs rioted to protest the move. In fact, the Balkans historically have been one of the world's hotspots, as the region contains a highly volatile mix of ethnic groups, nationalities, and religions. Conflict in the area has led to the phrase "the balkanization of politics" (see Comparative Perspective 18.1).

In the Middle East, ethnic and national violence has been one of the problems holding back democracy in the region. The conflict between Israel and the Palestinians has destabilized the region for more than half a century. The Kurdish minority problem in Turkey has been violent at times and remains a troublesome issue today. And even within the realm of Arabic-speaking Muslims, there are violent clashes between Sunni and Shiite Muslims in Iraq.

In all of these cases one can understand why it is difficult to facilitate a transition to democracy while violence is prevalent. It is almost impossible to entrench constitutional limitations on the state, carry on a public dialogue over policy issues, or administer the construction of roads, schools, hospitals, and health clinics when ethnic or national groups are struggling for autonomy or independence.

Religious Fundamentalism and Violence

Religious fundamentalism has emerged as a major difficulty in emerging democracies. This struggle is most obvious in countries where citizens practise the Islamic faith. There are more than one billion Muslims throughout the world, and they constitute

Comparative Perspectives 18.1

The Balkanization of Politics

The **balkanization of politics** means strong parochial ties between ethnic, religious, and national groups and the disintegration of political order caused by conflict among those groups. The Balkan peninsula is located in south-eastern Europe, between the Black and Aegean Seas to the east, the Adriatic and Ionian Seas to the west, and the Mediterranean Sea to the south. Yugoslavia before and after 1990

Federal People's Republic of Yugoslavia in 1945

Legend:
— Frontiers between countries that were states in federal Yugoslavia
— Other international frontiers
The remaining "Yugoslavia" comprises only Serbia.
Vojvodina and Kosovo are formerly autonomous regions in Serbia.

Source: Adapted from *An Atlas of World Affairs*, 10th ed., Andrew Boyd, © 1998 Routledge, p. 58. Reproduced by permission of Taylor & Francis Books UK.

Comparative Perspectives 18.1

presents a classic example of balkanized politics. In 1945, Marshal Josip Broz Tito, using the Communist Party, consolidated power in a centralized federal state. There were six republics: Slovenia and Croatia in the north, Serbia in the east, Bosnia-Herzegovina and Montenegro in the centre, and Macedonia in the south; Vojvodina and Kosovo became autonomous provinces (Kosovo is now an independent state). Within Yugoslavia, three faiths were practised: Roman Catholicism, Greek Orthodox Christianity, and Islam.

The federation lasted until 1991, when Croatia and Slovenia declared independence.

The intense and bitter strife in the region can be traced back to wars, occupations by the Ottoman and Austro-Hungarian Empires, and attempts by the European colonial powers to gain influence in the region. The violence may also be linked to low economic development. The gross national product per capita in U.S. dollars (2010) was as follows:

The Balkan Peninsula Today*

Source: Map from THE WORLD BOOK ENCYCLOPEDIA. © 2005 World Book, Inc. By permission of the publisher. www.worldbookonline.com. All rights reserved.

*Montenegro became independent from Serbia in 2006.

(continued)

PART 3

Comparative Perspectives 18.1   *(continued)*

Albania	$3 678	Kosovo	$3 080
Bosnia-	$4 491	Macedonia	$4 425
Herzegovina		Montenegro	$6 340
Bulgaria	$6 325	Romania	$7 538
Croatia	$13 754	Serbia	$5 366
Greece	$26 934	Slovenia	$23 267

a majority of the population in many countries from western Africa to Indonesia. Though Arabia was the cradle of Islam, most Muslims today are not Arabs; rather, they live in countries such as Bangladesh, India, Indonesia, and Pakistan. The problem is not with the Islamic faith itself but with the struggle going on within that faith. The split is between fundamentalist and more moderate Muslims. The way this conflict is playing out in Pakistan is an example of how it affects a struggling transitional democracy.

Pakistan is a country of about 174 million people, of whom about 97 percent are Muslims. Since gaining independence through partition from India in 1947, the country has alternated between democracy and dictatorships, mostly military. In 1988 Benazir Bhutto was chosen as prime minister, the first woman to serve as a head of government in an Islamic country. In 1990 her government was dissolved by the president. In the 1993 elections she was returned to power as prime minister, and remained in office until 1996. Again she was forced to resign; in the face of questionable accusations of corruption, she left the country. In 1999 General Pervez Musharraf led a coup and became president. In 2007 he agreed to return the government to elected officials, and elections were scheduled for early 2008. Benazir Bhutto returned to Pakistan to prepare for the election but was assassinated in early 2008.

Just before her death, Bhutto completed a book on the struggle between Muslim factions, explaining how this struggle could have profound implications for Pakistan's democracy. Her book describes the schism within the Islamic faith. "The battle for the hearts and soul of Islam today is taking place between moderates and fanatics, between democrats and dictators, between those who live in the past and those who adapt to the present."[32] The radical or fanatical Muslims are those

> who claim to speak for Islam who denigrate democracy and human rights, arguing that these values are Western values and thus inconsistent with Islam. These are the same people who would deny basic education to girls, blatantly discriminate against women and minorities, ridicule other cultures and religions, rant against science and technology, and endorse brutal totalitarianism to enforce their medieval views.[33]

These were the people who "attacked America, Spain, Britain, Indonesia, Afghanistan, and Pakistan and then attacked my supporters and me in Karachi on October 19, 2007"—their "ultimate goal: chaos."[34]

Bhutto goes on to suggest that these are not the Muslims she knows, that this is a "caricature" of the Islamic faith she knows. Islam

> is an open, pluralistic, and tolerant religion—a positive force in the lives of more than one billion people across this planet … It is a religion built upon the democratic principals of consultation (*shura*); building consensus (*ijma*); finally leading to independent judgement (*ijtibad*).[35]

While she argues that radical Muslims, such as the partisans of al-Qaeda, have "twisted the values of a great and noble religion," she does not feel that most Muslims agree with their position.[36] Therefore she is convinced that the Islamic religion and democracy can be reconciled.

In commenting on religious conflicts in the Islamic world, we should remember that the development of religious tolerance in Western Europe was a slow and in many cases a brutal process. In writing on religious pluralism in France, Joseph Lecler says:

> All those who were worried about the political unity of the kingdom (France), whether Catholics or Protestants, began therefore to think of granting the dissenters civil tolerance, either provisionally or for good. This solution prevailed, after many a struggle, with the promulgation of the Edict of Nantes (1598).[37]

But in 1685 Louis XIV revoked the Edict of Nantes and expelled the Protestants from France. Religious toleration was not achieved until the nineteenth century.

If the Western experience is an indicator, the transition to democracy may be slow and even violent. Religious fanatics can cause terrible disruptions in society and seriously impede its transformation to democracy. There is little opportunity for peaceful reconciliation of conflicts among different groups in society when little or no tolerance exists.

Strong Military or Paramilitary Forces and Corruption

A powerful military or paramilitary force can totally dominate politics in an emerging society. These forces can make it especially difficult for other segments of society such as labour, peasant farmers, businesspeople, religious groups, or educators to have any autonomy in the process. Military and paramilitary groups use the violent power of the gun to create fear and intimidation. As Daron Acemoglu and James A. Robinson suggest, "Many coups [and most coups are undertaken by the military], especially in Latin America, had reducing redistribution as one of their major objectives and, in most cases, proceeded to reduce redistribution and change the income distribution significantly."[38] These forces can be used to rig elections or to so intimidate groups that they fear for their lives and refrain from publicizing their cause or lobbying governments.

PART 3

Also, corruption can be a significant impediment to democratic transitions. Ronald Inglehart and Christian Welzel note that "the most serious violation of effective democracy is elite corruption." Using corruption,

> elites provide services only to privileged people who can afford to buy them by paying bribes or doing favors. This violates the rule of law and equal rights. Corruption tends to establish conspiratorial networks held together by mutual obligations, fueling nepotism, favouritism, and clientelism. Corruption distributes privileges in highly discriminatory ways disenfranchising the masses.[39]

But, in this elaborate study of cross-national cultural values, they see some hope. "If a society's mass culture becomes hostile to favouritism, corruption, and authoritarianism, elite culture is likely to do so as well."[40]

When one reviews the impediments to democratic transitions, it is easy to become pessimistic and think that democracy has no future in the Third World. However, the mass desire for participation in politics, for justice, equity, and the rule of law has had a profound impact upon governance. Democratic values, well articulated, plus strong institutions reinforcing those values, are crucial in attempting to overcome the impediments to democracy.

AP Photo/Pablo Martinez Monsivais

Canadian prime minister Stephen Harper, U.S. president Barack Obama, and former Mexican president Felipe Calderón leave their podiums after a joint news conference in the Rose Garden of the White House, Washington, D.C., 2 April 2012.

GLOBALIZATION

Globalization has obviously benefited countries such as India and China. They have been able to undertake extensive economic growth by rapidly expanding their industrial sector. But the issue of globalization is often interpreted differently in transitional democracies than in established democracies. Many non-industrial nations fear being "thrown into transitional lifestyles that they often neither want nor understand." They assume that globalization carries with it "waves of cultural transformation" leading to the convergence of a global culture—"the McDonaldization of the world."[41] This sort of fear creates a paradox in transitional democracies. Often the countries want foreign investment and the accompanying jobs but fear the loss of their cultural identity.

Some analysts have argued that these fears are not altogether justified. Ulrich Beck, for example, suggests that globalization is not a "linear convergence." He refers to it as a "dialectical" process whereby international and local forces combine, and the end result is not likely to be a monolithic world culture.[42] This is an interesting thesis, but it may be much later in the twenty-first century before it can be verified or refuted.

CONCLUSION

Manipulation of elections, violation of human rights, arbitrary use of force, lack of accountability, rampant nationalism, gross inequalities, and economic stagnation are some of the problems encountered in the transition to democracy. It is clear that developing democratic institutions and procedures, and engendering democratic values and beliefs, is a different process than maintaining established liberal democracies. The transition to democracy may involve destroying old methods of maintaining order and control and eliminating privilege and political immunity based on birthright or force. At the same time, transitions to democracy involve building anew, developing accountability for political leaders, and providing for equity in the system. Transitional systems need to provide opportunity for all, so that, as Soto and Sen advocate, a nation's human capital can be developed.

Will the democracies that emerge from transitions be similar to those that now exist? Will they follow the pattern of Western democracies, or will new forms emerge that reflect indigenous cultures and institutions? Indeed, not all Western democracies follow a single pattern. Democracy in France and democracy in the United States are very different. There are, however, common underlying principles that are followed wherever democracies have been established.

Howard Wiarda addresses this question in *Comparative Democracy and Democratization*, arguing that democracies will inevitably differ: "After all, different cultures and different societies at different levels of development do practice democracy in their own ways, and we should celebrate this diversity. Few countries practice democracy in the same way."[43] He goes on to say that democracy comes in "mixes, gradations, and distinct varieties," and that we should see the transition as a "continuum, a journey, and ongoing process."[44] Because of these differences,

> we need a set of categories—limited democracy, partial democracy, incomplete democracy, and the like—that enable us to comprehend and come to grips not only with the many gradations of democracy but also with the unique, culturally conditioned forms that democracy may take. Not only will that give us a useful and realistic way of measuring the condition and status of global democracy, but it also provides us with a base to encourage further evolution toward democracy in the future.[45]

Specifically, democracy still faces at least five huge challenges:

1. The world's largest country, the People's Republic of China, with an estimated population of 1.2 billion, remains firmly anti-democratic in politics, though it is experimenting with economic liberalization.

2. Democracy is superficial in many of the Soviet successor states in Eastern Europe and Central Asia. In countries such as Russia, Belarus, and Kazakhstan, recycled communists still hold power and the future of democracy is far from certain. In other new states, such as fragments of the former Yugoslavia, democratic elections have established a precedent but the system remains fragile.

3. The world of Islam, from Indonesia through the Middle East to North Africa, has been slow in embracing liberal democracy. Turkey, with its strong connections to Europe, is the main exception among the 46 Islamic states, and even Turkey's democracy has been broken by periods of military rule and is now challenged by Islamic fundamentalism. Elections take place in Indonesia, Bangladesh, and Pakistan, but the roots of democracy remain fragile in those countries. The Lebanese democratic experiment has been torn apart by internal religious rivalries and external political hostilities between Israel and the Arab states. And as F. Gregory Gause notes, "From Algeria to Saudi Arabia, Arab autocrats were able to stay in power over the past 40 years only by brutally suppressing popular attempts to unseat them."[46] In 2011, however, popular demonstrations did challenge autocratic rulers in Tunisia, Libya, Egypt, Syria, Yemen, and Bahrain. The fall of leaders in all the countries except Syria and Bahrain has been called the "Arab Spring." One of the most interesting and significant changes will be the form and speed with which transitions to democracy occur, although there is no guarantee they will occur. Read more on the characteristics of the Arab Spring in Chapter 19.

4. Democratic experiments in sub-Saharan Africa are in their earliest stages and are beset with difficulties. One of the largest and wealthiest countries in the region, Nigeria, is under civilian rule but hardly democratic. Tribal rivalries in Africa are a deeply rooted problem, and in the worst cases, such as Somalia and the Sudan, civil order has given way to civil war. However, the thus-far successful transition of the Republic

of South Africa from apartheid to a multiracial, multiparty democracy is a hopeful development. With its large population and (by African standards) highly developed economy, South Africa may be able to help show other countries the way toward liberal democracy. Indeed, some of its neighbours, such as Botswana and Namibia, are doing quite well, but another neighbour, Zimbabwe, has been plunged into turmoil by Robert Mugabe's efforts to hang on to power in the face of popular opposition.

5. Liberal democracies do not always "fit" local cultures. Liberal democracy is a value-laden process of government; if it is going to become universal, ways must be found to resolve conflicts between liberal democratic values and existing cultural values. For example, in most of the Islamic world, men and women do not enjoy political equality, and in certain societies throughout the world, traditional elites have governed for centuries. Few of those elites will willingly risk giving up power in free and fair elections. But we are not arguing that liberal-democratic values nurtured in the Western world should be imposed universally. The adoption of such a value system has to be the choice of the people in each society.

Questions for Discussion

1. Why does it take more than the imposition of democratic rules to make a state democratic? What are the most important factors for a successful transition to democracy? What is the role of civil society in stabilizing democratic government?

2. Is it inevitable that one day all systems of government will be democratic? Why or why not?

3. Which writer discussed in this chapter do you feel offers the most insight into the consolidation of transitional democracies? Which argument do you find the least convincing? Why?

Internet Links

1. Carter Center: **www.cartercenter.org**. A foundation established by former U.S. president Jimmy Carter to promote democratization.

2. Freedom House: **www.freedomhouse.org**. Annual rankings of freedom and democracy in all nations.

3. Gorbachev Foundation of North America: **www.gfna.net**. Established by Mikhail Gorbachev, the last leader of the Soviet Union, in order to promote worldwide democracy.

4. Institute for Liberty and Democracy: **www.ild.org.pe**. Hernando de Soto's foundation, based in Lima, Peru.

PART 3

Further Reading

Acemoglu, Daron, and James A. Robinson. *Economic Origins of Dictatorship and Democracy*. Cambridge: Cambridge University Press, 2006.

———. *Why Nations Fail: The Origins of Power, Prosperity and Poverty*. New York: Crown Publishers, 2012.

Badie, Bertrand. *The Imported State: The Westernization of the Political Order*. Translated by Claudia Royal. Palo Alto, CA: Stanford University Press, 2000.

Baker, Randall, ed. *Transitions from Authoritarianism: The Role of the Bureaucracy*. Westport, CT: Greenwood Publishing, 2002.

Baylis, John, and Steve Smith, eds. *The Globalization of World Politics*. 4th ed. Oxford: Oxford University Press, 2007.

Beck, Ulrich. *What Is Globalization?* Translated by Patrick Camiller. Cambridge, UK: Polity Press, 2000.

Bhutto, Benazir. *Reconciliation: Islam, Democracy, and the West*. New York: HarperCollins, 2008.

Clark, Terry D. *Beyond Post-communist Studies: Political Science and the New Democracies of Europe*. Armonk, NY: M. E. Sharpe, 2002.

Devins, Neal E. *The Democratic Constitution*. Toronto: Oxford University Press, 2004.

Diamond, Larry. *Developing Democracy: Toward Consolidation*. Baltimore: Johns Hopkins University Press, 1999.

Fairfield, Paul. *Why Democracy*. Albany: State University of New York Press, 2008.

Feldman, Noah. *What We Owe Iraq: War and the Ethics of Nation Building*. Princeton, NJ: Princeton University Press, 2004.

Fukuyama, Francis. *The Origins of Political Order: From Prehuman Times to the French Revolution*. New York: Farrar, Straus and Giroux, 2011.

Gause, F. Gregory, III. "Why Middle East Studies Missed the Arab Spring." *Foreign Affairs* 90, no. 4 (July/August 2011).

Giddens, Anthony, ed. *The Global Third Way Debate*. Malden, MA: Blackwell, 2001.

Haggard, Stephen, and Robert R. Kaufman. *The Political Economy of Democratic Transitions*. Princeton, NJ: Princeton University Press, 1995.

Handelman, Howard, and Mark Tessler, eds. *Democracy and Its Limits: Lessons from Asia, Latin America, and the Middle East*. Notre Dame, IN: University of Notre Dame Press, 1999.

Hollifield, James Frank, and Calvin C. Jillson. *Pathways to Democracy: The Political Economy of Democratic Transitions*. New York: Routledge, 2000.

Huntington, Samuel P. *The Clash of Civilizations and the Remaking of World Order.* New York: Simon and Schuster, 1996.

———. *The Third Wave: Democratization in the Late Twentieth Century.* Norman: University of Oklahoma Press, 1991.

Inglehart, Ronald, and Christian Welzel. *Modernization, Cultural Change and Democracy: The Human Development Sequence.* Cambridge: Cambridge University Press, 2005.

Keane, John. *Violence and Democracy.* Toronto: Cambridge University Press, 2004.

Pridham, Geoffrey, ed. *Transitions to Democracy: Comparative Perspectives from Southern Europe, Latin America and Eastern Europe.* Aldershot, UK: Dartmount, 1995.

Przeworski, Adam. *Democracy and the Market: Political and Economic Reforms in Eastern Europe and Latin America.* Cambridge: Cambridge University Press, 1991.

Przeworski, Adam, et al., eds. *Democracy and Development: Political Institutions and Well-Being in the World, 1950–1990.* New York: Cambridge University Press, 2000.

Reynolds, Andrew. *The Architecture of Democracy.* Toronto: Oxford University Press, 2002.

Schedler, Andreas, Larry Diamond, and Marc F. Plattner, eds. *The Self-Restraining State: Power and Accountability in New Democracies.* Boulder, CO: Lynne Rienner, 1999.

Sen, Amartya. *Development as Freedom.* New York: Anchor Books, 1999.

Shapiro, Ian, and Casiano Hacker-Cordon, eds. *Democracy's Value.* Cambridge: Cambridge University Press, 1999.

Sharansky, Natan. *The Case for Democracy: The Power of Freedom to Overcome Tyranny and Terror.* New York: Public Affairs, 2004.

Soto, Hernando de. *The Mystery of Capital: Why Capitalism Triumphs in the West and Fails Everywhere Else.* New York: Basic Books, 2000.

Sunstein, Cass R. *Designing Democracy.* Toronto: Oxford University Press, 2002.

Tilly, Charles. *Democracy.* Cambridge: Cambridge University Press, 2007.

Vanhanen, Tatu. *Prospects of Democracy: A Study of 172 Countries.* London: Routledge, 1997.

Whitehead, Laurence. *Democratization.* Toronto: Oxford University Press, 2002.

Wiarda, Howard J., ed. *Comparative Democracy and Democratization.* Orlando, FL: Harcourt College Publishers, 2002.

PART 3

CHAPTER 19

Autocratic Systems of Government

In spite of past trends toward democratic transitions, there remain many non-democratic systems of government. As noted in the previous chapter, Freedom House data for 2011 classified 47 of 194 nations as "not free" (24 percent).[1] Most of these states manifest some form of autocratic rule. The term **autocracy** is formed from two Greek stems: auto, meaning "self," and *kratia,* meaning "power" or "rule." It means, literally, "self-rule"—that is, doing whatever you want if you have the power. It represents absolute government by an individual or group that possesses unrestricted power, ruling according to their own desires rather than the rule of law. Such rulers are not responsible to anybody or any institution.[2]

Autocracy is essentially the same thing as tyranny or despotism. Aristotle defined tyranny as "the arbitrary power of an individual which is responsible to no one, and governs all alike … with a view to its own advantage, not to that of its subjects, and therefore against their will."[3] Montesquieu (1689–1755) said much the same thing when he defined **despotism** as one man ruling through fear without regard to law.[4] Such definitions of autocracy, tyranny, and despotism always point to certain similar and interrelated characteristics:

- Rule is arbitrary and not bound by law.

- Rule is exercised in the interest of the rulers and not in the common interest.

- Rule is based on coercion and fear.

These ideas are logically interlocked. People willingly submit to authority if it is exercised under genuine laws that are universal rules of conduct, and if those rules are binding on government and citizens alike for the common good. When these conditions are not met, fear must substitute for voluntary compliance.

Note that the essence of autocratic or tyrannical rule is found in the *how* of government, not in the *who.* It is not a question of numbers. A single individual who rules under law is a constitutional monarch; someone who rules arbitrarily, according to caprice, is a tyrant.

Autocracies can be further classified as either authoritarian or totalitarian. Even though these forms of government are decreasing in numbers, they are not likely to disappear from the globe, so it is important to understand their basic characteristics.

AUTHORITARIANISM

The concept of **authoritarianism** implies authority that may or may not rest on wide popular support but that is not put to the test of free elections. While that seems clear enough, a problem in speaking of authoritarian regimes is that the category includes such a wide diversity of types. Some regimes are civilian (Syria), others military (Myanmar); some are secular (Turkey's has been but faces pressures from Islamic fundamentalists), others avowedly religious (Iran); some are capitalist (Algeria), others socialist (Vietnam); some are traditional monarchies with few or none of the institutions of modern democracy (Gulf sheikhdoms); and others appear to have all the machinery of modern democracy but manipulated in such a way that there is no real democratic choice (Zimbabwe).

We cannot pursue all these differences here, but we will draw a distinction between right-wing, conservative regimes that interpret their mission as protecting society from harmful influences, and left-wing, revolutionary regimes that claim to be building a new society. Right-wing authoritarianism—for example, the government of General Pinochet in Chile (1973–90)—originally consisted of anti-communist regimes whose ostensible mission was to prevent a Marxist revolution. More recently, however, many conservative authoritarian regimes in Africa and the Middle East—for example, Algeria and Jordan—are directed not against communism but against Islamic radicalism. Similarly, on the left, authoritarian regimes used to be mainly socialist. That type still exists—as in the contemporary government of Hugo Chávez in Venezuela (1999–)—but there also are Islamic radical regimes such as the Islamic Republic of Iran, founded in 1979, and the Taliban regime in Afghanistan (1996–2001).

Right-Wing Authoritarianism

Drawing heavily on the example of Spain under Francisco Franco (in office 1936–75), Juan Linz developed a model of the **right-wing authoritarian** system of government that emphasized the following characteristics:

- limited political pluralism,

- no elaborate or guiding ideology,

- no extensive political mobilization, and

- leaders who exercise power within ill-defined yet predictable limits.[5]

One might add to these a bias toward statism and a major political role for the military.

PART 3

In most right-authoritarian systems there is no idea of a classless society or a master race. A substantial degree of social pluralism is tolerated. As the society grows more complex, a variety of organizations—business associations, labour unions, churches, peasant groups—can function with a minimum of interference from government. In fact, an authoritarian regime may use these organizations to achieve certain goals, such as the production of goods and services, or look to them for political support. These organizations can survive as long as they offer support or at least remain neutral politically. If, however, they become too critical of government policy or suggest fundamental societal change or a change in political leadership, they are expendable.

Right-authoritarian systems do not have an elaborate blueprint for utopian order. While the authoritarian ruler always advocates economic development, there is usually no doctrinaire plan to totally transform society to achieve that growth. Rather, economic development (the most common objective) is defined in terms of doing more of what is already being done and doing it within the existing structures of society.

The military regime that ruled South Korea from 1961 to 1988 is an excellent example. The government encouraged industrialization by creating favourable conditions for large companies to operate. Within two decades, South Korea became an international force in steel, shipbuilding, automobiles, clothing, electronics, and other industries. The country transformed itself in a very short period of time from a backward agricultural economy into a modern industrial power. Standards of living also rose dramatically, and continue to do so, although they are still below those in Japan or North America.

During those years of rapid development, the government tolerated token political opposition but manipulated elections to ensure its continued dominance. Social pluralism was allowed, but organizations that challenged government policy, such as labour unions, were severely repressed. The government often equated opposition to itself with communism—a tactic that retained some credibility because of the belligerence of North Korea. Right-wing authoritarianism in South Korea was typical in its political methods but exceptional in the success of its economic policies; few governments of this type have presided over such rapid and sustained industrial growth.

Another characteristic of the authoritarian model is that there is no great drive to mobilize the society in order to achieve utopian ends. In Chile, for example, all political parties were banned from 1973 until the closing years of General Pinochet's regime; the military government did not even maintain a party of its own, so great was its distaste for mass participation in politics. Mobilizing large numbers of people can nurture political instability by breaking down old patterns of living and stimulating the growth of new institutions. Unless the effects of these changes can be channelled or contained, they can be disastrous for a political leader. Few authoritarian leaders are willing to risk the consequences of drastic change. On the contrary, most cling to the stability of the status quo. However, they may undertake certain reforms, particularly in the interest of economic efficiency. South Korea redistributed much agricultural land—large holdings were appropriated from their owners, divided into smaller pieces, and given to peasants—and the late Shah of Iran confiscated large landholdings of the Islamic clergy. Improvements in non-political areas (for example, technical education) are also not uncommon in conservative authoritarian regimes. However, reform generally stops short of upsetting the balance of political power.

Rightist authoritarianism, even though broadly opposed to socialism, often leans toward **statism**. Rulers are usually unwilling to leave the process of economic development entirely to the private sector. While they may not impose state ownership of the economy, they see the state as a principal instrument in expanding the production of goods and services. The state becomes the driving force, influencing wages, employment, investment, and the development and management of natural resources and international trade. South Korea, for example, controlled exchange rates and restricted imports during its period of highest industrial growth, thus restricting opportunities for consumption and channelling savings into investment. This particular role of the state seems to be a significant characteristic of many authoritarian systems. Numerous authoritarian governments have used their concentrated political power to control many, if not all, aspects of a market economy. Examples are Taiwan, South Korea, Kenya, Brazil, and Chile. The last case is particularly instructive.

In 1973 a military revolt overthrew the socialist government of President Salvador Allende. The government of General Pinochet, tacitly supported by the United States, soon reversed many of Allende's socialist policies—most notably in the monetary field, where rampant inflation was reduced through application of conservative economic theories. Relative monetary stability resulted in an improved climate for business investment and the development of new industries such as production of fruit and wine for export. Yet the military government did not reverse Allende's decision to nationalize the copper industry. This illustrates the general rule that authoritarian rulers are often eclectic with respect to ideologies. They choose ideas from several sources; they don't commit themselves to a doctrine. In this sense, their approach remains statist, for the ultimate choice of policy is determined by the needs of the rulers rather than being left to spontaneous social evolution.

The military is usually the dominant institution in right-wing authoritarianism. Given its weapons and organizational capability, the military can intimidate political parties, interest groups, and the courts. Because authoritarian leaders have to rely on coercion rather than popular support, the military becomes the decisive force in the struggle for power. It often promises a return to civilian rule, but usually the date of free elections is repeatedly postponed until it vanishes into the indefinite future.

There are, however, cases in which military regimes have voluntarily relinquished power. In Brazil (1964), Uruguay (1973), and Argentina (1976), authoritarian military regimes ousted elected civilian governments. In each case they accused the civilian politicians of creating economic chaos and they pledged economic stability and development through efficient management. In 1984 each regime took steps to return the government to elected civilians. Interestingly, in each case the economy was in no better shape than it had been when the military seized power. These examples do not support the "efficient authoritarian" hypothesis; generals, like other mortals, do not necessarily have a quick fix for the complex economic problems of development.

That being said, the record of military regimes is not totally devoid of economic success stories. Pinochet's regime in Chile had a poor record on human rights; horrifying measures were used by the government as they tried to eradicate the socialist movement as a political force. At the same time it liberalized trade, reduced inflation, and reformed social programs. The result, after some years of austerity, was an export boom that continued through the transition to democracy and gave Chile one of the most dynamic economies in South America. Chile subsequently signed free-trade agreements with Canada, Mexico, and the United States, helping to lock in its internal reforms by tying them to external treaty commitments.

Using the South Korean and Chilean examples, it may be tempting to subscribe to the argument that dictatorships are efficient economically. However, the evidence is to the contrary. Adam Przeworski and his colleagues examined more than one hundred regimes, both authoritarian and democratic, between 1950 and 1990. Their findings:

> The main conclusion of this analysis is that there is no trade-off between democracy and development, not even in poor countries. Although not a single study published before 1988 found that democracy promoted growth, and not one published after 1987 concluded in favour of dictatorships (Przeworski and Limongi, 1993), there was never solid evidence that democracies were somehow inferior in generating growth—certainly not enough to justify supporting or even condoning dictatorships. We hope we have put that issue to rest.[6]

They go on to say, "The few countries that developed spectacularly during the past fifty years were as likely to achieve that feat under democracy as under dictatorship." Moreover, "per capita incomes grow faster in democracies." Finally, "these findings add up to a bleak picture of dictatorships. Although democracies are far from perfect, lives under dictatorships are grim and short."[7]

Left-Wing Authoritarianism

Left-wing authoritarian regimes seem very different from their right-wing counterparts, at least at first glance. They have an official ideology—either radical Islam or some variety of socialism other than orthodox Marxism-Leninism—combined with a strong element of nationalism. Tanzania had Nyerere's *ujamaa* socialism, a blend of British Labour ideology and indigenous African traditions. Iraq under Saddam Hussein and Syria under Hafiz al-Assad (who died in 2000) were mortal enemies, but both professed *ba'ath* ("renaissance") socialism. In Libya, Colonel Qaddafi, before he was removed from power and killed in 2011, propounded a unique mixture of revolutionary socialism and Islamic fundamentalism. His *Green Book*, like the "Little Red Book" of Chairman Mao, was prescribed ideological reading for a whole nation. In Afghanistan from 1996 to 2001, the Taliban took a certain interpretation of the Koran as their official ideology (see Historical Perspectives 19.1).

Though they differ in the details, the ideologies of all these regimes called for a fundamental social transformation and referred to revolution in all public discussion. In certain other ways, too, they seemed more totalitarian than authoritarian, at least at the rhetorical level. Political mobilization of the masses was a continuing theme, as was centralized economic planning under the control of a vanguard party.

Perhaps the difference between these left-authoritarian regimes and true totalitarianism is one of degree rather than of kind. If they had lived up to their stated goals, they might well have become totalitarian. But their revolutions have not been as thoroughgoing or as single-minded in pursuit of the stated utopian goals; there has been more compromise with present reality and more autonomy for groups in the society that do not oppose the leadership. In Libya, for example, Qaddafi nationalized the oil reserves previously owned by foreign oil companies, but he did not take the country out of the international network of the oil industry. Large numbers of managers and workers from other countries continue to operate the extraction and refining systems, and the products are exported to Western purchasers. Compare that to the autarchic policies of totalitarian states such as Albania and Cambodia, which excluded Western influences altogether, or to the Soviet Union, which tried to develop major industries—including a petroleum industry—without outside help, although it was willing to export surpluses for hard currency.

Lacking the full intensity of totalitarian regimes, left-authoritarian governments in practice often resemble right-authoritarian ones. Some social pluralism may be tolerated as long as it does not become politically dangerous. Police terrorism is used chiefly as a way of retaining power rather than as a means of inducing social change. The rigours of central planning are softened by bribery and corruption. Lip service is paid to ideological goals but the government does not enforce a monopoly of ideas. Foreign travel is allowed, as are foreign publications, and these things lead to some ideological diversification.

Whether of the left or right, authoritarian leaders tolerate little or no opposition and may do almost anything to remain in power. In virtually every case they reject the principles of liberal democracy, regarding it as too inefficient for the needs of developing nations. They argue that democracy promotes factions and that a faction-ridden society is unable to attain the mass unity required for social and economic development.

There is, no doubt, a great deal of truth in these criticisms. Liberal democracies are clumsy in their response to crisis and slow to implement public policies when a variety of interests must be considered. But the alleged efficiency of authoritarian rulers is often illusory. Their statist mentality often leads them to impose on society vast projects that seem no more productive than the pyramids of the pharaohs. Or they may embark on reckless international adventures: Iraq's invasion of Iran in 1981 was one of those, as was Argentina's attempt to take the Falkland Islands by force in 1982. When

PART 3

Historical Perspectives 19.1

Canada and the Taliban in Afghanistan

The Taliban regime in Afghanistan (1996–2001) manifested many totalitarian characteristics. In effect it established a theocratic state. Religious leaders' interpretation of the Koran served as an ideological basis for remaking society. Public punishment for violations of a strict form of shari'ah law was used to terrorize the people. Anything "Western," such as clothing, music, or communication devices, was prohibited. There were no schools for girls, and part of the training for boys included indoctrination against Western culture. The idea was to use Afghanistan as a base for the true Islamic state, from which to combat the evils of the Western world. That included providing shelter and assistance to al-Qaeda, which organized the attacks against New York City and Washington, D.C., on 11 September 2001.

With the approval of the United Nations Security Council, NATO, led by the United States, invaded Afghanistan in late 2001 and quickly overthrew the regime. The Taliban, however, were not totally defeated and sought refuge in neighbouring remote parts of Pakistan. From there they could send terrorists to attack targets in Afghanistan. Canada, along with other Western nations, was an integral part of this military mission in Afghanistan.

The first objective of the mission was to deny the Taliban a strategic base from which they could train terrorists for attacks on Western nations. A second objective was to assist in building the infrastructure required in any modernizing nation-state. A third objective was to train an Afghan army that could defend the sovereignty of the country. Western nations declared that they would withdraw from Afghanistan in 2014, and presumably the three objectives would be accomplished by then. Canada withdrew its combat military units in 2011, but approximately 1000 troops remained to assist in training the Afghan army.

The 2014 date triggered an intense debate. One question was whether Afghanistan would be able to defend itself against Taliban insurgents by that date. A second question was whether a central government in Afghanistan could overcome the difficulties of a patriarchal society, religious fundamentalism, corruption, great economic disparities, and powerful armed regional leaders. For more information on Canada's becoming involved in the Afghanistan war, see the so-called Manley Report, *Report of the Independent Panel on Canada's Future Role in Afghanistan* (Ottawa: Minister of Public Works and Government Services, 2008), http://dsp-psd.pwgsc.gc.ca/collection_2008/dfait-maeci/FR5-20-1-2008E.pdf.

only one will is obeyed, the chances of dramatic error are heightened. The presumed inefficiency of a liberal government is in the long run actually one of its virtues. By fragmenting power it allows many projects to compete with each other. Some will inevitably fail, but diversity increases the likelihood that solutions to the unexpected problems of the future will be found.

While liberal democracies have worked well for most Western societies, they are not easy to manage, and a certain democratic tradition may be required to make them work. The fact remains, however, that they are not designed to run efficiently. Internal checks are built into them to impede takeover by a powerful military leader. The processes are set up in such a way that a political leader cannot set a blind course and refuse to hear criticism or consider alternative courses. What seems like inefficiency in the short run may be the most efficient long-term method of governing in an ever-changing and unpredictable world.

Evidence of this can be seen in the fact that many authoritarian rulers enjoy power for only a short time, even where they were first greeted as saviours and later employed various tactics to maintain popular support. Leaders like this are frequently charismatic; they often articulate nationalist goals (mostly economic) that have mass appeal. In time, however, enthusiasm wanes as the leader is unable to perform those economic miracles. Time seems to erode initial support for authoritarian dictators, and to remain in power, they begin to rely more on coercion than on popular support. Often they are overthrown in a ***coup d'état*** organized by a faction within the military or the ruling party. In many authoritarian systems the *coup d'état* has been virtually institutionalized as a means of changing officeholders, playing a role analogous to elections in a liberal democracy. The system remains authoritarian but there is rotation of personnel at the top. The distinction between authoritarian and totalitarian rule will become clearer after the following discussion of the fundamental characteristics of a totalitarian system.

TOTALITARIANISM

Many scholars argue that the twentieth century witnessed a new form of autocratic rule: **totalitarianism**. The word was coined by Benito Mussolini to describe his system of government. He summarized his views in a speech in 1925: "Everything in the state, nothing outside the state, nothing against the state."[8] The term was soon accepted by the Nazi regime in Germany and was later applied by external observers to the Stalinist regime in the Soviet Union and the People's Republic of China under Mao Zedong. It was also used to classify the Soviet Union's Eastern European satellites and smaller communist states such as Yugoslavia, Albania, North Korea, Vietnam, Cambodia, Laos, and Cuba. With the collapse of international communism, much of this description became recent history rather than current politics. The Soviet Union and Yugoslavia no longer exist as multinational communist states. China and Vietnam

PART 3

are still nominally communist but are encouraging a market economy and foreign investment. With the retirement of Fidel Castro in 2008, Cuba also began to experiment with market reforms in its economy. This leaves North Korea as the only full-fledged totalitarian state in the contemporary world.

Totalitarianism is a way of organizing tyrannical or despotic rule in a modern society. In a perceptive analysis of the way totalitarian leaders manipulate the masses, use political organization and the power of the state, and apply ideology and terror, Hannah Arendt noted that

> totalitarianism differs essentially from other forms of political oppression known to us such as despotism, tyranny, and dictatorship. Wherever it rose to power, it developed entirely new political institutions and destroyed all social, legal, and political traditions of the country.[9]

Some scholars have held that the concept is merely propaganda—that totalitarianism exists more in the minds of analysts who are anticommunist or antifascist than as a real political system. This issue could be debated forever. That being said, the term is still used by politicians, journalists, and scholars; because totalitarian regimes may arise again in the future, it is important to analyze the principles on which they operate.[10]

Arendt restricts the term *totalitarian* to a small number of regimes—to those that combine an all-powerful political leader and an almost messianic sense of historical mission. Two distinguishing features of totalitarianism are, first, the existence of a revolutionary movement that claims to base itself on nature or history; and, second, the use of terror as an integral tactic in maintaining the momentum of a society in transformation. The leader uses systematic terror as a means of atomizing individuals and keeping the entire population off balance. Arendt describes this use of terror:

> Under conditions of total terror not even fear can any longer serve as an advisor of how to behave, because terror chooses its victims without reference to individual actions or thoughts, exclusively in accordance with the objective necessity of the natural or historical process.[11]

In Arendt's analysis, the arbitrary use of terror on any and all segments of the population becomes an institutionalized way of preventing the development of political forces opposed to the leader's vision of a new society.

Carl Friedrich and Zbigniew Brzezinski offer a broader definition of totalitarianism. To them it is a "syndrome," or "pattern of interrelated traits," that includes the following six elements: an official ideology; a single party typically led by one man; a terroristic police; a communications monopoly; a weapons monopoly; and a centrally directed economy.[12] One or more of these elements may be found individually in other forms of government; totalitarianism exists when they all come together.

The analysis of totalitarianism presented here is based on the historical reality of fascist and communist regimes. Even if the concept is temporarily in eclipse, totalitarianism is a real and recurrent possibility, and as such it cannot simply be tucked away into the history books along with descriptions of the Greek *polis* and the Mongol Empire.

Below we describe the "totalitarian syndrome" under eight headings, derived primarily from Arendt and Friedrich and Brzezinski:

1. Attempt to remake society

Central to totalitarianism, and distinguishing it from simple tyranny, is the attempt to remake society on a grand scale, to produce a condition of utopian perfection. These blueprints for the future are usually part of the official ideology, and they refute the notion of a plural society. Communists, for example, claimed to be working toward a classless society and the withering away of the state.

2. One-party state

Totalitarianism imposes a single mass political party that penetrates all aspects of state and society, including the army, schools, trade unions, churches, and leisure organizations. This disciplined party, controlled from above, monopolizes political power. Social organizations may be formally distinct from government, but the leaders of all institutions are either members of the party or acceptable to it. All other political parties are either outlawed, as was the case in the Soviet Union, or carefully manipulated in a common front, as was the case in East Germany. Never is real opposition tolerated.

3. All-powerful leader

Domination of the party by an all-powerful charismatic leader is an integral part of totalitarianism. Lenin, Stalin, Mao, Ho Chi Minh, and Tito are examples of this type of leadership. All of them passed away without leaving replacements of comparable stature, yet their regimes endured—at least for a time. It may be that charismatic leadership is a phenomenon of the early stages of totalitarianism, a requirement for transmitting the energy necessary to seize and consolidate power.

4. Pseudo-democratic rule

The leader and party maintain their power by force but rationalize their rule with pseudo-democratic arguments. Hitler argued that he represented the people (*Volk*) in such a special way that elections were unnecessary. Communism relied on Lenin's theory of democratic centralism. Elections took place, but the party nominated or approved all candidates. Usually there was only one candidate per position, and voting was more ratification than selection.

5. Control of communications

The totalitarian state seeks to monopolize the flow of ideas. This means that the physical bases of communication—newspapers, radio stations, publishing houses—are either owned or completely controlled by the state. One primary purpose of control over communications is to support an official ideology.

PART 3

6. Use of terror

Totalitarian rule is supported by the terroristic activities of a special political police. The Nazi Gestapo and the Soviet kgb were two such forces. A political police force reports directly to the leader and is under no legal restraint. It may use intimidation, arbitrary arrest, torture, and execution. It infiltrates other coercive agencies of the state, such as the regular police and the armed forces, to ensure their compliance.

7. Subordination of the law to the state

In a totalitarian state, law is a tool. It is only what the state says today and it may speak differently tomorrow. Law is subordinate to the state, not the other way around. There is no concept such as "higher law," or the rule of law, to which political leaders must respond and that protects the "rights" of citizens. Constitutions may exist as part of pseudo-democracies, but they are not formal checks on the power of political leaders.

8. Planned economy

The totalitarian state aspires to control a planned economy. This may entail public ownership, as in communism, or state supervision of private enterprise, as in Nazi Germany or fascist Italy. It does not allow a liberal economy, in which individuals or groups pursue private interests and coordination is left to the undirected market process symbolized by Adam Smith's "invisible hand."

The above characteristics combined make for a very forceful political system. They represent a vastly improved apparatus of autocratic rule that has become available over the past hundred years. Innovations in mass communication make it possible to saturate the population with propaganda to an unprecedented degree. Inventions in weaponry and new forms of organization provide means to coerce people on a much vaster scale. Totalitarianism is in one sense a bigger and better despotism, implemented by the most up-to-date means. It differs from authoritarianism in the importance it places on ideology and in its single-minded urge to remake society according to a utopian vision. Perhaps because of this absolute rule from the top, most "not-free" governments today remain authoritarian.

AUTOCRATIC GOVERNMENTS CHALLENGED

Today significant challenges are occurring for many autocratic political leaders. In Africa, Asia, Eastern Europe, Latin America, and the Middle East, leaders have, in certain instances, bowed to popular pressures. For example, in Africa, the Sudanese leadership agreed to hold a plebiscite on separating the northern and southern parts of the country. The subsequent division of the country in 2011 separated regional, sectarian, and tribal groups that had been fighting since independence in

Comparative Perspectives 19.1

Life and Death in Shanghai

The nature of totalitarian regimes is expressed most vividly not in textbooks but in the memoirs and autobiographies of people who have lived under such governments. A fine example of this type of literature is Nien Cheng's best-selling book *Life and Death in Shanghai*.

Cheng was born in Beijing in 1915, studied at the London School of Economics, married a Chinese diplomat, and lived in Australia from 1941 to 1948. After the communist revolution, she and her husband returned to China because they supported the new regime. The government found it in its interest to let a few Western corporations continue to operate in China, so her husband became the local manager for Shell Oil in Shanghai. After his death, Cheng took over as an adviser to the company, until she was caught up in the Cultural Revolution in 1966.

The Cultural Revolution was a complex series of events—partly a youth protest movement unleashed by Chairman Mao Zedong in an attempt to renew the Communist Party, partly a naked power struggle among different factions within the party. Cheng, though not a political activist, quickly became suspect because of her association with a Western corporation. After the Red Guard youth militia invaded her house and destroyed most of her possessions, she was accused of being a British spy and locked up in solitary confinement for six and a half years. She was cruelly mistreated through denial of proper food, clothing, and medical care, amounting in effect to severe torture. Although repeatedly interrogated for months at a time, she never confessed to anything.

When she was finally released after internal changes in the political power structure, Cheng learned that her only child, an actress not involved in politics, had also been arrested by the Red Guards and had died in custody after being pressured to incriminate her mother. The death had been falsely reported as suicide. With incredible courage, Cheng worked to expose the truth about her daughter's fate. She then took advantage of a temporary political thaw in 1980 to leave China and go to the United States, where two of her sisters lived. Her book, first published in 1986, is not only a moving account of one woman's suffering and heroism but also an incisive portrait of a political system not subject to the rule of law.

1956. In Asia, the powerful military government in Myanmar (Burma) has agreed to relax restrictions on political parties and has permitted parliamentary elections. In Eastern Europe, an autocratic president in Kyrgyzstan was forced out of the country in 2010 and credible elections followed; this action may set an example in a region that is having difficulties shaking authoritarian traditions. Cuba, formerly under a strict communist system, has made moves toward adopting aspects of a market economy.

Nowhere are these challenges more significant, and perhaps surprising, than in the Middle East. They are significant and surprising because most political analysts believed autocratic rule in the region to be solidly entrenched. Kings and dictators had strong military systems to support their regimes and used brutal tactics against any opposition.[13] As mentioned in Chapter 18, popular uprisings in Tunisia, Libya, Egypt, Syria, Yemen, and Bahrain have become known as the "Arab Spring." At the time of writing, four of the leaders had been deposed and Colonel Muammar al-Qaddafi killed. In Bahrain, Saudi Arabian support enabled the government to remain in office; in Syria, the Assad family, with support from the military, held on to power, at least for the time being. How does one explain the success of popular protests in the four cases?

If the cases of Libya and Egypt are used as examples, then the role of the military was crucial. In Libya, Qaddafi's rule over an array of tribes and interests relied on the power of the military. As popular protests formed, cracks developed in the ranks of the military, with some individuals and units supporting the insurgents. After NATO forces reduced the effectiveness of loyal military supporters, the protesters were able to prevail. And in Egypt, Hosni Mubarak had ruled for 30 years with the support of a loyal military. However, when the military refused to intervene and put down the protests, Mubarak was left without the power to maintain rule. It is obvious that, in most cases, autocratic rule relies on the power of the gun. In the first case, a split in the ranks of the military led to the ruler's downfall; in the second case, it was the refusal of the generals to support the leader that led to his demise.

But the above does not explain why the popular uprisings occurred at this time. Why did thousands of people rally in the streets in the face of possible brutal suppression? These are not easy questions to answer, as one can see in Chapter 18. Francis Fukuyama does offer a plausible explanation; in drawing on Huntington's ideas, he suggests that "political decay ... occurred when economic and social mobilization outran political development, with the mobilization of new social groups that could not be accommodated within the existing political system."[14] One lesson to be drawn from the Arab Spring is that if political institutions do not adapt to societal changes, then political decay may be inevitable.

Questions for Discussion

1. Why do authoritarian systems sometimes have a certain popular appeal? Does totalitarianism have a similar appeal?

2. What is the fundamental difference between authoritarian and totalitarian systems? Why do you think totalitarianism is no longer as prominent as it was in the middle of the twentieth century? Do you think a resurgence in totalitarianism is likely? Why or why not?

3. What is the most common way in which authoritarian systems try to build polit-ical legitimacy? Is it similar to or different from the way totalitarian regimes claim legitimacy?

Internet Links

1. "Black Book of Communism": Use this as a search term. This large book, origi-nally published in France in 1997, documents totalitarian atrocities in great detail. Using the title as a search term will lead you to useful reviews and discussions.

2. Hoover Institution: **www.hoover.org**. This famous research institute at Stanford University has sponsored many studies of totalitarian governments.

3. Internet Guide for Chinese Studies: **sun.sino.uni-heidelberg.de/igcs**. Established by the Institute for Chinese Studies, Heidelberg University, this is a gateway to information about the world's largest remaining quasi-totalitarian system.

4. National Committee on North Korea: **www.ncnk.org**. An American non-profit group that has collected a large databank of information on North Korea. Contains many resources and links to government and NGO websites on North Korea.

Further Reading

Authoritarianism

Acemoglu, Daron, and James A. Robinson. *Economic Origins of Dictatorship and Democracy.* New York: Cambridge University Press, 2006.

Angell, Alan, and Benny Pollack. *The Legacy of Dictatorship: Political, Economic and Social Change in Pinochet's Chile.* Liverpool: Institute of Latin American Studies, University of Liverpool, 1993.

Boron, Atilio C. *State, Capitalism, and Democracy in Latin America.* Boulder, CO: Lynne Rienner, 1995.

Casper, Gretchen. *Fragile Democracies: The Legacies of Authoritarian Rule.* Pittsburgh: University of Pittsburgh Press, 1995.

———. *Negotiating Democracy: Transitions from Authoritarian Rule.* Pittsburgh: University of Pittsburgh Press, 1996.

Dominguez, Jorge I., ed. *Authoritarian and Democratic Regimes in Latin America.* New York: Garland, 1994.

Hogman, David E. *Neo-liberalism with a Human Face? The Politics and Economics of the Chilean Model.* Liverpool: Institute of Latin American Studies, University of Liverpool, 1995.

PART 3

Jalal, Ayesha. *Democracy and Authoritarianism in South Asia: A Comparative and Historical Perspective.* New York: Cambridge University Press, 1995.

Linz, Juan J., and H. E. Chehabi. *Sultanistic Regimes.* Baltimore: Johns Hopkins University Press, 1998.

Moore, Barrington Jr. *Social Origins of Dictatorship and Democracy: Lord and Peasant in the Making of the Modern World.* Boston: Beacon Press, 1993.

Nelson, Daniel N., ed. *After Authoritarianism: Democracy or Disorder?* Westport, CT: Greenwood Press, 1995.

Ottaway, Marina. *Democracy Challenged: The Rise of Semi-authoritarianism.* Washington, DC: Carnegie Endowment, 2003.

Roller, Matthew B. *Constructing Autocracy: Aristocrats and Emperors in Julio-Claudian Rome.* Princeton, NJ: Princeton University Press, 2001.

Scott, James C. *Seeing Like a State: How Certain Schemes to Improve the Human Condition Have Failed.* New Haven, CT: Yale University Press, 1999.

Seligman, Adam B. *The Transition from State Socialism in Eastern Europe: The Case of Hungary.* Greenwich, CT: JAI Press, 1994.

Shain, Yossi, with Juan J. Linz. *Between States: Interim Governments and Democratic Transitions.* Cambridge: Cambridge University Press, 1995.

Shapiro, Ian, and Russell Hardin, eds. *Political Order.* New York: New York University Press, 1996.

Totalitarianism

Arendt, Hannah. *The Origins of Totalitarianism.* Rev. ed. Cleveland, OH: World Publishing, 1958.

Beilharz, Peter, Gillian Robinson, and John Rundell, eds. *Between Totalitarianism and Postmodernity: A Thesis Eleven Reader.* Cambridge, MA: MIT Press, 1992.

Boesche, Roger. *Theories of Tyranny: From Plato to Arendt.* University Park: Pennsylvania State University, 1996.

Brooker, Paul. *Non-democratic Regimes: Theory, Government, and Politics.* New York: St. Martin's Press, 2000.

———. *Twentieth-Century Dictatorships: The Ideological One-Party States.* New York: New York University Press, 1995.

Conquest, Robert. *Reflections on a Ravaged Century.* New York: W. W. Norton, 2000.

Daniels, Robert Vincent. *The Stalin Revolution: Foundations of the Totalitarian Era.* 3rd ed. Lexington, MA: D. C. Heath, 1990.

Gleason, Abbott. *Totalitarianism: The Inner History of the Cold War.* New York: Oxford University Press, 1995.

Linz, Juan J. *Totalitarian and Authoritarian Regimes.* Boulder, CO: Lynne Rienner, 2000.

O'Kane, Rosemary H. T. *Paths to Democracy: Revolution and Totalitarianism.* New York: Routledge, 2004.

Pauley, Bruce F. *Hitler, Stalin, and Mussolini: Totalitarianism in the Twentieth Century.* Wheeling, IL: Harlan Davidson, 1997.

Roberts, David D. *The Totalitarian Experiment in Twentieth-Century Europe: Understanding the Poverty of Great Politics.* New York: Routledge, 2006.

Rousso, Henry, and Richard Joseph Golsan, eds. *Stalinism and Nazism: History and Memory Compared.* Lincoln: University of Nebraska Press, 2004.

Shlapentokh, Vladimir. *A Normal Totalitarian Society: How the Soviet Union Functioned and How It Collapsed.* Armonk, NY: M. E. Sharpe, 2001.

Thurston, Robert W. *Life and Terror in Stalin's Russia, 1934–1941.* New Haven, CT: Yale University Press, 1996.

Tiruneh, Andargachew. *The Ethiopian Revolution, 1975–1987: A Transformation from an Aristocratic to a Totalitarian Autocracy.* Cambridge: Cambridge University Press, 1993.

Unger, Aryeh L. *The Totalitarian Party: Party and People in Nazi Germany and Soviet Russia.* Cambridge: Cambridge University Press, 2010.

PART 3

CHAPTER 20

Parliamentary and Presidential Systems

Of the many possible models for organizing the apparatus of representative government, the two most important are the parliamentary and presidential systems. Both trace their origins to Britain in the seventeenth and eighteenth centuries and are now found everywhere in the world, even in societies that owe relatively little to Anglo-American traditions. They exist in their pure form only in liberal democracies, though many autocratic systems have "borrowed" them to create a veneer of legitimacy.

The difference between the parliamentary and presidential systems can be understood only in the context of **separation of powers**, a doctrine that has a long history in political science. All governments, no matter how they are organized, have to perform certain functions and exercise certain powers. The most common approach is to divide these powers into three categories: legislative, executive, and judicial. The **legislative** power makes general laws of conduct for members of the community and establishes policies such as health care and education. Included are matters of both private law (such as rules about property, contracts, and marriage) and **public law** (such as rules governing voting, military service, and payment of taxes). The **executive** power does not make general rules but proposes policies and administers the state's resources. For example, the executive commands the army (which was created by the legislative power), oversees the monetary system, and raises and spends taxes that the legislative power has authorized. This entails making many discretionary decisions, such as where to locate post offices and military bases. The executive power enforces the rules of conduct by administering police forces and prisons to ensure that laws are obeyed. The judicial power, or **judiciary**, resolves conflicts that arise when laws are not obeyed or when there is disagreement over what the law means.

Early liberal thinkers such as John Locke argued that these powers of state should be distributed among different hands rather than concentrated in one institution because dispersion lessens the temptation to use power arbitrarily. "In all moderated monarchies and well-framed governments," wrote Locke, "the legislative and executive power are in distinct hands."[1] In its simple form, this view tends to equate each power with one branch of government that specializes in it. In *The Spirit of the Laws* (1748), Montesquieu analyzed British government in this way; he wrote that Parliament constituted the legislative branch, the monarch and ministers the executive branch, and the courts the judicial branch. The separation of powers into distinct branches of government was, in Montesquieu's opinion, the secret of the excellence of the British constitution, which made Britain the freest and most enviable country in Europe. Soon afterward, the doctrine of separation of powers became an integral part of liberal thinking, providing a structural and legal way of limiting the power of government.

Although certainly true in part, Montesquieu's analysis was too simple. He overlooked the fact that the courts had a large share of legislative power, to the extent that the common law evolved through their decisions. This was not deliberate making of law (which was Parliament's function) but it was equally significant as a source of rules of conduct. Even more important, Montesquieu did not fully appreciate the custom—increasingly observed since the Glorious Revolution—that ministers of the Crown had to be members of Parliament, in either the Commons or the Lords. The executive and legislative branches were more closely connected than Montesquieu thought.

Since the publication of *The Spirit of the Laws*, British-style representative government has evolved in two different directions. The United States retained institutions modelled on those of Britain, but the division between the president and Congress was made sharper than the one between the Crown and Parliament. This American model is the source of most contemporary presidential systems, in which the separation of powers is still maintained. In Britain, however, and in colonies such as Canada that stayed within the Empire, political evolution has brought the legislative and executive branches closer together. In modern parliamentary systems, the executive (**cabinet**) and the legislature work closely together because of the practice of political party discipline. We will discuss the parliamentary system first and then return to the presidential model.

THE PARLIAMENTARY SYSTEM

After the Norman Conquest, all three powers of government were united in the monarchy. The king was the "font of justice" and the supreme military commander and could also legislate by royal proclamation. Parliament, which was first convened by Edward I in 1295, was originally not a legislative body at all. Its major functions were to advise the monarch and to approve the taxes necessary to support government. Over time, Parliament increased its power by refusing to grant revenue unless the monarch fulfilled its desires, which were drawn up in "bills," or lists of requests. This ancient practice is the reason why a statute under consideration by Parliament is known today as a **bill**. Another reminder of this early period is that all legislation is still proclaimed by the monarch "with the advice and consent" of Parliament. Though Parliament long ago captured the legislative power, this verbal formula shows that it once belonged to the Crown.

The Glorious Revolution brought about a separation of powers that had until then been united. But the settlement of 1689, although it made Parliament supreme, still left the monarch with considerable prerogative powers. The king or queen remained a true chief executive, with the discretionary right to appoint and dismiss officials, declare war, conduct foreign relations, command the armed forces, pardon convicted criminals, and—as a remnant of lost legislative power—withhold assent to legislation.

Further political evolution reunited the legislative and executive powers under the control of a new executive: the prime minister and Cabinet. At first this trend seemed to be a further victory of Parliament over the Crown; the custom grew that ministers had to be members of parliament (MPs) and had to have the political support of a working majority in the House of Commons. This mechanism of **responsible government** meant that the Crown could act only on the advice of those who had the confidence of Parliament. Parliament, by the middle of the nineteenth century, appeared to have captured the executive power just as it had previously captured the legislative. But, before long, the new practice of **party discipline** made it clear that the Cabinet, led by the prime minister, was the real victor. As long as the supporters of the prime minister in the House of Commons vote as directed, the executive and legislative powers are fused and separation of powers no longer acts as a check. Instead, the check in a parliamentary system comes when the prime minister loses majority support and the opposition can withdraw confidence from the government.

The Westminster Model

The political machinery of the British parliamentary system, referred to as the Westminster model, consists of the Crown, the Cabinet, the House of Commons, and the House of Lords.

The British Parliament is a **bicameral** institution, consisting of the House of Commons and the House of Lords. The Commons is structured in a hierarchical fashion. The prime minister, who is leader of the majority party, was originally thought to be *primus inter pares*—"first among equals." Now, however, he or she is much more: the first minister of Cabinet, the party leader, and the leader of government. Cabinet ministers of the governing party manage the legislative process, with some cooperation from opposition parties. Those who do not belong to Cabinet are referred to as **private members**, whether they sit on the side of the government or in the opposition. The British House of Commons has 650 members: 533 from English constituencies, 40 Welsh, 59 Scottish, and 18 from Northern Ireland.

The House of Lords began as a largely hereditary body of more than 1000 members, but recent reforms have reduced that number. Of the 830 members today, 712 are life peers—distinguished men and women appointed by the Crown on the recommendation of the prime minister, who is in turn advised by an appointments commission. There are also 26 archbishops and bishops of the Church of England, plus 92 hereditary peers. The powers of the two houses of Parliament were originally equal, but since the Parliament Acts of 1911 and 1949 were passed, the Lords have become subservient to the Commons. They may initiate and amend legislation but they cannot veto acts of the Commons and can only delay bills, for approximately one year. Reforms currently being considered include reducing its size to 300 members, of which 80 percent would be elected and 20 percent appointed.

With all of these changes, the parliamentary system today has become what some observers refer to as "prime-ministerial government." No one—not the monarch, not private members in the Commons, not members of the House of Lords—is as powerful as the prime minister supported by the cabinet, whose members he or she chooses.

The Parliament of Canada

Canada was one of the first colonies in modern history to peacefully attain independence from a colonial power. Its Parliament developed within the British tradition. Before 1867, colonial governors representing the Crown existed alongside locally elected legislatures, but one Parliament was created for all the colonies in 1867. This institution, like the British Parliament, was a bicameral legislature containing two houses, the Senate (which now has 105 seats) being the upper house and the Commons (which now has 308 members) being the lower one.

Canada is a federal system, but otherwise the Canadian parliament operates in principle like the British. The British monarch is our **head of state.** The Crown's representative in Canada is the governor general, who is appointed by the monarch on the advice of the prime minister of Canada. Lieutenant-governors, who are appointed by the governor general (also on the advice of the prime minister), play the role of head of state in provincial governments. The Queen, the governor general, and the lieutenant-governors together represent the Crown in Canada. The prime minister and the provincial premiers are the **heads of government.**

The heads of state normally do not exercise actual political power; they "reign rather than rule." Most functions of a head of state are symbolic in nature. The duties include selecting or dismissing a head of government; performing certain ceremonial functions—for example, greeting foreign dignitaries; assenting to and proclaiming legislation; formally appointing judges and other public officials; dissolving Parliament and calling elections; and exercising certain emergency powers if and when there is a leadership crisis or when government is deadlocked. In normal circumstances the representative of the Crown carries out these functions without making real prerogative choices. The monarch or governor general must take the advice of the cabinet as long as there is a government in office. No executive action is taken without the signature of one or more ministers. Even in selecting a new government, the head of state normally has no real choice because the person to become head of government has already been determined by the voters.

By constitutional convention, the leader of the political party with a majority of seats in the House of Commons is asked by the governor general to form the government of Canada. The prime minister then nominates the rest of the cabinet for appointment by the governor general. If there is no single party with a majority of seats, the party leader with the largest plurality of seats or who has received sufficient indications of support from other parties is asked to form a government.

The Crown

The constitution almost always dictates the actions of the Crown. In rare circumstances there might not be a constitutionally clear course of action—for example, if a prime minister were to die unexpectedly in office and the party had not agreed on a successor. Then the head of state might have to use discretion in asking someone to form an interim government until the majority party could sort out its affairs. In general the Crown acts unilaterally only if a crisis immobilizes responsible political institutions. In times of emergency there is a role to be played by the head of state; this has been one of the principal arguments made by those who favour retaining the Crown as an integral part of Canadian government.[2]

A case in point involves events in Canada in 2008. Stephen Harper was just weeks into his second minority government when the opposition parties indicated to the governor general, Michaëlle Jean, that the government had lost their confidence because of elements in the fiscal update. The Liberals, led by Stéphane Dion, and the New Democrats, led by Jack Layton, had signed an accord stating they would enter into a formal coalition with Dion as prime minister, and with the support of the Bloc Québécois on confidence votes. Using control of the agenda to delay the vote of non-confidence, however, Harper asked the governor general to prorogue (adjourn) parliament. Some commentators at the time argued that because the government was threatened with losing the confidence of the House, the governor general should refuse the prime minister's request for prorogation, forcing him to face possible defeat at that time. However, she chose to accept the prime minister's advice. The cooling-off period provided by the prorogation, combined with concessions by the Harper government on its fiscal plans, led to the breakup of the coalition and a continuation of the minority government. The head of state's role, although often largely symbolic, can on occasion be of tremendous importance and provides a potential check on the power of the prime minister.

The House of Commons

The second major component of the parliamentary system is the House of Commons. The government of the day is formed mostly from the House. The leader of the majority party, or of a party that has a working majority, becomes prime minister and chooses ministers from among members of the House or the Senate. Technically a prime minister may choose an individual who is not a member of either house to become a member of the cabinet, but the practice is rare; when it is followed, that person is expected to obtain a seat in the House or the Senate within a matter of months. Under modern practice, almost all cabinet members come from the House of Commons, with only one or two senators.

The Senate

The third component of the Canadian parliamentary system is the Senate. Under the Constitution Act, 1867, the passage of legislation requires the approval not only of the House of Commons but also of the Senate. The Senate has exactly the same legislative power as the House of Commons except that bills involving taxes or expenditures must originate in the House.[3] The Senate, however, is not a confidence chamber. When it rejects a bill from the Commons, the government does not have to resign.

Senators are chosen by personal decision of the prime minister. This method of appointment tends to produce a Senate dominated by the opposition party when power shifts in the House of Commons after one party has been in power for a long time. Because the Liberals had been in power almost continuously from 1935 to 1984, Liberal prime ministers had chosen almost all those sitting in the Senate by the time Brian Mulroney became prime minister. In 1989, in order to ensure passage of the GST legislation, which the Liberals were blocking in the Senate, he resorted to an obscure provision of the Constitution that allows the governor general, with the prior approval of the Queen, to appoint eight extra senators.[4] The shoe was on the other foot when the Liberals returned to power in 1993. At the time, Prime Minister Chrétien had to deal with a holdover Conservative majority in the Senate, which succeeded in blocking several pieces of Liberal legislation. By 1996, however, Chrétien had restored the Liberal majority in the Senate by appointing a Liberal every time a vacancy occurred.

Canada's difficulties with the Senate are unique because it is a centrally appointed upper house in a federal system of government, but other parliamentary systems have also experienced problems with an upper house. In 1975, Australia's House of Representatives passed a money bill that the Senate refused to approve. The conflict evolved into a fiscal and constitutional crisis. The government would not budge and neither would the Senate, which in Australia is popularly elected. Finally the governor general dismissed the prime minister, dissolved both houses, and issued the writs for a new election. The prime minister was furious and accused the governor general of overstepping his powers and precipitating a constitutional crisis by permitting the upper house to bring down the government. The election that followed resolved the political issue with the defeat of the government, which vindicated the governor general to some degree.

Fusion of Powers

As Figure 20.1 indicates, the prime minister cannot function without support in the House of Commons, and ultimately it is the electorate that provides this support by determining the balance of partisan power in the House of Commons. Three election outcomes are possible. One party may win a majority of seats in the House, in which case its leader will form a **majority government.** If no party wins a majority, the leader of one party—usually but not necessarily the party with the largest number of seats—can form a **minority government.** Such a minority government can stay in office only if the other parties refrain from defeating it. Finally, two or more parties

Figure 20.1 The Canadian Parliamentary System

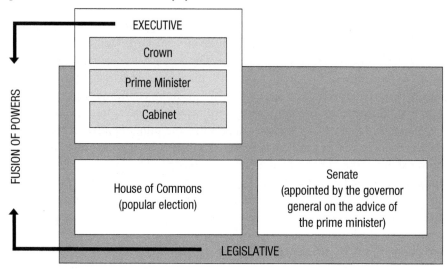

may join forces to form a **coalition government,** dividing ministerial appointments between them. The leader of the larger partner in the coalition normally becomes prime minister.

There has never been a true coalition government at the national level in Canada. The "Union Government" that ruled during World War I under Robert Borden consisted of breakaway Liberals who had joined with the Conservatives; it was not a genuine coalition of the two parties. However, there have been a number of coalitions at the provincial level, including most recently an NDP–Liberal coalition in Saskatchewan (1999–2003).

Cabinet and the Legislative Process

In forming the federal cabinet, the prime minister chooses the other ministers from MPs in his or her political party, who are then officially appointed by the governor general. The governor general would also dismiss them on the advice of the prime minister, although the usual course is for the prime minister to request and receive a resignation from a minister whose presence is no longer desired in the cabinet. The prime minister and the cabinet ministers, along with the Crown, form the political executive. Including Prime Minister Harper, the cabinet in 2011 consisted of 27 ministers plus 12 junior ministers, who do not attend meetings of the full cabinet but may serve on cabinet committees.

The cabinet determines legislative priorities and sets the legislative agenda. The cabinet has aptly been called "a combining committee—a hyphen which joins, a buckle which fastens, the legislative part of the state to the executive part."[5] It is the institution

---

Canadian Focus 20.1

How Cabinet Worked Under Prime Minister Jean Chrétien

He [Chrétien] was comfortable knowing that Cabinet decisions are the sole prerogative of the prime minister; there are no votes taken in Cabinet, and decisions aren't dependent on the number of ministers who have spoken on one side of an issue or another. As soon as discussion ended on an issue, he usually called his deci-sion and moved onto the next item. Occasionally, where there was no apparent consensus and where he had no strong views, Chrétien would take an issue under advisement and would decide at a later date.

Source: Eddie Goldenberg, *The Way It Works: Inside Ottawa* (Toronto: McClelland & Stewart, 2006), 99.

---

that most clearly distinguishes the modern parliamentary system from the presidential form of government. It is a collective decision-making body, but dominated by the prime minister and run according to his or her particular style (see Canadian Focus 20.1). After extensive discussion, the prime minister usually summarizes the arguments and announces the action to be taken. Once a course is set, the principle of **cabinet solidarity** prevents ministers from differing with government policy in public, whatever their private reservations.

Private members' bills, which are introduced by members of parliament who are not ministers, may be numerous but they are seldom passed. The prime minister, the cabinet, and the leaders of the opposition parties, together with their chief advisers, are the dominant figures in the parliamentary process. However, various changes in the rules of procedure of the House of Commons adopted since 1986 have eased the way for private members' bills, and more are now passing than used to be the case.

The House functions according to strict procedures and rules that are observed most of the time by all parties and enforced by a Speaker who is elected by the House. Before 1986 it was customary for the prime minister to nominate the Speaker, and party discipline turned the election into a foregone conclusion. Now, however, the Speaker is chosen by secret ballot in a free election, without prime-ministerial nomination and party discipline.[6] In Great Britain the Speaker becomes an impartial figure who completely withdraws from party affiliation, runs unopposed for re-election, and serves as Speaker until retirement from the House. In Canada the Speaker is also supposed to conduct the affairs of the House impartially, but the divorce from partisan politics is not so complete. The opposition parties generally field candidates in the Speaker's constituency at election time, and a Speaker is selected each time a new Parliament convenes.

A proposed bill must go through three **readings** in both chambers. At the first reading, the bill's title is introduced; the text of the proposed legislation is then printed and distributed to members. After the second reading there is a full debate on the bill;

PART 3

the opposition and government backbenchers have a specified time to address different aspects of it. It may then go to a standing committee—or, more commonly, to a special legislative committee of the House. **Standing committees** are permanent committees appointed to study particular areas of public policy; their membership is proportional to party strength in the House. Examples include committees on finance, health, and citizenship and immigration. **Special** (or **ad hoc**) **committees** are established to deal with specific problems and are dissolved when their assignment is finished.

Backbenchers become involved in the legislative process by serving on parliamentary committees. Their power is very limited in a majority parliament because the government party will have a majority on all committees and bloc voting will prevail. But in a minority parliament, opposition members will outnumber government members on committees and may use their voting power to harass and frustrate the government. Committees sometimes produce amendments to government bills, but they do not reject them altogether. The bill then goes through the **report stage**, at which time the House receives the committee report and votes on any proposed amendments.

The bill as amended is received and voted on by the House in the third reading; no amendment is allowed at this final stage. The bill is then introduced in the Senate, whose deliberations may also involve committee action. The Senate may suggest changes and send its version of the bill back to the House. Occasionally the Senate tries to block legislation coming from the House, as described above, but more frequently it functions as a source of technical amendments. It may even finish considering a bill before the Commons does. When this happens, its suggested amendments may be incorporated by the Commons at third reading.

A bill passed by the Commons and the Senate then goes to the governor general for **royal assent** and **proclamation**. *Royal assent* means that the governor general approves the bill; *proclamation* involves setting the date on which the new law will take effect. There is generally a period of weeks or months—sometimes even years—between royal assent and proclamation.

Throughout the legislative process, the **opposition** parties (i.e., those parties that do not share ministerial appointments) criticize the government and sometimes win concessions from it, even if they do not have the voting strength to make their views prevail. For example, the government may feel that points raised by the opposition have merit or public support, or it may yield in order to avoid obstructive or disruptive behaviour.

In Canada and Britain, the largest of the opposition parties is singled out as the **Official Opposition** (or simply "the Opposition"). Such status entitles the party to preferential funding and certain privileges during debate. The leader of the Opposition assigns various party members to follow the activities of one or more cabinet ministers with particular attention. In Britain the leader of the Opposition and these specialist critics form a cohesive group, known as a **shadow cabinet,** that is ready to assume office if invited to do so by the head of state. Canadian opposition parties have not always had this degree of organization.

Confidence, Party Discipline, and Responsible Government

For its tenure, the government depends not just on support of the electorate at election time but also on its ability to maintain a majority on the floor of the House of Commons. In other words, the exercise of power hinges on the government's ability to maintain the **confidence** of the House. The idea of confidence is rooted in the principle of responsible government, which makes the cabinet accountable to the House of Commons. Every legislative proposal made by the government must go to the floor of the House. As long as these proposals are supported by a majority of those voting, the government enjoys the confidence of the House and is ruling "responsibly."

Note that the term *responsible government*—meaning that the cabinet must enjoy continued support of the popularly elected house of the legislative assembly in order to remain in office—is a concept associated with parliamentary government. It is an essential aspect of the parliamentary form of representative democracy, although not of representative democracy in general. In the governments of Switzerland and the United States, for example, the cabinet does not need legislative support to remain in power, but these governments are just as democratic as parliamentary ones because they are equally responsible or accountable to the people through elections. This broader sort of accountability should not be confused with the precise form of responsible government that characterizes the parliamentary system.

(CP PHOTO) 1997 (stf-Fred Chartrand)

The seats in the Canadian House of Commons, following the British model, are placed on two sides of a central aisle in order to emphasize the difference between government and opposition.

PART 3

Budgetary bills are always treated as confidence motions, but beyond that, the prime minister is free to decide whether any legislation or other motion should be a matter of confidence. Typically a majority government will treat all votes as confidence votes, but a prime minister in a minority situation will often declare that legislation (except the budget) is not a matter of confidence, meaning that his government does not need to resign or ask for an election even if its legislation does not pass.

A member who does not support his or her party's position on the floor of the House or in committee can be punished in various ways; for example, travel opportunities or choice committee assignments may be denied. At the extreme, a recalcitrant member may even be expelled from caucus, and the party may deny that individual the right to run in the next election under the party label. However, the role of coercion should not be overestimated. Caucus members vote together most of the time more or less voluntarily, for three reasons: they want to remain in the good graces of the party's leadership; they would like to benefit from political patronage; and they see themselves as part of a team, and understand that the parliamentary system of responsible government will not work unless parties exhibit some coherence. Contemporary Canadian practice allows members of parliament to deviate from the party line occasionally but not too often, especially if it might unseat the government.

Occasionally the government may allow a **free vote** on certain bills that are of a controversial nature. In such a situation, all members of the caucus do not have to vote with the party; they are free to "vote their conscience." The Mulroney government held free votes on the morally supercharged issues of capital punishment and abortion, the Chrétien government allowed free votes on religious educational rights in Newfoundland and Labrador and Quebec, and the Martin and Harper governments both held free votes on same-sex marriage.

Party Caucus

Party discipline does not necessarily mean that **backbenchers**—those who are not in the cabinet or the shadow cabinet and who therefore sit on the rear benches in the House—have no influence on their party leadership. One primary function of the party **caucus** is to give party members an opportunity to be heard by their leaders. A party caucus is a closed meeting of the members of a parliamentary party in the House and Senate. At caucus meetings, backbenchers can question their own leaders and suggest alternatives to the party's policies. Party leaders know that the support of backbenchers is required to maintain a majority position, and they must therefore take into account the nature and strength of backbench opinion. Unanimity seldom exists, so these meetings can be raucous affairs. However, once a given issue is settled and goes to the House, all members are expected to support the collective caucus position. The backbenchers of a majority party can bring down a government by failing to support their own leaders. Although this rarely happens, it does mean that the government's own party can provide an important check on political power.

A second check on government is the activity of the opposition parties. The development of an institutionalized practice of loyal opposition, in which one can legally challenge the government without fear of repression, is one of the significant achievements of liberal democracy. The rationale for an opposition is the liberal view that everyone has limited knowledge and that no government or governor is infallible.

The essence of the parliamentary process is the formal duel between the government and those forces unable to muster sufficient legislative seats to form a government. The opposition has three basic functions: to offer an alternative government, to offer alternative policies, and to question and call attention to controversial legislative proposals or government actions of any kind. If the opposition is a minority, it cannot by itself defeat the government; it does, however, have important opportunities to object to legislation to which it is opposed and to delay and obstruct legislative proposals it wants altered. Time is limited in the House, and parliamentary procedures protect the role of the opposition. Proceedings can be immobilized until the opposition and government come to a compromise agreement. A government that tries to run roughshod over the opposition parties may succeed in passing a particular piece of legislation, but it may well find other aspects of its program jeopardized by delaying tactics.

A final check on the government is the electorate. At least every five years, voters have an opportunity to pass judgment on the record of the party in power. This serves to remind us of the liberal-democratic principle that political power emanates from the people and rests upon the consent of the governed.

In times of minority government, such as ensued in Canada after the elections of 2004, 2006, and 2008, the government's power to control the House of Commons is considerably reduced. See the description in Canadian Focus 20.2 for more on minority governments.

Variations on the Westminster Model

We have used Britain and Canada as examples of the Westminster model of parliamentary government. In other countries, that basic model has been modified to meet the needs of different political environments.

Under the Weimar constitution of 1919, Germany had something close to the Westminster model of parliamentary government. But representation in the legislative body was so badly fragmented among a number of political factions that no political party commanded a majority. Weak coalition governments, many of them dependent on the support of extremist or splinter parties, proved unable to deal effectively with political crises. The system found itself unable to combat the economic crash of 1929, with the result that Hitler established the Third Reich in 1933.

After World War II, the Germans modified their parliamentary system in order to deal with the problem of instability. The constitution of the Federal Republic of Germany, known as the Basic Law, was adopted in 1949. Those who drafted the document instituted a positive or **constructive vote of confidence**. The chancellor (prime

PART 3

Canadian Focus 20.2

Minority Versus Coalition Government

Minority government is fairly common in Canada; since 1867, Canada has had 13 minority governments, three of them since 2004. Lasting on average about a year and a half, they can be stable, efficient, and relatively effective, as were Lester Pearson's minority governments in the 1960s that brought in the Canada Pension Plan and universal health care. On the other hand, only one government has ever come close to a true coalition—at the outbreak of World War I—and this was to broaden support for conscription rather than because of lack of a majority government.

The relative absence of coalition governments is due in part to a belief on the part of politicians that a minority government can be turned into a majority government in a subsequent election, notwithstanding recent evidence. It is also true that smaller parties are generally unwilling to enter into formal coalitions with larger parties. Such agreements are often perceived to result in a loss of identity for the smaller party, given the loss of a vocal and critical party leader in exchange for cabinet seats.

Party members are also likely to reject such agreements because of the concessions to party policy that they often require. Finally, coalition governments are most likely to occur between parties with similar policy platforms. The large number of seats held by the Bloc Quebecois in recent years, a separatist party, has made it an unlikely coalition partner.

The result is a tendency towards minority governments held up by informal or ad hoc agreements with smaller parties, who gain a degree of influence but without the loss of identity or member backlash to more formal coalitions. And although the media tend to focus on their potential for instability, minority governments governed by a culture of cooperation and accommodation, rather than conflict and partisanship, can be effective and stable.

See Mark Chalmers, "Canada's Dysfunctional Minority Parliament," in Robert Hazell and Akash Paun, eds. *Making Minority Government Work: Hung Parliaments and the Challenges for Westminster and Whitehall* (London: Institute for Government, 2009), www.instituteforgovernment.org.uk/pdfs/making-minority-gov-work.pdf.

minister) is the leader of the majority party, or of a coalition of parties making up a majority, in the Bundestag, the lower house of parliament. The government can be defeated on a non-confidence vote in the Bundestag; however, the vote defeats the government only if the chancellor's successor is chosen at the same time. A majority in the Bundestag can bring down the government, but not unless that same majority approves another government. This breaks with the British and Canadian custom of holding an election or forming a new government after defeat on a matter of confidence.

Israel has found yet another way of coping with cabinet instability. Because that country uses a pure form of proportional representation (see Chapter 25), there are so many political parties that all governments have to be coalitions. Israeli governments accept coalitions as a fact of life and treat cabinets almost as if they were legislatures. Cabinet secrecy has been abandoned, as has cabinet solidarity; formal votes are taken in Cabinet on important issues and the results are announced to the public. The result is that, having made their opposition to a policy known, coalition partners do not necessarily feel obliged to break up the coalition. Thus coalitions can survive tensions that would destroy cabinets operating on the Westminster model, and political instability can be avoided despite a proliferation of parties.

Evaluating Parliamentary Systems

Critics often argue that the problem with the parliamentary process is that the executive has become too powerful. Some analysts would go so far as to say that now we have prime-ministerial government. With reference to executive federalism (i.e., federal politics being monopolized by first ministers), Stephen Brooks suggests that "it is a process from which legislatures are almost entirely excluded, except when called upon to ratify an agreement reached between executives of the two levels of government."[7]

And, in regard to the policymaking process of the federal government, he says:

> The popular identification of "government" with the individual who occupies the position of prime minister and his team of cabinet colleagues entails an accurate assessment of where the centre of power lies in the state system. In parliamentary systems as different as those of Canada, Belgium, and France the political executive is that part of the state system best able to shape the direction of public policy.[8]

When the executive initiates party policy and caucus members are expected to support it, the executive has become in effect an almost autonomous force at the expense of the legislature. In the system, there is thus a need to balance the roles of the legislature and the executive. The executive must not operate as an autonomous force, and there must be a way to involve backbenchers—and the public, for that matter—in the process of formulating policy. The question is, how can this be accomplished without rendering the legislative process ineffectual? How can the process be made more open to differing points of view without making it unworkable?

If party discipline does in fact undermine representation, there are ways to relax that discipline, such as increasing the number of free votes or permitting party members to oppose the government on votes. The result might well be more open debate on issues within the governing party itself. A reduction of party discipline could also show the electorate that backbenchers are not just puppets of the leadership; the party's rank and file would in fact have an opportunity to more openly represent constituents. However, too much autonomy of the legislature could lead to gridlock, as is sometimes the case in the presidential system.

THE PRESIDENTIAL SYSTEM

The presidential system of government was first devised in the United States in 1787, as an alternative to the monarchical system. It is used today chiefly in areas of the world where American influence has been particularly strong, as in Latin America and the Philippines. In some cases it may simply be a guise for an autocratic dictatorship. Nevertheless, the basic model is distinctive; the principle of separation of powers and the lack of responsible government set it apart from the parliamentary system.

While the parliamentary system is known for its fusion of powers and for cabinet government, the presidential system is known for the separation of powers and for the congressional committee system. The executive branch, although instrumental in the legislative process, is physically separated from the legislative branch. While the separation is real (each branch has veto powers), cooperation is required to pass legislation. In this system of government, the committees of both houses of congress dominate the legislative process. Figure 20.2 depicts the presidential system of the United States.

The customary term used to describe the presidential system—separation of powers—is somewhat misleading. James Madison, the chief draftsman of the American constitution, explicitly criticized the oversimplified view that the legislative, executive, and judicial powers of government ought to be absolutely separated within the distinct institutions or branches of government. In No. 47 of the *Federalist* papers, a series of essays he wrote with Alexander Hamilton and John Jay to persuade the American public to ratify the new constitution, Madison outlined the ideal of placing each power in the custody of the branch of government primarily concerned with it, while allowing the other two branches a secondary role in exercising it. Neither the president nor Congress nor the courts would be able to follow a course of action for very long without the cooperation of the other branches. A modern scholar has suggested that "separated institutions sharing powers" is a more apt description of the Madisonian system than "separation of powers."[9] Figure 20.3 illustrates this complex balance.

Figure 20.2 The American Presidential System

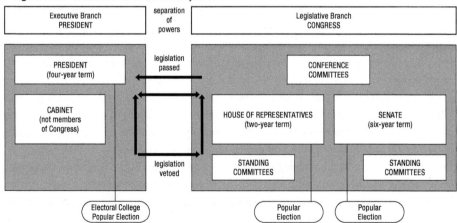

Figure 20.3 Balance of Powers in the American Presidential System

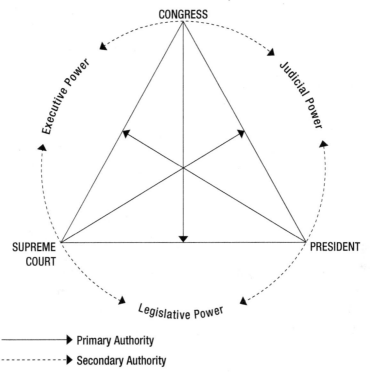

```
                    Primary Authority
                    Secondary Authority
```

The President

The president, the only elected official on the ballot across the entire nation, is elected for a four-year term and is both head of state and head of government. As head of state, the president greets foreign dignitaries and performs other ceremonial functions. As head of government, the president is the chief executive officer. The constitution grants the president powers that are, on the whole, rather similar to the ancient prerogative powers of the British Crown. In Britain these are now wielded by the prime minister, with relatively little interference by Parliament as long as party discipline holds; in the United States the president's powers are restricted by his or her not being a member of Congress and, as a result, limited to exercising influence rather than authority over its members.

The president has the power to appoint the highest officials of government: cabinet secretaries, ambassadors, federal judges, senior civil servants, and members of regulatory commissions. But all these appointments rely on the advice and consent of the Senate, the upper house of Congress; a simple majority suffices. As chief executive, the president directs the manifold business of government, but this power is dependent for revenue on appropriations from Congress. Although the president submits a budget to Congress, that body can and does alter it freely. Congress also has the power to investigate the administrative activities of government, in either closed or public hearings.

The president is responsible for the general conduct of foreign affairs and, in particular, is authorized to negotiate treaties with other states. But these treaties must also receive the advice and consent of the Senate—in this instance, a qualified majority of two-thirds. The dynamic of the presidential system is that the president checks Congress and Congress checks the president.

The president is commander-in-chief of the armed forces, but this coercive power is also subject to congressional limitation. The armed forces can be paid only with revenue voted by Congress, and a declaration of war requires approval in both houses of Congress. This constitutional provision has not been invoked since 1941; the Korean and Vietnam wars were waged as "police actions" under presidential authorization and were not declared by Congress. The war in Afghanistan (2001) and the two wars with Iraq (1990 and 2003) were approved by majority resolutions in both houses of Congress, but these were not official declarations of war.

Technically, the **Electoral College** chooses the president. Some delegates to the constitutional convention of 1787 wanted the president to be elected by Congress. Others, fearing the demise of state power in the federal system, wanted the president to be chosen by state legislators. A few others considered a more radical move—direct election by all voters. The Electoral College was the compromise. This was a group of electors, each supposedly an upstanding and respected individual of independent mind. They would be chosen by voters within the states and would in turn formally elect the president. The number of electors from each state was determined by adding the number of representatives from the state in the federal House of Representatives (determined by the population of the state) and the number of senators from the state (two). The total number of Electoral College votes in the United States is now 538: 435 for the number of members of the House, 100 for the number of senators, and an additional three electors from the District of Columbia.

In each state, the political parties select slates of electors who are pledged to cast their votes in the Electoral College for their party's candidate. When voters cast their ballot for president, they are, strictly speaking, voting for one of these slates. The electors assemble in their respective states in December to cast their votes. Technically the vote remains secret until January, when the vice-president, in the presence of the Speaker of the House of Representatives, counts votes. In fact, usually everyone knows the outcome of the race on election night, because the popular vote in each state on election night determines the Electoral College vote. Members of the Electoral College usually vote according to the popular vote in the state. In some states this is a legal requirement, but in most states it is merely a well-observed practice. For a discussion of the importance of the Electoral College on the outcome of the 2000 presidential election, see Comparative Perspectives 20.1.

Comparative Perspectives 20.1

The 2000 Presidential Election in the United States

Since the candidate who gets a plurality of popular votes in a state gets all of that state's electoral votes, there is often a marked difference between the percentage of popular votes and the percentage of electoral votes that candidates obtain. Table 20.1 shows how 55 or 60 percent of the popular vote can translate into 80 or 90 percent of the electoral votes.[10]

However, the November 2000 election between Texas governor George W. Bush (Republican) and Vice President Al Gore (Democrat) was very close, both in the popular vote and in the Electoral College. Out of approximately 103 million voters, Gore won the popular vote by 540,000. But Bush received a majority of the Electoral College votes, 271 to Gore's 267. The result was not decided until weeks after the election, after the Supreme Court of the United States rejected appeals from Florida courts.

The Florida dispute reflected two important points. First, state governments are responsible for conducting federal elections. This fact goes back to the original compromise on adopting the 1789 Constitution, when the states held out for a strong role in the governing process. Second, not all states have consistent standards for conducting elections; the quality of voting machines, for example, varied considerably from county to county in Florida. Old voting machines led to a high number of spoiled ballots (ballots that could not be counted). Vice President Gore tried to get the courts to order a recount in counties where disputes were obvious. In the end, the Supreme Court rejected the appeal and Governor Bush was elected president. Ultimately it was the courts that decided the outcome.

Electoral College Votes, American Presidential Election, 2000

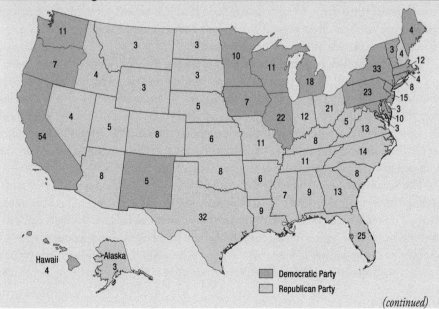

Democratic Party
Republican Party

(continued)

PART 3

Comparative Perspectives 20.1   *(continued)*

Table 20.1

Landslide Presidential Elections in the United States

Winner	Year	Popular Vote (%)	Electoral Vote	States Won
Warren G. Harding (R)	1920	60.3	404 (76.1%)	37
Franklin D. Roosevelt (D)	1936	60.8	523 (98.5%)	46
Lyndon B. Johnson (D)	1964	61.1	486 (90.3%)	44
Richard M. Nixon (R)	1972	60.7	520 (96.7%)	49
Ronald Reagan (R)	1984	58.9	525 (97.6%)	49

In the November 2008 election, Democratic Senator Barack Obama won 52 percent of the popular vote and 364 Electoral College votes—a robust victory but not a landslide—while Senator John McCain won 46 percent of the popular vote and 163 Electoral College votes. The Democrats also increased their majorities in the House of Representatives and the Senate.

The Congress

Congress, like the Canadian Parliament, is a bicameral legislature. The House of Representatives has 435 members, all elected in constituencies based on population. Each elected member represents a constituency called a congressional district. The boundaries of these districts are redrawn periodically to reflect population shifts, and attempts are made to keep these districts approximately equal in size. Each state, no matter how small, gets at least one representative.

The term of office of a member of the House is two years. Unlike the parliamentary system, the presidential system does not provide for the government to call elections. Rather, the dates are fixed. Election day in the United States is on the Tuesday after the first Monday in November. At that time, voters select all elected officials at the federal level, as well as many at the state and local level. This system of fixed dates for elections prevents the president from dissolving Congress at a politically opportune time and going to the people for a new mandate.

The Senate has 100 members (two from each state), each elected for a six-year term. Senators were originally chosen by state legislatures, but the Seventeenth Amendment changed this process in 1913 so that they are now directly elected. At the constitutional convention in 1787, equal representation of states in the Senate and representation by population in the House represented a trade-off between the populous states (which wanted to emphasize numbers as the basis of representation) and the thinly populated states (which wanted to emphasize territory). The Senate is considered the upper house and has more functions than the House of Representatives; most notably, it confirms presidential appointments and ratifies treaties. However, all money bills (i.e., those involving revenue or appropriations) must originate in the House of Representatives. This echoes the ancient British practice whereby revenue bills must originate in the House of Commons.

Congress is the chief repository of legislative power, but as Congress checks the president in the executive area, so the president checks Congress in the legislative area. All bills passed by Congress are sent to the president, who then has three options: to sign the bill, at which time it becomes law; not to sign the bill (after ten days it becomes law without the signature if Congress remains in session); or to **veto** the bill. In the event of a veto, the bill returns to Congress. If the bill passes again with a two-thirds majority in each house, the president's veto is overridden and the bill becomes law. This latter contingency is rather rare; the president's veto is usually final except on occasional highly charged issues.

The veto power is especially important because the president must approve or veto a bill as a whole. Most American state constitutions give the governor an **item veto**—the power to reject only certain clauses within a bill—but the president must approve or reject an entire package. Knowing this, Congress often puts together omnibus legislation, containing items that the president is known to oppose along with those he is known to like. Such tactics, coupled with the inevitable shortage of legislative time, often manoeuvre the president into signing legislation that he would not otherwise approve.

The president cannot actually introduce a bill into Congress—that task must be performed by a senator or representative—but he can have legislation drafted to submit to Congress, and in fact a large majority of American legislation originates this way. However, it is subject to amendment as it goes through Congress, and the final result may differ greatly from the original draft.

There are other important ways in which the presidential machinery of government differs from the parliamentary model. Neither the president nor the cabinet secretaries may hold a seat in Congress. The American cabinet, furthermore, is not a collective decision-making body. The main relationship is between the president and the secretaries individually. Under some presidents the cabinet seldom or never met as a group. The number of cabinet secretaries varies with the administration—between 14 and 16 in recent decades.

Another essential feature of the presidential system is that there is no vote of confidence and thus no principle of responsible government. No matter how votes go on the floor of either house, there is nothing comparable to the non-confidence motion or the dissolution of Parliament. Barring death, resignation, or removal for misconduct, the president is in office for four years, members of the House of Representatives for two years, and senators for six years. Since the executive is not responsible to the legislature, there is less need to practise party discipline, and party solidarity is not crucial for survival. In such a system the individual's first loyalty can be to the

PART 3

constituency rather than to the party. Party leaders in Congress try to invoke party discipline on votes, but they simply do not have the power that they would in the parliamentary system.

This generalization admits certain exceptions. Appointments to congressional standing committees are made along party lines at the opening of each session. If, for example, 60 percent of the membership of a chamber is Republican, the partisan division of members constituting committees will be 60 Republicans to 40 Democrats. Party positions often, though not invariably, count in these committees. Still, the necessity for strong party ties that exists in the parliamentary system does not hold in the presidential system.

A final feature of the presidential system is the importance of congressional committees. The number of committees may vary slightly, but it is usually around 20 in each house of Congress. These committees are almost little legislatures in themselves. After a bill is introduced in either house, it goes immediately to a committee. In most instances, if a bill is to reach the floor of either house, a committee must first approve it.

A bill that has successfully passed through a committee usually passes on the floor vote in the House or Senate. Conversely, bills can sometimes be bottled up in committee by influential members, such as the chairman of the whole committee or of a powerful subcommittee. A great deal of vote trading, or **log-rolling**, develops among committee members in the process of getting legislation passed. Deals arise in committee that in the parliamentary system would be hidden in cabinet proceedings.

Judicial Review

Although the American constitution does not explicitly mention **judicial review**—the power to declare legislation or executive action unconstitutional—the U.S. Supreme Court quickly asserted this role for itself and the lower courts. Judicial review means that in constitutional matters the courts have, in effect, the power to veto legislation, which amounts to a share of legislative power. As well, they share executive power to the extent that they rule on the legality of administrative actions when these are challenged. This power helps keep executive discretion within the bounds of the law.

Court decisions are final in the short run; in the long run, the other branches of government balance the judiciary. Because federal judges must be appointed by the president and confirmed by the Senate, the political complexion of the courts can be changed gradually as retirements open vacancies on the bench.

Even when the courts declare a piece of legislation unconstitutional, their ruling may not be the end of the story because Congress can introduce an amendment to the constitution. The amending process is complex: an amendment must be approved by two-thirds of the members of Congress and then ratified by three-quarters of the state legislatures. Nevertheless, the amending process serves as a potential check on the judiciary by the legislative branch.

Legislation, therefore, involves all three branches of government. Congress must pass it, the president has to sign it (unless a veto is overridden), and the courts need to interpret it and may sometimes even strike it down.

Checks and Balances

The system of **checks and balances**, as the Americans call it, gives the many interest groups of a pluralistic society marvellous opportunities to find friends in government. Cotton-growers, to select an example at random, make a special effort to maintain good relations not only with the chairs of the Senate and House agriculture committees but also with the chairs and members of the subcommittees that deal primarily with fibre crops. Even if the president or a congressional majority has pledged to do something that may reduce cotton-growers' incomes—for example, end a price-support program—they may be able to hold their ground by getting a strategically placed senator or representative to arrange for the bill to die a lingering death in committee. Or if a group cannot get Congress or the president to act upon its demands, as was true of Blacks seeking civil rights in the 1950s, it may turn to the courts to accomplish by litigation what it could not achieve by legislation. In the more narrowly focused power configuration of the parliamentary system, it is much harder to influence government in this manner.

Clearly the presidential system is highly decentralized, almost fragmented. Power, instead of being concentrated in the hands of a prime minister and cabinet, is divided among many offices. The reason for this was explained by James Madison in No. 51 of the *Federalist* papers:

> Ambition must be made to counteract ambition ... If men were angels, no government would be necessary. If angels were to govern men, neither external nor internal controls on government would be necessary. In framing a government which is to be administered by men over men, the great difficulty lies in this: you must first enable the government to control the governed; and in the next place oblige it to control itself.[11]

Separation of the legislative, executive, and judicial branches is one way of organizing government so as to "oblige it to control itself."

PARLIAMENTARY VERSUS PRESIDENTIAL SYSTEMS

Whether the parliamentary system is preferable to the presidential system as a form of liberal democracy is interesting to debate in the abstract but not of much practical relevance unless a new constitution is being designed. Interestingly, those who live under one system and become critical of it often wish to make it more like the other. For

PART 3

example, it is sometimes said in Canada that the prime minister's power of appointment is too unrestricted and that there should be a body like the American Senate to confirm appointments to the bench or other high office, and that party discipline is too strict, that members of parliament should be free to vote according to their conscience or the wishes of their constituents.

But the separation of powers creates problems of its own, as illustrated by the ongoing deadlock in the United States over balancing the budget. To simplify a bit, the Republicans want to reduce expenditures while the Democrats want to raise taxes on higher-income earners. With the Republicans controlling the House of Representatives since 2010 and the Democrats in control of the Senate and presidency, a coherent policy has been impossible to achieve. Perhaps the conclusion must be drawn that the grass is always greener elsewhere. Once a system is solidly established, it has so much inertia and weight of tradition behind it that the benefit of a wholesale change is unlikely to be worth the cost, although piecemeal reforms may transfer to one system some of the advantages of the other.

The two systems, while more or less equally viable, have different strengths and weaknesses, which can be summarized as follows. While both are effective forms of liberal democracy, the presidential system is more liberal and the parliamentary system is more democratic. By "more liberal" we mean that the presidential system has more internal checks on the exercise of power, which is in line with the classical liberal fear of excessive state control of society. By "more democratic" we mean that the parliamentary system is more effective in expressing the will of the majority because it allows the electorate to choose a government that can govern with relatively little hindrance from countervailing power.

This democratic potential of the parliamentary system raises problems for a country such as Canada, in which a national majority is often difficult to form because of regional and linguistic fragmentation. In such situations the parliamentary system may confer tremendous power on the governing party, even though it represents not a true majority but only the largest single minority. For example, the Conservatives won a solid majority of 169 seats in the House of Commons in the 1988 election, but with only 43 percent of the popular vote. They then used their majority to push through the Free Trade Agreement and the goods and services tax (GST), even though the former might well have been defeated, and the latter certainly would have been defeated, in a popular referendum. Although the government was much criticized by the opposition parties for legislating contrary to the "will of the people," it was not acting any differently from other governments before or after. It is part of the logic of the parliamentary system that the representatives of the largest voting minority act as if they represent a majority, at least for a period of time (see Comparative Perspectives 20.2).

One of the recurrent themes of Canadian politics is protest by minorities who feel that their rights have been ignored or curtailed by overwhelming parliamentary majorities. One thinks immediately of the resistance of French Canadians against

Comparative Perspectives 20.2

Comparing the Parliamentary and Presidential Systems

Parliamentary	Presidential
Strengths	
1. With a majority, the government has the power to govern.	1. Separation of powers discourages concentration of power.
2. The non-confidence vote provides a check on the government.	2. Checks and balances limit the power of branches of government.
3. The lines of responsibility for passage or defeat of legislation are clear. A voter can make decisions on the basis of party stance.	3. Without strict party discipline, members can be more constituency-oriented.
Weaknesses	
1. The system may be unstable if a majority is not obtained.	1. Separation of powers fragments the system, often rendering it immobile.
2. The power of a government with a large majority is very great—it is possibly insensitive to public desires.	2. Voters cannot pin responsibility on any one party.
3. Because party loyalty is necessary, individual members may have to vote against the wishes of their constituents.	3. Without a non-confidence vote, the electorate must wait for an election to unseat an unpopular president or member of Congress.

conscription in the two world wars, the demands of Aboriginal peoples for self-government, and the constant struggle of the Western provinces against Ottawa during the Trudeau years. These considerations lead to the discussion of the centralization and decentralization of government in Chapter 21.

SEMI-PRESIDENTIAL SYSTEMS

That parliamentary and presidential systems operate differently has inevitably led constitution-makers to try to combine the advantages of both in the so-called **semi-presidential system**. The prototype of the semi-presidential system is France, which experienced extreme political instability during the Fourth Republic (1946–58). Numerous political parties were represented in the National Assembly but none

PART 3

could command a majority of the seats, and governments were founded on loose and generally short-lived coalitions. In the constitution of the Fifth Republic (1958), General Charles de Gaulle remedied this instability by modifying the political executive. To the prime minister and the cabinet he added a president who is elected directly by the people for a seven-year term of office. The president is the actual head of government, not just a titular head of state. One responsibility is to appoint the prime minister, who is traditionally the leader of the majority party or of the senior party in a coalition in the National Assembly. The president also appoints the cabinet, although the prime minister can propose candidates for the positions. The National Assembly can still pass a non-confidence motion—or **vote of censure**, as it is called—and defeat the government, but this right can be exercised only once in a year. When the government is censured, only the prime minister and the cabinet must resign; the president remains because the incumbent has been popularly elected for a specific term of office.

Because the president remains in office in spite of government turnovers, the executive branch of government is stabilized. However, the value of this stability should be weighed against the possibility of deadlock. A French president may belong to a different party than the majority in the National Assembly. Under these circumstances, which the French call *cohabitation*, the president and the majority in the National Assembly must each put a little water in their wine and arrive at compromises in order to get anything done. Although such power sharing seems awkward, the French have made it work. The two most important semi-presidential countries are France and Russia, but the model has also been adopted in the developing world by states seeking to import more stability into parliamentary systems.[12]

Questions for Discussion

1. What problems can the parliamentary system of government cause in a pluralistic country such as Canada? Can you think of examples when, in your opinion, a majority government in Canada was insensitive to public desires? Why might the presidential system of government also be problematic in light of Canadian pluralism?

2. If you were a political engineer advising a transitional democracy in a non-industrial society, would you recommend the parliamentary or presidential system of government? Why?

3. What are the advantages and disadvantages of a disciplined party system in a parliamentary democracy? Why is party discipline more prevalent in the parliamentary system than it is in the presidential system?

Internet Links

1. Commonwealth Parliamentary Association: **www.cpahq.org**. The Canadian region of this international organization publishes the *Canadian Parliamentary Review.*

2. Parliament of Canada: **www.parl.gc.ca**. This website is a gateway to both the Senate and the House of Commons, with information on members, bills, procedures, and so on.

3. Parliament of the United Kingdom: **www.parliament.uk**.

4. United States House of Representatives: **www.house.gov**.

5. United States Senate: **www.senate.gov**.

Further Reading

Parliamentary Systems

Beyme, Klaus von. *Parliamentary Democracy: Democratization, Destabilization, Reconsolidation, 1789–1999.* New York: St. Martin's Press, 2000.

Bowler, Shaun, David M. Farrell, and Richard S. Katz, eds. *Party Discipline and Parliamentary Government.* Columbus: Ohio State University Press, 1998.

Docherty, David. *Legislatures.* Vancouver: University of British Columbia Press, 2004.

Franks, C. E. S. *The Parliament of Canada.* Toronto: University of Toronto Press, 1987.

Goldsworthy, Jeffrey. *Parliamentary Sovereignty.* Toronto: Oxford University Press, 2001.

Herman, V. *Parliaments of the World.* London: Macmillan, 1976.

Jennings, W. Ivor. *Parliament.* 2nd ed. Cambridge: Cambridge University Press, 1957.

Laver, Michael, and Kenneth A. Shepsle. *Making and Breaking Governments: Cabinets and Legislatures in Parliamentary Democracies.* Cambridge: Cambridge University Press, 1996.

MacKinnon, Frank. *The Crown in Canada.* Toronto: McClelland & Stewart, 1976.

Mackintosh, John P. *The Government and Politics of Great Britain.* 5th ed. London: Hutchinson, 1982.

March, Roman R. *The Myth of Parliament.* Scarborough, ON: Prentice-Hall Canada, 1974.

Marleau, Robert, and Camille Montpetit. *House of Commons Procedure and Practice.* Ottawa: House of Commons, 2000.

PART 3

Marshall, Edmund. *Parliament and the Public*. London: Macmillan, 1982.

Martin, Lanny W., and Georg Vanberg. *Parliaments and Coalitions: The Role of Legislative Institutions in Multiparty Governance*. Oxford: Oxford University Press, 2011.

Rose, Richard, and Ezra N. Suleiman, eds. *Presidents and Prime Ministers*. Washington, DC: American Institute for Public Policy Research, 1980.

Rush, Michael. *The Cabinet and Policy Formation*. London: Longman, 1984.

Russell, Peter H. *Two Cheers for Minority Government: The Evolution of Canadian Parliamentary Democracy*. Toronto: Emond Montgomery, 2008.

Russell, Peter, and Lorne Sossin, eds. *Parliamentary Democracy in Crisis*. Toronto: University of Toronto Press, 2009.

Smith, David E. *The Invisible Crown: The First Principle of Canadian Government*. Toronto: University of Toronto Press, 1995.

————. *The People's House of Commons*. Toronto: University of Toronto Press, 2007.

Presidential Systems

Bessette, Joseph M., and Jeffrey Tulis, eds. *The Presidency in the Constitutional Order*. Baton Rouge: Louisiana State University Press, 1981.

Burns, James MacGregor. *Presidential Government*. Boston: Houghton Mifflin, 1965.

Califano, Joseph A. Jr. *A Presidential Nation*. New York: W. W. Norton, 1975.

Cheibub, José Antonio. *Presidentialism, Parliamentarism, and Democracy*. New York: Cambridge University Press, 2007.

Cronin, Thomas E., and Michael A. Genovese. *The Paradoxes of the American Presidency*. 2nd ed. Toronto: Oxford University Press, 2003.

Edwards, George C. *Presidential Leadership: Politics and Policy Making*. Toronto: Thomson Nelson, 2003.

Fisher, Louis. *Constitutional Conflicts Between Congress and the President*. 5th ed. Lawrence: University Press of Kansas, 2007.

Genovese, Michael A. *The Presidential Dilemma: Revisiting Democratic Leadership in the American System*. 3rd ed. Piscataway, NJ: Transaction Publishers, 2011.

Goldwin, Robert A., and Art Kaufman. *Separation of Powers: Does It Still Work?* Washington, DC: American Enterprise Institute, 1986.

Heclo, Hugh, and Lester M. Salamon, eds. *The Illusion of Presidential Government*. Boulder, CO: Westview Press, 1981.

Henderson, Phillip G., ed. *The Presidency Then and Now*. Lanham, MD: Rowman and Littlefield, 2000.

Lijphart, Arend, ed. *Parliamentary versus Presidential Government*. Oxford: Oxford University Press, 1992.

McDonald, Forrest. *The American Presidency: An Intellectual History*. Lawrence: University Press of Kansas, 1994.

Mainwaring, Scott, and Matthew Soberg Shugart, eds. *Presidentialism and Democracy in Latin America*. Cambridge: Cambridge University Press, 1997.

Nwabueze, B. O. *Presidentialism in Commonwealth Africa*. New York: St. Martin's, 1974.

Wilson, James Q., and John J. Dilulio Jr. *American Government: Institutions and Policies*. 12th ed. Boston: Cengage Learning, 2011.

PART 3

CHAPTER 21

Unitary and Federal Systems

Governments can also be classified according to the degree of centralization they exhibit. The two main types applicable to modern circumstances are the **unitary system**, in which a single sovereign government controls all regions of the country, and **federalism**, in which sovereignty is divided between a central government and several regional or provincial governments. Two other types, of less practical significance, are **devolution** and **confederation**.[1] The former is a variant of the unitary state in which the central government creates regional governments but can override them as it wishes, even to the point of abolishing them. The latter is an inherently unstable arrangement in which sovereign constituent governments create a central government, but one without sovereign power of its own.

These types can be arranged as follows on a continuum of centralization:

Sovereign State	Confederation	Federalism	Devolution	Unitary State
No central government	Central government exists, but sovereignty retained by constituent governments	Sovereignty shared between central and constituent governments	Constituent governments exist, but sovereignty monopolized by central government	No constituent governments

As with most other classifications, these types represent points on a continuum, and existing political systems may fall between types. One federal system may be so centralized as to approach devolution, while another may be so decentralized that it almost amounts to a confederation. With this qualification in mind, let us discuss the major types.

THE UNITARY SYSTEM

In a unitary system, powers and responsibilities are concentrated within central governmental authorities. Constitutionally, the central government is sovereign. Municipal or county governments may exist, but their responsibilities are delegated by statute from the central government. Their functions are more administrative than legislative, much of their revenue comes from grants made by the central government, and in general they depend heavily on the central government. In a unitary system, no attempt is made to create provinces or states with specific powers established in a constitution. Ireland, France, Colombia, Japan, Sweden, and more than 150 other contemporary states are unitary. In each case a national assembly, congress, parliament, or diet is responsible for governing the entire nation. The power of local governments varies considerably, depending on the extent to which central authorities have delegated responsibilities of government and administration.

Devolution—the granting of governmental responsibilities, including limited legislative responsibilities, to regional governments—is a step toward decentralization. The powers of regional governments, however, are not entrenched in the constitution. They are created by statute of the central government and as a result can be modified or abolished in the same way. An example would be the government of Northern Ireland from 1921 to 1972. Under the Government of Ireland Act of 1920, the British established at Stormont in Belfast a parliament with local responsibilities. This legislative body had a great deal of autonomy in domestic matters such as housing, services, and public employment. The experiment was terminated in 1972, however, because violence between the Protestant majority and the Roman Catholic minority had made regional government unworkable.[2] This example illustrates the utter dependence of regional governments upon the central government in a devolved system. There was no constitutional barrier to the British cabinet's unilateral decision to dissolve the Stormont Parliament and place Northern Ireland under direct control of a Secretary of State for Northern Ireland. For a more contemporary description of devolution in Britain, see Comparative Perspectives 21.1.

FEDERALISM AND CONFEDERATION

In a federal system, powers and responsibilities are divided between a federal (or national) government and various regional governments. The federal government, for example, may be responsible for minting money and raising an army, while the provinces (or states, cantons, or departments) may be responsible for education and public works. Constitutionally, sovereignty is divided between different levels of government instead of being concentrated in one central government. Both levels of government are mentioned in a constitutional document, and neither level can unilaterally modify

PART 3

Comparative Perspectives 21.1

The Evolution of Devolution

When the first edition of this textbook was published in 1982, devolution appeared to be pretty much a thing of the past. The Stormont Parliament in Northern Ireland had been dissolved in 1972 and Scottish voters had rejected devolution in a 1979 referendum. But things change . . .

Tony Blair's Labour government was elected in 1997 on a program that included modernizing the British constitution, which in turn included consideration of devolution for Scotland, Wales, and Northern Ireland. Later that year, referendums were held in Scotland and Wales. Devolution passed with enthusiasm in Scotland (almost 75 percent) and barely in Wales (just over 50 percent). Scottish voters also approved giving their new parliament the ability to levy taxes.

In 1998 the Parliament of the United Kingdom passed the Scotland Act and the Government of Wales Act to create the Scottish Parliament and the Welsh National Assembly. Both bodies have a legislature and a cabinet, but their powers are somewhat different, reflecting different political aspirations in the regions.

The Northern Ireland Assembly, created after the 1998 Good Friday agreement among the various political forces, was created by British legislation and also approved by referendum. It was suspended in 2002 because of continuing communal violence but restored in 2007 after the Belfast Agreement made free and peaceful elections possible.

Representing a pragmatic tradition of politics, British devolution is a complex system of different arrangements for different parts of the United Kingdom. There are now three regional governments, each with different powers, while the main region—England—has no regional government of its own. The residents of the regions still elect members to the Parliament at Westminster, and Parliament is still sovereign; that is, it still retains unilateral legal authority to amend or abolish devolution. There will undoubtedly be further changes as conditions evolve, particularly in Scotland: the Scottish Nationalist Party won control of the Scottish Parliament in the 2011 election on the promise of a referendum for Scottish independence, likely to take place in 2014 or 2015.

or abolish the other. In reality, however, it is virtually impossible to divide powers neatly so that the responsibilities of one level of government are totally independent of the other. This means that disputes, overlapping jurisdictions, and joint efforts are commonplace in any federal system.

Although Switzerland has a history of confederation dating back to 1291, it was the American Constitution of 1789 that created the world's first modern federal system. The model has since been imitated in about 24 states, including Brazil, Mexico, Venezuela, Canada, Switzerland, Australia, Nigeria, India, Germany, and Russia. The invention of federalism was precipitated by the inadequacy of confederation as a form of government. After winning its independence from Britain, the United States adopted the **Articles of Confederation** in 1781, the first American constitution. The states retained sovereignty and the federal Congress was little more than a meeting place for ambassadors of the state governments. Congress could not levy taxes, raise an army, regulate commerce, or enforce law within the states, nor was there a national executive authority. General recognition that this system could not last very long led to the constitutional convention of 1787.

As with many important political innovations, the invention of modern federalism was almost accidental. According to the conventional wisdom of the eighteenth century, sovereignty was indivisible. Those who supported the Articles of Confederation saw sovereignty as lodged in the 13 sovereign states; those who criticized the Articles wanted to create a new, unitary state that possessed sovereignty at the centre. Both sides agreed that sovereignty had to be in one place or the other. James Madison broke the deadlock by suggesting that two levels of government could each have legislative authority secured by the constitution. Declaring that the people were sovereign solved the logical puzzle of sovereignty. The state and federal governments were instruments of the people, created and restrained by the constitution, which the people could alter according to prescribed methods. Few people at the time saw this as a new type of government; most thought of it as a constitutional marriage of two existing and well-understood forms of government: confederation and the unitary state. But it subsequently became conventional in political science to emphasize the division of sovereignty and to speak of federalism as a distinct form of government rather than a combination of other types. The rise of federalism has largely driven confederation from the field as a serious alternative.

We may see a resurgence of confederations as the world economy becomes more tightly interconnected. When the **European Union** was founded in 1956, it was little more than a free-trade zone. In governmental terms it represented six sovereign states agreeing to specific forms of cooperation under the Treaty of Rome. Today there are 27 member states (as of 2012), and the cooperation has become so massive and complex that use of the term *confederation* may one day be justified. There is as yet nothing resembling a European cabinet or head of state, but there are European prototypes of the other main governmental institutions— for example, the European Parliament at Strasbourg, a European bureaucracy at Brussels, and a European Court of Justice in Luxembourg—as well as regular meetings of first ministers. There have been so many attempts to harmonize policy in so many areas, such as labour codes, human rights, consumer standards, and the environment, that the legislative discretion of member states is now substantially

PART 3

reduced, particularly now that the euro has been adopted as a common currency for many member nations. Whether or not we call the European Union a confederation may be only a semantic quibble.

Because of its special relevance to Canadians, let us return to a more extended discussion of federalism. Federal systems have emerged for at least three important reasons. First, federalism has been argued to provide a structural mechanism for integration, an element of particular importance in geographically dispersed states. Decentralization allows far-flung regions to feel that not all decisions are being made for them and imposed on them by a government in a distant capital. Not surprisingly, most federal states are geographically large, including Russia, Mexico, Australia, and India.

Second, federal systems are often established in societies where a substantial degree of linguistic, religious, or cultural diversity exists. This explains the development of federalism in Switzerland, which is geographically small but linguistically and religiously diverse. Linguistic division is not a factor in Germany, but the circumstances of history have promoted federalism there. Because Germany was not fully united until 1871, some of the German *Länder* (provinces) such as Bavaria were sovereign states until relatively recently, and they still have important historical traditions of their own. Federalism can accommodate this sort of diversity. In practice, a large land area and cultural pluralism often go together, which means that federalism is doubly explained in such countries as India and Canada.

Third, federal systems provide one way of checking governmental power. When powers are divided among levels of government, absolute power is not concentrated within a single unit. The logic is much the same as in Madison's justification of the separation of powers—in a federation, government in effect "controls itself" because the ambitions of one group of politicians can never entirely defeat the ambitions of another. When the provinces check the federal government and the federal government checks the provinces, a balance may well result.

There are other advantages to the federal system of government. A larger state probably has greater human and natural resources with which to defend itself against foreign enemies. A larger nation-state also provides the possibility for greater economies of scale. It should be cheaper to administer public services on a large scale where costs can be spread among more people. As well, when governments are located at a regional level, people tend to feel closer to the decision-making process, and the decision-makers tend to be more aware of local needs and better able to respond to them. Finally, constituent governments can often establish innovative programs and policies aimed at particular problems. These experiments may prove valuable for the entire country once they are tested. For example, Saskatchewan enacted hospital insurance in 1946 and medical-care insurance in 1961; in each case that province anticipated federal legislation by a decade.

In spite of these advantages, as Garth Stevenson states, "One is tempted to conclude that both the arguments against federalism and the arguments in its favour can be as easily refuted as supported."[3] Having several layers of government involves financial costs that may outweigh any economies of scale. And while governments at the local or provincial level are closer to the people, this is no guarantee that they are any more responsive to local needs than a federal government would be. Moreover, the federal system may foster divisive intergovernmental conflict.

Obviously the division of sovereignty in a federal system reduces the power of the central government, thus taking away some of its ability to oppress the people. Less obvious but equally true is that the existence of two levels of government is a check on tyrannical tendencies in the constituent governments. James Madison pointed this out brilliantly in his contributions to *The Federalist*. He showed that in a small democracy there is a strong likelihood of some group's gaining the upper hand and practising a tyranny of the majority. A small jurisdiction is usually homogeneous in social composition, and this makes it easy for a majority to form. But in a large country there is such a diversity of classes and interests—farmers, workers, merchants, and so forth—that there is "in the society so many separate descriptions of citizens as will render an unjust combination of a majority of the whole very improbable."[4] While the following example dates from 150 years later, it indicates that Madison may have had a point. In the 1930s in Alberta, William Aberhart's Social Credit government, elected by a majority that included many debtors, passed laws against banks that amounted to confiscation of property. When the newspapers criticized Aberhart harshly, he tried to impose a form of censorship on them. The federal government protected the rights of both banks and newspapers by disallowing the provincial legislation and exercising judicial review.

The situation with Blacks in the American South is also a case in point, but from a different perspective. For almost 100 years, state governments in the decentralized American federal system had been able to pass laws that discriminated against Blacks. For instance, laws were passed limiting voting rights and segregating schools. By 1965, with the U.S. Supreme Court leading the way, the federal government was finally able to override the legal structure of racial segregation. The point is that, in a decentralized federal system, power at the constituent level (in this case, the state level) can be used to restrict the social, economic, and political rights of minorities. The genius of federalism lies in its recognition that power at any level is subject to abuse and in the way that it establishes layers of government with enough power to balance one another.

STRUCTURAL FEATURES OF FEDERALISM

Although each federal system must be uniquely adapted to the pluralistic conditions of its society, certain structural features are universal, or very nearly so. First, there must be a written document that explicitly assigns powers to the two levels of government. In Canada, Section 91 of the Constitution Act, 1867, grants power to the federal government, while Sections 92 and 93 spell out the powers of the

PART 3

provinces. Section 95 assigns concurrent jurisdiction over agriculture and immigration to the two levels of government. The powers of the federal or national Parliament include, for example, control of trade and commerce, maintenance of a postal service, and responsibility for navigation and shipping. Provincial powers under Section 92 include control of the sale of alcoholic beverages, responsibility for the solemnization of marriage, and management of hospitals. Section 93 makes provincial governments responsible for education "in and for each province"—this wording is open enough to allow the federal government to help support universities, whose research role transcends provincial boundaries.

The constitution of a federal system also has to say something about **residual powers**—that is, those powers of government that are not specifically mentioned in the text. No list of functions can ever be complete, if only because situations unforeseen at the time of drafting are bound to arise. In Canada, residual powers were given to the federal government by Section 91 of the Constitution Act, 1867:

> It shall be lawful for the Queen, by and with the Advice and Consent of the Senate and House of Commons, to make Laws for the Peace, Order, and good Government of Canada, in relation to all Matters not coming within the Classes of Subjects by this Act assigned exclusively to the Legislatures of the Provinces … .

In contrast, the Tenth Amendment to the American Constitution took the opposite approach: "The powers not delegated to the United States by the Constitution or prohibited by it to the States, are reserved to the States respectively, or to the people."

Second, almost all federal systems have bicameral legislatures in the central government, although in some the powers of the upper house have atrophied over the years. The rationale behind federal bicameralism is to provide the provinces or regions with a special form of representation within the central government. This is supposed to ensure that regional voices are heard in the capital and to prevent regional interests from being overridden by a numerical majority in the nation as a whole.

Germany is a good example of federal bicameralism. The upper house, or Bundesrat, is composed of delegates chosen by and responsible to the governments of the *Länder*, with the number of delegates being roughly in proportion to the size of the *Land* (province). The federal cabinet is responsible only to the lower house, or Bundestag, but the Bundesrat, unlike the Canadian Senate, often exercises its power of refusing to pass legislation. The American Senate is another good example. Senators, now democratically elected, were once chosen by state legislatures, and they still feel responsible for seeing that their state's interests are respected in Washington. Having two senators per state, regardless of the state's size, guarantees equal state representation.

In comparison, Canada has a weaker form of federal bicameralism, because the power of the Canadian Senate is quite limited in practice. Section 22(4) of the amended Constitution Act, 1867, specifies a certain regional distribution of senators (24 each from Quebec, Ontario, western Canada, and the Maritimes; 6 from Newfoundland and Labrador; and 1 each from Yukon Territory, the Northwest Territories, and Nunavut).

But this distribution makes senators only marginally regional representatives, since they are appointed by the governor general on the advice of the prime minister. From the beginning, the cabinet, which has traditionally included ministers from most provinces, has been a stronger instrument of federalism in Canada than the Senate.

Not surprisingly, most of the recent proposals to reform the Canadian constitution have involved changing the Senate to make it a more active representative of provincial interests. The 1987 Meech Lake Accord would have required the prime minister to choose senators from among names submitted by the governments of the provinces. The 1992 Charlottetown Accord would have gone even further, by giving each province an equal number of popularly elected senators.

Without reform, Canada's upper house will never be as effective as similar bodies in most federal states. Even when it is active, as in recent decades, when Liberals and Conservatives have taken turns using the Senate to block or delay legislation coming from the House of Commons, it does not effectively represent regional or provincial interests. The fact that the Senate does not speak for the regions undoubtedly contributes to the feeling among such provinces as Alberta and Newfoundland and Labrador that their interests are not effectively represented in Ottawa. Although abolition of the Senate has been suggested, this position seems a bit facile, in that Canada would then be the only federal system in the world without an upper house. Most federalists argue that an upper house is an integral part of our federal system, and that what we need is a Senate that is democratic, has real power vis-à-vis the House of Commons, and represents all provinces and territories without entirely disregarding population differences.

The weakness of regional representation in Ottawa has encouraged Canadian federalism to develop an *inter*state (activity between provinces and the federal government) rather than an *intra*state (activity within the nation-state) character.[5] Provincial governments have become the main advocates of regional interests and now deal with each other and with the federal government in quasi-diplomatic fashion. The most visible manifestations of this **executive federalism** are the periodic first ministers' conferences, which are conducted very much like international conferences—that is, with public posturing, secret negotiations, and final communiqués. These sessions are only the most visible meetings in the ceaseless round of federal–provincial talks at various levels among cabinet ministers, deputy ministers, and officials. This cycle of negotiations and meetings occurs outside parliamentary government in Ottawa. There is nothing like it in other major federal polities such as Australia, the United States, and Germany.

In federal systems, constituent governments often clash with each other and with the national government, and the courts often become the arbiters of these conflicts. Judicial review—the power to declare legislation unconstitutional—is an important feature of most federal constitutions. Curiously, judicial review in federalism issues is now said to be relatively unimportant in the United States, where federalism originated.[6] But it is still generally true, and certainly true in Canada, that federalism gives the courts a higher profile than in most unitary states. This in turn makes judicial appointments politically sensitive.

PART 3

Prime Minister Paul Martin, along with his provincial and territorial counterparts, takes part in a session of the First Ministers' Conference on health in Ottawa in September 2004. The Conservative government of Stephen Harper has held fewer of these meetings since coming to power in February 2006.

In the United States, Senate confirmation of presidential appointments to the bench helps raise the legitimacy of the federal judiciary in the eyes of the states. In Canada, judicial appointments are made by the governor general on the advice of the minister of justice, with the prime minister playing a special role by nominating members of the Supreme Court of Canada and the chief justices of the other courts. At present the provinces play no role in appointing judges, even though the Supreme Court's decisions can have a major impact on provincial powers. The Meech Lake Accord and the Charlottetown Accord tried to address this problem by providing that Supreme Court judges be chosen from lists submitted by the provinces. Since the defeat of both amendment packages, the status quo has prevailed; undoubtedly the provinces will continue to feel that the Supreme Court of Canada is too much an instrument of the federal government.

Until 1949 the highest Canadian appeals court was the **Judicial Committee of the Privy Council (JCPC)**, a special British court that heard appeals from the whole Empire. The provinces never considered this a problem, because the JCPC had rendered a long series of decisions favourable to the provinces in their disputes with Ottawa. But when appeals to the Committee were abolished in 1949, the Supreme Court of Canada, which was appointed solely by federal authorities, became the ultimate interpreter of the Constitution. Since that time, the provinces have increasingly desired a role in choosing judges, and something in that direction will probably happen sooner or later.

Constitutional amendment is another contentious subject in federal systems. There must be some sort of balance between the two levels of government. If the central government can change the constitution at will without the consent of the regional governments, the system is tantamount to devolution, because the central government could modify or even abolish the regional governments by unilateral constitutional amendment. Before 1982, the legal method for amending the Canadian Constitution was for the British Parliament, acting on a joint address from the Canadian Senate and House of Commons, to amend the British North America Act (as it was then called). In most, but not all, instances in which provincial rights were affected, the federal government obtained prior consent of all the provinces before requesting constitutional amendments. An all-Canadian amending formula was introduced as part of the Constitution Act, 1982. Under the general procedure of Section 38, amendments require approval by the House of Commons, the Senate, and the legislative assemblies of two-thirds of the provinces that have at least 50 percent of the population of all the provinces; amendments in certain matters require the agreement of all provinces. These provisions institutionalized the roles of the federal and provincial governments in amending the Constitution and excluded Great Britain altogether. In the United States, all constitutional amendments must receive approval from two-thirds of both houses of Congress and three-quarters of state legislatures. Again there is a balance of power between the central and constituent governments.

At the time of Confederation, the Canadian system had a feature that is unusual in federal states: the right of the central government to nullify the legislation of the constituent governments, even when they are acting within their proper constitutional sphere. There are two mechanisms by which this can happen. In the first, known as **reservation,** the lieutenant-governor of a province can refuse royal assent to a bill and refer it to the federal cabinet for a final decision. In the second, known as **disallowance,** the federal cabinet can nullify a provincial act within one year of passage, even though it has received royal assent from the lieutenant-governor of the province. These powers of the federal government were used frequently in the early years of Confederation and are still constitutionally alive, though they are now in abeyance. No provincial act has been disallowed since 1943, although Ottawa has sometimes threatened such action. In 1961, Saskatchewan's lieutenant-governor reserved a bill without seeking prior advice from Ottawa, much to the embarrassment of Prime Minister John Diefenbaker. In practice, court challenges have replaced reservation and disallowance in Canada. In the United States, as in most federal systems, there is no parallel to this constitutional dominance by the central government.

This review shows that Canadian federalism was originally so highly centralized as to border on devolution. In other words, a very centralized federal system may resemble a unitary system that has undergone devolution. The federal right to appoint judges and senators, nullify provincial legislation, amend the constitution, and exercise residual powers far outweighed the provincial powers. This was by design. The Fathers of Confederation could not ignore the American Civil War (1861–65). Most believed that the American constitution had granted too much power to the states. Sir John A. Macdonald would have preferred a unitary state, then known as a "legislative union" (i.e., only one legislature for all of Canada), but he realized that some form of federalism was required to entice Quebec and the Atlantic provinces into association with Ontario. The solution that emerged was, in legal terms, a strong central government with minimal concessions to the provinces.

The subsequent evolution of Canada has undone much of this work. The forces of decentralization were simply too strong to be contained within the centralizing constitution of 1867. The JCPC rendered a long series of decisions that circumscribed the legislative powers given Ottawa under Section 91 and expanded provincial powers under Section 92. Ottawa also gradually relinquished the use of centralizing powers such as reservation and disallowance.

There was, to be sure, a centralizing trend that began in World War II and carried on into the postwar period. The federal government acquired the important new jurisdictions of unemployment insurance and old-age pensions through constitutional amendment. It also used its extensive revenues to create national welfare programs such as health-care insurance and the Canada Assistance Plan. But this centralizing thrust in turn gave rise to a countermovement of decentralization. As the provinces expanded their tax base in the late 1950s and 1960s, they became less dependent on the federal government for financial support, which encouraged a new dynamic in the federal system. The Meech Lake and Charlottetown Accords contained provisions that would have enhanced provincial at the expense of federal jurisdiction. Quebec, motivated by linguistic and cultural factors, is at the forefront of provinces seeking more power, but it is not the only such province.

There have been many proposals for reforming the federal system, of which the Meech Lake and Charlottetown Accords, arrived at by the first ministers, received the most attention. Proposals have dealt with almost every conceivable topic, including multiculturalism, Senate reform, immigration policy, Supreme Court nominations, and the use of referendums. Almost invariably there has been a clear recommendation to expand the role of the provinces in the federation.

One interesting product of these constitutional discussions was the concept of **asymmetrical federalism,** a term used to convey the idea of powers being divided unevenly among provinces, of some provinces choosing to have greater responsibilities or more autonomy than others. Of course, a degree of asymmetry already exists in Canadian federalism. Quebec, for instance, collects its own income tax, operates its own provincial pension plan, and exercises more control over immigration than do the other provinces, which have been content to let Ottawa perform these functions. The transfer of powers to the provinces envisioned in the Meech Lake and Charlottetown Accords would have led to more of these asymmetrical arrangements. Many Canadians feared that, as a result, Canada would be "balkanized," that is, reduced to a patchwork of different programs in different jurisdictions across the country.

Proponents of asymmetrical federalism are willing to run this risk. They believe that greater flexibility in federalism will accommodate the differing needs of the provinces, especially those of Quebec, and thus reduce the threat of separatism.

Opponents question whether pushing asymmetry too far might not lead to the disintegration of federalism as we know it. They fear that too much decentralization would so weaken the federal government that Canada would be left with only a very loose confederation. This debate was not really resolved with the rejection of the Charlottetown Accord; it continues to bubble beneath the surface of Canadian politics (see Canadian Focus 21.1).

Curiously, American political evolution has moved in the direction of greater centralization, with power shifting steadily toward the federal government. International crises—two world wars, the Cold War, and the Korean, Vietnam, and Gulf Wars—and the nationalization of domestic issues such as racial disparities and inflation have

---

Canadian Focus 21.1

Quebec and Canadian Federalism

In November 2006, the House of Commons passed a motion introduced by Prime Minister Stephen Harper to "recognize that the Québécois form a nation within a united Canada." This motion rekindled old and very emotional feelings about Canada's federal system and Quebec's place in it.

Many "nationalists," particularly in English Canada, have argued that Canada is "one nation" with a predominantly symmetrical federalist structure, for the most part granting equal powers to all provinces. This model of federalism was reinforced with the Charter of Rights and Freedoms, which affirmed equality individually for all Canadians. In this perspective, no formal recognition of a dual society or a "distinct society" is needed; in fact, that kind of recognition could threaten unity or even break up the Canadian nation. Symmetrical federalism within one nation is seen as the model for a successful system of government.[7]

On the other hand, many "federalists," particularly in Quebec, have argued that our federal system of government should reflect our binational, or even multinational, character. They argue that the Meech Lake and Charlottetown Accords were attempts to create a more dynamic federal system— an experiment unique to Canada. It is worthwhile to examine the basis for this argument as articulated by three prominent political analysts:

Charles Taylor suggests the importance of a "unique identity" for "French Canadians, and particularly Quebeckers … and aboriginal peoples." The "survival" of this identity is important so that the society will not lapse into uniformity and all people become assimilated into a single culture. Thus there is a threat to recognizing "the equal value of different cultures" under the idea of one nation.[8]

Guy Laforest argues that Trudeau's constitutional changes represented the end of a Canadian dream. Part of the

(continued)

dream for the Québécois was a belief in the "duality" of Canadian society, that the sense of a distinct "nationalism" in Quebec was the basis for a belief in "two majorities" in Canada.[9] And for him the idea was to have asymmetrical powers in a federal constitution where national differences could be enshrined.[10]

Kenneth McRoberts claims that for French Canadians, "federalism had a different purpose, the defence of culture as opposed to regional or economic interests." He notes that asymmetry began under Prime Minister Lester Pearson's government but was halted by Trudeau.[11] McRoberts sees an option for accommodating Quebec: "an alternative strategy based on constitutional recognition of duality … ; asymmetry in federal-provincial relations; and territoriality in language policy." And the strategy could be modified to "incorporate the objectives of aboriginal peoples."[12]

One can see that the place of Quebec in Canadian federalism is an emotional issue—both for nationalists and for federalists. But one of the strengths of a federal system is that it can adapt to diversity and at the same time retain unity. It can adapt to regional differences as well as multinational, multi-ethnic, and multi-religious differences. It is a supple form of government for large and diverse societies.

tended to make all eyes focus on Washington for solutions. The federal government totally overshadows any state or group of states in its ability to confront national issues. An abstract reading of the American and Canadian constitutions would suggest that American states are far more powerful than Canadian provinces, but this is in fact a highly distorted picture of the current reality.[13] The constitutional allocation of residual powers to the federal government in Canada and to the states in the United States has had little long-term practical effect.

Assessing Federal Systems

While federal systems have enabled the building of large nation-states, they have not provided a cure for all political ills. Indeed, separatist movements have plagued many countries with a federal form of government. The Civil War in the United States was fought over the South's claim of a right to secede from the Union. In Nigeria in 1967, Biafrans, with their strong tribal identity and oil resources, tried to secede from the federation. The Chechens are still fighting Russia in their attempt to found an independent republic. Separatists in the Parti Québécois continue to push for sovereignty in Quebec. And the Scottish Nationalist Party's recent gain of a solid majority in the Scottish Parliament virtually guarantees that a referendum on Scottish independence will take place in the near future.

A basic challenge for all federal systems is establishing a workable balance acceptable to all levels of government. It was once believed that a central government was best suited to cope with national problems. Over the past 60 years there have been two conflicting trends: one toward centralizing power at the national level, because governments have expanded their functions to meet economic crises and have become involved in international conflicts, and the other toward decentralizing power, because national and ethnic feelings are running strong and because many people feel that regional governments can best deal with individual citizens. There seems to be much appeal in the thesis "Small is beautiful." Indeed, many federal systems of government are using decentralization as a way of countering separatist movements.

In Canada we are also getting mixed signals about our federation. The provinces have become more powerful in the federal system, and the Meech Lake and Charlottetown Accords were proposals to institutionalize that trend. However, for a variety of reasons, both accords failed to pass. With Quebec separatism at least temporarily in eclipse, the most important contemporary debate is over fiscal concerns, and in particular, which level of government ought to pay for program responsibilities. The Conservatives campaigned in 2006 on a promise to end the "fiscal imbalance" by transferring more money to the provinces, a pledge that was redeemed to some extent in their 2007 budget. But the squabbling over money continues as strongly as ever, particularly in light of the rising cost of health care. Such debates seem to be part of the very fabric of Canadian federalism.

Questions for Discussion

1. In your opinion, has the expanded provincial power that resulted from early JCPC decisions helped or hurt Canada? Is federalism properly balanced in Canada today, or do you see either the provinces or the federal government as having too much power? If there is an imbalance, what could be done to fix it?

2. Why do you think there are many more unitary than federal states in the world? Can you think of any positives that would result if Canada had a unitary government as Macdonald wanted? What about negatives?

3. Compare British devolution to Canadian federalism. Does federalism or devolution tend more to asymmetry? Why or why not?

Internet Links

1. European Union: **europa.eu**. Official website of the European Union.

2. *Federations*: **www.forumfed.org/en/products/federations.php**. A magazine published by the Forum of Federations on current events related to federal systems of government.

PART 3

3. Forum of Federations: **www.forumfed.org**. A Canadian group dedicated to dialoguing with other federal states on issues related to federalism and governance. Many links to resources on federalism.

4. Institute of Intergovernmental Relations, Queen's University: **www.queensu.ca/iigr**. Conducts research on federal systems worldwide.

5. *Publius, the Journal of Federalism*: **www.oxfordjournals.org/our_journals/pubjof/index.html**. A peer-reviewed journal that publishes recent academic work on federalism.

Further Reading

Anderson, George. *Federalism: An Introduction*. Don Mills, ON: Oxford University Press, 2008.

Bakvis, Herman, ed. *Canadian Federalism*. Toronto: Oxford University Press, 2001.

Bogdanor, Vernon. *Devolution in the United Kingdom*. Toronto: Oxford University Press, 2001.

Cairns, Alan C. *Charter versus Federalism: The Dilemmas of Constitutional Reform*. Kingston: McGill-Queen's University Press, 1992.

Conlan, Timothy J. *From New Federalism to Devolution: Twenty-Five Years of Intergovernmental Reform*. Washington, DC: Brookings Institution Press, 1998.

Elazar, Daniel J., ed. *Federal Systems of the World: A Handbook of Federal, Confederal and Autonomy Arrangements*. Harlow, UK: Longman, 1991.

Feeley, Malcolm M., and Edward Rubin. *Federalism: Political Identity and Tragic Compromise*. Ann Arbor: University of Michigan, 2008.

Gagnon, Alain-G., ed. *Contemporary Canadian Federalism: Foundations, Traditions, Institutions*. Toronto: University of Toronto Press, 2009.

Gibbins, Roger. *Regionalism: Territorial Politics in Canada and the United States*. Toronto: Butterworths, 1982.

Gutmann, Amy. *Multiculturalism*. Princeton, NJ: Princeton University Press, 1994.

Harrison, Kathryn. *Passing the Buck: Federalism and Canadian Environmental Policy*. Vancouver: University of British Columbia Press, 1996.

Hueglin, Thomas O. *Early Modern Concepts for a Late Modern World: Althusius on Community and Federalism*. Waterloo, ON: Wilfrid Laurier University Press, 1999.

Hueglin, Thomas O., and Alan Fenna. *Comparative Federalism: A Systematic Inquiry*. Peterborough, ON: Broadview Press, 2006.

Laforest, Guy. *Trudeau and the End of a Canadian Dream*. Translated by Paul Leduc and Michelle Weinroth. Montreal: Mcgill-Queen's University Press, 1995.

LaSelva, Samuel V. *The Moral Foundations of Canadian Federalism: Paradoxes, Achievements, and Tragedies of Nationhood.* Montreal: McGill-Queen's University Press, 1996.

McRoberts, Kenneth. *Misconceiving Canada: The Struggle for National Unity.* Don Mills, ON: Oxford University Press, 1997.

Murphy, Michael, ed. *Canada: The State of the Federation, 2005. Quebec and Canada in the New Century.* Montreal: McGill-Queens University Press, 2007.

Nagel, Robert F. *The Implosion of American Federalism.* New York: Oxford University Press, 2001.

Riker, William H. *Federalism: Origin, Operation, Significance.* Boston: Little, Brown, 1964.

Rocher, François, and Miriam Smith, eds. *New Trends in Canadian Federalism.* 2nd ed. Peterborough, ON: Broadview Press, 2003.

Saywell, John T. *The Lawmakers: Judicial Powers and the Shaping of Canadian Federalism.* Toronto: University of Toronto Press, 2002.

Smiley, D. V. *The Federal Condition in Canada.* Toronto: McGraw-Hill Ryerson, 1987.

Smith, Jennifer. *Federalism.* Vancouver: University of British Columbia Press, 2004.

———. *The Meaning of Provincial Equality in Canadian Federalism.* Kingston, ON: Institute of Intergovernmental Relations, Queen's University, 1998.

Stevenson, Garth. *Unfulfilled Union: Canadian Federalism and National Unity.* 5th ed. Montreal: McGill-Queen's University Press, 2009.

Ter-Minassian, Teresa, ed. *Fiscal Federalism in Theory and Practice,* Washington, DC: International Monetary Fund, 1997.

Watts, Ronald L. *Comparing Federal Systems.* 2nd ed. Kingston, ON: Institute of Intergovernmental Relations, Queen's University, 1999.

———. *The Spending Power in Federal Systems: A Comparative Study.* Kingston, ON: Institute of Intergovernmental Relations, Queen's University, 1999.

Westmacott, M. W., and Hugh Mellon. *Challenges to Canadian Federalism.* Scarborough, ON: Prentice Hall, 1998.

Wheare, K. C. *Federal Government.* New York: Oxford University Press, 1964.

Wildavsky, Aaron B., Brendon Swedlow, and David Schleicher, eds. *Federalism and Political Culture.* Piscataway, NJ: Transaction Publishers, 1997.

PART 3

PART 4

THE POLITICAL PROCESS

CHAPTER 22
The Political Process

In Part One we discussed politics in abstract terms, associating it with functions such as the exercise of authority, the allocation of values, and the settling of disputes. In Part Four we want to move from the level of abstraction to the level of concrete reality and be much more specific about the political process. Our objective is to explain politics as an institutionalized process for making public decisions. Our hope is that politics and the political process become a vivid and concrete idea in your mind.

INSTITUTIONS AND INSTITUTIONAL PROCESSES

It is important for all citizens of a polity to be able to conceptualize the process of politics in some way. When one speaks of the game of hockey, for example, one has no problem visualizing the sport and understanding all its complexities. When one thinks of politics, however, many things come to mind: a parliament, a prime minister or premier, corruption, lobbying, or perhaps elections. In fact, all these impressions can be part of the political process. The problem is that we need some way to pull all of these impressions together—and that is what a concept does for us. Therefore, if as citizens we talk politics, evaluate it, criticize it, or even participate in it, it is important to be able to see the whole process, all its actors and institutions, and understand how they interact in the process. In this chapter we offer two different ways of conceptualizing politics: politics as a comprehensive systemic process and politics as a "problem-oriented" policy process. Understanding either—or, hopefully, both—will be a first step in understanding the complexities of the political process.

The task may be easier to state than to accomplish. While all of us know that the process exists and that it works, it is still difficult to describe in precise terms. The political process is the complex activity of making public decisions for a society. In modern democracies it involves institutions of government (structures such as interest groups, political parties, and legislatures) and institutional processes (such as the confidence vote in Parliament or the annual transparent budget process). Politics is the interplay of all these components in devising public laws and policies, selecting and rejecting rulers, and shaping public opinion. Finding a successful course of action that can withstand the scrutiny of public dialogue is an art that requires a particular intuitive sense. It is probably true that the greater the freedom in society, the greater the participation in politics; and the greater the participation in politics, the more complex the political process. It is, then, a challenge to be able to understand this dynamic aspect of public life in an open society.

There is in all societies an endless and ongoing **political process** by which public decisions are made in response to claims and counterclaims from elements of that society. This political process produces not only decisions but also patterns of support for and resistance to those decisions. The process can be conceived as a system. In the cybernetic sense, a system is a connected set of functions that converts inputs into outputs and feeds the results back as data for future rounds of decision-making.[1]

POLITICS AS A SYSTEMIC PROCESS

David Easton specifically applied systems analysis to politics in a well-known book, *A Systems Analysis of Political Life* (1965). He showed that the **political system** in its simplest form is a process of authoritative decision-making,[2] as illustrated in Figure 22.1. Consider politics as a systemic flow. Specific inputs (demands and supports) are generated in society. Demands are what people would like government to do for them; supports are the approbation they bestow on a government they consider legitimate. These demands and supports are transformed or converted into outputs: laws and policies. This conversion takes place in what Easton calls the "black box," which is made up of the various branches and layers of government. He calls it the black box because at this point he is not concerned with the internal mechanisms by which conversion is accomplished; he is just noting that conversion occurs and is trying to situate it in a systemic context. The box is black because he does not yet look inside it. The impact

Figure 22.1 The Systemic Flow of Politics

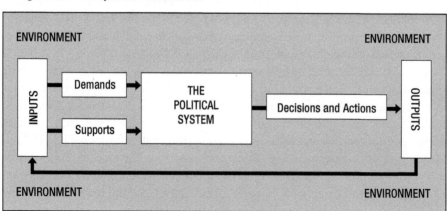

of laws and policies on society takes place through feedback, which generates new demands and supports. Easton was one of the first to apply the term *political system*, which is now used extensively in the political science literature to refer to the process of government and politics in any state.

An influential book by Gabriel Almond and G. B. Powell, *Comparative Politics* (1966), takes a similar approach.[3] Almond and Powell also adopted the fundamental notions of input, conversion, output, and feedback. However, they provide a more detailed analysis of the conversion process in the modern democratic state—an analysis that is at the same time compatible with traditional ideas in political science such as the separation of powers into legislative, executive, and judicial branches. They point to six important **structures** that carry out necessary functions: interest groups, political parties, the mass media, legislatures, executives, and the judiciary. The corresponding **functions** in the political process are interest articulation (making the position of the group known), interest aggregation (combining the positions of a number of interests), communication, making laws, administering laws, and adjudicating disputes.

Our model, shown in Figure 22.2, portrays politics as a process in which information flows from left to right. The process begins with the plural society (one composed of many interests) and converts political inputs (demands, expectations, and supports) into political outputs (laws and policies). Institutions, both formal and informal, interact to achieve this conversion and produce laws and public policies. Laws and policies can be classified as *regulative, extractive, distributive,* and *symbolic.* They are **regulative** when they control individual and group behaviour in society; speed limits are a regulative law. They are **extractive** when taxes are taken from citizens to pay for government; requirements to pay personal and corporate income taxes are extractive laws. They are **distributive** when they extend payments and services to individuals; public education, health care, and even garbage collection exemplify distributive

Figure 22.2 The Political Process

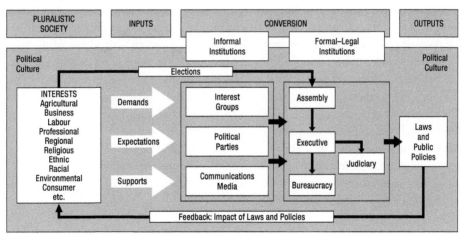

policies. They are **symbolic** when they represent the community with images such as a flag or national anthem. Feedback allows the system to adjust spontaneously to ever-changing conditions as outputs are evaluated and give rise to new inputs.

In society, conflicts inevitably develop among groups with different interests, goals, and expectations. For example, environmentalists have been demanding the reduction of greenhouse gas emissions. One of the methods to achieve that goal, supported by both the Liberal government of Paul Martin (2004–06) and the Conservative government of Stephen Harper (2006–), was to require gasoline sold at the pump to contain 5 percent ethanol, which is manufactured from corn or other grains. The regulation was accompanied by special tax incentives for ethanol producers. Farmers liked the policy because it created new markets and higher prices for the grains they grow, but by 2008 it was becoming apparent that consumers would likely have to pay higher prices for food as a result of diverting grains into fuel production. That might not matter too much in a wealthy country such as Canada, but it could have serious consequences in famine-prone Third World countries, where many people live on the edge of hunger. Environmentalists, farmers, and consumers represent different groups with partially conflicting, partially overlapping interests. In such circumstances, any governmental decision is an output that affects these groups. Even a decision to postpone a decision is in effect an output that ratifies the status quo.

Nothing in the model assumes that all groups will be equally powerful or have an equal chance of advancing their interests. Depending on the social structure, some groups will have command over greater resources or will be more strategically positioned. Rather than being egalitarian, the outcomes of the political process tend to reflect the inequalities of the existing social structure.

Not all political activity is necessarily conflict-oriented; many actions by individuals and groups support the political process. Taxes are paid and speed limits are observed. For society to be orderly, there must be compliance with authority. In fact, without compliance, the entire process would become oppressive. The point is that the political behaviour of individuals and groups involves both demands and supports. For example, people usually pay taxes voluntarily. If, however, tax rates go beyond what people consider a just proportion, tax avoidance and evasion may reduce the amount of revenue collected. Clearly, government cannot function without a basis of support.

Public participation by individuals and groups in the political process follows certain patterns. Most of it is organized around the various intermediate institutions that link people and their governors: interest groups, political parties, and the media. These are frequently referred to as the **informal institutions** of government. While they are an integral part of the process, they are informal (as opposed to formal–legal) because they are not established by a constitution. Yet they have power because they tend to coordinate and channel the activities of people in a concerted way. The development of these intermediate institutions has facilitated participation by large numbers of people in the modern political process.

Other institutions are **formal–legal**. That is, they are created explicitly by a constitution, which provides the rules of the political game. One of the primary functions of a constitution is to grant power to various institutions that formalize laws and policies for a society. These institutions include elected assemblies, executives, and the judiciary. A final formal–legal institution is, of course, the election—the means by which society's members choose their governors and express their opinion of past governmental performance. The activities of these formal–legal organizations are the most visible part of the political process.

The systemic view of politics is one way of conceptualizing the process of politics. While it includes most political institutions and suggests that the interaction of these institutions creates a political "flow" (from input to output), it can never capture the dynamic of a charismatic leader and his/her influence on the process, or the impact of corruption on the system. Nevertheless, a systemic view of politics does offer a way of pulling together a complex process of public decision-making.

POLICY COMMUNITIES AND NETWORKS

The political process can also be examined in the context of public policy. Political scientists study topics such as the politics of energy, health care, unemployment insurance, transportation, and defence. Instead of focusing on the role of particular institutions such as interest groups, political parties, the cabinet, the bureaucracy, and the courts, political scientists may analyze the interactions of the major players involved in enacting or rejecting a specific policy or set of policies.

Paul Pross enhanced this approach to political analysis by formulating the idea of a **policy community**. William Coleman and Grace Skogstad suggest that the policy community includes "all actors or potential actors with a direct or indirect interest in a policy area or function who share a common 'policy focus,' and who, with varying degrees of influence shape policy outcomes over the long run."[4] The policy community forms once a particular policy becomes an issue. Within the policy community there are sub-government groups and the attentive public. Sub-governments include "government agencies, interest associations, and other societal organizations such as business firms." The attentive public includes "relevant media and interested and expert individuals."[5]

The policy community is interactive and dynamic (see Figure 22.3). For example, once the federal government begins to consider a clean-air standards act, an environmental policy community emerges. Agencies of the state involved in this policy decision will include the cabinet, the departments of environment and industry, agencies concerned with interprovincial and international trade, Parliament, and perhaps the courts. Other groups with a stake in this process will also become involved:

PART 4

Figure 22.3 The Policy Community

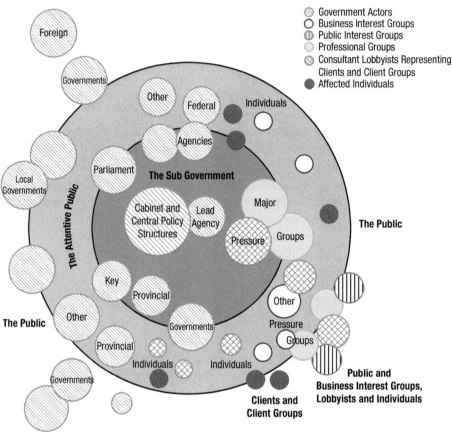

Legend:
- ⊚ Government Actors
- ○ Business Interest Groups
- ⦿ Public Interest Groups
- ○ Professional Groups
- ⊗ Consultant Lobbyists Representing Clients and Client Groups
- ● Affected Individuals

Foreign

Governments

Local Governments

The Attentive Public

Parliament

Other

Federal

Individuals

Agencies

The Sub Government

Cabinet and Central Policy Structures

Lead Agency

Major

Pressure

Groups

The Public

Key

Provincial

Other

Provincial

Governments

Pressure

Groups

The Public

Other

Individuals

Individuals

Individuals

Governments

Public and Business Interest Groups, Lobbyists and Individuals

Clients and Client Groups

Source: © A.P. Pross October 14, 2011. Contact: 220 Indian Path Rd., R.R. 2, Lunenburg, NS B0J 2C0, Canada. From *Group Politics and Public Policy* (Oxford, 1992) by A. Paul Pross. Reprinted by permission of the author.

environmental groups and provincial governments, as well as actors in the private sector such as business firms and labour unions. Presumably the interaction of these organizations will produce some kind of policy.

Thus the policy approach to politics is, according to Les Pal, a "problem"-oriented approach: "Existing policies therefore contain some definition of a problem; designing new policies depends initially on recognizing and defining public problems."[6] Focusing on societal problems offers another way of conceptualizing the process of politics. And we feel it is important for everyone to have some way of visualizing the process, especially if one is to discuss, evaluate, and criticize politics.

In the rest of Part Four, we examine the informal and formal–legal institutions and their role or function in a modern democratic process.

Questions for Discussion

1. How would you conceptualize the process of politics? What are the main differences between the systemic and policy approaches to politics? Which do you think better illuminates the political process? Why?

2. Choose a current policy issue and analyze its development using the systemic approach. Does it provide a convincing explanation for the policy's development? What are some of the advantages of taking a systemic or structural approach to politics?

3. Now analyze the same issue using the policy approach. Does your explanation change? Is it more or less convincing than the systemic explanation? What are some of the advantages of taking a policy or "problem" approach to politics?

Internet Links

1. *Canadian Public Policy:* **economics.ca/cpp**. Canada's leading peer-refereed academic journal for the study of public policy.

2. C.D. Howe Institute: **www.cdhowe.org**. One of Canada's leading public policy think-tanks.

3. Institute for Research on Public Policy (IRPP): **www.irpp.org**. The IRPP's *Policy Options* publishes shorter, less technical articles than *Canadian Public Policy*.

4. National Association of Schools of Public Affairs and Administration: **www.naspaa .org**. Provides accreditation to American graduate public-policy programs. The website provides links to a list of public-policy schools in the United States.

Further Reading

Andrain, Charles F. *Comparative Political Systems: Policy Performance and Social Change.* Armonk, NY: M. E. Sharpe, 1994.

Birkland, Thomas A. *An Introduction to the Policy Process: Theories, Concepts, and Models of Public Policy Making.* 2nd ed. Armonk, NY: M. E. Sharpe, 2005.

Brooks, Stephen, and Lydia Miljan. *Public Policy in Canada: An Introduction.* 4th ed. Toronto: Oxford University Press, 2003.

Campbell, Robert M., Michael Howlett, and Leslie A. Pal. *The Real World of Canadian Politics: Cases in Process and Policy.* 4th ed. Peterborough, ON: Broadview Press, 2004.

PART 4

Doern, G. Bruce, Leslie A. Pal, and Brian W. Tomlin. *Border Crossings: The Internationalization of Canadian Public Policy.* Toronto: Oxford University Press, 1996.

Doern, G. Bruce, and Richard W. Phidd. *Canadian Public Policy: Ideas, Structure, Process.* 2nd ed. Scarborough, ON: Nelson Canada, 1992.

Doern, G. Bruce, and Christopher Stoney, eds. *How Ottawa Spends, 2012–2013: The Harper Majority, Budget Cuts and the New Opposition.* Montreal and Kingston: McGill-Queen's University Press, 2012.

Dunn, William N. *Public Policy Analysis: An Introduction.* 3rd ed. Englewood Cliffs, NJ: Prentice-Hall, 2003.

Easton, David. *The Analysis of Political Structures.* New York: Routledge, 1990.

Hajer, Maarten A., and Hendrick Wagenaar, eds. *Deliberative Policy Analysis: Understanding Governance in the Network Society.* Cambridge: Cambridge University Press, 2003.

Homer-Dixon, Thomas. *The Ingenuity Gap: Can We Solve the Problems of the Future?* Toronto: Alfred A. Knopf, 2000.

Howlett, Michael, and M. Ramesh. *Studying Public Policy: Policy Cycles and Policy Subsystems.* 2nd ed. Toronto: Oxford University Press, 2003.

Kingdon, John W. *Agendas, Alternatives, and Public Policies.* 2nd ed. Boston: Addison-Wesley, 1997.

Lilleker, Darren G. *Key Concepts in Political Communication.* London: Sage, 2006.

March, James G., and Johan P. Olson. *Democratic Governance.* New York: Free Press, 1995.

Munger, Michael C. *Analyzing Policy: Choices, Conflicts, and Practices.* New York: W. W. Norton, 2000.

Pal, Leslie A. *Beyond Policy Analysis: Public Issue Management in Turbulent Times.* 3rd ed. Scarborough, ON: Thomson Nelson, 2006.

Peters, B. Guy. *Institutional Theory in Political Science: The "New Institutionalism."* 2nd ed. London: Continuum, 2005.

Savoie, Donald J. *Breaking the Bargain: Public Servants, Ministers, and Parliament.* Toronto: University of Toronto Press, 2003.

Shapiro, Ian. *Rethinking Political Institutions: The Art of the State.* New York: New York University Press, 2006.

Stone, Deborah. *Policy Paradox: The Art of Political Decision Making.* 3rd ed. New York: W. W. Norton, 2011.

Stoney, Christopher, and G. Bruce Doern, eds. *How Ottawa Spends, 2011–2012: Trimming Fat or Slicing Pork?* Montreal and Kingston: McGill-Queen's University Press, 2011.

CHAPTER 23

Political Parties, Interest Groups, and Social Movements: The Organization of Interests

Political parties, interest groups, and social movements are vital parts of the political process. Each provides a function essential to the conversion stage of the political process (refer to Figure 22.2). Political parties try to capture the reins of power of government; they want to control the institutions of government by winning a majority in elections. Interest groups, on the other hand, attempt to influence governments; they try to persuade public officials to enact legislation in their or the public's interest. Like interest groups, social movements attempt to influence governments, but they go beyond this in attempting to bring about some type of wider social change. In this chapter, political parties, interest groups, and social movements will be discussed separately.

POLITICAL PARTIES

Political parties are an essential feature of politics in the modern age of mass participation. In liberal-democratic systems they help to keep governments accountable to public opinion. Even in autocratic systems of government, they help the government maintain its hold on power. In either case, political parties are an important link between government and the people.

Political parties evolved with the extension of the franchise. In the eighteenth century, the Tories and Whigs dominated the British Parliament as political clubs of the upper class. They had little in the way of strong connections with the general population. But as suffrage was extended to most adult males, these clubs were transformed to accommodate the influx of voters, and the Conservative and Liberal Parties were formed. As reforms expanded the electorate in liberal democracies, political parties were viewed as the primary political organization facilitating mass politics. Political parties not only were the vehicle through which individuals could become involved in politics but also were considered the primary institutions shaping public policy.

A political party performs so many tasks in the political process that it is difficult to establish a simple definition. However, Joseph LaPalombara's working definition can serve as a point of departure: "A political party is a formal organization whose self-conscious, primary purpose is to place and maintain in public office persons who will control, alone or in coalition, the machinery of government."[1] These organizations are not usually part of the formal–legal machinery of government. In most Western nations, they do not derive power from a constitution. Any power they have depends on how the electorate responds in elections. However, there is an increasing tendency in many countries for political parties to be drawn into the formal sphere of government. In Canada, for instance, donations to parties are eligible for tax credits, while party finances are regulated by government and subject to disclosure laws. Their very success as informal institutions is pushing them toward formal–legal status.

The Roles of Political Parties

The first and most important goal of the political party in a democratic system is electoral success. An election win entitles the party to dominate the governmental machinery and perhaps enact some of the proposals to which it is committed. Electoral success short of outright victory may enable it to participate in a coalition government and thus achieve at least some of its aims.

A number of other roles complement the primary objective of winning power. A political party is the mechanism by which candidates are chosen to run for public office. A person may choose to run as an independent, but almost all successful candidates for public office are members of an organized party. A related role is to influence voters during campaigns. A great deal of the work of a party organization involves trying to get voters to support its candidates.

At the governmental level, the members elected with the support of the party put forward and pass legislative proposals in the assembly. Given the size of assemblies, there is a need for some kind of organization. The cabinet of the governing party determines which legislative proposals are to be considered, drafted, debated, and—the governing party hopes—passed. The party also acts as an intermediary between elected members and the public, that is, between people and their government. While the bulk of party activity occurs at election time, this continuous interchange between people and government can be an important function of the party.

Finally, the political party provides a training ground for political leaders. The party ranks are a pool from which political leaders are recruited. Party workers in constituency organizations often choose to run for office; if elected, they may work their way up from the backbenches to a ministerial post. Stephen Harper, for example, got his start in politics by joining the youth wing of the Progressive Conservative constituency association in Calgary West. In Canada, however, there has been some tendency in recent decades for leaders of the major national parties to be brought in "sideways."

Michael Ignatieff was persuaded by admirers to return to Canada specifically to lead the Liberal Party, and he became a candidate for leadership only a few months after the Liberal defeat in 2004.

Political leadership means building coalitions. For example, in the 2000 and 2004 elections, President George W. Bush pulled together a winning coalition of conservative Republicans, large business interests, and fundamentalist Christians in the southern, Midwestern, and northern industrial states. In 2008 Barack Obama mobilized moderate Democrats as well as black and Hispanic voters, and he was able to make inroads in the South (Florida, North Carolina, and Virginia), the Midwest (Iowa, Colorado, New Mexico, and Nevada), and Ohio. This aggregation of specific and regional interests enabled Obama to win the presidency over John McCain.

Another important function of the democratic political party is aggregation of interests. Various groups make a great many demands on government; it is never possible for a government to meet all of them, mainly because many of the demands are mutually incompatible. For example, organized consumer groups will demand that import quotas on shoes be abolished, while manufacturers will demand that those quotas be made more restrictive. The political party is a forum in which conflicting interests may be at least partially reconciled, where compromises can be reached and then bundled into a program that most party supporters can accept.

In autocratic systems, the party also aggregates demands to some extent, although because of the lack of political freedom this must be done behind the scenes. Specialists in Soviet politics often suggested that the monolithic façade of the Communist Party concealed squabbling factions representing such interests as the military and agriculture. More obvious is the totalitarian party's function of promoting support for the regime. The party is the government's instrument for enhancing popular acceptance of its policies. To this end, the party coordinates publicity in the mass media, organizes meetings and demonstrations, and carries out persuasion through its cells in workplaces.

It must be remembered that we are speaking of political parties in general. Not all parties perform all of the above roles, and the roles may be played out in different ways. For example, the role of political parties in the Canadian system has changed over time. They remain the primary vehicle through which politicians are recruited and they continue to mobilize the electorate at election time, but their function has changed in the area of policy formation. Most policy proposals come from the political executive—the prime minister and other cabinet ministers and their personal advisers—or from the permanent administration. The work of developing policy proposals is not so much an effort of the party faithful as it is of the senior people working for members of Cabinet, some of whom may not even belong to the party organization. Thus, while local, regional, provincial, and national party organizations meet and make policy recommendations to the party leadership, the policy proposals that emerge from the government may not reflect opinions at the grassroots level of the party. This is why

PART 4

most analysts now agree that the role of political parties in the legislative process has declined and that the executive and bureaucracy are now more influential (more on this issue in Chapter 27).

Because no two parties function in the same way, it is necessary to have a scheme of classification. Without pretending to be definitive, the following typology captures some of the main types: pragmatic, ideological, interest, personal, and movement parties.

The Pragmatic Party

One of the more common party types in Western society is the **pragmatic party**. The dictionary defines *pragmatism* as a "philosophy that evaluates assertions solely by their practical consequences and bearing on human interests."[2] In other words, a pragmatist's actions are less likely to be driven by a set of basic principles and doctrine than by a concern for the consequences of those actions. The pragmatic political party gears its campaign promises not to beliefs founded on doctrine but to programs that it believes have the greatest appeal to the public. It is thus open to the criticism of having no principles and of moving with the wind, and its programs sometimes appear to reflect nothing more than a cynical desire for power.

The mass parties in the Anglo-American tradition are generally classified as pragmatic: Conservatives and Labour in Great Britain, Conservatives and Liberals in Canada, Republicans and Democrats in the United States. The pragmatism of such parties always generates confusion about where they stand. Stephen Harper's Conservatives, for example, are attacked by voices on the left for pursuing a "right-wing, neoconservative" agenda, yet organizations on the right, such as the Fraser Institute and the Canadian Taxpayers Federation, criticize Harper for failing to implement a conservative agenda. Pragmatic parties sometimes appear more ideological— as the British Conservatives did under Margaret Thatcher—but this usually reflects not so much a fundamental change in the party as the temporary ascendancy of one faction within it. With the passage of time, the party usually reverts to a more pragmatic and less ideological stance, as happened when John Major replaced Thatcher as leader.

When pragmatic parties compete head to head, they characteristically make overlapping proposals, even to the extent of borrowing each other's ideas. For example, the proposal for a comprehensive free-trade agreement with the United States arose from a royal commission, appointed by the Liberal government of Pierre Trudeau and chaired by Donald Macdonald, a former Liberal cabinet minister. Brian Mulroney opposed the idea when he was running for leadership of the Conservatives, but he later adopted it as the most important policy initiative of his first term in office. The Liberals strenuously opposed the Free Trade Agreement (FTA) while it was being negotiated, but Jean Chrétien's government gave it final approval for implementation.

This mutual borrowing is not confined to particular policies; it also extends to broader party positions. Between the 1950s and 1970s, the welfare state and government interventionism were dominant ideas, and the pragmatic parties of the right had to accept them or face electoral extinction. "We are all Keynesians now," said Republican Richard Nixon when he was president of the United States. More recently, mirror-image claims have been made about Barack Obama. Having to cope with the revenue limits brought about by tax cuts adopted under George W. Bush, his limited record to date in implementing a stronger welfare state led to his being labelled the Democrats' Richard Nixon.

The Ideological Party

The **ideological party,** in contrast, emphasizes ideological purity more than the immediate attainment of power. Party doctrine takes precedence over electoral success. Such parties are criticized, of course, for their inflexibility. Often they put doctrine before the wishes of the voters, convinced that in time voters will come around to their way of thinking. The Communist Party is a good example of an ideological party, as are socialist parties and even some social-democratic parties. On the right, some conservative parties are as doctrinaire as any on the left.

The New Democratic Party is the most ideological of the traditional Canadian parties. As a party of the left, its major policy commitments have focused on social rights (e.g., opposition to the privatization of health care) and economic rights (e.g., review of NAFTA to achieve fairer trade). The Reform Party (1987–2000) was understood by most observers to be an ideological party of the right, in that it presented a simple, doctrinaire program: balance the federal budget, reduce taxes and government spending, abolish official bilingualism, introduce recall legislation, and so on. More careful observers, however, noted that Reform positions were often phrased with a "calculated ambiguity," suggesting a pragmatic party in waiting.[3] When the Reform Party merged itself into the Canadian Alliance in 2000, it abandoned or watered down a number of its more radical positions, thus taking further steps toward becoming a pragmatic party. That process was completed in 2003 when it merged with the Progressive Conservatives to form the Conservative Party of Canada.

When pragmatic parties adopt policies that are very similar, they run the risk that new parties may appeal to voters who perceive the pragmatic parties as no longer standing for anything. In Canada, Brian Mulroney's success at adopting many positions previously associated with the Liberals (bilingualism, multiculturalism, employment equity) led many ideological conservatives to defect from the Progressive Conservatives in favour of the Reform Party, which offered a more consistent ideological stance. The Reform Party, however, found its potential limited because it was perceived by many voters as excessively ideological. The point is not that pragmatic parties are good and ideological parties are bad, or vice versa; it is that each type of party offers something different to voters and may fail or succeed under various sets of circumstances.

PART 4

The Interest Party

Another type of party is the **interest party.** Here we find people converting their interest group into a full-fledged political party that runs candidates and attempts to obtain power. Such a group feels that it can best achieve its ends by acting as a party rather than trying to influence existing parties, but its narrow basis of support makes it hard for it to win control of the state. In Australia, the National Party (once known as the Country Party) began as a farmers' party. There have also been peasants' parties in Eastern Europe and Latin America. In Scandinavia, industrialists have formed conservative parties. Around the world, Green parties developed from environmental movements when they became convinced of the need to have political parties win seats in legislatures to fight for environmental issues from within rather than outside government. In Canada the Green Party was established in 1983; in the 2006, 2008, and 2011 general elections it won less than 7 percent of the popular vote share, earning only one seat, the leader's, in 2011.

There is vigorous debate about the merits of pragmatic, ideological, and interest parties. Some believe that pragmatic parties contribute to the stability of the political system—that they cover the waterfront, so to speak, in their response to demands made by groups in society. These parties endeavour to include something for everyone in their platforms. They appeal to diverse groups—employers and labour unions, farmers and consumers, conservationists and developers. Many people see pragmatic parties as mechanisms for aggregating interests and mending the fault lines in a pluralistic society.

Those who advocate the virtues of interest and ideological parties make their arguments from the standpoint of representation. They are quite critical of pragmatic parties, suggesting that, by making broad appeals to all groups, such parties dilute their platforms so that in the end they represent no one. This is the position taken by Maurice Duverger, a noted authority on political parties whose comparative work is still basic in the field.[4] An interest or ideological party, according to this view, can cater its platform to a specific interest or to a group with a defined ideology. Political parties of this type are able to offer voters a clear choice, and elected members have a responsibility to a specific clientele. But what is made up in representation could be lost in stability. The advocates of pragmatic parties suggest that interest and ideological parties tend to intensify cleavages in society rather than reconcile them. Moreover, when these parties are unwilling to compromise at the legislative level, little is accomplished, and governmental instability and inaction may well result.

In fact, both pragmatic parties and interest or ideological parties have shown themselves capable of aggregating interests and reconciling conflicts. In the Anglo-American model of pragmatic parties, the resolution of conflicts takes place within the party. Labour, business, and agricultural organizations come to some sort of compromise with the government of the day, which is almost always formed by a single party. In contrast, in democracies where coalition governments of ideological or interest parties are the norm, interest reconciliation takes place among parties. Parties do not have to surrender their principles internally, but they have to make compromises to keep a coalition cabinet in power. This illustrates the general principle that the necessary functions of the political process may be accomplished in quite different ways in different systems. Any successful political system must resolve conflicts of interest among different social groups, but this task can be carried out within parties, among parties, or by other institutions in the governmental process.

The Personal Party

Another type of party is the **personal party,** which is founded around a single influential political leader. After World War II, supporters of General Charles de Gaulle formed the Gaullist Party, which became the strongest political force in France after de Gaulle established the Fifth Republic in 1958. With the support of this party, renamed the Union for the Defence of the Republic (UDR), de Gaulle was elected president in 1958 and 1965. The Gaullists, under a variety of party names, survived the General's retirement in 1969 and today represent a coalition of moderate conservatives. Juan Perón of Argentina also developed a political party from his personal following; his supporters elected him president in 1946 and 1951. Perón, however, was removed from office after a *coup d'état* in 1955. The Peronistas were the main force behind the election of President Carlos Menem in 1989 and 1995, reinforcing the fact that personal parties need not die with their founders.

Personal parties have been common in the Global South particularly in Africa. For years Robert Mugabe of Zimbabwe dreamed of establishing his Zimbabwe African National Union–Patriotic Front (ZANU-PF) as the single party under which racial and ethnic groups would be united. This was accomplished in December 1987; he was re-elected president in 1990, 1996, and 2002. In the 2008 election, however, Morgan Tsvangirai, leader of the Movement for Democratic Change (MDC), earned a sufficient number of votes to force a runoff election for the presidency. Mugabe won the runoff when Tsvangirai withdrew, accusing the government of mounting a campaign of violence against his supporters.

All these examples show that the personal party, like the other types of parties, is not an entirely clear-cut category. All parties have leaders who are usually quite prominent even in a thoroughly democratic party, and even the most dominating leader has to have an organization to be effective. Thus parties that may be considered personal vehicles at the outset often evolve into long-lasting pragmatic, ideological, or interest parties.

PART 4

The Movement Party

A **movement party** is a political movement that evolves into a party apparatus. A movement is a union of people that aims at a profound social change, such as national independence, but does not itself aspire to govern. A movement sometimes is converted into a party when the prestige it gains by achieving its goals makes it a logical choice to become the government. The Indian National Congress, organized in 1885, became the instrument by which Indians sought independence from Great Britain. The party became the focus of nationalist feeling throughout India and mobilized popular pressure against the British. After achieving independence in 1947, it became the dominant political force in the federal parliament, a position that it long maintained, although it slipped a good deal during the 1990s.

In Canada the Bloc Québécois could be considered a movement party. Its only real program is the sovereignty of Quebec. If it ever achieves that goal, it will probably break up into ideological factions. In the meantime, it uses the House of Commons as a forum for promoting the independence of Quebec. For a list of other movement parties throughout Canadian history, see Canadian Focus 23.1.

POLITICAL PARTY SYSTEMS

Political party systems also influence the manner in which parties carry out their roles. There are basically three types of party systems: one-party, two-party, and multiparty.

The One-Party System

This one-party system includes true **single-party systems** and **one-party-dominant systems.** In the former there is only one party in the political system, and no political alternative is legally tolerated. The former Communist Party of the Soviet Union, whose leading role was guaranteed in the constitution, was the classic example. Where political leaders are building a utopian order according to an ideological blueprint, political opposition becomes heresy. Under such conditions any political alternative is prohibited.

In a one-party-dominant state, a single political party dominates the political process without the official support of the state. While a number of minor parties offer political alternatives, the electorate usually votes overwhelmingly for the dominant party. The Institutionalized Revolutionary Party (PRI) of Mexico was an example until the 2000 elections. The PRI maintained power by clever use of the state apparatus, especially through patronage and corruption. Electoral reforms initiated under President Ernesto Zedillo (1994–2000) played a role in the victory of the National Action Party under the leadership of Vicente Fox in 2000.

Canadian Focus 23.1

New Political Parties in Canada

For a long time, the two regions of Canada most dissatisfied with the status quo in Canada have been Quebec and the West. It is not surprising, then, that these two regions, so different in other ways, have both given rise to a long series of political parties challenging the constitutional order in fundamental ways. Below are lists of the main parties created in these two regions. The symbol P means provincial party, F means a federal party, and F+P indicates that the party operated at both levels.

New Political Parties Founded in Western Canada

Provincial Rights Party (P)	1905
Non-Partisan League (P)	1916
Progressives (including United Farmers' parties) (F+P)	1919
Co-operative Commonwealth Federation (F+P)	1932
Social Credit (F+P)	1935
Social Credit Party of British Columbia (P)	1952
Western Canada Concept (F+P)	1980
Western Canada Federation (F+P)	1980
Confederation of Regions (F+P)	1983
Reform Party of Canada (F)	1987
Reform Party of British Columbia (P)	1989
National Party (F)	1992
Progressive Democratic Alliance of British Columbia (P)	1993
Saskatchewan Party (P)	1997
British Columbia Unity Party (P)	2001
Alberta Alliance (P)	2002
Wildrose Alliance Party (P)	2008

New Political Parties Founded in Quebec

Parti National (P)	1885
Nationalist League (as political party) (F)	1911
Action Libérale Nationale (P)	1934
Union Nationale (P)	1935
Union des Electeurs (F+P)	1939
Bloc Populaire Canadien (F+P)	1942
Ralliement des Créditistes (F)	1957

(continued)

PART 4

Canadian Focus 23.1 *(continued)*	
Parti Québécois (P)	1968
Ralliement Créditiste du Québec (P)	1970
Equality Party (P)	1989
Bloc Québécois (F)	1990
Action Démocratique du Québec (P)	1994
Québéc Solidaire (P)	2006
Coalition Avenir Québec (P)	2011

Finally, there are times when one party dominates without in any way using the state machinery to support its position. For whatever reason, voters seem content with a single party for long periods of time. The Democrats dominated the American South for a century after the Civil War. In Canada, the province of Alberta has had the curious habit of endorsing one party for long periods, then suddenly turning to another. Since 1905, no party in Alberta, having once formed a government and then lost an election, has ever returned to power. The result has been a sequence of one-party-dominant situations rather than sustained competition between two or more credible contenders. This assertion was reinforced in 2012 when the Progressive Conservatives won their twelfth consecutive majority government since 1971.

The Two-Party System

A **two-party system** exists when two parties are credible contenders for power and either is capable of winning any election. The United Kingdom and the United States are commonly cited as illustrations, but neither is literally a two-party system. In Britain, the Liberal Democrats, plus several regional parties operating in Scotland, Wales, and Northern Ireland, have challenged the two major parties, the Conservatives and Labour. In the American election of 2000, Ralph Nader ran for the Green Party and received only about 3 percent of the popular vote and no Electoral College votes. However, it has been argued that Nader's candidacy was significant because the approximately 100 000 votes he took in Florida might otherwise have tipped the balance in favour of Al Gore. This is an example of how even a minor third party may influence a close political race.

In systems where third parties receive a significant but minor share of the vote, it might be more accurate to call these systems **two-party-plus systems,** as some observers do. Germany furnishes an example of two-party-plus politics. The Christian Democrats and Social Democrats there are so evenly matched at the polls that the small Free Democratic Party, the Left, and/or the Greens can determine who will govern by throwing their parliamentary weight to one side or the other. The current government is a coalition between the Christian Democrats and the Free Democrats.

Canada was close to a strict two-party system during the first 50 years after Confederation, when only the Conservatives and Liberals mattered in federal politics. But from 1921 onward there have always been more than two parties represented in the House of Commons. The Progressives were the first successful third party, followed by Social Credit and the CCF, which both entered the House of Commons in 1935. The CCF continues in the form of the NDP, while more recently we saw the rise of the Bloc Québécois and the Reform Party/Canadian Alliance.

The two-party system is widely praised as a source of political stability, especially in parliamentary systems, in which the cabinet must maintain the confidence of an elected assembly. A two-party system is likely to yield majority governments that can hold office for a respectable length of time. Less convincing is the common argument that a two-party system serves the interests of voters by offering them a clear choice between two responsible aspirants to power. Parties in two-party systems are often highly pragmatic; for long periods of time their platforms may greatly resemble each other, giving voters little real choice. American and Canadian politics are like this at most elections. This is not to say that the two-party system is necessarily worse than the multiparty alternative, only that it is not as obviously superior as newspaper editorials in the Anglo-American democracies often maintain.

The Multiparty System

In a **multiparty system**, three or more political parties have a realistic chance of participating in government. In most cases the parties are either interest parties or ideological parties that consider the interests of their supporters their first priority. Sweden has a multiparty system. From left to right on the political spectrum, one could find eight political parties represented in the Riksdag (parliament) after the 2010 election: Left, Greens, Social Democrats, Centre, Christian Democrats, Liberals, Moderates, and Sweden Democrats. The Left Party is the residue of the old Communist Party and is supported by workers; the Greens, as their name implies, are an expression of the environmentalist movement; the Social Democrats are a pragmatic socialist party; the Centre is an agrarian party with some urban support; Christian Democrats advocate Christian values; the Liberals represent professionals and intellectuals; the Moderates represent free-enterprise financial and business interests; and the Sweden Democrats are a far-right nationalist party.

Cabinet instability sometimes occurs in parliamentary systems in which there are many parties. When representatives are drawn from a number of parties, majority governments may be difficult to come by, and coalition governments may become the norm. Where the parties in a coalition government hold to principle and refuse

PART 4

to compromise, governments tend to change frequently. This was the case in the Fourth Republic of France in the 1950s, which saw 13 governments in one period of 18 months. The same was true of Italy from the end of World War II until the 1990s.

However, in political science, generalizations seldom apply without exceptions. Instability does not occur in all multiparty systems. The multiparty systems of Denmark, Norway, and Sweden, for example, have usually produced durable coalitions that cannot be characterized as unstable. The difference has an interesting and logical explanation. Italy and France at various times had large extremist parties of both the left and the right. Because some of these parties were fundamentally opposed to the constitution, they were not acceptable coalition partners, which restricted the number of possible coalitions. Under such conditions, when a working partnership among parties breaks down, there may be no alternative to re-establishing it, except perhaps by replacing the cabinet. The result is a game of political musical chairs in which cabinets succeed one another with monotonous regularity. In contrast, the Scandinavian countries do not have large extremist parties. All important parties are acceptable coalition partners, so there is more room to manoeuvre and create durable coalitions.

Assessing Political Parties

Political parties developed in concert with the extension of the franchise and they have helped to legitimize mass democracy. But this does not mean that all political parties are mass organizations with every voter holding a membership; on the contrary, in most Western societies the actual number of party members is very small. In Canada, fewer than 5 percent of voters belong to any federal or provincial party. Moreover, most of those who do are in the middle and upper-middle income brackets, are relatively well educated, and generally feel they have something at stake in the political process. For this reason, political parties have been criticized as representing not the masses but the social and economic elite in society. Indeed, when one examines a sociological profile of party activists, that criticism may seem valid. Oligarchies of a kind do run political parties.

This point was made early in the century by Roberto Michels, in his classic work *Political Parties*. Michels argued that even the parties that talked the most about democracy, such as the social-democratic parties of his day, inevitably fell under the control of small, self-perpetuating elites. He went so far as to state that an "iron law of oligarchy" represented the real truth about democracy.[5]

However, the charge of elitism conveys the idea of a group closed off from the rest of society by restricted membership; this is not really the case with political parties in most Western democracies. While there may be only a few militants and they may represent the upper echelons of society, the doors of party organizations are not closed. On the contrary, anyone who pays the nominal membership fee is welcomed with open arms, and anyone who volunteers for party work is quickly inundated with tasks. A few middle-class activists may fill the ranks of political parties because they are the ones who choose to become involved. Many people simply do not have an interest in the mundane tasks that accompany political party membership.

In another sense, parties are elitist. Modern political competition depends heavily on public relations, advertising, polling, and fundraising—the so-called "black arts" of politics. These tasks require special skills and connections that are possessed by only a few insiders. While there may be many ordinary people serving as foot soldiers in the trenches of political warfare, the commanders and strategists are well-paid, well-connected people who possess unusual skills. This makes it difficult for the rank and file to feel they have any impact on policy directions of the party.

Be that as it may, we are seeing a remarkable proliferation of new political parties in Western Europe and North America. On the left, the main entrants are the Green parties, which represent environmentalism as a rising political issue. There are also a number of "new" socialist parties, which are actually recycled versions of older communist parties. On the right, the picture is even more complex. New **"populist"** conservative parties emerged recently in several countries; for example, New Democracy in Sweden and the Reform Party/Canadian Alliance in Canada had temporary but important life spans. These parties tended to be market-oriented, to advocate direct democracy, to be opposed to large-scale immigration, and to be rather antagonistic to corporations, trade unions, government bureaucracies, and other large organizations. Farther to the right are nationalistic, even racist, parties such as the National Front in France, the Republicans in Germany, and the Freedom Party in Austria.

At one level, these new parties are responding to emerging issues. Green parties are responding to environmental concerns; populist conservative parties are driven by the fiscal problems of the welfare state; and nationalist–racist parties represent a backlash against the flood of refugees and other immigrants into Western Europe. Also involved is the rise of post-materialism, as discussed in Chapter 5. Voters influenced by the post-materialist political culture are more concerned about self-expression and less willing to defer to the compromises engineered by political brokers. This may point toward the emergence of new political parties catering to the demands of a more diverse, opinionated, and fractious electorate. However, pragmatic centre parties remain the key to electoral success in most liberal democracies.

INTEREST GROUPS

In addition to political parties, particular social groups, usually called interest groups, also undertake the articulation of interests. An **interest group** is defined as "any organization that seeks to influence government policy, but not to govern."[6] It represents

PART 4

In 2003, the Progressive Conservative Party of Canada merged with the Canadian Alliance. This cartoon, showing PC leader Peter MacKay and Alliance leader Stephen Harper, poses the question—widely asked at the time—whether the two parties could be successfully merged.

people who band together to accomplish specific objectives. Because interest groups exert political pressure to achieve their ends, they may also be called pressure groups. Obviously, not all groups are political; people may organize for any number of reasons. There are social groups such as bridge and dance clubs, sports clubs, community associations, and professional organizations. Most of these voluntary organizations will never become involved in politics; however, if they do, they become interest groups in the political process. By coordinating political activities, they offer individuals an opportunity to become involved in the complex process of politics. Politics is an endless cycle because there are always new demands, generated by a variety of interests, with which government must deal.

Unlike political parties, interest groups do not seek to control the entire machinery of government; they seek merely to influence the political process with the goal of achieving certain legislative or policy ends. Interest groups may work with political parties and may even become affiliated with them—as in the relationship between the New Democratic Party (NDP) and some, but not all, member unions of the Canadian Labour Congress (CLC). Generally, however, parties and interest groups are conceptually distinct, even if their activities sometimes overlap.

Interest groups can be categorized according to the degree to which the benefits they seek largely benefit their own members (selective benefits) or the wider community more generally (diffuse benefits). While the distinction is not watertight and is sometimes subjectively determined, it is important nonetheless to understand that not all interest groups are motivated by self-interest.[7]

The function of an interest group in politics is to articulate the interest of its members, with the goal of changing laws and influencing policies. Interest groups seek to achieve their ends by persuading public officials. Land developers may try to influence a city council's decisions on planning and zoning; labour unions may try to persuade the provincial cabinet to amend collective bargaining legislation; conservation organizations may seek to influence public policies relating to national or provincial parks. Interest groups also address themselves to public opinion; in the Canadian election of 1988, business, labour, and other groups all spoke out vigorously about free trade, although the business community, led by the Canadian Council of Chief Executives (formally the Business Council on National Issues) and the Canadian Manufacturers' Association, had much more money to spend on advertising. In all such cases, citizens with a common goal band together in an effort to shape legislation that they believe affects their lives.

In the second half of the twentieth century, one of the great developments in the political process in Western democracies was the proliferation of organized interest groups. Before World War II, organized interest groups were relatively few in number and consisted chiefly of economic producer groups with a specific focus: business and industrial associations, labour unions, farmers' associations, and the organized professions, such as doctors, lawyers, and teachers. Because groups had to operate with whatever resources they could collect from their members, those representing a well-to-do clientele tended to be most effective.

The present-day picture is radically different. First, there are now many more politically active groups. Second, there are politically effective groups representing not only traditional producers but also diverse consumer interests (e.g., consumer associations, environmental protection groups), as well as a host of moral, cultural, and symbolic causes. Social movements arise (as discussed at greater length later) and organizations are created in rapid succession; witness the way in which the original liberation movements of the 1960s (epitomized by Black civil rights in the United States) have been followed by environmental, feminist, gay liberation, and animal-rights movements. Each of these movements has stimulated the growth of a number of organized interest groups to formulate and express distinct political views in the contemporary political process.

Many reasons are suggested as causes for interest-group proliferation. One is the expansion of formal education. More people now have the skills required to run an organization—public speaking, keeping minutes and financial records, doing research on political issues, writing and submitting briefs to public officials. Another is the ongoing revolution in transportation and communication, which has dramatically

PART 4

Figure 23.1 Attitudes on the Most Effective Way to Work for Change by Age Group, Canada: Strengthening Canadian Democracy Survey, 2000

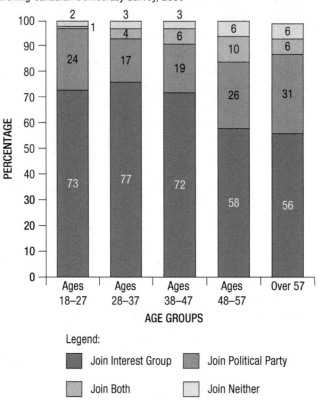

Legend:
- Join Interest Group
- Join Political Party
- Join Both
- Join Neither

Source: Adapted from Brenda O'Neill, "Generational Patterns in the Political Opinions and Behaviours of Canadians," *Policy Matters* 2001, 2(5), p. 14. Used with permission of the Institute for Research on Public Policy, www.irpp.com.

lowered the costs of building and maintaining a national organization. Modern communication technology, especially via the Internet, makes possible the creation of organizations that could not have existed 50 years ago. The same technology has also revolutionized fundraising methods. Even relatively small groups can raise significant amounts of money through telephone solicitation, direct mailings driven by computerized lists of target recipients, and credit card donations on the Internet. Finally, with the declining role of political parties as formulators of public policy, individuals may be more inclined to associate with and work for interest groups that support causes with which they identify, because they are perceived to be more effective. This trend is especially true of recent generations (see Figure 23.1).

A number of political scientists have argued that interest groups provide an important opportunity for political participation. Participating in an interest group not only provides members with an opportunity for acquiring civic skills and knowledge, but it can also provide the "glue" that makes for stronger communities (in political science terminology, this glue is referred to as "social capital").[8]

A standard typology for classifying interest groups is the fourfold division of anomic, associational, institutional, and nonassociational groups.[9] For more detail on these group types, see Concept Box 23.1.

A number of issues arise when considering just how interest groups work as part of the political process. For example, an important theoretical analysis by Mancur Olson suggests that the costs in time and money of organizing for political action often outweigh the benefits that an individual can expect to gain by lobbying, especially when

---

Concept Box 23.1

Interest-Group Typology

Anomic Groups. Spontaneous groups formed by citizens concerned about a specific issue. They usually disband after resolution of the single issue. *Example*: Fight HST.

In 2009 the British Columbia government agreed to adopt the harmonized sales tax, which would have applied to a wider selection of goods and services than the PST and GST in existence, a decision that caused considerable controversy. A group formed spontaneously, with former Premier Bill Van der Zalm as its most visible leader, to fight the decision by using the citizen initiative, a direct-democracy instrument that gives organizers 90 days to collect the signatures of at least 10 percent of voters in each of B.C.'s electoral districts, which they did. As it was the first successful initiative since the legislation enabling such actions had been introduced, the decision was sent to the Select Standing Committee on Legislative Initiatives, which then referred the issue to the Chief Electoral Officer for a province-wide binding mail-in referendum on the issue. It was held in the summer of 2011, and the proposal to end the HST was endorsed by 54.7 percent of voters, with a turnout of 52 percent. The B.C. government then announced it would return to the combined PST/GST within 18 months. Its goal achieved, the Fight HST group disbanded.

Associational Groups. Formal organizations set up to articulate the interests of their members over a long period of time. *Examples*: Canadian Labour Congress, Canadian Manufacturers and Exporters, Canadian Medical Association.

Associational groups are established to further the interests of their members or the public interest. They usually charge their members a fee and use the proceeds to support a permanent staff to conduct the business of the organization. Most of the large associational groups have representatives in provincial capitals and in Ottawa to lobby for their organizations.

Institutional Groups. Organizations closely associated with government that act internally to influence public decisions. *Examples*: Canadian Union of Public Employees, National Council of Veterans' Associations of Canada.

(continued)

PART 4

Concept Box 23.1 *(continued)*

While people in these groups are part of government and in theory politically neutral, they have interests to articulate and seek specific goals. Like associational groups, they have the advantage of large memberships, permanent organizations, and continuity. There are certain associational groups that, according to this classification, might almost be labelled institutional because of their close association with governments. Such ties are usually financial. Aboriginal associations are examples, as are francophone and anglophone minority-language associations and multicultural ethnic societies. All such groups receive substantial financial support from the federal government, from departments such as Indian Affairs and Northern Development or Canadian Heritage. This funding is often crucial to their existence.

Non-associational Groups. Unorganized groups made up of individuals who perceive a common identity on the basis of culture, religion, or some other distinctive quality. *Examples:* youth, Catholics, Westerners, Maritimers.

Non-associational groups lack formal organizations designed for political activity, even though often they are considered as if they were organized. The term *latent groups* captures the significance of these people—at any time, given the right issue, they could mobilize and possibly become a political force. For that reason, politicians take the interests of such groups into account.

---

the potential benefits are diffuse.[10] This is another aspect of the free-rider problem discussed in Chapter 10. Why should I spend my time, for example, working in an environmental association when all who live in the community, whether or not they contribute to the movement, will enjoy the benefits of cleaner air and water?

One answer is that when a group is already organized for other reasons, its incremental costs of entry into the political system may be much lower. A group may also provide nonpolitical benefits, such as the recreational activities sponsored by the Sierra Club.[11] In both these ways, pre-existing associations have an advantage in undertaking pressure-group activity. The expectation that pre-existing associations such as labour unions and professional associations should be formidable lobbyists seems to be borne out empirically.

Government support of interest groups first became important in Canada as part of Pierre Trudeau's "Just Society." The rationale was that Aboriginal peoples, women, and ethnic and linguistic minorities were disadvantaged or even oppressed groups that could not hope to compete on equal terms in the political marketplace. It was thought that giving them financial assistance to form interest groups would enable them to exert political pressure for economic and social reforms, and thereby improve their position over the long run. Public support of interest groups was thus a logical corollary of reform liberalism. The public funding of interest groups has declined significantly, however, beginning with the Mulroney government in the 1980s.[12]

It is perhaps surprising that such federally funded interest groups often became the severest critics of federal policy, sometimes in unexpected ways. For example, the National Action Committee on the Status of Women actively opposed most of the initiatives of the Mulroney government, including the FTA and NAFTA, the Charlottetown Accord, and many changes in social policy. But if one considers that such groups received funding because of their relative disadvantage and oppression, then their criticisms are perhaps easier to understand.

Public funding of interest groups raises a number of questions. While the funding provides some groups with their only possibility for participating effectively in the political system, it can also compromise their ability to protect the interests of their members. Government funding also means that certain interests are provided the means with which to organize while others are not; government, in effect, can directly determine which marginalized interests are voiced and heard through its funding decisions. If, however, one accepts that not all interests are equally capable of mobilizing, then public funding remains an important mechanism for ensuring the articulation of a diversity of interests.

Political Consultants and Lobbying

The expansion of interest-group activity has given rise to a new profession, that of the **political consultant**.[13] Consultants are often former politicians, public servants, or military officers who see the opportunity to put their expertise to work in the private sector. For a fee, they keep clients informed of new developments within government and advise them on how to pursue their goals effectively. After consultants have been retired from the public service long enough to avoid charges of conflict of interest, they may also engage in lobbying.

The term **lobbying** is derived from the old practice of individuals and groups buttonholing MPs in the lobby of the British House of Commons. The practice now involves many different methods for influencing decisions: arranging an interview with a cabinet member, submitting a brief to a royal commission or parliamentary committee hearing, writing letters to elected representatives, and advertising in the media to generate public pressure over an issue. In every case the objective is the same: to influence governors and the public so that they will be favourably disposed to the interest group's position on an issue.

Lobbying has become an accepted part of today's political process. In 2011, more than 5000 lobbyists were registered under Canada's federal Lobbying Act, a number that has remained relatively unchanged in recent years.[14] While the term carries certain derogatory connotations, many public officials admit that they depend on lobbyists as a source of information. Typically, elected officials depend on members of

PART 4

the administration or bureaucracy to supply the facts they require to make a political decision. But the administration has its own views and biases, or it may not have all the information pertinent to a decision; as a result, resorting to lobbyists for a range of views has become a recognized part of politics. In this sense, interest-group lobbying can be seen as a positive part of politics, in that it counters the entrenched views of bureaucrats or cabinet members.

The focus of lobbying depends on the institutional arrangements of government. In the United States, where Congress is a more autonomous body and is not controlled by party discipline, lobbyists concentrate on swaying the minds of individual representatives and senators. Such a strategy would have little payoff in Canada, or in other parliamentary systems in which elected representatives must vote according to party discipline. In the parliamentary milieu, the ultimate goal is to influence members of Cabinet and the senior advisers of the prime minister. In practice, however, these people are extremely difficult to reach, so Canadian lobbyists do much of their work with the civil servants who offer advice to politicians over the long term. And in countries such as the United States and Canada, where judicial review is an important factor in the political process, interest groups may also devote resources to sponsoring litigation.

Determinants of Influence

An important question is why some groups are more influential in their lobbying than others. What makes an interest group powerful? A number of factors have been suggested: the size and cohesion of the group; its wealth, organizational abilities, and leadership; and the nature of the issue at hand. For a further discussion, see Concept Box 23.2, on determinants of interest-group influence.

Interest groups tend to be particularly influential when several of these factors coincide. Provincial medical associations are an example. While their members are few in relation to the larger society, the associations are cohesive because their members share a common education and body of professional practices. They have great financial resources as well as excellent leaders and organizational capabilities. All this has made them effective lobbyists on the political scene.

Interest Groups and the Political System

Let us make some general observations about the place of interest groups in contemporary liberal democracies. First, there is a correlation between interest-group activity and the guarantee of political freedom in a society. Without constitutional guarantees of free speech, a free press, and the right to assemble, the political activities of interest groups would be seriously jeopardized. Governments seldom cherish criticism, and a good portion of an interest group's activities involves criticizing proposed or existing laws and policies. Without immunity from reprisal, there would be considerably

Concept Box 23.2

Determinants of Interest-Group Influence

Numbers. The size of the group cannot help but count in democratic politics. Legislators listen when a group represents a large membership. Numbers, however, do not tell the whole story.

Cohesion. To be effective, members of a group must act cohesively. Organized labour, for example, is one of the largest groups in Canada, and if its members voted as a bloc they could carry many ridings. While labour organizations often endorse political party candidates, the members usually vote across the party spectrum.

Organizational Skills. Effective groups maximize their use of human resources and have the ability to translate emotion into action. No matter how strongly individuals feel about an issue, ad hoc and sporadic complaints may be ineffective. Coordinating individual responses under an effective organization is more likely to have an impact on public policy.

Financial Support. It costs money to set up an organization, monitor government decisions, and engage in lobbying. The main sources of support are large contributions by corporations or unions, small contributions by grassroots members, grants from foundations, and subsidies from government.

Interest groups vary greatly in how they combine these sources of revenue, but none can function without money.

Leadership. Good leadership can mobilize concerned individuals and make a difference by inspiring coordinated action on the part of the group.

Nature of the Issue. The issue must have significant appeal to legislators and to the public, or there is little chance of obtaining results in politics. Over time, however, appeal for an issue can develop. For example, when the anti-smoking movement began in the 1970s, it seemed to have little chance of success. More than half of North American adults smoked, and not only was smoking in public taken for granted, but also it was on the increase. There was already substantial medical evidence about the harmful effects of smoking, but it had made little impact on the public consciousness. Then, as part of wider trends involving diet, fitness, health, and the environment, the medical evidence began to register, public opinion began to turn against smoking, and anti-smoking groups became highly successful lobbyists, achieving higher taxes on tobacco products, limitations on tobacco advertising, and restrictions on smoking in public places.

less enthusiasm for this type of public participation. Even in our own, relatively free society, governments are sometimes accused of withholding vital information and even using intimidation.

PART 4

Second, interest-group activity may be good "therapy" in the participatory society. While all groups cannot achieve all their ends in the political process, most of them are successful at least occasionally. The theory of group politics suggests in part that successful participation in the political process through interest-group activity reinforces confidence in the system. Group politics thus has the potential to enhance the legitimacy of the system in the minds of citizens. To deny groups an opportunity to participate in politics would be to undermine this perceived legitimacy.

The increase in the activity of interest groups is a fact, but it is also a fact that only a small number of people become activists in interest-group politics. Are non-participants—those not affiliated with an interest group—excluded from the benefits of public decisions? Certainly to some extent but perhaps not entirely, because the unorganized still have the potential to organize and therefore constitute latent interests.[15] In other words, when public officials distribute benefits through the political process, they cannot afford to bypass unorganized interests totally—the unorganized are voters and have the potential to become organized into effective groups.

Political freedom has nurtured a great deal of interest-group activity, with the benefits described above, but there are ways in which interest groups may damage the community. For one thing, interest-group activity is closely interwoven with a distributive approach to politics, in which political activity represents an exchange: voters render their support (votes) to politicians, and politicians in turn enact programs and policies for the benefit of those groups that support them. Although this may reflect much that occurs in the politics of liberal democracy, it is hard to view it without concern. Liberal democracy as a form of government rests ultimately on the notion that its laws are universal laws that apply equally to all citizens. It is this general equality before the law that justifies equal political rights for all citizens. But aggressive interest-group activity may easily become a pursuit of special privileges, which is inimical to equality before the law. Manufacturers of certain products lobby for protective tariffs to prevent consumers from buying cheaper foreign versions. Organized labour uses collective bargaining legislation to win benefits denied to the rest of the workforce. Organized farmers use their political power to get government to set up marketing boards to raise prices in their favour. As one special-interest group succeeds in its objectives, other interests may be stimulated to organize themselves for entry into the lobbying contest. If this process continues over many decades, a society of equality before the law can transform itself into a society of entrenched privilege, with each interest group jealously defending its special prerogatives.

A related phenomenon is the tendency to politicize issues. Once groups learn that they can use government to their particular advantage, they tend to begin looking for political rather than economic or social solutions to problems. For example, owners of declining industries, faced with severe competition from foreign producers, may seek protective tariffs and quotas rather than new outlets for their capital. Similarly, the workers in such industries may pressure government to protect their jobs by propping up or even nationalizing faltering companies. What were once economic matters decided in the marketplace can become political issues decided by a preponderance of power. Politicization can jeopardize the fundamental liberal concept of the limited state by injecting government into more and more realms of social activity. If each group single-mindedly pursues its own interests, all the groups together may bring about a general situation that none of them would ever have chosen in the first place.

The Dilemma of Interest-Group Politics

Interest-group politics can be seen positively as part of the tendency toward democratization in modern society. The increase in the number of effective interest groups has likely produced a more level playing field in politics. As more people participate in politics, the number of interest groups grows accordingly. Environmental and anti-globalization groups are current examples of different segments of the population organizing around new political issues.

But interest-group politics also has a negative aspect. The playing field in the competition of interest groups is not perfectly level. Some have greater financial resources or better access to the levers of power and therefore get more than their fair share of benefits. Others, such as business groups, occupy a privileged position relative to other groups in pluralist societies, and governments are generally more responsive to their interests than to other groups.[16] This reflects the overall importance of the economy on the political agenda rather than anything more sinister, but it highlights the fact that structural factors can limit the effectiveness of certain groups.

Yet imagining modern participatory politics without interest groups is difficult. So, to curb the possibility of unfairness in the operations of interest groups, there has been a growing tendency toward public regulation of interest-group activity, including public identification as well as tighter definitions of conflict of interest on the part of politicians and civil servants.

Such problems cause some analysts to see interest-group politics as a long-term threat to liberal democracy. Legislators at all levels of government have voiced the concern that powerful lobbying by special interests can dominate the process for distributing public goods and services. Mancur Olson suggests that small but cohesive organizations with a single purpose have a great capacity for influencing public officials. Because the goals of these groups are usually self-centred, they may create economic inefficiency for the larger society.

Political thinkers at the dawn of the democratic era were acutely aware of these problems. Rousseau went as far as wishing to outlaw organized groups.[17] His view was that individuals could exercise their political responsibilities in the spirit of what he called the "general will"—that is, the good of the whole community—but that the formation of groups fostered a selfish spirit of particular advantage. Rousseau's diagnosis was undoubtedly shrewd, but his remedy of banning private associations was extreme and perhaps totalitarian in its implications. James Madison suggested a more moderate approach in *The Federalist*, where he discussed interest groups

PART 4

(then called **factions**).[18] Madison realized that factions could not be banned without destroying liberty itself. His remedy (which Rousseau had also accepted, as a second-best solution) was to promote the existence of a great number and variety of factions, so as to maintain an approximate balance or equilibrium among them. This fundamentally defensive strategy is based on the hope that a drive for special privilege by one group will generate contrary political pressure from other groups that stand to be adversely affected.

SOCIAL MOVEMENTS

While interest groups continue to play an important role in political systems, **social movements** have become increasingly important political actors. Interest groups are often elements of social movements, but movements encompass more than these traditional political organizations. Social movements are identified by their form (relatively unorganized and fluid), goals (sweeping political, social, and cultural change), structure (non-hierarchical and participatory), and techniques (often non-traditional, including protests—both legal and illegal—and boycotts).[19] An interest group is a hierarchical organization working to influence public policy on issues of concern to its members, while social movements are loose organizations of groups and individuals working to bring about wholesale change by influencing multiple actors, including governments, business, and individuals. For social movements, the objective is to change not only public policy and legislation but also political priorities, social values, and individual values and behaviour. And their focus often extends beyond national borders toward transnational actors.

Social movements are not a recent phenomenon, but contemporary movements can be distinguished from earlier ones. "Old" social movements include agrarian, labour, and religious reform movements, spurred in part by the processes of industrialization and urbanization. Examples of "new" social movements, on the other hand, include those that focus on the environment, women's equality, peace, and, most recently, anti-globalization. In line with post-materialism, new social movements focus on issues of identity and non-material goals rather than on questions of redistribution and class. The 1960s are normally identified as the years during which new social movements appeared. Societal changes taking place at that time furnish part of the explanation for their rise, including increased secularization, access to higher education, and the availability of the birth control pill. In 1970, for example, in one of the first examples of national feminist protests, Canadian women organized the Abortion Caravan, which travelled from Vancouver to Ottawa and ended with demonstrators chaining themselves to the gallery in the House of Commons, to protest amendments made a year earlier to Section 251 of the Criminal Code, dealing with abortion.

Political parties frequently emerged from old social movements—for example, the CCF, the British Labour Party, and Christian Democratic parties in a number of Latin American countries. The same is true of new social movements; Green parties have grown out of environmental movements in many countries, including Canada. And as support for the cause grows, existing political parties attempt to adopt the programs of new social movements as part of their party policy.

Social movements often develop from grassroots efforts directed at a particular issue. Interest groups can develop from the efforts, or existing organizations can join in the effort. Mentioned earlier, the Sierra Club lobbies the American government on a number of environmental issues, including the building of dams and carbon emissions. These organizations can also be involved in activities besides lobbying and advocacy, such as direct action (e.g., Earth First! employs tree-sits and illegal tree-spiking in its conservation efforts), conducting research to better understand issues (e.g., Earthwatch supports scientific research around the world to assist sustainability), and changing public attitudes (e.g., the Friends of Nature encourage green tourism to develop an increased love and understanding of nature). Importantly, movements also include unorganized individuals whose behaviour and attitudes reflect the goals of the movement, such as the many individuals who use blue boxes to collect recyclables.

The fluid and relatively unorganized nature of social movements means that, while there is general agreement on goals (the transformation of community and society), there is often much less agreement on how best to pursue them. Some of the organizations and individuals within a movement may seek change by working with governments to influence policies and legislation (sometimes referred to as "mainstreaming" or "large P" politics). Others will argue that working with governments can lead to co-optation by requiring that the organizational goals be compromised to some degree to win concessions, an option they flatly reject; instead, their position is one of disengagement, or a focus on "small p" politics. Some will argue that actions should always and everywhere be legal, in part to ensure that public support for the movement remains strong; others argue that the slow pace of change and the consequences of non-action demand the use of illegal means to raise awareness and increase the speed of change. Yet others will adopt a mix of approaches, their pragmatic positions responding to changing circumstances.[20]

Anti-globalization protestors provide a current example of a new social movement. They have organized demonstrations, sometimes violent ones, in cities around the world to oppose what they see as the anti-democratic practices of economic globalization. Maude Barlow's Council of Canadians is an important interest group that takes this position. Proponents of globalization argue that reduced trade restrictions will stimulate the economies of all countries, especially the industrializing transitional democracies, and that this economic growth will in turn enhance democratization. The forces of anti-globalization counter with three points: the process of globalization is undemocratic because discussions on its particulars are closed to the public; the economic growth experienced in industrializing transitional democracies is uneven, creating great disparities of wealth; and the lack of a regulatory process leads to environmental degradation and poor working conditions.[21]

The anti-globalization movement presents an important example of contemporary interest mobilization. It is transnational; it fights for increased citizen access to decision-making processes; it focuses on the media, corporations, and international trade organizations in addition to states; and it combines the use of "old" techniques (demonstrations and protests) with new mechanisms for mobilization (cellphones, text messaging, and the Internet).[22] Many major political issues of the past and present, such as feminism, gay and lesbian rights, and environmentalism, started with the noisy protests of relatively small numbers of people and went on from there to enter the political mainstream.

Questions for Discussion

1. Which political party comes closest to your political positions on issues? Which political issues do you consider to be priorities? Would you be more likely to work with a political party or with an interest group? Why?

2. Have you ever taken part in non-traditional political action? If so, what did you do (e.g., sign a petition, participate in a boycott, participate in a protest, etc.)? If not, would you, if given the opportunity? When (if ever) is illegal political protest defensible?

3. Are interest groups and social movements a response to increasing political complexity or do they unnecessarily complicate politics?

Internet Links

1. Assembly of First Nations: **www.afn.ca**.

2. Canadian Council of Chief Executives: **www.ceocouncil.ca**.

3. Canadian Labour Congress (CLC): **http://canadianlabour.ca**.

4. Conservative Party of Canada: **www.conservative.ca**.

5. Global Greens Charter: **http://www.globalgreens.org/globalcharter**. A statement of the values and principles of Green parties and movements.

6. Greenpeace: **www.greenpeace.org/international**.

7. Liberal Party of Canada: **www.liberal.ca**.

8. National Organization for Women: **www.now.org**.

9. New Democratic Party of Canada: **www.ndp.ca**.

10. United States Democratic National Committee (DNC): **www.democrats.org**.

11. United States Republican National Committee (RNC): **www.rnc.org**.

Further Reading

Interest Groups and Social Movements

Baumgartner, Frank R., and Beth L. Leech. *Basic Interests: The Importance of Groups in Politics and Political Science.* Princeton, NJ: Princeton University Press, 1998.

Berry, Jeffrey M., and Clyde Wilcox. *The Interest Group Society.* 5th ed. New York: Pearson Longman, 2009.

Chong, Dennis. *Collective Action and the Civil Rights Movement.* Chicago: University of Chicago Press, 1991.

Della Porta, Donatella, and Mario Diani. *Social Movements: An Introduction.* 2nd ed. Malden, MA: Blackwell, 2006.

Duverger, Maurice. *Party Politics and Pressure Groups: A Comparative Introduction.* New York: Thomas Y. Crowell, 1972.

Hein, Gregory. Interest *Group Litigation and Canadian Democracy.* Montreal: Institute for Research in Public Policy, 2000.

Kingdon, John W. *Agendas, Alternatives and Public Policies.* 2nd ed. New York: HarperCollins, 1995.

Kwavnick, David. *Organized Labour and Pressure Politics: The Canadian Labour Congress,* 1956–1968. Montreal and Kingston: McGill-Queen's University Press, 1972.

Montpetit, Eric. *Misplaced Distrust: Policy Networks and the Environment in France, the United States and Canada.* Vancouver: University of British Columbia Press, 2003.

Olson, Mancur. *The Logic of Collective Action.* Rev. ed. Cambridge, MA: Harvard University Press, 1971.

Petracca, Mark P., ed. *The Politics of Interests: Interest Groups Transformed.* Boulder, CO: Westview Press, 1992.

Pross, Paul A. *Governing under Pressure.* Toronto: Institute of Public Administration of Canada, 1982.

———. *Group Politics and Public Policy.* 2nd ed. Toronto: Oxford University Press, 1992.

Sawatsky, John. *The Insiders: Government, Business, and the Lobbyists.* Toronto: McClelland & Stewart, 1987.

Smith, Miriam, ed. *A Civil Society?* Collective Actors in Canadian Political Life. Peterborough, ON: Broadview Press, 2005.

———. *Group Politics and Social Movements in Canada.* Peterborough, ON: Broadview Press, 2008.

Staggenborg, Suzanne. *Social Movements.* 2nd ed. Toronto: Oxford University Press, 2011.

PART 4

Tarrow, Sidney. *Power in Movement: Social Movements, Collective Action, and Politics.* New York: Cambridge University Press, 1994.

Truman, David B. *The Governmental Process.* New York: Knopf, 1958.

Wright, John R. *Interest Groups and Congress: Lobbying, Contributions, and Influence.* Boston: Allyn and Bacon, 1996.

Young, Lisa, and Joanna Everitt. *Advocacy Groups.* Vancouver: University of British Columbia Press, 2004.

Political Parties

Ajzenstat, Janet, and Peter J. Smith, eds. *Canada's Origins: Liberal, Tory, or Republican?* Ottawa: Carleton University Press, 1995.

Archer, Keith, and Alan Whitehorn. *Canadian Trade Unions and the New Democratic Party.* Kingston, ON: Industrial Relations Centre, 1993.

Bashevkin, Sylvia B. *Toeing the Lines: Women and Party Politics in English Canada.* 2nd ed. Toronto: Oxford University Press, 1993.

Bickerton, James, Alain-G. Gagnon, and Patrick J. Smith. *Ties That Bind: Parties and Voters in Canada.* Toronto: Oxford University Press, 1999.

Brodie, M. Janine, and Jane Jenson. *Crisis, Challenge and Change: Party and Class in Canada, Revisited.* Rev. ed. Ottawa: Carleton University Press, 1988.

Campbell, Colin, and William Christian. *Parties, Leaders, and Ideologies in Canada.* Toronto: McGraw-Hill Ryerson, 1996.

Carty, R. Kenneth, William Cross, and Lisa Young. *Rebuilding Canadian Party Politics.* Vancouver: University of British Columbia Press, 2000.

Courtney, Johon. *Do Conventions Matter? Choosing National Party Leaders in Canada.* Toronto: Macmillan, 1995.

Cross, William. *Political Parties.* Vancouver: University of British Columbia Press, 2004.

Dalton, Russell J., David M. Farrell, Ian McAllister, and Martin P. Wattenberg. *Political Parties and Democratic Linkage: How Parties Organize Democracy.* Oxford: Oxford University Press, 2011.

Duverger, Maurice. *Political Parties.* 3rd ed. New York: Wiley, 1978.

Flanagan, Tom. *Harper's Team: Behind the Scenes in the Conservatives' Rise to Power.* 2nd ed. Montreal: McGill-Queen's University Press, 2009.

———. *Waiting for the Wave: The Reform Party and Preston Manning.* Toronto: Stoddart, 1995.

Gagnon, Alain-G., and A. Brian Tanguay, eds. *Canadian Parties in Transition.* 3rd ed. Peterborough, ON: Broadview Press, 2007.

Ingle, Stephen. *The British Party System: An Introduction.* London: Routledge, 2008.

Katz, Richard S., and William Croty, eds. *A Handbook of Party Politics*. Thousand Oaks, CA: Sage, 2006.

Laver, Michael, and Norman Schofield. *Multiparty Government: The Politics of Coalition in Europe*. New York: Oxford University Press, 1990.

Michels, Robert. *Political Parties*. New York: Free Press, 1962. First published 1911.

Piven, Frances Fox, ed. *Labour Parties in Postindustrial Societies*. Cambridge, UK: Polity Press, 1991.

Rose, Richard. *Do Parties Make a Difference?* 2nd ed. London: Macmillan, 1984.

Rose, Richard, and Neil Munro. *Elections and Parties in New European Democracies*. 2nd ed. Washington, DC: CQ Press, 2009.

Sáez, Manuel Alcántara. *Politicians and Politics in Latin America*. Boulder, CO: Lynne Rienner, 2008.

Sartori, Giovanni. *Parties and Party Systems: A Framework for Analysis*. Colchester, UK: ECPR, 2005.

Sayers, Anthony M. *Parties, Candidates, and Constituency Campaigns in Canadian Elections*. Vancouver: University of British Columbia Press, 1999.

Scarrow, Susan E. "Political Parties and Party Systems." *In Comparing Democracies 3: Elections and Voting in the 21st Century,* edited by Lawrence LeDuc, Richard G. Niemi, and Pippa Norris. London: Sage Publications, 2010.

Thorburn, Hugh G., and Alan Whitehorn, eds. *Party Politics in Canada*. 8th ed. Scarborough, ON: Prentice Hall Canada, 2000.

Webb, Paul, David Farrell, and Ian Holliday, eds. *Political Parties in Advanced Industrial Democracies*. Oxford: Oxford University Press, 2002.

Young, Walter D. *Democracy and Discontent: Progressivism, Socialism and Social Credit in the Canadian West*. 2nd ed. Toronto: McGraw-Hill Ryerson, 1978.

PART 4

CHAPTER 24

Communications Media

Communications media include all means of transmitting, exchanging, and receiving communication. These currently range from the very traditional—television and newspapers—to the more modern—smartphones and tablet PCs. These media are not political institutions in the same way as political parties, interest groups, and social movements, which have an overt political purpose—that is, to influence or control government. The media's purpose is to inform or entertain. However, the media have such vast influence on the political process that we must consider them an integral part of it. They are vital transmission channels for both articulating demands and expressing support. Communications media are particularly important if democratic government is to be meaningful, for they provide much of the information by which citizens evaluate governments and assess political options.

Most people involved in traditional media would deny that their work is political in a partisan sense. Their job, so they claim, involves reporting facts, political events, and circumstances without political bias. Yet whether or not bias exists, the media are political institutions—not necessarily in partisan terms, but as important two-way links between people and government. News outlets broadcast election results as the votes are counted, allowing voters to feel that they are part of the process. In addition, the media provide the basis for public discussion of issues. They not only report political events but also provide the means for individuals, groups, and government to state positions that can be aired before the public.

We often take the political importance of the media for granted. Representative government, having been established before the age of mass media, was originally based on face-to-face contact between representatives and their electors, who were few in number. Voters personally knew their representatives and the election was held by a show of hands at a public meeting of electors convened for that purpose. Rival candidates would be present at this meeting to speak before the vote was taken. This method of election persisted well into the nineteenth century, until democratic extension of the franchise so expanded the electorate that it became impossible for representatives and electors to know each other personally. The introduction of the secret ballot made the electoral process more anonymous and impersonal, so that images conveyed by the mass media have now almost entirely replaced direct human contact. The consequences for democratic government are complex, but it is clear that representative democracy as we know it could not possibly exist without the mass media.

Political communication through the media takes many forms. For one, governments use the media to transmit information to the public. A prime minister or president may call a press conference or choose to address a national audience via radio or television. The press agents of important ministers make news releases available on particular issues. Governments employ websites as a way of informing people about public hearings or petitions for rezoning. Some of this flow of information is purely factual, but much of it contains implicit or explicit pleas for support of government policy. The flow of information also moves in the opposite direction. While a letter to the editor of a newspaper remains a possibility for voicing support or opposition to specific policies, a blog or an email to an MP or MLA are now also options.

Where political information was once relatively limited in its accessibility, it is now readily available. Most homes today have access to around-the-clock news sources. Ninety-nine percent of North American households include a television set, and recent statistics suggest that over 78 percent of North Americans use the Internet, which provides a channel of convergence for all other media.[1] And more than half of all cellphones in North America are smartphones, increasing our connectivity to media even further.[2]

Increased access has been matched by growth in the number of news sources. Gone are the days when news was available only in 30-minute television slots a few times a day on a handful of stations or in one's morning newspaper. An array of television channels, including 24-hour news channels such as CNN, the CBC News Network, and the CTV News Channel, and an unlimited number of news sources on the Internet, including BBC News and automated news aggregators such as Google News, provide access to a wealth of political information from around the world. Add to this the number of the world's newspapers now available online and the vast number of podcasts available for downloading, and the sheer quantity of available political information is staggering.

Not all are convinced, however, that the changes have been positive. Television news coverage has been criticized for having "dumbed down" content to too great an extent. According to David Taras, "television news stories are so visual, so sensational, so fixated on personalities, so fast-moving, so fleeting, and so intent on entertaining that they give viewers almost nothing tangible to hold on to."[3] News coverage of politics is likely to give more time to analysts and commentators than to politicians, whose comments are now limited to sound bites rather than speeches.[4] Others argue that the abundance of information has created a type of overload, with few citizens being able to process it.[5]

A positive aspect of the growth of the electronic media, and in particular the Internet, is the ability it affords citizens to become producers as well as consumers of information.[6] Citizens have at their fingertips access to an unlimited array of political information from

PART 4

more traditional sources such as newspapers, which remain a vital source of information, to more modern ones such as political party and interest-group websites, political blogs, and Twitter, which provide not only information but social networking possibilities. YouTube, for instance, have provided a powerful counter to the controlled media message of political candidates and parties. Each provides users with the possibility of sharing information, and for creating networks and "virtual communities." The importance of such technology and **social media** as mobilizing tools for new social movements was identified earlier (see Chapter 23). But it also opens up multiple opportunities not only for communicating with the "commons" but also for individual citizen engagement. For more on the implications of media development, see World View 24.1.

World View 24.1

Blogs and Politics

How important are blogs for politics? Do they make politics better or worse overall? Researchers in the United States have started to tackle these questions in light of the rise of this newest media form.

Blog is a contraction of two terms, *web* and *log*. A blog consists of a web page with online commentary on a topic, presented in reverse chronological order, and often with hyperlinks to other online sources. Bloggers can be independent, although many traditional media have adopted the form by sponsoring individual bloggers or by hiring in-house bloggers in their own right. The growth of the medium has been tremendous: one estimate suggests that there were 70 million blogs online in 2007.

Do blogs matter? Many would argue that they do and point to examples of the key role they have played in certain political events. In the United States, for example, Trent Lott resigned as Senate majority leader in 2002 following intense blog attention to inflammatory statements he had made, which led to increased media attention that could then not be ignored. Another example is Howard Dean, who is argued to have been, in 2004, the first politician to successfully harness the potential of blogs for rallying activists and raising money.

Blogs have also launched targeted campaigns and networks—Netroots, Google-bombing, and Porkbusters are but a few—the latter successfully limiting the degree to which House and Senate members could earmark extra funding to bills for districts or states. Not all blogs and blog campaigns are successful, however, which this type of anecdotal evidence-building misses.

Are they good for politics? Although it is still a bit early to tell, while many underscore the independent source of information they provide, others note that blogs can be less about the exchange of ideas and more about like-minded people expressing and reinforcing their views to each other, referred to as "cocooning" and

---

World View 24.1

"cyberapartheid." Still others have noted that bloggers tend to be predominantly white, male, and well educated, reinforcing the norm for politics more generally. Additional research will help to shed light on these questions.

A special issue of the journal *Public Choice* titled "Blogs, Politics and Power" (vol. 134, 2008) offers more on the question of the role and impact of blogs in politics.

CAMPAIGNS AND THE MEDIA

Political parties and election campaigns have been particularly affected by developments in the communications media. In all industrial democracies, electoral politics is now conducted primarily in the media. One result of this has been the rise to prominence in political parties of communications consultants, who are now indispensable. Four types of activities deserve particular mention.

The first is public relations, as managed by the so-called "spin doctors" whose job is to release news stories to and answer questions from print and electronic reporters. Insiders refer to the world of daily news coverage as the "unpaid media." Every day there is a tremendous volume of potential free publicity in the form of political news coverage, and political leaders have to ensure that their activities are represented as favourably as possible. Amateurism in this enterprise can be dangerous, since reporters are quick to pounce on any error or misstatement. Add to this the latest technologies, which provide an instant and widely available record of candidate missteps via media-sharing sites such a YouTube that can effectively kill a campaign. Thus all major parties now place great emphasis on "quick response" and "damage control" to reduce the negative effects of poorly worded statements or unflattering video clips.

A special form of unpaid media is the televised debate among party leaders. In 1984 the Canadian leaders' debate was a key turning point in the campaign for the Conservatives, when Brian Mulroney effectively attacked Prime Minister John Turner over patronage appointments. More recently, the first leaders' debate to be broadcast live in the United Kingdom likely led to the surprising showing of the Liberal Democrats in the 2010 election. A relative unknown, leader Nick Clegg's strong performance provided an opportunity to reach a huge audience in an unprecedented manner. The main purpose of the debate is to generate powerful short stretches of political theatre that can be played over and over on news programs and be incorporated into advertising. To make sure they generate the right sound bites, leaders prepare for days with their professional advisers.

The second great branch of media politics is the world of paid media, or advertising. Political parties advertise in all media during election campaigns, but television now gets the lion's share of expenditures. As in the realm of unpaid media,

PART 4

professionals have come to dominate. Political advertising campaigns are prepared by advertising executives who lend their services to political parties out of a mixture of motives such as ideology, personal friendship, and loyalty—and the hope of future patronage contracts. Ads are carefully tested in focus groups before they are run, and their performance is monitored equally carefully. If they do not seem to be working, they are pulled and replaced.

In spite of this research-and-development process, disastrous mistakes can occur. Late in the 1993 election campaign, the Conservatives started running television ads attacking Jean Chrétien's leadership ability. The ads featured close-up pictures of Chrétien that drew attention to the fact that one side of his mouth is partially paralyzed. When the ads were tested, members of the focus groups had not perceived them as making fun of Chrétien's disability, but the ads had this effect on the public at large when they were broadcast. The Conservatives had to pull them amid great embarrassment.

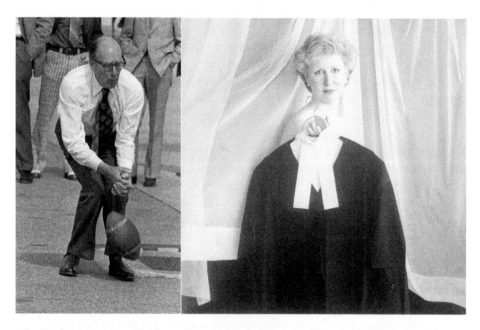

How leaders are portrayed by the media can have significant consequences. In 1974 a newspaper photo of Canadian Progressive Conservative leader Robert Stanfield fumbling a football was seen by many to epitomize the state of the party's campaign. The response to a 1992 photo of a bare-shouldered Kim Campbell was less clear-cut.

Photos: Left: (CP Photo) 1974 (Stf-Doug Ball). Right: © Barbara Woodley/Labatt Breweries of Canada/Library and Archives Canada/PA-186869. Source: Woodley, Barbara, *Portraits: Canadian Women in Focus*. Toronto: Doubleday Canada. © 1992, Image 64. Used with permission of Barbara Woodley.

The third activity that has become indispensable to modern politics is **public-opinion polling.** With the development of survey techniques and computer analysis, it is now possible to get fast and accurate information about the views of the public on any issue. Polling data now drive both public relations and advertising, and pollsters have become key figures in most parties' campaign-management committees. The goal of such committees is to produce a seamless interface between the party's and politicians' activities as reported in the news and the themes that are repeated in the paid advertising, while at the same time addressing concerns that polling has discovered among the voters. An important development in polling technology is the rolling or tracking poll, which most parties now use during campaigns. The pollster surveys a small new sample every night and averages those data with the results of (usually) the preceding two nights' surveys. The aggregate is large enough to be statistically reliable, and the averaging smooths out day-to-day fluctuations. Those in charge of the campaign receive a report every morning and can change course if it suggests that things are not going well.

The Internet is also becoming an important medium of political communication. All parties and candidates now maintain websites, which they use for fundraising, enlisting volunteers, and publishing information that they want to place before voters. The 2008 U.S. presidential election showed the contemporary importance of the Internet in politics (see Figure 24.1). Forty percent of Americans went to the Internet for news and information on the campaign in the spring of 2008, compared to only 16 percent in the spring of 2000.[7] The greatest change is in the viewing of online videos related to the campaign and the use of social networking sites for engaging in political activity, particularly by younger voters.[8]

Some observers are concerned about the overwhelming importance of the media and related technology in contemporary public life, fearing that it makes politics too professionalized, expensive, and manipulative, effectively reinforcing the strength of already powerful players. Others, however, argue that the Web provides an opportunity for greater equalization by, for example, allowing small political parties to bypass traditional media altogether and speak directly to the public. The reality is likely some mixture of the two, dependent in part on national context and the institutional and regulatory frameworks that structure election campaigns.

Content analysis of political party websites during the 2004 Canadian general election suggests that the power differential between minor and major parties is largely replicated on the Web: major parties' websites "have more visual appeal and entertainment features; they are easier to find and updated more frequently."[9] In short, major political parties such as the Conservatives and Liberals were able to develop more sophisticated websites, with more features and greater information. Importantly, however, minor parties provided greater levels of interactivity on their sites. Theory suggests that major parties employ the Web as a top-down mechanism of power-seeking and controlled communication; smaller parties are more likely to use it as a form of bottom-up grassroots communication with their membership, in part because of their more limited organizational structure.

PART 4

Figure 24.1 Internet Use in the U.S. Election by Age Group, Spring 2008

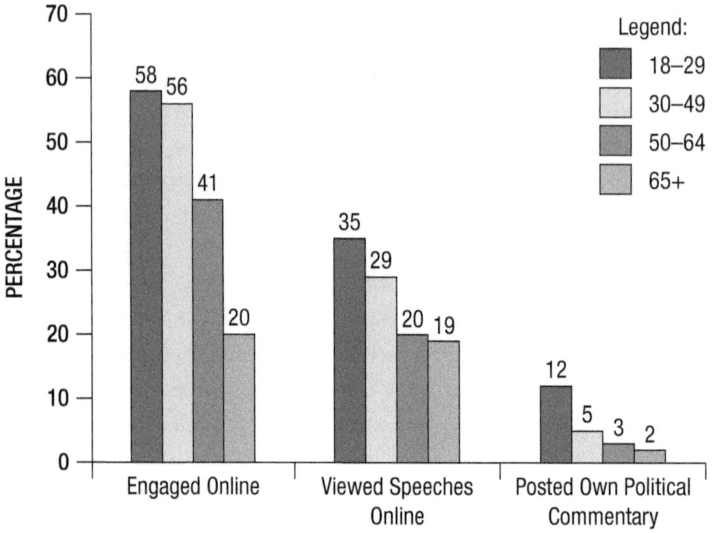

Note: Online engagement includes using the Internet, email, or text messaging to get news or exchange views about the race among all adults surveyed. "Viewed speeches online" and "Posted own political commentary" were within the past few months and included only those respondents who were Internet users.
Source: Adapted from Aaron Smith and Lee Rainie, "The Internet and the 2008 Election," *Pew Internet & American Life Project*, 15 June 2008, 5, 10.

PRIMING AND AGENDA-SETTING

Besides playing a large—and increasingly larger—role in political campaigns, the media actively participate in the day-to-day dissemination of political information, opinion, and symbolism. To some extent they do this openly, in editorials where they take explicit stands on various issues. However, people have minds of their own and are not necessarily persuaded by editorials. More important than editorials is the "objective" task of factual news reporting. Reporters strive for objectivity, but like the rest of us they work within intellectual and emotional constraints of which they may not be fully aware. Probably more profound in its effects than personal bias is the media's internal logic. We need not subscribe fully to Marshall McLuhan's famous dictum "the medium is the message" to see that news reporting has certain basic and sometimes conflicting requirements. While appearing to be accurate and objective, it must also be concise, interesting, and even entertaining. If it is too detailed, complex, or subtle, it will lose its mass audience. The audience will also evaporate if news reporting is too far at variance with the fundamental values and opinions of the political culture.

One way for journalists to reconcile these various demands is to focus on conflict. Arguments, debates, fights, strikes, boycotts, wars, and revolutions are far more exciting to report than cooperation, agreement, consensus, and quiet compromise. There is, therefore, an understandable tendency for almost all news to be recast according to a conflict model. Journalists play a large role in setting up conflicts, by choosing the authorities whose conflicting opinions they cite. They also heighten conflicts by actively seeking out controversial opinions about matters on which there is in fact a high degree of consensus. However, none of this is to say that journalists possess sinister powers of persuasion. Repeated studies of the effects of the mass media on opinion have shown that people tend to pick out reported facts that reinforce their deeply held beliefs. There is no guarantee that even deliberately slanted stories will have the desired effect on their audience.

But if news reporting does not change people's opinions in a direct way, it plays an extremely important role in **agenda-setting.**[10] Attention is a scarce resource, for people cannot think about everything at once. The media do not tell people what to think, but they may tell people what to think *about*.[11] This is of the highest importance in politics, because interest groups, parties, and ideologists often differ profoundly in their assessment of what constitutes a problem worth thinking about. The role of the media in setting the agenda will vary with the type of issue in question. The importance of some issues, such as inflation and unemployment, is less likely to be driven by the media because they are ones that the public is confronted with directly, through their pocketbooks. But the prominence of other issues—AIDS and crime, for example—is more susceptible to media effects. The importance that the public attaches to such issues is more likely to be driven by media coverage, because fewer people experience them directly and they seem relatively easy to understand.[12]

A concept related to agenda-setting is **priming**, which "brings to the top of one's head certain pieces of information that then shape one's opinion on a specific issue."[13] Because political events and personalities are always too complicated to be reported in their totality, journalists must be selective in the portraits they present. Inevitably they produce stereotypical images by attaching key words to names. For example, it matters a great deal politically whether the oil deposits of northern Alberta are called the "oil sands" or the "tar sands." The labels employed to describe political events or policies are part of the information that the public uses to evaluate them. Even though reporters usually refrain from open editorializing, the way they prime their messages has an effect upon public opinion.

Those who engage in politics are quite aware of the ways in which the media actively create rather than passively report news, so they do their best to manipulate the media. Mass public demonstrations that are supposed to be spontaneous expressions of demand or support are sometimes carefully staged events that depend on the cooperation of the mass media. This was more common in the past; the arrival of smartphones with video capability has provided an important check on such scripted and staged events.

The media also shape political reality through their investigative or watchdog activities. With the help of the opposition, reporters often uncover inconvenient facts that governments or powerful interest groups would like to suppress. The most famous example of this activity is, of course, the Watergate affair, when American reporters uncovered the misdeeds of officials in Richard Nixon's administration. As a result of

PART 4

their efforts, Nixon was forced to resign in 1974. This episode elevated the media to new heights of prestige. More recently the "Cablegate" affair saw WikiLeaks collaborate with media outlets in 2010 to release thousands of classified U.S. State Department diplomatic cables related to the war in Afghanistan, an event that continues to generate intense debate over the importance of and limits to the freedom of press.

The media's investigative role is less highly developed in Canada than it is in the United States and Great Britain. One reason is the state of Canadian media law. Access-to-information laws requiring governments to disclose information are relatively weak in this country, and when combined with a governmental culture that is more prone to delay information disclosure than to encourage it, journalists often resort to American sources to discover information about Canada.[14] Also, libel laws are so strong that the rich and powerful can effectively use the legal system to discourage reporters from pursuing controversial stories.[15] Another layer of silence arises in the judicial system itself. There is a strong Canadian tradition, enforced by judicial findings of contempt of court, that limits media discussion of cases before the courts. This allows the rich and the powerful to avoid disclosure by launching a libel action and dragging it out for years, during which time the information usually loses its relevance to political action.

INFLUENCE, OWNERSHIP, AND CONTROL

Most of the media are skilled at continuously reporting a flow of news but do not involve themselves in a thorough analysis of issues. In many countries, therefore, one or two newspapers have emerged as particularly important in politics because they provide both good coverage and sharp analysis. In Britain, almost everyone involved in government or observing it seriously reads *The Times, The Guardian, or The Independent*. Letters to the editors of these papers are often carefully thought-out statements written by important people and meant to be read by other important people. The papers in general serve as a handy means of communication among the political elite of the country. In France, *Le Monde* and *Le Figaro* are read in the same way. In the United States, the *New York Times* and the *Wall Street Journal* have this position in national politics, although many other papers have regional importance. For years Canada did not really have an equivalent, except for *Le Devoir* in Quebec; however, in English Canada, the Toronto-based *Globe and Mail*, using satellite technology, was the first to stake a claim to be a national newspaper. Subsequently the *National Post* challenged the *Globe's* claim. Both newspapers can be purchased in every province and territory and are engaged in a bitter struggle for subscribers. The absence until recent years of a truly national newspaper in Canada may have contributed to the fragmentation of Canadian political culture. Politicians and leaders in other walks of life in different parts of the country often lack a common frame of reference and information that might have been supplied in part if they were reading the same paper.

The Print Media

The print media—newspapers, magazines, publishing houses—took shape in the eighteenth and nineteenth centuries, before the socialist idea of state ownership had become influential. These media receive government subsidies in some countries; however, in the Western world they remain almost entirely in private hands and are run as profit-making businesses. Governments do not license or otherwise regulate them, except for enforcing laws against libel, pornography, false advertising, and so on. Underlying this arrangement is the classical liberal philosophy that holds that the public good is best served through competition of private actors following their own interests. Newspapers, magazines, and books constitute a mass market of profit-seeking interests in the field of ideas, information, and entertainment.

Does competition among newspapers still contribute to an open marketplace of ideas? On the one hand, the number of local independently owned and operated newspapers declined drastically throughout the twentieth century, so that today corporations and large chains are the rule. On the other hand, these large companies can compete with one another across Canada. Hence one might argue that readers have more effective choice than ever. Someone wanting to pick up a daily newspaper on the streets of Toronto can choose among the *Globe and Mail*, the *National Post,* the *Toronto Sun*, and the *Toronto Star*. Each of these newspapers offers a distinctive product that serves a different market niche and espouses different political sympathies. There is also a choice among two national and two local dailies in Vancouver, Edmonton, Calgary, Winnipeg, and Ottawa. Readers in Montreal have an even greater range of options because of the competitive coexistence of French and English newspapers. It seems that the world of Canadian newspapers is more vigorously competitive than ever, even if the competitors are large corporations rather than local proprietors. On the other side—and there is always another side to political questions—fierce competition among newspapers may lead to staff cuts and more reliance on advertising to maintain profits. There may be intense competition to attract readers but less emphasis on quality, scope, and depth of reporting.

The Electronic Media

The electronic media, born as they were in the twentieth century, when public ownership was becoming a powerful idea, have been involved with government almost from the start. There are technical aspects of broadcasting that invite public regulation. A radio or television signal is a public good, available to anyone with an antenna and a receiver. Broadcasters can seriously interfere with competitors' transmissions unless they respect the concept of reserved frequencies. In many European countries—for example, England, France, and Germany—radio and television are dominated by public corporations. Private enterprise is permitted, but only in a secondary role. In the United States private ownership is the rule, but—unlike the print media—the electronic media are subject to government licensing. Canada combines both models. There are publicly owned English and French networks of radio and television stations (such as the CBC, Radio-Canada, and some smaller provincial networks), but they do not dominate the market, which consists mostly of privately owned, governmentally licensed stations. Advocates of public owner-ship say that a network supported by taxes rather than advertising revenue is able to offer news and public affairs in greater depth—an argument that surely has some merit. Perhaps there is something to be said for the Canadian arrangement, which provides the benefits of a subsidized non-profit system but does not give government a predominant role in the electronic media.

In Canada, electronic media enterprises are increasing rapidly, and ownership of them is becoming concentrated in a few large corporations such as Bell, Rogers, Shaw, and Quebecor. The most significant development here is the rise of large communica-tions corporations that combine newspapers, radio and television, and Internet ser-vice providers—a phenomenon often called "convergence." As a result, the Canadian Radio-television and Telecommunications Commission (CRTC), which regulates media in Canada, recently imposed new rules on media ownership: a market-share cap that restricts broadcasting assets to no more than 45 percent of Canada's total viewing hours and a limit of two media types in any given market.[16]

Not everyone is happy with convergence and other new developments in media ownership and operation. David Taras, a political scientist at the University of Calgary who specializes in the study of Canadian media, offers a comprehensive critique. Taras argues that the current media universe is depriving citizens "of the vital information they need to make decisions about their communities and their lives."[17] He builds his argument on five contemporary developments: corporate convergence in the com-munications industry; fragmentation in the media, illustrated by the "500-channel universe" and the Internet; the relative decline of publicly owned broadcasting in the industry; a decline in the quality of journalism, including a heavy reliance on rebroadcasting American programs; and the dominance of right-wing perspectives in the Canadian media. He concludes: "The Canadian public is being betrayed by those who care much more about lining their pockets than about the survival of a distinct Canadian culture or serving the needs of citizens."[18]

Outside the liberal democracies, almost all mass media, whether print or electronic, are owned or controlled by the state. In totalitarian systems the mass media are quite simply an instrument used by the state to transform society. Communication with the masses is considered too important to be left to independent organizations in society, so state control is total. Authoritarian states also supervise the mass media, but not quite to the same extent: their chief concern is usually to ensure that the government is not criticized in public. Criticism may result in the imprisonment or exile of writers or the closing of newspapers, journals, and radio and TV stations. Independent units of the media may exist and operate as long as their political reporting is neutral or complimentary to the government. In both totalitarian and authoritarian systems, the media are viewed more as means of generating support for the regime than as means of articulating demands by the public or serving as an independent source of information.

However, the pace of technological advancement is now making it increasingly difficult for any kind of government to maintain monopolistic control over what is reported in the country. Satellite dishes, smartphones, and the Internet are now available almost everywhere in the world, making it harder for anyone to control the flow of information. Protests in 2011 in Tunisia and Egypt succeeded in part because of the use and availability of new media: blogs, Facebook, and YouTube, in particular, provided networking and organizational capabilities that could not be controlled, despite attempts by both governments to shut down the Internet for that very reason. A bystander holding a camcorder or mobile phone can videotape examples of police brutality and upload them to the Web in a matter of seconds. Yet those very videos can also be used by authoritarian states to identify protesters—the new technology can be a tool for whoever wishes to use it.

Questions for Discussion

1. From what sources do you acquire information on politics? Which source is most significant, and why?

2. How has the Internet changed politics? How has it changed liberal democracy?

3. In your opinion, are news media biased? Can you think of some examples of left- and right-wing biases in contemporary news media? Does ownership in the communications industry really matter?

4. What do you like and dislike about the media in Canada today? What changes would you make, and why?

Internet Links

1. *The Globe and Mail:* **www.theglobeandmail.com**. One of Canada's two national newspapers.

2. *Guido Fawkes' Blog:* **order-order.com**. "Tittle Tattle, gossip and rumours about Westminster's Mother of Parliaments."

3. *The Huffington Post:* **www.huffingtonpost.ca**. The Canadian edition of the American online news website.

4. Institute for Politics, Democracy and the Internet, George Washington University: **gspm.gwu.edu/ipdi**.

5. *National Post:* **www.nationalpost.com**. Canada's other national newspaper.

PART 4

Further Reading

Alexander, Cynthia, and Les Pal, eds. *Digital Democracy: Policy and Politics in the Wired World*. Don Mills, ON: Oxford University Press, 1998.

Arutunyan, Anna. *The Media in Russia*. New York: Open University Press, 2009.

Bain, George. *Gotcha! How the Media Distort the News*. Toronto: Key Porter, 1994.

Baker, William, and George Dessart. *Down the Tube: An Inside Account of the Failure of American Television*. New York: Basic Books, 1998.

Barney, Darren. *Communication Technology*. Vancouver: University of British Columbia Press, 2005.

Braun, Stefan. *Democracy Off Balance: Freedom of Expression and Hate Propaganda Law in Canada*. Toronto: University of Toronto Press, 2004.

Capella, Joseph, and Kathleen Hall Jamieson. *Spiral of Cynicism: The Press and the Public Good*. New York: Oxford University Press, 1997.

Chadwick, Anthony, and Philip N. Howard, eds. *The Routledge Handbook of Internet Politics*. New York: Routledge, 2009.

Cobb, Chris. *Ego and Ink: The Inside Story of Canada's National Newspaper War*. Toronto: McClelland & Stewart, 2004.

Curran, James, and Jean Seaton. *Power Without Responsibility: The Press, Broadcasting and New Media in Britain*. 6th ed. London: Routledge, 2003.

Fraser, Matthew. *Free-for-All: The Struggle for Dominance on the Digital Frontier*. Toronto: Stoddart, 1999.

Gibson, Rachel, Paul Nixon, and Stephen Ward. *Political Parties and the Internet: Net Gain?* New York: Routledge, 2003.

Gibson, Rachel, Andrea Römmele, and Stephen Ward. *Electronic Democracy: Mobilisation, Organisation and Participation via new ICTS*. New York: Routledge, 2004.

Hackett, Robert A., and Yuezhi Zhao. *Sustaining Democracy? Journalism and the Politics of Objectivity*. Toronto: Garamond, 1997.

Holmes, H., and David Taras, eds. *Seeing Ourselves: Media Power and Policy in Canada*. Toronto: Harcourt Brace Jovanovich, 1992.

Iyengar, Shanto. *Is Anyone Responsible? How Television Frames Political Issues*. Chicago: University of Chicago Press, 1991.

Jamieson, Kathleen Hall, ed. *The Media and Politics*. Thousand Oaks, CA: Sage, 1996.

Kenski, Kate, Bruce W. Hardy, and Kathleen H. Jamieson. *The Obama Victory: How Media, Money and Message Shaped the 2008 Election*. New York: Oxford University Press, 2010.

Kingdon, John W. *Agendas, Alternatives, and Public Policies*. 2nd ed. New York: HarperCollins, 1995.

Kuhn, Raymond. *Politics and the Media in Britain*. New York: Palgrave Macmillan, 2007.

Lorimer, Rowland, Mike Gasher, and David Skinner. *Mass Communication in Canada*. 6th ed. Don Mills, ON: Oxford University Press, 2008.

Miljan, Lydia, and Barry Cooper. *Hidden Agendas: How Journalists Influence the News*. Vancouver: University of British Columbia Press, 2003.

Norris, Pippa. *Digital Divide:* Civic *Engagement, Information Poverty, and the Internet Worldwide*. London: Cambridge University Press, 2001.

Purvis, Hoyt. *The Media, Politics, and Government*. Toronto: Thomson Nelson, 2001.

Taras, David. *The Newsmakers*. Scarborough, ON: Nelson Canada, 1990.

———. *Power and Betrayal in the Canadian Media*. 2nd ed. Peterborough, ON: Broadview Press, 2001.

West, Darrell M. *Air Wars: Television Advertising in Election Campaigns*. 5th ed. Washington, DC: Congressional Quarterly Press, 2009.

PART 4

CHAPTER 25

Elections and Electoral Systems

Protests that took place throughout the "Arab Spring" of 2011 asserted the fundamental democratic right of citizens to select their leaders. The protesters understood that elections are central to democratic political systems. **Elections** provide an opportunity for changing political leaders without bloodshed, an important historical accomplishment. More important, competitive political elections are the basis of democratic legitimacy. Political leaders can claim the right to power when their selection takes place in a fair and free manner. As this book was being written, protesters in Russia were rallying against alleged ballot-box tampering in the state Duma elections of December 2011, underscoring their belief in the significance of the conditions under which elections take place.

Elections have been defined as the "formal expression of preferences by the governed, which are then aggregated and transformed into a collective decision about who will govern—who should stay in office, who should be thrown out, who should replace those who have been thrown out."[1] But the responsibilities of those choosing governments do not end at the ballot box; the opportunity to participate in choosing rulers confers on the participants an obligation to obey the laws made by those who are chosen. Citizens are presumed to consent to laws to the extent that they have participated in choosing the lawmakers (see Figure 25.1). Disagreement with the substance of lawmakers' decisions is not normally sufficient reason for disobedience, because an opportunity will soon arise (i.e., another election) to vote for other lawmakers who are willing to alter the disliked rule or policy. Of course, if an elected government repeatedly ignores the will of most citizens on issues of vital concern, it is likely to provoke mass demonstrations and even violent protest. In any case, the replacement of traditional with legal authority resulted in the collapse of traditional theories of obligation based on the will of God or on inherited position; democratic elections provide an alternative theory of obligation that is compatible with the legal concept of authority.

In a simpler world, public officials might be elected with a mandate to do certain things and thus implement popular desires in a direct and unambiguous way. If that were the case, elections could be considered a mechanism for articulating demands.

Figure 25.1 Elections Legitimize

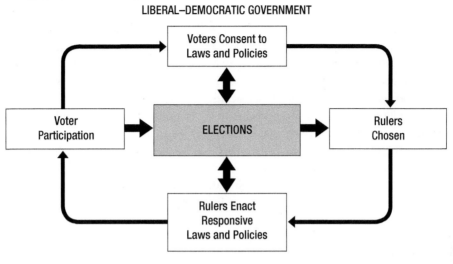

LIBERAL–DEMOCRATIC GOVERNMENT

However, elections are rather inefficient mechanisms for determining the policy preferences of the electorate, because elections are about more than a single policy: they involve an aggregated judgment on multiple issues, parties, candidates, and leaders. Elections are more like a judgment of the record of those in office, whose actual performance may have had little to do with the promises they made when elected, given unanticipated events or changes in economic forces. If voters generally like what has happened, they can vote for a continuation; if not, they can vote for a change, without being quite sure what the alternative will be. In this way elections are an ingenious mechanism for coping with an uncertain and ever-changing future. Elected rulers are allowed periods of creativity during which they seek to cope with the unexpected problems that always present themselves; afterwards, the voters decide whether they will be allowed to continue their efforts. Dealing with dilemmas gradually as they appear provides greater flexibility than trying to work out far in advance the answers to problems that may never arise in their expected form. The greatest strength of liberal democracy may well be the sophistication of its institutions that link the rulers and the ruled. Among these, elections are paramount.

For elections to provide this link, a number of conditions must be present.[2] First, elections must occur at regular intervals and under free and fair conditions. Usually their frequency is specified in a constitution and ranges from every two years (the House of Representatives in the United States) to every seven years (the president of France). The point is that elections must be institutionalized so that a head of government cannot arbitrarily cancel or postpone them in order to rule indefinitely. They must be regular and reasonably frequent if they are to be effective in a democratic system. If the

PART 4

opportunity is taken away, the democratic system loses its grounds for legitimacy. Free and fair elections are those that allow voters to cast their ballots secretly and safely—without violence or intimidation—and with sufficient information to make informed choices. They also guarantee that cast ballots are counted and reported honestly.

Second, there must be wide opportunity for all to run for office so that voters have a genuine choice across candidates and parties. If restrictions are placed on who can run for office, elections cannot be democratic. Some argue that a one-party system can be democratic if there is competition among factions within the party. If the party nomination process is relatively open, there may be a choice of candidates. But the choice in this case is made by party members, not by all voters, so the process is democratic only in a very restricted sense.

Third, the limits on universal adult suffrage must be minimal; practically all adults should have the right to participate in the selection of those who will govern. Restricting the franchise to a select group of voters limits the degree to which those who govern can respond to the desires of the masses. Various devices have been used to limit mass participation. Under the property franchise, for example, an individual was required to own assets of a certain value before being allowed to vote. Poll taxes, which had to be paid as a prerequisite for voting, also limited participation by the poor. More recently, age and residency requirements have been manipulated to influence voter turnout, and literacy requirements are still used in many developing nations to restrict full participation in elections. As discussed earlier, the long-term trend of liberal democracy has been to erase or minimize all such restrictions.

Finally, there must be a high degree of political freedom. If freedom of speech or of the press is limited, the electoral campaign cannot function as it must, and voters are unable to make fully informed decisions. The rights to express political ideas and critiques, to form independent associations and groups, and to receive political information from independent sources are essential to ensuring that elections provide an effective accountability mechanism.

In autocratic governments, elections have little or nothing to do with the give-and-take between rulers and the ruled; rather, they are means of mobilizing support for the regime. Voters ratify lists of selected candidates and often are penalized for not participating in the election. Token opposition is sometimes permitted by authoritarian regimes when they have a firm grip on the government, as a way of enhancing the external legitimacy of the electoral result. This mobilization of support for the government also attaches legitimacy to elections in liberal democracies. National elections are quasi-sacred occasions during which the participants reaffirm their commitment to constitutional procedures. This comparison of liberal-democratic with authoritarian and totalitarian elections again shows how seemingly similar institutions can perform quite different functions in different systems.

An election is a complex procedure, and countries use many different methods to conduct elections. A bewildering variety of electoral systems have been tried at one time or another. Below we describe some of the more common types and point out a few of the consequences of each type for the democratic process. Political scientists are aware, now more than ever, that the choice of electoral procedures is a crucial variable in political systems.

ELECTORAL SYSTEMS

Electoral systems involve a set of rules that deal specifically with the process of turning votes into seats: how many votes citizens will have and whether they will vote for candidates, a political party, or both; how the ballots will be counted; and how the count will be translated into seats. On election night, these rules establish the number of seats won by each political party.

Electoral systems involve a number of rules that can be combined in multiple ways; the result is that no two electoral systems function in quite the same manner. This complexity can be managed, however, by categorizing them into three broad types: plurality/majority, proportional, and mixed systems (see Concept Box 25.1). Plurality/majority systems place importance on ensuring that the governing party holds a majority of seats, a criterion that can help to provide for strong and stable governments. Proportional systems, on the other hand, place more weight on ensuring the **proportionality** of electoral results—the percentage of votes that each party earns should correspond closely to the percentage of seats it is awarded in the legislature. The distortion in the seat-to-vote ratio under Canada's electoral system has been one of the incentives for considering electoral reform, a topic revisited further on in this chapter. Finally, mixed systems attempt to minimize the problems associated with the plurality/majority and proportional systems by combining them into a hybrid form.

Concept Box 25.1

Typology of Electoral Systems

Category	Dominant Types	Description	Examples
Plurality/ majority	Employs single-member districts; individual candidates are elected. Emphasis on creation of stable majority governments.		
	Single-member plurality (SMP)	Candidate with the most votes in a district wins the seat.	Canada (legislative); United Kingdom (legislative); United States (legislative)

(continued)

PART 4

Concept Box 25.1   *(continued)*

	Majority-runoff	Candidate must win a majority of votes to win the election. If not obtained on first ballot, the two leading candidates compete in a second round of balloting.	Brazil (presidential); France (presidential); Portugal (presidential)
	Majority-plurality	Candidate must win a majority of votes to win the election. If not obtained on first ballot, candidate with a plurality of votes in second round wins the seat.	France (legislative); Mexico (presidential)
	Alternative vote (AV)	Voters rank their preferences across the candidates on one ballot. A majority of first preferences is required to win the seat. If not obtained, second preferences of the bottom candidate are reallocated to the remaining candidates. The process continues until a majority of first preferences is obtained.	Australia (legislative); Ireland (presidential)
Proportional	Employs multi-member districts; seats are distributed to parties; employs various formulas for allocating seats within districts (e.g., largest-remainder and highest-average methods); employs thresholds (minimum percentage of votes required to be allocated a seat); voters face closed (no choice of candidates) or open (choice of candidate) lists. Emphasis on proportionality of election results.		
	List (single or multiple multi-member districts)	Voters cast a ballot for a party's list of candidates. Percentage of votes won by a party determines the number of seats that party wins.	Argentina (legislative); Israel (legislative); Netherlands (legislative); South Africa (legislative)

Concept Box 25.1

	Single transferable vote (STV)	Voters rank preferences for candidates across all parties. Candidates whose number of first preferences meets a minimum quota are elected. Remaining seats are filled by transferring the unallocated votes of winning candidates and those of the weakest candidates.	Australia (legislative); Ireland (legislative)
Mixed	Combines elements of plurality/majority and proportional systems.		
	Corrective	Two tiers of members across the country, some elected by proportional system and some by plurality/majority. Voters are allocated two votes: one for a party (proportional) and one for a candidate (plurality/majority). Distribution of seats occurs so as to correct any distortion in proportionality introduced by the plurality/majority allocation.	Germany (legislative); New Zealand (legislative)
	Superposition or parallel	Same as in the corrective system except that distribution of seats occurs independently in each tier.	Japan (legislative); South Korea (legislative)

Source: Adapted from André Blais and Louis Massicotte, "Electoral Systems." Reproduced by permission of SAGE Publications, London, Los Angeles, New Delhi and Singapore from L. LeDuc, R.G. Niemi and P. Norris, eds., *Comparing Democracies 2* Copyright © Sage Publications, 2003, pp. 40–69. www.sagepub.co.uk.

PLURALITY/MAJORITY SYSTEMS
The Single-Member-Plurality System

The **single-member-plurality system (SMP)**, popularly known as "first past the post," is familiar from its use in Britain, Canada, and the United States. One candidate is elected in each **constituency**—that is, in each geographical district that has a representative—and each voter has one vote to cast. This vote is cast for an

PART 4

individual candidate rather than a party and the winning candidate is the one who receives a plurality of valid ballots—that is, more votes than any other candidate. If there are only two candidates, the winner automatically gets a majority, but if there are several candidates who split the vote fairly evenly, the winner's plurality may be far less than a majority.

The SMP method is a natural partner to the two-party system because it does not distort electoral results when there are only two candidates. In that case, a plurality is also a majority and the democratic criterion of majority rule is unambiguously satisfied. However, when social cleavages are such that a two-party system cannot be maintained, SMP can have peculiar and even distorting consequences. In the 1996 British Columbia election, for example, the Liberals led in the popular vote (42 percent), the NDP came second (39 percent), and the provincial Reform Party finished third overall (9 percent). However, the NDP took a majority of seats (39 out of 75, or 52 percent) and thus formed the government, even though the Liberals had won substantially more votes.

In SMP systems a single seat in each constituency means that votes cast for unsuccessful candidates are "wasted," in that there is no seat reward for the votes obtained. As a result, the relationship between votes and seats can often be very disproportional, as happened in New Brunswick in 1987 and in British Columbia in 2001 (see Table 25.1). A party that finishes second in every constituency and earns 25 percent of the national vote can fail to gain a single seat in the legislature in spite of having earned a significant level of popular support. As shown in Table 25.2, using data from the 2006 election, voters in a constituency can be divided fairly evenly among two or three political parties but, because SMP allows only a single winner, the losing parties earn no reward for the votes they have garnered. The reality of "wasted votes" under SMP has been argued to favour a two-party system, by reducing the number of parties with seats in the legislature and by pushing voters to support larger parties to avoid throwing away their vote.[3]

In general, SMP penalizes parties that earn a solid but small percentage of the vote share. The NDP at the federal level in Canada is a good example; in the 2004 and 2006 elections the party earned 15.7 and 17.5 percent of the national vote but WAS allocated only 6.2 and 9.4 percent of legislative seats. The one exception to this relates to parties that are regionally concentrated, such as the Bloc Québécois at the federal level in Canada. It is thus almost a general law of politics that no new party can break into a system based on SMP voting unless it achieves territorial concentration.

SMP also magnifies relatively small shifts in the popular vote. In a two-party system, an increase in a party's popular vote from 50 to 60 percent of the total will produce a landslide in parliamentary seats. And if there are three or more competitive parties, anything over 45 percent for one will probably produce a landslide.

Particularly in ethnically segmented societies, the first-past-the-post method can lead to permanent underrepresentation of minorities, given the winner-take-all nature of the system. During the years of the Stormont Parliament, the Catholics of Northern

Table 25.1

New Brunswick (1987) and British Columbia (2001) Provincial Elections

	Percentage of Popular Vote	Seats	Percentage of Seats	Seat-to-Vote Ratio
NEW BRUNSWICK, 1987				
Liberals	60.4	58	100	1.66
Conservatives	28.6	0	0	0
NDP	10.6	0	0	0
BRITISH COLUMBIA, 2001				
Liberals	57.6	77	97.5	1.69
NDP	21.5	2	2.5	0.12
Greens	12.3	0	0	0

Note: The seat-to-vote ratio is calculated by dividing the percentage of seats won by the percentage of votes earned. Values greater than 1 indicate that the party was over-rewarded and values less than 1 that it was under-rewarded.

Table 25.2

Winner-Take-All Effects of SMP: Three Ridings, 2006 Federal Election

	Liberals	New Democrats	Conservatives
Brant	36.9%*	21.3%	36.0%
Fleetwood–Port Kells	31.6%	25.2%	33.5%*
South Shore–St. Margaret's	28.4%	28.5%	36.8%*

(* denotes winner)

Ireland constituted about one-third of the population, but they never came close to winning one-third of the seats in the assembly. This result was reinforced by the use of **gerrymandering,**[4] that is, deliberately drawing constituencies so as to favour one side—in this case the Protestant majority—over the other. Blocks of Catholic voters were divided up so as to form permanent minorities within Protestant-dominated

PART 4

constituencies, thus restricting their ability to elect sympathetic candidates. Such long-standing underrepresentation can destroy the legitimacy of government in the minds of the aggrieved minority. Countries such as Canada and Great Britain have given responsibility for electoral redistricting to **non-partisan** bodies in order to reduce the likelihood of gerrymandering. Plurality/majority systems, including SMP, have also been linked to the underrepresentation of women in legislatures; the ability to nominate only one candidate per constituency appears to lower the overall chances that a woman will be chosen to run for a party.[5]

Because of these many difficulties, SMP has been falling out of favour over the past hundred years. It was originally used quite widely, but among the world's major democracies it is now used only in Great Britain, the United States, Canada, and India. However, SMP is a relatively simple electoral system that has a tendency to produce single-party majority governments (hence, strong and stable governments) and maintains a clear link between the legislator and his or her constituency.

Majority Systems

Like SMP, majority systems employ single-member constituencies, but they "raise the bar" by requiring that the winning candidate earn a majority rather than a plurality of valid votes. There are various ways of meeting this requirement. The **majority-runoff system** is favoured in countries that elect their president directly, such as France. In French presidential elections, two rounds of voting take place on two separate dates. The first round of voting is exactly like that held under SMP. If no candidate receives a majority of votes in the first round, only the candidates with the highest and second-highest number of votes run in the second round, which takes place two weeks later. By reducing the number of candidates to two, a majority of votes for the winner is virtually guaranteed. The **majority-plurality system** proceeds much like the runoff system, except that to win on the second ballot, a candidate needs only a plurality of valid votes cast.

Another variant of plurality/majority systems is the **alternative (or preferential) vote system** (AV), which attempts to capture information not only about voters' first choices but also about their second, third, and further choices. Electors are given a form on which they rank candidates in order of preference. Voters' first preferences are tabulated on the first count. If no one has a majority, the candidate with the least number of first-preference votes is dropped and a second count is taken. The eliminated candidate's votes are distributed to the other candidates according to the second preferences expressed on the ballots. The process continues until a majority is reached. The objective of the system is similar to that of a runoff: to ensure that the victor has majority support. The difference is that the alternative vote system collects the necessary information in advance and thus dispenses with further rounds of balloting. In a sense, it is a condensed runoff system.

In practice, AV, like the runoff system, allows parties to retain a separate existence while forming coalitions with each other for electoral advantage. In Australia, the Liberal Party and the National (previously Country) Party have maintained a working coalition for decades, and together they dominate the conservative side of the ideological spectrum. The electoral system favours their coalition because a conservative-minded voter who tilts toward one party or the other can rank the Liberal (or National) candidate first and the National (or Liberal) candidate second. At some point in the vote-counting process, the trailing candidate will be dropped, but those votes will be transferred rather than wasted. As a voter on the right, you can vote for your favourite party without fearing that you will "split the right-wing vote" and thus help to elect a left-wing candidate. The same logic would apply on the left, but thus far the large Labour Party has been able to go it alone without a coalition partner.

PROPORTIONAL REPRESENTATION SYSTEMS

Plurality/majority systems have as one of their goals the creation of stable, strong governments. **Proportional representation (PR)** systems, on the other hand, strive to ensure proportionality; that is, they seek to reward parties with a percentage of seats in the legislature that reflects the percentage of votes earned in the election. To do so requires multi-member constituencies, for a single seat cannot be divided between two or more parties.

There are two main forms of proportional representation: the list system and the much less common single-transferable-vote (STV) system (sometimes called the Hare system after its inventor, Thomas Hare). Both have the same aim: to ensure that representatives are elected in numbers proportional to the share of votes that their parties receive in the balloting.

List System

The **list system** is the easier of the two to grasp. The elector votes not for individuals but for parties. Each party has a list of as many candidates as there are seats to be awarded. If a party gets x percent of the popular vote, then the top x percent of its list is declared elected. This system gives great power to the party leaders, who in most cases determine the candidates' positions on the list. Being high on the list of a major party is tantamount to election; being low on the list of any party is tantamount to defeat. Minimum thresholds are usually adopted in such systems to keep splinter parties from gaining seats, such as the German requirement to earn a minimum of 5 percent of the list vote in order to be awarded any seats at all. The higher this threshold, the less proportional the election results, as smaller parties are under-rewarded.

The purest examples of the list system in practice are found in Israel and the Netherlands. In each case the entire country is treated as a single constituency, and there is a very low threshold (around 1 percent of the vote) for obtaining representation in the legislature. The result is a faithful translation of the popular vote into the proportion of parliamentary seats, as well as a proliferation of parties and a permanent situation of coalition government. Variations in this list system can move electoral results away from the goal of proportionality. Imposing thresholds, referred to above, is one variation. Another is the district magnitude, or number of seats awarded in each constituency. As the number of constituencies increases, the number of seats awarded per constituency decreases, and with it the likelihood of proportionality.

Variations in the ballot structure affect the control provided to voters over parties in the selection of candidates. The open ballot structure allows voters to allocate their votes to candidates within party lists, thus removing power from political parties. The closed ballot structure allows them only to select a party and leaves candidate selection entirely in the parties' hands.

List systems require the use of electoral formulas for determining seat allocation after the election has taken place. Although a number of variations exist in their use, the two main formulas are the *largest remainder* and the *highest average*. The first employs a quota, most often the total vote count divided by the number of seats to be allocated, to allocate seats. If a party's vote count exceeds the quota, it is allocated a seat and the quota is removed from its total vote count. This allocation continues until no party's vote count exceeds the quota, at which point the remaining seats are allocated to the parties with the largest remainders. The second formula—both more common and more complicated—divides each party's vote count by a series of divisors (the simplest being 1, 2, 3, 4, and so on) to produce a set of average votes. The highest average is allocated to the first seat, the second-highest average is allocated to the second seat, and so on until all the seats are allocated. Variations in these formulas affect the system's proportionality. Importantly, not all PR systems are more proportional than plurality/majority systems. The list system is widely used, with various modifications, in many European and Latin countries, and in a number of newer African democracies.

Single-Transferable-Vote System

The less common **single-transferable-vote (STV) system** of proportional representation requires only brief mention. It is best understood as an extension of the alternative, or preferential, ballot from single-member to multi-member constituencies. Electors vote for individuals rather than party lists, but they do so preferentially—that is, by ranking the candidates in their order of choice. Thus the proportionality of PR systems is combined with increased voter choice and constituency representation. A formula establishes the quota of votes required to win, and each victor's surplus votes are transferred according to lower preferences. STV produces a more or less proportional result without providing the party leadership with the extraordinary power given it by the list system.

Proportional representation tends to promote the existence of small parties, although proliferation of parties can be controlled by the use of thresholds. It is not necessary to come anywhere close to a majority to attract voters, as in a first-past-the-post situation. A party only has to be able to retain the support of its loyalists. Thus, proportional representation tends to encourage relatively small or medium-sized interest or ideological parties—for example, Catholic parties, farmers' parties, workers' parties, Green parties. Such alignments can be stable over long periods of time, creating a distribution of representatives in the assembly that changes very little from election to election. This is the contemporary situation in many European states.

When the distribution of support is stable and no single party commands a majority, the result must be prolonged coalition government. This in itself is not a bad thing, though it is somewhat alien to the British tradition. It can work well—as it has in most Scandinavian countries and in the recent U.K. coalition between the Conservative Party and the Liberal Democrats—but in cases such as Italy from the late 1940s until the fall of communism, when the presence of large extremist parties severely limited the choice of coalition partners, the result was cabinet instability.

Proportional representation has often been attacked for encouraging the proliferation of parties, thus balkanizing politics and making majority government impossible. The criticism is not without merit, but it is often true that social cleavages exist that will produce a multi-party system regardless of the electoral method. In those circumstances, proportional representation is a way of keeping civil peace by allowing all significant minorities to feel represented. A first-past-the-post system might extinguish the smaller parties and leave certain minorities permanently underrepresented.

MIXED SYSTEMS

One type of electoral system saw considerable growth in the 1990s: the mixed electoral system. Such systems combine the proportionality of PR systems with the constituency representation of single-member districts, but in a simpler system than STV. The two dominant types of mixed systems are the corrective and the superposition. Germany provides an example of the corrective system (called the **mixed-member proportional system,** or MMP). On election day voters cast two ballots, one for a local candidate running in a territorial constituency and the other for a national list of candidates put forward by a political party. The winner of each constituency seat is determined

PART 4

by SMP. After the local constituency winners are known, members from the lists are added to the territorial members in the numbers needed to ensure proportionality based on the percentage of votes cast for each party on the national list ballot. The superposition system is similar to the corrective except that the list seats are awarded independently of those awarded in the districts. This results in reduced proportionality in the system.

ELECTIONS: WHO VOTES AND WHY

Attempting to explain why people vote the way they do is an integral part of political science. For years there existed an underlying assumption that democracies relied upon the participation of an informed citizenry. It was assumed that when citizens went into the voting booth, they made rational choices based on knowledge of the issues. However, modern survey research methods have shown that people make voting decisions for a whole variety of reasons, some of which appear rational and some of which may seem irrational. Factors such as religion, class, ideology, party identification, region, education, and gender have been shown to play a role in shaping voting choices.

There are three distinct approaches to research examining voting behaviour. The *sociological approach* focuses on socio-demographic characteristics such as ethnicity and gender for explaining voting decisions. Our backgrounds play a role in shaping our values and priorities, and our social groups provide important political cues and reference points for evaluating our political preferences. The *psychological approach* emphasizes attitudes and beliefs as explanations but emphasizes the importance of short-term factors in the vote decision, issue positions, candidate evaluations, and in particular party identification—the party that an individual normally feels closest to. The campaign period is also considered an important element in voting behaviour in that it provides the material from which evaluations and attitudes stem. The *rational-choice approach,* derived from Anthony Downs's An *Economic Theory of Democracy,* assumes that voters evaluate party promises and governmental performance and make their choices according to which best serve their self-interest. Contemporary political scientists usually draw on all three approaches for an integrated causal model of voting behaviour.

In an analysis of the 2000 Canadian election, Blais and colleagues developed a model describing the "variables" that explain vote choice (Figure 25.2). The variables closest to the vote decision are those that are closest to it in time; leader evaluations, for example, will have a direct impact on vote decisions but are likely to take place some time during the election campaign, when voters get a chance to assess party leaders. Variables further away from the vote decision are more distant in time from it; the greater the distance, the more likely it is that the variable will work indirectly through more proximate factors in shaping the vote choice. Party identification, for

Figure 25.2 The Multi-stage Explanatory Model

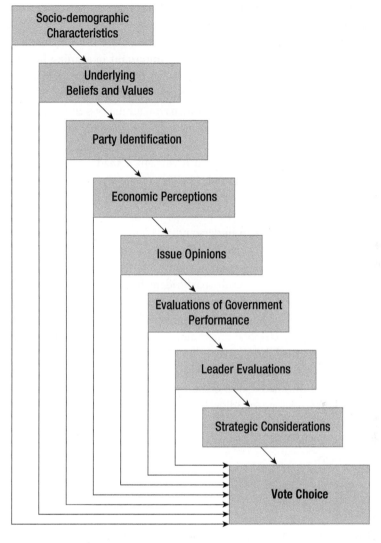

Source: André Blais, Elisabeth Gidengil, Richard Nadeau, and Neil Nevitee, *Anatomy of a Liberal Victory: Making Sense of the Vote in the 2000 Canadian Election* (Peterborough: Broadview, 2002), p. 84. Copyright © 2002 by André Blais, et al. University of Toronto Press Higher Education Division. Reprinted with permission of the publisher.

example, is likely to shape how voters evaluate party leaders and thus will indirectly influence their vote decision. While the model provides a clear picture of the many factors that can influence vote decisions, the authors also point out that the context of an individual election is likely to cue individual elements of the model differently. Some elections may emphasize the importance of issue positions for the vote

PART 4

calculus; opinion on free trade, for example, was an important determinant of voting in the 1988 election. In other elections, evaluations of government performance may play a leading role.

Evaluation of survey data collected at the time of the 2000 Canadian election suggests that four sets of factors were especially important in shaping how Canadians voted. First, socio-demographic characteristics, including region, religion, ethnicity, gender, and community type (urban versus rural), cannot be ignored. Canadian politics has long had a regional and religious dimension; ethnicity, gender, and community type are more recent additions to the voting calculus. Second, values and beliefs are another important part of the voting story in Canada. According to the authors, "Our results indicate that the main ideological divide, in Canada as elsewhere, concerns orientations towards markets. Those who believe in the virtue of the market tend to support right-wing parties, and those who are more sceptical about market values, tend to vote for center or left-wing parties."[6]

The third important factor in understanding Canadian voting behaviour is party identification. Conventional academic wisdom has argued that Canadian voters have "flexible" **partisan** loyalties—voters do not normally align themselves with one party over all others—and that, as a result, party identification plays relatively little role in shaping their vote choices.[7] Blais and colleagues suggest that while the number of strong partisans in Canada may be comparatively low, they nevertheless play an important role in shaping electoral outcomes. More than half of those with a partisan loyalty identified with the Liberal party in 2000, a fact that helps to explain that party's dominance at the time. It also helps to explain the importance of some of the socio-demographic factors outlined above: certain groups, including certain ethnic minorities and Catholics, have long-standing loyalties to the Liberal party. The final factor identified as playing an important role in the vote choice is political leaders. Blais et al. estimate that one in five Canadians voted the way they did because of how they felt about party leaders.

Turnout

One of the hallmarks of modern democratic systems is the opportunity for all adult citizens to participate in choosing their governors. This political right is a fundamental principle that fires the hearts and minds of our many, some of whom have gone to the streets to gain the right to vote. However, in many contemporary nation-states that qualify as liberal democracies, the **voter turnout** rate is far from 100 percent.

In Figure 25.3, election turnout rates since 1980 are plotted for Canada and the United States. One immediately sees an apparent difference between the two countries: prior to 2000, turnout in Canada was usually about 10 to 15 percentage points higher than in the United States. Since then, however, increased turnout in the United States has closed that gap. Indeed, by 2008, turnout in the United

Figure 25.3 Voter Turnout Percentages in Canadian Federal and U.S. Presidential Elections, 1980–2012

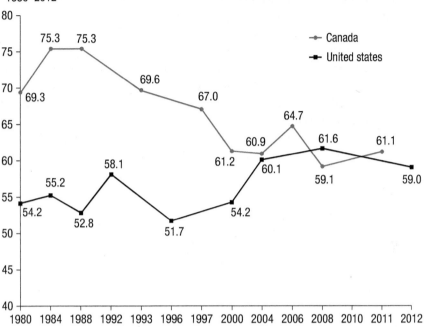

Note: Percentages for Canada were calculated using a denominator of number of registered voters and for the United States using the voting eligible population, or VEP (see the United States Elections Project website). The turnout figure for the 2012 U.S. presidential election is an estimate rather than an actual figure, given the limited data available as of December 19, 2012.

Sources: Elections Canada, www.electionscanada.ca; United States Elections Project, elections.gmu.edu /voter_turnout.htm.

States had surpassed that in Canada. Importantly, the gap in turnout between the two countries is an actual one; turnout figures in Figure 25.3 for both countries are calculated by dividing the number of voters by the number of eligible voters (in Canada, those on the permanent voters list; in the United States, the voting-age population minus non-citizens, ineligible felons, and overseas citizens who are ineligible to vote). Turnout figures in the United States were previously calculated by dividing the number of voters by the number of adult citizens eligible, a practice that artificially deflated the rate.

According to the Institute for Democracy and Electoral Assistance, voter turnout rates in Canada and the United States have been relatively low by world standards for elections since 1945.[8] Compared with 172 other states, Canada ranks 77th and the United States 139th overall, with average turnout rates of 68.4 and 48.3 percent respectively. Top spot goes to Italy, with an overall average turnout of 92.5 percent; Mali comes in last with an average turnout rate of 21.7 percent. If we evaluate regions of the world, Western Europe has the highest average turnout and South and Central

PART 4

America the lowest, but regional trends do not appear to be directly related to overall wealth. The Middle East and Asia, for example, come in as the regions with the fourth and fifth highest turnout levels, while North America ranks sixth overall.

The most important question arising from these figures is why citizens in a democracy today would choose not to exercise their franchise. Some may not vote because they are satisfied with what is going on and so do not bother, having decided not to let elections get in the way of their busy lives. If that is the case, there may not be much to worry about. But others may not vote because of **political alienation**; that is, they feel estranged from the process or have become quite cynical about it. These feelings are often driven by a sense that voters are not effective in the process: if voting is unlikely to make a difference to the political outcome, then why bother? If this is the situation, democracy may be in danger of losing its essential popular support.

In a number of countries, including Canada and the United States, young people are becoming less likely to vote. There is no evidence that young people are any more alienated from the system—they simply do not vote. The reasons for this trend are not entirely clear. Age has always been connected to voter turnout; life-cycle explanations point out that as young people age they take on increasing responsibilities, such as parenthood and mortgages, that increase their stake in political outcomes and thus increase their likelihood of participating. Recent research, however, suggests that the transition to adulthood has been extended over a long period of time. On average, young people today spend more years in school and wait much longer to marry, have children, and enter stable employment. Participation in politics is probably part of adopting a full adult role. If this line of thought is correct, people in their late teens and twenties who do not now vote will probably do so when they reach their thirties and forties. Other research has identified the increasing importance of education for voter turnout: those without a university education are much less likely to vote than those with a degree. Some have argued that increasing political complexity and access to political information through the Internet serve to overwhelm those without an advanced education. If this line of thought is correct, these voters are unlikely to begin voting as they age.

Beyond a question of attitudes, which vary greatly from one country to another, political scientists have learned a lot about factors that contribute to higher turnout rates everywhere. Some factors, such as the weather, are beyond control; others, such as the relative ease with which one can register to vote, can be manipulated.

Questions for Discussion

1. Would you support a shift away from SMP? What would be your main reasons for advocating electoral reform? What system should Canada adopt in SMP's place?

2. Do you vote? Why or why not? Do you think that this will change in the future?

3. Why does voter turnout matter in a liberal democracy? Why do you think that voter turnout has been on the decline in Canada? What institutional reforms do you think might reverse this trend?

Internet Links

1. Administration and Cost of Elections: **www.aceproject.org**. An encyclopedia of everything you could possibly want to know about electoral systems and the administration of elections around the world.

2. Elections Canada: **www.elections.ca**.

3. International Foundation for Election Systems: **www.ifes.org**.

4. International idea (Institute for Democracy and Electoral Assistance): **www.idea .int**.

5. United States Elections Project: **elections.gmu.edu**.

Further Reading

Blais, André, Elisabeth Gidengil, Richard Nadeau, and Neil Nevitte. *Anatomy of a Liberal Victory: Making Sense of the Vote in the 2000 Canadian Election.* Peterborough, ON: Broadview Press, 2002.

Brennan, Geoffrey, and Loren E. Lomasky. *Democracy and Decision: The Pure Theory of Electoral Preference.* Cambridge: Cambridge University Press, 1993.

Clarke, Harold D., Jane Jensen, Lawrence LeDuc, and Jon H. Pammett. *Absent Mandate: Canadian Electoral Politics in an Era of Restructuring.* 3rd ed. Vancouver: Gage, 1996.

Clarke, Harold D., David Sanders, Marianne C. Stewart, and Paul Whiteley. *Political Choice in Britain.* Oxford: Oxford University Press, 2004.

Conway, M. Margaret, Gertrude A. Steuernagel, and David W. Ahern. *Women and Political Participation: Cultural Change in the Political Arena.* 2nd ed. Washington, DC: CQ Press, 2005.

Courtney, John C. *Elections.* Vancouver: University of British Columbia Press, 2004.

Dalton, Russell J. *Citizen Politics: Public Opinion and Political Parties in Advanced Industrial Democracies.* 5th ed. Washington, DC: CQ Press, 2008.

———. *Democratic Challenges, Democratic Choices: The Erosion in Political Support in Advanced Industrial Democracies.* Oxford: Oxford University Press, 2004.

Everitt, Joanna, and Brenda O'Neill, eds. *Citizen Politics: Research and Theory in Canadian Political Behaviour.* Don Mills, ON: Oxford University Press, 2002.

Farrell, David M. *Electoral Systems: A Comparative Introduction.* New York: Palgrave, 2001.

Gidengil, Elisabeth. "Canada Votes: A Quarter Century of Canadian National Election Studies," *Canadian Journal of Political Science* 25, no. 2 (June 1992): 219–48.

PART 4

Ginsburg, Benjamin, and Alan Stone, eds. *Do Elections Matter?* Armonk, NY: M. E. Sharpe, 1993.

Harrop, Martin, and William L. Miller. *Elections and Voters: A Comparative Introduction.* London: MacMillan, 1987.

Johnston, Richard, et al. *Letting the People Decide: Dynamics of a Canadian Election.* Montreal: McGill-Queen's University Press, 1992.

Kavanagh, Dennis, ed. *Electoral Politics.* Oxford: Clarendon Press, 1992.

Law Commission of Canada. *Voting Counts: Electoral Reform for Canada.* Ottawa: Minister of Public Works and Government Services, 2004.

LeDuc, Lawrence. *The Politics of Direct Democracy.* Peterborough, ON: Broadview Press, 2003.

LeDuc, Lawrence, Richard G. Niemi, and Pippa Norris, eds. *Comparing Democracies 3: Elections and Voting in Global Perspective.* Thousand Oaks, CA: Sage, 2009.

Leighley, Jan E., ed. *The Oxford Handbook of American Elections and Political Behavior.* New York: Oxford University Press, 2011.

Milner, Henry, ed. *Making Every Vote Count: Reassessing Canada's Electoral System.* Peterborough, ON: Broadview Press, 1999.

———. *Steps Toward Making Every Vote Count: Electoral System Reform in Canada and Its Provinces.* Peterborough, ON: Broadview Press, 2004.

Nevitte, Neil, André Blais, Elisabeth Gidengil, and Richard Nadeau. *Unsteady State: The 1997 Canadian Federal Election.* Toronto: Oxford University Press, 2000.

Norris, Pippa. *Democratic Phoenix: Reinventing Political Activism.* Cambridge: Cambridge University Press, 2002.

———. *Electoral Engineering: Voting Rules and Political Behavior.* Cambridge: Cambridge University Press, 2004.

Polsby, Nelson W., Aaron Wildavsky, Steven E. Schier, and David A. Hopkins. *Presidential Elections: Strategies and Structures of American Politics.* 13th ed. Lanham, MD: Rowman & Littlefield, 2012.

Posado-Carbo, Eduardo. *Elections before Democracy: The History of Elections in Europe and Latin America.* New York: St. Martin's Press, 1996.

Reeve, Andrew, and Alan Ware. *Electoral Systems: A Comparative and Theoretical Introduction.* London: Routledge, 1992.

Shugart, Matthew Soberg, and Martin P. Wattenberg, eds. *Mixed-Member Electoral Systems.* Toronto: Oxford University Press, 2003.

Tremblay, Manon, and Linda Trimble. *Women and Electoral Politics in Canada.* Toronto: Oxford University Press, 2003.

CHAPTER 26
Representative Assemblies

The preceding three chapters focused on citizen participation as a part of the political process. Citizens in a democracy can participate, joining interest groups to push for policies and legislation, joining political parties to develop policies and select candidates to run for public office, electing representatives to the legislature, and using the communication media for information about government and politics.

The following four chapters focus on the managerial side of the political process, describing how government officials—some elected, some appointed, some hired—manage the public business of a society. These officials include legislators, who make laws and policies; members of the executive, who organize the legislative process and supervise the administrators; and judges, who adjudicate disputes arising over laws and policies of the government.

According to liberal-democratic theory, the representative assembly should be the central institution for converting political inputs into outputs. Through the mechanism of elections, the sovereign people have delegated to the assembly their power to rule—that is, to make decisions about public business. In the political system, these decisions constitute conversion. Conversion that takes place in the elected assembly meets the standard of democratic legitimacy because representatives of the people perform it.

This ideal, which gives central importance to the assembly, must be heavily qualified in reality, because a great deal of decision-making also occurs in the executive and judicial branches of government, and this decision-making is often beyond the effective control and supervision of the assembly. However, we discuss the assembly first because of its special importance in the theory of liberal democracy. Representative assemblies perform a number of functions in liberal democracies, but these functions vary considerably between legislatures in parliamentary and those in presidential systems.

FUNCTIONS

The most visible function of the democratic assembly is to legislate. This is so true that a representative assembly is commonly referred to as a **legislature**. The terminology is misleading, however, given that modern assemblies do much more than legislate, and their influence in this role is more often than not limited.

There is symbolic importance in the idea that assemblies composed of the people's representatives are given the power to make laws. In parliamentary systems where the executive branch dominates the legislative assembly, the reality is that this role amounts to little more than one of providing a final "quality control" check on bills initiated and drafted by the executive. Where the executive is less dominant and/or where party discipline is weaker, however, assemblies in parliamentary systems can assume a greater role in initiating and shaping bills that subsequently come before the assembly for approval. In contrast, presidential systems, with their separation of powers, afford the greatest role to assemblies in legislating. In the U.S. system, although many bills originate in the executive, the particularly strong committee system in Congress ensures that many are significantly modified prior to their passage, or that they simply die. The importance of ten anti-abortion Democrats in the American Congress for the passage of President Obama's health-care reform in 2010 makes this clear: in order to win their votes, which were crucial to approval, the bill had to be modified to ensure that public funds would not be used for abortions, except in the case of incest or rape.

Assemblies in both parliamentary and presidential assemblies undertake the function of deliberation. This involves publicly discussing and deliberating on measures drafted by the executive or the assembly, a function made all the more public with the introduction of television cameras into assembly chambers. In parliamentary assemblies, deliberation is epitomized by question period, the point in the daily calendar when the opposition has an opportunity to question the executive in an effort to acquire information and call it to account for its actions. In presidential assemblies, deliberation takes place largely within committees and, except for very public issues, is less theatrical. In both systems, however, deliberation provides an opportunity for scrutiny. The increased complexity of modern politics, the global interdependence of states, and the rise of disciplined parties have made it increasingly difficult for legislatures to play an effective role in governing. Where they do continue to be effective, however, is in scrutinizing the actions of executives, whether through questions on the floor of the assembly or in committee. And nowhere is this scrutiny more important than in the review of the budget, one of the core duties of assemblies in liberal democracies.

The assembly ensures that the executive branch carries out the business of government: that laws are enforced, taxes collected, roads paved, and so forth. The assembly cannot perform such tasks but it can cause them to be performed, investigate their performance, and debate the results. In the parliamentary system, responsible government is the chief mechanism by which the assembly retains some control over the business of government. The highest executive officers of the state must be members of the assembly, must be answerable to their colleagues in the assembly for the conduct of business, and must retain the confidence of a working majority. Members of the assembly have an obligation to ask questions of the executive, request disclosure of documents, and even conduct special investigations into governmental business. Assemblies in presidential systems do not have such intimate ties with the executive, but they possess other powers of control, such as the power to alter budgets. In various ways, all democratic assemblies seek to influence the administration of public business.

Responsible government in parliamentary systems links to an additional function exclusive to assemblies in these systems: making a government. The executive remains in power only so long as it retains the confidence of the assembly; once that confidence is lost, it is expected to resign and the focus moves again to the assembly for the formation of a new executive. In those systems with a plurality/majority electoral system (see Chapter 25) where majority governments are the norm, the inability of opposition parties to form a coalition that could secure the support of a majority of the assembly's members often triggers an election. In those employing a more proportional electoral system, bargaining begins anew between the parties in the search for a viable governing coalition—often a protracted and fractious affair. Election is triggered only when majority support for a party or coalition of parties cannot be found among the parties in the assembly. The executive in parliamentary systems emerges through parliament rather than from elections, as in the presidential model.

Other functions of the assembly can be more briefly described. One is local representation, which has two aspects. At the collective level, representatives speak in the assembly for the interests of their constituents. Representatives from Newfoundland and Labrador and coastal British Columbia take a special interest in fisheries, those from Saskatchewan have to be vitally concerned with agriculture, and so on. At the individual level, elected representatives, with the aid of their paid staff, spend a great deal of time acting as virtual ombudsmen for the voters in their constituencies. When citizens experience problems with government services—anything from pension cheques to passports—they may ask their representative to intervene on their behalf.

Still another function is to provide opposition. Members of the assembly who are not on the government's side of the house criticize policies and programs, ensuring that governments cannot sweep issues or incidents under the rug. The organized opposition within the assembly may also be ready to offer an alternative government if necessary, so that changes in power can take place without a period of confusion. This is part of the genius of liberal democracy—to make opposition a part of the system of government rather than drive it outside government. It recognizes that, in a world where everyone's knowledge is limited and everyone is fallible, public opinion benefits by institutionalizing a clash of perspectives.

An assembly plays two additional roles. It educates the public in the sense that its debates and discussions draw the public's attention to certain issues. And it also socializes the public, because as it attempts to wrestle with public problems, it can stimulate the formation of public opinions, attitudes, and beliefs about the nature of the governmental process.

As the scope of state activity has expanded, the limitations on what the assembly can accomplish by itself have also grown. During the period of classical liberalism, government was relatively small and the assembly could debate most legislation at length and monitor all the administrative activities of the state. But the welfare state has grown so large that this is impossible today. This is why there has been a trend in all countries toward greater responsibility of the executive at the expense of the assembly.

PART 4

This tendency is particularly noticeable in parliamentary systems. Through party discipline, the modern cabinet exercises a high degree of control over the majority caucus and thus over the assembly as a whole. Under these conditions, individual members of the assembly have little effective control over legislation and particularly over governmental revenues and expenditures. The assembly still links the executive to the electorate, but it has lost much of its power to initiate legislation. This is less true in presidential systems, where the assembly is not so subject to party discipline. But even in the United States, which probably has the most independent assembly among important democracies, political observers have repeatedly commented on how the president's power has grown at the expense of Congress. (Recall the discussion in Chapter 20 about the autonomy of Congress in the presidential system.)

To grasp the complexity of the Canadian legislative process and the extent to which the executive dominates it, consider Figure 26.1. The chart begins with a minister submitting a legislative proposal to Cabinet. Probably this proposal has already been discussed at length within the minister's department. If the proposal survives consideration in a cabinet committee and receives the formal approval of the whole cabinet, it goes for legal drafting by officials of the Department of Justice. It must then be approved by another cabinet committee and again by the whole cabinet. By this time members of Cabinet will have developed firm views about the draft legislation and will not want to see it greatly altered in Parliament.

There are, of course, opportunities for further discussion and amendment in Parliament. The bill must go through floor debate and committee discussion in both the House of Commons and the Senate, and groups affected by the bill can try to get MPs and senators to introduce amendments favourable to their interests. Changes to bills do take place, but party discipline generally ensures that these changes are within limits acceptable to the cabinet. The chief power of the opposition is that it can exploit the complexity of the process to create delay and force the government to set priorities on its objectives. A determined government can have virtually anything it wants, but it cannot have everything it wants.

Although that is the usual situation, things can be somewhat different when the government does not have a parliamentary majority. Under those conditions, the government may have to accept that some of its bills may be defeated, amended, or delayed for long periods of time. Its main weapon is to make a bill a matter of confidence, which means that the opposition will precipitate an election if it defeats that bill. That tactic worked well for the minority Conservative government in Canada in late 2007 and 2008, because the Liberals, fearing they would not do well in a general election, repeatedly abstained on or even voted for government bills, thus enabling them to pass.

The decline of assemblies has long been noted by political scientists but has perhaps not been fully grasped by the public. Many naïve views still exist about how assemblies work. People often visualize the elected assembly as the focal point at which all issues are raised, debated, and voted on. Visitors to Ottawa and to the provincial capitals frequently express disillusionment when they see a single speaker talking to an almost empty House. The fact is that much of the work of the assembly

Figure 26.1 Overview of the Legislative Process

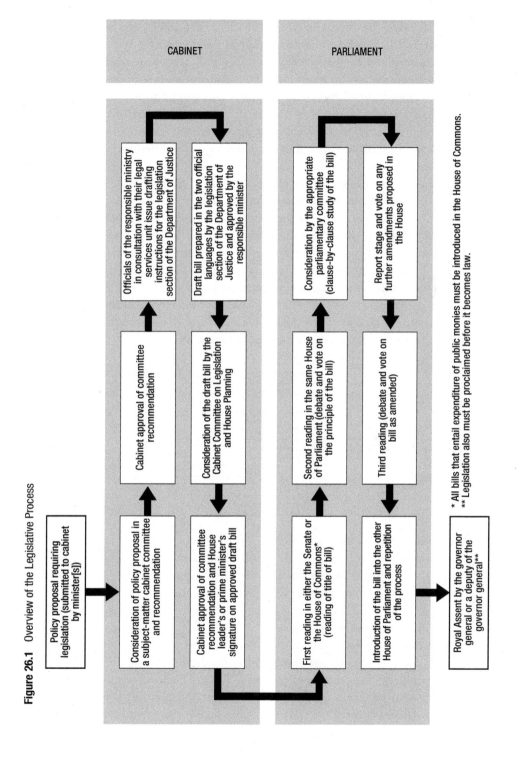

is done elsewhere: in the parliamentary system, by Cabinet, the bureaucracy, the caucus, and parliamentary committees, and in the presidential system, by Cabinet, the bureaucracy, and congressional committees. Full debates from which significant decisions follow are rare. In many cases, full debates come after most of the wrinkles have been ironed out of legislative proposals and compromises have already been struck. In effect, the assembly is putting its stamp of approval on a bill that has already been subjected to a great deal of discussion and scrutiny; individual members, by making speeches pro and con, are staking out political turf for possible use in the next election.

It would be impossible for the entire assembly to handle all the intricate details involved in working out a compromise among conflicting interests. This is why the executive is responsible for preparing most of the assembly's business and handling the administrative details of bills the assembly passes. But again, the executive must have the support of a majority of members of the assembly before establishing laws or policies. To that extent the assembly retains real power in the conversion part of the political process. It remains a check on executive power.

The long-term decline of the assembly relative to the executive arm of government has been accompanied by the decline of bicameralism. Many assemblies today are at least nominally bicameral, as shown by the following list.

Country	Lower House	Upper House
United Kingdom	House of Commons	House of Lords
Canada	House of Commons	Senate
Australia	House of Representatives	Senate
United States	House of Representatives	Senate
Japan	House of Representatives	House of Councillors
Germany	Bundestag	Bundesrat
France	National Assembly	Senate

Unicameral assemblies have become more common over time and are far more common overall at the sub-national level. They exist, for example, in Denmark, Finland, New Zealand, Venezuela, and all the Canadian provinces. Unicameralism is more common in homogeneous societies or in societies where a deliberate attempt is being made to avoid fragmenting government when the society is already divided along cultural, regional, or racial lines.

Most commonly, upper houses have been allowed to atrophy rather than being abolished outright. They do not fit well with either the logic of majoritarian democracy or the machinery of responsible government. The experience of Canada's Parliament, which has seen the Senate decline in both power and prestige, is typical of many countries. Generally speaking, the only upper houses that have been able to retain their vitality are in presidential systems (for example, the United States) or in federal parliamentary systems (for example, Germany). In the former instance, the voters of the states elect senators; in the latter, the governments of the Länder appoint them. In both instances they are seen to represent important and durable interests of particular regions of the country. This principle, which in the end comes down to protecting the minority rights of different regions, has been able to maintain itself against the democratic legitimacy of majority rule. In contrast, other ways of choosing a second chamber, such as heredity (the House of Lords, prior to the latest reforms) or appointment as a reward for service (the contemporary House of Lords and the Canadian Senate), provide those bodies so chosen with little force in a direct conflict with democratically elected lower chambers. However, the expertise of an appointed body can make it a legitimate source of technical amendments to legislation.

These considerations lead directly to the question of how to reform Canada's Senate. Three main options have been put forward in the constitutional debates of the past 30 years. The first is simply to abolish the Senate. This has long been the official position of the NDP, although individuals in that party have sometimes supported other options. In concise terms, the case for abolishing the Senate is that it does not do anything very important, so we should end it and save the cost of running it. The second option is to make the Senate a "house of the provinces"—that is, to let senators be appointed by provincial cabinets or elected by provincial legislators and serve in Ottawa as acknowledged ambassadors of provincial interests. This model, which is loosely based on the German Bundesrat, would extend the interstate approach to

Figure 26.2 Selection Methods of the World's Upper and Lower Legislative Chambers, 2011

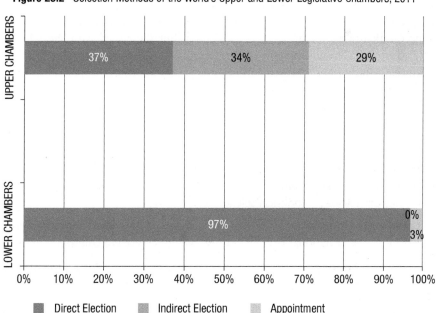

Source: Inter-Parliamentary Union, "Parliaments at a Glance: Mode of Designation of Members—All Regions" (2011), www.Ipu.org/parline-e/ModeofDesignation.Asp?REGION=All&typesearch=1&LANG=ENG. Copyright IPU.

federalism that has characterized recent Canadian political history, as well as legitimize the growing tendency for provinces to deal with each other and with Ottawa almost as though they were sovereign states.

The third option is the "triple-E" proposal, which originated in Alberta and has sometimes received support from other provinces. The second chambers in Australia, Switzerland, and the United States serve as models for this approach. In those countries, each constituent government has the same number of representatives (*equal*); the members are elected by the people, not by the provincial legislatures (*elected*); and the second chamber has the same, or almost the same, legislative power as the lower house (*effective*). The triple-E proposal represents the intrastate model of federalism, in which the interests of the various regions of the country are given effective representation within the machinery of the central government, as well as through constituent governments. It has been argued that Canadian federalism has veered too much toward the interstate model and that a triple-E Senate would help to restore this country's intrastate character by establishing a federal institution based on provincial interests.

The Conservative government of Stephen Harper, first elected in 2006, is committed to what might be called a double-E, rather than a triple-E, approach to Senate reform. Harper wants senators to be elected and to retain their constitutional powers, but he no longer insists that every province should have exactly the same number of senators. Prime Minister Harper originally refused to appoint senators who had not been elected, but then he did just that in 2008 to fill 18 open seats in the Senate—to avoid risking that they be filled by a possible Liberal-NDP coalition government—and then again in May 2011, following the election. The Harper government introduced bills to limit terms for senators and to set up a procedure for nominating them from among candidates elected at the provincial level, but these died with the 39th and 40th Parliaments. The government tried again with the Senate Reform Act (Bill C-7), introduced in June 2011.

REPRESENTATION

Before continuing this discussion of representative assemblies, we must re-examine the basic concept of representation.[1] The word *representation* has three different meanings, all of which are relevant to political science:

1. A representative may be a symbol—that is, a sign by which something else is known. A flag or national anthem may be said to represent a country.

2. A representative may be an agent who is empowered to act for a principal, as a lawyer represents a client in the courtroom. In a similar sense, city councillors, members of provincial legislative assemblies, and members of parliament are representatives because they are agents who act on behalf of their electors, who are the principals.

3. A person who shares some of the typical characteristics of a group is sometimes said to represent it. At the collective level, a subset of items is said to be a representative sample if it accurately reflects selected characteristics of the population from which it is drawn. For example, feminists have said that the House of Commons is not truly representative of the Canadian people because only about 25 percent of its members are women, while more than half of the adult population is female.

We will not concern ourselves further with representation in the symbolic sense. Our focus will be on the latter two meanings, both of which have a bearing on the way people view the role of representatives. Representation is a universal fact of politics. Any system, except the smallest and simplest direct democracy, requires that some people act for others. And questions inevitably arise about whether the agents reflect the salient characteristics of their principals.

Theories of representation are as varied as theories of legitimacy. Autocratic governments of all sorts claim to represent their people in some way that does not need to be tested by competitive elections. We will confine ourselves here to discussing representation in liberal democracies.

There are four different ways in which agents represent those who elect them to a representative assembly. Three concern the individual representatives; the fourth concerns representatives as a collective body. To put it another way, representatives may play any one of four different roles, as follows.

Trustee

The role of trustee demands that representatives rely on their personal judgment when deciding what is in the best interests of the community as a whole. The people elect them and may refuse to re-elect them if they do not like what they do, but in the meantime representatives act independently. Edmund Burke gave this theory its classic formulation in 1774, in a speech to the electors of Bristol: "Your representative owes you, not his industry only, but his judgement, and he betrays, instead of serving you, if he sacrifices it to your opinion."[2]

It is important to remember that Burke spoke at a time when the right to vote was still extremely limited. Burkean trusteeship is essentially a pre-democratic theory of representation. It gives representatives almost carte blanche to carry on the business of government, subject to the sole constraint of facing periodic elections. It does not conceive of democracy as an ongoing process in which the people are actively involved in governing themselves. Interestingly, in 1780 Burke lost his race for re-election in Bristol because he refused to accept instructions from his constituents.

In any event, party discipline in parliamentary systems has largely destroyed trusteeship. Canadian MPs are free to use their own judgment only in rare free votes or in caucus meetings, whose proceedings are confidential. However, cabinet members might be considered trustees to the extent that they deliberate to determine policy positions that are then imposed on backbenchers. City councillors may act as trustees because parties do not normally function at that level in Canada. American representatives may also act as trustees because party discipline in the United States is rather weak.

Delegate

Representatives are **delegates** if they subordinate their own views to those of their constituents and act as instructed by them. Party discipline largely excludes this role along with that of trustee. But city councillors often act as delegates when they vote in accord with the wishes of their ward on such issues as road location and the granting of building permits. American representatives also sometimes act as delegates. A famous example was Senator William Fulbright from Arkansas: although he privately claimed to be an integrationist, he voted against civil rights bills because of the wishes of the majority of his constituents. The delegate model is also used in many private associations, such as trade unions, political parties, and churches; in those cases, representatives chosen to attend national conventions go armed with specific instructions. In Canada the delegate model was revived by the Reform Party, which made a point of claiming that it wanted MPs to be free to vote as their constituents wished. However, it slipped from view as Reform morphed into the Canadian Alliance and then merged with the Progressive Conservatives to form the Conservative Party of Canada.

Although the delegate model is attractive to voters in an era when elitism is under attack, there are some major problems in applying it to the running of a large country. Typically the Parliament of Canada passes dozens of bills every year, sometimes more than one hundred. Is it practical for MPs to find out what the voters think about all, or even many, of them? If opinion in a constituency is divided, how would the "majority" be determined? If consultation is required, how should it be organized—town-hall meetings, mail-in ballots, surveys? Should we ensure that only voters who are sufficiently informed on an issue have a say? And who will interpret the "will" of the constituency? Since there are more than two alternatives on most issues of public policy, a majority within the constituency may not result for any particular position. All in all, MPs would have considerable room to create the appearance of consulting their constituents while in fact predetermining the outcome through manipulation of the process.

Note also that the delegate model requires representatives to pursue the special interests of their constituents, not the general good of the community. This limitation suggests that representatives cannot always be delegates. There are occasions when the general interest must be paramount over sectional concerns and representatives must rise above the wishes of their electors.

Party Member

Representatives who are **party members** may vote and act only as loyal members of their caucus, following the instructions of the leadership. The underlying assumption is that parties are teams that work together collectively and that people make a choice between these teams when they vote, even though in a legal sense they are voting for individual representatives. Since representatives are team players in this model, they have to vote together in the assembly and be judged on the party's collective record at election time. Party discipline made this the dominant form of representation in parliamentary systems in the twentieth century. However, it is a lesser feature of American politics and does not apply at all to the non-party systems found in most municipal governments.

The party model assumes that the policy of the party takes account of the general interest as well as of special interests. In a sense the party leaders act as trustees, using their own judgment and drawing on their own consciences to determine what is best for the community. Thus the notion of trusteeship appears somewhere in each of these three models.

The party-member model of representation has become the norm in parliamentary systems, particularly in Canada, where party discipline is stronger than in almost any other democracy, and politicians and political scientists generally accept it as indispensable to responsible government. The public, however, has never really accepted it. A survey of Canadians taken in 2011 revealed the extent of the public's unhappiness with the importance of the party for members of parliament: While 24 percent of those sampled believed that MPs spend their time representing the views of their party, only 1 percent agreed that that was how they *should* spend their time.[3] Instead, 27 percent thought they should spend their time representing the interests of local people.

Politicians, of course, are aware of the state of public opinion. The Reform Party tried to capitalize on it by calling on party leaders to allow more free votes in Parliament and calling on MPs to vote according to the "consensus of the constituency."[4] Many in the other parties have also called for a relaxation of party discipline, but so far nothing much has happened. The reality is that the incentives created by the parliamentary system lead inevitably to the party-member model of representation, and the behaviour of MPs will not change without major changes in the system.

University of Dalhousie political scientist Jennifer Smith has argued that reforming the system is more complicated than just abolishing party discipline. The problem with delegate representation in our system is that it will "destabilize" party discipline and responsible government—the genius of the parliamentary process. Party discipline and responsible government are ways of realizing the larger national interest rather than local interests. Thus the way to achieve something closer to delegate representation is to either move to a congressional system (which she suggests "is out of the question") or move to a form of proportional representation (PR). A PR electoral system would enable a closer connection between "like-minded voters" and their representatives.[5] Therefore, one way to improve the parliamentary system might be to change the electoral system.

The Microcosm

Whatever role representatives play, a qualitatively different question is bound to arise: Are they similar to those they represent? In other words, do they reflect the characteristics of ethnicity, language, religion, gender, class, income, and occupation that are found in the population at large? A common feeling today is that representatives must be similar to their constituents in order to have their best interests at heart. We can call this the **microcosm theory**—the idea that a governing body should be a miniature replica of those it represents, similar to the argument for a representative bureaucracy (see Chapter 28). John Adams the second president of the United States as well as a political philosopher, wrote 200 years ago that the representative assembly "should be in miniature an exact portrait of the people at large. It should think, feel, reason, and act like them."[6]

Obviously the microcosm theory cannot be applied too literally, for any number of characteristics might be considered politically relevant. It is impossible to get a working body of a reasonably small size that will have just the right proportions of every conceivable characteristic. But the theory can be given a more sensible interpretation. While exact proportionality is not important, no significant group of people should be left without a voice. This ties in well with the view of Bernard Crick, discussed in Chapter 1, that politics involves the reconciliation of differences. For example, the precise proportion of French- and English-speaking judges on the Supreme Court of Canada is not critical, but it is important that there be some of each. A more complex example is the Canadian cabinet. In choosing ministers, the prime minister usually tries to select about three-quarters anglophones and one-quarter francophones, including anglophones from inside Quebec and francophones from outside Quebec whenever possible. In addition, the prime minister wants to have at least one minister from each province, as well as some representation for women, ethnic groups, and regions. It is a complicated balancing act with a double purpose: to allow all significant groups to be heard and to convince the population that no sector has been omitted from consideration. Image is as important as reality. For more on this topic, see Canadian Focus 26.1.

Politics is always a matter of trade-offs between competing values. Both representing the whole country in the cabinet and maintaining party unity seem like desirable goals to the prime minister, but pursuing one may interfere with the other. Political leadership requires the ability to manage such inevitable trade-offs and conflicts.

Although microcosmic representation in the cabinet seems necessary in a pluralistic country such as Canada, there can be political costs, as illustrated by the story of Brian Mulroney's first cabinet. Because of the long years of Liberal dominance in Quebec, the 58 Conservative MPs from that province were relatively inexperienced when they came to Ottawa in 1984. Many had not been active in politics before or had been associated with other Quebec parties, such as the Union Nationale or the Parti Québécois. In appointing 11 Quebec ministers to his first cabinet, Mulroney had to draw from a less experienced pool of talent than is usual and desirable. Several of his original appointments did not turn out well, and a few ministers were forced from the cabinet under embarrassing circumstances. All of this contributed substantially to the Mulroney government's image problems in its first term. However, the long-term political consequences of under-representing Quebec in the cabinet might have been much worse than the effects of these passing embarrassments.

Canadian Focus 26.1

The Fine Art of Composing a Cabinet

On 18 May 2011, Prime Minister Stephen Harper announced his cabinet, which had grown in size to 39 ministers. Nine of them—23 percent—were women. Every province and region had at least one minister, including one from the North, and the larger provinces had more than one each:

Ontario 15
Quebec 4
Alberta 6
British Columbia 4

The prime minister would have liked to appoint more members from Quebec, but despite winning his first majority government, he was limited by the composition of the Conservative caucus and in particular the small number of Conservatives elected in Quebec. Winning a majority government and increasing the overall size of Cabinet did provide some flexibility in making the appointments. A 167-member caucus, one that includes members from every province and region, 28 women, and some ethnic diversity, provides a greater likelihood of forming a cabinet that is balanced. The degree to which the balance is matched by experience is another question altogether.

In composing a cabinet, a prime minister uses the microcosm theory of representation, within the limitations provided by his caucus and consistent with the need to appoint cabinet members who have the executive ability to run departments of government. There are, however, always many trade-offs involved in making these choices, and a larger caucus does not always mean greater balance on all fronts.

Stephen Harper faced a similar dilemma after the 2006 election, when the Conservatives elected only 10 MPs from Quebec, most of them with little political experience. He was taking a chance by appointing six Quebeckers to his cabinet, and indeed one of them, Maxime Bernier, was forced to resign in 2008 under embarrassing circumstances: dating a woman with prior connections to biker gangs and organized crime, as well as leaving confidential cabinet papers at her house.

Another problem with the microcosm theory of representation is that, if pushed hard enough, it can conflict with the ordinary democratic understanding of elected representation. Those with the desired demographic characteristics of race or gender may not win nominations and elections. This conflict has bedevilled recent discussions about how the proportion of women in the House of Commons can be increased. That proportion has been rising—from less than 1 percent as recently as 1968 to a high of 24.6 percent after the election of 2 May 2011—but it is still much less than the

PART 4

percentage of women in the voting-age population (which is greater than 50 percent because, on average, women live longer than men). Leaders can set goals for the proportion of female candidates, but in order to reach those goals, a leader might have to appoint women to run in some ridings or the party adopt gender quotas, thus circumventing an unrestricted process of local nomination races. One can imagine similar difficulties arising in attempts to fix the gender ratio of elected MPs. Such changes have been employed elsewhere, however, with a measure of success.

One proposal, however, would at least partially circumvent these difficulties. It has been suggested by the National Action Committee on the Status of Women that single-member constituencies could be turned into dual-member constituencies, and that one member would have to be a woman and the other a man. Voters would have two ballots, one of which they would cast in the women's contest, the other in the men's contest. In this scheme, men and women elected to public office would not represent just their own sex, for each would have been elected by voters of both sexes. In that respect the proposal would not divide the electorate into opposed camps based on gender. It is true that men would run only against men and women only against women, but that might not be such a grave drawback when we think of the overall contest as one of party against party, for the candidates of all parties would be composed equally of men and women. A proposal similar to this was advanced for the new territory of Nunavut, but it was defeated in a referendum in the spring of 1997.

Each of the four models of representation has its own strengths and weaknesses. Trustees are a bit removed from popular pressure and can thus take a more independent view. The result of the free vote on capital punishment in the House of Commons was that MPs voted to abolish it, even though public-opinion polls showed that most people wanted to reinstate the death penalty. While the trustee role offers an opportunity for independence, it may also lead to representatives voting according to their own particular biases. Conversely, a close adherence to public opinion, which is the virtue of the delegate role, may blind representatives to the long-range general interest. Party discipline restricts representatives' initiative but it tends to produce a more coherent and intelligible set of policies. Local politics often degenerates into a name-recognition or popularity contest because councillors act individually as delegates or trustees but rarely as cohesive, identifiable groups. Finally, the microcosm theory has its own special problem: it can clash with democracy. The person with the right demographic characteristics of gender, language, region, and ethnicity may not be the person that the voters select in open democratic contests.

Perhaps there is no simple solution to these problems. It may be that all the modes of representation are useful in varying circumstances and that each can compensate for the drawbacks of the other three. Regardless of what may be best in some abstract sense, the tendency in parliamentary democracies is clear. The roles of trustee and delegate have declined; the party-member role and the microcosm idea now predominate. These latter two are more compatible with the parliamentary system. Where there is greater opportunity for autonomy in representation is in the presidential–congressional system.

ASSESSING REPRESENTATIVE ASSEMBLIES

In theory one might assume representative assemblies to be the cornerstone of democratic government. In practice, however, things are different. In parliamentary systems, and particularly in Canada, members of parliament have their roles limited in two ways. First, the executive dominates the legislative process: the prime minister and the central agencies of the government control the legislative agenda. Second, with political party discipline, elected representatives cannot freely represent their constituents. As one critic of the system puts it,

> Democracy teaches that they [members of parliament] receive their authority from the people and are thus the representatives of people. However, parliamentary democracy teaches us that they are instead the representatives of their parties. It is the party that nominates them as candidates, guides them and assists them financially during election campaigns. They are elected under the party banner. The party dictates their behaviour in the House and, in short, structures electoral competition and dominates parliamentary life. There is little room for independent members in this kind of system.[7]

On the other side of the issue, supporters of the existing system of representation argue that executive dominance and party discipline are required to make responsible government work. Representatives in assemblies mirror the people they represent; therefore, any assembly will be divided into factions. The executive, with political party discipline, is then able to craft a legislative agenda that is a compromise in the public interest. These supporters of the representative system argue that the more independent assemblies within the presidential system are torn by factionalism and often end up in gridlock. Under that process, essential legislation may be delayed or never passed.

The debate over the proper role of representative assemblies in modern government has gone on for quite some time and will continue. It appears to be one of those situations where both sides have something worthwhile to say and the truth—if there is such a thing—lies in a balance of the opposed views.

Questions for Discussion

1. What are two criticisms of parliamentary representative assemblies? What are two strengths?

2. What are two criticisms of presidential representative assemblies? What are two strengths?

3. Which form of representation—trustee, delegate, or party member—would you prefer that your member of parliament take in representing you? Why? Which best describes what actually happens in Canada? What could be done to implement change?

PART 4

Internet Links

1. Inter-parliamentary Union: **www.ipu.org/english/home.htm**.
2. Parliament of Canada: **www.parl.gc.ca**.
3. Parliament of the United Kingdom: **www.parliament.uk**.
4. United States House of Representatives: **www.house.gov**.
5. United States Senate: **www.senate.gov**.

Further Reading

Arnold, R. Douglas. *The Logic of Congressional Action*. New Haven, CT: Yale University Press, 1990.

Close, David, ed. *Legislatures and the New Democracies in Latin America*. Boulder, CO: Lynne Rienner, 1995.

Docherty, David. *Legislatures*. Vancouver: University of British Columbia Press, 2004.

Franks, C. E. S. *The Parliament of Canada*. Toronto: University of Toronto Press, 1987.

Gallagher, Michael, Michael Laver, and Peter Mair. *Representative Government in Modern Europe*. 5th ed. New York: McGraw-Hill Education, 2011.

Jackson, Robert J., and Michael M. Atkinson. *The Canadian Legislative System*. Rev. ed. Toronto: Macmillan, 1980.

Loewenberg, Gerhard, Peverill Squire, and D. Roderick Kiewiet. *Legislatures: Comparative Perspectives on Representative Assemblies*. Ann Arbor: University of Michigan Press, 2002.

March, James G., and Johan P. Olsen. *Democratic Governance*. New York: Free Press, 1995.

Mezey, M. L., and David M. Olson, eds. *Legislatures in the Policy Process: The Dilemmas of Economic Policy*. Cambridge: Cambridge University Press, 1991.

Norton, Philip, ed. *Legislatures*. Oxford: Oxford University Press, 1990.

Pitkin, Hanna F. *The Concept of Representation*. Berkeley: University of California Press, 1967.

Remini, Robert Vincent. *The House: The History of the House of Representatives*. New York: HarperCollins, 2006.

Schroedel, Jean Reith. *Congress, the President, and Policymaking: A Historical Analysis*. Armonk, NY: M. E. Sharpe, 1994.

Seidle, F. Leslie, and Louis Massicotte, eds. *Taking Stock of 150 Years of Responsible Government in Canada*. Ottawa: Canadian Study of Parliament Group, 1999.

Smith, David E. *The Canadian Senate in Bicameral Perspective*. Toronto: University of Toronto Press, 2003.

———. *The People's House of Commons: Theories of Democracy in Contention*. Toronto: University of Toronto Press, 2007.

Strom, Kaare. *Minority Government and Majority Rule*. Cambridge: Cambridge University Press, 1990.

Thurber, James A. *Rivals for Power: Presidential–Congressional Relations*. Lanham, MD: Rowman & Littlefield, 2009.

Weaver, R. Kent, and Bert A. Rockman, eds. *Do Institutions Matter? Government Capabilities in the United States and Abroad*. Washington, DC: Brookings Institution, 1993.

White, Randall. *Voice of Region: The Long Journey to Senate Reform in Canada*. Toronto: Dundurn Press, 1990.

PART 4

CHAPTER 27

The Political Executive

The executive branch of government includes not only highly visible officials, such as the prime minister or president, but also the many anonymous officials who labour in the civil service. We will discuss the latter group in the next chapter, under the heading of administration; here we will confine our attention to those at the top of the executive pyramid—those officers of state who are in some sense politically responsible (as opposed to politically neutral, which most public employees are supposed to be). This category includes the head of state, the head of government, and the ministry or cabinet. It also includes the personal advisers and assistants to these officers. We shall refer to all these people as the **political executive.**

THE PARLIAMENTARY EXECUTIVE

We have already discussed the head of state and head of government at some length, but relatively little has been said about other ministers. In Britain the cabinet is relatively small by Canadian standards; it usually consists of 22 or 23 members.[1] However, the British prime minister also appoints dozens of junior ministers, who have specific responsibilities but do not sit in the cabinet. The whole group, which includes but is not limited to cabinet members, is known as the **ministry.**

In nineteenth-century Canada, Sir John A. Macdonald could make do with a cabinet of 12; in the late 1940s, Louis St. Laurent's cabinet had only 19 ministers, but membership grew steadily larger with the expansion of the welfare state. Brian Mulroney governed with 39 or 40 ministers in his cabinet, until he reduced the size to 35 in January 1993. By that time the size of the Canadian cabinet had become a political issue in its own right.

Comparisons with the American cabinet of 16 are perhaps unfair because of other differences between presidential and parliamentary government; all the same, Canada's cabinets of three dozen or more ministers were very large by the standards of other parliamentary systems. Nations such as Great Britain, Australia, France, and Germany got along perfectly well with about two dozen or even fewer ministers (although in some of these cases junior ministers perform executive functions but do not sit in the cabinet). When Kim Campbell became prime minister in June 1993, she reduced the size of Cabinet from 35 to 25, but numbers have gradually rebounded since then. After the 2011 election, Prime Minister Harper appointed 27 ministers, 12 junior ministers, and 28 parliamentary secretaries, so the Canadian cabinet is now back to the size it had attained before the modest reduction efforts of the early 1990s.

Canadian cabinets are oversized for political rather than administrative reasons. The extra appointments are made to place MPs from various regions and demographic categories in positions of prominence and to promote and reward members of caucus whom the prime minister wishes to advance because of perceived talent or loyalty. As Canadian cabinets grew in size under Pierre Trudeau and Brian Mulroney, they almost ceased to function as a unit. The important work was done in cabinet committees and ratified, when necessary, in the increasingly infrequent meetings of the whole cabinet.

Each prime minister will establish a different set of cabinet committees, but some structure is indispensable for a body of this size. At the time of publication, the main cabinet committees were Priorities and Planning, Operations, and Treasury Board (this last is required by statute to oversee government spending). In addition there were several specialized committees for various areas of policy. Most of the work is done in these committees, whose recommendations are then ratified in meetings of the cabinet as a whole.

The Role of Cabinet

Political executives in a liberal democracy perform much the same tasks as executives in any organization—they manage the business of the enterprise. But this is management on a grand scale. The budget of the federal government is larger than that of the 20 largest Canadian corporations combined.

The political executive has two main functions: to initiate policy proposals for the assembly and to supervise the administration of laws passed by the assembly. The first function is a necessity. A session of Parliament would never end if the entire body had to develop its own policy proposals, debate those proposals, consider amendments, and vote on the final versions. Thus the executive formulates legislative proposals to be submitted to the entire assembly. In parliamentary systems, of course, the executive goes farther and actually controls the deliberations of the assembly, at least when there is a majority government.

Administration of existing laws is also the responsibility of the executive. Ministers run the different departments in their particular areas of responsibility. A minister of agriculture, for example, is responsible for all federal activities that fall under the department of agriculture. This will include keeping trained agricultural agents in the field, running experimental farms, providing loans to farmers in special situations, and keeping statistics on farm production. The same applies to the fisheries, transport, and labour departments, and so on. Each minister, along with the cabinet collectively, is responsible to the House (and ultimately to the people) for the business of a specific administrative department.

PART 4

It should be noted again that structural differences exist between parliamentary and presidential executives. Because the executive and the legislature in the parliamentary process are fused, all ministers answer to the House for the work of their departments. The institution of **question period** allows backbenchers to pose questions directly to ministers, sometimes putting them under intense political pressure. Steering legislation through the House and the committees is the responsibility of the house leader, who is also a member of the ministry. In the presidential system, the president and cabinet secretaries are not members of the legislative assembly, because those institutions are separated. While the executive formulates policy proposals, it is up to the party leaders and committee chairs to manage the flow of legislation. And since cabinet members do not hold seats in the legislature, they cannot be subjected to routine questioning there; no equivalent to question period exists in the presidential system.

The members of the executive also perform symbolic and ceremonial functions, provide party and national political leadership, make government appointments to the judiciary and regulatory agencies, and exercise military power. The expanding role of the political executive has influenced the governmental process in two important ways. First, there has been dramatic growth in the administrative arm of government. Departments, agencies, boards, and commissions have increased in number and size because of the need to carry out more and more administrative responsibilities. This growth is manifested in the size of the civil service at the federal, provincial, and municipal levels. Second, there has developed a very significant organizational tier of advisers to the government. While the advisers are part of the executive, they are separate from the traditional civil service. These personal advisers to the prime minister and the cabinet are important not in terms of numbers but in terms of their influence on the governmental process.

In Canada the management of government involves half a dozen so-called **central agencies**, of which four are particularly important: the Department of Finance; another government department, the Treasury Board, which is supervised by the cabinet committee of the same name; and two staff organizations, the Prime Minister's Office (PMO) and the Privy Council Office (PCO). All four of these bodies are deeply involved in initiating, implementing, and monitoring policy proposals; they are sometimes called the "exclusive club" of central agencies.[2]

The **Department of Finance** is important because the minister of finance, advised by officials from the department, prepares the annual budget of the federal government. There may be some discussion in cabinet or in cabinet committees, but under current practice the minister of finance makes decisions about how much money each department gets. Only the prime minister can give direction to the minister of finance, and that happens very rarely. That is why, in the Chrétien government of the 1990s, it was Paul Martin, then minister of finance, who received so much credit for moving toward a balanced budget and who would have received the blame if no progress had been made.

Eddie Goldenberg, a long-time policy adviser to Prime Minister Jean Chrétien, explains that decisions over how much to allocate to each department cannot be made by the cabinet collectively. Ministers are simply too caught up in the priorities of their own departments. When ministers spoke at meetings,

> they began their remarks by paying lip service to the importance of fiscal discipline. Then they immediately endorsed a variety of policy ideas, each of which they believed clearly deserved funding by the minister of finance. Unfortunately, the ideas always required the expenditure of billions of dollars of public funds. No one ever suggested cuts to existing programs, or tradeoffs that might make some of their ideas affordable.[3]

Budgetary allocation elevates the minister of finance over all other cabinet members except the prime minister. Several ministers in the Chrétien government learned to their sorrow that they would have to give up cherished spending projects because they could not get Paul Martin's support. Control of the budget is the single most important management tool exercised over the entire range of government activities.

The **Treasury Board,** which has been separate from the Department of Finance since 1967, is responsible for public administration in general terms. Its minister, known as the president of the Treasury Board, presides over a large bureaucracy, the most important function of which is to provide central control over expenditures. Proposals from departments to spend money must be approved by the Treasury Board, which verifies that they conform to government policy. The Department of Finance prepares the budget and allocates money to the various departments, while the Treasury Board ensures that the money is spent for approved purposes.

The **Prime Minister's Office** came into its own under Pierre Trudeau and has continued to be important under every prime minister since then. Directed by the prime minister's chief of staff, the PMO includes political operatives as well as advisers on various policy areas. These people are hired and fired by the prime minister and serve without the career security of civil servants. In particular, the prime minister relies on the PMO for political advice that neutral public servants should not be asked to give. The highest appointments in the PMO are usually personal friends or political associates of the prime minister; the junior appointments are usually young people who put in a few years of extremely concentrated work before going on to something more regular (and probably less exciting).

The **Privy Council Office** is a special organization designed to serve the cabinet and cabinet committees. First, a word about the **Privy Council**. It is made up of all present and former cabinet ministers, as well as a few other individuals who have received the special honour of membership. However, the cabinet is the only working part of the Privy Council, and it acts in its name; the council as a whole does not meet. R. MacGregor Dawson, a political scientist whose textbook on Canadian government was standard reading for a whole generation, explained it this way:

PART 4

The Privy Council ... performs no functions as a Council, despite the fact that it is mentioned a number of times in the British North America Act as an advisory body to the Governor. Such functions have been assumed by that small portion of the Council which constitutes the Cabinet of the moment.[4]

The PCO, however, is very much alive. As the secretariat to the cabinet, it is responsible for helping that body to manage overall government priorities and for coordinating the process by which those priorities are achieved. Cabinet relies on the PCO as a source of advice independent of the permanent departments, which ministers often perceive as captive to tradition and special interests. The PCO can be considered the control centre for the government; its chief executive, the Clerk of the Privy Council, is the head of the whole civil service. Conservative Prime Minister Stephen Harper's first appointment to that position was Kevin Lynch, even though Lynch had once been deputy minister to Liberal Finance Minister Paul Martin; that illustrates the nonpartisan character of the Clerk's position.

These and other central agencies do not themselves provide services to the public. Rather, they are instruments by which the prime minister and cabinet attempt to manage the entire public service. The formal lines of responsibility are shown in Figure 27.1.

This structure complements the older direct relationship between the prime minister, the cabinet, and the bureaucracy, and it also acts as a counterweight to the growing permanent bureaucracy. At the same time, however, it has led critics to suggest that cabinet ministers and senior bureaucratic officials, such as **deputy ministers** and assistant deputy ministers, have taken a back seat to the prime minister's personal advisers. Critics contend that central agencies have given the prime minister an inordinate amount of power in the legislative arena. With the support of the PMO, PCO, the Treasury Board, and the Finance Department, the prime minister can dominate the process by which public-policy proposals are developed and priorities assigned. The expansion of these organizations reinforces the argument that the collegiality of cabinet government has given way to prime-ministerial government, which is highly focused on the person of the prime minister.

Figure 27.1 The Political Executive and the PCO

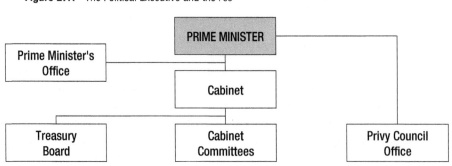

Canadian Focus 27.1

Prime-Ministerial Government?

One significant criticism of the parliamentary system is that prime ministers now dominate the governmental process. Donald Savoie makes this argument in two books (see Further Reading for this chapter). He suggests that political power has shifted to the "centre" and that we now have what he calls "court government": "By *court government* I do not mean the rise of judicial power. Rather, I mean that effective political power now rests with the prime minister and a small group of carefully selected courtiers." He goes on to say that this process of government is different from an older process whereby policy proposals and public decision-making were done by cabinets, cabinet committees, and civil servants.

Today, for example, "Authority is highly concentrated in the hands of prime ministers and their courtiers. Courtiers are drawn from the cabinet, from partisan political staffers, from the bureaucracy, and from outside, including lobbyists and think tanks." Thus, currently "cabinets in both Canada and Britain scarcely participate in determining the expenditure budget. Prime ministers and the minister of finance or the chancellor of the exchequer, together with key advisors, will determine the broad outline of the expenditure budget and decide which new major initiatives the government will support." In Canada this "court" process began with Pierre Trudeau and has been practised by all prime ministers since.

Savoie also suggests there may be significant consequences for court governments. "This study … documents the tendency of citizens of Canada and Britain to be less involved in political parties and less inclined to vote."

Source: Donald J. Savoie, *Court Government and the Collapse of Accountability in Canada and the United Kingdom* (Toronto: University of Toronto Press, 2008), 16, 330, 328.

THE PRESIDENTIAL EXECUTIVE

Comparisons are sometimes drawn between the contemporary situation of the prime minister, who has a phalanx of personal advisers in the PMO and PCO, and that of an American president, who has an admittedly much larger staff. The comparison is worrisome in that the president, because of the separation of powers, does not control Congress to the extent that the prime minister controls Parliament. The power of the parliamentary executive is less balanced by an independent legislative assembly.

The executive branch in the United States is also responsible for initiating legislation. The president has some 4000 staff members, who are the organizational network supporting domestic and foreign policy initiatives. The president, like the prime minister, is the chief executive officer and is responsible for choosing cabinet secretaries to direct the administrative departments of government, such as agriculture, defence, foreign affairs, and transportation. In addition, the president has two offices that assist in setting the policy direction of the government: the **White House** staff and the **Executive Office.**

The White House staff is composed of the personal advisers to the president—the kind of people depicted in the television series *West Wing*. This description by two writers on American politics conveys the flavour of this group:

> It is not accidental that journalists have come to popularize the staff of each president with such names as the "Irish Mafia" (Kennedy), the "Georgia Mafia" (Carter), and the "California Mafia" (Reagan). Every modern president has gathered around himself those people who fought most of the battles with him during his long struggle for ultimate political success. These are his trusted political friends, and their value to him has been proven over time. But this group of trusted cronies is now only the small core of a large personal staff, the White House staff.[5]

Prominent figures in the White House staff of any president include the chief of staff, the communications director, and the special legal counsel. The president's wife (until now all presidents have been men and almost all have been married) may also be an influential figure. Clinton put his wife, now Secretary of State Hillary Rodham Clinton, in the public eye by appointing her to head a special task force on health-care issues. George W. Bush's wife, Laura, a teacher and librarian, took a special interest in education and literacy. Michelle Obama, a lawyer who still has two young daughters to look after, has advocated for the poor and for the cause of healthy nutrition.

The Executive Office is located in the building adjacent to the White House. It comprises a number of agencies that are vital to the president's policymaking role, for example, the Office of Management and Budget, the Council of Economic Advisors,

Figure 27.2 Presidential Executive

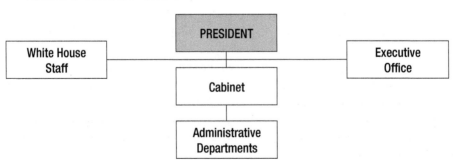

the Office of the United States Trade Representative, and the National Security Council. This latter body, chaired by the president, brings together the secretary of state, the secretary of defence, the heads of intelligence agencies, and other senior officials concerned with foreign affairs and national security.

The individuals and organizations that make up the executive in the presidential system do not merely initiate policy; they also have the formidable job of selling their policy proposals to Congress. They must get a majority of those voting in both the House of Representatives and the Senate on their side to get the legislation through Congress. This means that much of their work involves finding ways to get members of Congress of whatever party to support their initiatives. This work is part of the dynamic of **log-rolling** or **pork-barrelling,** as this kind of vote-trading politics is sometimes called. "You scratch my back and I'll scratch yours," says the old adage. By any name, it involves devising trade-offs that will lead to a majority vote for legislation in Congress. The president may also appeal to the American public, usually on television, if he still lacks a majority even after working members of Congress, in an attempt to persuade Americans to pressure their representatives in the House and the Senate to support his proposed legislation.

RESPONSIBLE GOVERNMENT AND MINISTERIAL RESPONSIBILITY

Returning to the parliamentary system, two mechanisms were traditionally thought to make the assembly the ultimate master of the political executive. Under the principle of responsible government, the cabinet is collectively accountable to the House, because the prime minister and the cabinet cannot remain in office without the support of a working majority in the popularly elected branch of the assembly. But we have seen how party discipline has weakened, if not completely destroyed, the meaning of responsible government. (Recall the discussion in Chapter 20 about the dominance of the executive in the modern parliamentary system.)

The second great check on the political executive was supposed to be the individual responsibility of every minister to the assembly. Most ministers receive a **portfolio** containing one or more departments or agencies (there may also be one or two ministers without a portfolio). Under the doctrine of **ministerial responsibility,** when there is a serious problem in a department—such as dishonesty, mismanagement, or gross incompetence—a minister should offer to resign. This idea developed in the age of smaller government, when it was reasonable to assume that ministers could keep in touch with everything being done by the employees of their departments. It is somewhat unrealistic to expect the same today, given the far-flung activities of departments that may have thousands of employees and budgets of billions of dollars. Thus, ministers in Canada today do not usually offer their resignation unless they are personally implicated in a breach of trust, even if the opposition parties demand that they step down.

PART 4

All recent ministerial resignations under the doctrine of ministerial responsibility have involved personal actions. During Brian Mulroney's first term, eight ministers resigned from Cabinet for personal indiscretions. For example, Robert Coates was careless with official documents when he visited a strip bar in West Germany while on an official trip, and Sinclair Stevens did not insulate himself completely enough from his private business affairs. In contrast, Michael Wilson rejected calls for his resignation as finance minister when the 1989 budget was leaked to the press before it was read to the House of Commons. Wilson, supported by the prime minister, said he could not be expected to resign because of an error by an unknown employee far down the chain of command.

The same pattern prevailed during the term of the Liberal government of Jean Chrétien that came to power in 1993. The prime minister accepted the resignation of Sheila Copps because she had publicly promised to resign if the goods and services tax was not repealed; she then won a hastily called by-election and was reappointed to the cabinet. During the Somalia inquiry, David Collenette's position as minister of defence steadily became more untenable as revelations mounted about military mis-conduct, but in spite of many calls from the opposition benches for his resignation, he did not resign over this issue. He did resign, however, after newspaper publication of a letter that had gone out with his signature; the letter concerned an immigration problem in his own riding and had nothing to do with his ministerial responsibilities. Later Collenette was brought back into the cabinet as minister of transport. In 2005, when Paul Martin was prime minister, Immigration Minister Judy Sgro resigned over charges that she had inappropriately used her personal authority in immigration cases. In 2008, under Prime Minister Harper, Maxime Bernier resigned as foreign minister when his girlfriend Julie Couillard revealed that he had left official documents at her home.

Ministerial responsibility remains, as the aforementioned cases illustrate, but it has lost much of its effectiveness: it is now in practice limited to the minister's personal actions and no longer includes the actions of departmental officials. Nonetheless, the assembly still has the power to inquire, expose, and accuse. Ministers do not wish to appear in a bad light, for even if their jobs are not immediately threatened, their long-term political future could be jeopardized. Thus most executive functions are tempered by regard for the assembly.

In spite of the trend toward executive power, the executive and the assembly remain interdependent. Checks on the executive exist today as they always have. Votes of confidence, the opinions of caucus, and regular elections are only three of these checks. The power of the executive, while great, is not absolute, and the health of democracy depends on such checks for balancing executive and legislative powers. For more on ministerial responsibility, see Canadian Focus 27.2.

Canadian Focus 27.2

The Problem of Ministerial Responsibility

The sponsorship scandal that arose in 2004 with the auditor general's report raises an important problem with ministerial responsibility. For example, is the head of government or a cabinet minister to be held responsible for actions that occur "on their watch" if these actions are deemed to be criminal? In other words, if a civil servant or an appointed adviser to the government is charged with some criminal activity, should the head of government or the minister resign? Former deputy prime minister Sheila Copps touches on the complexity of this issue in trying to explain the actual role of a cabinet minister in conducting the day-to-day business of a government department, in this case Heritage Canada. It is interesting to note her view of the responsibilities of the minister and the deputy minister:

> In fact, a government minister is more like the chairman of the board. The deputy minister is the chief executive officer: All hiring, firing, and day to day operations are managed by the deputy, with the minister giving overall direction. All personnel decisions are handled by the deputy—but

when somebody screws up, it's up to the minister to answer publicly for the mistake.

When I managed Canadian Heritage and crown agencies associated with it, I gave direction for an operation totalling over 25,000 employees. I certainly could not know what was going on in every area under my jurisdiction. Yet by the old-fashioned ministerial code, I was responsible for every mistake made in every part of the department and 18 associated crown agencies. I had to answer in the House of Commons for everything from a Don Cherry rant (courtesy of the CBC) to a salacious Canada Council–funded work called *Bubbles Galore.* It didn't matter that there were thousands of grants given out every year through the Canada Council, and that I had absolutely no say over a single grant. It would have been impossible to explain that I didn't make the decision on grants under my jurisdiction— even though it was the truth.

Source: Excerpt from Sheila Copps, "Don't Believe the Spin on Gomery," *National Post*, February 4, 2005. Used with permission of Hon. Sheila Copps.

Questions for Discussion

1. In the parliamentary system, what has caused power to move to the prime minister? Why do the institutions of parliamentary government make it difficult to reverse the trend?

PART 4

2. In the presidential system, why was the executive separated from the legislature? What are the benefits of this separation? What are the drawbacks?

3. Would it be practical in the modern world for cabinet ministers to be required to resign over all the mistakes made in their departments? Can you think of any situations in which you think a cabinet minister should have resigned and did not?

Internet Links

1. Executive Office of the President of the United States: **www.whitehouse.gov**.

2. Office of the Prime Minister, Canada: **www.pm.gc.ca**.

3. Office of the Prime Minister, United Kingdom: **www.number-10.gov.uk**.

4. Privy Council Office, Canada: **www.pco-bcp.gc.ca**.

Further Reading

Bakvis, Herman. *Regional Ministers: Power and Influence in the Canadian Cabinet.* Toronto: University of Toronto Press, 1991.

Band, John R., and Richard Fleisher. *The President in the Legislative Arena.* Chicago: University of Chicago Press, 1990.

Bernier, Luc, Keith Brownsey, and Michael Howlett, eds. *Executive Styles in Canada: Cabinet Structures and Leadership Practices in Canadian Government.* Toronto: University of Toronto Press, 2005.

Blondel, Jean, and Ferdinand Müller-Rommel. *Cabinets in Eastern Europe.* New York: Palgrave, 2001.

Campbell, Colin, and M. J. Wyszomirski, eds. *Executive Leadership in Anglo-American Systems.* Pittsburgh, PA: University of Pittsburgh Press, 1991.

Davis, James W. *The President and Party Leader.* New York: Greenwood Press, 1992.

Delacourt, Susan. *Juggernaut: Paul Martin's Campaign for Chrétien's Crown.* Toronto: McClelland & Stewart, 2003.

Dunn, Christopher J. C. *The Institutionalized Cabinet: Governing the Western Provinces.* Kingston, ON: Institute of Public Administration of Canada, 1995.

Gardner, John William. *On Leadership.* New York: Free Press, 1990.

Goldenberg, Eddie. *The Way It Works: Inside Ottawa.* Toronto: McClelland & Stewart, 2006.

Hennessy, Peter. *The Prime Minister: The Office and Its Holders since 1945.* New York: Palgrave, 2001.

James, Simon. *British Cabinet Government.* 2nd ed. New York: Routledge, 1999.

Keyes, John Mark. *Executive Legislation: Delegated Law Making by the Executive Branch.* Toronto: Butterworths, 1992.

Laver, Michael, and Kenneth A. Shepsle. *Cabinet Ministers and Parliamentary Government.* Cambridge: Cambridge University Press, 1994.

—————, eds. *Making and Breaking Governments: Cabinets and Legislatures in Parliamentary Democracies.* New York: Cambridge University Press, 1996.

LeLoup, Lance T. *The President and Congress: Collaboration and Combat in National Policymaking.* Upper Saddle River, NJ: Allyn and Bacon, 1999.

Linz, Juan J., and Arturo Valenzuela. *The Failure of Presidential Democracy.* Baltimore, MD: Johns Hopkins University Press, 1994.

Neustadt, Richard E. *Presidential Power and the Modern Presidents: The Politics of Leadership from Roosevelt to Reagan.* New York: Free Press, 1990.

Savoie, Donald J. *Court Government and the Collapse of Accountability in Canada and the United Kingdom.* Toronto: University of Toronto Press, 2008.

—————. *Governing from the Centre: The Concentration of Power in Canadian Politics.* Toronto: University of Toronto Press, 1999.

Shapiro, Robert Y., Martha Joynt Kumar, and Lawrence R. Jacobs, eds. *Presidential Power: Forging the Presidency for the Twenty-First Century.* Irvington, NY: Columbia University Press, 2000.

Simpson, Jeffrey. *The Friendly Dictatorship.* Toronto: McClelland & Stewart, 2001.

Smith, David E. *The Invisible Crown: The First Principle of Canadian Government.* Toronto: University of Toronto Press, 1995.

Warwick, Paul. *Government Survival in Parliamentary Democracies.* Cambridge: Cambridge University Press, 1994.

White, Graham. *Cabinets and First Ministers.* Vancouver: University of British Columbia Press, 2005.

PART 4

CHAPTER 28

The Administration

The modern state requires a large administrative apparatus to implement its legislation and policies. The assembly and the executive would be powerless without the support of a massive **administration**, a term that is used here interchangeably with **bureaucracy.** The latter word has acquired many negative connotations relating to delay, inflexibility, and red tape, but it has a particular and indispensable meaning in social science.

THE BUREAUCRATIC ORGANIZATIONAL FORM

Bureaucracy is a particular kind of social structure for carrying out organized work, a structure that has the following characteristics:

- The work is divided into impersonal roles or offices that may be filled by different people as the need arises. Bureaucracies always have job descriptions to ensure that the functions of the positions are stable over time.

- These positions tend to be specialized—another way of saying that there is a high degree of division of labour.

- This specialization demands a career commitment from employees because complex roles can be learned only through long experience.

- Careers are protected by some form of job security or tenure. Usually this means that employees can be dismissed only for designated cause.

- Positions are filled by **merit recruitment,** which normally means competitive examinations. The opposite is recruitment by **political patronage,** which means that jobs are distributed according to kinship, friendship, or personal favour.

- Ideally a bureaucracy is supposed to be a neutral instrument in the hands of those who command it; in this regard it is organized as a hierarchy, with authority flowing from the few at the top to the many at the bottom.

- A bureaucracy minimizes the discretion of its employees, who must work within policies and rules laid down by authority. Found in every bureaucracy are an administrative manual, a rulebook, a policy manual, and extensive written records; all of these help to make administration regular and predictable.

The bureaucratic form of organization is not confined to government. The Roman Catholic Church, as well as General Motors and other large and small corporations, are examples of private bureaucracies. Although bureaucracies were known in ancient empires such as Rome, Egypt, and China, they have been perfected and widely used in the West only in recent times. The absolute monarchs of the eighteenth century created bureaucratic armies, but government administration did not become fully bureaucratized until the late nineteenth and early twentieth centuries. The principle of merit recruitment was not fully accepted in Canada until passage of the Civil Service Act of 1918.

Bureaucracy has many advantages when it runs smoothly—that is why it has been so widely adopted as both a private and public organizational form. When adopted by governments, it ought ideally to exhibit honesty, impartiality, professionalism, stability, predictability, and competence. It has been critiqued, however, for being short on imagination, innovation, and compassion, but presumably these qualities can be found elsewhere in the political system. In theory it should be politically neutral, responding to directions from the assembly and the political executive but not itself making political decisions, and it should enjoy anonymity, with ministers fielding public scrutiny and criticisms for departmental decisions. As we shall see, complete political neutrality is not wholly realistic. The bureaucracy must be considered an independent element in the conversion phase of the political process, not just a passive adjunct to the political executive. The level of anonymity enjoyed by bureaucrats, moreover, has diminished as a result of recent reforms.

The bureaucracy has two fundamental roles in the governmental process: it advises the political executive and it administers the laws and policies enacted by the assembly. Under the first heading, whenever the cabinet wishes to introduce legislation, the preparatory work and the drafting are always done by civil servants. In its administrative role, the bureaucracy is responsible for such matters as distributing child-benefit cheques and veterans' pensions, staffing customs and immigration offices in Canada and abroad, monitoring environmental conditions, regulating transportation, and performing myriad other tasks in the modern welfare-service state.

TYPES OF STATE AGENCIES

The bureaucratic structure is enormously complex. In 2010 there were about 283 000 core employees in the federal public service, excluding the employees of Crown corporations and uniformed military personnel in the Canadian Forces. The budget cuts made by the Chrétien government in the mid-1990s reduced the number of employees over a period of several years, but growth has since resumed. If one counts the number of people working directly or indirectly for the federal government in departments, agencies, boards, Crown corporations, and the military, the total may be more than 500 000. If one adds provincial and municipal employees, including teachers, nurses, police, and firefighters, the total climbs to around three million people. This is undoubtedly a large figure, but whether it is too large is a matter of some debate.

Canadian governments have created several kinds of bureaucracies. Most completely under government control is the public service in the narrow sense; this includes the line departments and other agencies that are directly supervised by ministers, such as Transport Canada and the Canada Border Services Agency. Less thoroughly controlled are the many autonomous or semiautonomous boards, commissions, and Crown corporations. It is difficult to generalize about these bodies because their structures and responsibilities vary greatly with the statutes by which they were created. Students will be most familiar with those Crown corporations that are essentially business enterprises owned by the government, such as Canada Post, Via Rail Canada, and the Canadian Broadcasting Corporation (CBC). Other boards, commissions, and Crown corporations are more regulatory in character—that is, they do not operate large programs of their own but monitor and control the activities of others. Examples of regulatory bodies include the Canadian Radio-television and Telecommunications Commission (CRTC) and the Canadian Transport Commission. **Regulatory agencies** impose public policies on the market in a bid to change personal and organizational behaviours without resorting to public ownership.

The term **Crown corporation** is unique to Canada, but public corporations can be found in almost every nation-state. They used to be numerous in Great Britain, where a great wave of nationalization of key resource and transport industries occurred after World War II. Between 1946 and 1951 the Labour government created the National Coal Board, the British Railways Board, the National Bus Company, the National Freight Corporation, the British Gas Corporation, and the British Steel Corporation. Between 1971 and 1977 the government also acquired a number of ailing industries: Rolls-Royce, British Leyland, the British National Oil Corporation, British Shipbuilders, and British Aerospace. By 1976, nationalized public corporations "accounted for 9.6 percent of GNP and 6.9 percent of employment."[1] But under Margaret Thatcher's Conservative governments, privatization policies adopted in the 1980s resulted in the sale of almost all of these corporations, as well as many others, to the private sector.

Public corporations in the United States are mostly public utilities—for example, electric power companies—managed by independent commissions. These are usually authorized under state law. Amtrak (the national railway passenger service) and the U.S. Postal Service are two public corporations responsible to the federal government. In all cases the public corporation, as an alternative to the conventional civil service, is supposed to offer more business flexibility while remaining linked to the political executive.

At the provincial level in Canada, the same distinction exists between the public service in the narrow sense and semi-independent agencies and Crown corporations. For example, most provinces have monopolistic agencies to market alcoholic beverages;

from a functional point of view, these are businesses that happen to be owned by government. Provincial governments also own, or have owned in the past, a wide range of businesses such as railways, airlines, natural resource companies, utilities, and financial institutions. At the provincial and municipal levels many service agencies have been established by government, and are largely funded by it, but operate more or less autonomously under elected or appointed boards of directors. Public schools, universities, hospitals, and police forces are in this category.

CONTROL OF THE ADMINISTRATION

The basic principle of control of the public service in a parliamentary system is that the bureaucracy should be responsible to the political executive and, through it, to the elected assembly. A minister of the Crown heads each department. Quasi-independent agencies and boards, such as the Canadian Human Rights Commission and the National Parole Board, as well as Crown corporations such as Via Rail and the Bank of Canada, are not directly under ministerial authority but rather are kept at arm's length and simply report to a minister. If the operations of a commission or Crown corporation do not please the cabinet or the assembly, different personnel may be appointed to leadership positions or legislation may be introduced to change the body's terms of reference. The underlying principle is hierarchical control and responsibility, modelled on a pyramid of authority delegated from the sovereign. Power is held in the positions at the top of the hierarchy and flows downwards to positions and levels below.

This political control of bureaucracy in the public sector contrasts with the competitive balance of bureaucracies in the private sector. Private bureaucracies are to some extent a check on each other as corporations compete for dollars and markets. When government offers a non-monopolistic public service, competition provides some control, as in the case of the CBC, but some governmental services are monopolistic, so the competitive model is inapplicable. What remains is the model of authoritative hierarchy and responsibility.

In the British parliamentary tradition, Canada has tried to control the public service by ensuring that it is firmly subordinated to Parliament, as illustrated in Figure 28.1. The basis of the Canadian system is that all executive power emanates from the Crown. The Crown acts only through ministers, who in turn are supposed to be accountable to the House of Commons for their actions. These ministers supervise the machinery of government under their respective portfolios and thus share responsibility for the management of the entire public service. The bureaucracy, as a hierarchy, responds to this direction from above. In this way popular sovereignty is ultimately served and the public service remains a servant of the people, not its master.

Ministers are politicians, not specialists in the business of their portfolios, and they often possess limited managerial expertise. They seldom serve in any one position long enough to build up much technical expertise—in fact, many prime ministers

PART 4

Figure 28.1   Subordination of Bureaucracy to Parliament

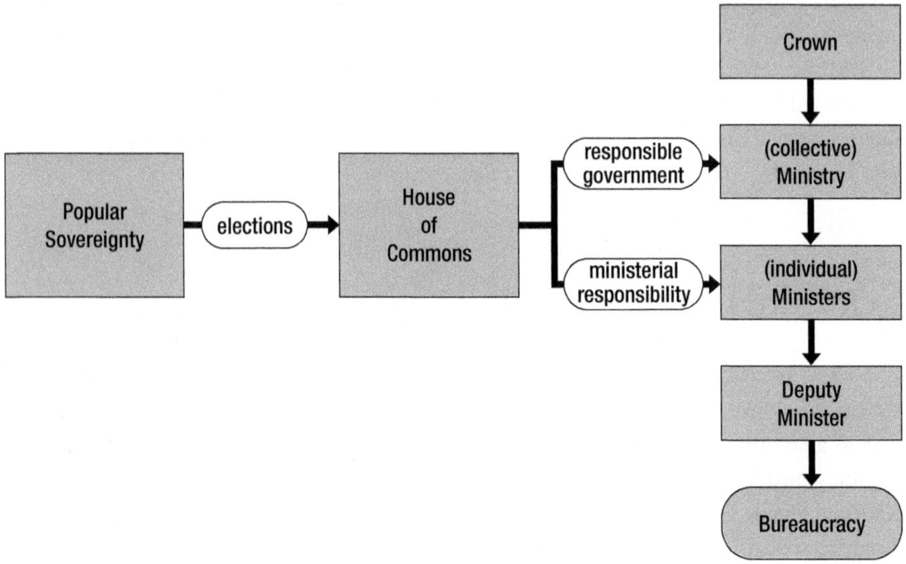

deliberately rotate their ministers to prevent them from becoming too identified with a particular aspect of government. Deputy ministers, in contrast, are not politicians but career civil servants (or, occasionally, administrative experts brought in from the private sector). The prime minister's power to appoint deputy ministers is an important lever for controlling the public service.

Deputy ministers have reached the apex of the bureaucracy; they have been promoted for competence. They run their departments, issuing instructions through assistant deputy ministers down the whole chain of command. Their role is also to offer advice to their ministers, explaining what is or is not administratively feasible. Because of this huge responsibility, deputy ministers serve at the pleasure of the Crown and can be dismissed at any time, but it is not Canadian practice to fire deputy ministers very often. They may be transferred from one department to another, but they are seldom dismissed unless they have been politically indiscreet. This is in sharp contrast to the American custom, which is for the incoming president to make wholesale changes in the top ranks of the federal civil service.

When Barack Obama assumed office in 2009, the transition was overseen by a team of 450 people with a budget of $12 million, and one of its responsibilities was to find ideologically and politically suitable people to fill the more than 3000 appointments he would make, including White House staff, Cabinet, and a number of top advisors. In the United States this so-called transition represents a complete housecleaning; the Democratic transition team presented thousands of new faces for appointment.

In the American system, the changeover in personnel goes far beyond the equivalent of the deputy-minister level; it reaches down five or six layers into the bureaucracy. To some extent the American practice is a survival of the nineteenth-century **spoils system** ("To the winners belong the spoils," President Andrew Jackson is reputed to have said) but it represents more than pure patronage. It is based on the assumption that the political executive—which includes the president and the cabinet—cannot really control the bureaucracy unless it has the support of like-minded administrators at the pinnacle of the civil service. The result is a frank and open politicization of the upper levels of the bureaucracy.

In contrast, Canadian civil servants are assumed to be politically neutral and able to work under a minister from any party. After coming to power in 1984, the new Conservative government of Brian Mulroney threatened to implement an American-style turnover in the civil servants by giving them "pink slips and running shoes," a threat that was never carried out. At the end of nine years in government, Mulroney concluded that he had been well served by the Canadian bureaucracy. When the government of Jean Chrétien came to power in 1993–94, it offered generous early-retirement incentives to the bureaucracy, although this was done more to reduce the size of the civil service than to change its political complexion. For his part, Prime Minister Stephen Harper has made numerous changes at the deputy-minister level, but quietly and gradually, so as not to create an impression of political intrusion.

The Canadian model of administrative control assumes that there is a clear distinction between politics and administration, referred to as the "politics–administration dichotomy." Politics is supposed to be the realm where goals are set and choices are made between options; administration is supposed to be the realm where settled policy is carried into effect. Politics is the business of ministers and administration is the business of deputy ministers—the latter are clearly subordinate to the former. The reality is much less clear-cut than this. Politicians in power depend on information and expert advice from the public service. These administrative officials, with their knowledge and experience, wield real power in the political process. Furthermore, even when legislation is adopted, it will have to be put into effect by the public service, a function that affords a certain amount of discretion. Much may depend on the way a law is put into practice. Modern legislation can provide only a broad framework for implementing programs and policies; the overall impact of this discretion becomes clear only as administrative decisions accumulate.

Equally important in the politics–administration dichotomy to the power of the administration is the power of the politician in the relationship. In order to deliver programs and implement policies in an impartial and neutral manner, administrators must be free from political interference. Neutral application of rules and policies is the cornerstone of predictability and regularity, important objectives in liberal democracies; the bending of rules for political benefit undermines the legitimacy of the administrative arm of the state.

The British television series *Yes Minister* derived its popularity from the way it portrayed the efforts of Jim Hacker, a new and bumbling minister, to control Sir Humphrey Appleby, his cunning and experienced **permanent secretary** (the British

PART 4

equivalent of a deputy minister). Hacker loses almost all the battles, for many reasons. He cannot deal directly with the civil service but must work through the permanent secretary. Sir Humphrey is far more experienced and knowledgeable about the affairs of the department than is Hacker, and he knows that Hacker is likely to last no more than a year or two at this particular ministry. While exaggerated for effect, the underlying premise bears remembering.

We have focused on controls because the civil service is an institution that is difficult to manage, in part because of its size and also given its discretionary power. In an ideal world it is designed to serve the people of its society: the goal is to provide public services for citizens of the society. However, like any large organization, public or private, it may develop internal goals that do not always square with this ideal goal. These internal goals may deviate from the governing body's ideas of the public interest. A police force and prosecutors, for example, may be more interested in conviction than justice. In the transport department, the goal may be to serve the clientele rather than public safety. Keeping the bureaucracy focused on government objectives is fundamental.

Some observers of politics fear that too much power is vested in the public service and that it is not as subordinate as it should be to Cabinet and Parliament. Various reforms have been adopted in an effort to address this issue. As previously mentioned, prime ministers have greatly enlarged their personal staff in the Prime Minister's Office and cabinet staff in the Privy Council Office, with the goal of depending less on the regular public service for advice. As an external control, the federal House of Commons has appointed an independent **auditor general** to review the annual expenditures and activities of the public service. The Public Accounts Committee of the House, to which the auditor general reports, is chaired by a member of the opposition, which gives it greater latitude in investigating possible administrative misuse of funds.

The importance of this type of independent audit was very clear in the "Adscam" scandal. A 2004 report of the auditor general at the time, Sheila Fraser, exposed political improprieties and administrative laxity in the Chrétien government's sponsorship program, a program that ran for several years, beginning in the late 1990s, that tried to combat separatism in Quebec by sponsoring events and public relations campaigns in support of Canadian unity. The auditor general's report showed that, among other things, much of the program spending was poorly documented and monitored, a finding that was supported by the subsequent Gomery Commission of Inquiry. The auditor general's findings were instrumental in uncovering significant problems in the program, which was possible because of the position's political independence.

Over the past 30 years, all provinces except Prince Edward Island have established an **ombudsman** to deal with complaints from individual citizens who feel that bureaucrats have not treated them properly. Typically the ombudsman does not have the authority to grant relief to a complainant. Even so, the power to investigate and expose may be enough to goad the bureaucracy into taking another look at the matter.

The pressure toward a large and powerful bureaucracy stems partly from the public demand for a service-oriented state. Public-opinion polls reveal that while the public believes the bureaucracy to be too large, it is also likely to agree that additional programs are necessary. And while early theories of public administration suggested that the self-interest of bureaucrats was responsible for continued growth and expansion, more recent evidence suggests that top-level bureaucrats are better described as "budget-minimizers" rather than "budget-maximizers," given their attitudes toward checking spending in their own departments.[2] Others have highlighted the potential for control that exists in ensuring that the bureaucracy is representative of the public from which it is drawn: a representative bureaucracy is likely to hold values and beliefs in line with the general public's and as a result will make decisions that are broadly in line with public opinion.[3]

While the tendency toward growth in the bureaucracy is equally strong in private and public bureaucracies, there are stronger countervailing tendencies in the former than in the latter. Business corporations cannot pursue growth to the neglect of profitability; expansion for its own sake will lead to lower rates of return on investment, declining dividends on shares, falling prices on the stock market, and possibly even bankruptcy. The existence of market competition—to the extent that it is effective—is one way to discipline the internal tendencies of the bureaucracy toward expansion for its own sake. Both the McDonald's and Starbucks chains have felt the pain of overexpansion and the pressure of competition in recent years and have responded appropriately. Public bureaucracies, absent the profit-and-loss feedback mechanism, lack this particular countervailing force. If there are checks on this tendency toward self-aggrandizement, one that has been particularly powerful in recent years stems from the financial restrictions placed on bureaucracy by governments.

New Public Management

The traditional model of bureaucracy adopted in Western states has undergone significant reform since the 1980s. The problem came to a head as public spending exceeded public revenues. With the election of Margaret Thatcher (1979), Ronald Reagan (1980), and, to a lesser extent, Brian Mulroney (1984), a philosophical change led to re-evaluation of the role of the state and questioned the need for a large bureaucracy to deliver public services. The conclusion of many governments was that they were trying to do too much and that the administrative arm of government was bloated, inefficient, and ineffective. This triggered the downsizing, privatizing, and deregulation of governments.

In Canada the fiscal crisis of the 1980s and 1990s dictated the necessity of government reforms. These reforms sparked a philosophical debate over their direction and how to continue providing services without public spending deficits. This led the Liberal government to initiate the 1993 "Program Review." This shaped changes within the government of Canada and led to the adoption of balanced budgets in the 1997–98 fiscal year, largely through a 12 percent drop in federal program spending that ended only as a result of the global fiscal crisis in 2008.[4]

Along with these changes came the introduction of managerial reforms in the public service, referred to as **new public management** (NPM). These reforms in the public service were extensive and spawned a significant addition to the public

PART 4

administration literature. One influential book was David Osborne and Ted Gaebler's *Reinventing Government,* which argued for the adoption of a more entrepreneurial, private-sector spirit in the public sector.[5] One of the core principles underlying the reforms was to move away from the idea that bureaucrats ought simply to apply fixed rules to cases, toward the idea that they ought rather to be provided with greater degrees of flexibility, authority, and discretion. Stated differently, the idea was to "let the managers manage" and to encourage them to "steer rather than row."

New public management reforms were adopted to address what were seen as the key problems associated with the traditional bureaucratic model. One was the existence of constraints on efficiency, effectiveness, and economy stemming from a too highly centralized and uniform management structure. Another was the lack of public accountability for public servants' actions and performance. A final concern was the "lethargy that invariably sets in when the management of an organization has a government-imposed monopoly control over the provision of public service."[6]

According to Pollitt and Bouckaert, new public management reforms have included a range of practices and concepts, including

- greater emphasis on performance, through the measurement of outputs;
- a move toward lean, small, flat, and specialized organizational forms over the traditional organizational hierarchy;
- the increased use of contracts over traditional lines of hierarchical control;
- the adoption of market-type mechanisms such as performance pay and competitive tendering; and
- an emphasis on treating service users as customers rather than clients in an effort to adopt a more service-oriented model of delivery.[7]

Since its adoption, NPM reforms have restructured the public service in most Western democracies, although the reforms vary significantly across states and have generated criticisms. Reforms in Canada have been much less dramatic than those of Australia, New Zealand, and Britain, where devolution, external recruitment, and contracting out are the new standard; they have been more dramatic, however, than in states such as Japan with a strong professional bureaucracy that is less amenable to reform. Canada has been identified as a leader in its use of e-government and citizen-centred service-delivery mechanisms—focused on paying serious attention to citizen priorities as defined by citizens—made possible by NPM reforms.[8]

NPM may solve a number of problems in government, but it is not likely to resolve the problem of the role of the state in society. According to one scholar, "In the modern (or para- or post-modern) state, bureaucracy has continued to be, as it has been historically, both solution and problem, an apparatus that provides structure, stability and capacity to modern states but, at the same time, poses challenges to institutions of democratic control and participation."[9]

Questions for Discussion

1. How does the role of public administration differ from that of the political executive?

2. How, if at all, can "success" be measured in the delivery of public goods? What approach have NPM reforms taken to this question?

3. What difficulties do you think accompany the move to make the bureaucracy follow a private-sector management model? Are NPM reforms a positive development? Why or why not?

Internet Links

1. American Society for Public Administration: **www.aspanet.org**.

2. Canada, Departments and Agencies: **www.canada.gc.ca/depts/major/depind-eng .html**.

3. Canada School of Public Service: **www.csps-efpc.gc.ca/index-eng.asp**.

4. Institute of Public Administration of Canada (IPAC): **www.ipac.ca**.

5. United Nations Public Administration Network: **www.unpan.org**.

Further Reading

Albelda, Randy, and Ann Withorn, eds. *Lost Ground: Welfare Reform, Poverty and Beyond.* Cambridge, MA: South End Press, 2002.

Aucoin, Peter. *The New Public Management: Canada in Comparative Perspective.* Montreal: Institute for Research on Public Policy, 1995.

Barzelay, Michael. *The New Public Management: Improving Research and Policy Dialogue.* Berkeley: University of California Press, 2001.

Campbell, Robert Malcolm, Leslie A. Pal, and Michael Howlett. *The Real Worlds of Canadian Politics: Cases in Process and Policy.* 4th ed. Toronto: University of Toronto Press, 2004.

Dilulio, John J. Jr., ed. *Deregulating the Public Service: Can Government Be Improved?* Washington, DC: Brookings Institution, 1994.

Downs, Anthony. *Inside Bureaucracy.* Boston: Little, Brown, 1967.

Dunn, Christopher, ed. *The Handbook of Canadian Public Administration.* 2nd ed. Don Mills, ON: Oxford University Press, 2010.

Dwivedi, O. P., and James Iain Gow. *From Bureaucracy to Public Management: The Administrative Culture of the Government of Canada.* Peterborough, ON: Broadview Press, 1999.

PART 4

Gormley, William T., and Steven J. Balla. *Bureaucracy and Democracy: Accountability and Performance*. Washington, DC: CQ Press, 2003.

Hodgetts, J. E. The *Canadian Public Service: A Physiology of Government, 1867–1970*. Toronto: University of Toronto Press, 1973.

Johnson, David. *Thinking Government: Public Administration and Politics in Canada*. 3rd ed. Toronto: University of Toronto Press, 2011.

Kauffman, Franz-Xavier, ed. *The Public Sector: Challenge for Coordination and Learning*. Berlin: Walter de Gruyter, 1991.

Lynn, Laurence E. Jr. *Public Management: Old and New*. New York: Routledge, 2006.

Miljan, Lydia. *Public Policy in Canada*. 6th ed. Don Mills, ON: Oxford University Press, 2012.

Morgan, Nicole S. *Implosion: An Analysis of the Growth of the Federal Public Service in Canada, 1945–1975*. Montreal: Institute for Research on Public Policy, 1986.

Osbaldeston, Gordon F. *Keeping Deputy Ministers Accountable*. Toronto: McGraw-Hill Ryerson, 1988.

Osborne, David, and Ted Gaebler. *Reinventing Government: How the Entrepreneurial Spirit Is Transforming the Public Sector*. Reading, MA: Addison-Wesley, 1992.

Peters, B. Guy. *The Politics of Bureaucracy*. 2nd ed. New York: Longman, 1984.

Peters, B. Guy, and Donald J. Savoie, eds. *Governance in a Changing Environment*. Montreal: McGill-Queen's University Press, 1995.

———. *Governance in the Twenty-First Century: Revitalizing the Public Service*. Montreal: McGill-Queen's University Press, 1998.

———. *Taking Stock: Assessing the Public Sector Reforms*. Montreal: McGill-Queen's University Press, 1998.

Pollitt, Christopher, and Geert Bouckaert. *Public Management Reform: A Comparative Analysis—New Public Management, Governance and the Neo-Weberian State*. 3rd ed. New York: Oxford University Press, 2011.

Savoie, Donald J. *Breaking the Bargain: Public Servants, Ministers, and Parliament*. Toronto: University of Toronto Press, 2003.

———. *Court Government and the Collapse of Accountability*. Toronto: University of Toronto Press, 2008.

———. *The Politics of Public Spending in Canada*. Toronto: University of Toronto Press, 1990.

Vigoda, Eran, ed. *Public Administration: An Interdisciplinary Critical Analysis*. Boca Raton, FL: CRC Press, 2002.

CHAPTER 29
The Judiciary

Although the judicial system was originally intended to be apolitical, it has now become a key part of the political process. After more than 25 years of living with the Charter of Rights and Freedoms, Canadians have grown to see the courts as an integral part of politics. Political actors now view the courts as an alternative (usually the last alternative) to the legislature, the political executive, and the bureaucracy in matters of achieving policy objectives. We will describe some of the less political functions of the judiciary before returning to its role in political decision-making.

JUDICIAL STRUCTURES

The rule of law is a cornerstone of civilized life. Institutionalized rules (i.e., laws), when applied equally, discourage both public authorities and private individuals from using power arbitrarily. An extension of the rule of law is the court system, where legal disputes are adjudicated. The adjudication of disputes between individuals, between individuals and the state, and between different levels of government within the state takes place within the boundaries of a single country. There are also disputes involving two or more states, and individuals or corporations and other states, which concern breaches of international law. Such disputes may be brought before the International Court of Justice, but the decisions of that body are not binding because no power exists to enforce them; compliance in such cases is voluntary. In this chapter we will not look further at international courts but will confine ourselves to a discussion of domestic law and court systems.

There is no single model for a system of courts; rather, every country seems to adopt a structure of courts in response to its particular needs. In particular, court systems tend to vary between federal and unitary states. In a unitary system there is typically a single set of laws passed by the national legislature and a single system of courts administering justice. In a federal system, in which laws are made by different levels of government, there may be more than one tier of courts: federal courts with responsibility for federal laws and provincial or state courts for provincial or state laws. Moreover, specialized courts may be established to deal with specific laws; for example, tax, labour, family, and juvenile courts can be found in many countries.

Figure 29.1 The American Court System

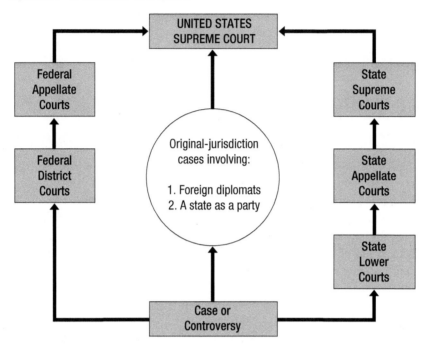

The British courts are an example of court organization in a unitary state. There is a single, unified system and all judges are appointed by the Crown on the advice of the prime minister and/or the Lord Chancellor. Historically the highest court of appeal was the House of Lords, the work being left to a special committee of the Lords with legal expertise. In 2009 the "Law Lords," as they were informally known, were reorganized as the new Supreme Court of the United Kingdom, in order to emphasize the independence of the judiciary from the legislative and executive powers.

The American system makes an instructive contrast to the British because federalism has had such a strong impact on how American courts are organized. As shown in Figure 29.1, the United States has a dual system of courts. Disputes under federal law go before a system of federal courts. The president appoints federal judges, subject to the advice and consent of the Senate. In addition, each of the 50 states maintains its own system of courts, with a state supreme court at the top. There is great diversity among these systems: in some judges are appointed by the state governor; in others, they are popularly elected. Although federal and state courts are organizationally distinct, they are not completely isolated from one another. For one thing, many cases can go to either federal or state court because federal and state laws overlap. Kidnapping, for example, is an offence in all states and also becomes a federal crime if state lines are crossed, so an accused kidnapper may often be tried in either system. Also, the federal Supreme Court exercises appellate jurisdiction over the supreme courts of the states if federal or constitutional questions are involved.

Figure 29.2 The Canadian Court System

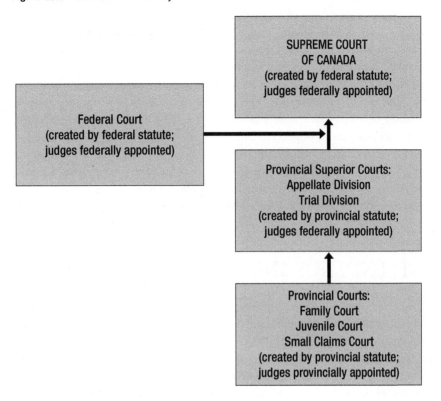

The Canadian arrangement falls between the British and the American. Figure 29.2 shows that the system is fundamentally unified. The Federal Court of Canada deals with certain specialized matters of federal administrative law: claims against the Crown, taxation, customs duties, immigration, and so on. All other cases are heard in the provincially organized courts at one level or another. The provinces maintain their own **provincial courts** for such matters as small claims and minor criminal offences. The judges of the **superior courts** are all appointed by the governor general on the advice of the cabinet. According to long-standing practice, the prime minister personally selects the members of the Supreme Court of Canada and the chief justices of the other superior courts, while the minister of justice selects all other federally appointed judges.

Each province organizes its superior courts in a distinctive way. The provinces also provide the support personnel and services required by the courts. Canada's courts are thus a practical compromise between the unitary and federal approaches to court organization. The power of the provinces to organize their provincial and superior courts as they wish recognizes the diversity of local conditions, but the system is pushed toward uniformity of interpretation by the federal power of appointment and by the overall appellate jurisdiction of the Supreme Court of Canada.

PART 4

The apex of the Canadian court system is the Supreme Court of Canada, which is the highest court of appeal. This does not mean that every appeal will reach the Supreme Court, for the justices often deny leave to appeal, allowing the decisions of lower courts to stand. The Supreme Court has not always been the highest court of appellate jurisdiction. Before 1949 its decisions could be appealed to the Judicial Committee of the Privy Council in Britain, the highest court of appeal for the British Empire and the Commonwealth. The removal of the Judicial Committee's appellate jurisdiction over Canadian cases was another step in Canada's gradual emancipation from British institutions of government.

The Supreme Court is made up of nine justices, of whom one is the chief justice. Three of the justices must be from Quebec, a stipulation that reflects a previously discussed peculiarity in that province's legal system—while other provinces rely on the British common-law tradition, Quebec has its own *code civil* for matters of private law.

INDEPENDENCE AND ACCESS

The professed object of a court system in a liberal democracy is to administer justice equally to all citizens. Unequal treatment before the law constitutes a violation of one of the fundamental principles of liberal democracy. Here we can mention some of the main factors that determine whether equality before the law is realized in practice.

There must be **judicial independence** from direct political interference, which can be guaranteed in a number of ways. The principle of tenure in office (serving "during good behaviour") ensures that judges cannot be discharged except for violation of law or gross impropriety of conduct. In the United States, Congress is constitutionally barred from lowering judges' salaries while they are in office (although neglecting to grant periodic raises may have the same effect in an inflationary age). In Canada, independent commissions now make recommendations to cabinets on judicial salaries. In spite of such safeguards, politicians may still try to influence judges, either by criticizing them in public or through more subtle private communications. In Canada in the 1970s and 1980s, several ministers had to resign from the federal cabinet after trying to influence judges. Judicial independence, probably the single greatest institutional support of the rule of law, can never be taken for granted.

The courts must be efficient. Cases before the courts must be handled expeditiously. Lives can be ruined if individuals are held in custody for a long time awaiting a criminal trial, or if payment of compensation in a civil suit is indefinitely postponed by legal manoeuvres. Court rulings must also be consistent, so that similar punishment is imposed for similar crimes. The sentencing practices of judges have long been debated by law-reform commissions. There is no way to guarantee that judges in Halifax and in Toronto, or even two judges in the same city, will apply the same penalty for similar crimes. Penalties written into the law contain some latitude, and for good reason: judges usually take account of the particular circumstances surrounding a crime, and their interpretations of the severity of a crime may vary greatly. We will undoubtedly never find uniformity when punishing violators of the law, but there must be some common denominator or, again, the system will be questioned.

A final problem involves the cost of obtaining justice in the court system. Lawyers, especially good ones, are expensive—much too expensive for all except the very wealthy or those with corporate backing. The poor can get free or inexpensive legal services through legal aid, but this helps only the very poor, leaving ordinary people of modest resources facing a legal system that is often far too costly for their use. In practice, lawyers' fees for litigation that goes on for any length of time are often paid by governments or by other organizations that have deep pockets and are interested in the outcome.

THE JUDICIARY IN THE POLITICAL PROCESS

Canadian courts are strictly neutral with respect to partisan politics, but they still play an important role in the political process. Their decisions about cases sometimes have the same effect as legislative outputs from Parliament or policy outputs from the executive or bureaucracy, or even amendments to the Constitution. Of course, most cases that come before the courts do not have such sweeping implications; they merely require the application of a known principle of law to a particular situation. But occasionally there is no precedent that really applies to the case, or perhaps the dispute hinges on interpretation of the wording of statutory or constitutional language. In such instances the court's decision—in that it becomes a precedent for subsequent decisions of other courts—is a source of law just as if a statute had been passed or amended.

A good example of the potential importance of statutory construction is furnished by a series of court decisions in Manitoba in the late 1970s and early 1980s that had the effect of abolishing mandatory retirement in that province. The courts held that the wording of the prohibition of age discrimination in the Manitoba Human Rights Act made it illegal for employers and unions to negotiate contracts with a fixed age of retirement. Public statements from members of the cabinet who had brought in the legislation made it clear that they had not intended it to have any effect on retirement plans, but courts construe the words of statutes, not the statements of politicians. The effect was a major change in public policy brought about without any of the normal processes of study by experts and debate in the legislature.[1]

An important example of constitutional interpretation is the celebrated *Persons* case of 1929. Section 24 of the Constitution Act, 1867, allows "qualified persons" to be appointed to the Senate. At the time the Act was passed, *persons* was a technical legal

PART 4

term that generally referred only to adult males. When Prime Minister Mackenzie King wanted to appoint the first woman to the Senate, it was not clear whether the words "qualified persons" included women, but the Judicial Committee of the Privy Council held that women were persons within the meaning of the Act.[2] The case was political in at least two ways: because it changed law and policy to allow women to sit in the Senate, it was virtually the equivalent of a constitutional amendment; because it signalled a remarkable victory for women as a group, it helped lead to subsequent improvements in their status. In this instance, a judicial decision provided an easier means than formal constitutional amendment for recognizing the emerging social consensus in favour of equal political rights for women.

Judicial Review

Another political role of the courts is judicial review. Essentially, judicial review is a court ruling on the constitutionality of legislation or executive action. The concept was mentioned in our earlier discussion of federalism because disputes often arise in federal systems, where legislative powers are granted to different levels of government. Because the distribution of powers is often not entirely clear or there may be overlapping responsibilities, jurisdictional disputes invariably arise between levels of government.

Judicial review exists in both Canada and the United States, as in most federal systems. However, it has had a different character in each country—at least it did before the adoption of the **Canadian Charter of Rights and Freedoms**. Before 1982, judicial review in Canada mainly involved the courts' deciding which assembly, provincial or federal, possessed legislative power under the Constitution Act, 1867. Having decided which was the appropriate legislature, the Canadian courts seldom used judicial review to challenge legislative wisdom. Also before 1982, there was no Canadian equivalent to a constitutional bill of rights placing limits on what any legislature, provincial or federal, could do. The United States has long had such an entrenched document, and it has made American courts more self-confident about ruling legislation *ultra vires*— that is, beyond the constitutional power of a legislature to enact.[3]

The power of the courts to interpret and even set aside legislation, coupled with their relative independence from the assembly and the executive, makes them an attractive alternative for interest groups that lack influence with other decision-making bodies. In the United States, the National Association for the Advancement of Colored People (NAACP) pursued litigation for decades to challenge legal segregation of the races. The case of *Brown v. Board of Education* (1954), in which the Supreme Court held segregated schools to be unconstitutional, is the most famous result of their work. Similar strategies have also paid off in Canada. In Manitoba, the trivial matter of a parking ticket became the case of *Forest v. the Queen*, which led to the ruling that Manitoba, established as an officially bilingual province by the Manitoba Act, 1870, must publish all its statutes in both English and French—an extraordinary victory that the francophone minority of that province could never have won in the legislature.[4]

Interest groups now pursue strategies of litigation as calculatingly as they lobby the assembly for legislation. The four basic steps of such strategic litigation are described in a document produced by the Canadian Advisory Council on the Status of Women:

1. defining a goal in terms of the desired principle of law to be established;

2. plotting how the principle of law can be established from case to case in incremental, logical, and clear steps;

3. selecting winnable cases suitable for each stage taken to achieve the goal; and

4. consolidating wins of each stage by bringing similar cases to create a cluster of cases in support of the principle established.[5]

The most successful practitioner of strategic litigation in Canada has undoubtedly been the feminist Legal Education and Action Fund. LEAF has been associated with most of the major cases involving the legal rights of women in areas such as abortion, employment opportunities, and protection against violence. In some cases LEAF has actually sponsored the litigation (i.e., paid for legal representation); more frequently, though, it has **intervened**—with the permission of the court, it presents its views on the law without actually representing a client. LEAF has also supported research useful to its cause and offered orientation sessions to judges to sensitize them to women's issues.

Aboriginal people are also making sophisticated use of strategic litigation. The *Delgamuukw* decision (1997) established that Aboriginal rights and title had never been extinguished in the province of British Columbia because no land-surrender treaties had been signed there.[6] The province and the federal government are now engaged in a complicated process of negotiation with British Columbia First Nations to sign modern treaties. In 1999 the Supreme Court held in the two *Marshall* decisions that "status Indians" in Atlantic Canada have a treaty right to fish commercially for eels, and by implication to participate in other fisheries.[7] This ruling touched off violent confrontations between Native and non-Native fishers before the federal government could sort out their relative shares in the lucrative lobster fishery.

Judicial Activism

Strategic litigation dovetails well with the growing activism of courts. **Judicial activism**, defined as the willingness of judges to overturn legislation or executive action, has been a feature of American politics for decades. In the 1930s the U.S. Supreme Court initially ruled much of Franklin Roosevelt's New Deal legislation unconstitutional. In one period from 1935 to 1937, the court held 12 acts of Congress *ultra vires*. There was then a sudden shift in the court's decisions after the president threatened to "pack" it by expanding its size and appointing members who shared his ideology of reform liberalism. In this instance judicial activism was a weapon of the ideological right, but it can be used equally to forward the aims of the left.

PART 4

The U.S. Supreme Court was particularly active between 1954 and 1969, while Earl Warren was chief justice. The Warren court struck down racial segregation, compelled the states to draw constituency lines to approximate "one man, one vote," greatly enhanced the rights of those accused of crimes, outlawed prayer in public schools, and in many other ways wrought unprecedented changes in the social fabric of the United States. When courts begin to decide so many questions of policy, they have plainly become politicized. There is in all of this a difficult question of democratic theory, for judges, after all, are appointed, not elected. Is it compatible with the idea of representative government to have so many questions settled by appointed officials who serve for life and never have to confront the voters?[8]

Since adoption of the Charter of Rights and Freedoms in 1982, Canadian courts have become more "constitutionalized"; that is, many more court cases involve constitutional disputes over the rights of women, immigrants, and gays and lesbians and in the fields of language and education, as well as over the powers of the federal and provincial governments. Alan Cairns even suggests that the Charter "is a consciousness-raising instrument that has profoundly changed Canadian constitutional culture." And this prominent place of the Charter in our politics has produced both critics, who feel that it has "shifted more public policy powers to an unelected legal elite," and supporters, who feel it "is a progressive change" that has improved "the quality of laws and state actions."[9]

Often we label judges who offer broad interpretations of the constitution as being liberal and judges who narrowly define the constitution as being conservative. In his book *The Judge in a Democracy,* Aharon Barak, a Supreme Court justice in Israel, explains the problem with using these labels:

> It would be a mistake to define an activist judge as a liberal judge and a restrained judge as a conservative judge. Liberal and conservative are appropriate terms to evaluate the results of the judicial activity. For example, from the turn of the twentieth century until the end of the 1930s, the United States Supreme Court was an activist conservative court that invalidated a number of statutes that sought to recognize individual rights. The Warren Court of the 1970s was an activist liberal court. And today's United States Supreme Court, whose majority is conservative, behaves as an activist court in many areas of law. A liberal judge like Brandeis was viewed as a judge who exercised self-restraint; a conservative judge like Scalia is seen as an activist judge. Definitions of activism and self-restraint should therefore address the way judicial discretion is exercised, irrespective of the evaluation of the outcome.

Barak goes on to say that "we should not assume that judges can be divided according to those who are always activists and those who always exercise self-restraint. This absolute approach is inconsistent with a judge's need to act within the framework of his zone of discretion, which at various times will demand more or less activism and more or less self-restraint."[10]

In any case, the Canadian courts are heavily involved in political decision-making, and that gives new urgency to debates over how judges, who now have so much decision-making power, should be appointed. The process for appointing judges to the Supreme Court of Canada concentrates power in the hands of the prime minister, leading to calls for reform.

Appointments to the Supreme Court of Canada

Political scientist Ted Morton has written that "Canada now has an American style Supreme Court with an unreformed British style appointment system."[11] The appointment system is a contentious issue because we straddle two conflicting principles. On the one hand, democracy today requires an independent judiciary that can render objective, unbiased decisions free of interference by legislators. On the other hand, in selecting individuals for the judiciary, we are choosing people who may have been active in partisan politics and who have discretionary powers as members of the judiciary. As Peter Russell says, "The one clear conclusion to be taken from the accounts of appointing judges … is that no matter how the process is constructed it always has a political dimension."[12]

In the United States, the problem is addressed in part by the constitutional requirement that the Senate approve the federal judges nominated by the president. Because of the acknowledged policymaking role of the courts, and particularly of the Supreme Court, it is now commonly accepted that the Senate will interrogate nominees to that body about their political philosophy as well as about their legal competence and personal character. In 1987 the Senate rejected Ronald Reagan's nomination of Robert Bork to the Supreme Court. No one could impugn Bork's character or competence, but the Senate found him to be too conservative. George H. W. Bush's nomination of Clarence Thomas precipitated yet another bitter Senate hearing; Thomas's character and competence were challenged along with his conservative ideology. Ironically, Thomas was confirmed and Bork was not, at least partly because Bork's prolific writings had made his views abundantly clear, whereas Thomas's were less well documented. Whatever one may think of these hearings, they at least draw attention to the political consequences of judicial appointments and bring political factors into the process.

In Canada, transparency has been the problem with Supreme Court appointments. The tradition has been for superior court judges to be appointed by order-in-council without any public hearings. In practice that means selection by the minister of justice for most appointments and by the prime minister for members of the Supreme Court of Canada and the chief justices of other courts. In 2004 Paul Martin introduced a new wrinkle by allowing a parliamentary committee to review the names of two new appointees to the Supreme Court of Canada. Prime Minister Harper continued the practice in 2006, when he appointed Marshall Rothstein to fill a vacancy on the Supreme Court. In that instance Rothstein appeared in person before a House committee and answered questions from the members.

PART 4

In 2011 two Supreme Court justices, Ian Binnie and Louise Charron, resigned. In May 2011 the Prime Minister's Office announced the process for filling these vacancies. The process can be summarized as follows:

1. The minister of justice and the attorney general consult with leading members of the legal community and invite members of the public to submit names of qualified candidates who merit consideration for the appointment.

2. The list of qualified candidates is reviewed by a Supreme Court selection panel made up of five members of parliament: three members from the government caucus and one member each from the recognized opposition caucuses.

3. The panel assesses the candidates and provides an unranked short list of six qualified candidates to the prime minister and the minister of justice for consideration.

4. The two selected nominees appear before a public hearing of an ad hoc parliamentary committee to answer questions from members of parliament.

The prime minister's choices, Andromache Karakatsanis and Michael Moldaver, appeared before parliamentary hearings in October 2011 and their swearing-in ceremony took place in November 2011. The process was similar to the one used in the appointment of Marshall Rothstein in 2006. While this process is no direct check on the power of the prime minister, it does appear that the selection of Canadian Supreme Court justices is becoming more transparent.

The Notwithstanding Clause

There is an additional form of political balance in Canada, namely Section 33 of the Charter, the so-called **notwithstanding clause**. This clause allows Parliament and the provincial legislatures to enact legislation even if the courts hold it to be in conflict with certain sections of the Charter (Sections 2 and 7–15). This "legislative review of judicial review," as Peter Russell has called it, is a unique way of elevating democratic government over the decisions of unelected judges. However, this tool has not been used very frequently. The fact that the override can be applied for only five years at a time, after which it expires unless it is passed again by the legislature, creates difficulties for governments seeking to get around a court decision. It might buy a little time to bring in some other legislation, but it is not an attractive long-term solution.

In 1989 Quebec's National Assembly invoked the notwithstanding clause to protect its language legislation from judicial review. This use of Section 33 was subject to the five-year limitation in Section 33(3). The Supreme Court had held that the law violated freedom of speech inasmuch as it prohibited the posting of commercial signs in languages other than French. In response, Premier Robert Bourassa's government introduced Bill 178, to allow commercial signs inside buildings in languages other than French, as long as French signs were also present and at least equally prominent. It then invoked the notwithstanding clause to make sure this "inside/outside" legislation would not be upset in the courts.

In 1993 Bourassa introduced more permissive legislation, hoping that it would survive judicial challenges so that use of the notwithstanding clause would not be necessary. This illustrates the importance of the five-year limitation. If there had been no such limitation, it would have been easier for the Quebec government to leave Bill 178 on the books; under Section 33 it was forced to review the matter.

LIFE IN CHARTERLAND

The adoption in 1982 of the Canadian Charter of Rights and Freedoms as part of the Constitution accelerated the growth of judicial activism. The guarantee of individual rights and freedoms now depends on the Constitution and on the courts' protection of the Charter's principles. Constitutional sovereignty has challenged parliamentary sovereignty because the courts can declare laws *ultra vires*—that is, unconstitutional. Parliament, however, can fight back. If the government or members of parliament feel the courts are invading their jurisdiction, they can, with popular support, change the Constitution. However, as was mentioned in Part One, formally changing the Constitution is no easy task. Additionally, Parliament or a provincial legislature may invoke the notwithstanding clause, although this is done only in rare cases. This fundamental change in constitutional law in Canada will by no means work itself out overnight. Individuals and groups now use the courts frequently to challenge the constitutionality of particular federal and provincial laws.

The reason for adopting the Charter, it was explained to the Canadian public, was to advance toward the ideal of rule of law in a liberal democracy. The Charter would prevent governments, no matter how strong their majority support, from violating the rights of individuals or minorities. While this is undoubtedly true, there is another aspect of the Charter that cannot be overlooked: it involves an extensive transfer of decision-making power from legislatures to the courts. The rights enunciated in the Charter are necessarily described in such broad language that they become meaningful only through judicial interpretation.

To take one example, Section 10 of the Charter reads in part: "Everyone has the right on arrest or detention ... (b) to retain and instruct counsel without delay and to be informed of that right." The *Therens* case, decided in 1985 by the Supreme Court of Canada, hinged on the precise meaning of the word *detention*.[13] After an automobile accident in Moose Jaw, Saskatchewan, Therens was requested by a police officer to come to the police station to take a breathalyzer test (to refuse this request is itself a violation of the Criminal Code). Therens complied and was later prosecuted for driving while impaired. At the trial, Therens's counsel moved for dismissal of the breathalyzer evidence because the police constable had not informed Therens of his right to retain counsel. The legal question—ultimately decided in the affirmative by the Supreme Court—was whether being asked to go to the police station to give a breath sample amounted to detention.

PART 4

A related question was whether evidence obtained in violation of Section 10(b) might be introduced anyway. Section 24(2) of the Charter states that "the evidence shall be excluded if it is established that, having regard to all the circumstances, the admission of it in the proceedings would bring the administration of justice into disrepute." Again the courts were required to interpret abstract words. The Supreme Court upheld the view of the lower courts that to admit such evidence would in fact bring the administration of justice into disrepute.

The point here is not whether the decision was right or wrong but where decision-making power is located. Parliament, in providing for check-stop procedures under the Criminal Code, had not explicitly said that those requested to "breathe into the box" should be informed of their right to retain counsel. By interpreting the generalized language of the Charter, the courts laid down a new rule that is just as binding as if it had been legislated by Parliament. See Canadian Focus 29.1 for more on rights.

Canadian Focus 29.1

The Rights Revolution

The growing importance of the courts in Canadian politics is not an isolated phenomenon. In the period since World War II, many other countries have also adopted bills of rights, enlarged the scope of judicial review, and in other ways transferred more decision-making power to courts. Many authors refer to these developments as part of a "rights revolution."

In the 2000 Massey Lectures, Canadian-born author Michael Ignatieff (leader of the Liberal Party 2009–11) developed an interesting thesis on human rights. The "rights revolution," he said, has grown with democracy; in fact, "rights talk" in society "has transformed how we think about ourselves as citizens, as men and women, and as parents." The revolution is making "our democracy more inclusive by incorporating groups and individuals who were marginalized or excluded." At the same time, attaining human rights is a difficult task, one not easy to achieve in the best of democracies. One problem is that we are "enhancing our right to be equal and protecting our right to be different. Trying to do both—that is enhancing equality, while safeguarding difference—is the essential challenge of the rights revolution."

Thus the rights revolution does not make democracy any easier. Indeed, it "makes society harder to control, more unruly, more contentious." Nevertheless, there are certainly benefits. Today "we have learned that the preconditions of order are simple: equal protection under the law, coupled with the capacity for different peoples to behave towards each other not as members of tribes or clans, but as citizens."

Source: Michael Ignatieff, *The Rights Revolution* (Toronto: Canadian Broadcasting Corporation and House of Anansi Press, 2000), 1, 2, 6, 14, 141.

After its proclamation on 17 April 1982, the Charter's effects were at first felt largely in the field of criminal law. Most frequently litigated in the early years were such rights as the right to security against unreasonable search or seizure and the right to counsel. Numerically, the main groups resorting to Charter arguments in the courts were those accused either of driving while impaired or of selling illegal drugs.[14] Because the courts obviously have great expertise in criminal law, the transfer of decision-making power from government and Parliament did not seem problematic. Outside the field of criminal law, only a few early Supreme Court decisions based on the Charter had broad consequences.

This situation, however, has gradually been changing since the proclamation on 17 April 1985 of the **equality rights** section of the Charter, Section 15(1), which reads: "Every individual is equal before and under the law and has the right to the equal protection and equal benefit of the law without discrimination and, in particular, without discrimination based on race, national or ethnic origin, colour, religion, sex, age or mental or physical disability." Federal and provincial statute books contain literally thousands of clauses authorizing differential treatment based on the criteria mentioned in Section 15(1). To mention only a few examples, one generally has to be 16 to obtain a driver's licence and 18 to vote; publicly supported athletic competitions are usually divided into classes by sex; physically and mentally disabled children are subject to special treatment of many kinds in the public schools. Proclamation of Section 15 was delayed for three years, from 1982 to 1985, in order to give Parliament and the provincial legislatures time to amend such laws so that they conformed to the Charter, but many of them remain on the books because they seem reasonably justifiable. (Is it really age discrimination to require a minimum age to obtain a driver's licence?) However, since Section 15 has been proclaimed, the courts are inevitably drawn into deciding whether particular rules or policies are discriminatory.

As mentioned previously, some analysts, such as political scientists Ted Morton and Rainer Knopff, are critical of judicial activism and fear that Canadian democracy will be undermined by too much reliance on the rulings of unelected judges. On the other side of the debate, Peter Hogg, dean of Osgoode Hall Law School, and his student Allison Thornton developed a counter-argument around the concept of **dialogue**. In their view, court decisions are seldom final in any practical sense; they almost always leave room for the government of the day to take further action if it wishes. At the extreme, the government can invoke the notwithstanding clause, or, more moderately, it can revise existing statutes or introduce new legislation that will withstand judicial scrutiny. Thus judicial review under the Charter does not mean unchecked judicial supremacy. In the words of Hogg and Thornton,

> A critique of the Charter of Rights based on its supposed usurpation of democratic legitimacy simply cannot be sustained. To be sure, the Supreme Court of Canada is a non-elected, unaccountable group of middle-aged lawyers. To be sure, from time to time the Court strikes down statutes enacted by accountable, representative legislative

PART 4

The Supreme Court of Canada.

bodies. But the decisions of the Court almost always leave room for a legislative response, and they usually receive a legislative response. In the end, if the democratic will is there, a legislative way will be found to achieve the objective, albeit with some new safeguards to protect individual rights. Judicial review is not "a veto over the politics of the nation" but rather the beginning of a dialogue on how best to reconcile the individualistic values of the Charter with the accomplishment of social and economic policies enacted for the benefit of the community as a whole.[15]

Because the courts are now so much a part of the political system, students of political science cannot help but hear more of this debate in years to come.

Questions for Discussion

1. What is judicial review and what is its significance in liberal democracies?

2. Why is judicial independence critical to democracy? In what case does judicial accountability become similarly critical? Given its function, has the Canadian judiciary struck the appropriate balance between judicial independence and judicial accountability?

3. Do you think Canadian courts are too activist? How can Parliament respond to a judicial ruling it disagrees with?

Internet Links

1. The Court: **www.thecourt.ca**. Osgoode Hall Law School's blog on recent Supreme Court of Canada decisions.

2. Jurist Canada: **http://jurist.law.utoronto.ca**. The Canadian version of the U.S. "Legal Education Network."

3. Lexum: scc.lexum.org. Full texts of all Supreme Court decisions as well as decisions of some other courts, plus various other forms of legal information.

4. *Osgoode Hall Law Journal*: **www.ohlj.ca**.

5. Supreme Court of Canada: **www.scc-csc.gc.ca**.

6. Supreme Court of the United States: **www.supremecourt.gov**.

Further Reading

Baker, Dennis. *Not Quite Supreme: The Courts and Coordinate Constitutional Interpretation*. Montreal and Kingston: McGill-Queen's University Press, 2010.

Barak, Aharon. *The Judge in a Democracy*. Princeton, NJ: Princeton University Press, 2006.

Bateman, Thomas M. J., Janet L. Hiebert, Rainer Knopff, and Peter H. Russell. *The Court and the Charter: Leading Cases*. Toronto: Emond Montgomery, 2008.

Bogart, W. A. *Courts and Country: The Limits of Litigation and the Social and Political Life of Canada*. Toronto: Oxford University Press, 1994.

Cairns, Alan C. *Charter versus Federalism: The Dilemmas of Constitutional Reform*. Montreal: McGill-Queens University Press, 1992.

———. *Disruptions: Constitutional Struggles, from the Charter to Meech Lake*. Toronto: McClelland & Stewart, 1991.

Epp, Charles R. *The Rights Revolution: Lawyers, Activists, and Supreme Courts in Comparative Perspective*. Chicago: University of Chicago Press, 1998.

Geyh, Charles Gardner. *When Courts and Congress Collide: The Struggle for Control of America's Judicial System*. Ann Arbor: University of Michigan Press, 2006.

Hiebert, Janet L. *Charter Conflicts: What Is Parliament's Role?* Montreal and Kingston: McGill-Queen's University Press, 2002.

Horner, Jessie. *Canadian Law and the Canadian Legal System*. Toronto: Pearson Education Canada, 2006.

Ignatieff, Michael. *The Rights Revolution*. Toronto: Canadian Broadcasting Corporation and House of Anansi Press, 2000.

Knopff, Rainer, and F. L. Morton. *Charter Politics*. Scarborough, ON: Nelson Canada, 1992.

PART **4**

Kulchyski, Peter, ed. *Unjust Relations: Aboriginal Rights in Canadian Courts*. Toronto: Oxford University Press, 1994.

Malleson, Kate, and Peter H. Russell, eds. *Appointing Judges in an Age of Judicial Power: Critical Perspectives from around the World*. Toronto: University of Toronto Press, 2006.

Mandel, Michael. *The Charter of Rights and the Legalization of Politics*. Toronto: Thompson Educational, 1994.

Manfredi, Christopher P. *Feminist Activism in the Supreme Court: Legal Mobilization and the Women's Legal Education and Action Fund*. Vancouver: University of British Columbia Press, 2004.

———. *Judicial Power and the Charter: Canada and the Paradox of Liberal Constitutionalism*. Toronto: Oxford University Press, 2000.

Martin, Robert Ivan. *The Most Dangerous Branch: How the Supreme Court of Canada Has Undermined Our Law and Our Democracy*. Montreal and Kingston: McGill-Queen's University Press, 2003.

McCormick, Peter. *Canada's Courts: A Social Scientist's Ground-Breaking Account of the Canadian Judicial System*. Toronto: James Lorimer, 1994.

———. *Supreme at Last: The Evolution of the Supreme Court of Canada*. Toronto: James Lorimer, 2000.

McCormick, Peter, and Ian Greene. *Judges and Judging: Inside the Canadian Judicial System*. Toronto: James Lorimer, 1990.

Morton, F. L. *Law, Politics and the Judicial Process in Canada*. 3rd ed. Calgary: University of Calgary Press, 2002.

———. *Morgentaler v. Borowski: Abortion, the Charter, and the Courts*. Toronto: McClelland & Stewart, 1992.

Morton, F. L., and Rainer Knopff. *The Charter Revolution and the Court Party*. Peterborough, ON: Broadview Press, 2000.

Perry, Michael J. *The Constitution in the Courts: Law or Politics?* New York: Oxford University Press, 1994.

Powers, Stephen, and Stanley Rothman. *The Least Dangerous Branch? Consequences of Judicial Activism*. Westport, CT: Greenwood, 2002.

Roach, Kent. *The Supreme Court on Trial: Judicial Activism or Democratic Dialogue*. Toronto: Irwin Law, 2001.

Russell, Peter H., and Paul Howe, eds. *Judicial Power and Canadian Democracy*. Montreal: McGill-Queen's University Press, 2001.

Saywell, John T. *The Lawmakers: Judicial Power and the Shaping of Canadian Federalism*. Toronto: University of Toronto Press, 2002.

Notes

PREFACE

1. E. D. Hirsch Jr., *The Schools We Need: And Why We Don't Have Them* (New York: Doubleday, 1996), 156.

INTRODUCTION

1. David M. Ricci, *The Tragedy of Political Science: Politics, Scholarship, and Democracy* (New Haven: Yale University Press, 1984), 60–61.

2. Alan C. Cairns, "Political Science in Canada and the Americanization Issue," *Canadian Journal of Political Science* 8 (1975): 196.

3. Thomas Flanagan, *Game Theory and Canadian Politics* (Toronto: University of Toronto Press, 1998).

4. Donald P. Green and Ian Shapiro, *Pathologies of Rational Choice Theory: A Critique of Applications in Political Science* (New Haven: Yale University Press, 1994).

CHAPTER 1: GOVERNMENT AND POLITICS

1. "Politics," Wikipedia, http://en.wikipedia.org/wiki/Politics.

2. Lewis Carroll, *Through the Looking Glass (and What Alice Found There)*, chap. 6, http://www.alice-in-wonderland.net/books/alice-in-wonderland-quotes.html.

3. Thomas Hobbes, *Leviathan* (New York: E. P. Dutton, 1950), chap. 4, 27.

4. Frans de Waal, *Chimpanzee Politics: Power and Sex among Apes* (Baltimore: Johns Hopkins University Press, 1982).

5. Bertrand de Jouvenel, *The Pure Theory of Politics* (New Haven, CT: Yale University Press, 1963), 30.

6. J. D. B. Miller, *The Nature of Politics* (Harmondsworth, UK: Penguin, 1965), 14.

7. Alan R. Ball, *Modern Politics and Government* (London: Macmillan, 1971), 20.

8. Harold D. Lasswell, *Politics: Who Gets What, When, How* (New York: Peter Smith, 1950). First published in 1936.

9. David Easton, *A Systems Analysis of Political Life* (New York: John Wiley and Sons, 1965), 21.

10. Jouvenel, *Pure Theory of Politics,* 204–12.

11. Bernard Crick, *In Defence of Politics,* rev. ed. (Chicago: University of Chicago Press, 1972), 22.

12. Alexander H. Harcourt and Frans B. M. de Waal, eds., *Coalitions and Alliances in Humans and Other Animals* (Oxford: Oxford University Press, 1992), 3.

13. Brian Topp, *How We Almost Gave the Tories the Boot: The Inside Story behind the Coalition* (Toronto: James Lorimer, 2010).

14. Norman Cohn, *The Pursuit of the Millennium,* rev. ed. (New York: Oxford University Press, 1970).

15. John Gray, *Black Mass: Apocalyptic Religion and the Death of Utopia* (Toronto: Doubleday Canada, 2007).

16. V. I. Lenin, "The State and Revolution," in *Selected Works*, vol. 2 (Moscow: Progress Publishers, 1967), 345.

17. Marx himself did not use the term "withering away of the state"; it was popularized by his collaborator Friedrich Engels. See his "Socialism: Utopian and Scientific," in Karl Marx and Friedrich Engels, *Selected Works* (Moscow: Progress Publishers, 1968), 417–36.

CHAPTER 2: POWER, LEGITIMACY, AND AUTHORITY

1. Stuart Schram, ed., *The Political Thought of Mao Tse-tung* (New York: Praeger, 1963), 209.

2. R. M. MacIver, *The Web of Government,* rev. ed. (New York: Free Press, 1965), 64.

3. Carl J. Friedrich, *Man and His Government: An Empirical Theory of Politics* (New York: McGraw-Hill, 1963), 225.

4. H. H. Gerth and C. W. Mills, eds. and trans., *From Max Weber*, part 2 (New York: Oxford University Press, 1950).

5. Alexis de Tocqueville, *Democracy in America,* ed. Andrew Hacker (New York: Washington Square Press, 1964), 9–10.

6. Cited in Reinhard Bendix, *Max Weber: An Intellectual Portrait* (Garden City, NY: Doubleday, 1960), 88 n. 15.

7. Cited in J. G. Ismael and T. Y. Ismael, "Social Change in Islamic Society: The Political Thought of Ayatollah Khomeini," *Social Problems* 27 (1980): 614.

8. Gerth and Mills, *From Max Weber,* 297.

CHAPTER 3: SOVEREIGNTY, STATE, AND CITIZENSHIP

1. Cited in Jacques Maritain, "The Concept of Sovereignty," in W. J. Stankiewicz, ed., *In Defence of Sovereignty* (New York: Oxford University Press, 1969), 44–46.

2. Jean-Jacques Rousseau, *The Social Contract* (New York: Hafner, 1947), 85.

3. H. H. Gerth and C. W. Mills, eds. and trans., *From Max Weber*, part 2 (New York: Oxford University Press, 1950), 78.

4. Robert L. Carneiro, "A Theory of the Origin of the State," *Science* 169 (21 August 1970): 733–38; Jared Diamond, *Guns, Germs, and Steel: The Fates of Human Societies* (New York: W. W. Norton, 1997), 265–92.

5. The literature is summarized in Fred H. Wilhoite Jr., "Political Evolution and Legitimacy: The Biocultural Origins of Hierarchical Organizations," in Elliot White and Joseph Losco, eds., *Biology and Bureaucracy: Public Administration and Public Policy from the Perspective of Evolutionary, Genetic, and Neurobiological Theory*, 193–231 (University Press of America, 1986).

6. I Kings 11:3.

7. Rogers Brubaker, *Citizenship and Nationhood in France and Germany* (Cambridge, MA: Harvard University Press, 1992).

CHAPTER 4: THE NATION

1. Cited in Hans Kohn, ed., *Nationalism: Its Meaning and History* (New York: Van Nostrand Reinhold, 1965), 1.

2. Louis L. Snyder, *Global Mini-Nationalism: Autonomy or Independence* (Westport, CT: Greenwood Press, 1982).

3. Michael Ignatieff, *Blood and Belonging: Journeys into the New Nationalism* (Toronto: Penguin Books Canada, 1993).

4. Will Kymlicka, *Contemporary Political Philosophy: An Introduction*, 2nd ed. (Oxford: Oxford University Press, 2002), 348–55.

5. Theodore Draper, *The Rediscovery of Black Nationalism* (New York: Viking Press, 1969), chap. 5.

6. Mel Watkins, ed., *Dene Nation: The Colony Within* (Toronto: University of Toronto Press, 1977), 3.

7. Menno Boldt and J. Anthony Long, "Tribal Traditions and European–Western Political Ideologies: The Dilemma of Canada's Native Indians," *Canadian Journal of Political Science* 17 (1984): 537–53; Thomas Flanagan, "Indian Sovereignty and Nationhood: A Comment on Boldt and Long," *Canadian Journal of Political Science* 18 (1985): 367–74.

8. *Renewal: A Twenty-Year Commitment*, Report of the Royal Commission on Aboriginal Peoples, vol. 5 (Ottawa: Minister of Supply and Services Canada, 1996), 5.

9. Tom Flanagan, "Harper and the N-Word," *Maclean's,* December 11, 2006.

10. Michael Asch, *Home and Native Land* (Toronto: Methuen, 1984), 34.

11. P. B. Waite, *The Confederation Debates in the Province of Canada, 1865* (Toronto: McClelland & Stewart, 1963), 50.

CHAPTER 5: POLITICAL CULTURE AND SOCIALIZATION

1. Raymond Williams, *Keywords: A Vocabulary of Culture and Society* (Glasgow: Fontana, 1976), 76.

2. Richard Simeon and D. J. Elkins, "Provincial Political Cultures in Canada," in D. Elkins and R. Simeon, eds., *Small Worlds: Provinces and Parties in Canadian Political Life* (Toronto: Methuen, 1980), 31–76.

3. Ailsa Henderson, "Regional Political Cultures in Canada," *Canadian Journal of Political Science/Revue canadienne de science politique* 37 (2004): 595–615.

4. Gabriel A. Almond and G. Bingham Powell Jr., *Comparative Politics: A Developmental Approach* (Boston: Little, Brown, 1966), 23.

5. See Abacus Data, "Public Opinion on the Occupy Canada Protests," October 26, 2011, available online at http://abacusdata.ca/2011/10/26/public-opinion-on-the-occupy-canada-protests/.

6. Howard J. Wiarda, "Toward a Framework for the Study of Political Change in the Iberic-Latin Tradition: The Comparative Model," *World Politics* 25 (1973): 206–35.

7. For information on the Latin American Public Opinion Project at Vanderbilt University, go to http://www.vanderbilt.edu/lapop/.

8. Edward N. Muller and Mitchell A. Seligson, "Civic Culture and Democracy: The Question of Causal Relationships," *American Political Science Review* 88 (1994): 635–52.

9. Gabriel A. Almond and Sydney Verba, *The Civic Culture: Political Attitudes and Democracy in Five Nations* (Boston: Little, Brown, 1963), chap. 1.

10. Oliver H. Woshinsky, *Explaining Politics: Culture, Institutions and Political Behaviour* (New York: Routledge, 2008).

11. Ronald Inglehart, *Culture Shift in Advanced Industrial Society* (Princeton, NJ: Princeton University Press, 1990). For a summary, see Neil Nevitte, "New Politics," in Mark O. Dickerson, Thomas Flanagan, and Neil Nevitte, eds., *Introductory Readings in Politics and Government,* 4th ed. (Toronto: Nelson Canada, 1991), 145–54.

12. See Ronald Inglehart and Pippa Norris, *Rising Tide: Gender Equality and Cultural Change around the World* (New York: Cambridge University Press, 2003) and Ronald Inglehart and Christian Welzel, Modernization, *Cultural Change and Democracy: The Human Development Sequence* (New York: Cambridge, 2005).

13. Neil Nevitte, *The Decline of Deference* (Peterborough, ON: Broadview Press, 1996).

14. Robert D. Putnam, *Bowling Alone: The Collapse and Revival of American Community* (London: Simon and Schuster, 2000).

15. Robert Putnam, "*E Pluribus Unum*: Diversity and Community in the Twenty-first Century. The 2006 Johan Skytte Prize Lecture," *Scandanavian Political Studies* 30 (2007): 137–74.

16. For background information, see CBC News, "France Riots: Understanding the Violence," November 28, 2007, available online at http://www.cbc.ca/news /background/paris_riots/.

17. Tina Chui, Kelly Tran, and Hélène Maheux, *Immigration in Canada: A Portrait of the Foreign-Born Population, 2006 Census: Findings*, Social and Aboriginal Statistics Division, Statistics Canada, available online at http://www12.statcan.ca/english /census06/analysis/immcit/index.cfm.

18. Ronald Inglehart and Pippa Norris, *Sacred and Secular: Religion and Politics Worldwide* (New York: Cambridge, 2004).

19. Marc Hooghe, "Political Socialization and the Future of Politics," *Acta Politica* 39 (2004): 331–41.

20. W. A. Galston, "Political Knowledge, Political Engagement, and Civic Education," *Annual Review of Political Science* 4 (2001): 217.

21. Sidney Verba, Kay Lehman Schlozman, and Henry E. Brady, *Voice and Equality: Civic Voluntarism in American Politics* (Cambridge, MA: Harvard University Press, 1995).

22. Galston, "Political Knowledge," 217–34.

23. Dietland Stolle and Marc Hooghe, "The Roots of Social Capital: Attitudinal and Network Mechanisms in the Relation between Youth and Adult Indicators of Social Capital," *Acta Politica* 39 (2004): 422–41.

24. Michael X. Delli Carpini, "Gen.com: Youth, Civic Engagement, and the New Information Environment," *Political Communication* 17 (2000): 341–49.

CHAPTER 6: LAW

1. Exodus 34: 27–33.

2. F. A. Hayek, *Law, Legislation and Liberty*, vol. 1 (Chicago: University of Chicago Press, 1973–79), 81.

3. John Henry Merryman, *The Civil Law Tradition: An Introduction to the Legal Systems of Western Europe and Latin America* (Palo Alto, CA: Stanford University Press, 1969).

4. John E. C. Brierly, "Quebec's Civil Law Codification Viewed and Reviewed," *McGill Law Journal* 14 (1968): 521–89.

CHAPTER 7: CONSTITUTIONALISM

1. Ivor Jennings, *The Law of the Constitution,* 5th ed. (London: University of London Press, 1959), 136.

2. Andrew D. Heard, "Recognizing the Variety among Constitutional Conventions," *Canadian Journal of Political Science* 22 (1989): 63–82.

3. Rainer Knopff, "Legal Theory and the 'Patriation' Debate," *Queen's Law Journal* 7 (1981): 54.

4. *Plessy v. Ferguson*, 163 U.S. 537 (1896).

5. *Brown v. Board of Education*, 437 U.S. 483 (1954).

6. *Marbury v. Madison*, 1 Cranch 137 (1803).

7. Peter Russell, "The Anti-Inflation Case: The Anatomy of a Constitutional Decision," *Canadian Public Administration* 20 (1977): 635–65.

8. F. L. Morton, ed., *Law, Politics and the Judicial Process in Canada* (Calgary: University of Calgary Press, 1984), 262–67.

9. J. R. Lucas, *The Principles of Politics* (Oxford: Clarendon Press, 1966), 106.

10. Jennings, *Law of the Constitution*, 52.

11. *Roncarelli v. Duplessis*, [1959] S.C.R. 121.

12. *Operation Dismantle v. the Queen*, [1985] 1 S.C.R. 441.

CHAPTER 9: IDEOLOGY

1. Lyman Tower Sargent, *Contemporary Political Ideologies,* 4th ed. (Homewood, IL: Dorsey Press, 1978), 3.

2. Philip Converse, "The Nature of Belief Systems in Mass Publics," in David Apter, ed., *Ideology and Discontent* (Glencoe, IL: Free Press, 1964), 206–61.

3. Karl Marx, "A Contribution to the Critique of Political Economy" (1859), in Lewis S. Feuer, ed., *Marx and Engels: Basic Writings on Politics and Philosophy* (Garden City, NY: Doubleday, 1959), 44.

4. Karl Mannheim, *Ideology and Utopia* (New York: Harcourt, Brace and World, n.d.). First published 1936.

5. Jeremy Bentham, "An Introduction to the Principles of Morals and Legislation" (1789), in Jeremy Bentham and John Stuart Mill, *The Utilitarians* (Garden City, NY: Anchor Books, 1973), 73.

6. Karl Marx, "Introduction to the Critique of Hegel's Philosophy of Right" (1843), in T. B. Bottomore, ed., *Karl Marx: Early Writings* (New York: McGraw-Hill, 1963), 44.

7. Bill Devall, *Deep Ecology: Living As If Nature Mattered* (Salt Lake City, UT: Peregrine Smith Books, 1985), 67.

8. http://www.ikhwanweb.com/article.php?ID=813&LevelID=2&SectionID=116.

9. Marci McDonald, *The Armageddon Factor: The Rise of Christian Nationalism in Canada* (Toronto: Random House Canada, 2010).

10. David Caute, *The Left in Europe Since 1789* (New York: McGraw-Hill, 1966), chaps. 1 and 2.

CHAPTER 10: LIBERALISM

1. Pierre Berton, *The Smug Minority* (Toronto: McClelland & Stewart, 1968), 42–43. Reprinted by permission of McClelland & Stewart.

2. Bertrand de Jouvenel, *Sovereignty: An Inquiry into the Political Good*, trans. J. F. Huntington (Chicago: University of Chicago Press, 1957), 247–59.

3. John H. Schaar, "Equality of Opportunity and Beyond," in J. Roland Pennock and John W. Chapman, eds. *Equality* (New York: Atherton, 1967), 242.

4. John Locke, *The Second Treatise of Government* (Indianapolis: Bobbs-Merrill, 1952), 5.

5. Ibid., 76.

6. Ibid., 114.

7. Carl L. Becker, *The Declaration of Independence,* 2nd ed. (New York: Random House, 1942), 8.

8. J. Salwyn Schapiro, ed., *Liberalism: Its Meaning and History* (New York: Van Nostrand Reinhold, 1958), 129.

9. John Locke, *A Letter Concerning Toleration,* 2nd ed. (Indianapolis: Bobbs-Merrill, 1955), 18.

10. Schapiro, *Liberalism,* 126.

11. Ibid., 129.

12. John Stuart Mill, *On Liberty* (Indianapolis: Bobbs-Merrill, 1956), 13.

13. Adam Smith, *The Wealth of Nations*, vol. 1 (Chicago: University of Chicago Press, 1976), 477–78.

14. See especially Milton and Rose Friedman, *Free to Choose* (New York: Harcourt Brace Jovanovich, 1970), and Friedrich A. Hayek, *The Constitution of Liberty* (Chicago: University of Chicago Press, 1960).

15. David Hume, *A Treatise of Human Nature* (1739), cited in James Moore, "Hume's Theory of Justice and Property," *Political Studies* 24 (1976): 108.

16. Friedrich A. Hayek, *Law, Legislation and Liberty*, vol. 1 (Chicago: University of Chicago Press, 1973–79), 35–54.

17. Smith, *Wealth of Nations*, vol. 2, 208–9.

18. The discerning reader will see that the street light is a collective good because streets are publicly owned. If the streets were turned over to an entrepreneur who could find an appropriate way of charging for their use, lighting could be furnished as part of the overall service.

19. It is now recognized that many collective goods can be offered in some way in the market. See the essays in Tyler Cowen, ed., *The Theory of Market Failure* (Fairfax, VA: George Mason University Press, 1988).

20. Paul Starr, *Freedom's Power: The True Force of Liberalism* (New York: Basic Books, 2007), 3.

21. John Stuart Mill, *The Collected Works of John Stuart Mill*, vol. 2, *Principles of Political Economy* (Toronto: University of Toronto Press, 1965), 207.

22. T. H. Green, "Liberal Legislation and Freedom of Contract" (1881), in John R. Rodman, ed., *The Political Theory of T. H. Green* (New York: Appleton-Century-Crofts, 1964), 51–52.

CHAPTER 11: CONSERVATISM

1. Michael Oakeshott, *Rationalism in Politics and Other Essays* (London: Methuen, 1962), 169.

2. W. L. Morton, "Canadian Conservatism Now" (1959), in Paul W. Fox, ed., *Politics Canada,* 3rd ed. (Toronto: McGraw-Hill, 1970), 233.

3. Edmund Burke, *Reflections on the Revolution in France* (Indianapolis: Liberal Arts Press, 1955), 99.

4. Gordon W. Allport, *The Nature of Prejudice* (Reading, MA: Addison-Wesley, 1954), 20.

5. Ibid., 9.

6. Edmund Burke, "Letter to Sir Hercules Langrische on the Catholics" (1792), cited in Russell Kirk, *The Conservative Mind* (Chicago: Henry Regnery, 1960), 99.

7. Burke, *Reflections*, 110.

8. Russell Kirk, *The Conservative Mind* (Washington, DC: Regnery Publishing, 1985), 8–9.

9. Clinton Rossiter, "Conservatism," in David L. Sils, ed., *International Encyclopedia of the Social Sciences*, vol. 3 (New York: Macmillan and Free Press, 1968), 294.

10. Edmund Burke, "Thoughts and Details on Scarcity" (1795), cited in C. B. Macpherson, *Burke* (Oxford: Oxford University Press, 1980), 58.

11. Rod Preece, "The Political Wisdom of Sir John A. Macdonald," *Canadian Journal of Political Science* 17 (1984): 479.

12. George Grant, *Lament for a Nation: The Defeat of Canadian Nationalism* (Toronto: McClelland & Stewart, 1965), 68.

13. Private Willis's song from W. S. Gilbert and A. Sullivan, *Iolanthe*, http://math.boisestate.edu/gas/iolanthe/web_op/iol14.html.

CHAPTER 12: SOCIALISM AND COMMUNISM

1. Mikhail Heller, *Cogs in the Wheel: The Formation of Soviet Man* (New York: Alfred A. Knopf, 1988). As far as we know, Marx first used the phrase "socialist man" in 1844 in "Economic and Philosophical Manuscripts." See T. B. Bottomore, ed., *Karl Marx: Early Writings* (New York: McGraw-Hill, 1963), 166.

2. Acts of the Apostles 4: 32–33.

3. J. L. Talmon, *The Origins of Totalitarian Democracy* (New York: Praeger, 1960), 167–247.

4. John Anthony Scott, ed., *The Defense of Gracchus Babeuf* (New York: Schocken Books, 1972), 68. Copyright University of Massachusetts Press, 1967.

5. Ibid., 62–63.

6. Mark Holloway, *Heavens on Earth: Utopian Communities in America, 1680–1880*, 2nd ed. (New York: Dover, 1966).

7. Karl Marx, "Contribution to the Critique of Hegel's Philosophy of Right" (1843), in Bottomore, *Karl Marx: Early Writings*, 58–59.

8. Marx, "Economic and Philosophical Manuscripts" (1844), in Bottomore, *Karl Marx: Early Writings*, 132.

9. Ibid., 124.

10. M. M. Bober, *Karl Marx's Interpretation of History*, 2nd ed. (New York: W. W. Norton, 1965), chap. 12.

11. Friedrich Engels, "Socialism: Utopian and Scientific" (1892), in Karl Marx and Friedrich Engels, *Selected Works* (Moscow: Progress Publishers, 1968), 432.

12. Karl Marx, "Critique of the Gotha Programme" (1875), in Lewis S. Feuer, ed., *Marx and Engels: Basic Writings on Politics and Philosophy* (Garden City, NY: Doubleday, 1959), 119.

13. Karl Marx and Friedrich Engels, *The Communist Manifesto* (Harmondsworth, UK: Penguin Books, 1967), 104–5.

14. Karl Marx and Friedrich Engels, *The German Ideology* (Moscow: Progress Publishers, 1968), 45.

15. On anarchism, see James Joll, *The Anarchists* (London: Methuen, 1964).

16. James Joll, *The Second International* (London: Routledge and Kegan Paul, 1955).

17. Alfred G. Meyer, *Marxism: The Unity of Theory and Practice* (Ann Arbor: University of Michigan Press, 1963), 122–26.

18. Lenin's seminal work on party organization is *What Is to Be Done?* (1902). On democratic centralism, see Alfred G. Meyer, *Leninism* (New York: Praeger, 1962), 92–103.

19. V. I. Lenin, *Selected Works*, vol. 1 (Moscow: Progress Publishers, 1967), 680.

20. Michael S. Cross, ed., *The Decline and Fall of a Good Idea: CCF–NDP Manifestoes, 1932–1969* (Toronto: New Hogtown Press, 1974), 19.

21. Ibid., 33–42.

22. Quoted in Charlotte Gray, "Designer Socialism," *Saturday Night,* August 1989, 8.

23. See http://www.ndp.ca/platform.

24. Cross, *Decline and Fall,* 19.

25. Gregory C. Chow, "The Integration of China and Other Asian Countries into the World Economy," paper presented to the Mont Pelerin Society, Vancouver, BC, 31 August 1992.

26. Research Committee of the League for Social Reconstruction, *Social Planning for Canada* (Toronto: University of Toronto Press, 1975). First published in 1935. The League for Social Reconstruction was an intellectual study group founded in 1932 on the model of the British Fabian Society. It was not, strictly speaking, affiliated with the CCF, but members of the LSR were usually CCF activists.

27. Cross, *Decline and Fall,* 20.

28. The "Waffle Manifesto" (1969), in Cross, *Decline and Fall,* 45.

29. David Lane, *The End of Inequality? Stratification under State Socialism* (Harmondsworth, UK: Penguin, 1971), and Mervyn Matthews, *Privilege in the Soviet Union* (London: George Allen and Unwin, 1978), chap. 2.

30. Charles E. Lindblom, *Politics and Markets: The World's Political–Economic Systems* (New York: Basic Books, 1977). Lindblom adds a third alternative, exhortation, which does not seem to be even close to the other two in long-term effectiveness.

31. See Richard N. Hunt, *The Political Ideas of Marx and Engels*, vol. 1 (Pittsburgh: University of Pittsburgh Press, 1974), chap. 9.

32. N. S. Khrushchev, "Report on the Program of the Communist Party of the Soviet Union, October 17, 1961," in *Documents of the 22nd Congress of the CPSU*, vol. 2 (New York: Crosscurrents Press, 1961).

CHAPTER 13: NATIONALISM

1. Aristotle, *Nicomachean Ethics*, 1155a, in Richard McKeon, ed., *The Basic Works of Aristotle* (New York: Random House, 1941), 1058.

2. Quoted in Ramsay Cook, ed., *French-Canadian Nationalism: An Anthology* (Toronto: Macmillan, 1969), 95.

3. Ibid., 98.

4. Seymour Martin Lipset, "Canada and the United States: The Cultural Dimension," in Charles F. Doran and John H. Sigler, eds., *Canada and the United States* (Englewood Cliffs, NJ: Prentice Hall, 1985).

5. Letter to Joseph Priestley, 19 June 1802, cited in Saul K. Padover, ed., *Thomas Jefferson and the Foundations of American Freedom* (Princeton, NJ: D. Van Nostrand, 1965), 120–21.

6. Benedict Anderson, *Imagined Communities: Reflections on the Origin and Spread of Nationalism,* 2nd ed. (London: Verso, 1991).

7. Edward A. Tiryakian and Neil Nevitte, "Nationalism and Modernity," in Edward A. Tiryakian and Ronald Rogowski, eds., *New Nationalisms of the Developed West* (Boston: Allen and Unwin, 1985), 67.

8. John Stuart Mill, *Considerations on Representative Government* (Chicago: Henry Regnery, 1962), 309.

9. Lord Acton, "Nationality" (1862), in Gertrude Himmelfarb, ed., *Essays on Freedom and Power* (New York: Free Press, 1949), 193.

10. Pierre Elliott Trudeau, "The New Treason of the Intellectuals," in *Federalism and the French Canadians* (Toronto: Macmillan, 1968), 177–78.

11. Edward McWhinney, *Constitution-Making* (Toronto: University of Toronto Press, 1981), 206.

12. Kenneth Woodside, "The Canada–United States Free Trade Agreement," *Canadian Journal of Political Science* 22 (1989): 155–70.

13. Hans Kohn, ed., *Nationalism: Its Meaning and History,* 2nd ed. (Princeton, NJ: D. Van Nostrand, 1965).

14. Richard Wagner, "Judaism in Music" (1850), in ibid., 165.

15. On the *Protocols,* see Norman Cohn, *Warrant for Genocide,* 2nd ed. (New York: Harper and Row, 1969).

16. An elaborate exposition of "Holocaust revisionism" is Arthur Butz, *The Hoax of the Twentieth Century* (Brighton, UK: Historical Review Press, 1977).

17. Benito Mussolini, "The Doctrine of Fascism" (1932), in Department of Philosophy, University of Colorado, *Readings on Fascism and National Socialism* (Denver: Alan Swallow, n.d.), 15.

18. A convenient overview of fascism is Eugen Weber, *Varieties of Fascism* (New York: Van Nostrand Reinhold, 1964).

CHAPTER 14: FEMINISM

1. See BBC News, "Slutwalk marches sparked by Toronto officer's remarks," May 8, 2011, available online at http://www.bbc.co.uk/news/world-us-canada-13320785.

2. See Brenda O'Neill, "On the Same Wavelength? Feminist Attitudes across Generations of Canadian Women," in Manon Tremblay and Linda Trimble, eds., *Women and Electoral Politics in Canada* (Don Mills, ON: Oxford, 2003), 178–91.

3. Quoted in Margaret Tims, *Mary Wollstonecraft: A Social Pioneer* (London: Millington, 1976), 135–36.

4. Quoted in Josephine Donovan, *Feminist Theory: The Intellectual Traditions of American Feminism* (New York: Frederick Ungar, 1985), 6.

5. John Stuart Mill, *The Subjection of Women*, ed. Sue Mansfield (Arlington Heights, IL: AHM Publishing, 1980), 1.

6. Ibid., 5.

7. Ibid., 11.

8. Ibid., 18.

9. Ibid., 26.

10. Ibid., 47.

11. Betty Steele, *The Feminist Takeover* (Toronto: Simon & Pierre, 1987), 36–37.

12. Betty Friedan, *The Feminine Mystique*, 2nd ed. (New York: Dell, 1983), 15.

13. Ibid., 384–85.

14. Betty Friedan, *The Second Stage* (New York: Summit Books, 1981), 16.

15. Ibid., 41.

16. Jonathan Beecher and Richard Bienvenu, eds., *The Utopian Vision of Charles Fourier* (Boston: Beacon Press, 1971), 195.

17. Robert Owen, *A New View of Society and Other Writings* (London: Dent, 1927), 45.

18. Quoted in Donovan, *Feminist Theory*, 70.

19. Quoted in ibid., 75.

20. Frederick Engels, *The Origin of the Family, Private Property and the State* (New York: International Publishers, 1972), 137–38.

21. Quoted in Donovan, *Feminist Theory*, 76.

22. Quoted in ibid., 145.

23. Quoted in ibid., 144.

24. Quoted in Elaine Storkey, *What's Right with Feminism* (London: SPCK, 1985), 94.

25. Quoted in ibid., 100.

26. Quoted in Donovan, *Feminist Theory*, 146.

27. Quoted in ibid., 147.

28. Quoted in ibid., 152.

29. Donovan, *Feminist Theory*, 147; Storkey, *What's Right*, 98–99.

30. See Mary O'Brien, *The Politics of Reproduction* (Boston: Routledge and Kegan Paul, 1981).

31. Roxanne Dunbar, quoted in Donovan, *Feminist Theory*, 142.

32. Elisabeth Gidengil, André Blais, Neil Nevitte, and Richard Nadeau, *Citizens* (Vancouver: UBC Press, 2004), 23–24, 51–54.

33. Ronald Inglehart and Pippa Norris, "The Developmental Theory of the Gender Gap: Women's and Men's Voting Behavior in Global Perspective," *International Political Science Review* 21 (October 2000): 441–63.

34. Elisabeth Gidengil, Matthew Hennigar, André Blais, and Neil Nevitte, "Explaining the Gender Gap in Support for the New Right: The Case of Canada," *Comparative Political Studies* 38 (December 2005): 1171–95.

CHAPTER 15: ENVIRONMENTALISM

1. Robyn Eckersley, *Environmentalism and Political Theory: Toward an Ecocentric Approach* (Albany: State University of New York Press, 1992), 38.

2. Brundtland Commission report, *Our Common Future* (United Nations World Commission on Environment and Development, 1987), quoted in http://geneva-international.org/GVA3/WelcomeKit/Environnement/ chap_5.E.html.

3. Quoted in Bill Devall and George Sessions, *Deep Ecology: Living As If Nature Mattered* (Layton, UT: Gibbs Smith, 1985), 70.

4. Neil Carter, *The Politics of the Environment*, 2nd ed. (New York: Cambridge University Press, 2007), 161.

5. Ibid., 48.

CHAPTER 16: CLASSIFICATION OF POLITICAL SYSTEMS

1. Aristotle, *Politics*, 3.16, in Richard McKeon, ed., *The Basic Works of Aristotle* (New York: Random House, 1941), 1202.

2. John Stuart Mill, *On Liberty* (Indianapolis: Bobbs-Merrill, 1956), 7; Alexis de Tocqueville, *Democracy in America,* ed. Andrew Hacker (New York: Washington Square Press, 1964), 102.

3. Aristotle, *Politics*, 4.11, in McKeon, *Basic Works*, 1221.

CHAPTER 17: LIBERAL DEMOCRACY

1. Dorothy Pickles, *Democracy* (London: B. T. Batsford, 1970), 11.

2. R. MacGregor Dawson, *The Government of Canada,* 4th ed., rev. Norman Ward (Toronto: University of Toronto Press, 1963), 351.

3. Ibid.

4. Terence H. Qualter, *The Election Process in Canada* (Toronto: McGraw-Hill, 1970), 9.

5. *Sauvé v. Canada (Chief Electoral Officer),* [2002] 3 S.C.R. 519.

6. Constitution Act, 1982, ss. 38, 41.

7. J. A. O. Larsen, "The Judgment of Antiquity on Democracy," *Classical Philology* 49 (1954): 1–14.

8. James Mill, *An Essay on Government* (Indianapolis: Bobbs-Merrill, 1955), 66.

9. Patrick Boyer, *The People's Mandate: Referendums and a More Democratic Canada* (Toronto: Dundurn, 1992), 23–26. See also David Butler and Austin Ranney, eds., *Referendums* (Washington, DC: American Enterprise Institute, 1978).

10. Boyer, *People's Mandate*, 113–16. The argument actually originates with A. V. Dicey.

11. Particulars of the initiative, referendum, and recall can be found in J. A. Corry and Henry J. Abraham, *Elements of Democratic Government,* 4th ed. (New York: Oxford University Press, 1964), 410–22.

12. *Quebec v. Ford,* [1988] 2 S.C.R. 712.

13. Cited in F. A. Hayek, *Law, Legislation and Liberty,* vol. 3 (Chicago: University of Chicago Press, 1973–79), 1.

14. John Adams, "A Defense of the American Constitutions" (1787), in George A. Peek, ed., *The Political Writings of John Adams* (Indianapolis: Bobbs-Merrill, 1954), 148.

15. Geraint Parry, *Political Elites* (London: George Allen and Unwin, 1969), 30.

16. Raymond Aron, "Social Structure and the Ruling Class," *British Journal of Sociology* 1 (1950): 10, quoted in T. B. Bottomore, *Elites and Society* (Harmondsworth, UK: Penguin, 1966), 115.

17. Leo Panitch, "The Development of Corporatism in Liberal Democracies," in Schmitter and Lehmbruch, Trends, 63–94.

18. Robert A. Dahl, *A Preface to Democratic Theory* (Chicago: University of Chicago Press, 1956), 133.

19. Philippe C. Schmitter, "Still the Century of Corporatism," in Philippe C. Schmitter and Gerhard Lehmbruch, eds., *Trends Toward Corporatist Intermediation* (Beverly Hills, CA: Sage Publications, 1979), 13.

20. Arend Lijphart, *Democracy in Plural Societies: A Comparative Exploration* (New Haven, CT: Yale University Press, 1977), 25.

21. Kirstin Seefeldt, Gordon Abner, Joe A. Bolinger, Lanlan Xu, and John D. Graham, *At Risk: America's Poor During and After the Great Recession* (Bloomington: School of Public and Environmental Affairs, Indiana University, January 2012), http://www.indiana.edu/~spea/pubs/white_paper_at_risk.pdf.

22. Charles A. Kupchan, "The Democratic Malaise," *Foreign Affairs* 91, no. 1 (January/February 2012): 62.

23. Lisa Anderson, "Demystifying the Arab Spring," *Foreign Affairs* 90, no. 3 (May/June 2011): 2.

24. See Jack Goldstone, "Understanding the Revolutions of 2011," *Foreign Affairs* 90, no. 3 (May/June 2011), 8–16.

CHAPTER 18: TRANSITIONS TO DEMOCRACY

1. Samuel P. Huntington, *The Third Wave: Democratization in the Late Twentieth Century* (Norman: University of Oklahoma Press, 1991).

2. Larry Diamond, *Developing Democracy: Toward Consolidation* (Baltimore: Johns Hopkins University Press, 1999), 1.

3. Freedom House, "Freedom in the World, 2000–2001," http://www.freedomhouse.org.

4. Freedom House, "Freedom in the World, 2011 Edition," http://www.freedomhouse.org.

5. Larry Diamond, "Democracy in Retreat," *Foreign Affairs* 87, no. 2 (March/April 2008): 36.

6. Ibid., 43.

7. Paul Fairfield, *Why Democracy?* (Albany: State University of New York Press, 2008), 91.

8. Francis Fukuyama, *The Origins of Political Order: From Prehuman Times to the French Revolution* (New York: Farrar, Straus and Giroux, 2011), 4.

9. Ibid., 15–16.

10. Ibid., 7.

11. Ibid., 16.

12. Peter Frank, "Problems of Democracy in Post-Soviet Russia," in Ian Budge and David McKay, eds., *Developing Democracy* (Thousand Oaks, CA: Sage Publications, 1994), 284–85, 290.

13. Andrew Schedler, "Conceptualizing Accountability," in Andrew Schedler, Larry Diamond, and Marc F. Plattner, eds., *The Self-Restraining State Power and Accountability in New Democracies* (Boulder, CO: Lynne Rienner, 1999), 18.

14. Diamond, *Developing Democracy*, 221.

15. Iris Marion Young, "State, Civil Society, and Social Justice," in Ian Shapiro and Casiano Hacker-Cordon, eds., *Democracy's Value* (Cambridge: Cambridge University Press, 1999), 153.

16. S. M. Lipset, *Political Man: The Social Basis of Politics* (New York: Doubleday, 1960).

17. World Bank, *World Development Report, 2000/2001* (New York: Oxford University Press, 2001), 35.

18. Tatu Vanhanen, *Prospects of Democracy: A Study of 172 Countries* (London: Routledge, 1997), 4.

19. Ibid., 23.

20. Ibid., 99.

21. Amartya Sen, *Development as Freedom* (New York: Anchor Books, 2000), 18.

22. Ibid., 36, 144.

23. Ibid., 262.

24. Ibid., 263.

25. Ibid., 295.

26. Hernando de Soto, *The Mystery of Capital* (New York: Basic Books, 2000).

27. Ibid., 209.

28. Ibid., 5.

29. Ibid., 8.

30. Severine Autesserre, "The Trouble with Congo: How Local Disputes Fuel Regional Conflict," *Foreign Affairs* 87, no. 3 (May/June 2008): 94.

31. Ibid.

32. Benazir Bhutto, *Reconciliation: Islam, Democracy and the West* (New York: HarperCollins, 2008), 19.

33. Ibid.

34. Ibid., 20.

35. Ibid., 18.

36. Her argument is essentially that radical Islamic "reformers" have hijacked the Muslim religion and that these people are not representative of most Muslims.

37. Joseph Lecler, *Toleration and the Reformation*, trans. T. L. Westow, vol. 2 (New York: Association Press, 1960), 3.

38. Daron Acemoglu and James A. Robinson, *Economic Origins of Dictatorship and Democracy* (Cambridge: Cambridge University Press, 2006), 224.

39. Ronald Inglehart and Christian Welzel, *Modernization, Cultural Change, and Democracy* (Cambridge: Cambridge University Press, 2005), 192–93.

40. Ibid., 219–20.

41. Central Intelligence Agency, The World Factbook, 2000, http://www.cia.gov/cia/publications/factbook.

42. Ulrich Beck, *What Is Globalization?* (Cambridge: Polity Press, 2000), 20, 42.

43. Howard J. Wiarda, ed., *Comparative Democracy and Democratization* (Toronto: Harcourt College Publishers, 2001), 171.

44. Ibid., 172.

45. Ibid., 172–73.

46. F. Gregory Gause III, "Why Middle East Studies Missed the Arab Spring," *Foreign Affairs* 90, no. 4 (July/August 2011), 83.

CHAPTER 19: AUTOCRATIC SYSTEMS OF GOVERNMENT

1. Freedom House, "Freedom in the World, 2011 Edition," http://www.freedomhouse.org.

2. For a discussion of autocracy, see *International Encyclopedia of the Social Sciences*, vol. 1 (New York: Macmillan and Free Press, 1968), 478–80.

3. Aristotle, *Politics*, 4.10, in Richard McKeon, ed., *The Basic Works of Aristotle* (New York: Random House, 1941), 1219.

4. Baron de Montesquieu, *The Spirit of the Laws* (New York: Hafner, 1949), 26.

5. Juan J. Linz, "An Authoritarian Regime: Spain," in Erik Allardt and Stein Rokkan, eds., *Mass Politics: Studies in Political Sociology* (New York: Free Press, 1970), 255.

6. Adam Przeworski et al., *Democracy and Development: Political Institutions and Well-Being in the World, 1950–1990* (Cambridge: Cambridge University Press, 2000), 178.

7. Ibid., 271.

8. Giorgio Pini, *The Official Life of Benito Mussolini* (London: Hutchinson, 1939), 149.

9. Hannah Arendt, *The Origins of Totalitarianism,* 2nd ed. (New York: World Publishing, 1958), 460.

10. Carl J. Friedrich and Zbigniew K. Brzezinski, *Totalitarian Dictatorship and Autocracy,* 2nd ed. (New York: Praeger, 1965); Waldemar Gurian, "The Totalitarian State," *Review of Politics* 40 (1978): 514–27.

11. Arendt, *Origins of Totalitarianism,* 467.

12. Friedrich and Brzezinski, *Totalitarian Dictatorship,* 9.

13. See F. Gregory Gause III, "Why Middle East Studies Missed the Arab Spring: The Myth of Authoritarian Stability," *Foreign Affairs* 90, no. 4 (July/August 2011): 81–90.

14. Francis Fukuyama, *The Origins of Political Order: From Prehuman Times to the French Revolution* (New York: Farrar, Straus and Giroux, 2011), 458.

CHAPTER 20: PARLIAMENTARY AND PRESIDENTIAL SYSTEMS

1. John Locke, *The Second Treatise of Government* (Indianapolis: Bobbs-Merrill, 1952), 91.

2. Frank MacKinnon, *The Crown in Canada* (Toronto: McClelland & Stewart, 1976).

3. Constitution Act, 1867, s. 53.

4. Ibid., s. 26.

5. Walter Bagehot, cited in R. MacGregor Dawson and Norman Ward, *The Government of Canada*, 5th ed. (Toronto: University of Toronto Press, 1970), 168.

6. C. E. S. Franks, *The Parliament of Canada* (Toronto: University of Toronto Press, 1987), 122.

7. Stephen Brooks, *Public Policy in Canada: An Introduction* (Toronto: McClelland & Stewart, 1989), 135.

8. Ibid., 136.

9. Richard Neustadt, *Presidential Power*, 2nd ed. (New York: Wiley, 1964), 42.

10. *Congressional Quarterly Almanac* 40 (1985): 48.

11. Alexander Hamilton, John Jay, and James Madison, *The Federalist* (New York: Modern Library, n.d.), 337.

12. James Q. Wilson, *American Government: Brief Version*, 10th ed. (Boston, MA: Wadsworth, 2012): 244

CHAPTER 21: UNITARY AND FEDERAL SYSTEMS

1. Canadian Confederation (with a capital C) is an example of federalism. The general term *confederation* is an abstract concept of political science not particularly associated with Canada.

2. Vernon Bogdanor, *Devolution* (New York: Oxford University Press, 1979), chap. 3.

3. Garth Stevenson, *Unfulfilled Union: Canadian Federalism and National Unity* (Toronto: Macmillan, 1979), 23.

4. Alexander Hamilton, John Jay, and James Madison, *The Federalist* (New York: Modern Library, n.d.), 339.

5. Alan Cairns, "From Interstate to Intrastate Federalism," *Bulletin of Canadian Studies* 2 (1979): 13–34.

6. Robert C. Vipond, "From National League of Cities to Garcia: The Framers' Intentions and the Rhetoric of Rights," paper presented at the Conference on Adaptive Federalism, Dartmouth College, Hanover, NH, June 1989.

7. Discussions of different versions of federalism are found in Alan C. Cairns, *Charter versus Federalism: The Dilemmas of Constitutional Reform* (Montreal: McGill-Queen's University Press, 1992); Guy Laforest, *Trudeau and the End of a Canadian Dream*, Paul Leduc and Michelle Weinroth, trans. (Montreal: McGill-Queen's University Press, 1995); and Kenneth McRoberts, *Misconceiving Canada: The Struggle for National Unity* (Toronto: Oxford University Press, 1997).

8. Charles Taylor, "The Politics of Recognition," in Amy Gutmann, ed., *Multiculturalism* (Princeton: Princeton University Press, 1994), 38, 52, 61, 64.

9. Laforest, *Trudeau*, 4, 86.

10. Ibid.

11. McRoberts, *Misconceiving Canada*, 30, 249.

12. Ibid., 275–76.

13. Roger Gibbins, Regionalism: Territorial Politics in Canada and the U.S. (Scarborough, ON: Butterworths, 1982).

CHAPTER 22: THE POLITICAL PROCESS

1. Ludwig von Bertalanffy, *General System Theory* (New York: George Braziller, 1968); James A. Bill and Robert L. Hardgrave, *Comparative Politics: The Quest for Theory* (Columbus, OH: Charles E. Merrill, 1973), chap. 4.

2. David Easton, *A Systems Analysis of Political Life* (New York: Routledge, 1990), 32.

3. Gabriel Almond and G. B. Powell, *Comparative Politics: A Developmental Approach* (Boston: Little, Brown, 1966), 16–41.

4. William D. Coleman and Grace Skogstad, eds., *Policy Communities and Public Policy in Canada: A Structural Approach* (Mississauga, ON: Copp Clark Pitman, 1990), 25.

5. Ibid.

6. Leslie A. Pal, *Public Policy Analysis,* 2nd ed. (Toronto: Nelson Canada, 1992), 7.

CHAPTER 23: POLITICAL PARTIES, INTEREST GROUPS, AND SOCIAL MOVEMENTS: THE ORGANIZATION OF INTERESTS

1. Joseph LaPalombara, *Politics Within Nations* (Englewood Cliffs, NJ: Prentice Hall, 1974), 509.

2. *Canadian Oxford Dictionary* (Toronto: Oxford University Press, 1998), 1137.

3. Murray Dobbin, *Preston Manning and the Reform Party* (Toronto: James Lorimer, 1991), 215.

4. Maurice Duverger, *Political Parties,* 3rd ed. (New York: Wiley, 1978).

5. Roberto Michels, *Political Parties* (1911; New York: Free Press, 1962).

6. Lisa Young and Joanna Everitt, *Advocacy Groups* (Vancouver: University of British Columbia Press, 2004), 5.

7. Ibid., 6.

8. Sidney Verba, Kay Lehman Schlozman, and Henry E. Brady, *Voice and Equality: Civic Voluntarism in American Politics* (Cambridge, MA: Harvard University Press, 1995); Jane Mansbridge, "A Deliberative Theory of Interest Representation," in Marc Petracca, ed., *The Politics of Interests* (Boulder, CO: Westview Press, 1992); Robert D. Putnam, *Bowling Alone: The Collapse and Revival of American Community* (New York: Touchstone, 2000).

9. Gabriel A. Almond and James S. Coleman, eds., *The Politics of Developing Nations* (Princeton, NJ: Princeton University Press, 1960), 33–34.

10. Mancur Olson, *The Logic of Collective Action* (Cambridge, MA: Harvard University Press, 1965).

11. Russell Hardin, *Collective Action* (Baltimore: Johns Hopkins University Press, 1982).

12. Young and Everitt, *Advocacy Groups,* 79.

13. John Sawatsky, *The Insiders: Government, Business, and the Lobbyists* (Toronto: McClelland & Stewart, 1987).

14. Canada, Office of the Registrar of Lobbyists, *Annual Report, 2010–2011* (Ottawa: Office of the Registrar of Lobbyists, 2011), http://www.ocl-cal.gc.ca/eic/site/lobbyist-lobbyiste1.nsf/eng/nx00591.html#s1 (accessed 16 December 2011).

15. David B. Truman, *The Governmental Process* (New York: Alfred A. Knopf, 1951).

16. Thomas Ferguson, *Golden Rule: The Investment Theory of Political Parties and the Logic of Money-Driven Political Systems* (Chicago: University of Chicago Press, 1995); William D. Coleman, *Business and Politics: A Study of Collective Action* (Kingston and Montreal: McGill-Queen's University Press, 1988).

17. Jean-Jacques Rousseau, *The Social Contract* (New York: Hafner, 1947).

18. Alexander Hamilton, John Jay, and James Madison, *The Federalist* (New York: Modern Library, n.d.).

19. Jacquetta Newman and A. Brian Tanguay, "Crashing the Party: The Politics of Interest Groups and New Social Movements," in Joanna Everitt and Brenda O'Neill, eds., *Citizen Politics: Research and Theory in Canadian Political Behaviour* (Don Mills, ON: Oxford University Press, 2002), 387–412.

20. Miriam Smith, *A Civil Society? Collective Actors in Canadian Political Life* (Peterborough, ON: Broadview Press, 2005), 36.

21. See Russell J. Dalton and Manfred Kuechler, eds., *Challenging the Political Order: New Social and Political Movements in Western Democracies* (New York: Oxford University Press, 1990); John Baylis and Steve Smith, eds., *The Globalization of World Politics: An Introduction to International Relations* (New York: Oxford University Press, 1997); and R. J. Barry Jones, *The World Turned Upside Down? Globalization and the Future of the State* (New York: Manchester University Press, 2000).

22. Smith, *A Civil Society?*, 78.

CHAPTER 24: COMMUNICATIONS MEDIA

1. Television Bureau of Advertising Online, "TV Basics," http://www.tvb.org/media/file/TV_Basics.pdf (accessed 14 December 2011); Internet World Stats, "Internet Usage and Population Statistics for North America," http://www.internetworldstats.com/stats14.htm (accessed 13 December 2011).

2. Sarah Perez, "It's Still a Feature Phone World: Global Smartphone Penetration at 27%," *Tech Crunch*, 28 November 2011, http://techcrunch.com/2011/11/28/its-still-a-feature-phone-world-global-smartphone-penetration-at-27/ (accessed 14 December 2011).

3. David Taras, *Power and Betrayal in the Canadian Media,* 2nd ed. (Peterborough, ON: Broadview Press, 2001), 33.

4. Shanto Iyengar, "The Media Game: New Moves, Old Strategies," *The Forum,* 9, no. 1 (2011): 4.

5. Russell J. Dalton, *Citizen Politics: Public Opinion and Political Parties in Advanced Industrial Democracies*, 4th ed. (Washington, DC: CQ Press, 2006), 21–22.

6. See Taras, *Power and Betrayal,* 104–6.

7. Aaron Smith and Lee Rainie, *The Internet and the 2008 Election* (Washington, DC: Pew Internet and American Life Project, 2008), 3.

8. Ibid., 10–11.

9. Tamara A. Small, "Unequal Access, Unequal Success: Major and Minor Canadian Parties on the Net," *Party Politics* 14, no. 1 (2008): 65.

10. John W. Kingdon, *Agendas, Alternatives and Public Policies,* 2nd ed. (New York: HarperCollins, 1995).

11. This hypothesis was first stated in Bernard C. Cohen, *The Press and Foreign Policy* (Princeton, NJ: Princeton University Press, 1963), 13.

12. Stuart Soroka, *Agenda-Setting Dynamics in Canada* (Vancouver: UBC Press, 2002).

13. Clyde Wilcox and Barbara Norrander, "Introduction: The Diverse Paths to Understanding Public Opinion," in Barbara Norrander and Clyde Wilcox, eds., *Understanding Public Opinion,* 2nd ed. (Washington, DC: CQ Press, 2002), 5.

14. Gil Shochat, "The Dark Country: The Afghan Torture Scandal. The Arar Affair. Adscam. The Bush Years. Given So Many Cautionary Tales, Why Are Canadians Still Letting the Government Hide Public Information?" *The Walrus,* January/February 2010, http://www.walrusmagazine.com/articles/2010.01 -national-affairs-the-dark-country/1/ (accessed 15 December 2011).

15. Kimberley Noble, *Bound and Gagged: Libel Chill and the Right to Publish* (Toronto: HarperCollins, 1992).

16. Grant Robertson, "New Rules to Crimp Broadcast Mergers," *Globe and Mail,* 16 January 2008, B1.

17. Taras, *Power and Betrayal,* 219.

18. Ibid., 195.

CHAPTER 25: ELECTIONS AND ELECTORAL SYSTEMS

1. Martin Harrop and William L. Miller, *Elections and Voters: A Comparative Introduction* (London: Macmillan Education, 1987), 2.

2. Michael Saward, *Democracy* (Cambridge, UK: Polity Press, 2003), 49.

3. Maurice Duverger, *Political Parties: Their Organization and Activity in the Modern State* (London: Methuen, 1954).

4. The term *gerrymander,* which means to draw constituency lines so as to achieve a deliberate result, comes from Elbridge Gerry, governor of Massachusetts in 1812, who tried to favour his party at the time of redistricting. The constituency that he drew looked to some like a salamander, and thus the practice was named. See David M. Farrell, *Electoral Systems: A Comparative Introduction* (New York: Palgrave, 2001), 14.

5. Heather MacIvor, "Women and the Canadian Electoral System," in Manon Tremblay and Linda Trimble, eds., *Women and Electoral Politics in Canada* (Don Mills, ON: Oxford University Press, 2003), 22–36.

6. André Blais, Elisabeth Gidengil, Richard Nadeau, and Neil Nevitte, *Anatomy of a Liberal Victory: Making Sense of the Vote in the 2000 Canadian Election* (Peterborough, ON: Broadview Press, 2002), 191.

7. Harold D. Clarke, Jane Jensen, Lawrence LeDuc, and Jon H. Pammett, *Absent Mandate: Canadian Electoral Politics in an Era of Restructuring* (Toronto: Gage, 1996).

8. Institute for Democracy and Electoral Assistance, *Turnout in the World: Country by Country Performance*, www.idea.int/vt/survey/voter_turnout _pop2.cfm.

CHAPTER 26: REPRESENTATIVE ASSEMBLIES

1. See, in general, Hanna Pitkin, *The Concept of Representation* (Berkeley: University of California Press, 1967), and A. H. Birch, *Representation* (London: Macmillan, 1971).

2. Edmund Burke, *Burke's Speeches and Letters on American Affairs* (London: E. P. Dutton, 1908), 73.

3. "Politicians Must Reach out to Jaded Voters," TheStar.com, 7 July 2011, http://www.thestar.com/opinion/editorials/article/1021515--politicians-must-reach-out-to-jaded-voters (accessed 6 December 2011).

4. Reform Party of Canada, *Principles and Policies* (1991), 39.

5. Jennifer Smith, "Democracy and the Canadian House of Commons at the Millennium," *Canadian Public Administration* 42 (Winter 1999): 418.

6. John Adams, "Thoughts on Government," in George A. Peek, ed., *The Political Writings of John Adams* (Indianapolis: Bobbs-Merrill, 1954), 86.

7. Réjean Pelletier, "Responsible Government: Victory or Defeat for Parliament?" in F. Leslie Seidle and Louis Massicotte, eds., *Taking Stock of 150 Years of Responsible Government in Canada* (Ottawa: Canadian Study of Parliament Group, 1999), 66.

CHAPTER 27: THE POLITICAL EXECUTIVE

1. Peter Hennessy, *Cabinet* (Oxford: Basil Blackwell, 1986).

2. Donald J. Savoie, *Governing from the Centre: The Concentration of Power in Canadian Politics* (Toronto: University of Toronto Press, 1999), 12.

3. Eddie Goldenberg, *The Way It Works: Inside Ottawa* (Toronto: McClelland & Stewart, 2006), 107.

4. R. MacGregor Dawson, *The Government of Canada,* 4th ed. (Toronto: University of Toronto Press, 1963), 185.

5. Theodore Lowi and Benjamin Ginsberg, *American Government: Freedom and Power* (New York: W. W. Norton, 1990), 273.

CHAPTER 28: THE ADMINISTRATION

1. Colin Leys, *Politics in Britain* (Toronto: University of Toronto Press, 1983), 269.

2. For a discussion of the budget-maximizing behaviour of bureaucrats, see William A. Niskanen Jr., *Bureaucracy and Representative Government* (Chicago: Aldine-Atherton, 1971). For recent research on the budget-minimizing tendencies of senior administrators, see Julie Dolan, "The Budget-Minimizing Bureaucrat? Empirical Evidence from the Senior Executive Service," *Public Administration Review* 62, no. 1 (2002): 42–50.

3. John J. Hindera and Cheryl Young, "Representative Bureaucracy: The Theoretical Implications of Statistical Interaction," *Political Research Quarterly* 51, no. 3 (1998): 655–71.

4. "Insight: Lessons for U.S. from Canada's 'Basket Case' Moment," Reuters online (U.S. edition), 21 November 2011, http://www.reuters.com/article/2011/11/21 /us-crisis-idUSTRE7AK0EP20111121 (accessed 21 November 2011).

5. David Osborne and Ted Gaebler, *Reinventing Government: How the Entrepreneurial Spirit Is Transforming the Public Sector* (Reading, MA: Addison-Wesley, 1992).

6. Peter Aucoin, "New Public Management and the Quality of Government: Coping with the New Political Governance in Canada," paper presented at the Conference on New Public Management and the Quality of Government, 13–15 November 2008, http://www.qog.pol.gu.se/working_papers/SOG%20papers/Aucoin%20 -%20SOG%20Conference%20Nov08.pdf (accessed 25 November 2011).

7. Christopher Pollitt and Geert Bouckaert, *Public Management Reform: A Comparative Analysis—New Public Management, Governance and the Neo-Weberian State,* 3rd ed. (New York: Oxford University Press, 2011), 10, 33.

8. Aucoin, "New Public Management," 5.

9. Laurence E. Lynn Jr., *Public Management: Old and New* (New York: Routledge, 2006), 177.

CHAPTER 29: THE JUDICIARY

1. Thomas Flanagan, "Policy-Making by Exegesis: The Abolition of 'Mandatory Retirement' in Manitoba," *Canadian Public Policy* 11 (1985): 40–53.

2. *Edwards et al. v. Attorney General of Canada et al.*, [1930] A.C. 124.

3. Originally the Bill of Rights applied only to the federal Congress, but the Supreme Court held that it was extended through the Fourteenth Amendment to the state legislatures.

4. *Forest v. the Queen,* [1979] 2 S.C.R. 1032.

5. M. Elizabeth Atcheson, Mary Eberts, and Beth Symes, *Women and Legal Action: Precedents, Resources and Strategies for the Future* (Ottawa: Canadian Advisory Council on the Status of Women, 1984), 166–67.

6. *Delgamuukw v. British Columbia*, [1997] 3 S.C.R. 1010.

7. *R. v. Marshall*, [1993] 3 S.C.R. 456; *R. v. Marshall*, [1993] 3 S.C.R. 533.

8. See, for example, Theodore J. Lowi, *The End of Liberalism*, 2nd ed. (New York: W. W. Norton, 1979), chap. 11.

9. Alan Cairns, *Charter versus Federalism: The Dilemmas of Constitutional Reform* (Montreal: McGill-Queen's University Press, 1992), 125.

10. Aharon Barak, *The Judge in a Democracy* (Princeton, NJ: Princeton University Press, 2006), 265–66.

11. Ted Morton's chapter is an excellent discussion of attempts at reforming the judicial appointment process.

12. Peter Russell, "Conclusion," in Kate Malleson and Peter Russell, eds., *Appointing Judges in an Age of Judicial Power: Critical Perspectives from around the World* (Toronto: University of Toronto Press, 2006), 420.

13. *R. v. Therens*, [1985] 1 S.C.R. 613.

14. F. L. Morton and M. J. Withey, "Charting the Charter, 1982–1985: A Statistical Analysis," in Human Rights Research and Education Centre, University of Ottawa, *Canadian Human Rights Yearbook* (Toronto: Carswell, 1987).

15. Peter W. Hogg and Allison A. Thornton, "The Charter Dialogue Between Courts and Legislatures," *Policy Options* (April 1999): 19–22.

Constitution Act, 1867

(formerly British North America Act, 1867)

Below are a few sections of the Act of particular interest to Canadian students of political science at the introductory level.

. . . .

Preamble

WHEREAS the Provinces of Canada, Nova Scotia and New Brunswick have expressed their Desire to be federally united into One Dominion under the Crown of the United Kingdom of Great Britain and Ireland, with a Constitution similar in Principle to that of the United Kingdom:

And whereas such a Union would conduce to the Welfare of the Provinces and promote the Interests of the British Empire:

And whereas on the Establishment of the Union by Authority of Parliament it is expedient, not only that the Constitution of the Legislative Authority in the Dominion be provided for, but also that the Nature of the Executive Government therein be declared:

And whereas it is expedient that Provision be made for the eventual Admission into the Union of other Parts of British North America:

. . . .

VI. DISTRIBUTION OF LEGISLATIVE POWERS.

Powers of the Parliament

Legislative Authority of Parliament of Canada

91. It shall be lawful for the Queen, by and with the Advice and Consent of the Senate and House of Commons, to make Laws for the Peace, Order, and good Government of Canada, in relation to all Matters not coming within the Classes of Subjects by this Act assigned exclusively to the Legislatures of the Provinces; and for greater Certainty, but not so as to restrict the Generality of the foregoing Terms of this Section, it is hereby declared that (notwithstanding anything in this Act) the exclusive Legislative Authority of the Parliament of Canada extends to all Matters coming within the Classes of Subjects next herein-after enumerated; that is to say,—

1. The amendment from time to time of the Constitution of Canada, except as regards matters coming within the classes of subjects by this Act assigned exclusively to the Legislatures of the provinces, or as regards rights or privileges by this or any other Constitutional Act granted or secured to the Legislature or the Government of a province, or to any class of persons with respect to schools or as regards the use of English or the French language or as regards the requirements that there shall be a session of the Parliament of Canada at least once each year, and that no House of Commons shall continue for more than five years from the day of the return of the Writs for choosing the House: provided, however, that a House of Commons may in time of real or apprehended war, invasion or insurrection be continued by the Parliament of Canada if such continuation is not opposed by the votes of more than one-third of the members of such House.

1A. The Public Debt and Property.

2. The regulation of Trade and Commerce.

2A. Unemployment insurance.

3. The raising of Money by any Mode or System of Taxation.

4. The borrowing of Money on the Public Credit.

5. Postal Service.

6. The Census and Statistics.

7. Militia, Military and Naval Service, and Defence.

8. The fixing of and providing for the Salaries and Allowances of Civil and other Officers of the Government of Canada.

9. Beacons, Buoys, Lighthouses, and Sable Island.

10. Navigation and Shipping.

11. Quarantine and the Establishment and Maintenance of Marine Hospitals.

12. Sea Coast and Inland Fisheries.

13. Ferries between a Province and any British or Foreign Country or between Two Provinces.

14. Currency and Coinage.

15. Banking, Incorporation of Banks, and the Issue of Paper Money.

16. Savings Banks.

17. Weights and Measures.

18. Bills of Exchange and Promissory Notes.

19. Interest.

20. Legal Tender.

21. Bankruptcy and Insolvency.

22. Patents of Invention and Discovery.

23. Copyrights.

24. Indians, and Lands reserved for the Indians.

25. Naturalization and Aliens.

26. Marriage and Divorce.

27. The Criminal Law, except the Constitution of Courts of Criminal Jurisdiction, but including the Procedure in Criminal Matters.

28. The Establishment, Maintenance, and Management of Penitentiaries.

29. Such Classes of Subjects as are expressly excepted in the Enumeration of the Classes of Subjects by this Act assigned exclusively to the Legislatures of the Provinces.

And any Matter coming within any of the Classes of Subjects enumerated in this Section shall not be deemed to come within the Class of Matters of a local or private Nature comprised in the Enumeration of the Classes of Subjects by this Act assigned exclusively to the Legislatures of the Provinces.

Exclusive Powers of Provincial Legislatures

Subjects of exclusive Provincial Legislation

92.   In each Province the Legislature may exclusively make Laws in relation to coming within the Classes of Subject next herein-after enumerated; that is to say,—

1. The Amendment from Time to Time, not withstanding anything in this Act, of the Constitution of the Province, except as regards the Office of Lieutenant Governor.

2. Direct Taxation within the Province in order to the raising of a Revenue for Provincial Purposes.

3. The borrowing of Money on the sole Credit of the Province.

4. The Establishment and Tenure of Provincial Offices and the Appointment and Payment of Provincial Officers.

5. The Management and Sale of the Public Lands belonging to the Province and of the Timber and Wood thereon.

6. The Establishment, Maintenance, and Management of Public and Reformatory Prisons in and for the Province.

7. The Establishment, Maintenance, and Management of Hospitals, Asylums, Charities and Eleemosynary Institutions in and for the Province, other than Marine Hospitals.

8. Municipal Institutions in the Province.

9. Shop, Saloon, Tavern, Auctioneer, and other Licences in order to the raising of a Revenue for Provincial, Local, or Municipal Purposes.

10. Local Works and Undertakings other than such as are of the following Classes:—

    (a) Lines of Steam or other Ships, Railways, Canals, Telegraphs, and other Works and Undertakings connecting the Province with any other or others of the Provinces, or extending beyond the Limits of the Province;

(b) Lines of Steam Ships between the Province and any British or Foreign Country;

(c) Such Works as, although wholly situate within the Province, are before or after their Execution declared by the Parliament of Canada to be for the general Advantage of Canada or for the Advantage of Two or more of the Provinces.

11. The Incorporation of Companies with Provincial Objects.
12. The Solemnization of Marriage in the Province.
13. Property and Civil Rights in the Province.
14. The Administration of Justice in the Province, including the Constitution, Maintenance, and Organization of Provincial Courts, both of Civil and of Criminal Jurisdiction, and including Procedure in Civil Matters in those Courts.
15. The Imposition of Punishment by Fine, Penalty, or Imprisonment for enforcing any Law of the Province made in relation to any Matter coming within any of the Classes of Subjects enumerated in this Section.
16. Generally all Matters of a merely local or private Nature in the Province.

. . . .

For section 92A, see sections 50 and 51 of the Constitution Act, 1982, in Appendix B in this volume.

. . . .

Education

Legislation respecting Education

93. In and for each Province the Legislature may exclusively make Laws in relation to Education, subject and according to the following Provisions:—

(1) Nothing in any such Law shall prejudicially affect any Right or Privilege with respect to Denominational Schools which any Class of Persons have by Law in the Province at the Union:

(2) All the Powers, Privileges, and Duties at the Union by Law conferred and imposed in Upper Canada on the Separate Schools and School Trustees of the Queen's Roman Catholic Subjects shall be and the same are hereby extended to the Dissentient Schools of the Queen's Protestant and Roman Catholic Subjects in Quebec:

(3) Where in any Province a System of Separate or Dissentient Schools exists by Law at the Union or is thereafter established by the Legislature of the Province, an Appeal shall lie to the Governor General in Council from any Act or Decision of any Provincial Authority affecting any Right or Privilege of the Protestant or Roman Catholic Minority of the Queen's Subjects in relation to Education:

(4) In case any such Provincial Law as from Time to Time seems to the Governor General in Council requisite for the due Execution of the Provisions of this Section is not made, or in case any Decision of the Governor General in Council on any Appeal under this section is not duly executed by the proper Provincial Authority in that Behalf, then and in every such Case, and as far only as the Circumstances of each Case require, the Parliament of Canada may make remedial Laws for the due Execution of the Provisions of this Section and of any Decision of the Governor-General in Council under this Section.

. . . .

Old Age Pensions

Legislation respecting old age pensions and supplementary benefits

94A. The Parliament of Canada may make laws in relation to old age pensions and supplementary benefits, including survivors and disability benefits irrespective of age, but no such law shall affect the operation of any law present or future of a provincial legislature in relation to any such matter.

. . . .

Agriculture and Immigration

Concurrent Power of Legislation respecting Agriculture, etc.

95. In each Province the Legislature may make Laws in relation to Agriculture in the Province, and to Immigration into the Province, and it is hereby declared that the Parliament of Canada may from Time to Time make Laws in relation to Agriculture in all or any of the Provinces, and to Immigration into all or any of the Provinces; and any Law of the Legislature of a province relative to Agriculture or to Immigration shall have effect in and for the Province as long and as far only as it is not repugnant to any Act of the Parliament of Canada.

. . . .

Use of English and French Languages

133. Either the English or the French Language may be used by any Person in the Debates of the Houses of the Parliament of Canada and of the Legislature of Quebec; and both those Languages shall be used in the respective Records and Journals of those Houses; and either of those Languages may be used by any Person or in any Pleading or Process in or issuing from any Court of Canada established under this Act, and in or from all or any of the Courts of Quebec.

The Acts of the Parliament of Canada and of the Legislature of Quebec shall be printed and published in both those languages.

APPENDIX B

Constitution Act, 1982

Schedule B to Canada Act 1982 (U.K.)

PART I

CANADIAN CHARTER OF RIGHTS AND FREEDOMS

Whereas Canada is founded upon principles that recognize the supremacy of God and the rule of law:

Guarantee of Rights and Freedoms

Rights and Freedoms in Canada

1. The *Canadian Charter of Rights and Freedoms* guarantees the rights and freedoms set out in it subject only to such reasonable limits prescribed by law as can be demonstrably justified in a free and democratic society.

Fundamental Freedoms

Fundamental freedoms

2. Everyone has the following fundamental freedoms:
(a) freedom of conscience and religion;
(b) freedom of thought, belief, opinion and expression, including freedom of the press and other media of communication;
(c) freedom of peaceful assembly; and
(d) freedom of association.

Democratic Rights

Democratic rights of citizens

3. Every citizen of Canada has the right to vote in an election of members of the House of Commons or of a legislative assembly and to be qualified for membership therein.

Maximum duration of legislative bodies

4. (1) No House of Commons and no legislative assembly shall continue for longer than five years from the date fixed for the return of the writs at a general election of its members.

Continuation
in special
circumstances

(2)   In time of real or apprehended war, invasion or insurrection, a House of Commons may be continued by Parliament and a legislative assembly may be continued by the legislature beyond five years if such continuation is not opposed by the votes of more than one-third of the members of the House of Commons or the legislative assembly, as the case may be.

Annual sitting of
legislative bodies

5.   There shall be a sitting of Parliament and of each legislature at least once every twelve months.

Mobility Rights

Mobility of citizens

6.   (1) Every citizen of Canada has the right to enter, remain in and leave Canada.

Rights to move and
gain livelihood

(2)   Every citizen of Canada and every person who has the status of a permanent resident of Canada has the right

(a)   to move to and take up residence in any province; and

(b)   to pursue the gaining of a livelihood in any province.

Limitation

(3)   The rights specified in subsection (2) are subject to

(a)   any laws or practices of general application in force in a province other than those that discriminate among persons primarily on the basis of province of present or previous residence; and

(b)   any laws providing for reasonable residency requirements as a qualification for the receipt of publicly provided social services.

Affirmative action
programs

(4)   Subsections (2) and (3) do not preclude any law, program or activity that has as its object the amelioration in a province of conditions of individuals in that province who are socially or economically disadvantaged if the rate of employment in that province is below the rate of employment in Canada.

Legal Rights

Life, liberty and
security of person

7.   Everyone has the right to life, liberty, and security of the person and the right not to be deprived thereof except in accordance with the principles of fundamental justice.

Search or seizure

8.   Everyone has the right to be secure against unreasonable search or seizure.

Detention or
imprisonment

9.   Everyone has the right not to be arbitrarily detained or imprisoned.

Arrest or detention

10.   Everyone has the right on arrest or detention

(a)   to be informed promptly of the reasons therefore;

(b)   to retain and instruct counsel without delay and to be informed of that right; and

(c)   to have the validity of the detention determined by way of *habeas corpus* and to be released if the detention is not lawful.

Proceedings in criminal and penal matters

11. Any person charged with an offence has the right

(a)   to be informed without unreasonable delay of the specific offence;

(b)   to be tried within a reasonable time;

(c)   not to be compelled to be a witness in proceedings against that person in respect of the offence;

(d)   to be presumed innocent until proven guilty according to law in a fair and public hearing by an independent and impartial tribunal;

(e)   not to be denied reasonable bail without just cause;

(f)   except in the case of an offence under military law tried before a military tribunal, to the benefit of trial by jury where the maximum punishment for the offence is imprisonment for five years or a more severe punishment;

(g)   not to be found guilty on account of any act or omission unless, at the time of the act or omission, it constituted an offence under Canadian or international law or was criminal according to the general principles of law recognized by the community of nations;

(h)   if finally acquitted of the offence, not to be tried for it again and, if finally found guilty and punished for the offence, not to be tried or punished for it again; and

(i)   if found guilty of the offence and if the punishment for the offence has been varied between the time of commission and the time of sentencing, to the benefit of the lesser punishment.

Treatment or punishment

12. Everyone has the right not to be subjected to any cruel and unusual treatment or punishment.

Self-crimination

13. A witness who testifies in any proceedings has the right not to have any incriminating evidence so given used to incriminate that witness in any other proceedings, except in a prosecution for perjury or for the giving of contradictory evidence.

Interpreter

14. A party or witness in any proceedings who does not understand or speak the language in which the proceedings are conducted or who is deaf has the right to the assistance of an interpreter.

Equality Rights

Equality before and under law and equal protection and benefit of law

15. (1) Every individual is equal before and under the law and has the right to the equal protection and equal benefit of the law without discrimination and, in particular, without discrimination based on race, national or ethnic origin, colour, religion, sex, age or mental or physical disability.

Affirmative action programs

(2)   Subsection (1) does not preclude any law, program or activity that has as its object the amelioration of conditions of disadvantaged individuals or groups including those that are disadvantaged because of race, national or ethnic origin, colour, religion, sex, age or mental or physical disability.

Official Languages of Canada

Official languages of Canada

16. (1) English and French are the official languages of Canada and have equality of status and equal rights and privileges as to their use in all instructions of the Parliament and government of Canada.

Official languages in New Brunswick

(2)   English and French are the official languages of New Brunswick and have equality of status and equal rights and privileges as to their use in all institutions of the legislature and government of New Brunswick.

Advancement of status and use

(3)   Nothing in this Charter limits the authority of Parliament or a legislature to advance the equality of status or use of English and French.

Proceedings of Parliament

17. (1) Everyone has the right to use English or French in any debates and other proceedings of Parliament.

Proceedings of New Brunswick legislature

(2)   Everyone has the right to use English or French in any debates and other proceedings of the legislature of New Brunswick.

Parliamentary statuses and records

18. (1) The statutes, records and journals of Parliament shall be printed and published in English and French and both language versions are equally authoritative.

New Bruswick statutes and records

(2)   The statutes, records and journals of the legislature of New Brunswick shall be printed and published in English and French and both language versions are equally authoritative.

Proceedings in courts established by Parliament

19. (1) Either English or French may be used by any person in, or in any pleading in or process issuing from, any court established by Parliament.

Proceedings in New Brunswick courts

(2)   Either English or French may be used by any person in, or in any pleading in or process issuing from, any court of New Brunswick.

Communications by public with federal institutions

20. (1) Any member of the public in Canada has the right to communicate with, and to receive available services from, any head or central office of an institution of the Parliament or government of Canada in English or French, and has the same right with respect to any other office of any such institution where

(a)   there is a significant demand for communications with and services from that office in such language; or

(b)   due to the nature of the office, it is reasonable that communications with and services from that office be available in both English and French.

Communications by public with New Brunswick institutions

(2)   Any member of the public in New Brunswick has the right to communicate with, and to receive available services from, any office of an institution of the legislature or government of New Brunswick in English or French.

Continuation of existing constitutional provisions

21. Nothing in sections 16 to 20 abrogates or derogates from any right, privilege or obligation with respect to the English and French languages, or either of them, that exists or is continued by virtue of any other provision of the Constitution of Canada.

Rights and privileges preserved

22. Nothing in sections 16 to 20 abrogates or derogates from any legal or customary right or privilege acquired or enjoyed either before or after the coming into force of this Charter with respect to any language that is not English or French.

Minority Language Educational Rights

Language of instruction

23. (1) Citizens of Canada

(a)   whose first language learned and still understood is that of the English or French linguistic minority population of the province in which they reside, or

(b)   who have received their primary school instruction in Canada in English or French and reside in a province where the language in which they received that instruction is the language of the English or French linguistic minority population of the province, have the right to have their children receive primary and secondary school instruction in that language in that province.

Continuity of language instruction

(2)   Citizens of Canada of whom any child has received or is receiving primary or secondary school instruction in English or French in Canada, have the right to have all their children receive primary and secondary school instruction in the same language.

Applications where numbers warrant

(3)   The right of citizens of Canada under subsections (1) and (2) to have their children receive primary and secondary school instruction in the language of the English or French linguistic minority population of a province

(a)   applies wherever in the province the number of children citizens who have such a right is sufficient to warrant the provision to them out of public funds of minority language instruction; and

(b)   includes, where the number of those children so warrants, the right to have them receive that instruction in minority language educational facilities provided out of public funds.

Enforcement

Enforcement of guaranteed rights and freedoms

24. (1) Anyone whose rights or freedoms, as guaranteed by this Charter, have been infringed or denied may apply to a court of competent jurisdiction to obtain such remedy as the court considers appropriate and just in the circumstances.

Exclusion of evidence bringing administration of justice into disrepute

(2)   Where, in proceedings under subsection (1), a court concludes that evidence was obtained in a manner that infringed or denied any rights or freedoms guaranteed by this Charter, the evidence shall be excluded if it is established that, having regard to all the circumstances, the admission of it in the proceedings would bring the administration of justice into disrepute.

General

Aboriginal rights and freedoms not affected by Charter

25. The guarantee in this Charter of certain rights and freedoms shall not be construed so as to abrogate or derogate from any aboriginal treaty or other rights or freedoms that pertain to the aboriginal peoples of Canada including

(a) any rights or freedoms that have been recognized by the Royal Proclamation of October 7, 1763; and

(b) any rights or freedoms that now exist by way of land claims agreements or may be so acquired.[1]

Other rights and freedoms not affected by Charter

26. The guarantee in this Charter of certain rights and freedoms shall not be construed as denying the existence of any other rights or freedoms that exist in Canada.

Multicultural heritage

27. This Charter shall be interpreted in a manner consistent with the preservation and enhancement of the multicultural heritage of Canadians.

Rights guaranteed equally to both sexes

28. Notwithstanding anything in this Charter, the rights and freedoms referred to in it are guaranteed equally to male and female persons.

Rights respecting certain schools preserved

29. Nothing in this Charter abrogates or derogates from any rights or privileges guaranteed by or under the Constitution of Canada in respect of denomination, separate or dissentient schools.

Application to territories and territorial authorities

30. A reference in this Charter to a province or to the legislative assembly or legislature of a province shall be deemed to include a reference to the Yukon Territory and the Northwest Territories, or to the appropriate legislative authority thereof, as the case may be.

Legislative powers not extended

31. Nothing in this Charter extends the legislative powers of any body or authority.

Application of Charter

Application of Charter

32. (1) This Charter applies

(a) to the Parliament and government of Canada in respect of all matters within the authority of Parliament including all matters relating to the Yukon Territory and Northwest Territories; and

(b) to the legislature and government of each province in respect of all matters within the authority of the legislature of each province.

Exception

(2) Notwithstanding subsection (1), section 15 shall not have effect until three years after this section comes into force.

Exception where express declaration

33. (1) Parliament or the legislature of a province may expressly declare in an Act of Parliament or of the legislature, as the case may be, that the Act or a provision thereof shall operate notwithstanding a provision in section 2 or sections 7 to 15 of this Charter.

Operation of exception

(2)   An Act or a provision of an Act in respect of which a declaration made under this section is in effect shall have such operation as it would have but for the provision of this Charter referred to in the declaration.

Five year limitation

(3)   A declaration made under subsection (1) shall cease to have effect five years after it comes into force or on such earlier date as may be specified in the declaration.

Re-enactment

(4)   Parliament or the legislature of a province may re-enact a declaration made under subsection (1).

Five year limitation

(5)   Subsection (3) applies in respect of a re-enactment made under subsection (4).

Citation

Citation

34.   This Part may be cited as the *Canadian Charter of Rights and Freedoms.*

PART II

RIGHTS OF THE ABORIGINAL PEOPLES OF CANADA

Recognition of existing aboriginal and treaty rights

35.   (1) The existing aboriginal and treaty rights of the aboriginal peoples of Canada are hereby recognized and affirmed.

Definition of "aboriginal peoples of Canada" Land claims agreement

(2)   In this Act, "aboriginal peoples of Canada" includes the Indian, Inuit and Métis peoples of Canada.

(3)   For greater certainty, in subsection (1) "treaty rights" includes rights that now exist by way of land claims agreements or may be so acquired.

Aboriginal and treaty rights are guaranteed equally to both sexes

(4)   Notwithstanding any other provision of this Act, the aboriginal and treaty rights referred to in subsection (1) are guaranteed equally to male and female persons.[2]

Commitment to participation in constitutional conference

35.1 The government of Canada and the provincial governments are committed to the principle that, before any amendment is made to Class 24 of section 91 of the "Constitution Act, 1867," to section 25 of this Act or to this Part,

(a)   a constitutional conference that includes in its agenda an item relating to the proposed amendment, composed of the Prime Minister of Canada and the first ministers of the provinces, will be convened by the Prime Minister of Canada; and

(b)   the Prime Minister of Canada will invite representatives of the aboriginal peoples of Canada to participate in the discussion on that item.[3]

PART III

EQUALIZATION AND REGIONAL DISPARITIES

Commitment to promote equal opportunities

36.   (1) Without altering the legislative authority of Parliament or of the provincial legislatures, or the rights of any of them with respect to the exercise of their legislative authority, Parliament and the legislatures, together with the government of Canada and the provincial governments, are committed to

(a)   promoting equal opportunities for the well-being of Canadians;

(b)   furthering economic development to reduce disparity in opportunities; and

(c)   providing essential public services of reasonable quality to all Canadians.

Commitment respecting public services

(2)   Parliament and the government of Canada are committed to the principle of making equalization payments to ensure that provincial governments have sufficient revenues to provide reasonably comparable levels of public services at reasonably comparable levels of taxation.

PART IV

CONSTITUTIONAL CONFERENCE

Constitutional conference

37.   (1) A constitutional conference composed of the Prime Minister of Canada and the first ministers of the provinces shall be convened by the Prime Minister of Canada within one year after this Part comes into force.

Participation of aboriginal peoples

(2)   The conference convened under subsection (1) shall have included in its agenda an item respecting constitutional matters that directly affect the aboriginal peoples of Canada, including the identification and definition of the rights of those peoples to be included in the Constitution of Canada, and the Prime Minister of Canada shall invite representatives of those peoples to participate in the discussions on that item.

Participation of territories

(3)   The Prime Minister of Canada shall invite elected representatives of the governments of the Yukon Territory and the Northwest Territories to participate in the discussion on any item on the agenda of the conference convened under subsection (1) that, in the opinion of the Prime Minister, directly affects the Yukon Territory and the Northwest Territories.

PART IV.1

CONSTITUTIONAL CONFERENCES

Constitutional conferences

37.1 (1) In addition to the conference convened in March 1983, at least two constitutional conferences composed of the Prime Minister of Canada and the first ministers of the provinces shall be convened by the Prime Minister of Canada, the first within three years after April 17, 1982 and the second within five years after that date.

Participation of aboriginal peoples

(2)   Each conference convened under subsection (1) shall have included in its agenda constitutional matters that directly affect the aboriginal peoples of Canada, and the Prime Minister of Canada shall invite representatives of those peoples to participate in the discussions on those matters.

Participation of territories

(3)   The Prime Minister of Canada shall invite elected representatives of the governments of the Yukon Territory and the Northwest Territories to participate

in the discussions on any item on the agenda of a conference convened under subsection (1) that, in the opinion of the Prime Minister, directly affects the Yukon Territory and the Northwest Territories.

Subsection 35(1) not affected

(4)   Nothing in this section shall be construed so as to derogate from subsection 35(1).[4]

PART V

PROCEDURE FOR AMENDING CONSTITUTION OF CANADA

General procedure for amending Constitution of Canada

38. (1) An amendment to the Constitution of Canada may be made by proclamation issued by the Governor General under the Great Seal of Canada where so authorized by

(a)   resolutions of the Senate and House of Commons; and

(b)   resolutions of the legislative assemblies of at least two-thirds of the provinces that have, in the aggregate, according to the then latest general census, at least fifty per cent of the population of all the provinces.

Majority of members

(2)   An amendment made under subsection (1) that derogates from the legislative powers, the proprietary rights or any other rights or privileges of the legislature or government of a province shall require a resolution supported by a majority of the members of each of the Senate, the House of Commons and the legislative assemblies required under subsection (1).

Expression of dissent

(3)   An amendment referred to in subsection (2) shall not have effect in a province the legislative assembly of which has expressed its dissent thereto by resolution supported by a majority of its members prior to the issue of the proclamation to which the amendment relates unless that legislative assembly, subsequently, by resolution supported by a majority of its members, revokes its dissent and authorizes the amendment.

Revocation of dissent

(4)   A resolution of dissent made for the purposes of subsection (3) may be revoked at any time before or after the issue of the proclamation to which it relates.

Restriction on proclamation

39. (1) A proclamation shall not be issued under subsection 38(1) before the expiration of one year from the adoption of the resolution initiating the amendment procedure thereunder, unless the legislative assembly of each province has previously adopted a resolution of assent or dissent.

Idem

(2)   A proclamation shall not be issued under subsection 38(1) after the expiration of three years from the adoption of the resolution initiating the amendment procedure thereunder.

Compensation

40. Where an amendment is made under subsection 38(1) that transfers provincial legislative powers relating to education or other cultural matters from provincial legislatures to Parliament, Canada shall provide reasonable compensation to any province to which the amendment does not apply.

Amendment by unanimous consent

41. An amendment to the Constitution of Canada in relation to the following matters may be made by proclamation issued by the Governor

General under the Great Seal of Canada only where authorized by resolutions of the Senate and House of Commons and of the legislative assembly of each province:

(a)   the office of the Queen, the Governor General and the Lieutenant Governor of a province;

(b)   the right of a province to a number of members in the House of Commons not less than the number of Senators by which the province is entitled to be represented at the time this Part comes into force;

(c)   subject to section 43, the use of the English or the French language;

(d)   the composition of the Supreme Court of Canada; and

(e)   an amendment to this Part.

Amendment by general procedure

42. (1) An amendment to the Constitution of Canada in relation to the following matters may be made only in accordance with subsection 38(1):

(a)   the principle of proportionate representation of the provinces in the House of Commons prescribed by the Constitution of Canada;

(b)   the powers of the Senate and the method of selecting Senators;

(c)   the number of members by which a province is entitled to be represented in the Senate and the residence qualifications of Senators;

(d)   subject to paragraph 41(d), the Supreme Court of Canada;

(e)   the extension of existing provinces into the territories; and

(f)   notwithstanding any other law of practice, the establishment of new provinces.

Exception

(2)   Subsections 38(2) to (4) do not apply in respect of amendments in relation to matters referred to in subsection (1).

Amendment of provisions relating to some but not all provinces

43. An amendment to the Constitution of Canada in relation to any provision that applies to one or more, but not all, provinces, including

(a)   any alteration to boundaries between provinces, and

(b)   any amendment to any provision that relates to the use of the English or the French language within a province, may be made by proclamation issued by the Governor General under the Great Seal of Canada only where so authorized by resolutions of the Senate and House of Commons and of the legislative assembly of each province to which the amendment applies.

Amendments by Parliament

44. Subject to sections 41 and 42, Parliament may exclusively make laws amending the Constitution of Canada in relation to the executive government of Canada or the Senate and House of Commons.

Amendments by provincial legislatures

45. Subject to section 41, the legislature of each province may exclusively make laws amending the constitution of the province.

Initiation of amendment procedures

46. (1) The procedures for amendment under sections 38, 41, 42 and 43 may be initiated either by the Senate or the House of Commons or by the legislative assembly of a province.

Revocation of authorization

(2)   A resolution of assent made for the purposes of this Part may be revoked at any time before the issue of a proclamation authorized by it.

Amendments without Senate resolution

47. (1) An amendment to the Constitution of Canada made by proclamation under section 38, 41, 42 or 43 may be made without a resolution of the Senate authorizing the issue of the proclamation if, within one hundred and eighty days after the adoption by the House of Commons of a resolution authorizing its issue, the Senate has not adopted such a resolution and if, at any time after the expiration of that period, the House of Commons again adopts the resolution.

Computation of period

(2)   Any period when Parliament is prorogued or dissolved shall not be counted in computing the one hundred and eighty day period referred to in subsection (1).

Advice to issue proclamation

48. The Queen's Privy Council for Canada shall advise the Governor General to issue a proclamation under this Part forthwith on the adoption of the resolutions required for an amendment made by proclamation under this Part.

Constitutional conference

49. A constitutional conference composed of the Prime Minister of Canada and the first ministers of the provinces shall be convened by the Prime Minister of Canada within fifteen years after this Part comes into force to review the provisions of this Part.

PART VI

AMENDMENT TO THE CONSTITUTION ACT, 1867

Amendment to Constitution Act, 1867

50. The Constitution Act, 1867 (formerly named the British North America Act, 1867) is amended by adding thereto, immediately after section 92 thereof, the following heading and section:

*"Non-Renewable Natural Resources, Forestry Resources
and Electrical Energy*

Laws respecting non-renewable natural resources, forestry resources and electrical energy

92A. (1) In each province, the legislature may exclusively make laws in relation to

(a)   exploration for non-renewable natural resources in the province;

(b)   development, conservation and management of non-renewable natural resources and forestry resources in the province, including laws in relation to the rate of primary production therefrom; and

(c)   development, conservation and management of sites and facilities in the province for the generation and production of electrical energy.

Export from provinces of resources

(2)   In each province, the legislature may make laws in relation to the export from the province to another part of Canada of the primary production from non-renewable natural resources and forestry resources in the province and the production from facilities in the province for the generation of electrical energy, but such laws may not authorize or provide for discrimination in prices or in supplies exported to another part of Canada.

Authority of Parliament

(3)   Nothing in subsection (2) derogates from the authority of Parliament to enact laws in relation to the matters referred to in that subsection and, where such

a law of Parliament and a law of a province conflict, the law of Parliament prevails to the extent of the conflict.

Taxation of resources

(4) In each province, the legislature may make laws in relation to the raising of money by any mode or system of taxation in respect of

(a) non-renewable natural resources and forestry resources in the province and the primary production therefrom, and

(b) sites and facilities in the province for the generation of electrical energy and the production therefrom, whether or not production is exported in whole or in part from the province, but such laws may not authorize or provide for taxation that differentiates between production exported to another part of Canada and production not exported from the province.

"Primary production"

(5) The expression "primary production" has the meaning assigned by the Sixth Schedule.

Existing powers or rights

(6) Nothing in subsections (10) to (5) derogates from any powers or rights that a legislature or government of a province had immediately before the coming into fore of this section."

Idem

51. The said Act is further amended by adding thereto the following Schedule:

"THE SIXTH SCHEDULE

Primary Production from Non-Renewable Natural Resources and Forestry Resources

1. For the purposes of section 92A of this Act,

(a) production from a non-renewable natural resource is primary production therefrom if

(i) it is in the form in which it exists upon its recovery or severance from its natural state, or

(ii) it is a product resulting from processing or refining the resource, and is not a manufactured product or a product resulting fro refining crude oil, refining upgraded heavy crude oil, refining gases or liquids derived from coal or refining a synthetic equivalent of crude oil; and

(b) production from a forestry resource is primary production therefrom if it consists of sawlogs, poles, lumber, wood chips, sawdust or any other primary wood product, or wood pulp, and is not a product manufactured from wood."

PART VII

GENERAL

Primacy of Constitution of Canada

52. (1) The Constitution of Canada is the supreme law of Canada, and any law that is inconsistent with the provisions of the Constitution is, to the extent of the inconsistency, of no force or effect.

Constitution of
Canada

(2)   The Constitution of Canada includes

(a)   The Canada Act 1982, including this Act;

(b)   the Acts and orders referred to in the schedule; and

(c)   any amendment to any Act or order referred to in paragraph (a) or (b).

Amendments to
Constitution of
Canada

(3)   Amendments to the Constitution of Canada shall be made only in accordance with the authority contained in the Constitution of Canada.

Repeals and new
names

53. (1) The enactments referred to in Column I of the schedule are hereby repealed or amended to the extent indicated in Column II thereof and, unless repealed, shall continue as law in Canada under the names set out in Column III thereof.

Consequential
amendments

(2)   Every enactment, except the *Canada Act 1982,* that refers to an enactment referred to in the schedule by the name in Column I thereof is hereby amended by substituting for that name the corresponding name in Column III thereof, and any British North America Act not referred to in the schedule may be cited as the *Constitution Act* followed by the year and number, if any, of it enactment.

Repeal and
consequential
amendments

54. Part IV is repealed on the day that is one year after this Part comes into force and this section may be repealed and this Act renumbered, consequentially upon the repeal of Part IV and this section, by proclamation issued by the Governor General under the Great Seal of Canada.

Repeal of Part IV.1
and this section
French version of
Constitution of
Canada

54.1 Part IV.1 and this section are repealed on April 18, 1987.[5]

55. A French version of the portions of the Constitution of Canada referred to in the schedule shall be prepared by the Minister of Justice of Canada as expeditiously as possible and, when any portion thereof sufficient to warrant action being taken has been so prepared, it shall be put forward for enactment by proclamation issued by the Governor General under the Great Seal of Canada pursuant to the procedure then applicable to an amendment of the same provisions of the Constitution of Canada.

English and French
version of certain
constitutional texts

56. Where any portion of the Constitution of Canada has been or is enacted in English and French or where a French version of any portion of the Constitution is enacted pursuant to section 55, the English and French versions of that portion of the Constitution are equally authoritative.

English and French
versions of this Act
Commencement

57. The English and French versions of this Act are equally authoritative.

58. Subject to section 59, this Act shall come into force on a day to be fixed by proclamation issued by the Queen or the Governor General under the Great Seal of Canada.

Commencement of
paragraph 23(1)(a)
in respect of Quebec

59. (1) Paragraph 23(1)(a) shall come into force in respect of Quebec on a day to be fixed by proclamation issued by the Queen or the Governor General under the Great Seal of Canada.

Authorization of
Quebec

(2)   A proclamation under subsection (1) shall be issued only where authorized by the legislative assembly or government of Quebec.

Repeal of this
section

(3)   This section may be repealed on the day paragraph 23(1)(a) comes into force in respect of Quebec and this Act amended and renumbered, consequentially upon the repeal of this section, by proclamation issued by the Queen or the Governor General under the Great Seal of Canada.

Short title and
citations

60.   This Act may be cited as the *Constitution Act, 1982*, and the Constitution Acts 1867 to 1975 (No. 2) and this Act may be cited together as the *Constitution Acts, 1867 to 1982.*

References

61.   A reference to the *"Constitution Acts, 1867 to 1982"* shall be deemed to include a reference to the *"Constitution Amendment Proclamation, 1983."*[6]

For an online version of Appendices A and B, plus the SCHEDULE to the Constitution Act, 1982: Modernization of the Constitution, visit the text's website at **www.nelson.com/intropolitics9e.**

---

[1]Paragraph 25(b) was repealed and the present paragraph 25(b) was substituted by the Constitution Amendment Proclamation, 1983.

[2]Subsections (3) and (4) of s. 35 were added by the Constitution Amendment Proclamation, 1983.

[3]Section 35.1 was added by the Constitution Amendment Proclamation, 1983.

[4]Part IV.1, consisting of s. 37.1, was added by the Constitution Amendment Proclamation, 1983.

[5]Section 54.1 was added by the Constitution Amendment Proclamation, 1983.

[6]Section 61 was added by the Constitution Amendment Proclamation, 1983.

Glossary

(Numbers in parentheses refer to the chapter(s) and page(s) containing the main discussion of the term.)

aboriginal (indigenous) peoples Inhabitants of the Americas prior to the arrival of European settlers. (4, p. 43)

ad hoc committees Legislative committees appointed for special temporary purposes, such as to investigate a problem before the government prepares legislation on the subject. (20, p. 282)

administration The organized apparatus of the state for preparation and implementation of legislation and policies, also called the bureaucracy. (28, p. 420)

agenda-setting Controlling the focus of attention by establishing the issues for public discussion. (24, p. 365)

alpha male The highest-ranking male in a chimpanzee troop. The key to moving up the dominance hierarchy is not physical strength but rather building a supporting coalition, that is, a cooperative group that can intimidate even the fiercest opponent. (1, p. 4)

alternative vote system An electoral system in which voters rank the candidates. (25, p. 380)

anarchist One who advocates anarchy. Also refers to the followers of Mikhail Bakunin, who opposed Marx's focus on the state. (9, p. 107; 12, p. 151)

anarchy Order resulting from mutual coordination in the absence of a higher, coercive authority. (8, p. 83)

animal liberation A movement that proposes to ban hunting, the raising of domestic livestock for food and other economic purposes, and the use of animals in laboratory experiments. (15, p. 201)

anomic group A spontaneously formed interest group with concerns over a specific issue. (23, p. 345)

Arab Spring The name given to the collection of revolutions that took place beginning early in 2011 and to date have resulted in governments being overthrown in Tunisia, Egypt, and Libya; in significant governmental change in Yemen, and Bahrain; civil war in Syria; and in more minor governmental change and protest in a number of other countries in the region. (17, pp. 234)

aristocracy A form of government in which a minority rules under the law. (16, p. 210)

Articles of Confederation The first American constitution, ratified in 1781, replaced by the U.S. Constitution in 1789. (21, p. 305)

associational group A formally organized group that articulates the interests of its members over long periods of time. (23, p. 345)

asymmetrical federalism A federal system of government in which powers are unevenly divided among provinces so that some provinces have greater responsibilities or more autonomy than others. (21, p. 312)

auditor general An official of Parliament whose staff audits the expenditures of government departments and who provides an annual report on selected programs. (28, p. 426)

authoritarianism A system of government in which leaders are not subjected to the test of free elections. (19, p. 259)

authority A form of power based on agreement regarding the right to issue commands and make decisions. (2, p. 16)

autocracy   An arbitrary system of government unconstrained by the rule of law and the consent of the governed. (19, p. 258)

autonomy   A state of independence from outside control. (17, p. 230)

backbenchers   Members of parliament on the government side who sit on the back benches and are not in Cabinet, or those similarly distant from shadow-cabinet posts in opposition parties. (20, p. 284)

balance of power   The theory that international security is best maintained when all states have comparable military strength, so that no individual state can dominate the others. (8, p. 88)

balkanization of politics   Named for the Balkan region in Eastern Europe, denotes strong parochial ties within ethnic, religious, and national groups and the disintegration of political order due to conflict among the groups. (18, p. 248)

behavioural revolution   Introduction of more empirical, especially quantitative, analysis into the study of government and politics. (Introduction, p. xxv)

bicameralism   A system of government in which the legislature is divided into two chambers, an upper and a lower house. (20, p. 276)

bilateral procedure   A procedure for amending certain sections of the Canadian Constitution in which approval is required only from Parliament plus the legislature(s) of the province(s) affected by the amendment. (7, p. 74)

bilingualism   In the Canadian context, the fact that Canada has two official languages, English and French. (13, p. 167)

bill   A piece of legislation under consideration by a legislative body. (20, p. 275)

binational state   Two nations coexisting within one state. (4, p. 45)

bourgeoisie   A Marxist term referring to those who own the means of production. (12, p. 148)

bureaucracy   A type of administration characterized by specialization, professionalism, and security of tenure. (28, p. 420)

by-laws   Legal enactments, such as parking regulations or zoning ordinances, passed by local government under provincial authority. (6, p. 65)

cabinet   Along with the Crown and the prime minister, the cabinet forms the executive branch of government. In the parliamentary system it is composed of the prime minister and chosen members of the legislative branch; in the presidential system it is made up of the president and chosen advisors from outside the legislature. (20, p. 275)

cabinet solidarity   The convention by which all members of the cabinet support government policy and do not criticize it or each other in public. (20, p. 281)

Canadian Charter of Rights and Freedoms   The first 34 sections of the Constitution Act, 1982. (29, p. 436)

Canadian politics   The study of federal, provincial, and municipal politics in Canada. (Introduction, p. xxix)

capitalism   A political and economic system defined by private ownership and the pursuit of profit in a free-market economy. (18, p. 245)

caucus   A meeting of legislators of any one party to discuss parliamentary strategy and party policy. (20, p. 284)

central agencies   Government agencies, such as the Prime Minister's Office, the Privy Council Office, the Treasury Board, and the Department of Finance, that have certain coordinating functions across the whole federal public service. (27, p. 410)

charismatic authority   Authority based on admiration of the personal qualities of an individual. (2, p. 22)

checks and balances   A system of government in which power is divided among the executive, legislative, and judicial branches of government so that those powers check and balance one another. (20, p. 295)

citizenship   Legal membership in the state. (3, p. 34)

civic nation (nationalism)   National identity based on loyalty to the state rather than on ethnic factors. (4, p. 42)

civil disobedience   Voluntary acceptance of the legal penalties that may be imposed for breaking unjust laws in order to highlight the coercive nature of a regime; typified by passive resistance. (7, p. 79)

civil society   The network of self-generating, autonomous social organizations bound by shared rules. (18, p. 243)

classical liberalism   A liberal ideology entailing a minimal role for government in order to maximize individual freedom. (10, p. 113)

coalition   Alliance between two or more political units in response to opposing forces. (1, p. 7)

coalition government   A parliamentary government in which the cabinet is composed of members of more than one party. (20, p. 280)

code   A comprehensive set of interrelated rules intended to reduce uncertainty in interpretation of the law by systematizing and making explicit legal precedents. (6, p. 63)

code civil   The unique system of civil law used in Quebec. (6, p. 64)

coercion   A form of power based on forced compliance through fear and intimidation. (2, p. 14)

Cold War   A period of antagonism between the Western powers, consisting of the United States and its allies, and the Soviet bloc, beginning after World War II and persisting until the breakup of the USSR in the early 1990s. (8, p. 89)

collective (public) goods   Goods and services enjoyed in common and not divisible among individuals. (10, p. 120)

collective security   Commitment by a number of states to join in an alliance against member states that threaten the peace. (8, p. 88)

collectivist culture   A political culture that combines broad agreement on basic social values with limited civic and political engagement. (5, p. 52)

Cominform Short for Communist Information Bureau, an international communist organization formed after World War II. (12, p. 152)

Comintern   Short for Communist International, also known as the Third International, the communist international organization between the two world wars. (12, p. 152)

common law   The accumulation of judicial precedents as a basis for court decisions. (6, p. 62)

communications (mass) media   General term for all modern means of conveying information. (24, p. 358)

communism   A political ideology characterized by a belief in eliminating exploitation through public ownership and central planning of the economy. (12, p. 149)

communist   One who advocates communism. (12, p. 152)

comparative politics   An area of political study concerned with the relative similarities and differences among political systems. (Introduction, p. xxix)

confederation   A federal system of government in which sovereign constituent governments create a central government but the balance of power remains with the constituent governments. (21, p. 302)

confidence   Support for a government by the majority of members of (usually) the lower house of parliament. (20, p. 283)

consent of the governed   People's acceptance of the form of government under which they live. (10, p. 112)

conservationism   Attempts to manage natural resources in order to maximize benefits over a long period of time. (15, p. 195)

conservatism   A political ideology generally characterized by belief in individualism and minimal government intervention in the economy and society. Also a belief in the virtue of the status quo and general acceptance of traditional morality. (11, p. 131)

consociationalism   A form of democracy in which harmony in segmented societies is maintained through the distinctive roles of elites, the autonomy of organized interests, and a balance of power among those interests. (17, p. 232)

constituency   An electoral district with a body of electors who vote for a representative in an elected assembly. (25, p. 377)

constitution   The fundamental rules and principles by which a state is organized. (7, p. 68)

constitutional democracy   See *liberal democracy*.

constitutionalism   The belief that governments will defer to the rules and principles enshrined in a constitution and will uphold the rule of law. (7, p. 75)

constructive vote of confidence   A system in which the majority in the lower house can bring down a government, but not until that majority approves another government—for example, Germany. (20, p. 285)

content analysis   Systematic analysis of printed text or images. (24, p. 363)

convention   A practice or custom followed by those in government even though not explicitly written in the constitution or in legislation. (7, p. 68)

corporatism   Organization of a liberal democracy in such a way that the state is the dominant force in society and the activities of all interests in society are subordinate to that force. (17, p. 231)

coup d'état   A quick, forcible, and unconstitutional change of government, often by a faction within the military or the ruling party. (19, p. 265)

crisis of governability   The inability of representative governments to respond to the demands of their citizens in the wake of the Great Recession of 2008. (17, p. 230)

Crown corporations   Corporations owned by the government that assume a structure similar to that of a private company and operate semi-independently of the cabinet. (28, p. 422)

culture   The pattern of beliefs and behaviour of a people, including the place of the family, the role of religion, and the influence of economics and politics. (5, p. 49)

custom   A generally accepted practice or behaviour developed over time. (6, p. 60)

customary law   Rules of conduct developed over time and enforceable in court. (6, p. 61)

deep ecology   A form of environmentalism holding that nature and the natural order should be valued over individual human happiness. (15, p. 200)

deficit   A surplus of annual expenditures over revenues. (10, p. 124)

delegate   A representative role in which the individual subordinates his or her views to those of his or her constituents. (26, p. 400)

democracy   In the original sense of the term, a system of government in which the majority rules without legal restraint. Compare *liberal democracy*. (16, p. 210)

democratic centralism   Concentration of power among the leadership of the Communist Party, which in theory acts in the interests of the people. (12, p. 151)

Department of Finance   The government department that has overall responsibility for the government's finances and its role in the economy. (27, p. 410)

deputy minister   A Canadian public servant who heads a government department, manages the department, and advises the minister. (27, p. 412)

deregulation   A government policy designed to remove regulations on market activity. (11, p. 140)

despotism   A form of government in which an individual rules through fear, without regard to law, and is not answerable to the people. (19, p. 258)

deux nations   The view that Canada is a partnership of two nations, English and French. (4, p. 45)

devolution   A system of government in which the sovereign central government devolves (delegates) power to regional governments, subject to its overriding control. (21, p. 302)

dialogue theory   The concept that constitutional principles are developed over time through repeated interchanges among the executive, legislative, and judicial branches of government. (29, p. 443)

dictatorship of the proletariat Revolutionary seizure of power by the "vanguard" of society, the Communist Party, which then rules in the name of the working class. (12, p. 149)

diplomacy A system of formal, regularized communication that allows states to peacefully conduct their business with one another. (8, p. 84)

direct democracy A system of government based on public decisions made by citizens meeting in an assembly or voting by ballot. (17, p. 221)

disallowance A power given to the federal government in the Constitution Act, 1867, under which the cabinet can nullify any provincial law, even though it has received royal assent from the lieutenant-governor of the province. (21, p. 311)

discretion The flexibility afforded government to decide something within the broader framework of rules. (7, p. 77)

distributive laws Laws designed to distribute public goods and services to individuals in society. (22, p. 323)

downsizing Reduction of the size and scope of government. (11, p. 140)

election A process by which electors cast votes to choose governmental office-holders. (25, p. 372)

Electoral College The body that formally chooses the president of the United States. (20, p. 290)

electoral system A set of rules that deal specifically with the process of turning votes into seats: how many votes citizens will have; whether they will vote for the candidates, a political party, or both; how the ballots will be counted; and how the count will be translated into seats. (25, p. 374)

elite A small group of people with a disproportionate amount of public decision-making power. (17, p. 227)

empirical Political analysis based on factual and observable data in contrast to thoughts or ideas. (Introduction, p. xxvi)

environmentalism A family of ideologies in which human damage to the natural world is the central concern. (15, p. 196)

equality of opportunity Equalization of life chances for all individuals in society, regardless of economic position. (10, p. 115)

equality of result Equalization of the outcomes of social and economic processes. (10, p. 114)

equality of right Application of the law in the same way to all. (10, p. 112)

equality rights Refers to Section 15 of the Charter of Rights and Freedoms, which prohibits governments from discriminating against certain categories of people. (29, p. 443)

ethnic group A subgroup within a nation categorized by objective factors of common ancestry, language, religion, customs, and so on. (4, p. 43)

ethnic nation (nationalism) National identity based on objective factors of common ancestry, language, religion, customs, and so on. (4, p. 42)

ethnonational violence Concern for preservation of ethnic or national identity made manifest in violent conflicts within or between nation-states. (18, p. 246)

executive The person or persons responsible for managing the business array of government. (20, p. 274)

European Union An economic and political organization composed of 27 states (as of 2012), with its own currency, parliament, bureaucracy, and court. (21, p. 305)

executive federalism A federal process directed by extensive federal-provincial interaction at the level of first ministers, departmental ministers, and deputy ministers. (21, p. 309)

exclusive economic zone (EEZ) The oceanic water column extending 200 nautical miles from a state's shores, over which a state has resource control. (8, p. 87)

Executive Office The Executive Office of the President made up of White House offices and agencies that help develop and implement the policies and programs of the president. (27, p. 414)

extractive laws   Laws designed to collect taxes to pay for governing society. (22, p. 323)

faction   An association of individuals organized for the purpose of influencing government actions favourable to their interests. Now known as an *interest* (pressure) group. (23, p. 352)

failed state   A state suffering from conflict, political instability, economic collapse, inability to provide services to its people, or some combination of these factors. (3, p. 31)

fascism   An extreme form of nationalism that played on fears of communism and rejected individual freedom, liberal individualism, democracy, and limitations on the state. (13, p. 171)

federalism   A system of government in which sovereignty is divided between a central government and several provincial or state governments. (21, p. 302)

feminism   Belief that society is disadvantageous to women, systematically depriving them of individual choice, political power, economic opportunity, and intellectual recognition. (14, p. 177)

First International   A loose association of socialist parties and labour unions in Western Europe, organized in 1864. (12, p. 151)

fiscal policy   Policy related to government spending. (10, p. 124)

formal–legal institutions   Institutions explicitly created by a constitution. (22, p. 325)

fragmented culture   A political culture where there is a high degree of citizen engagement but little agreement on the rules of the game. Disagreements, disunity, and violence often lead to instability in such cultures. (5, p. 51)

franchise   The right to vote. (17, p. 218)

free-market environmentalism   The view that environmental problems are best solved by property rights and markets. (15, p. 198)

free riders   Those who enjoy a collective good without helping to pay for it. (10, p. 119)

free vote   A legislative vote in which members are not required to toe the party line. (20, p. 284)

functions   Special activities or purposes that *structures* serve in the political process; for example, interest groups function to articulate interests. (22, p. 323)

gender gap   A difference between men and women on a political measure, for instance in voting for political parties. (14, p. 190)

general procedure   A procedure for amending the Canadian Constitution, requiring the approval of Parliament plus the legislatures of two-thirds of the provinces, having among them at least half of the population of the provinces. (7, p. 74)

gerrymander   To manipulate constituency boundaries for partisan election purposes. (25, p. 379)

globalization   The processes and consequences of increasing the scope of exchange in goods and services, money, people, and ideas. (17, p. 232)

government   A specialized group of individuals, institutions, and agencies that makes and enforces public decisions. (1, p. 3)

Green parties   Political parties or movements dedicated to environmental protection. (15, p. 201)

habit   A personal rule of conduct. (6, p. 60)

head of government   The person in effective charge of the executive branch of government; in a parliamentary system, the prime minister. (20, p. 277)

head of state   An individual who represents the state but does not exercise political power; in Great Britain and Canada, the Queen. (20, p. 277)

human rights   Rights thought to belong to all people simply because they are human beings. (6, p. 65)

human welfare ecology   An offshoot of the conservation movement that addresses the value of the environment to human health and happiness. (15, p. 196)

ideological party   A type of political party that emphasizes ideological purity over attainment of power. (23, p. 333)

ideology   A system of beliefs and values that explains society and prescribes the role of government. (9, p. 99)

immigrants   Individuals who have voluntarily moved to another country. (4, p. 43)

indigenous peoples   See *Aboriginal peoples.*

influence   A form of power based on the ability to persuade others to pursue a desired objective. (2, p. 13)

informal institution   An institution that is an integral part of the political process but not established by a constitution. (22, p. 324)

initiative   Initiation of legislative action on a particular issue by way of a voters' petition. (17, p. 222)

institutional group   A group closely associated with some part of the government that acts internally to influence public decisions. (23, p. 345)

interest party   A political party with a single interest or purpose, such as the Green Party. (23, p. 334)

interest (pressure) group   An organization whose members act together to influence public policy in order to promote their common interest. (23, p. 341)

international law   The body of rules governing the relationships of states with one another. (8, p. 83)

international organization   An organization composed of states, non-government organizations (NGOs), and/or other international actors. (8, p. 83)

international regime   A pattern of regular cooperation governed by implicit and explicit expectations between two or more states. (8, p. 84)

international relations   An area of political study concerned with the interaction of independent states. (Introduction, p. xxx)

intervention   In a court case, presentation of a view on the law without representing one of the parties in the litigation. (29, p. 437)

irredentism   A nationalistic desire to recover lost territory adjacent to the boundaries of a state. (13, p. 168)

item veto   The power of some American state governors to veto particular components of a bill rather than reject the entire legislation—a power not available to the president. (20, p. 293)

judicial activism   The willingness and inclination of judges to overturn legislation or executive action. (29, p. 437)

Judicial Committee of the Privy Council (JCPC)   The highest appellate court for the British Empire, which functioned as Canada's final court of appeal until 1949. (21, p. 310)

judicial independence   The principle that judges should be insulated from direct political influence. (29, p. 434)

judicial review   The power of the courts to declare legislation unconstitutional, or *ultra vires*. (20, p. 294)

judiciary   The branch of government with the power to resolve legal conflicts that arise between citizens, between citizens and governments, or between levels of government. (20, p. 274)

junta   A Spanish word meaning a group of individuals who form a government, especially after a revolution or *coup d'état*. (17, p. 216)

jus sanguinis   A Latin phrase literally meaning "right of blood," used to describe legal systems that grant citizenship automatically to the children of citizens, no matter where they are born. (3, p. 35)

jus soli   A Latin phrase literally meaning "right of place," used to describe legal systems that grant citizenship automatically to all those born within state territory. (3, p. 35)

laissez-faire   Non-intervention of the state in the economy. (Introduction, p. xxiv; 10, p. 118)

law   Enforceable rules of conduct. (6, p. 60)

Law of the Sea   The treaty that informs coastal states and states with vessels sailing the seas of their rights and obligations. It also gives coastal states a complex set of jurisdictional zones that overlap both physically and in terms of their other legal properties. See also *exclusive economic zone*. (8, p. 86)

left-wing authoritarianism An official ideology that has a vision of fundamental social transformation, extensive political mobilization, and centralized economic planning but lacks the full intensity of totalitarian regimes. (19, p. 262)

legal authority A system of authority based on general rules rather than inheritance or personal qualities. (2, p. 20)

legislation Consciously formulated and deliberately constructed law. (6, p. 61)

legislative The branch of government responsible for making laws for the society. (20, p. 274)

legislature A representative assembly responsible for making laws for the society. (26, p. 391)

legitimacy Belief in the "rightness" of rule. (2, p. 18)

liberal democracy A system of government characterized by universal adult suffrage, political equality, majority rule, and constitutionalism. (17, p. 218)

liberal feminism Advocacy of equal rights between men and women. (14, p. 179)

liberalism A family of ideologies that emphasizes individual freedom, a limited state, constitutionalism, and the rule of law. (10, p. 112)

libertarianism A contemporary ideology that advocates maximum individual freedom in all spheres of life, social as well as economic. (11, p. 139)

limited government A state restricted in its exercise of power by a constitution and the rule of law. (7, p. 75; 10, p. 112)

limited state See *limited government*.

list system A form of proportional representation in which the elector votes not for individuals but for parties, which make lists of the candidates running for office. (25, p. 381)

lobbying Activities of interest groups aimed at influencing governors and the public

to achieve favourable policy decisions. (23, p. 347)

log-rolling The act of vote-trading among legislators in the process of getting legislation passed. (20, p. 294, 27, p. 415)

Magna Carta ("Great Charter") A document signed by King John of England in 1215, conceding that the king is subject to law. (7, p. 69)

majority Fifty percent plus one of those voting. Also called a simple majority. (17, p. 220)

majority-plurality system An electoral system in which there are two rounds of voting. Candidates who do not achieve some minimum proportion of votes on the first ballot are dropped from the second. On the second ballot, the winning candidate needs only a plurality of valid votes cast. (25, p. 380)

majority-runoff system An electoral system in which there are two rounds of voting. The first round of voting is held as in a *single-member-plurality (SMP) system*. If no candidate earns a majority of votes in that round, the two candidates with the highest vote totals advance to the next round, where the winner is guaranteed to have the support of the majority. (25, p. 380)

majority government A parliamentary government in which the party in power has more than 50 percent of the seats in the legislature. (20, p. 279)

materialist The term used by Ronald Inglehart to describe those who are motivated primarily by personal and economic security. See also *post-materialist*. (5, p. 52)

merit recruitment A system of hiring public servants on the basis of qualifications rather than on party preference or personal connections. (28, p. 420)

microcosm theory The idea that a governing body should be a miniature replica of the society it represents. (26, p. 402)

ministerial responsibility The principle that cabinet ministers are individually responsible to the House of Commons for everything that happens in their department. (27, p. 415)

ministry   The entire group of MPs appointed by the prime minister to specific executive responsibilities. (27, p. 408)

minority government   A parliamentary government in which the government party has less than 50 percent of the seats in the legislature. (20, p. 279)

mixed economy   An economy based on both private and public (government-controlled) enterprises. (12, p. 153)

mixed-member proportional (MMP) system   An electoral system in which voters cast two ballots, one for a local candidate running in a territorial constituency (first-past-the-post system) and the other for a list of candidates put forward by a political party (list system). (25, p. 383)

modernization   In economics, refers to the adoption of markets and sophisticated technology in place of barter and subsistence production. In politics, the replacement of traditional authority with legal authority. (2, p. 21)

monarchy   A form of government in which a single person rules under the law. (16, p. 210)

monetary policy   Governmental control over the supply of money. (10, p. 124)

movement party   A type of political party that emerges from a political movement such as a national liberation movement. (23, p. 336)

multiculturalism   A policy adopted by Prime Minister Pierre Trudeau in 1971 to promote cultural pluralism in Canada. (13, p. 167)

multinational state   Three or more nations coexisting under one sovereign government. (4, p. 45)

multiparty system   A party system in which there are three or more major contenders for power. (23, p. 339)

nation   Comprises individuals whose common identity creates both a psychological bond and a political community. (4, p. 40)

nationalism   A feeling of loyalty and attachment to one's nation or nation-state, and strong support for its interests. (13, p. 163)

national mythology   A set of stories about the common history and destiny of a nation. (13, p. 163)

nation-state   A state with a single predominant national identity. (4, p. 39)

natural authority   Authority based on spontaneous deference to an individual's knowledge or social position. (2, p. 17)

naturalization   The process of acquiring citizenship not by birth but by grant from the state. (3, p. 35)

natural law   Rules of conduct binding by virtue of human rationality alone. (6, p. 64)

neo-fascist   A term used to describe contemporary anti-democratic, racist parties of the far right. (13, p. 172)

new public management   A recent approach to public administration that emphasizes efficiency and accountability to the public. (28, p. 427)

non-associational (latent) group   A group that lacks formal organization but has potential for mobilizing politically. (23, p. 346)

non-governmental organization (NGO)   A not-for-profit organization that is not associated with a government. (8, p. 83)

non-partisan   Neutral or objective, specifically with reference to political preference. (25, p. 380)

normative   Describes political analysis based on values, commitments, and ideas. (Introduction, p. xxvi)

notwithstanding clause   Section 33 of the Charter of Rights and Freedoms, which allows federal or provincial legislatures to pass laws that may violate certain sections of the Charter. (29, p. 440)

Official Opposition   In a parliamentary system, the largest of the opposition parties, which is given a special role to play in the legislative process. (20, p. 282)

oligarchy   A form of government in which a minority rules outside the law. (16, p. 210)

ombudsman   An official with the power to investigate complaints against government administration. (28, p. 426)

one-party-dominant system A party system in which there are political alternatives, but a single political party dominates the political process as a result of overwhelming support from the electorate. (23, p. 336)

opposition Those members of parliament who are not part of the government of the day. See also *Official Opposition*. (20, p. 282)

order-in-council In the British parliamentary tradition, a decision by Cabinet that carries legal force. (6, p. 65)

parliamentary sovereignty The supreme authority of parliament to make or repeal laws. (3, p. 28)

parochial culture A type of political culture that emphasizes local grievances and benefits rather than the broader concerns of the entire society or nation. (5, p. 51)

participatory culture A type of political culture combining active participation in politics with a responsive government. (5, p. 51)

partisan A supporter of a particular political party. (25, p. 386)

party discipline The convention that all members of parliament within one party vote together, as predetermined in caucus and enforced by the party whip. (20, p. 276)

party member Describes a form of representation in which a representative votes with the party to whom he or she belongs. (26, p. 400)

patriarchy The domination of society by men. (14, p. 185)

peacekeeping The interposition of lightly armed outside military forces between combatants who have agreed to stop fighting. (8, p. 90)

permanent secretary The British equivalent of a Canadian deputy minister. (28, p. 425)

personal freedom Absence of coercion in various aspects of life. (10, p. 112)

personal party A type of political party founded around a single, overwhelmingly influential political leader. (23, p. 335)

philosopher-king Plato's view of the ideal individual who rules in the common interest and is directed by wisdom and virtue rather than the constraint of law. (16, p. 211)

planning Production and allocation of resources as determined by a central authority. (12, p. 154)

plebiscite An advisory referendum. (17, p. 222)

pluralism Open competition of political interests. (17, p. 231)

plurality A voting decision based on assigning victory to the largest number of votes but not necessarily a majority. (17, p. 220)

policy community The network of individuals and organizations that are deeply involved in a particular area of public policy. (22, p. 325)

polis The Greek city-state. (1, p. 3)

political alienation A sense of estrangement from political power. (25, p. 388)

political consultant A professional adviser who puts his or her political expertise to work in the private and public sectors. (23, p. 347)

political culture Attitudes, values, beliefs, and orientations that individuals in a society hold regarding their political system. (5, p. 49)

political economy Study of the involvement of the state in the economy. (Introduction, p. xxiii)

political executive The politically accountable heads of government. (27, p. 408)

political party An organized group that makes nominations and contests elections in the hope of gaining control of government. (23, p. 329)

political patronage Government appointments made as rewards for loyal partisan activity. (28, p. 420)

political philosophy An area of political study based on historical, reflective, and conceptual methods. (Introduction, p. xxix)

political police A police force that reports directly to a political leader, who uses it for political control rather than law enforcement. (19, p. 268)

political process The interaction of organized political structures in making and administering public decisions for a society. (22, p. 322)

political science The systematic study of government and politics. (Introduction, p. xxii)

political socialization The process by which political culture is transmitted from generation to generation. (5, p. 56)

political system The process of government and politics in any state. (22, p. 322)

politics A process of conflict resolution in which support is mobilized and maintained for collective action. (1, p. 3)

polity A form of government characterized by *popular sovereignty* but exercised within a constitutional framework to prevent oppression of the minority by majority rule. (16, p. 211)

polyarchal culture A political culture exhibiting broad agreement on basic social values and active citizen engagement based on a strong sense of efficacy. (5, p. 51)

polyarchy Robert Dahl's term for pluralist forms of liberal democracy, in which many different interests complete. (17, p. 231)

popular sovereignty Supreme authority residing in the consent of the people. (3, p. 28)

populist Describes a political party that endeavours to connect with ordinary people, often by advocating market-oriented policies and direct democracy, by opposing large-scale immigration, and by displaying antagonism to corporations, trade unions, government bureaucracies, and other large organizations. (23, p. 341)

pork-barrelling Using governmental power to do favours for particular groups or constituencies in return for promises of political support. (27, p. 415)

portfolio The administrative responsibility carried by a minister, usually some combination of departments and other agencies. (27, p. 415)

positive law A law that is formally made or put into place ("posited") by state authority. (6, p. 64)

post-materialism The shift in values since the late 1940s from public order and material prosperity to self-fulfillment. (5, p. 52; 14, p. 177)

post-materialist The term used by Ronald Inglehart to describe those who are motivated primarily by self-fulfillment and self-expression. (5, p. 52)

power The ability to get other individuals to do what one wants them to do. (2, p. 13)

pragmatic party A type of political party concerned primarily with winning elections. (23, p. 332)

precedent A previous judicial case used as an example for deciding the case at hand. (6, p. 62)

prerogative The residual powers of the Crown that can be exercised at its own discretion. (7, p. 69)

Prime Minister's Office (PMO) Support staff appointed by the prime minister to carry out political functions. (27, p. 411)

priming Selective portrayal of political events and personalities by the media, which in turn affects public opinion. (24, p. 365)

primus inter pares A Latin phrase meaning "first among equals." (20, p. 276)

private law Laws controlling relationships between individuals. (6, p. 64)

private member A member of parliament who is not in the cabinet. (20, p. 276)

private member's bill A public bill introduced in the legislature by a member who is not in the cabinet. (20, p. 281)

privatization The sale of government-owned assets or activities to the private sector. (11, p. 140)

Privy Council A ceremonial body made up of all present and former cabinet ministers. (27, p. 411)

Privy Council Office (PCO) A governmental department that supports the prime minister, cabinet, and cabinet committees in devising government policy. (27, p. 411)

proclamation   Announcement of the official date on which a new law will take effect. (20, p. 282)

progressive tax   A tax rate that increases as the amount of one's income increases. (10, p. 127)

proletariat   A Marxist term referring to those who sell their labour to the bourgeoisie; the working class. (12, p. 147)

property franchise (suffrage)   The requirement that citizens own a stipulated amount of property in order to receive the right to vote. (10, p. 115)

proportionality   Refers to how closely the percentage of seats awarded to a party corresponds with the percentage of votes earned. Where these percentages match closely, the results are considered to be proportional. (25, p. 375)

proportional representation (PR)   An electoral system in which the share of seats won closely matches the share of popular votes received. (25, p. 381)

proportional tax   A tax rate that is the same for everyone. (10, p. 127)

provincial courts   Courts created by provincial statute and staffed by judges appointed by the province to deal with matters such as small claims and minor criminal offences. (29, p. 433)

public authority   Authority based on institutional office-holding. (2, p. 17)

public law   Laws controlling the relations between the state and individuals in society. (20, p. 274)

public-opinion polling   A random sample survey of the population to determine public opinion on a particular issue. (24, p. 363)

qualified majority   In which a simple majority requirement of "50 percent plus one" is raised to a higher level in order to protect the rights of minorities. (17, p. 220)

question period   The daily session in the House of Commons during which the opposition parties are given an opportunity to pose questions to the government. (27, p. 410)

radical feminism   A belief that men and women constitute "sexual classes" and that women's subordinate status is the result of a system controlled by men. (14, p. 185)

readings   First, second, and third readings of a bill represent the introduction, debate, and approval of laws in the legislative chambers. (20, p. 281)

recall   The ability of voters in a constituency to remove their elected representative from office by means of a petition. (17, p. 223)

redistribution   Reallocating wealth and income to achieve an economic or social objective. (10, p. 121)

Red Tory   A conservative with collectivist leanings. (11, p. 137)

referendum   A decision on policy proposals by a direct vote of the electorate. See also *initiative* (17, p. 221)

reform liberalism   A liberal ideology that advocates a larger role for the state in providing equality of opportunity. (10, p. 113)

regulations   Legal enactments made by a minister, department, or agency acting under legislative authority. (6, p. 65)

regulative laws   Laws that control individual and organizational behaviour. (22, p. 323)

regulatory agencies   Government agencies established to administer laws in certain fields—for example, the Canadian Human Rights Commission. (28, p. 422)

rehabilitation   A function of law enforcement encouraging a change in conduct that will prevent lawbreaking in the future. (6, p. 61)

report stage   The stage in the legislative process after the second reading, when the House debates the committee's report on a proposed bill. (20, p. 282)

representative democracy   A system of government based on election of decision-makers by the people. (17, p. 221)

reservation   A mechanism by which the lieutenant-governor of a province can refuse royal assent to a bill and refer it to the federal cabinet for a decision. (21, p. 311)

residual powers   The powers in a federal system of government that are not explicitly allocated in its constitution. (21, p. 308)

responsible government   A form of parliamentary democracy in which the political executive must retain the confidence of a majority of the elected legislature or assembly; it must resign or request an election if defeated on a vote of non-confidence. (20, p. 276)

restitution   A function of law enforcement that provides compensation to those who have been harmed by lawbreakers. (6, p. 61)

restraint   A function of law enforcement designed to instill fear in those who cannot be swayed by influence or authority. (6, p. 61)

retribution   A function of law enforcement that results in the punishment of those who violate the norms of society. (6, p. 61)

right-wing authoritarianism   An authoritarian regime with limited political pluralism and little guiding ideology or political mobilization, combined with a statist bias and a major political role for the military. (19, p. 259)

royal assent   Approval of a bill by the Crown. (20, p. 282)

rule of law   Belief that all actions, both of individuals and of governments, are subject to an institutionalized set of rules and regulations. (7, p. 75)

runoff system   An electoral system in which additional rounds of balloting are held, with trailing candidates dropped until a candidate receives a majority of the votes cast. (25, p. 380)

satyagraha   Gandhi's "the power of truth." As with *civil disobedience,* the point is not to defeat one's opponents but to convert them through non-resistance, thus demonstrating the power of moral conviction. (7, p. 79)

scientific socialism   The term Marx and Engels used to stress that their ideology was based on an analysis of class conflict. (12, p. 148)

Second International   The organization of socialist and labour parties in Europe—with the absence of anarchists—established in 1889. (12, p. 151)

Secretary-General   The chief administrative officer of the United Nations, who is appointed by the UN General Assembly on the advice of the Security Council (8, p. 90)

secularization   Process through which decreasing importance is assigned to religious values and institutions in modern states. (5, p. 54)

Security Council   The primary organ of the United Nations responsible for maintenance of international peace and security, made up of five permanent members—the United States, Russia, France, England, and China—who have a veto over any UN military action, plus 10 elected members that serve two-year terms. (8, p. 89)

self-government   The right of members of a group to control their own collective affairs. (13, p. 167)

semi-presidential system   A system of governance that combines features of both parliamentary and presidential systems, with a strong, popularly elected president as well as a prime minister responsible to a parliament. (20, p. 297)

separation of powers   Assignment of different powers to the executive, legislative, and judicial branches of government. (20, p. 274)

shadow cabinet   A cohesive group of specialized critics in the Official Opposition. (20, p. 282)

single-member-plurality (SMP) system   An electoral system in which the candidate with the most votes wins, even though that win may not represent 50 percent plus one of the votes. (25, p. 377)

single-party system   A party system in which there is only one party, and no political alternatives are legally tolerated. (23, p. 336)

single-transferable-vote (STV) system   A form of proportional representation in which electors vote for individuals rather than party lists, but they do so by ranking the candidates in order of choice. (25, p. 382)

social capital   The levels of trust and reciprocity and strength of social networks that exist in a community. (5, p. 53)

social conservatives   Conservatives who advocate restraint of individual desire on behalf of the common good. (11, p. 139)

social democrats   Socialists who emphasize popular consent, peaceful change, political pluralism, and constitutional government. (12, p. 152)

social media   Social networking sites, such as Facebook, YouTube, and Twitter, that allow users to share information and create networks, and in so doing facilitate interaction between individuals and organizations such as interest groups or political parties. (24, p. 360)

socialism   A leftist political ideology that emphasizes the principle of equality; it usually prescribes a large interventionist role for government in society and the economy, via taxation, regulation, redistribution, and public ownership. (12, p. 144)

social justice   Equalization of wealth and income to reach a more desirable outcome. (10, p. 127)

social movement   Loose organizations of groups and individuals working to bring about wholesale change—of policies, priorities, values and behaviour—by influencing multiple actors, including governments, business, and individuals. (23, p. 352)

sovereign   The highest or supreme political authority. (3, p. 27)

sovereignty   Internally, refers to the highest governmental authority in a territorial state; externally, refers to independence from control by other states. (3, p. 27)

special committee   An ad hoc legislative committee, appointed for special temporary purposes such as to investigate a problem before the government prepares legislation on the subject. (20, p. 282)

spoils system   A system based on the assumption that, after successfully winning an election, the political executive is entitled

to appoint large numbers of supporters to the bureaucracy. (28, p. 425)

spontaneous order   The pattern of mutual coordination that emerges as individuals pursue their own interests in society. (10, p. 119)

standing committee   A legislative committee set up permanently to parallel government functions. (20, p. 282)

stare decisis   The legal principle that precedents are binding on similar subsequent cases; the basis of the common-law system. (6, p. 62)

state   A combination of people, territory, and sovereign government. (3, p. 30)

stateless society   A society without a sovereign government. (3, p. 31)

statism   Heavy intervention of the state in societal affairs, especially in the economic system. (19, p. 261)

statute   A specific piece of legislation. (6, p. 63)

structures   In social science jargon, organizations or organized patterns of behaviour. Compare *functions*. (22, p. 323)

subject culture   A political culture that emphasizes obedience to authority. (5, p. 51)

substate nation   An ethnic group that could potentially have developed into a sovereign nation had they not been outnumbered by waves of new settlers. (4, p. 43)

suffragism   A political movement by women to obtain the right to vote. (14, p. 181)

suffragists   Advocates of extension of the franchise, particularly to women. (7, p. 79)

superior courts   In Canada, courts organized by provincial statute and staffed by judges appointed by the federal government. (29, p. 433)

sustainable development   An environmentalist concept that economic development should not outstrip available natural resources. (15, p. 198)

symbolic laws   Laws designed to create special meaning for society, such as the adoption of a national anthem. (22, p. 324)

syndicalism   A variation of socialism in which workers own or control the factory or workplace. (12, p. 157)

Third International   The worldwide association of communist parties established in 1921. (12, p. 152)

totalitarianism   A modern form of despotic rule in which the state undertakes to remake society according to an ideological design. (19, p. 265)

traditional authority   Authority based on birthright and custom. (2, p. 19)

Treasury Board   A cabinet committee and government department whose primary responsibility is to oversee government spending. (27, p. 411)

treaty   An international agreement concluded between states in written form and governed by international law. (8, p. 83, 85)

trustee   A representative who acts independently in deciding what is in the best interests of his or her constituents. (26, p. 399)

two-party-plus system   A party system in which there are two major contenders for power of approximately equal strength, plus one or more minor parties able to win seats but not to control the government. (23, p. 338)

two-party system   A party system in which there are two credible contenders for power and either is capable of winning an election. (23, p. 338)

typology   A broad classification scheme. (16, p. 209)

tyranny   A form of government in which one person rules arbitrarily. (16, p. 210)

ultra vires   Literally, "beyond the power," used to describe an action that exceeds the conferred constitutional powers of the actor. (29, p. 436)

unanimity   A decision rule in which any action must be approved by all participants. (17, p. 220)

unanimous procedure   A procedure for amending the Canadian Constitution in which approval from Parliament plus the legislatures of all provinces is required. (7, p. 73)

unicameral   Describes a legislature with a single legislative chamber. (26, p. 396)

unitary system   A system of government in which a single sovereign government rules the country. (21, p. 302)

unwritten constitution   An uncodified constitution established through traditional practice. (7, p. 69)

utopian socialism   Early-nineteenth-century socialism based on a universal appeal to reason. (12, p. 147)

veto   In the United States, the authorized power of a president to reject legislation passed by Congress. (20, p. 293)

violence   The use of physical force or power as a means of achieving ends. (2, p. 15)

vote of censure   A motion of non-confidence that requires the prime minister and cabinet to resign. (20, p. 298)

voter turnout   The percentage of eligible citizens that vote in a particular election, calculated by dividing the number of actual voters by the number of eligible voters. (25, p. 386)

welfare state   Provision for redistribution of benefits, such as education and health services, by the state. (10, p. 123)

White House staff   Special advisers to the U.S. president; part of the Executive Office and similar to the Canadian Prime Minister's Office. (27, p. 414)

Zionism   The Jewish nationalist movement advocating establishment of a Jewish nation-state. (13, p. 171)

Index